FREE SPEECH

Timothy Garton Ash is the prize-winning author of nine previous books of political writing, including, *The Magic Lantern*, *The File* and *Facts Are Subversive*. He is Isaiah Berlin Professorial Fellow at St Antony's College, Oxford, Senior Fellow at the Hoover Institution, Stanford University, and a regular contributor to the *Guardian* and the *New York Review of Books*. He was awarded the 2017 Charlemagne Prize and has won the Orwell Prize for Journalism.

'A major piece of cultural analysis, sane, witty and urgently important. Timothy Garton Ash exemplifies the "robust civility" he recommends as an antidote to the pervasive unhappiness, nervousness and incoherence around freedom of speech, rightly seeing the basic challenge as how we create a cultural and moral climate in which proper public argument is possible and human dignity affirmed.' Rowan Williams, Master of Magdalene College, Cambridge, and former Archbishop of Canterbury

'Particularly timely . . . Garton Ash argues forcefully that . . . there is an increasing need for freer speech . . . A powerful, comprehensive book' *The Economist*

'Garton Ash has two virtues that are rarely combined. The ability to theorise and the ability to work. His research is wide-ranging. He covers all the great controversies of our time and many more illuminating conflicts you are unlikely to know about... An urgent and encyclopedic work' Nick Cohen, *Observer*

'Illuminating and thought-provoking . . . Garton Ash's larger project is not merely to defend freedom of expression, but to promote civil, dispassionate discourse, within and across cultures, even about the most divisive and emotive subjects.' Faramerz Dabhoiwala, *Guardian*

'*Free Speech* is a resource, a weapon, an encyclopedia of anecdote, example and exemplum that reaches toward battling restrictions on expression with mountains of data, new ideas, liberating ideas.' Diane Roberts, *Prospect*

'Admirably clear . . . wise, up-to-the-minute and wide-ranging . . . *Free Speech* encourages us to take a breath, look hard at the facts and see how well-tried liberal principles can be applied and defended in daunting new circumstances.' Edmund Fawcett, *New York Times Book Review*

'An informative and bracing defense of free speech liberalism in the Internet age . . . In a world where free speech can never be taken for granted, Garton Ash's free speech liberalism is a good place to start any discussion.' David Luban, *New York Review of Books*

'Timothy Garton Ash rises to the task of directing us how to live civilly in our connected diversity.' John Lloyd, *Financial Times*

'A brave and admirable attempt to construct a platform on which more people can find common ground, even if only on how to disagree without killing each other. Whether the ten principles are used or not, they are a considerable achievement.' George Brock, *Times Literary Supplement*

'Timothy Garton Ash aspires to articulate norms that should govern freedom of communication in a transnational world. His work is original and inspiring. *Free Speech* is an unfailingly eloquent and learned book that delights as well as instructs.' Robert Post, Dean and Sol & Lillian Goldman Professor of Law, Yale Law School

'There are still countless people risking their lives to defend free speech and struggling to make lonely voices heard in corners around the world where voices are hard to hear. Let us hope that this book will bring confidence and hope to this world-as-city. I believe it will exert great influence.' Murong Xuecun, author of *Leave Me Alone: A Novel of Chengdu*

'Garton Ash impresses with fact-filled, ideas-rich discussion that is routinely absorbing and illuminating.' Malcolm Forbes, *American Interest*

'Timothy Garton Ash's new book *Free Speech: Ten Principles for a Connected World* is a rare thing: a worthwhile contribution to a debate without two developed sides. Ash does an excellent job laying out the theoretical and practical bases for the western liberal positions on free speech.' Malcolm Harris, *New Republic*

'A thorough and well-argued contribution to the quest for global free speech norms.' *Kirkus Reviews*

'A master class in political and historical analysis' *Publishers Weekly*

Also by Timothy Garton Ash

Facts Are Subversive
Free World
History of the Present
The File
In Europe's Name
The Magic Lantern
The Uses of Adversity
The Polish Revolution

FREE SPEECH

Ten Principles for a Connected World

Timothy Garton Ash

ATLANTIC BOOKS
London

First published in hardback in the United States of America in 2016 by
Yale University Press.

First published in hardback in Great Britain in 2016 by Atlantic Books, an imprint of
Atlantic Books Ltd.

This paperback edition first published in Great Britain in 2017 by Atlantic Books.

A catalogue record for this book is available from the British Library.

E-book: 978-1-78239-031-2
Paperback: 978-1-84887-094-9

Printed in Great Britain by CPI Group (UK) Ltd, Croydon CR0 4YY

Atlantic Books
An Imprint of Atlantic Books Ltd
Ormond House
26–27 Boswell Street
London

www.atlantic-books.co.uk

To
All contributors to Free Speech Debate
freespeechdebate.com

CONTENTS

POST-GUTENBERG

We are all neighbours now. There are more phones than there are human beings and close to half of humankind has access to the internet.[1] In our cities, we
rub shoulders with strangers from every country, culture and faith. The world is
not a global village but a global city, a virtual cosmopolis. Most of us can also be
publishers now. We can post our thoughts and photos online, where in theory
any one of billions of other people might encounter them. Never in human
history was there such a chance for freedom of expression as this. And never
have the evils of unlimited free expression—death threats, paedophile images,
sewage-tides of abuse—flowed so easily across frontiers.

This unprecedented world-as-city has been shaped by the United States, that
liberal leviathan, and to a lesser extent by other countries of the historic West.
Today, however, both the right and the power of the West to set the terms for
cosmopolis are being fiercely contested—by China above all, but also by rising
powers such as India and Brazil. Each new-old power brings to the discussion of
free speech its own cultural heritage and historical experience, the lessons from
which are themselves hotly contested inside each of those countries.

When it comes to enabling or restricting global freedom of expression, some
corporations have more power than most states. Were each user of Facebook
to be counted as an inhabitant, Facebook would have a larger population than
China.[2] What Facebook does has a wider impact than anything France does,
and Google than Germany. These are private superpowers. Yet, like the giant
figure of the sovereign in the frontispiece to Thomas Hobbes's *Leviathan*, they
are composed of countless individual people.[3] Without their users—us—these
giants would be nothing.

This book lays out an argument for, and invites a conversation about, free speech in our new cosmopolis. I start from the history of dramatic transformations—technological, commercial, cultural and political—that have occurred since the mid-twentieth century, and with particular intensity since 1989. That year saw no less than four developments that would prove seminal for free speech in the twenty-first century: the fall of the Berlin Wall, the invention of the World Wide Web, the Ayatollah Khomeini's fatwa on Salman Rushdie and the strange survival of Communist Party rule in China. History's horse has not stopped galloping since, and I am always conscious of Walter Raleigh's injunction that 'who-so-euer in writing a modern Historie, shall follow truth too neare the heeles, it may happily strike out his teeth'.[4] Nonetheless, I maintain that the basic character of the challenges we face in this world of neighbours is now clear.

What is more, this transformation of communication itself offers new possibilities for addressing changes as they happen. When I started writing this book, I thought I was just going to write a book. Some nine months after I delivered it to my publishers—'delivery' has traditionally been to typescripts what conception is to babies—a pleasing little object, wrapped in swaddling cloth, would plop through the letterbox. What Johann Gutenberg called 'the work of books' would carry on as it had for centuries.[5] But as I pursued my research at Stanford University, in the heart of Silicon Valley, I asked myself: If your subject is the post-Gutenberg world, how can you rest content with writing about it only in the old Gutenberg way? If the internet gives unprecedented opportunities for people across the world to speak freely, and to debate free speech, why not explore those opportunities as an integral part of writing this book?

I therefore turned aside to develop, with a team at Oxford University, an experimental website called freespeechdebate.com. It presents case studies, video interviews, analyses and personal commentaries from around the world, and invites online debate. Much of its content is translated into thirteen languages, which makes it linguistically accessible to some two thirds of the world's internet users.[6] It has been made possible by an inspiring group of graduate students, native speakers of those languages, all fizzing with ideas, examples and objections. Along the way, I have travelled to speak about the project and to listen carefully to the views of others, from Cairo to Berlin, Beijing to Delhi, New York to Yangon. That experience has both informed and transformed this book. As a result of those debates, both live and online, the ten principles originally suggested on the site have been reworded and reordered.[7] Quite a few of the illustrative stories I tell, especially those from countries beyond the West, were thrown up in the course of this experiment.

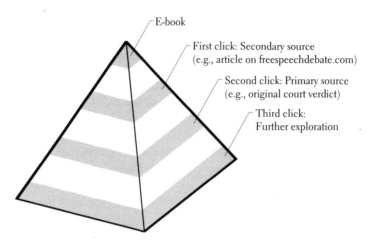

E-book

First click: Secondary source
(e.g., article on freespeechdebate.com)

Second click: Primary source
(e.g., original court verdict)

Third click:
Further exploration

Figure 1. A post-Gutenberg book

If you are reading these words in the traditional Gutenberg form, printed on paper, then endnotes point you to material on the site, amongst many other sources. If you are reading them on a connected device, then what you have in your hands is a post-Gutenberg book. Future post-Gutenberg books will doubtless take many forms, but I visualise this one as an electronic pyramid (see Figure 1).

Thus, for example, clicking at this point in the online text will take you to an essay on freespeechdebate.com which notes that in 1995 a French court convicted the American historian Bernard Lewis of violating a French memory law because he had questioned, in an interview with Le Monde, whether what happened to the Armenians in the last years of the Ottoman Empire was, strictly speaking, genocide. Click on a further link in that essay and you can read the original French court verdict.[8] For other subjects, the process may require another click or two, depending how many levels or hidden chambers inside the pyramid you wish to explore. The click-through model is entirely familiar in online journalism but has yet to become the norm for e-books, so embedding links in the main text is itself an exploration of the possibilities of a connected world.

I contend that the way to live together well in this world-as-city is to have more and better free speech. Since free speech has never meant unlimited speech—everyone spouting whatever comes into his or her head, global logorrhea—that entails discussing where the limits to freedom of expression and information should lie in important areas such as privacy, religion, national security and the ways we talk about human difference. As important, it means identifying positive methods and styles that will enable us to use this defining gift of humankind to best advantage, in these conditions of unprecedented opportunity and risk.

The philosopher Michel Foucault tells us that the Epicurean thinker Philodemus (himself reporting the lectures of Zeno of Sidon) argued that the use of free speech should be taught as a skill, like medicine or navigation. I don't know how much of that is Zeno or Philodemus, and how much Foucault, but it seems to me a vital thought for our time.[9] In this crowded world, we must learn to navigate by speech, as ancient mariners taught themselves to sail across the Aegean Sea. We can never learn if we are not allowed to take the boat out.

The goal of this journey is not to eliminate conflict between human aspirations, values and ideologies. That is not just unachievable but also undesirable, for it would result in a sterile world, monotonous, uncreative and unfree. Rather, we should work towards a framework of civilised and peaceful conflict, suited to and sustainable in this world of neighbours.

I do not pretend to offer some kind of detached, universal view from no-where—or everywhere. I have a firm standpoint, one that I am proud to call liberal, and I argue for it. That strong individual standpoint is entirely compatible with a commitment to go beyond the confines of a purely intra-Western debate. I can discern no better way to proceed towards a more universal universalism—essential if we are to live together well in this twenty-first century world-as-city—than to spell out what we believe are the standards that, were they applied by all, would be best for all. Then let others dispute our claims and advance their own.

The philosopher Isaiah Berlin famously insisted that there is a plurality of values and these cannot all be fully realised at the same time. Personally, Berlin was always fascinated by the differences between thinkers and cultures. Yet towards the end of his long life he observed that 'more people in more countries at more times accept more common values than is often believed'.[10] Maybe he was right: that is certainly my own conclusion from travels to many countries over many years. When you first arrive in another place, you are struck by everything that is different and strange. Stay a little longer, and you discover the all-human under the skin. Or maybe he was wrong, and what has been called 'moral globalisation' is a naïve liberal pipe dream. One thing is certain: we will never know unless we try to find out.

Part I

COSMOPOLIS

SPEECH

Something like human speech probably emerged at least 100,000 years ago, as a result of evolutionary developments in the brain, chest and vocal tract.[1] To speak, in this most elemental meaning, is to modulate the airflow from our lungs by movements of the chest, jaw, tongue and lips, producing sequences of distinct sounds with recognisable meanings. When we say of a toddler 'she's talking now', that is what she has learned to do.

A highly developed ability to communicate, involving the use of language and abstract thought, is what distinguishes human beings from our nearest relatives, such as the chimpanzee and the bonobo. The more we learn about the animal world, the more we appreciate the level of communication between dolphins or chimps. Online, you can watch videos showing the understanding of human speech achieved by the world's most language-proficient bonobo, Kanzi, and his ability to 'speak' back by tapping lexigrams on a computer screen. Kanzi has reportedly learned to 'say' some 500 words and understand as many as 3,000. Yet, even leaving aside the fact that his chest and vocal tract do not allow him to produce sustained sequences of recognisable sounds as humans do, there is still a qualitative gulf between what Kanzi has achieved and what most human beings can express.[2]

Towards the end of a lifetime spent studying the animal kingdom, the broadcaster David Attenborough was asked what he found the most astonishing creature on earth. He replied: 'The only creature that really makes my jaw sag so much that I find it hard to stop looking is a nine-month-old human baby. The rate at which it grows. The rate at which it learns. The rate at which it acquires nerves. It is the most complex and the most extraordinary of all creatures.

Nothing compares to it'.[3] Amongst the things it learns, like no other animal, is language. The evolutionary psychologist Robin Dunbar notes that by age 3 an average child can use about 1,000 words (double Kanzi's bonobo world record); by age 6, around 13,000; and by age 18, some 60,000: 'that means it has been learning an *average* of 10 new words a day since its first birthday, the equivalent of a new word every 90 minutes of its waking life'.[4]

Speech is not just one among many human attributes; it is a defining attribute of the human. When motor neurone disease was slowly robbing the historian Tony Judt of the power of intelligible communication, he unforgettably told me, through breaths artificially induced by a breathing machine strapped into his nostrils: 'So long as I can communicate, I am still alive'. Pause for machine-induced breath. 'When I can no longer communicate'—pause for machine-induced breath—'I will no longer be alive'.[5] I communicate, therefore I am.

Human communication has never been confined to speech. Physical contact, hand gestures and facial expressions must have played an important role even before chest, tongue and brain got their act together. In a sketch of what he calls Universal People, summarising what he considers anthropologically established human universals, Donald Brown dwells at length on speech and language, but includes physical gestures and the range of messages that we convey through the expressions on our faces.[6]

From the earliest times, we have also reached beyond our own bodies in the effort to communicate. The oldest known cave paintings have been dated to some 40,000 years ago. There is evidence of musical instruments that are probably as old and jewellery that is much older.[7] These are distant predecessors of the artworks, cartoons, YouTube clips, demo placards, flag burnings, theatrical performances, songs, tattoos, forms of dress, dietary choices, Instagram and GIF pictures, Second Life avatars, emojis and myriad other contemporary forms of expression that are all embraced in the English-language phrase 'free speech'. As the poet John Milton says in *Areopagitica*, his appeal for freedom from censorship in mid-seventeenth-century England, 'what ever thing we hear or see, sitting, walking, travelling or conversing may be fitly call'd our book'.[8]

The transformed context in which the question of free speech is posed today is, however, the result of more recent developments in communication. The acceleration of communication can be tracked along two main vectors: the physical and the virtual.[9] A highly selective timeline of the means human beings have found to transport themselves into physical proximity with each other could go: walk, run, swim, dugout canoe, ride on other animals, wheels, river boat, ocean-going ship, train, motor car, airplane, jet. For now, the technological advance of mass transport has paused with the jet airplane, but, as Figure 2

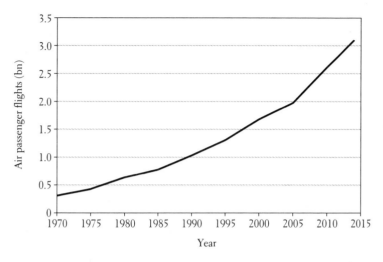

Figure 2. Growth in air passenger flights
Source: World Development Indicators, 2014.

shows, ever more people are jetting around. In 1970, just over 300 million air passenger flights were recorded. Today, it is more than 3 billion a year, or nearly one flight for every two people on earth.[10]

Most of those who fly are visitors, but some go to stay. A UN estimate of 'world migrant stock' suggests that roughly one in every 30 people has moved to a new country of residence within a single lifetime.[11] A Vatican document describes this as 'the vastest movement of people of all times'.[12] Ours is now a city planet. In 2014, more than half the world's population already lived in cities, and UN projections suggest that the world's cities will add another 2.5 billion people by 2020.[13] These will be men, women and children from everywhere, especially in the 'megacities' with more than 10 million inhabitants. There are already at least 25 world cities where more than one out of every four residents was born abroad, and the 2011 Canadian census revealed that an astonishing 51 percent of the population of Toronto was foreign-born.[14] This is before you even get to 'postmigrants', the children and grandchildren of migrants. In such cities, you routinely rub shoulders with men and women from every country, culture, faith and ethnicity. Figure 3 shows the hyperdiversity of Toronto. Step into the métro, tube, U-Bahn or subway: all humankind is there.

Advancing technologies of physical communication did not by themselves cause this unprecedented diversity. Its deeper sources include postcolonial

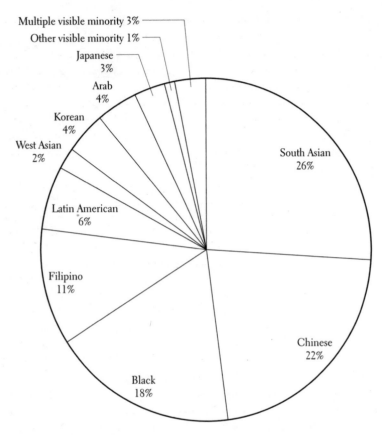

Figure 3. Hyperdiversity: Toronto's visible minorities
This shows the breakdown of what are counted as 'visible minorities', which in 2011
composed 49 percent of Toronto's total population.
Source: Canadian National Household Survey, 2011.

legacies, the impact of war, revolution and famine, a yawning economic gulf between rich global north and poor global south, the attraction of open societies and the repulsion of closed ones. Now, as 5,000 years ago, people still walk hundreds of miles and swim perilous waters in the hope of better lives for themselves and their kin. But these technologies of physical transport have made it easier for them to move.

They also enable migrants, and their postmigrant children and children's children, to travel frequently to their own or their parents or grandparents' country of origin: from Spain to Morocco, from Britain to Pakistan or from Australia to Vietnam.[15] As important for our subject: through satellite television, the internet, email and mobile phones, migrants and postmigrants have intensive virtual contact with the people, culture and politics of their other homelands. It is only a slight exaggeration to say that, through the physical and virtual reduction of distance, they live in two countries at once.

The digital age brings both acceleration along and convergence of two previously distinct lines of communication: one-to-one and one-to-many. Key advances in the history of one individual communicating with another include the development of postal services, the telegraph, the telephone, the mobile phone, email and the smartphone. The smartphone has given access to the 'mobile internet', where one-to-one converges with one-to-many and all other variants, including many-to-many and many-to-one.

One-to-many has a long prehistory in the invention of writing, inscribed on tablets of stone or clay (as were, for example, the edicts of the third-century-B.C.E. Indian emperor Ashoka), on paper (in China, around the second century C.E.), the handwritten scroll and, by the third century C.E., the codex—a handwritten book with pages you turn. A great leap forward along this line was the development of printing with movable type, which was originally invented in China in the eleventh century, using ceramic type, with metal type being developed in Korea some two centuries later. However, what changed the world was the (re)discovery by the German inventor and entrepreneur Johann Gutenberg of printing with movable metal type in the 1440s, and its diffusion across Europe in the second half of the fifteenth century.[16] The spread of radio and television marked another significant leap in communication from one person to many, which is the basic meaning of 'broadcast'. (The word was originally used in nineteenth-century English to describe scattering seed by hand.) Yet there is no way round what has become a breathless commonplace: yes, the invention of the internet inaugurated the greatest advance in human communication since Gutenberg.

On 29 October 1969 a message was sent from a computer at the University of California, Los Angeles, to one at the Stanford Research Institute. What may be considered the first message of the internet age read simply 'Lo'.[17] This was not a crypto-biblical welcome to the internet as messiah (Lo! It comes!), nor the casual argot of an American cartoon character, but the result of the Stanford computer crashing before it received the final g of 'Log'. A December 1969 map of what would eventually develop into the internet shows four computers.[18] The *Oxford English Dictionary* dates the word 'internet' to 1974.[19] In August 1981 there were just 213 internet hosts.[20] The idea of the World Wide Web was proposed by Tim Berners-Lee in 1989, and he created the first ever website at the end of 1990.[21]

Then it was fast forward. As Figure 4 shows, what is known as 'Moore's Law'—predicting a regular doubling of the number of transistors you can fit on a microchip, and hence an exponential growth in computing power—has held roughly true for 50 years, since the chipmaker Gordon Moore first made that prediction in 1965, although it appears the rate of growth is now finally slowing.[22]

New words must be coined to describe the number of bytes—the basic unit of digital memory, usually consisting of an 'octet' string of eight 1s and 0s—of information stored online: from the megabytes (MB, or $1,000^2$ bytes) and gigabytes (GB, or $1,000^3$ bytes) we have on our personal computers, all the way to the exabyte, zettabyte and yottabyte, or 1,000,000,000,000,000,000,000,000 individual bytes.[23] According to an estimate by Cisco, it would take you about 6 million years to watch all the videos crossing global networks in a single month.[24]

As of 2015, there are already somewhere around 3 billion internet users, depending exactly how you define internet and user, and that number is growing

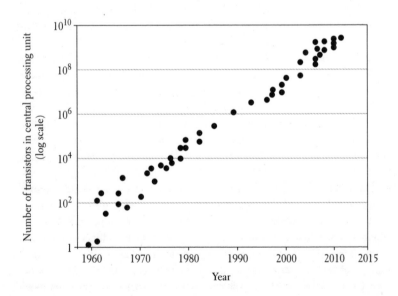

Figure 4. Moore's Law
Source: Intel/The Economist, 2015.

rapidly.[25] The fastest growth will come in the non-Western world, in wireless rather than wired and especially on mobile devices. There are perhaps 2 billion smartphones across the world and that is projected to reach 4 billion by 2020.[26] Some 85 percent of the world's population is within reach of a mobile phone tower which has the capacity to relay data. Tim Berners-Lee and Mark Zuckerberg have been among those campaigning to achieve internet access for all.[27]

Billions of people are still excluded from this unprecedented network of communication. As Map 1 shows, internet access is very unevenly distributed across the globe.

Even if you have regular, affordable access to the internet, which so many still do not, you need a minimum level of education to use it. According to UN estimates, some 900 million of the world's people are still illiterate, and that is using the minimal literacy criterion that a person 'can with understanding both read and write a short simple statement on his or her everyday life'. As can be seen from Map 2, in several African countries more than half the population is illiterate even by this minimal standard.[28]

The level of education needed to join in a wider online conversation, let alone a global one, is clearly higher than that. You also need basic facilities such as light to read by. I have neither the space nor the professional competence to examine these human development preconditions for free speech, but they are clearly vital. Thus, much of what I write in this book currently applies only to about half of humankind, although that proportion is increasing.

Technologically, however, there is no longer any reason why everyone in the world should not in future be connected with everyone else, and with almost everything known, through a small handheld box. In his satirical novel *Super Sad True Love Story*, Gary Shteyngart calls such a box 'the äppärät'. (The plural, in case you were wondering, is 'äppäräti'.)[29] For our purposes, it is both futile and unnecessary to speculate, gush or moan about the next phases of this great convergence. Fortunes will be made and lost, commercial empires rise and fall, the latest innovation be lauded to the skies even as its nemesis is being developed by someone even younger, working down the road in Palo Alto, Bangalore or the Haidian district of Beijing.

Without slavering over the technical details, we can safely say that in the second decade of the twenty-first century anyone with a smartphone, sufficient education to use it and money to get data access has already reached the converged world of the äppärät. Every traditionally distinct medium of expression ('newspaper', 'radio', 'film', 'television', 'orchestra'), source of information and ideas ('book', 'archive', 'journal') and channel of communication ('phone', 'email', 'text message', 'videoconference') is or soon will be available through

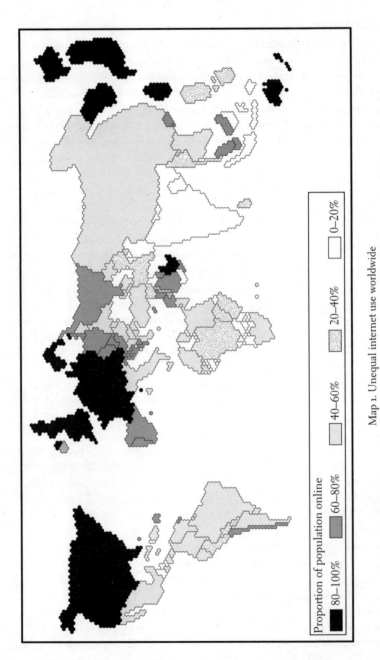

Map 1. Unequal internet use worldwide

Country sizes are proportionate to absolute numbers of users. Countries with fewer than 470,000 people online are omitted.

Source: Oxford Internet Institute, 2013.

Proportion of population online

80–100% 60–80% 40–60% 20–40% 0–20%

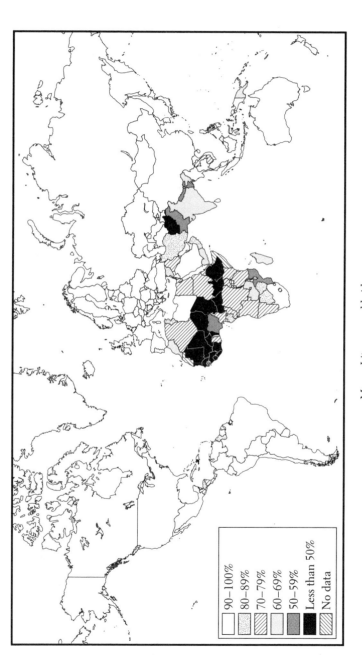

Map 2. Literacy worldwide
The map shows adult literacy according to the minimal definition explained in the text.
Source: UNESCO Institute for Statistics, 2013.

90–100%
80–89%
70–79%
60–69%
50–59%
Less than 50%
No data

that box in your hand. Or if you prefer it another way, it may be a large screen in the corner of your living room, or a small device attached to your wrist or a chip implanted inside your skull. Figure 5 shows, in round figures, the main stages on this path to a connected world.

Since the satirical umlauts of Shteyngart's äppäräti could begin to pall, I refer throughout this book to that universal communication device simply as your 'box'. And I use the word 'internet', with a lowercase *i*, in a deliberately broad sense, to denote the whole of this worldwide information and communications network—its universality still seriously limited by political, legal, cultural and economic constraints, but not by technological ones.

The internet subverts the traditional unities of time and space. It telescopes space, making us virtual neighbours, but it also concertinas time. Once something is up there online, it is usually there forever. Whether an ill-advised remark was made this morning or 20 years ago, if it comes up in an online search it is still, in some important and novel sense, part of the here and now. Only with the greatest difficulty can stuff be entirely removed, the published unpublished.

One further technological possibility demands a mention: that of computers achieving a level of artificial intelligence at which they may be judged themselves to speak. While cyberutopians join Ray Kurzweil in envisaging the glorious moment when artificial and human intelligence merge into one transformative 'singularity', cyberdystopians fear machine intelligence first overtaking

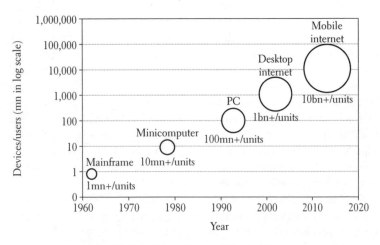

Figure 5. More devices than people
Source: Adapted from Mary Meeker, Internet Trends 2014.

and then taking over humans—like the mesmerically voiced computer HAL in Stanley Kubrick's '2001: A Space Odyssey', but this time with HAL coming out on top.[30]

We are not there yet, even if the hypnotic lady speaking from the GPS in your car adjusts her instructions as you change your route, and your handheld box, using software such as Apple's Siri, can respond to your spoken requests exploiting all the information she's got on you. Already in the 1960s, the computer scientist Joseph Weizenbaum developed a computer programme named Eliza, after Eliza Doolittle in George Bernard Shaw's *Pygmalion*—better known as Julie Andrews in 'My Fair Lady'.[31] Eliza was capable of having rudimentary conversations with people, of a vacuously sympathetic kind ('I am sorry to hear you are depressed'). More recently, a chatbot called Eugene Goostman was alleged by its developers to have passed the Turing test—can you tell if you are talking to a human or machine?—although that claim was soon disputed.[32] Many Chinese have apparently found comfort in talking to a purportedly female Microsoft chatbot called Xiaoice.[33]

Leading scientists have argued that artificial intelligence may be upon us sooner than we think and that we should address the issue seriously.[34] Since, however, there is still a little while to go until that singular moment, this book is concerned only with human speech—not that attributed to other animals or to machines. There are, to be sure, already important questions to be asked about what the legal scholar Tim Wu has called 'machine speech', and I return to them under principle 9, when considering the ethics of algorithms. Thus far, however, the pertinent questions mainly concern what human programmers set machines to do algorithmically, rather than what an evolved machine intelligence has, in some significant sense, decided to say for itself. The greater the input of human opinion or value judgement, the clearer the free speech issue.[35]

Moreover, even the most astonishing communication technology caters for just two of our five senses: smell, touch and taste currently remain almost entirely beyond their reach. An online banquet will not fill your stomach, and virtual sex is not the real thing.[36] (Some phones and game consoles offer rudimentary touch experiences. There is also a field called teledildonics, involving devices that claim to purvey sexual satisfaction without direct physical contact, but I leave in-depth research on that to others.)

For all the wonders of the online world, the fullest range of human communication is still achieved only in a direct personal encounter. Here, the original power of speech combines with physical signals that we aptly call 'body language'. Face to face, subtle variations of vocal timbre, a tilt of the head, a softening of the eyes and a touch of the hand, all complement those modulations of air pumped through the vocal tract. It is in such unmediated human encounters that words come closest to deeds, and sometimes the word becomes flesh. Who knows, perhaps bioengineering and communications technology will one day combine to reproduce cybercognitively, at a distance of thousands of miles, the incomparable richness of that experience. In the meantime, what characterises our transformed world is external combinations of the virtual and the physical, as a result of developments that I summarise as 'mass migration and the internet'.

COSMOPOLIS

In a book called *The Gutenberg Galaxy*, published in 1962, the media guru Marshall McLuhan declared that 'the new electronic interdependence recreates the world in the image of a global village'.[37] This was an extraordinary seerlike insight, well ahead of its time, but McLuhan's simile of 'global village' is inadequate, both as description and prescription. Villages are small, usually homogeneous and conformist places. Tolerance is not their hallmark. When things get rough, villagers who have been neighbours all their lives can end up murdering each other: Serb and Bosniak, Hutu and Tutsi. 'Global village' is neither where we are nor where we should want to be.

Being electronic neighbours is more like living in a global city. Most of the time we encounter people from different cultures and backgrounds only superficially, in the subway, bus or shop. We can choose to visit that Indian, Chinese or French restaurant down the road, or not. Occasionally, we come together for a big shared occasion: a football game, perhaps, a concert or a rally. Sometimes, however, a more or less chance encounter can lead to a life-changing interaction, be it a business partnership, an exhilarating romance or a traumatic assault. So it is online. This is the world-as-city.

'City air makes free', says a medieval German proverb. 'By its nature', wrote the theologian Paul Tillich, 'the metropolis provides what otherwise could be given only by travelling; namely, the strange. Since the strange leads to questions and undermines familiar tradition, it serves to elevate reason to ultimate significance'.[38] This is an inspiring thought, but cities inhabited by people from everywhere, and their descendants, also have furious rows about Islamic centres, sectarian marches and controversial plays and books. These cities are buffeted by the hatred of neighbours, intolerance of difference, calls for censorship and self-censorship. They are shaken by race and faith riots, and by a young Muslim man who calmly goes out to murder a Dutch filmmaker on an Amsterdam winter's morning in 2004. At his trial, the assassin said that divine law did not allow him to live 'in any country where free speech is allowed'. But instead of returning to his parents' country, Morocco, where free speech was distinctly limited, he tried to strangle free speech in the Netherlands, where he lived. Mohammed Bouyeri, the young man who murdered the filmmaker Theo van Gogh, was a frequenter of, and contributor to, jihadi websites. Now more than ever, sentences typed on keyboards can become sentences of death.[39]

Since the term 'global city' is already in use to describe big, multicultural cities like London, New York or Tokyo, and it would be clumsy to repeat the phrase 'world-as-city' every time, I have revised and extended an old word, 'cosmopolis', using it to embrace the entirety of this mixed-up, connected world-as-city.[40]

Cosmopolis is the transformed context for any discussion of free speech in our time. Cosmopolis exists in the interconnected physical and virtual worlds and is therefore, to borrow a phrase from James Joyce's *Finnegans Wake*, 'urban and orbal'. The taxi driver parked outside my home in Oxford reads a paper that carries news from Britain in English and from Pakistan in Urdu. Thanks to electronic communication, what is published in Bradford will often be accessible in Lahore and vice versa. If the norms for freedom of expression differ starkly between the two places—if, for example, it is normal to question Islam in one place and unacceptable in the other—then violent responses become more likely, in one country or both.

Many of the defining free speech moments of our time have precisely this dual, urban-orbal character. In 1989, the novelist Salman Rushdie's life was endangered because an ayatollah in distant Tehran issued a fatwa ('what's a fatwa?' exclaimed Rushdie's American publisher, back in those innocent days) and the news travelled rapidly around the world.[41] The threat had to be taken seriously, not least because Rushdie lived in a city (London) and a country where many Muslims now also lived, and it would take only one of them to carry out Ayatollah Khomeini's injunction. A study of the worldwide storm that followed the publication in 2005 of cartoons of Muhammad by the Danish newspaper Jyllands-Posten—the 'Danish cartoons'—estimates that more than 240 people died in the course of demonstrations against them.[42] None of those deaths was in Denmark, and only one was in Europe; most were in countries such as Nigeria, Pakistan, Libya and Afghanistan. At the end of this chapter, I tell the tragifarcical story of how in 2012 a ridiculous anti-Islamic YouTube video clip posted by a convicted fraudster in southern California occasioned the death of more than 50 people—none of them in the United States. In 2015, people rioted and died in Pakistan and Niger over cartoons published in Charlie Hebdo, a French satirical magazine that the protesters had never seen.[43]

A man publishes something in one country and a man dies in another. Someone threatens violence in that other country and a performance or publication is halted in the first. In this disturbing way, too, we are all neighbours now.

CYBERSPACE, CA 94305

Vaulting political and moral claims have often been made for new technologies of communication. Martin Luther said printing was 'God's highest and extremest act of grace'.[44] In 1881, Scientific American magazine hailed 'the moral influence' of the telegraph.[45] 'The fax will set you free', the American nuclear strategist Albert Wohlstetter proclaimed in an article published in 1990.[46] Equally vaulting claims have been made for the internet: some suggest that it will inevitably produce a heaven of free speech and political liberation, others, a hell of corporate exploitation and totalitarian surveillance.

Here is the fallacy of technological determinism. The fax never set anyone free. People set people free. The telegraph, like the printing press, was used to transmit the best and the worst of which humans are capable. But equally, we should not fall for the opposite fallacy: that technologies are entirely neutral. Rather, they possess what have been called affordances.[47] New technologies afford possibilities that were not there before, or not in the same degree. To be sure, if someone gives you a wheel, you can lay the wheel on its side and sit on it, but the new possibility it affords is for you to travel farther, faster and carrying a heavier load than you could before.

What are the most characteristic affordances of the internet? Put most simply: it is easier to make things public and more difficult to keep things private. The first affordance has a great liberating potential, especially for free speech; the second harbours an oppressive potential, including a threat to free speech. If a state or corporation knows everything that we express to everyone, we will be less free. That includes things we don't even intend to say, but reveal through our online search histories. Even if we merely fear that some governmental or corporate Big Brother knows what we express in private, we will speak less freely. (I explore the relationship between privacy and free expression more fully under principle 7.)

All such artefacts and systems were designed by particular men and women, in a particular time and place, and bear the marks of those origins. In the case of the internet, those men and women were mostly Americans, or English speakers working in America, from the 1950s to the 1990s.[48] The Internet, in the original, more specific sense, with a capital *I*, is not as American as motherhood and apple pie. The Internet is more American than motherhood and apple pie—both of which are, after all, occasionally to be found in other civilisations. It is a product of Cold War America at the height of its power, self-confidence and capacity for innovation.

Generous funding from the Pentagon's Advanced Research Projects Agency, which was originally set up in response to the Soviet Union's launch of the Sputnik satellite, brought together a strange but dynamic ménage-à-trois of government agencies, private corporations and computer engineers.[49] These engineers did not just have tools, they also had views—and generally their views had a strong libertarian strain. 'We reject: kings, presidents, and voting', one of them famously observed. 'We believe in: rough consensus and running code'. So they made it up as they went along. 'Ready, fire, aim!' was another of their mottoes.[50] An informal organisation called the Internet Engineering Task Force has played an important role in shaping the internet ever since.

The word 'Internet' originally derived from 'internetworking' between three Pentagon-funded computer networks, and it won out over the alternatives precisely because it was designed to operate between differently configured machines and networks.[51] The defining feature of the internet is not any physical object but a software protocol suite called TCP/IP, which has allowed millions of computers across the planet to connect and route what a British scientist christened 'packets' of information between them.[52] For some of those involved, one reason for developing a 'distributed network', in which packets could reach their destinations via multiple alternative routes, was to increase the chances of information still getting through after a first nuclear strike.[53] But their American libertarian convictions also fed into this notion of free passage irrespective of content: you pass my packets, I'll pass yours. Later, this would be elaborated into the broader principle of 'net neutrality', rejecting any discrimination on grounds of the content of the packet, the identity of its sender or the application used.[54] (More on this under principle 9.) So the deep architecture of the internet was also culturally determined. It seems a fair guess that Soviet or Iranian engineers would have come up with something so different that we would not recognise it as 'the internet'.

The private enterprises that first seized the chances offered by the internet were equally American. I am writing these words just up the road from the original location of the Stanford Research Institute, where that first message of the internet age ('Lo') was delivered. Within a radius of forty miles from Stanford, I can visit Google, Facebook, Twitter, Intel, Oracle, Cisco and Wikipedia. While these private superpowers differ from each other in many respects, they are all the products of a unique American conjuncture of innovation, power and ideology.

'Cyberspace' is a word coined by the science fiction writer William Gibson in a short story published in 1982 ('Burning Chrome') and subsequently used in his novel *Neuromancer*. In the 1990s, as science fiction seemed to be becoming fact, American cyberlibertarian hopes for a global newfoundland of freedom soared to giddy heights. John Perry Barlow, a passionate advocate for internet freedom and former lyricist of the rock band the Grateful Dead, produced in 1996 a Declaration of the Independence of Cyberspace, with obvious echoes of the 1776 Declaration of Independence. It even denounced 'hostile and colonial measures', as if King George III were about to dispatch his redcoats into cyberspace.

'Governments of the Industrial World', the declaration began, 'you weary giants of flesh and steel, I come from Cyberspace, the new home of Mind. On behalf of the future, I ask you of the past to leave us alone. You are not welcome among us. You have no sovereignty where we gather'. Heralding a 'global social space' and 'a great and gathering conversation', Barlow wrote, 'We are creating a world where anyone, anywhere may express his or her beliefs, no matter how singular, without fear of being coerced into silence or conformity'. Governments, he boldly claimed, did not 'possess any methods of enforcement we have true reason to fear'.[55]

This rousing piece of American prose perfectly expresses the hopes of freedom, and free speech in particular, attached to the internet. It also exemplifies a profound illusion. For the internet never has been independent of the influence of governments, corporations and other terrestrial powers. Rather, it has been decisively shaped by them—and is now being fought over by them.

Its initial development was paid for by the US Department of Defense. Since 1998, new top-level domain names (such as .com, .net, .org), and the numerical IP addresses that underpin the whole worldwide system, have been assigned by a supposedly multistakeholder Internet Corporation for Assigned Names and Numbers, ICANN. But ICANN is a nonprofit corporation registered in the state of California, and its naming power long remained ultimately subject to a US government contract. (The Obama administration finally decided to change this as a symbolic concession to a changing world.)[56] Across the planet, .gov refers to just one national government. Guess which. Everyone else has to be .gov.cn, .gov.br, .gov.uk and so on. You could not ask for a better ostensive definition of hegemony.

The global free speech opportunities offered by the first decades of the internet also have much to do with its American origins and location. Its founders lived, and their operations enjoyed the protection of, the most systematically pro–free speech jurisdiction in the world. This tradition is classically identified with the 1791 First Amendment to the US Constitution, the relevant words of which read 'Congress shall make no law . . . abridging the freedom of speech, or of the press'. But America's First Amendment culture, as we know it today, is in fact the product of judicial rulings, laws and political decisions over the 100 years since the First World War, and mainly from the last half century.

One that has been crucial to global internet freedom is buried away in section 230 of the Communications Decency Act, the very law against an earlier, more restrictive version of which Barlow's broadside was directed. Section 230 states that 'no provider or user of an interactive computer service shall be treated as the publisher or speaker of any information provided by another information content provider'.[57] So the intermediary is not responsible. This exclusion is so sweeping that some American legal scholars have argued that it should be amended or even repealed.[58] Yet it is thanks to these 26 words of US law that every month many millions of people around the world can access on google.com (the US mother site, not to be confused with google.fr, google.de etc., which are subject to local laws) such a large proportion of everything ever said, thought, sung or depicted by humankind. At the same time, if there is something you are looking for and cannot find, it may well be because a copyright holder has successfully demanded that it be taken down under another US law, the 1998 Digital Millennium Copyright Act. Whether you are in Yangon, Accra or Sao Paolo, if you can get unrestricted access to google.com it is as if, for the hours that you are online, you have virtually emigrated to the United States. Provided only—and there's the rub—that your own government, or another local power, does not catch and punish you for doing so.

In its purest form, this freedom of virtual emigration to the US can be seen in the multiple language, user-generated encyclopaedia Wikipedia, one of the world's most visited online resources. Mike Godwin, a pioneering American cyberlawyer and for some years the online encyclopaedia's senior legal counsel, argued that so long as Wikipedia kept all its servers, legal entities, funds and staff in the United States, it would be, as he expressed it to me, 'behind a legal firewall'.[59] It could therefore be a global First Amendment space, in all its many languages. For any Wikipedia entry in any language, the rule is the same: only if you can get a US court to say that an American law has been broken will you have legal redress. If you raise a reasonable objection, you may secure an editorial correction from the community of Wikipedia editors in your language. If you are a Wikipedia contributor—a 'Wikipedian'—in a less free country, you may get called in for questioning, or worse, by local powerholders. But legally speaking, this worldwide information trove is answerable only in the United States. Tellingly, when the Wikimedia foundation briefly opened an office in

India it soon closed it again, after coming under pressure from the Indian authorities over maps depicting Kashmir—accurately—as divided between India and Pakistan.

Thus, while the Grateful Dead lyricist of cyberspace crooned that governments 'have no sovereignty where we gather', it is precisely the old-fashioned territorial sovereignty of the United States that underpinned this great leap forward in global freedom of expression. To capture the dualistic nature of this American-rooted global realm I call it 'Cyberspace, CA 94305'. 94305 is the zip code of Stanford University. Google's original web address was google.stanford.edu. When President Barack Obama casually told a tech journal interviewer that 'we have owned the internet' he was perhaps being a little impolitic, but not inaccurate—so long as one notes the past tense.[60]

Future historians may count these global networks of electronic communication, and their deliberate openness, among the most important legacies of the 'liberal leviathan'.[61] In the twenty-first century, however, previously open, free-wheeling technologies of communication are being reined in and constrained by both public and private powers—as happened to all their predecessors, from printing to radio.[62] And the United States is no longer the digital hegemon it was in the 1990s, at what was perhaps the apogee of American power.[63] Today, cyberspace has multiple zip codes and every aspect of global communication is contested.

THE STRUGGLE FOR WORD POWER

Unnoticed by many of us, a great power struggle over the shape, terms and limits of global freedom of expression is raging around us, inside that box in your pocket and perhaps even inside our heads. I call it the struggle for *word power*. Like the 'speech' in 'free speech', the 'word' in 'word power' obviously involves much more than words. It includes images, sounds, symbols, information and knowledge, as well as structures and networks of communication. Manuel Castells talks of 'communication power', but I prefer the short word to the long, especially since any label will only capture part of the whole.[64]

The nature of the power involved here is complex. One of the simplest definitions of power is the ability to get what you want. That in turn leads us to ask who gets what, how, where and when. Joseph Nye and Steven Lukes have helpfully identified three dimensions of power. First, and most obviously, there is getting someone to do something that is not his or her initial preference. You make me do it. Second, there is agenda-setting, or 'the power to decide what is decided', as Lukes puts it. Third, and most subtly, there is the capacity to shape people's initial preferences, so they don't even realise that the choices they make result from the prior exercise of power by others. Many observers would instinctively assign word power to the realm of 'soft power', but Nye, the scholar who has most rigorously defined soft power, rightly notes that when it comes to cyberpower you can find examples of hard and soft in all three dimensions.[65]

Clearly, the control of knowledge and information is a vital part of the second and third dimensions. Francis Bacon famously observed that knowledge is power, while Michel Foucault turned that round to assert that power 'determines what counts as knowledge'. Given the now well-established plasticity of the brain, the impacts of new information and communication technologies, and how we use them, arguably go even deeper, changing the way we think and feel. In his wonderful essay *Petite Poucette* (Little Thumbelina), the French academician Michel Serres writes of the thumbelinas and thumbelins, the generations who live toggling their thumbs on a smartscreen. 'They no longer have the same head' (i.e., as us oldies), he says.[66] A delightful exaggeration.

I am very far from dismissing the importance of a theoretical analysis of the kinds of power involved here, but that would require another book. Moreover, it may help to gather more evidence of what actually goes on in this transformed world before ascending to the heights of system analysis. So I shall not offer any elaborate typology, such as Castells's mind-stretching distinction between networking power, network power, networked power and network-making power (the last being the highest level, exercised only by 'meta-programmers').[67] Instead, I shall identify the main players in this power struggle and let its character emerge through examples.

Plainly, this is no longer just a matter of a single national government telling you what you may or may not publish or broadcast in one country, or a single newspaper proprietor deciding what it will or will not print—the classic territory of twentieth-century literature on free speech. Even these old-fashioned print matters are not as clear-cut as they once seemed. For example, in 2005 an American author, Rachel Ehrenfeld, was held liable for libel by an English court. A Saudi businessman had sued her in London, and the English court accepted that it had jurisdiction because 23 copies of her book on the funding of Islamist terrorism, published only in the United States, had been sold via the internet to addresses in Britain.[68] In response, the New York State legislature passed an act—informally known as 'Rachel's Law'—that protected US citizens within its jurisdiction from the enforcement of foreign libel judgements that did not meet American First Amendment and due process standards.[69] In 2010, President Barack Obama signed into law a so-called SPEECH Act which had the same effect across the United States. (In the cringe-making acronymics beloved of the US Congress, SPEECH stood for 'Securing the Protection of our Enduring and Established Constitutional Heritage'.)

In practice, however, the law of every country struggles to keep up with the latest technical innovation, like an elderly gentleman puffing along the pavement to catch his bus. With three clicks of my computer mouse, I can have delivered to my home in England, from amazon.com or another foreign-based website, a printed book that the government or courts in London would otherwise forbid me to see. Milton, whose *Areopagitica* is one great broadside against the English authorities restricting what printed matter can be read in their realm, will be cheering from beyond the grave. In fact, after writing these words I just ordered Rachel's book from amazon.com: click-click-click and so much for that English judge. Or you can download the e-book. (As we will see, a subsequent reform of English libel law significantly reduced the possibilities for egregious 'libel tourism'.)

Online, the struggle is more complicated still. A plethora of international organisations, national governments, parliaments, companies, engineers, media outlets, celebrity tweeters and physical and virtual mass campaigns through social networks all now compete in a multilevel, multidimensional game. The outcome often hinges on intricate intersections between business, politics, law, regulation and rapidly developing technologies of communication. One of the pioneers in this area, Lawrence Lessig, identifies four different kinds of constraint acting on any given point in the global information system: law, the market, norms and the architecture of the internet. 'Code is law', he said, in perhaps his most famous apothegm, explaining that 'the software and hardware (i.e., the 'code' of cyberspace) that make cyberspace what it is also regulate cyberspace as it is'.[70] The internal, sometimes secret, operational practices of private superpowers may be more influential than the decisions of lawmakers and regulators.

For all this complexity, we can get a long way with the analogy of dogs, cats and mice.[71] Governments are the dogs, companies are the cats and we are the mice. The biggest cats are more powerful than all but the very biggest dogs. The fascination of Google clashing with China, as it did in 2010 when it withdrew its mainland-based search engine google.cn, citing Chinese online censorship and hacking into Gmail accounts, is that this was one of the world's biggest cats facing one of the world's biggest dogs. At least as common, however, is close, sometimes covert collaboration between governments and the internet service providers, publishers, and media and data companies active in their territories. This I call 'power squared' or P^2 for short. Meanwhile, both governments and companies work to influence international organisations that set rules or technical standards for global communications.

Cyberspace is not a separate, unitary state, with its own laws, courts and police, but neither is it simply a patchwork quilt of national jurisdictions. It is something in between, with many mongrel forms of life—a confused reality inadequately papered over by such labels as 'multistakeholder' or 'the internet community'. Dismayed by American dominance of key areas of the internet, albeit in 'multistakeholder' community-wrapping, other states, and especially emerging powers such as China, have for years tried to assert the control of a UN agency called the International Telecommunication Union.

Of course the UN's role in influencing and to some extent regulating global freedom of expression is not confined to the internet. Article 19 of the 1948 UN Declaration of Human Rights proclaimed that 'Everyone has the right to freedom of opinion and expression: this right includes freedom to hold opinions without interference and to seek, receive and impart information and ideas through any media and regardless of frontiers'. At a time when international broadcasting was still in its infancy and the internet barely a twinkle in a science fiction writer's eye, this last phrase was groundbreaking in its explicit defiance of national borders. 'Regardless of frontiers'![72]

The original 1948 version was elaborated into Article 19 of the 1966 International Covenant on Civil and Political Rights. (To avoid an eczema of acronyms, I shorten that mouthful throughout this book to 'the Covenant', although this is not the only International Covenant.)[73] Its central formula is similar, but more detailed: 'Everyone shall have the right to freedom of expression; this right shall include freedom to seek, receive and impart information and ideas of all kinds, regardless of frontiers, either orally, in writing or in print, in the form of art, or through any other media of his choice'. But it is more explicit in spelling out legitimate restrictions, 'such as are provided by law and are necessary: (a) for respect of the rights or reputations of others; (b) for the protection of national security or of public order (*ordre public*), or of public health or morals'. It is further qualified by Article 20, which demands that both 'any propaganda for war' and 'any advocacy of national, racial or religious hatred that constitutes incitement to discrimination, hostility or violence' shall be 'prohibited by law'.

I'll have more to say about these canonical texts and their fiercely contested interpretation. The point here, as we discern the outlines of the struggle raging around our heads, is that—as Map 3 shows—this is an international treaty which most states in the world have signed and ratified.

Of the few that have not, the most important is China, which has signed but not yet ratified. Saudi Arabia has not even signed. Nor has the Vatican. (What is it about these guardians of holy places?)[74] Once ratified, the Covenant is in theory 'legally binding' on the signatory state. This means a state is supposed

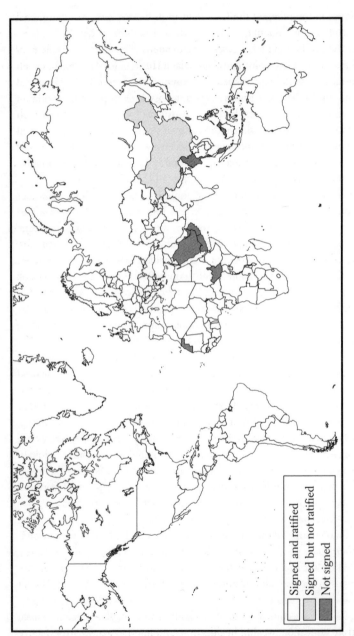

Map 3: A world notionally signed up to free speech

States that have signed and in most cases ratified the International Covenant on Civil and Political Rights, Article 19 of which promises free speech.

Signed and ratified

Signed but not ratified

Not signed

to guarantee and implement the Covenant in its domestic political and legal system.[75] But what if it doesn't?

The UN has a Human Rights Committee to interpret and monitor implementation of this Covenant. Confusingly, it also has a Human Rights Council, which nominates a UN special rapporteur on freedom of expression. Both the special rapporteur and the Human Rights Committee issue detailed reports and can point the finger at errant states. In 2011, the Human Rights Committee, which at that time included representatives from Egypt, Algeria and Colombia, as well as those from established democracies, produced a so-called General Comment on Article 19.[76] This is a clear, remarkably liberal and in some sense authoritative interpretation of what the words of Article 19 should be taken to mean.

In addition, as you can see in Map 4, some 115 states have signed another international agreement, catchily named the First Optional Protocol.[77] This provides that individual men and women, once they have exhausted all domestic remedies, can take their complaint directly to the UN Human Rights Committee, arguing that their Article 19 rights have been violated by their own authorities. In response to such individual appeals, the committee has ruled that the Uzbek and Belarussian governments were wrong to refuse the registration and distribution of particular newspapers, that South Korea should not have arrested a painter who depicted his country as an American puppet and so on.[78] But this committee has no means of compelling a government to mend its ways.

The moral and symbolic importance of this canopy of international law and accompanying institutions should not be dismissed. It provides a universal frame of reference for embattled individuals and groups as well as for national and international campaigners. The news that a UN committee or rapporteur has condemned or praised this or that action of a government may be noted, and occasionally carry weight, in the media and parliaments of countries where such statements are allowed to be quoted. Even where they are not, the globalisation of electronic communications allows the message to flow across national borders more than it could when that resonant phrase 'regardless of frontiers' was coined, in the first fine rapture of post-1945 liberal internationalism.

Yet the governments most likely to take note of such UN admonitions are the ones that incline to adhere to those values anyway. Those that don't, won't. Worse, their sleek plenipotentiaries will pay lip service to freedom of expression at endless international meetings, even as, back home, their torturers are strangling it. As the poet James Fenton advises: 'Listen to what they did. / Don't listen to what they said'.[79]

So we do, after all, come back to the individual dogs and cats. If I do not have the requisite education, wealth, health, time and internet access, my effective

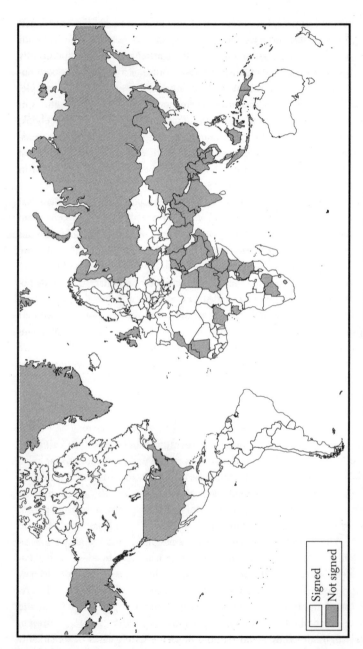

Map 4. But can I take my case to the UN Human Rights Committee?
States that have signed the First Optional Protocol to the International Covenant on Civil and Political Rights.
Source: UN.

freedom of expression will be severely curtailed by my personal circumstances. For the rest of us, who do have those basic capabilities, the main limits to our effective freedom of expression are set by the state in which we are currently located, the companies and organisations that control our mediums of communication and the interaction between that dog and those cats. If, for example, I live in Paris, my effective freedom of expression is a product of conditions in the real country of France, but also those in virtual countries called Facebook, Google and Twitter, and the other platforms, publishers, broadcasters, newspapers, universities and so on that function where I live. If I live in northeast Senegal, then what matters most to me are the conditions at this moment in northeast Senegal; if in Peru, those in Peru.

Each of us therefore needs his or her own freedom of expression map that includes, at a minimum, the country in which we currently reside and the main information platforms and media available to us there. That's close to 200 maps if you do it by country, or more than 7 billion by individual person, and the contours on each map keep shifting.

Yet there is a much smaller group of states and corporations that have the potential to shape the architecture, market, law and norms (to recall Lessig's fourfold distinction) of the global information and communications system which I call, in shorthand, the internet. Sometimes they have this effect without meaning to, just by being what they are and doing what they do, but often they are consciously competing to shape that system. The struggle for word power is also a struggle for world power.

BIG DOGS

In the second decade of the twenty-first century, the United States is still the biggest dog. It is the most powerful country in the world, is home to the most widely used global platforms of electronic communication and has the most explicit, systematically implemented commitment to free speech. These three dimensions account for the unique reach and character of American word power.

From Palo Alto to Washington and from New York to Seattle, whether in government, the press, information companies, nongovernmental organisations (NGOs) or academia, you encounter Americans who have imbibed a particular approach to free speech with mother's milk, at high school, university and law school—or, if they are more recent arrivals, have adopted it with varying degrees of enthusiasm. Terms of art derived from the judicial, political and journalistic elaboration of the First Amendment—'public forum', 'common carriage', 'fighting words'—and seminal Supreme Court cases of remarkably recent date—New York Times v Sullivan (1964), Brandenburg v Ohio (1969)—have acquired quasi-biblical status, and this approach has been extended to the analysis, design and operation of global information networks. Wherever you turn, these sons and daughters of the Church of the First Amendment are labouring in the virtual vineyard.

In the conditions of a global cosmopolis, what they do inside the United States has an impact far beyond the country's borders, even when that is not their intention. So far as the United States deliberately projecting American principles abroad is concerned, there is more than one tradition. Walter Russell Mead has identified four main schools of American foreign policy—Jeffersonian, Hamiltonian, Jacksonian and Wilsonian—and each suggests a somewhat different attitude to the global promotion of the American version of free speech.[80] Yet, painting with a broad brush, one can describe the most characteristic American approach as unilateral universalism. Essentially, the claim—and, so far as I can judge, usually also the genuine belief—is that the whole world would be better off if it adopted the First Amendment tradition. Lee Bollinger, a First Amendment scholar and longtime president of Columbia University, makes this explicit, arguing that 'we need to do on a global stage what was done on the US national stage over the 20th century'.[81]

In a speech delivered in 2010 at the Newseum, a museum of journalism in Washington, US Secretary of State Hillary Clinton drew a straight line from the First Amendment to what she called 'internet freedom'. Citing Franklin D. Roosevelt's 1941 speech enumerating four freedoms—of expression and of worship, from want and from fear—she effectively added a fifth, the freedom to connect. 'We stand', she said, 'for a single internet where all of humanity has equal access to knowledge and ideas'. Internet blocking firewalls should come down, as the Berlin Wall came down in 1989.[82]

The United States has long used respect for freedom of expression and worship as key criteria in rating other states. In 2012, a State Department spokesperson admonished India, the world's largest democracy, for blocking websites and social media platforms which the Indian government argued were helping to foment intercommunal violence.[83] The US government also developed a small programme to fund technologies that would help circumvent internet-blocking firewalls built by authoritarian regimes such as Iran and China. The American understanding of 'internet freedom' thus embraced two distinct but related ideas: a general principle that the internet should be open, free and neutral, as envisaged by its American libertarian inventors, and the specific idea that social networks, smartphones and the like could furnish 'liberation technology', helping people to challenge authoritarian regimes.[84]

American officials energetically promote these principles in international organisations and fora, citing the relevant international agreements, from Article 19 and on down. Yet there is a peculiarity which leads me to describe this American approach as unilateral universalism. While the liberal leviathan is keen for such international agreements to be as binding as possible on others, it is less keen to apply them to itself. The United States guards its own sovereignty as jealously as do China, India and other postcolonial states. One analyst uncharitably characterises the American attitude as 'our sovereignty is absolute, other people's is negotiable'.[85]

A small but telling example is the First Optional Protocol to the Covenant, which entitles individual citizens to take their cases to the UN Human Rights Committee if they feel their Article 19 rights have been violated by their government. The US government supported the adoption of this protocol but has not itself adopted it.[86] So the highest free speech commandment for all humankind must be Article 19, except in the United States, where no commandment may be higher than the First Amendment.

There is another ambivalence in the US position. Even as the State Department has funded the development of circumvention technologies, to help dissidents get round the firewalls of Iran or China, other arms of the US government, such as the Departments of Homeland Security, Defense and Commerce, have tried to prevent the use of such technologies against the US, or what they see as American interests. When Wikileaks published a vast trove of State Department diplomatic despatches, one of the tools it used was Tor, a software to facilitate online anonymity developed with US government funding. Washington was, so to speak, hoist with its own cyberpetard.

It is, of course, possible to claim consistency in this position. The US supports such technologies to promote the spread of good things (democracy, human rights, free speech) and opposes them to prevent the spread of bad ones (terrorism, cybercrime, child pornography, infringements of intellectual property). But who decides what is good or bad? The United States. A State Department spokesperson, asked to explain the apparent inconsistency between her criticism of the Indian government for blocking sites the Indian government considered dangerous and Washington's own stance on Wikileaks, said: 'WikiLeaks didn't have to do with freedom of the internet. It had to do with . . . the compromise of US Government classified information'.[87] While governments must naturally assert perfect consistency, there is a tension here, as America's left hand points in a different direction to and sometimes wrestles with its right. In a reference to Hillary Clinton, this has been called the Clinton Paradox.[88]

With these reservations, it is nonetheless fair to say that the United States remains at once the most powerful and the most consistently pro–free speech state in the early-twenty-first-century world.

The second biggest dog in the West, which goes by the name of Europe, is not really a single dog but rather an intercanine league. In fact, to make things simple, it is three distinct intercanine fraternities, the largest of which, the 56-state Organisation for Security and Cooperation in Europe (OSCE), includes the United States and Canada. These three Europes overlap, as can be seen in Map 5.

The largest is, however, the least effective of the trio. The OSCE's monitoring bodies, and especially its representative on freedom of the media, play a mainly admonitory role. They can, for instance, criticise member states such as Russia and Uzbekistan for allowing their journalists to be murdered or tortured. Like the work of the special rapporteurs of other regional organisations, such as the Organisation of African States and the African Commission on Human and People's Rights, this may have some impact if it is picked up by national and international media, domestic political forces and external powers with leverage in the country concerned, but its direct effect is modest.

What makes Europe a superpower in this global struggle is the combined effect of two other leagues: the 47-state Council of Europe and the 28-state European Union (EU). They work in different ways. The Council of Europe is the guardian of the European Convention on Human Rights, which came into force in 1953. 'Everyone has the right to freedom of expression', declares its Article 10, which uses language similar to the original Article 19 of the UN Declaration of Human Rights — including that futuristic phrase 'regardless of frontiers'. However, the second part of Article 10 specifies that restrictions may be made 'as are prescribed by law and are necessary in a democratic society, in the interests of national security, territorial integrity or public safety, for the prevention of disorder or crime, for the protection of health or morals, for the protection of the reputation or rights of others, for preventing the disclosure of information received in confidence, or for maintaining the authority and impartiality of the judiciary'.

Article 10 of the European Convention on Human Rights is both Europe's specific version of Article 19 and the closest thing Europeans have to a First Amendment.[89] It differs from it, however, in one important respect. If you say 'First Amendment', most Americans will know roughly what you are talking about. If you say 'Article 10', most Europeans won't have the first idea what you're on about. Nonetheless, as with the First Amendment, a large body of literature and practice across Europe is devoted to debating what is, or should be,

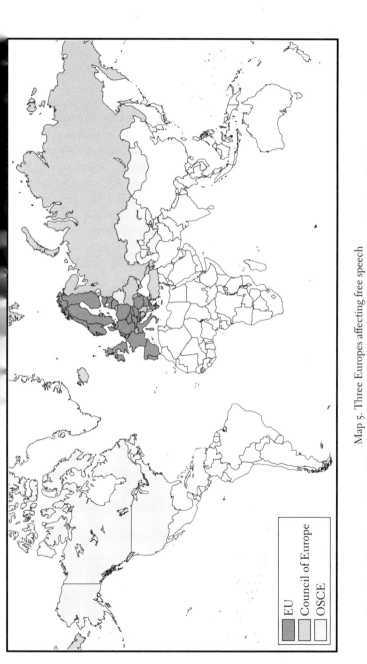

Map 5. Three Europes affecting free speech

All members of the European Union (EU) are members of the Council of Europe, and all members of the Council of Europe are members of the Organisation for Security and Cooperation in Europe (OSCE).

Source: EU, CoE, OSCE.

the precise meaning of Article 10, how the restrictions in its second part should be interpreted in today's new circumstances and how the rights of more than 800 million people under Article 10 should be balanced against those under its other provisions, such as Article 8 on privacy.

As with the First Amendment, these rights are ultimately adjudicated by a supreme court—in this case, the European Court of Human Rights, based in Strasbourg. Its not always consistent judgements are supposed to be binding on all member states of the Council of Europe.[90] In practice, the more law-abiding and democratic among those 47 still-sovereign states go to considerable lengths to abide by those judgements, while the more lawless and authoritarian, such as Russia or Azerbaijan, ignore them. The judgements of the Strasbourg court are therefore significantly less effective than those of the US Supreme Court, but they have more force than the admonitions of the Organisation for Security and Cooperation in Europe or the UN Human Rights Committee. Importantly, individuals, groups or organisations can take their cases to the Strasbourg court. In this sense it is every individual European's highest court of appeal.

The smaller and more integrated European Union formally requires all of its member states to sign up to the European Convention. It also requires adherence to Article 11 of its own more recent Charter of Fundamental Rights, which adds an explicit mention of respect for 'freedom and pluralism of the media'.[91] Yet the EU's real power in this struggle derives not from all these noble words but from the fact that it represents and regulates the largest, richest multinational single market in the world. Anyone who wants to operate in that market must play by EU rules. The responsibility to enforce those rules lies with member states. If they fail to do so, they risk being taken to another European supreme court, the European Court of Justice, based in Luxembourg.

Thus, for example, when we set up freespeechdebate.com at Oxford University, we had to comply with a British statutory instrument giving force to the EU's Electronic Commerce directive. Article 19 (coincidence, one assumes) of this British European regulation provides that an information service intermediary such as freespeechdebate.com, on which others can freely post, is not liable if the service provider—in our case, Oxford University—'does not have actual knowledge of unlawful activity or information' or 'upon obtaining such knowledge or awareness' acts expeditiously to remove or disable access to that information'. In shorthand, this is known as 'notice and take down'.[92] Freespeechdebate .com may be a globally accessible platform, but our physical location in the EU determines the legal limits of our freedom to debate free speech.

So important is the European market that it can have, across the world, what inside the United States is known as the 'California effect'.[93] (When California sets exhaust emissions standards, American manufacturers usually build their cars to that standard for the whole US market.) Thus, when Microsoft introduced its dot-NET passport to make navigation between password-protected websites easier, it ended up making it conform with EU privacy and data protection standards not just in Europe but across the globe. A new EU data protection regulation, embodying European privacy standards stronger than those prevailing elsewhere, is as much a concern for Google or Facebook as it is for a company operating solely in Belgium. With conscious exaggeration, two leading legal scholars describe the EU as 'the effective sovereign of global privacy law'.[94] In his history of copyright, Peter Baldwin talks of 'America being carried along in Europe's wake' and the 'Europeanisation of American policy' on intellectual property.[95]

Now someone sitting in Tehran, Nairobi or Shanghai might say: 'these are fine distinctions you are making between Europe and the US, but the reality is that there's one overwhelming global actor, which we call the West. Whether from Washington or Brussels, the West pushes a liberal agenda on free speech'. A disgruntled observer would call that agenda 'imperialist' or 'neo-colonial'.

It is true that in matters of free speech there is an extended family of the West, centred upon but stretching well beyond Europe and North America. To an extent insufficiently acknowledged in the US—where the free speech bible opens with the words 'In the beginning was the First Amendment'—American ideas about free speech had their roots in the English revolution of the seventeenth century. And two years before the First Amendment, the French revolution of 1789 produced, in its Declaration of the Rights of Man and Citizen, this Article 11: 'The free communication of ideas and opinions is one of Man's most precious rights: every citizen is therefore free to speak, write and publish freely, except to answer for abuses of this liberty, in cases determined by the law'.[96]

In the international and European covenants and their implementation, the Anglo-American and continental European traditions intertwine. British officials played a leading role in the drafting of what became the European Convention, yet it and the subsequent jurisprudence of the European Court of Human Rights also embody distinctive French and German ideas of honour, dignity and a 'right of personality'.[97]

This is one conversation in an extended family, but there is no single big dog called 'the West'. There are two giant powers, the United States and Europe, and then a host of other Western or more or less strongly Western-influenced states. Only the most incorrigible ideological fantasist could claim that they always act as one. Moreover, some of the issues on which Western states differ most sharply with each other, such as how far the law should go to protect privacy or curb hate speech, are crucial ones for an emerging cosmopolis in which privacy has been eroded and people from all cultures are becoming physical and virtual neighbours. A simplistic dichotomy of West-East or West-Rest does not hold up either philosophically or in the realities of global power relations.

That said, the fastest-growing dog in this fight is also the one that can plausibly claim the largest cultural, geographical and political distance from the West. China represents the most formidable attempt to show that a powerful, determined state can still control the flow of information, ideas and images across and within its frontiers. In 2000, president Bill Clinton scoffed that curbing the internet in China would be like trying to 'nail Jell-O to the wall'.[98] China's leaders replied, in effect, 'just watch us'.

When we say 'China' it is vital to distinguish between the state controlled by the Communist Party of China (hereafter the Party) and the entirety of its people. Many Chinese are constantly pushing the limits of free speech, especially on the internet. They use the Chinese word for 'netizen', *wang min*, which often carries clear implications of independence from if not active opposition to the authorities. The struggle, in this case, is at least as much inside China and between the Chinese—including those living outside mainland China, whether in Taiwan, Singapore, elsewhere in Asia or the West—as it is between China and the West. And more than anything I have said about the United States and Europe, everything I say about China is subject to this proviso: 'At the moment, but it will change'.

The Chinese party-state claims the right to control all expression within its frontiers on three grounds, which we might call Westphalian, Huntingtonian and Orwellian.[99] Like other postcolonial states, it places a high value on the kind of sovereignty that scholars have traditionally associated with Europe's 1648 Peace of Westphalia—hence 'Westphalian'. It promotes the idea of 'information sovereignty', and its national security law passed in 2015 specifically includes 'maintaining cyberspace sovereignty'. The official news agency Xinhua quoted an expert's comment that 'cyberspace now constitutes the fifth dimension of the nation's sovereignty, in addition to land, sea, air and space'.[100]

It also justifies its different standards on the kind of deep-seated civilisational difference that Samuel Huntington emphasised in his influential book *The Clash of Civilisations*—hence 'Huntingtonian'. The term 'Orwellian' is overused, but appropriate here. The Party insists that it knows best what it is good for its people to know. In line with the Orwellian motto 'who controls the past controls the future', this applies particularly to controversial events in the Party's own history, such as the Great Famine caused by Chairman Mao, the Cultural Revolution and the killing of citizens who had been peacefully protesting in

Tiananmen Square in June 1989. These three arguments—from sovereignty, civilisation and ideology—are mutually reinforcing.

Not that the Chinese party-state declares itself opposed to free speech. China is, as we have seen, a signatory to the Covenant—although, at this writing, it is one of very few UN member states not to have ratified it. Article 35 of its constitution declares that 'citizens of the People's Republic of China enjoy freedom of speech, of the press, of assembly, of association, of procession and of demonstration'. Its 2010 white paper on the internet has a whole section devoted to 'Guaranteeing Citizens' Freedom of Speech on the Internet'.

All it is doing, says China's government, is what other governments do: impose legal limits for the sake of higher interests. When, after riots in British cities in the summer of 2011, British prime minister David Cameron talked about restricting people's access to mobile and social networks, and when authorities in San Francisco actually did shut down wireless service at several subway stations to prevent a planned protest, Xinhua commented, 'We may wonder why Western leaders, on the one hand, tend to indiscriminately accuse other nations of monitoring, but on the other, take for granted their steps to monitor and control the internet'.[101] So the official Chinese stance is not 'no to free speech in principle'—as it once used to be 'no to capitalism in principle'. It is 'yes to free speech in principle, but with certain necessary limits'. That said, the Chinese approach differs fundamentally in the extent and vagueness of the limits it invokes as legitimate, and the range of means used to enforce them.

Its 2010 internet white paper, for example, prescribed that

> no organisation or individual may produce, duplicate, announce or disseminate information having the following contents: being against the cardinal principles set forth in the Constitution; endangering state security, divulging state secrets, subverting state power and jeopardizing national unification; damaging state honour and interests; instigating ethnic hatred or discrimination and jeopardizing ethnic unity; jeopardising state religious policy, propagating heretical or superstitious ideas; spreading rumours, disrupting social order and stability; disseminating obscenity, pornography, gambling, violence, brutality and terror or abetting crime; humiliating or slandering others, trespassing on the lawful rights and interests of others; and other contents forbidden by laws and administrative regulations.[102]

And who decides what is a heretical idea, a rumour, or a threat to social order and stability? The Party. Nor does a Chinese citizen have recourse to independent courts, ruling on the basis of clearly worded laws promulgated by a democratically elected parliament.

Where most of the world has or is rapidly developing widespread usage of American-made platforms such as Google, Facebook and Twitter, China has its own separate (though not precisely parallel) universe: Baidu instead of Google, RenRen for Facebook, Sina Weibo instead of Twitter, Tencent's Weixin/We-Chat rather than WhatsApp. Whereas in most areas of the Chinese economy, state-owned enterprises are dominant, some of the commanding heights of the Chinese internet are occupied by private, very much for-profit corporations such as Baidu, Alibaba and Tencent—sometimes collectively known as BAT—as well as Sina, Sohu and NetEase. Some of the leading figures in these companies are independent-minded as well as profit-oriented, but they operate under intense political supervision—and they know on which side their bread is buttered. Listening to leading editors of both print and online media at a workshop in Beijing, I was struck by their emphasis on the pressure to make a profit. Interestingly, this also applies to state-owned media. In a sense, China's media platforms have the worst of both worlds: commercial and political. The internet service providers and the mobile phone companies that serve more than 1.2 billion mobile phone users are largely state-controlled.[103] The authorities also ensure, with significant exertion of commercial and diplomatic muscle, that most Chinese citizens cannot see independent Chinese-language news and analysis beamed in by satellite television.[104]

China blocks, filters and directs at every level: from its self-styled Golden Shield (colloquially known as the Great Firewall of China), involving top-level internet service providers and internet exchange points, which bring information into the country through massive skeins of cable, down through a second level of automated keyword filtering, all the way to labour-intensive, selective human censorship.[105] To do this the party-state has a vast, multi-agency bureaucracy of censorship and propaganda. A major Harvard University study, which collected more than 11 million online posts inside the firewall, argues that the size and sophistication of the Chinese censorship operation is 'unprecedented in recorded world history'. It found that in 2011 some 13 percent of social media posts were censored. Estimates of the number of employees in the many agencies of internet control range from 20,000 to 50,000—and that's just for the internet, not for all media, publishing and propaganda. Individual online platforms have their own 'monitoring departments', with up to 1,000 in-house censors for the largest of them. When the Harvard research team established its own social media platform inside China, it was advised to have two or three in-house censors for every 50,000 users. That produces a guesstimate of 50,000 to 75,000 in-house internet censors for China as a whole, on top of those directly employed by the Party and state.[106]

The Harvard study finds that most online posts the apparatus decides should be censored are taken down within 24 hours, in an operation of 'large scale military-like precision'. It also suggests that online censorship sometimes anticipated, and so presumably was coordinated with, other state actions. For example, deletions of posts about the dissident artist Ai Weiwei increased sharply over the five days before his otherwise unheralded arrest in 2011.

Since 1989, 'guidance of public opinion' has been an official key phrase.[107] Detailed instructions are given daily, and sometimes hourly, to television, radio, print and online publishers and editors. The China Digital Times website, based in the United States, regularly publishes what it calls—with a hat tip to Orwell's *1984*—'Ministry of Truth' directives, leaked to it by Chinese colleagues. One from November 2014 read, 'all websites in all locales are forbidden from reporting on US President Obama's call at APEC for China to open the internet'.[108] Most revealing is the micromanagement of domestic news. After one of the country's vaunted high-speed trains crashed near the city of Wenzhou in 2011, the Central Propaganda Bureau issued numerous media directives, including this:

1. Release death toll only according to figures from authorities.
2. Do not report on a frequent basis.
3. More touching stories are to be reported instead i.e. blood donation, free taxi services, etc.
4. Do not investigate the causes of the accident; use information released from authorities as standard.
5. Do not reflect or comment.[109]

Meanwhile, perhaps as many as 300,000 so-called '50 cent party members' are paid to push the party line online. Prizes are also handed out to those who report 'illegal and unhealthy information' online.[110] Censorship and propaganda are two sides of the same coin: delete the wrong line, promote the right.

It would be a bold person who claimed that all this effort is motivated by ideological belief. I asked a fervent young Party member in what sense China is still a communist country. 'Well', he replied, 'it is ruled by the Communist Party'. He seemed to find that an entirely sufficient answer. Nonetheless, the terms of political debate are still defined ideologically, with concepts lurching in and out of favour.

In 2013 an internal Party document, which came to be known as Document Number 9, exhorted party members to beware of seven dangerous concepts, including Western constitutional democracy, civil society and neoliberalism. These became known as the Seven Don't-Mentions. One of them was 'promoting the West's idea of journalism, challenging China's principle that the media and publishing system should be subject to Party discipline'. Another, equally relevant to this book, was 'promoting "universal values" in an attempt to weaken the theoretical foundations of the Party's leadership'. The inadmissible proposition here was that 'Western freedom, democracy and human rights are universal and eternal'. This obscured 'the essential differences between the West's value system and the value system we advocate, ultimately using the West's value systems to supplant the core values of Socialism'.[111]

Such ideological directives have a measurable impact on what most Chinese see and hear. Using the advanced search function on the Baidu search engine, the veteran journalist and media analyst Qian Gang found that in 2012 there were 150 articles using the term 'universal values' in the headline, of which 78 percent presented the term in a positive light, and 400 having 'constitutionalism' in the headline, with all uses being positive. In 2013, by contrast, there were 500 articles using 'universal values' in the headline, of which 84 percent presented the concept in a negative light. Also, 1,200 articles used the term 'constitutionalism', 86 percent of them negatively.[112] In one notorious incident, the liberal Southern Weekly had 18 mentions of 'constitutionalism' removed from a 2013 New Year's editorial that was totally and crudely rewritten.[113]

This is China's domestic version of the struggle for word power. Qian Gang uses a four-colour system to analyse China's political discourse. Deep red, on the left of the spectrum, denotes political terms from the Maoist era; light red, those currently deployed by the Party leadership; light blue, those not encouraged; and dark blue, those denounced or banned. In just one year, 'constitutionalism' and 'universal values' moved sharply from light blue to dark, and every educated reader knew it.

Yet the society that lives with this whole astonishing apparatus is nothing like the Orwellian dystopia of *1984*. (As if to illustrate the point, one Chinese website lists no fewer than 13 editions of *1984* published in mainland China between 1985 and 2012).[114] It is precisely the potentially liberating technological affordances of the post-Gutenberg world that have compelled the creation of such a massive apparatus to restrict them. The more speech there is, the more effort is needed to control it. Back in the real-life year of 1984, when there was simply less 'speech' to control, it was so much easier to orchestrate the semantic occupation of the public sphere. Only if the Chinese party-state were prepared to stifle its economy by full-blown totalitarian regimentation, North Korean-style, could it perhaps put this genie back in the bottle.

Many Chinese show great creativity in finding ways to express themselves beyond the prescribed limits. For example, they use assemblages of characters that either look like, sound like or merely allude to banned terms and themes. These include online memes such as the now famous Grass Mud Horse, which in Chinese is a near-homophone with a phrase meaning 'fuck your mother', and was originally depicted defeating a river crab, itself a pun on 'harmony', a propaganda buzzword often used by Chinese leaders.[115] Censorship instructions recognize this subversive ingenuity. When the dissident writer Liu Xiaobo was awarded the Nobel Peace Prize in December 2010, an internal directive read:

> All media outlets are requested to strictly and rigorously examine and check images, videos, and web pages, and prevent acrostics, caricatures, and other forms of reporting that hype the news of Liu Xiaobo receiving the Nobel Peace Prize.[116]

I once heard a Chinese online editor explain how he would carefully edit and post articles which he knew for certain the censors would take down: 'but at least it will be up there for 10 minutes!' Ten minutes of free speech.

The battle lines of this daily online struggle are not drawn exactly where you might expect. Chinese leaders have acknowledged that they go online to find out what their people really think, which is always a challenge for dictatorships. Their own internet white paper talks of 'amass[ing] the public's wisdom'. Moreover, the Harvard study confirms that a lot of very direct criticism of government policies and officials is left online. (This does not apply to critical posts about top leaders and criticism of the censors themselves, which the censors vigorously remove.) What they systematically take down is anything that might lead people to organise any sort of independent collective action. For that is what the authorities fear most, even if it is not directly critical of them—as in the case of the Falun Gong movement.

I had a small taste of this everyday struggle for word power on a visit to Beijing in 2012. An adventurous publisher had commissioned a Chinese translation of *The File*, my book about reading my Stasi file and tracking down those who had spied on me for the East German secret police behind the Berlin Wall. (Ancient European history, you understand. Nothing at all to do with today's China.) The book had not yet appeared, but the publisher encouraged me to give some pre-publication interviews, including a live 'micro interview' on the then vibrant Sina Weibo microblogging site. The online interview was announced in advance and netizens could post questions on a dedicated page. One was: 'The Berlin Wall has already fallen. Is it possible that the Great Firewall of China will fall as well? If so, under what circumstances?'

By the time we got to the appointed chat time, that post had disappeared, presumably deleted by Sina's in-house censors. Nonetheless, there I sat at a coffee table in the lobby of my Beijing hotel, with an interpreter, a representative of my publisher and another colleague crouched over a laptop. Questions that were equally bold kept popping up on the laptop screen, minute by minute, translated to me by the interpreter, who was soon white-hot with the exertion. Questions like this: 'The restriction posed by the Chinese government on the state internet is in many ways similar to the restrictions posed by the Berlin Wall. What are your views on some of the people who have climbed over the wall?' And this: 'How to keep faith under the government's pressure?' And, amusingly, 'Do you see any prospects in joining the *wumaodang*?' (the ironically named '50 cent party' of those paid to peddle the Party line on comment threads.)

Rat-tat-tap went the keyboard, with my swiftly translated answers. There were 92 questions and we managed to answer 23. At one point, someone at Sina Weibo rang up to urge my publisher's representative not to have translated to me the 'sensitive' questions. Yet when I last looked, some pretty sensitive questions and answers remained on my Sina Weibo page.[117]

But that was 2012 and I a privileged foreigner. Over the period that I was writing this book and conducting the freespeechdebate.com experiment there was a major crackdown on free speech in China. When we launched the website in early 2012, one of the largest and fastest-growing groups of users was Chinese. But then—surprise, surprise—we were blocked. Our Sina Weibo page was taken down, all retweets removed and videos deleted, and for an extended period 'free speech debate' became a censored term on Weibo.

This was a tiny sideshow compared to what happened to Chinese writers and activists. The so-called 'Big V' Weibo bloggers—those with V-for-verified accounts reaching millions of readers—were given warnings, and many then had their accounts deleted. In total, more than 100,000 accounts were permanently shut down.[118] One of the most eloquent bloggers, Murong Xuecun, wrote an 'Open Letter to a Nameless Censor'. 'On May 11, 2013', it began, 'you ordered the termination of all my microblogs on Sina Weibo, Tencent, Sohu and Net-Ease, deleting every single entry I ever posted'. Over the last three years he had written about 200,000 characters, 'and every word was chosen with painstaking care'. All gone. Defiantly, Xuecun cried: 'you can delete my words, you can delete my name, but you cannot snatch the pen from my hand'.[119] A brave civil rights lawyer who specialised in free speech cases, Pu Zhiqiang, was arrested and put on trial under a law that forbids 'picking quarrels and provoking trouble'. The prosecution case against Pu was built around posts he had written on Weibo, and he received a three-year suspended sentence.[120]

Increasingly, people moved from the public Weibo blogs, which could be read by millions, to Tencent's innovative Weixin/WeChat app. By 2015, it counted more than half a billion users. This was partly because it was a highly ingenious, attractive product, arguably superior to the original American WhatsApp. It was also because those who wished to share their thoughts with others were frightened by what had happened to the Big V bloggers on Weibo. Whereas Weibo had created a real public sphere, with instantaneous, one-to-many broadcasting, the world of Weixin/WeChat was more fragmented, with most users being limited to discussion groups of not more than 500 members. Once again, Jell-O was being nailed to the wall. And yet, ways might still be found . . .

By the time you read these words, the boundaries of the permissible will certainly have moved again. Yet the arbitrary, unpredictable movability of these Chinese walls is itself a powerful deterrent. As David Bandurski observes: 'the government's primary means of control is the fuzzy line. No one ever knows exactly where the line is. The control apparatus is built on uncertainty and self-censorship, on creating this atmosphere of fear'.[121] The American scholar Perry Link famously compared it to an anaconda lurking in a chandelier hanging from the ceiling of your living room. The anaconda only has to shake the glass pendants a little and you will feel afraid.[122]

The evolution of this intra-Chinese struggle, in which the West plays at most a secondary role, matters to everyone in cosmopolis. It directly affects more than 1.3 billion Chinese, roughly one out of every six people on the planet. How their freedom of expression develops will be both a symptom and a cause of how their entire political system develops. Moreover, China presents such a massive, rapidly developing market that every Western communications and media company is seriously tempted to enter it. Whether Facebook ever goes into China, with its hope of profit prevailing over its fear of reputational damage, remains one of the more significant free speech questions of our time.[123]

China also has a growing impact abroad. China's giant communications and media companies play a major role in Africa, Latin America and the Middle East.[124] Such is the scale of its media investment in Africa, especially through state agencies such as Xinhua and CCTV, that it is already the leading international media player in countries like Kenya, gaining privileged access to official sources and shaping the local news agenda as well as views of the outside world. As its power grows, China is promoting a global norm of national, territorial control over the internet—and all other means of communication—effected both by domestic measures and through international organisations such as the International Telecommunication Union. (I say more about this under principle 9.) China's Westphalian-Huntingtonian insistence on 'information sovereignty' resonates with many postcolonial countries, as well as postimperial ones such as Russia, especially following Edward Snowden's revelations about the degree of US surveillance of international electronic traffic.

Graciously visiting a Snowden-shaken Brazil in 2014, president Xi Jinping inaugurated a Portuguese-language version of the Baidu search engine and smiled on Brazilian partnership agreements signed by Huawei and Alibaba. He then pronounced: 'In the current world, the development of the internet has posed new challenges to national sovereignty, security and development interests, and we must respond to this earnestly. Although the internet has the characteristic that it is highly globalised, no country should be subject to violations of their sovereign rights and interests in the area of information. However much internet technology develops, it cannot infringe upon the information sovereignty of other countries'.[125]

In theory, Beijing's position is not as missionary as Washington's. Rather than the American 'we do it this way over here, and we think you should over there too', it is 'you do it your way over there, and let us do it our way over here'. That is, in plain words, the compromise Samuel Huntington himself proposed: to avoid a 'clash of civilisations' by applying what he called the 'abstention rule'.[126] If the United States represents unilateral universalism, one might say that China stands for universal unilateralism. But Beijing is not consistent in this. When, for example, an independent committee in Oslo awarded Liu Xiaobo the Nobel Peace Prize, the Chinese authorities went to extraordinary lengths to prevent European ambassadors from attending the award ceremony in Oslo, and even claimed they had succeeded. In short, China tried to dictate to Europeans what they should say and hear in a European capital.[127] China's own sovereignty must be absolute, but other countries' was negotiable. (Now, where have we seen that before?)

The United States, Europe and China are the three biggest dogs competing to promote their norms across the world, but of course they are not the only ones. Arguably a handful of major regional powers, such as India, Brazil, Turkey, South Africa and Indonesia, will be decisive in the evolution of this global struggle. They may aptly be called the swing states for free speech.[128] If authoritarian regimes in Russia and Iran were to evolve in a more liberal direction, they too could have a significant effect on the balance of word power.

All these countries have a strong attachment to sovereignty and are therefore susceptible to the Chinese argument for 'information sovereignty'. On the other hand, each of them has its own distinctive free speech tradition and a substantial inheritance from the broader Western one. There is simply no clear-cut line between West and East, North and South: they come intermingled in every culture. Russia, for example, has for centuries lived its own cultural contest between two orientations which in the nineteenth century would come to be called Slavophiles and Westernisers. Brazil, like the rest of Latin America, has long seen itself as part of a wider West, as well as of a more recently conceptualised global south. Latin America also has regional institutions, weaker than those in Europe but far from irrelevant. A provision of the Chilean constitution was actually amended in response to a judgement of the Inter-American Court of Human Rights, which ruled that Chile should not have banned a film called 'The Last Temptation of Christ'.[129]

Some of these traditions and values may have come originally in the wake of European colonialism, but even where they did, they have taken root in local soil and been changed in the process. South Africa combines a Dutch and English legal heritage with strong native traditions, memorably evoked in Nelson Mandela's *Long Walk to Freedom*. A comparable blending can be observed in English-, French-, Spanish- and Portuguese-speaking countries around the world, from Australia to Chile and Kenya to Venezuela. India has an ancient, original heritage of religious and political thought relating to freedom of expression, yet its contemporary free speech debates often revolve around the proper interpretation of a penal code originally drafted by the nineteenth-century English historian and politician Thomas Babington Macaulay.[130] All are also influenced by the international legal and human rights framework developed since 1945. As with China, the decisive contest takes place between forces inside the country.

These swing states and their societies are not simply objects of a global struggle for word power. They are decisive actors in it. The argument of this book is in no small measure addressed to them.

BIG CATS

In 2010, when Google was confronting China, the company's then chief executive Eric Schmidt spoke to a small group of journalists at the World Economic Forum's annual meeting in Davos. 'Google is not a country', said Schmidt. It does not make laws. It does not do state-to-state diplomacy. But, he went on, 'we have to secure our borders'.[131]

Schmidt quickly corrected himself to 'secure our networks', but his slip of the tongue was revealing. Google may not be a country, but it is a superpower. So are Facebook, Twitter and a few other giant information businesses. They do not have the formal lawmaking authority of sovereign states. Their leaders are not accountable to their users as democratic governments are to voters. There is no constitution or formal mechanism for securing what the internet commentator

Rebecca MacKinnon calls 'the consent of the networked'.[132] Yet their capacity to enable or limit freedom of information and expression is greater than that of most states. The biggest of the private powers are something like virtual countries.[133] The French have given four of these 'Anglo-Saxon' giants the sinister label 'les Gafa' (Google, Apple, Facebook, Amazon).[134]

The term 'privately owned public spaces', POPS, has been coined to characterise a vital dimension of their power. This is not mere hyperbole. Map 6 shows the extraordinary predominance of Facebook as the leading social network in all but a handful of stand-out countries. British imperialists used to boast that the map of the world was 'painted red'. Now it is blue. In countries such as Indonesia and Thailand, surveys have found a larger number of respondents saying they use Facebook than say they use the internet. In Nigeria, Indonesia, India and Brazil, more than half those asked in a poll commissioned by Quartz magazine agreed with the statement 'Facebook is the internet'. Mark Zuckerberg's internet.org aims to 'bring the internet to the two thirds of the world's population that doesn't have it', but (at this writing) its showcase app only provides free access to Facebook, Facebook Messenger and a handful of other services. So is internet.org bringing the underprivileged of the world to the internet or just to Facebook?[135]

Beside the laws and policies of the sovereign states in which they operate, these corporations' choices result mainly from a combination of three factors: the affordances of ever more astonishing new technologies (the engineers are the Brahmins of Silicon Valley), the quest for profit and the preferences and quirks of their individual leaders.

Which private powers make the most difference to you personally still depends on where you live. If you are in China, Russia or Iran, the American online giants do not have the salience they enjoy in the rest of the world. The policies of Baidu, Alibaba and Tencent (the BAT), or those of the Russian search engine Yandex and social network VKontaktę (or 'VK'), will be more important for you. In Britain, Rupert Murdoch and a clutch of other newspaper proprietors have shaped the public debate over the last decades more than any online giant. In Brazil, as in many other countries, partisan private owners of dominant television channels have been crucial.[136]

Concern about the way ownership limits and distorts freedom of expression is nothing new. A. J. Liebling, who wrote about what was then still properly called 'the press' in the New Yorker of the 1940s and 1950s, famously observed that 'freedom of the press is guaranteed only to those who own one'.[137] And he highlighted a crucial dichotomy: 'the function of the press in society is to inform, but its role is to make money'.[138] Like newspapers in Liebling's day, today's

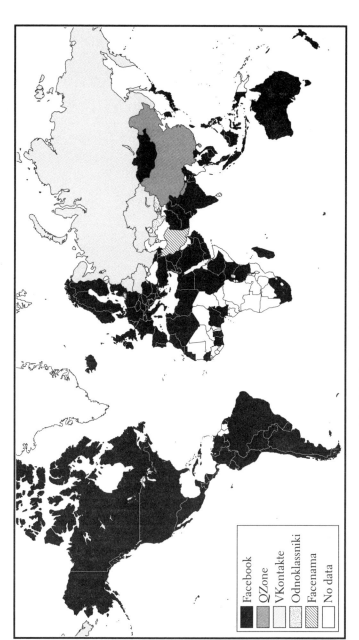

Map 6. Leading social network by country
Data is for December 2014.
Source: Vincenzo Cosenza, Vincos blog.

information businesses live in a constant tension between the public service they offer and the private profit they pursue. They report to shareholders, and the value of their stock seesaws with the latest results.[139]

This tension is especially acute in companies like Google, Facebook and Twitter, which see themselves as part of a global movement for 'internet freedom'. Google did, after all, employ one of the founding fathers of the internet, Vint Cerf, with the official title Chief Internet Evangelist.[140] When I talk to senior staff of these internet giants, I find their language lurches queasily between that of a First Amendment free speech scholar and that of a salesman. One minute, it is 'no prior restraint', the next 'our new product'. In the end, you are left wondering whether you are being sold freedom disguised as dishwasher powder or dishwasher powder disguised as freedom. Or perhaps it's just dishwasher powder 'with added freedom'.

Some have referred to this language as Siliconese. In any case, to assess the role these big cats play in the global struggle over free expression we have to understand how they make their money. The press, and traditional print publishing more broadly, have long relied on two main revenue sources: people paying to buy the publication and advertisers paying to advertise in it. The same is true on the internet, but since people are less inclined to pay for most kinds of information online, such businesses depend more on advertising: that is, on selling the value of their nonpaying users' attention to other companies who wish to persuade those people to buy other things. As one observer sharply comments: 'If you are not paying for it, you're not the customer; you're the product being sold'.[141]

This is mainly personalised advertising, customised to appeal to the individual user. These information giants have accumulated an astounding quantity of detailed, highly personal data on you. They use it not to oppress you politically but to sell you to advertisers as a potential consumer. Facebook, for example, shares your data with a company called Datalogix to establish what percentage of those who view an ad actually go on to buy a product from that advertiser.[142] In a bracing book called *You Are Not a Gadget*, the virtual reality pioneer turned cybersceptic Jaron Lanier describes Google and Facebook as 'spying/advertising empires'.[143]

These information businesses claim the data and results are all anonymised, but somewhere some machine and therefore potentially some person knows it is you. Hence the disconcerting experience that, minutes after searching for, buying online or simply emailing about, say, sandals, advertisements for sandals start popping up on our screens. (I choose a deliberately innocuous example.) Google's most famous slogan is 'Don't be evil'. Yet as one Google engineer confided to another author, with a smile: 'We're not evil. We try really hard not to be evil. But if we wanted to, man, could we ever!'[144]

Beside personalised advertising and the gargantuan collection of personal data that underpins it, there is customised search. An amusing academic experiment in 2009 set up Google identities for the philosophers Friedrich Nietzsche, Immanuel Kant and Michel Foucault, developed a search history for them by entering words from the indices of their books and then tracked how their personalised search results diverged. After a few thousand searches, more than half of Nietzsche's top ten search results differed from those offered to Kant and Foucault. If the three philosophers did not already have their heads in different clouds, they soon would have.[145] The situation is constantly evolving but, at this writing, Google will customise your search results on the basis of your location and—if you are logged in rather than actively opting to search anonymously—your personal search history, as well as information drawn from those of your email accounts and social networks to which it has access. The last is the 'social' component of customisation, including what your friends are interested in. If you and I search for exactly the same term, we will get different results. And if we are not careful, we will each hive off into our own individual 'filter bubble'.[146]

More broadly, across the internet there is a risk of fragmentation into thousands of tiny 'information cocoons': echo chambers where the news and opinions we see are only those favoured by the like-minded and our only newspaper is the Daily Me. At the extreme, you have the Norwegian mass murderer Anders Behring Breivik, whose anti-Muslim fury was reinforced by constantly revisiting a handful of hysterical sites about the threats Islam and multiculturalism posed to Europe and by his own tiny crowd of online correspondents. The same has happened, at the other extreme, with violent Islamists.[147]

Such online-reinforced groupthink is the precise opposite of a liberal ideal of an internet-enabled public sphere, where we are constantly confronted with inconvenient facts, contrary arguments and different values, and therefore, as John Stuart Mill argued in the great Chapter 2 of *On Liberty*, compelled to question and refine our own convictions. 'There is always hope', writes Mill, 'when people are forced to listen to both sides; it is when they attend only to one that errors harden into prejudices . . .'[148] Whether our online experience becomes that of a wider public sphere or a Balkanised patchwork of information hamlets will depend as much on the technological and commercial decisions of these private powers as on the legal and political ones of public powers and the personal choices of individual netizens.

Then there is the difference between platforms that are open and those that are closed—or, in Jonathan Zittrain's terms, generative versus tethered.[149] The tethered platform or device not only determines, by fiat of its controller, what you may or may not see there in the first place. It is also continually monitoring, and sometimes directly policing, what you view or download. One fine Friday in July 2009, some book lovers who had purchased an electronic version of George Orwell's *1984* from Amazon.com found that it had mysteriously disappeared from their Kindle reading devices. Amazon realised that this e-version of *1984* had been sold by a company that did not have rights to it and, without giving any warning to users, deleted it by remote control.[150] So *1984* was consigned to the memory hole. What is worrying here is not the substance of the case—the clumsy handling of a legitimate intellectual property concern—but the technical possibilities it reveals. In the wrong hands, used for the wrong purposes, these are, indeed, Orwellian. You think that äppärät in your hand is yours alone, but actually it is theirs as well. You are watching your tablet, but your tablet is also watching you.

Apple has become a byword both for brilliant, user-friendly design and for the closed, tethered device. Its App Store rejected the work of a Pulitzer prize–winning cartoonist, because it 'ridicule[d] public figures'. (After protests, the decision was reversed.) It turned down an app called Freedom Time, which counted the days until the end of George W. Bush's presidency, and instructed the German tabloid newspaper Bild to put a bikini on one of its topless girls. Amazon provoked a storm of protest when it attempted to strong-arm the publisher Hachette into accepting its commercial terms by discriminating against the books of all Hachette authors.[151]

Now you might say: what's the problem here? Doesn't a shop have the right to determine what it sells, and on what terms? But when a few companies have such a dominant market position, their policies—their private censorship, if you will—can be almost as limiting as state censorship. Tim Wu argues persuasively in his book *The Master Switch* that the structure of our information industries is a key determinant of our effective freedom of expression.[152]

These corporations' choices are shaped by the profit motive but also by the character of their founders. The influence of a Steve Jobs or a Mark Zuckerberg on their respective empires has been more like that of an idiosyncratic absolute ruler in some mediaeval principate than that of the head of government in a modern liberal democracy. Apple's tethered perfectionism has everything to do with Jobs's personality. If the other Apple-founding Steve—Wozniak—had become Apple's dominant figure, it might have remained the open, generative platform it was at the time of the 1982 Apple II desktop computer. For years, Google did not allow advertisements for cigarettes and hard liquor because Sergey Brin and Larry Page disapproved of them. Facebook's insistence on people using their real names is, to a significant degree, a result of Zuckerberg's personal attitude. If you have ever doubted the role of the individual in history, just look behind your screen.

P²

While a large, determined state or company can set the boundaries and terms of free expression within its own territorial or virtual realm, the strongest force is generated where public and private powers combine: 'power squared' or P² for short. The bigger the two powers, the larger the value of P². P² creates some of the greatest opportunities for free speech and some of the largest threats to it.

In the last decade of the twentieth century and the first of the twenty-first, the combination of the First Amendment legal tradition in the world's most powerful state and the pro–free speech cultures of private American platforms such as Wikipedia, Twitter and Google produced a great leap forward in transnational freedom of expression. Even when material was taken down to comply with US law on copyright or defamation, the fact of that deletion was usually noted on a website called chillingeffects.org (subsequently lumendatabase.org).[153]

Yet there are as many, if not more, examples of negative P²—and not only in authoritarian countries. One reason Silvio Berlusconi retained political power in Italy for so long is that he owned the most-watched private television stations but could also heavily influence the public television channels. This in a country where more than 80 percent of those asked said they got their news about the 2008 election campaign from television.[154] (More on this under principle 4.)

In many other places, the state or dominant political forces directly or indirectly control companies that have a major influence on what can be said, seen or heard in that territory. Politicians' hunger for media support puts the boot on the other foot. Through lobbying, be it in the US Congress, the Indian parliament, or EU offices in Brussels, companies can influence the supposedly neutral public rules that regulate their activities. At worst, in a process known as regulatory capture, they effectively write their own rules. The 'revolving door' of individuals moving from jobs in business to government and back again strengthens such incestuous ties.

Public and private power have also combined to formidable effect in the surveillance of those suspected of terrorist or criminal activity. In the wake of the 2001 terrorist attacks, American and British security agencies acquired powers to demand mountains of data and so-called metadata on individuals from private holders. They included mobile phone companies, search engines, online retailers like Amazon, internet service providers, credit rating agencies, medical insurance companies, libraries (in the United States), social networks and data storage companies such as Acxiom—which reportedly held an average of 1,500 data items on more than 95 percent of Americans.[155] Some corporations, such as the American telecommunications giant AT&T, secretly shared data on their customers with the National Security Agency well beyond what the law required.[156] (I consider the effects of this P^2 at length under principle 9, where I also scrutinise the collaboration of companies with authoritarian governments.)

There is an important debate to be had about the attitude such private powers should adopt to the demands of states. When Google was locked in its very public argument with China, Bill Gates said, not very sympathetically: 'You've got to decide: Do you want to obey the laws of the countries you're in or not?'[157] But that raises two further questions. First, how does a transnational platform or medium decide what country it is in? When, in 2000, Yahoo was instructed by a French court to remove from its globally accessible website some Nazi objects that were available for sale there, a Yahoo vice president exclaimed: 'OK, whose laws do I follow? We have many countries and many laws and just one internet'.[158] 'Just one internet' was the optimistic assumption of the time. In the second decade of the twenty-first century, the issue is whether there still is 'just one internet'—or are we rapidly getting not merely a bordered internet but a 'splinternet' containing a distinct Chinanet, Russianet, Brazilnet and so on?

The second question is this: are the 'laws' of North Korea laws in the same sense that we use that word for those of Sweden? Should not companies make some distinction between states where laws are promulgated by a democratically elected legislature—albeit subject to heavy lobbying, not least by companies—and interpreted by an independent judiciary, and states where, as in China, the words 'law' and 'administrative regulation' can be used interchangeably? To distinguish, in other words, between those places where you have at least an ideal (however debased in practice) of what the American founding father John Adams called 'a government of laws and not of men', and those where both the historical tradition and current practice are that, as the scholar Simon Leys summarises Confucius, 'the government is of men, not of laws'.[159]

One coherent position is that there should be a presumption of legitimacy for the laws of rule-of-law democracies but not for those of lawless dictatorships. Easily stated as theory, in the real world this is not a simple black-and-white dichotomy—to the left, the rule-of-law sheep, to the right, the lawless goats—but rather a sliding scale, with many countries located somewhere in the middle. And the practical working out of such a principle entails hard choices for both governments and companies.

Take, for example, the matter of Germany, Google and Holocaust denial. In Germany, denying the historical truth that Nazi Germany attempted to exterminate the Jews of Europe is a criminal offence. There being no doubt that Germany is a fully qualifying, democratic rule-of-law country, Google removes links to some explicit Holocaust denial material from its German domain, google.de. This is the domain to which searchers in Germany will be referred by default. If you google, say, '*Holocaust Lüge*' (Holocaust lie), a notice at the bottom of the google.de page indicates that a search result has been removed and directs you to a page on lumendatabase.org (previously chillingeffects.org) which explains, in English and German, that the link was 'reported as illegal by a German regulatory body'.[160] Yet by the simple expedient of typing in google.com/ncr, anyone in Germany can override the default google.de setting, transport themselves to that virtual America which is google.com and find the forbidden Holocaust denial site with a couple of mouse clicks.

Now you could argue that Germany's stance here is inconsistent. If the German government really believes its citizens should not be exposed to this poison, it should make sure they are not. To do this would, however, require a Chinese-scale apparatus of blocking and filtering, imposed on all internet service providers operating in the country: a virtual Berlin Wall. Germany seems to have quietly concluded that this would be a greater evil. The state has made its moral and symbolic point. Most internet users in Germany will not be exposed to this vile stuff, but they can find it if they really want to. This is a messy compromise but in my view a reasonable one.

More extreme has been the policy of Turkey, which blocked its citizens from accessing the entire YouTube platform for more than three years because YouTube would not take down a few offensive videos of the founder of the Turkish Republic, Kemal Atatürk, which are illegal under Turkish law. (In practice, Turks found ways around the block, a fact acknowledged even by the prime minister, Recep Tayyip Erdoğan, who in answer to a reporter's question in 2008 said, 'I can access [YouTube], you do it too'.)[161] Similarly, Thailand denied its citizens all access to YouTube because of a few videos about the Thai king, whose mystique is protected by the world's most ferocious lèse-majesté laws.[162] In both cases a deal was eventually reached in which YouTube blocked the offending videos for the IP addresses known to be in the respective country, and YouTube was then unblocked for users in Turkey and Thailand. Indeed, an unwritten convention by which content considered illegal in country X is blocked for users in country X seems gradually to be gaining wider acceptance. In 2012, Twitter announced that it would do the same, though only in response to a 'valid and applicable legal request'.[163]

By the time you read this, there will certainly be new twists in a developing tale but the basic issue will not have changed. The choices such information businesses make are at once commercial, technological, legal, ethical and political. The deals they arrive at with the states in which they operate are among the key determinants of our effective freedom of expression in our time. It is when the big cats and dogs get together that we must be most alert.

THE POWER OF THE MOUSE

Where does this leave us, the individual citizens and netizens? Cowering like mice in our holes, helplessly awaiting the outcome of the latest fight—or furtive coupling—between dog and cat? Seeing such large powers at work, we may feel that way, yet this would be quite wrong. It would be wrong morally: we should fight for what we believe is right even if the odds seem hopelessly stacked against us. But it would also be wrong analytically. To conclude that we are powerless in these transformed circumstances is to misunderstand our own position.

While we should always beware the technological determinism and visionary overstatement of 'the internet will set you free', the internet does afford new possibilities for individuals to broadcast, connect and organise. As I observed at the beginning of this book, most of us can now be authors, journalists and publishers. At relatively small expense, we can broadcast ourselves, in words, images or sounds that are theoretically accessible to billions of other human beings.

Most of them won't notice. As Figure 6 illustrates, the online world has a huge 'long tail' of individuals communicating to a tiny number of other individuals—or just to themselves. A blogger called Randi Mooney modestly comments that most blogs are a form of vanity publishing.[164]

The technical ease of self-broadcasting produces a Tower-of-Babel cacophony in which it can actually be more difficult than it was previously for the individual voice to be heard. In the 1970s, in eastern Europe, copies of the Russian writer Alexander Solzhenitsyn's Nobel Prize lecture on the power of 'one word of truth'—which, according to a Russian proverb, 'shall outweigh the whole world'—had to be typed in secret, with painful slowness, using carbon copy papers placed between individual sheets of wafer-thin ordinary paper in a typewriter.[165] This was called *samizdat*, a Russian coinage meaning clandestine self-publishing. If you hit the manual typewriter keys like a concert pianist playing Beethoven fortissimo, the maximum legible copies you could get from a single typing was about twelve: the *samizdat* dozen.[166] A reader would devour

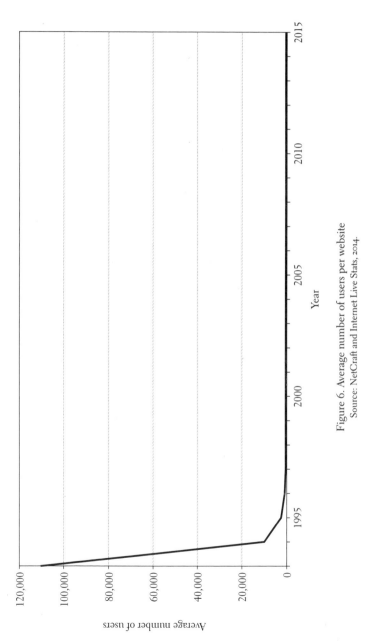

Figure 6. Average number of users per website
Source: NetCraft and Internet Live Stats, 2014.

the text in a single night's passionate reading, then pass it on to a friend. Amidst the silence and darkness of the pre-internet world, Solzhenitsyn's 'one word of truth' had a life-changing impact on the few it reached.

Yet we should not underrate the new potential for individual broadcasting. After that 2013 New Year editorial in the Chinese newspaper *Southern Weekly* was crudely censored, a well-known Chinese actress, Yao Chen, tweeted the logo of *Southern Weekly* on her Sina Weibo account, adding this line: 'one word of truth shall outweigh the whole world—Solzhenitsyn (Russia)'. At the time, she had more than 30 million followers. Despite the subsequent crackdown on Weibo, in autumn 2015 the comment was still there—and she had more than 78 million followers.[167]

Also transformed in both scale and kind are the opportunities to organise collective action. Email, social networks and everything now in your handheld box have been used to make things happen. A worldwide campaign that eventually resulted in an (albeit flawed) UN treaty to ban landmines was made possible by email.[168] Networks such as Avaaz and Change.org have shown what can be achieved by collective action that begins and spreads through online mobilisation. Social networks and text messages have played a vital role in demonstrations against authoritarian regimes from Egypt to Belarus—though the indispensable ingredient remains the courage of individual men and women prepared to gather in the face of violence.[169] If the Harvard analysis of Chinese internet censorship is correct, China's censors are telling us something important. What they most fear is the networking of voices that leads to collective action.

As citizens and netizens, we can influence the worldwide struggle for word power on at least four levels. The highest, though not necessarily the most decisive, is that of international treaties, organisations, networks and governance. Here, the individual's best chance is to work through one of the numerous nongovernmental organisations for freedom of expression, transparency, privacy, human rights and accountability, which operate to influence those often highly technical, acronym-laden debates. IFEX, an online global network for free expression, lists nearly 100 organisations in some 60 countries, and I can immediately think of several that are not there.[170]

Direct forms of collective action also play a part. One of central Europe's largest mobilisations of young people for many years happened in 2011/12 against the proposed Anti-Counterfeit Trading Agreement (ACTA), a secretly negotiated draft treaty which would have disproportionately restricted online freedom of expression in the name of protecting intellectual property rights.[171] They called themselves ACTAvists. A combination of street demonstrations in many European cities, online activism, coordinated lobbying by NGOs and the work of politicians from Europe's newly arrived Pirate parties resulted in the measure being voted down in the European parliament. Given the 'California effect' of Europe's market size, this effectively killed ACTA.[172]

The second level is that of national laws, policies and customs. The essence of being a citizen of a democracy is that you can work to change the laws under which you live. In the United States, another mobilisation in 2011/12 saw the defeat of the Stop Online Piracy Act and the Protect Intellectual Property Act— those two ugly sisters, SOPA and PIPA. Like ACTA, these overbroadly drafted bills would have sacrificed online freedom of expression to the demands of intellectual property owners. SOPA and PIPA largely resulted from intensive lobbying of the US Congress—where, as we shall see, money often speaks louder than words—by the movie and media businesses centred in Hollywood and Los Angeles. While netizens and NGOs played a part in the campaign against the ugly sisters, the key to its success was the engagement of the online giants of Silicon Valley and San Francisco. This included the first ever one-day blackout of the English-language version of Wikipedia, heartlessly ignoring the despair of thousands of students on essay deadlines.[173] With only slight exaggeration, one could say that, in the public power arena of Washington, the private powers of Northern California defeated those of Southern California.

At both these levels, there is a question about the efficacy of nongovernmental organisations, which see themselves as the organised form of civil society. For any issue discussed in this book, a quick online search will find at least one NGO and probably several. Many of them will be small, geographically limited and competing with each other for funds. And they are to influence those public and private superpowers? Where the tendency with information companies is clearly towards concentration, that of NGOs seems to be towards fragmentation. This has some advantages—diversity, originality, creativity—but it is far from obvious that small gaggles of mice are the best way to control big dogs and cats. Sometimes, concentrated power needs concentrated power to check it.[174]

Nonetheless, if you live in a democracy, it is possible to build coalitions to change laws, policies and customs. Once every few years, politicians will come looking for your vote. The ever more sophisticated ways in which politicians track and respond to public opinion, through polling, focus groups and the monitoring of social networks, mean that even the quietest private opinion may still count for something.[175]

The less democratic your political system is, the more difficult it becomes to influence it. Freedom of expression is both a cause and an effect of wider freedom. Yet even in authoritarian countries, the powerholders do sometimes respond to the voices of their people. An often-quoted example is the mass of individual posts on China's social network and especially Weibo sites following the deaths of schoolchildren in poorly constructed schools during the Szechuan earthquake of 2008, and again after a high-speed train crash in the neighbourhood of Wenzhou in 2011.[176] In both cases, there was an online flood not merely of popular indignation but of information that the authorities had tried to suppress. As we have seen, the Party subsequently cracked down on precisely the Weibo platform that had made this mass participation possible, but Chinese leaders should not underestimate the capacity of their people to find new ways to make their voices heard.

Our individual relationships with the private powers constitute a third level of influence. We may depend on them for what we can effectively see, hear and express, but they depend on us for their profits. If they have no users, viewers or readers, they will be dead. Many online platforms pay homage to what they call their 'community'—a term of truly alpaca woolliness. Who decides what 'the community' thinks? Who speaks for it? Yet individual members of those ill-defined 'communities' can make an impact in one of the three ways which the political scientist Albert O. Hirschman famously identified: exit, voice or loyalty.[177]

Voice, in Hirschman's triad, means speaking up to change policy or behaviour. Sometimes that works. In 2007, Facebook introduced a service called Beacon which, by default, shared information about your online purchases with your Facebook friends. Thus, for example, Beacon informed a woman called Shannon Lane that her husband Sean had just bought a white gold ring. 'Who is this ring for?' she messaged him, tartly. In fact, the ring had been intended not for some secret lover but as a surprise Christmas present for Shannon herself.[178] Protests against such automated intrusion grew rapidly, using Facebook pages to criticise Facebook. A movement called MoveOn.org turned aside from campaigning for a Democratic president of the United States to start a Facebook protest group. It also took out Facebook ads asking 'Is Facebook Invading Your Privacy?' Facebook withdrew Beacon.

Loyalty and exit, by contrast, usually don't involve conscious collective action. As we have seen, information companies obsessively follow the clickstream, watching where users go, for their own commercial reasons. This means they know an alarming amount about you, but it also means that we can vote with our mice. The naming of the computer mouse, incidentally, goes back to two American computer engineers, Doug Engelbart and Bill English, at the Stanford Research Institute in the 1960s.[179] You can see at the Computer History Museum in Mountain View (and admire online) the first, wonderfully DIY mouse, crudely carved from wood, with two metal wheels.[180] Nowadays, your 'mouse' is as likely to be your fingertip on a smartphone touchscreen, but the word endures. We, the mice, vote with our mice.

The same principle of aggregated individual action applies to newspapers that print topless photos of members of a royal family or hack into the mobile phones of abducted children. If, as an expression of their disgust, enough readers stopped buying such papers, they would soon change their editorial policy. But usually people don't. Michael Kinsley summarises his experience as editor of the online magazine Slate, where he received emails from readers protesting about its publication of salacious detail on Bill Clinton's sexual encounters with Monica Lewinsky: 'Their emails say no no, but their mouse clicks say yes yes'.[181]

Fourth, we can insert ourselves into the struggle by creating our own virtual and physical communities for the exchange of information and ideas. The earliest recorded Western debates around free speech, in ancient Greece, connected it directly to the idea of a self-governing and well-governed community, pooling collective wisdom to establish the facts and arrive at good decisions. 'There is this to be said for the many', Aristotle wrote in his *Politics*. 'Each of them by himself may not be of a good quality; but when they all come together it is possible that they may surpass—collectively and as a body, although not individually—the quality of the few best . . . For when there are many, each has his share of goodness and practical wisdom'.[182] The legal philosopher Jeremy Waldron calls this the 'doctrine of the wisdom of the many'.[183] Twenty-five hundred years ago, that was the original 'crowdsourcing'.

The internet offers us opportunities to create our own self-governing online communities and draw on the 'wisdom of crowds' across frontiers. Within the technical, legal and political outer limits set by the big cats and dogs, we can establish communities where we say: 'we wish to conduct this debate by certain rules. If you don't want to live by those rules, go somewhere else'. In the best case, what in the online world are usually called 'community standards' are exactly that—the self-determined standards of a self-governing community. (Freespeechdebate.com raises an interesting question in this respect: how freely can we speak about free speech? Our community standards explain our approach and the reasoning behind it.[184])

A book by Jeff Howe, who seems to have coined the term 'crowdsourcing', concludes with ten pieces of advice, one of which is 'pick the right crowd'.[185] This is a plain but useful truth. Although the number of potential members is huge, the active membership of such crowds typically is not. Howe quotes an estimate that the optimal user base for crowdsourcing is around 5,000 people. Interestingly, that is roughly the size of the crowd you might have got together in person at a typical assembly in ancient Athens.[186] As we shall see when we look more closely at free speech and knowledge, under principle 3, a few thousand very active editors have been the key to the success of Wikipedia.

Yet these new possibilities of communication can cut both ways. If the right crowds can find each other, so can the wrong ones: terrorists, paedophiles, criminals. They can successfully deploy the trans-frontier magnifying potential of the internet to spread hatred and violence. The power of the mouse may be used for good or ill, but who decides which is which? After all, one person's good is another's evil. This book is based on the premiss—spelt out under principle 10—that it is ultimately you, the individual woman or man, who must decide. A colleague of mine who has spent a lifetime studying the European and North American intellectual movement known as the Enlightenment summarises its message in three words: think for yourself.[187] Exactly so. We work it out for ourselves. Then we can use the possibilities of individual and collective action at any or all of these four levels to influence the struggle—and we take the consequences.

The next chapter is devoted to exploring the intellectual and moral foundations on which we may build our principles, and the extent to which the resulting values and ideals are universal or could become more so. But before moving on to questions of what should be rather than what is, I shall tell the story of one free speech controversy that erupted while I was writing this book. For it illustrates, in explosive miniature, the transformed world of human communication and the complex interplay of old and new players that I have thus far sketched in necessarily broad strokes.

'INNOCENCE OF MUSLIMS' AND
THE LOST INNOCENCE OF YOUTUBE

In July 2011, Lily Dionne, a young woman recently arrived in Hollywood to pursue an acting career, responded to a casting advertisement in Craigslist for a movie called 'Desert Warrior'. It turned out to be a strange movie shoot. 'We did wonder what it was about', she commented later. 'They kept saying "George". Like, this is the Middle East two thousand years ago. Who's "George"?' Later she and other cast members were called in to record 'specific words, like "Muhammad", for example'.[188]

Another recruit, Myles Crawley, turned up at an address in Duarte, near Los Angeles, where he was given a pair of sandals, a robe and a turban, and told to play a blind character called Amir who, amongst other things, kills a pregnant woman. 'The crew was in stitches as we shot the scene. How was I, a blind man, supposed to find a pregnant woman in the desert and stab her to death? It was decided that another actor, tattooed from head to toe, would lead me to my victim. I was told that when the woman fell dead I should turn to the camera, raise my bloody sword, and say, "George is the messenger and the book is our constitution"'.[189]

The director was one Alan Roberts, whose earlier credits included 'The Sexpert' and 'Young Lady Chatterley II'. According to several of the actors, Roberts received instructions on location from a man introduced to them as Sam Bacile. The records of the agency which licences film shootings in the L.A. area list the working title as 'Desert Warriors', the production organisation as Media for Christ and the producer as Sam Bossil.[190] On MySpace.com, Media for Christ declared itself dedicated 'to communicate and promote the word of Jesus Christ through attractive Christian media'.[191]

Some ten months later, on 1 July 2012, a video titled 'The Real Life of Muhammad' was posted on YouTube by 'Sam Bacile'. It was just over 13 minutes long. The next day, this 'Bacile' posted a marginally longer version, calling it 'Muhammad Movie Trailer'.[192] Like miles of other stuff uploaded every day, in an online universe of almost cost-free, pseudonymous self-publishing, this was malignant rubbish. None other than Salman Rushdie would later characterise it with one well-chosen word: 'crap'.

Its disjointed scenes include the following: A Muslim mob murders a Christian woman. (Presumably this was Myles Crawley's stitch-inducing scene.) A young Muhammad is invited by an attractive woman to put his head between her thighs. Muhammad then talks ecstatically to a donkey, saying 'and this shall be the first Muslim animal'. That attractive woman, now identified as Khadija—the name of the historical Muhammad's first wife—asks an elder man, dressed in what look like wizard's robes, to help this half-crazy young Muhammad. The wizard character says 'I will make a book for him. It will be a mix between some versions from the Torah and some versions from the New Testament, and will mix them into false verses'.

After six and a half minutes, a group of warlike men, brandishing swords, cry, 'Muhammad is our messenger and the Qur'an is our constitution'. (So that's what happened to Myles's line about 'George' and 'the book'. The sound is badly dubbed, with the warriors' lips visibly out of sync.) Muhammad has his wicked way with various women. His disciples ask, 'Is the messenger of God gay?' A noble Jew is murdered in front of Sophia, his understandably distressed wife. 'I'm late for the battle', cries Muhammad, after bedding Sophia too. His army is represented by a single shot of just six horses galloping across the desert—a very Craigslist jihad. A bloodstained Muhammad cries to the camera:

'Every non-Muslim is an infidel. Their lands, their women, their children are our spoils'. Then do-it-yourself, iMovie flames spurt up around the vengeful Prophet, aka 'George', in real life an unfortunate actor who for his own safety had best remain identified only as Michael. The End.

Nobody seems to have taken any notice of this rubbish until early September 2012, when an Arabic-dubbed version was apparently posted on YouTube and a Coptic Christian extremist named Morris Sadek promoted it on the blog of an outfit called the National American Coptic Assembly.[193] Sadek also drew it to the attention of a journalist at a Cairo-based newspaper, who wrote about it in inflammatory terms in an article published on 6 September.[194] Only then did the provocation succeed in eliciting a response. On 8 September, as the anniversary of the 11 September 2001 attacks on New York and Washington approached, an Egyptian Salafist rabble-rouser called Sheikh Khalid Abdullah appeared and denounced an extract from the video in the course of his chat show on Egypt's Al Nas satellite television channel. Posted on YouTube on 9 September, the Al Nas clip had harvested more than 2 million views by the end of the month.

Soon, the flames were real. On the anniversary of the 9/11 attacks, Egyptian Salafists demonstrated violently outside the US embassy in Cairo. Like all such protests, this one had its local politics. The Salafists were attempting to strengthen their street credibility as the true defenders of the Prophet and to put the Muslim Brotherhood, which was now in government, on the spot. Their provocation, too, succeeded. The first reaction of the Muslim Brotherhood's Mohammad Morsi, who had been elected president of the country, was evasive and ambiguous. Now these Salafist-led protesters chanted to Morsi: 'Why are you silent—is Muhammad not your Prophet?'[195]

Also on the 9/11 anniversary, Christopher Stevens, the US ambassador to Libya, was killed in an armed attack on the US consulate in Benghazi. Senior Obama administration officials said this had begun as a demonstration in response to the video—which by now had become known as 'Innocence of Muslims', the title given it on the most-viewed reposting on YouTube.[196] That interpretation subsequently became the subject of fiercely partisan controversy and congressional hearings in Washington, with some Republicans arguing that this had been an Al Qaeda attack unconnected to outrage at the video. However, a detailed New York Times investigation quoted Libyan witnesses saying they 'received lectures from the attackers about the evil of the film'.[197]

Demonstrations against the video erupted in many other places. Western news bulletins reported that protests spread across 'the Muslim world', and it is true that the largest and most violent were in majority Muslim countries. Yet Map 7 shows that there were also protests in Europe, India, Africa and Australia.[198]

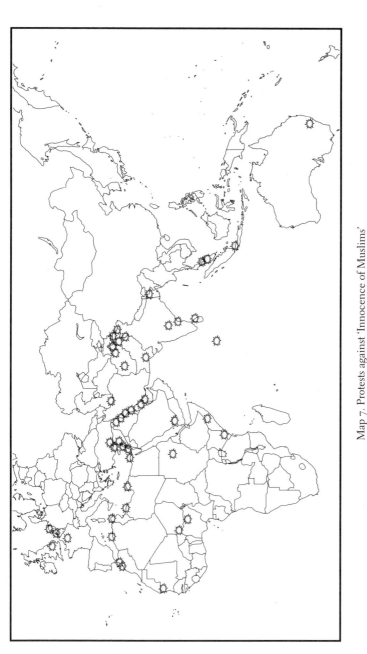

Map 7. Protests against 'Innocence of Muslims'

This map shows some of the reported protests against the 'Innocence of Muslims' YouTube video.

Source: Adapted from John Hudson, The Wire, 2012.

As we have seen, our new cosmopolis is defined by its combination of virtual and physical, global and local—and here was another urban-orbal free speech drama.

In a familiar ritual, protesters often gathered outside a US embassy to burn and stamp on American and Israeli flags, although neither the American nor the Israeli government had played any part in the production or distribution of the video. By the end of September, more than 50 people had died in the protests, mainly in majority Muslim countries such as Pakistan, Afghanistan and Libya. They included two Pakistani policemen who had been trying to control the crowd on a government-declared Day of Love for the Prophet.[199]

The US government distanced itself from the video, which Secretary of State Hillary Clinton called 'disgusting and reprehensible' but insisted that nothing justified the violent reaction to it.[200] President Barack Obama placed a reportedly frosty telephone call to Egypt's President Morsi, to ask why he had not more emphatically condemned the violent protests outside the US embassy.[201] In fact, not to be outdone by the Salafists, the Muslim Brotherhood had itself called a demonstration against the video on Tahrir Square, that historic centre of the Arab Spring. It subsequently cancelled it, although still suggesting a 'symbolic' protest.[202]

More remarkably, General Martin Dempsey, the chairman of the Joint Chiefs of Staff, got in touch with a Florida pastor called Terry Jones—who had himself sparked riots in 2010/11 by first threatening to burn and then actually burning a copy of the Qur'an—to ask him not to promote this video, as his fellow Christian extremist Morris Sadek had done.[203] Consider for a moment: the most senior officer of the mightiest armed forces the world has ever seen feels it necessary to contact some backwoods Florida pastor to beg him not to promote a 13-minute D-movie YouTube upload. Such are the power asymmetries in this connected world. The pen may not be mightier than the sword, but a video clip can be mightier than the US Fifth Fleet.

Meanwhile, the White House 'reached out', as a National Security Council spokesman delicately put it, to Google, which owns YouTube, 'to call the video to their attention and ask them to review whether it violates their terms of use'.[204] Here is another symptomatic feature of the case: the pivotal role of a private power. The occasion for violent protests that preoccupied the United States' highest leaders, as well as claiming many lives, was not anything done by the big dog USA but a video posted on a global platform owned by a big cat called Google. Google/YouTube declined the White House's request to review the video on the grounds that the company had already done so and found it 'clearly within our guidelines'.

Those YouTube Community Guidelines suggested that, beside gratuitous violence, sexually explicit content and 'bad stuff like animal abuse, drug abuse or bomb making', the platform does not permit 'hate speech (speech which attacks or demeans a group based on race or ethnic origin, religion, disability, gender, age, veteran status, and sexual orientation/gender identity)'.[205] Analysing the affair, the eminent First Amendment scholar Robert C. Post argued that 'Innocence of Muslims' did not violate this guideline because it 'does not attack a group (or an individual) "based upon" any such status category. Instead it directly quarrels with the authority of Muhammad, and hence derivatively with the status of Islam as a religion. In classic American fashion, Google regards the film as a debate about ideas rather than as a defilement of sacred ground'.[206]

This seems a somewhat lofty interpretation. Since, unlike the search facility on google.com, YouTube does not aspire to be a global First Amendment space but rather a welcoming 'community' with guidelines banning 'bad stuff', one could argue that they should have taken the video down when first it was flagged by users as offensive content, for it plainly was intended to demean Muslims as a group.[207] To take it down months later because it had become the subject of violent protests in front of US embassies would, however, send a very different message.

The American government was not the only one to 'reach out' to YouTube. Within a fortnight, Google/YouTube had received requests to block or review the video from at least 21 national governments.[208] In a number of countries, including India, Indonesia, Malaysia, Singapore, Jordan and Saudi Arabia, where YouTube is 'localised'—with a local legal presence and country-specific version—and the government said the video violated local laws or regulations, YouTube blocked it for IP addresses in that country. In Pakistan, Afghanistan and Bangladesh, where YouTube was not 'localised', Google refused removal requests. Those governments then blocked the whole of YouTube for users on their national IP addresses. (A contributor to freespeechdebate.com who was then in Pakistan gives a vivid account of spending hours getting round the censorship so as to view the video, but tellingly feels the need to use a pseudonym even when writing about the experience three years later.[209]) Bahrain and the United Arab Emirates did not bother to ask but filtered the video using their own means. In Russia it was partially blocked, while Russian Orthodox campaigners made rare common cause with Muslims to demand that material offensive to the 'feelings of believers' (a term used in Russian law) should be banned. In short, there was a hectic worldwide game of jurisdictional, political and technological Whac-A-Mole.[210]

More unusual was the fact that, after the US embassy in Egypt and consulate in Libya came under attack, YouTube blocked access to the video in those two countries without receiving any request from the Egyptian or Libyan governments. 'We work hard to create a community everyone can enjoy and which also enables people to express different opinions', YouTube said in a statement. 'This can be a challenge because what's OK in one country can be offensive elsewhere'. The video was 'clearly within our guidelines and so will stay on You-Tube. However, given the very difficult situation in Libya and Egypt we have temporarily restricted access in both countries. Our hearts are with the families of the people murdered in yesterday's attack in Libya'.[211]

While this reaction was understandable, it set a dangerous precedent. For YouTube to respond to requests from governments asserting that an item violates local laws—either by complying and blocking by IP address, or by refusing and risking the whole platform being blocked in that country—may raise questions about the differing quality of the laws in different states, but it has a transparent logic and consistency. To do so without any legal request from the relevant government has two worrying implications.

First, this private power, Google/YouTube, becomes the arbiter—a largely nontransparent, arbitrary arbiter—of what people in other countries may see. Yet on what grounds and by what right does a company executive sitting in Mountain View, California, determine that this is fit for the eyes of someone in Cupertino but not for someone in Cairo? Second, and more seriously, suggests that violent protest pays. What was justified by YouTube as an exceptional response, to minimise the clear and present danger of violence, actually becomes an implicit encouragement to such violence. The conclusion any extremist might reasonably draw is: just demonstrate violently enough outside a US embassy, preferably killing a few US diplomats, and YouTube will take the offending item down. (I say more about what I call the 'assassin's veto' under principle 2.)

While all this was roiling on, world leaders were gathering in New York for the UN General Assembly. President Barack Obama devoted a large part of his address to these events. He condemned the video but gave a robust defence of the First Amendment tradition of allowing offensive speech: 'We do so not because we support hateful speech, but because our founders understood that without such protections, the capacity of each individual to express their own views and practice their own faith may be threatened'. In a diverse society, he said, restating a classic American position, 'the strongest weapon against hateful speech is not repression, it is more speech—the voices of tolerance that rally against bigotry and blasphemy, and lift up the values of understanding and mutual respect'.[212]

Moreover, 'in 2012, at a time when anyone with a cell phone can spread offensive views around the world with the click of a button, the notion that we can control the flow of information is obsolete'. (Tell that to the Chinese Communist Party.) Not all countries shared this particular understanding of free speech, he acknowledged, but 'on this we must agree: There is no speech that justifies mindless violence. There are no words that excuse the killing of innocents. There is no video that justifies an attack on an embassy. There is no slander that provides an excuse for people to burn a restaurant in Lebanon, or destroy a school in Tunis, or cause death and destruction in Pakistan'. (Although, we might note in passing, he clearly did believe that a terrorist threat justified unmanned US drones causing death and destruction in Pakistan—a distinction between legitimate and illegitimate kinds of violence to which I will return under principle 2.)

President Mohammad Morsi of Egypt took a very different line. While condemning the use of violence 'in expressing objection to these obscenities' and stressing his country's (newfound and, in the event, short lived) respect for freedom of expression, Morsi said, 'the obscenities recently released as part of an organised campaign against Islamic sanctities is [*sic*] unacceptable and requires [*sic*] a firm stand. We have a responsibility in this international gathering to study how we can protect the world from instability and hatred'.[213]

What such international remedial action might consist of was spelled out by Pakistani President Asif Ali Zadari. After condemning 'the acts of incitement of hate against the faith of billions [*sic*] of Muslims of the world and our beloved prophet Muhammad (peace be upon him)', Zadari went on: 'The international community must not become silent observers and should criminalise such acts that destroy the peace of the world and endanger world security by misusing freedom of expression'.[214]

But who exactly should criminalise what acts? A member of the Pakistani government, the railways minister Ghulam Ahmad Bilour, helped flesh out his president's remarks. He personally offered a $100,000 reward to 'whoever kills the makers of this video'.[215] ('Sam Bacile' had in the meantime been identified as Nakoula Basseley Nakoula, a California-based Egyptian Coptic Christian who at the time of filming was out on parole, after serving time in prison for bank and credit card fraud. But the railway minister's wording presumably also put Alan Roberts, of 'Young Lady Chatterley II' fame, and 'Michael', a.k.a. 'George', a.k.a. the Prophet, in the firing line.) Challenged to explain himself by the BBC's Zubeida Malik, the Pakistani railways minister said, 'I feel that I have to do something because in Europe and America there is no law to stop this kind of activity. I think if they . . . America and the Western world . . . have some laws that our prophet, peace be upon him, is not disgraced, I would not have done this'.[216]

So the demand was not just that Pakistan should be able to impose its own cultural norms on all the information platforms accessible in its territory, where blasphemy against Muhammad is legally punishable by death. It was that America and Europe should change their laws to accommodate those norms — or else. This from a government minister in a country that annually received more than \$2 billion in aid from the United States. Bilour's contract death threat, or political fatwa, was condemned by his own prime minister, but he was not sacked. Analysts pointed out that the ruling Pakistan People's Party would not want to risk losing its coalition partner, Bilour's Awami National Party, in the run-up to a general election. Although the Awami National Party described itself as a secular, left-wing party, Bilour had apparently boosted his own popularity by taking this militant stance. Ironically enough, the Pakistani Taliban honoured him by declaring that he had been removed from their own hit list.[217] So all it takes to lift a death threat from the Taliban is for you to make a death threat to someone else. Mehfouz Jan, the organiser of Bilour's party in Britain, where at least 1.7 million people of Pakistani origin live, distanced himself from his colleague's remarks but demanded on BBC radio 'a once-for-all stop for this blasphemous action which is causing this day-by-day problem in the whole Islamic world'.[218]

Thus a sleazy little video posted on YouTube by a convicted fraudster in Southern California had dictated the agenda of the US president, secretary of state and chairman of the joint chiefs of staff; prompted YouTube to exercise arbitrary private censorship; given the Salafists a card to play against the Muslim Brotherhood in Egypt; become the occasion or pretext for violent demonstrations in many countries, resulting in the death of more than 50 people; and brought a \$100,000 price on the filmmaker's own head, offered for transparently political reasons by a Pakistani government minister. That in turn led a British-based Pakistani politician from the same party to demand 'a once-for-all stop for this blasphemous action' — presumably also in Britain, where I watched the video and wrote these lines. Welcome to cosmopolis.

The story did not end there. The Egyptian state prosecutor issued arrest warrants for seven Egyptian Coptic Christians allegedly involved in making the video and Florida pastor Terry Jones: an example of legal procedure as gesture politics if ever there was one. 'Sam Bacile' Nakoula was taken back into custody in California, on the grounds that he had broken his probation conditions by concealing and then lying about his role in making the video.[219] His defence lawyer said he should be allowed out on bail, arguing that Nakoula would be in danger at the downtown Los Angeles federal prison. Why? Because it has a large number of Muslim inmates.

Cindy Lee Garcia, a bit-part actress in what she had thought was 'Desert Warrior', sued the film's producer and YouTube on various grounds, including an unusual claim that her copyright in her own performance had been violated. Amazingly, in February 2014 an appeals court recognised her claim to copyright in her five-second appearance in the film and ordered Google to take down all copies of 'Innocence of Muslims' from YouTube and all other platforms. Thus, in the land of the First Amendment, a grossly tendentious claim for individual intellectual property rights succeeded where all other considerations had failed. More than a year later, the court reversed its judgement and the original video was reposted to YouTube.[220]

Back in the heat of controversy in autumn 2012, the pseudonymous individual who posted the most-watched version of 'Innocence of Muslims' changed his (or her) description of it. When I first looked, in mid-September, it was titled 'Innocence of Muslims—Muhammad Movie—Full HD' and there had already been around 10 million viewings. 'DarthF3TT', whose other uploads consisted mainly of clips from a computer sharpshooter video game called Sniper Elite V2—so, shall we boldly guess, he rather than she?—had put a strip message across the opening shot saying 'Thumbs up for Free Speech and Human Rights'. His introductory description read 'Innocence of Muslims is the movie by Sam Bacile that caused Muslims to kill United States ambassador, J. Christopher Stevens'. But by 4 October, when his upload had garnered more than 16 million viewings, 'DarthF3TT' had removed the 'thumbs up' strip and changed the headline to read 'A Stupid Movie Not Worthy of Global Turmoil'. Underneath he wrote: 'my reason for reposting this video was based on reports from US Media that Americans were killed over it. New information has come to light that shows these reports were FALSE. My reason for reposting is therefore no longer valid. I have disabled the comments because there was nothing new being said, and I cannot in good conscience allow all the hate and racism to continue here'. (So far as I can establish, he subsequently removed it altogether from his YouTube page.)[221]

Indeed, many of the comments on that thread made the graffiti on your bog standard men's lavatory wall look like lyric poetry. Yet by 14.59 UK time on 4 October 2012, the version he reposted had registered no fewer than 47,481 'likes' to 116,167 'dislikes'—though, given only that binary choice, it is not clear what exactly people were 'liking'. Darth now referred viewers back to Sam Bacile's original upload of 2 July, which was still there—for users in countries where it had not been blocked—and still called 'Muhammad Movie Trailer'. As the internet commentator Rebecca MacKinnon discovered by tweeting to ask anyone in Egypt to take a look, YouTube had quietly unblocked it for Egypt and Libya.[222]

But there was another video, high in the YouTube clickstream, which would give some encouragement to those who shared the classic liberal belief that the best answer to hateful speech is more and better speech. Titled 'A Muslim's reaction to Muhammad Movie Trailer', it was posted on 12 September, just a day after the first violent protests, by someone called Syed Mahmood.[223]

A quiet-spoken, bespectacled young man with a distinct British accent talks to his home computer camera. He says he has just viewed the video and is 'a bit upset' by it but urges his fellow Muslims not to react violently. For, he argues, that is exactly what 'this guy named imbecile, sorry, this imbecile named Sam Bacile' wants them to do. 'He wants Muslims to go crazy about this . . . so by reacting, I would say you are going to make him successful, you are going to make him happy actually'. In what seems an entirely spontaneous way, Mahmood suggests that his fellow believers should not again fall into the familiar role of the 'Offended Muslim'.[224] 'This movie is intended to hurt your feelings, so don't let it succeed', he appeals. 'Don't let it succeed by being violent'. By mid-October, this improvised message from a totally unknown young British Muslim, who according to his profile had only started uploading stuff to YouTube a fortnight before, had been viewed more than 485,000 times.

I managed to contact Syed Mahmood and we met for a coffee in London. He had grown up in Bangladesh and come to England in 2010. He now worked as an accountant. He had made the home video spontaneously and was astounded when it went viral: 30,000 hits on the first day, 100,000 on the second. A devout Muslim, adhering to the Hanafi school of Islamic jurisprudence, he cited to me several Qur'anic verses to underpin his argument that his fellow Muslims should not react violently. These things will happen, he said. 'If it's offensive, don't watch it, don't be offended'. If Muslims reacted calmly, relations between them and non-Muslims would get better over the next 30 years, 'and it's up to us Muslims to do that'. How had people responded to his appeal? 'Oh, some people inboxed me'. And yes, he'd had the odd death threat. How did that feel? 'To be honest, I don't really care . . . So long as I'm doing the right thing'.[225]

So if, as this affair once again demonstrated, the connected world can multiply a millionfold the snarls of obscurantist bigotry, to fatal effect, it can also amplify the quieter voices of courageous reason.

IDEALS

WHY SHOULD SPEECH BE FREE?

The fact that most states in the world have signed international treaties guaranteeing freedom of expression, and make such promises in their constitutions, does not answer the question: why should speech be free? As soon as we start trying to hold governments to their word, or debate the proper limits of free speech, we find ourselves reaching for arguments that either underpin or call into question the terms of such treaties, laws and policies. Even if your instinct, like mine, is to say, 'but of course speech must be free!' it is still important to spell out why.

The Western intellectual tradition has offered four main answers. Each comes with multiple philosophical, legal and literary variations, yet the basic thoughts are remarkably persistent. I call them in shorthand STGD: Self, Truth, Government, Diversity.

The first argument is that we need freedom of expression to realise our full individual humanity. The power of speech is what distinguishes us from other animals and, thus far, from computers. If we are prevented from exercising it freely, we cannot fully be ourselves. That includes revealing ourselves to others, insofar as we wish to. Strapped into a straitjacket with a hood over my head and lips taped shut, I may inwardly reflect 'my thoughts are free; you can't take that away from me'. Yet even that innermost freedom of thought cannot entirely be separated from the freedom of expression. As anyone who writes or speaks will know, often you discover what you really think only in the process of speaking or writing. 'The thought is made in the mouth', said the Dadaist Tristan Tzara.[1] Remember Syed Mahmood, spontaneously articulating to his home computer camera his reaction to the 'Innocence of Muslims' video.[2] I will know what I definitely want to argue in this book only when I have finished writing it and discussed the draft with friends and critics.

Moreover, even the most unbending liberal individualist must accept, as a description of lived reality, that I establish not just what I think but who I am through relations with other people. The Zulu proverb *umuntu ngumuntu ngabantu*, which roughly translates as 'a person is a person through other persons', is sometimes understood as an African communitarian rebuke to European individualism, but it can simply be taken as the description of a human universal.[3] It is precisely because we are not what Jeremy Waldron calls 'the self-made atoms of liberal fantasy' that we need the liberal good of freedom of expression, in communication with others, so as to be fully ourselves.[4]

I have been labouring to summarise this first answer in cold prose, but behind it is a truth that millions of people who have been denied freedom of expression know instinctively, feel passionately and articulate in ways such prose cannot capture. So, before proceeding a line further, please stop and listen on your box to Nina Simone's rendition of a song called 'I Wish I Knew How It Would Feel to Be Free', originally written in 1963, at a time when black Americans were still fighting to achieve the equal freedom they had been promised by Abraham Lincoln a hundred years before. To Billy Taylor's jazz melody, itself a musical embodiment of freedom of expression, Simone sings, in a contralto voice blending warmth and melancholy:

> I wish I knew how
> It would feel to be free
> I wish I could break
> All the chains holding me
> I wish I could say
> All the things that I should say
> Say 'em loud say 'em clear
> For the whole round world to hear

A little later come two lines as profound as they are simple:

> I wish you could know
> What it means to be me

Here is the most elemental argument for free speech.

Returning to cold prose, there is a philosophical variant of this answer that deserves a mention. Thomas Scanlon derives the case for free speech from the essential sovereignty of the individual. In order that we may regard ourselves as 'equal, autonomous, rational agents', Scanlon writes, we must be 'sovereign in deciding what to believe and in weighing competing reasons for action'.[5] Note that this focuses on the right of the listener to hear competing arguments and beliefs, rather than that of the speaker to express something. (Needless to say, 'speaker' and 'listener' are terms of art, embracing all forms of communication.) When we judge any claim for free speech, we have to keep in mind and some-times balance these two things: the rights of and consequences for the speaker, and the rights of and consequences for the listener. Simone's couplet brilliantly captures both: 'I wish *you* could know / what it means to be *me*'.

Scanlon takes us to the doorstep of a second classic argument for free speech, which is that it enables us to find the truth. Or at least it helps us to seek the truth. After a century of totalitarian lies, and faced with chronic media manipu-lation even in liberal democracies, we may no longer share the magnificent confidence of Milton's 'let her and Falsehood grapple; who ever knew Truth put to the worse in a free and open encounter?'[6] Even John Stuart Mill, who penned the most eloquent and influential version of the argument from truth in the Eng-lish language, acknowledged that 'it is a piece of idle sentimentality that truth, merely as truth, has any inherent power denied to error, of prevailing against the dungeon and the stake'. But Mill argues—against censorship—that a sup-pressed opinion may turn out to be true and that, even if not altogether true, it may yet contain some grain of truth. Even supposing the received wisdom is one hundred percent correct, if it is never challenged it will come to be held 'in the manner of a prejudice', or what another writer called 'the deep slumber of a de-cided opinion'. 'Both teachers and learners go to sleep at their post', writes Mill, 'as soon as there is no enemy in the field'.[7] So the good sword of truth will only be kept sharp if it is constantly tried against the axes and bludgeons of falsehood.

The philosopher Bernard Williams acutely describes Mill's notion as the 'survival of the true'. It has had a huge influence on the whole Western tradition of thinking about freedom of expression.[8] Together with his 'harm principle', it shapes free speech debates to this day.

In the United States, this approach is characterised with the aid of another metaphor: the 'marketplace of ideas'. The market comparison was popularised by the early-twentieth-century Supreme Court justice Oliver Wendell Holmes, although—as with so many famous quotations—he never used those exact words. But Holmes did argue, in a dissenting opinion in a 1919 Supreme Court case, 'that the ultimate good desired is better reached by free trade in ideas—that the best test of truth is the power of the thought to get itself accepted in the competition of the market'.[9] In a seminal article entitled 'The Use of Knowl-edge in Society', Friedrich Hayek made a lucid case for markets (as opposed to central planners) and especially what he called the 'marvel' of the price system being the best way to arrive at certain kinds of truth.[10]

In the early twenty-first century, following a historic crisis of unbridled free market capitalism, this image of the market as optimal truth-finder may seem somewhat less compelling—but the case does not stand or fall on a single metaphor. Our semantic armoury is brought up to date by a more recent writer on the First Amendment, Anthony Lewis, who refers to free speech as 'a search engine for truth'.[11] The future will surely throw up new metaphors for the same thought.

A third classic argument for free speech is that it is necessary for good government. Although American universities have discarded the teleological 'from Plato to NATO' self-congratulation of once-obligatory courses on 'Western Civ', it remains astonishing how the essence of our modern idea of free speech as a democratic public good is to be found almost fully formed 2,500 years ago, in Athens and some Greek colonies across the seas. Every citizen who desired to do so would gather in the designated assembly place of the city-state. In Athens, some 6,000 people came together on the gentle slopes of the pnyx, just off the Acropolis.[12] 'Who wishes to address the assembly?' cried the herald.[13] Then any free man could speak, outlining what he believed would be the best policy for that city-state and presenting his reasons for it. The best decisions and policies, it was claimed, would be arrived at by openly debating the alternatives, often ending with a vote. The ancient Greeks named this novel form of government 'democracy', meaning rule by the people.

To emphasise the speech element, modern scholars refer to 'deliberative democracy'.[14] First voice, then vote. The English word 'vote' derives etymologically from the Latin *votum*, meaning 'wish' or 'vow'. 'I do think', said the Leveller Thomas Rainsborough, in the great Putney debates of Oliver Cromwell's army during the English Civil War, 'that the poorest man in England is not at all bound in a strict sense to that government that he hath not had a *voice* to put himself under' (my italics).[15] It is no accident that, in several modern languages, the words for vote and voice are one and the same: *Stimme* in German, *stem* in Dutch, *stemme* in Danish, *głos* in Polish, *golos* in Russian, *sawt* in Arabic.

The ancient Greeks' innovation of free speech for deliberative democracy embraces not one but two ideals, which they called *parrhesia* and *isegoria*. *Parrhesia* meant speech that was both free and fearless. The playwright Euripides has a mother wish that her sons should return to 'glorious Athens, hold their heads high there, and speak their minds there like free men'.[16] While the etymology of the word—from *pan-rhesia*, to say everything—might suggest unlimited speech, there was a strong presumption that the parrhesiast, the free-speaker, should say things he believed to be true and for the good of the community.[17] The orator Demosthenes spoke of 'the truth spoken with all freedom, simply in goodwill and for the best'.[18] There was special licence for the arts, especially for comedy, but even Euripides deplored 'hectoring and untutored *parrhesia*'.[19]

As important was *isegoria*, which meant equality of speech — or what, in the modern language of rights, we would call an equal right to speak. In another of his plays, Euripides has Theseus, the mythical king of Athens, explain that 'freedom lives in this formula: "Who has good counsel which he would offer the city?" He who desires to speak wins fame; he who does not is silent. Where could greater equality be found?'[20] To be sure, this ur-equality applied only to free men, not to women, noncitizens or slaves, but the essential idea was there. Free and equal speech would allow deliberative democracy and that, the ancient Athenians believed, would produce better government. Indeed, the historian Herodotus maintained that it was because Athens had free speech that it became powerful and victorious.[21]

Fast-forward to modern Britain and America. This is exactly what the contemporaries of Mill and Holmes believed, and they did so as conscious heirs to ancient Greece. To this day, the triple linkage between free speech, democracy and — as the attributed result — good government remains a central tenet of Western liberal democracy. This can also be described as self-government, the system in which, to quote a fine formulation by the American scholar Alexander Meiklejohn, 'rulers and ruled are the same individuals'.[22] Ronald Dworkin articulates a contemporary liberal egalitarian version, arguing that free speech is a condition of legitimate government. Fair democracy, he says, requires 'that each citizen has not just a vote but a voice: a majority decision is not fair unless everyone has had a fair opportunity to express his or her attitudes or opinions or fears or tastes or presuppositions or prejudices or ideals, not just in the hope of influencing others (though that hope is crucially important), but also just to confirm his or her standing as a responsible agent in, rather than a passive victim of, collective action'.[23]

Pulling together some of these threads, an English judge wrote in a late-twentieth-century judgement that 'freedom of speech is the lifeblood of democracy'. As Stephen Sedley points out, the word 'lifeblood' is particularly apt, since 'free speech enables opinion and fact to be carried round the body politic'.[24]

While the connection with democracy is both classical and strong, there are also time-honoured arguments about the connection between free speech and good government that are not exclusively tied to democracy. A first-century-C.E. author has Diogenes say to Alexander the Great (hardly a model democrat), 'In view of what I say, rage and prance about . . . and think me the greatest blackguard and slander me to the world and, if it be your pleasure, run me through with your spear, for I am the only man from whom you will get the truth, and you will learn it from no one else'.[25]

Free speech is also required to check and control what your government does. This brings into play not just freedom of expression but freedom of information, and what has been called the right to know. The American founding father James Madison spoke of 'the right of freely examining public characters and measures'.[26] The economist and political theorist Amartya Sen famously pointed out that 'no famine has ever taken place in the history of the world in a functioning democracy'.[27] He explicitly connects this to the flow of information, both to the people and to their rulers, made possible by a free press. This is most fully articulated in liberal democracies, but the idea of enabling a degree of public scrutiny and access to information so as to improve the quality of government is far from unheard of in other political systems. As we have seen, China's rulers have allowed their censors to leave online, and even quietly encouraged, the exposure of local and provincial mismanagement. Traditionally, a 'right to know' has been asserted mainly against public powers, but since private powers are now so potent, it should surely be claimed against them too. If we have a right to know what the government knows about us, don't we have a right to know what Google knows about us?

A fourth major claim for free speech is particularly relevant to our emerging cosmopolis. Freedom of expression, it is argued, helps us to live with diversity. Although this strand does not figure so prominently in the modern Western classics on free speech, the germ of the idea is there at the very origins of modern liberalism. We can find it, for example, in the essays of John Locke and others about the need for 'toleration' in place of Europe's wars of religion. We find it also in Immanuel Kant's claim that human progress is best served not by the absence or suppression of conflict but by conducting that essential, creative conflict in peaceful, civilised ways.

The American scholar Lee Bollinger has developed this thought. Drawing on the experience of the United States, with its long history of religious and ethnic diversity, he suggests that freedom of expression 'tests our ability to live in a society that is necessarily defined by conflict and controversy; it trains us in the art of tolerance and steels us for its vicissitudes'.[28] One could put the same point more positively, circling back to the first argument for speech. If everyone living in the same place or space is free to express herself or himself, then we have a better chance of understanding what, in that memorable phrase sung by Nina Simone, 'it means to be me' — and you, and her, and him; John, Aisha or Ming. We will not all choose to live our lives in the same way. We will not all agree. As Kant observed, human society would be stagnant and bovine if we did. (Adam and Eve were probably bored stiff in the Garden of Eden.) But we can learn, by practice, how to live with irreducible difference and not come to blows. At best, we will agree on how we disagree.

These four classic Western arguments—STGD—are combined by the former German Constitutional Court judge Dieter Grimm into a single pregnant formula: individual self-development and collective self-determination.[29] Obviously my brief sketch does not begin to exhaust the many subtle answers that have been given over centuries to the question 'why should speech be free?' We should not exclude the possibility that others will find their strongest case for freedom of expression to rest on different grounds. The Chinese Communist Party, for example, might conclude that it needs more free speech in order to have the scientific and technological innovation that is essential to sustain the dynamism of a maturing economy—and hence for China to attain its ancient goal of 'wealth and power'.[30] So their instrumental justification would have little to do with individual human flourishing or popular self-government. Plainly, the version of free speech that followed from this rationale would be somewhat different from that justified on the classic liberal grounds.

Ultimately, each of us has to make up her or his own mind which arguments we find most persuasive—and produce our own. Yet this is only the beginning of the conversation. Although free speech debates may return to underlying justifications, they are not mainly about the question 'why?'. Rather, they are largely preoccupied with two questions that begin with the word 'how': 'How free should speech be?' and 'How should free speech be?'

HOW FREE SHOULD SPEECH BE? HOW SHOULD FREE SPEECH BE?

Most of the modern literature on free speech is devoted to the first of these questions. Typically it uses philosophical and legal arguments to ask, 'should the state allow this or ban that?' This is how free speech issues are often debated in the media, usually prompted by controversy around a particular book, film, cartoon, court case, proposed law or other measure. Vitally important though that question remains, too little attention is paid to the second: how should free speech be? In what style, with what conventions and mutual understandings, should we choose to express something (or not)? A right to say it does not mean that it is right to say it. A right to offend does not entail a duty to offend. This challenge goes beyond voluntary self-restraint to the active exploration of opportunities. What social, journalistic, educational, artistic and other ways are there of making free speech fruitful, enabling creative provocation without tearing lives and societies apart? How can we treat each other like grown-ups, exploring and navigating our differences with the aid of this defining human gift of self-expression?

In truth, the first question—how free should speech be?—cannot satisfactorily be answered without addressing the second. The less we want enforced by law, the more we need to do ourselves. The less we manage to achieve by our own voluntary, sovereign shaping of the ways we interact, the more call there will be for the police and courts to do the job for us.

This thought has been developed in different ways by two people with special authority to speak on the matter. The early-twentieth-century Harvard law professor Zechariah Chafee was one of the founding fathers—or at least, uncles—of the modern American First Amendment tradition. Oliver Wendell Holmes acknowledged the scholar's influence on his seminal judgements in the aftermath of the First World War. In the 1942 preface to the second edition of his book *Free Speech in the United States*, originally published in 1920, Chafee wrote that the law should lay few restraints on those who wish to speak, 'but that makes it all the more important for them to restrain themselves'. 'It is hopeless for the law to draw the line between liberty and license', he continued, but 'the man can look into his own heart and make that decision before he speaks out'.[31] In a new chapter written for that edition, he argued that we need to go beyond the confident assumption made by Milton and Mill that truth will win out if we simply remove the legal obstacles to open discussion. 'We must', he writes, 'take affirmative steps to improve the methods by which discussion is carried on'.[32]

Then there is Aung San Suu Kyi, the heroine of Burma's struggle for freedom and a political prisoner for nearly twenty years. In a manifesto written for the fortieth anniversary of the magazine Index on Censorship, Suu Kyi makes a powerful case for free speech. Noting someone else's observation that the vital thing is not so much freedom of speech as freedom *after* speech, she writes: 'Through long years of authoritarian rule, members of the movement for democracy in Burma have been punished for speaking out in protest against violations of human rights and abuses of power'.

Yet she also insists that freedom of speech can be abused, 'that words can hurt as well as heal'. 'Misusing the gift of speech to deceive or harm others is generally seen as unacceptable. Buddhism teaches that there are four verbal acts that constitute "tainted failure in living": uttering deliberate lies for one's own sake, for the sake of others, or for some material advantage; uttering words that cause dissension, that is, creating discord among those united and inciting still more those who are in discord; speaking harshly and abusively, causing anger and distraction of mind in others; indulging in talk that is inadvisable, unrestrained and harmful'. Here is the hugely demanding agenda of the Buddhist precepts traditionally summarised as 'right speech'.[33]

The legal philosopher Leslie Green has set out to explore how these Buddhist precepts of right speech might be applied in a Western liberal society.[34] Some notion of right speech or good speech is to be found in most cultures, and in the Western tradition too. One of the ancient Greek Nereids, daughters of the mythical Nereus, was called *Euagore* — 'good speech'.[35] Mill ends his great chapter on free speech with an eloquent description of how public debate should be conducted. He calls these habits and manners, which he insists cannot be legally enforced, 'the real morality of public discussion'.[36]

NOT BY LAW ALONE

A central contention of this book is that we should limit free speech as little as possible by law and the executive action of governments or corporations, but do correspondingly more to develop shared norms and practices that enable us to make best use of this essential freedom. I see three main reasons to focus on underlying principles or norms. The first is the nature of cosmopolis. As we have seen, this definitely does not render irrelevant the laws a single state tries to enforce in its own territory, as the early cyberlibertarians hoped ('Governments of the Industrial World . . . You have no sovereignty where we gather'.) But it does reduce the singular significance of sovereign states.

The old principle 'when in Rome do as the Romans do' loses much of its force when the Romans, many of whom retain close ties with family homelands far from Rome, are simultaneously — at the click of a mouse — also in San Francisco, Athens and Beijing. If our effective freedom of expression in a connected world is decided at the intersection of four different kinds of force — international bodies, nation states, private powers and electronically enabled networks of individuals — then it makes less sense to concentrate so heavily on the single question 'what should be the laws of this state?' Rather, we need to think about the underlying principles or norms that we hope to see realised at all those levels, and can try to realise ourselves by collective, aggregated and individual action.

The second reason for looking beyond the law is older, but even more relevant today. The eighteenth-century British author Samuel Johnson said it beautifully:

How small, of all that human hearts endure,
That part which laws or kings can cause or cure.[37]

It is both the strength and the weakness of the modern Western literature on free speech that it concentrates on questions of law within one, usually national, jurisdiction—or, as in Europe, a set of closely linked jurisdictions. This has the great virtues of rigour, precision and concreteness. It takes you to a series of real-life cases, in which courts had to decide whether it was legal or illegal for someone, in a particular place and time, to hold up a sign proclaiming 'homosexuality is a sin', shout 'Islam is of the devil', write 'President Bonjo is a liar', burn a national flag, wear the hijab or show a pornographic movie. If history is philosophy teaching by examples, law is philosophy tested by examples.

Yet this philosophical-legal literature also has the weakness of its strengths. It tends to reduce questions about free speech to the generic 'is/should this be illegal?' Yet in authoritarian states and what have been called 'illiberal democracies', laws are made of rubber. They are stretched this way and that by the powers that be. Even in mature liberal democracies, free speech is distorted by the immense and often hidden power of money, which both speaks and silences; by political manipulation; by popular prejudice; by media proprietors and bad journalism; by power relations in the workplace, communities and the home, as well as between sexes, classes and ethnic groups; and, not least, by the silencing force of the individual man or, less often, woman. In practice, religious, social and cultural norms can also be more compelling than the letter of the law.

Law comes into action mainly at the contested frontiers of speech. It covers—what? 0.1 percent? 0.01 percent?—of all human expression. Its effect is of course far larger than that figure suggests, but it does not directly impact most of us most of the time. Law's searchlights are trained on the cliff's edge; they do not routinely play over the huge inland of human communication. That does not mean this inland is a continent without standards. Far from it. With countless registers of frankness, politeness, irony, deference, joking and powerplay, we consciously, half-consciously and unconsciously self-regulate our freedom of speech a thousand times a day. This is the stuff of novels, poetry and everyday conversation the world over. It differs subtly from language to language, culture to culture, family to family. What is inoffensive in Italy may be deeply offensive in Tunisia. What is humorous joshing in an Irish pub in Toronto may be mortal insult in the Moroccan teahouse next door.

Some of these standards are written down. The editorial guidelines of the BBC, for example, are a theological compendium of responsible free speech in public service broadcasting.[38] Senior BBC executives agonise over them with the intellectual passion of a medieval Jesuit. (Should Hamas fighters be described as terrorists or insurgents? Can this politician be called gay?) Many of the nonlegal standards, however, are unwritten—which does not mean unspoken. We speak as we do today, and don't say what we don't say, partly because of many a word uttered years ago by mother to child, teacher to pupil, friend to friend.[39] Some of the lessons are not expressed in words but intimated by a raised eyebrow, a sudden coldness or an unwanted laugh. Other lessons you just work out for yourself, by trial and error. Mark Twain captured this customary self-restraint with glorious exaggeration when he observed of the United States, through the mouth of Pudd'nhead Wilson: 'It is by the goodness of God that in our country we have those three unspeakably precious things: freedom of speech, freedom of conscience, and the prudence never to practice either of them'.[40]

This brings me to the third main reason for concentrating on norms. I have touched on it already while summarising the case for free speech as a way of living with diversity. Recall the analogy with navigation: we will never learn how to sail if the state will not allow us to take the boat out. To discover and set limits for ourselves is what responsible adults do. And recall Kant's famous definition of Enlightenment: to emerge from our 'self-imposed immaturity'.[41] Kant contrasts enlightened maturity with the *Vormünder*, those who paternalistically control and presume to speak for others. *Bevormundung* in modern German means tutelage or the act of patronising. The overregulation of speech by law manifests precisely this tendency for the state to treat us as overgrown children, not mature enough to make such judgements for ourselves, incapable of coping with contrary or offensive views, forever needing to be ticked off by the teacher.

LAWS AND NORMS

Thus far, I have talked of laws and norms as if they were obviously distinct things, like fire and water. In truth, they are more like ice and water—two distinct states of the same H_2O, one hard, one soft, together with intermediate conditions such as slush, sleet and hail. The early-twentieth-century linguist Max Weinreich observed that 'a language is a dialect with an army and a navy'.[42] In the same spirit, one might say that a law is a norm with a court and a prison. It is a behavioural rule, specified in careful detail, by a combination of statute and court judgements, and then enforced within a jurisdiction—usually a state, or a clearly defined part of a state.

Yet this does not capture the full range of possibilities. When we say 'the law', we tend to think of the criminal law: say or do that and you'll be locked up. But there are other, progressively softer versions of law which shade into the realm of norms. There is civil law. There is the so-called expressive function of law, with wording that is designed to send a general message about how things should be in a given society.[43] There is 'soft law', a term which well describes the nonbinding character of most international agreements on freedom of expression.[44] There are regulations on nondiscrimination which affect what may or may not be said in hiring someone and at the workplace, and statutory regulation of the media. Beyond that, states may choose not to ban some form of expression but to tax it, or to give it financial assistance. Cheap postage was crucial to the spread of nineteenth-century American periodicals. To this day many countries exclude books and newspapers from value-added tax (VAT).

The political scientist Corey Brettschneider makes a useful distinction between the state's coercive and expressive functions. Quoting John Locke's observation that it 'is one thing to persuade, another to command', he argues that while the coercive power of the state should be used with extreme caution in relation to free speech, there is every reason for a state to use its expressive power for what he calls 'democratic persuasion'. Thus, for example, the state can 'speak' through designating an anniversary, a Holocaust Day or Martin Luther King Jr. Day, through monuments and museums, through parliamentary and presidential declarations, and, perhaps most important, through what is taught in state-regulated schools. There are difficult issues here too—for example, how far should teachers be encouraged directly to challenge the views of parents?—but the general principle is an important one.[45]

Moreover, it is a mistake to believe that self-regulation necessarily means less restriction. Take the Production Code (sometimes known as the Hays Code) that was adopted by Hollywood film studios in 1934 and remained largely in force until the early 1960s. Have you ever wondered why in old American movies married couples always seem to have twin beds? Because the code decreed it. No sex please, we're American. And that was not all. As Tim Wu observes,

> on the topic of dance in films, the Production Code set standards that might have satisfied the Taliban:
> DANCES
> 1. Dances suggesting or representing sexual actions or indecent passions are forbidden.
> 2. Dances which emphasise indecent movements are to be regarded as obscene.[46]

This purely private piece of self-regulation restricted what Americans—and everyone around the world who watched American movies—could see or hear as effectively as any federal law. Today's counterparts are the self-made rules of private powers such as Facebook, Google and Twitter.

Perhaps the most telling example of self-restraint is parliament. Harking back to ancient Athens, the special freedom of speech in a democratic parliament is one of the oldest established free speech rights. The very word 'parliament' has its roots in the French *parler*—to speak. A parliament is a place of speaking. A century before France's Declaration of the Rights of Man and Citizen offered a more comprehensive and egalitarian article on free speech, England's 1689 Bill of Rights proclaimed 'that the freedom of speech and debates or proceedings in Parliament ought not to be impeached or questioned in any court or place out of Parliament'.[47]

Yet the British parliament, like other parliaments, has elaborate rules and conventions governing what may or may not be said by members in its chambers. They are summarised in a mighty tome known as Erskine May, first published in 1844 and now in its 24th edition.[48] These rules are about exercising responsibly that special privilege a parliament enjoys, at what should be the heart of a democracy, and ensuring robust yet civilised debate. They are, in some respects, more restrictive than the laws prevailing outside. Thus, for example, in the British parliament you are not supposed to accuse another member of lying. That would be an 'unparliamentary expression'. Winston Churchill famously withdrew one such accusation, replacing it with a charge of 'terminological inexactitude'. In recent years, the weekly questioning of the prime minister, known as Prime Minister's Questions, has seen a sharp decline in these standards of robust civility, often descending into a puerile shouting match. British democracy is no stronger as a result.[49]

Universities, too, though dedicated to Kant's 'dare to know' (*sapere aude*), have their own free speech policies. Oxford's are rather legalistic for my taste, Stanford's elusive, Yale's magnificent.[50] Some of these policies are too restrictive, but no reasonable person would question the principle that a self-governing community of scholars and students has the right to set its own rules for civilised interaction. (I say more about this under principle 3.) So does any other club, society or community. One of my favourites is the German Chaos Computer Club, which describes itself as 'Europe's largest association of hackers'. These German hackers are nonetheless constituted in a registered association with a detailed set of statutes, as prescribed by German law, regulating what the Chaos Computer Club modestly calls its 'galactic community of living beings'.[51] In families, the rules are generally unwritten, yet they probably have more impact on what we do or do not say than the hardest injunction of criminal law.

In short, there are not two clearly delineated countries, with a single, sharp frontier between them: the Kingdom of Laws and the Republic of Norms. But neither is there a smooth continuum from hard law to soft norm. Rather, there is a series of discontinuities as you traverse from the firmest criminal law ('if you say that, you go to jail') to the most private norm ('please don't say that, it upsets me'). Think of it as a sprawling castle in the middle of an old town. There is the inner keep of criminal law and the outer castle of other kinds of law and regulation. There are multiple, overlapping norms beyond the castle walls, varying from village to village, church to church, field to field, house to house. And then there are the self-made rules and practices of private powers which stretch wirelessly across all the others.

So the question you have to ask of any free speech issue in our time is not just 'should our state allow or ban it?' It is: 'what, if any, is the appropriate form of constraint or convention, legal or nonlegal, written or unwritten, for this specific act of expression, or sharing of information, in this particular context?' The issue then becomes: on what grounds should we make such judgements?

OFFENDED? WHAT'S THE HARM IN THAT?

Where to begin? The legal philosopher Joel Feinberg produced a magisterial account of justifications for limiting liberty by the criminal law.[52] Although his purpose was at once broader and narrower than mine, it offers a helpful framework in which to think about justifications for restricting freedom of expression by any means, from hardest law to softest norm.[53] His first four justifications, to each of which he devotes a whole volume, are harm to others, offence to others, harm to self and harmless wrongdoing. He describes attempts to prevent the last two as legal paternalism and legal moralism. In legal paternalism, the state, acting like a father (Latin: *pater*) to his children, tries to prevent its subjects from doing harm to themselves. In legal moralism, the state uses the law to enforce what it deems to be a true morality.

Now contemporary Western liberal debates about free speech generally concentrate, as I will, on Feinberg's first two categories: harm to others and offence. But it is important to remember that through much of the history of the West, both paternalism and moralism played a huge role in limiting free speech — and in much of the world they still do. The attitude of many authoritarian regimes, and all totalitarian ones, is quintessentially paternalistic. The state says to its citizens: we know best what is best for you. It treats them like children, not Kant's enlightened adults. The approach of states identified with a single dominant religion or code of morality, found in its strongest form in theocracies, is also moralistic. It says: you may not express that, or see or hear that expressed, because it is contrary to true morality, as defined by our interpretation of sharia law, or the Bible, or a little green or red book, or whatever the acknowledged source of public morality may be.

We forget at our peril how much of both approaches was still accepted in Western societies until quite recently. In 1959, an influential British judge, Lord (Patrick) Devlin, argued that a proper function of the law was, in the words of his book title, *The Enforcement of Morals*. An organised society would be justified in banning private sexual immorality—in which category he included homosexual acts—if it felt that it jeopardised its integrity. As late as 1962, a British Law Lord could still approvingly quote a famous judgement from 1774: 'whatever is *contra bonos mores et decorum* the principles of our laws prohibit, and the King's Court as the general censor and guardian of the public morals is bound to restrain and punish'.[54] (Note the positive use of the word 'censor'.) In the early twenty-first-century West, there are both remaining traces of such paternalism and moralism and new versions of them. Article 10 of the European Convention still refers to 'public morals' and, as we shall see, European legislation on hate speech sometimes strays into paternalistic—or maternalistic— territory. Moreover, when the liberal mainstream in the West comes to engage with the rest of the world, ideas of the paternal role of the state (as in China) or the enforcement of morality (as in Saudi Arabia) are central to the resulting disagreements.

Most of the major contemporary Western debates about free speech can, nonetheless, be captured in terms of harm and offence. (Unless otherwise indicated, the words 'to others' should be understood to follow whenever I use the term 'harm'. Feinberg also says 'offence to others', but can I really offend myself? The comic potential seems considerable.) In John Stuart Mill's original formulation, the 'harm principle' says that 'the only purpose for which power can be rightfully exercised over any member of a civilised community, against his will, is to prevent harm to others'.[55]

Many contemporary liberals wish to draw the line at that. Freedom of expression, they say, should not be limited on the grounds of mere offence. No one has the right not to be offended. Yet, as Feinberg points out, serious modern liberals—including Mill himself—in fact stray across that apparently bright line, and concede some validity to limitations based on something being offensive rather than outright harmful. For example, in considering obscenity and film censorship a British committee chaired by the liberal philosopher Bernard Williams explicitly justified its proposed restrictions on the grounds not of Millian harm but of 'offensiveness'—although, as we shall see, the Williams committee used the term in a very distinct and limited sense.[56] At the very least, to capture the range of argument we have to look at both harm and offence.

But what is harmful? And what offensive? At once the difficulties begin. Take the ultimate harm: the unnatural termination of a human life. Who would disagree with the proposition that speech that leads to murder should not be allowed? But how do we know what speech 'leads to' murder? It all depends on the context. The very same words or images can be harmless in one context, fatal in another. We therefore have to look at the time, manner, place and medium of speech, an exercise significantly complicated by the fact that the internet telescopes both time and space.

When I was a child, my mother used sometimes to exclaim in exasperation, 'I could shoot him'. I heard her turn of phrase again on BBC Radio 4 the other day, when an older woman's voice said, 'I think they should be shot'. No one in their right mind would think these old-fashioned English ladies meant it seriously. Britain's Guardian newspaper once ran a strap headline across the top of its front page saying 'Charlie Brooker: Execute Simon Cowell and give away croissants'.[57] Charlie Brooker is known as a humorous writer, and this call for the killing of Cowell, a popular music impresario, was obviously a joke. But when the Libyan dictator Muammar Gaddafi threatened to 'cleanse the city of Benghazi . . . alley by alley', everyone knew it was no joke.[58]

Context is all. People endlessly cite Oliver Wendell Holmes's observation that one should not be free to shout 'Fire!' in a crowded theatre when there is no fire. The example given by John Stuart Mill is better. 'An opinion that corn-dealers are starvers of the poor', he writes, 'or that private property is robbery, ought to be unmolested when simply circulated through the press, but may justly incur punishment when delivered orally to an excited mob assembled before the house of a corn-dealer or when handed out among the same mob in the form of a placard'.[59]

And this is only the beginning. 'Sticks and stones may break my bones but words can never hurt me' says an English proverb. Taken literally, as a descriptive statement, that is plainly wrong. Words, images and other forms of expression can hurt, sometimes more than a mere physical assault. A leading academic authority on free speech, Frederick Schauer, offers a nice personal example. 'Disparaging comments about my scholarship by a universally respected scholar', he writes, 'would do me more harm than would be done if that same person kicked me, or even broke my arm'.[60] The harm here would be to his reputation—that is, to how others see him—and therefore in some sense objective. Yet there would also be a subjective component: he would feel bad and, in the worst case, might lose the confidence to pursue his work.

What seem like clear lines between physical and psychological, objective and subjective, turn out to be fluid and contestable. At the extreme, there are writers who argue that words and images do not merely incite to harmful deeds, they *are* those deeds. Thus, for example, the feminist philosopher Catherine MacKinnon famously wrote that 'pornography is masturbation material. It is used as sex. It therefore is sex'. Later in the same book, she refers to 'speech that is sex'.[61] Richard Delgado and Jean Stefancic have claimed that racist hate speech causes physical as well as psychological harm. 'The immediate short-term harms of hate speech', they write, 'include rapid breathing, headaches, raised blood pressure, dizziness, rapid pulse rate, drug-taking, risk-taking behaviour and even suicide'.[62] However thin the medical evidence may be for these sweeping claims, few would deny that there are psychological harms and these can be serious.

The distinction between objective and subjective, meanwhile, takes us to the frontier zone between harm and offence. Jeremy Waldron argues that the law should protect people's dignity but that it should not protect them from offence. He suggests that dignity concerns the 'objective or social aspects of a person's standing in society', but offence 'subjective aspects of feeling, including hurt, shock and anger'. 'Offence', he says, 'is inherently a subjective reaction'.[63]

But, what if I choose, like Nelson Mandela and many dignified African Americans in the last century, to maintain that those who are truly demeaned are not the targets of racist abuse but their abusers? Are we to say 'no, *objectively*, Comrade Mandela, your dignity has been demeaned, even if you maintain it has not. Who are you to say whether you have kept your dignity?' In the early 1960s, the African American writer James Baldwin proudly insisted, '*Whoever debases others is debasing himself.* That is not a mystical statement but a most realistic one, which is proved by the eyes of any Alabama sheriff—and I would not like to see Negroes ever arrive at so wretched a condition' (his italics).[64] To define harms to dignity as objective—irrespective of the recipient's subjective view—may actually be to deprive people of the most irreducible human dignity: that of making the sovereign decision on how to view their own situation.

This said, the transition from harm to offence clearly does involve a growing element of subjectivity. But here too there are important gradations. In a perhaps intentionally uproarious passage of *Offense to Others*, Joel Feinberg tells 31 stories of more or less offensive things that you might encounter as a passenger on a bus.[65] Story 6, for example, has a group of passengers eating a picnic lunch 'that consists of live insects, fish heads and pickled sex organs of lamb, veal and pork, smothered in garlic and onions'. Story 7 has the same picnickers practicing 'gluttony in the ancient Roman manner, gorging until satiation and then vomiting on their tablecloth. Their practice, however, is a novel departure from the ancient custom in that they eat their own and one another's vomit along

with the remaining food'. Story 8 is demurely described as 'a coprophagic se-
quel to Story 7'. ('Coprophagic' means 'eating excrement'.) Turning to sex, hap-
penings on the Feinberg Express include heavy petting and fondling (Story 15),
someone wearing a T-shirt depicting Jesus and Mary as a copulating couple
(Story 19), two lesbians performing cunnilingus (Story 22) and oral sex between
a passenger and her dog (Story 23). Whoever said legal philosophy was dull?

Feinberg's thoroughly serious point is that there are multiple kinds of offensiveness and states of being offended. It matters whether offence is intended. It
also matters whether the offended person cannot easily avoid seeing, hearing or
smelling what they find offensive (hence his chosen setting on a bus) or has voluntarily put himself or herself in, so to speak, offence's way. Feinberg wants to
add an 'offence principle' to the Millian harm principle, justifying some restrictions in the criminal law—but the offensiveness has to be intended, significant
and not reasonably avoidable.

In considering obscenity and film censorship, the British committee chaired
by Bernard Williams added another important qualification. The kinds of offensiveness with which it was concerned—delicately defined as portraying,
dealing with or relating to 'violence, cruelty or horror, or sexual, faecal or uri-
nary functions, or genital organs'—should be limited, only if the unrestricted
availability of such material would be 'offensive to reasonable people'.[66]

Of course that last phrase, familiar in philosophy and law, raises the question
of who is a reasonable person, what she or he might find offensive, and why a
judge or film censor is qualified to determine it. And in cosmopolis a phrase like
'contemporary community standards' raises the question of which among many
interconnected communities we are referring to. Nonetheless, Williams's careful, narrowly drawn standard is a long way from the kind of purely subjective act
of declaring 'I am offended', which is what defenders of free speech are mainly
worried about when they draw the line at 'offence'. Such 'taking offence' is, as
Frank Furedi writes, 'a privatised, subjective and arbitrary response to a feeling
of hurt by an individual'.[67] If you legitimise that as a justification for curbing
freedom of expression, then you are—taking this to its logical conclusion—
giving everyone a right to exercise a veto simply by pronouncing the words 'I am
offended', rather as a single seventeenth-century Polish nobleman could block
a piece of proposed legislation by pronouncing the words *'liberum veto!'*

Today's veto statements come most often in the form of claimed offence
to a group identity. Next to what Kamila Shamsie has dubbed the Offended
Muslim, there is the Offended Woman, the Offended Hindu, the Offended
Homosexual, the Offended Person of Colour, the Offended [fill in nationality,
creed or ethnicity to taste]—and, let us not forget, the Offended Liberal.[68] The

logic is the same: the legitimation, with negative consequences for others, of a purely subjective act of taking offence. Thus, for example, an ever longer list of terms and images may be ruled off limits because they might just be offensive to someone. In his novel *The Human Stain*, Philip Roth has a university professor's life unravel because he casually remarks of a couple of students who never turn up for his class 'Do they exist or are they spooks?' He means 'are they ghosts?' but 'spook' can also be an offensive term for black Americans, which these students, whom he has never seen, happen to be.[69] In real life, the actor Benedict Cumberbatch felt impelled to make a grovelling apology for using the word 'coloured' on US television, even though, far from intending to insult people of colour, his whole purpose was to express concern at how few non-white actors were given work in prominent theatrical roles.[70]

There are at least two mutually reinforcing reasons for refusing to limit freedom of expression on grounds of such purely subjective offensiveness. The first is a matter of, so to speak, moral psychology: Do we want to be the kind of human beings who are habitually at the ready to take offence, and our children to be educated and socialised that way? Do we wish our children to learn to be adults or our adults to be treated like children? Should our role model be the thin-skinned identity activist who is constantly crying, 'I am offended'? Or should it rather be the Mandela, Baldwin or Gandhi who says, in effect, 'although what I see written or depicted is grossly offensive, I hold it beneath my dignity to take offence. It is those who abuse me who are demeaning themselves'. 'Sticks and stones may break my bones but words can never hurt me' then becomes not a patently false description of reality but a precept for fortitude.

There is an obvious objection to this, which I will take head-on: 'It is easy for you, a white, middle-aged, male, comfortably-off professor at Oxford, and hence a member of a secure privileged group, to say this. If you were poor/black/lesbian/Muslim, you would feel differently. You have no right to speak for such vulnerable minorities'. To this there are several answers. If everyone is entitled only to talk about his or her own experience, or that of their group, any wider conversation becomes impossible. Indeed, this objection is itself a meta-version of the subjective, identity-based offence veto. It says: 'I am offended by you—you of all people—challenging my right to be offended!' (But then, by your own criterion, how dare you tell me how easy it is to be me? What can you possibly know of the inner suffering of white, middle-aged Western man?) Anyway, what I argue here is not a dictum, let alone a diktat. It is a proposition put forward for debate and disagreement. Moreover, the most inspiring examples of dignity come not from a secure, dominant majority, but from among the downtrodden who refused to be trodden down.

A further reason for refusing limits based on purely subjective taking offence is that we now live in cosmopolis, and in cosmopolis we are bound to encounter things that offend some of us. In a global city such as Toronto or London, different and sometimes mutually offensive ways of life necessarily exist cheek-by-jowl. A late-night city bus may not exhibit quite the baroque array of behaviours seen on the Feinberg Express, but it will throw up some which the proverbial man on the Clapham omnibus would find grossly offensive.

This is, of course, even more true on the internet. The British newspaper columnist Suzanne Moore found—online, of course—an image of a cat sitting in front of a computer screen.[71] It is captioned 'OMG. I have been offended. And on the internets of all places'.[72] ('The internets' is, I am reliably informed, cat-speak for 'the internet'.) Especially with the prevalence of anonymous posting, the internet has become a global anthology of the offensive.

It is tempting to suggest that the nature of the internet makes it impractical to control the dissemination of anything offensive at all, but that would be inaccurate. If something is considered unacceptable by almost everybody, in all countries and cultures, then an international collaboration of public and private powers can prevent most people from being exposed to it most of the time. Extreme, paedophile forms of child pornography are the best example. Some 140 states (including the Vatican) have signed up to the UN Convention on the Rights of the Child, and most governments take at least some measures against this filth.[73] The Council of Europe's Convention on Cybercrime, which has a section on 'content-related offences' entirely concerned with child pornography, has been signed or ratified not only by all members of the Council of Europe but by 11 other states, including Australia, Japan, Panama and Sri Lanka.[74] Significantly this is one major area in which Google voluntarily and actively filters its own search results and collaborates with law enforcement agencies to help track down paedophiles—for example, using sophisticated photographic analysis to identify their possible locations and scanning emails for child pornography.[75] Some mobile phone companies go to the very edge of legality (if not beyond) to help the authorities find paedophiles.

But child pornography is the exception that proves the rule: it is one of very few things that almost everyone agrees should not be allowed online. And it is, after all, not merely offensive to reasonable people; it is the gateway to an appalling harm—the sexual abuse of children. Yet even then, even with this almost universal condemnation, enforced by the active collaboration of public and private powers, some of the poison still gets through, not least because its purveyors flee to the so-called dark net.[76]

Faced with this new reality, there are, broadly speaking, three alternative routes we could take. One is for each government to try to impose its own limits on what it considers offensive within its frontiers. As we have seen, practice on the internet has moved in this direction since its Californian cyberlibertarian beginnings. Even in the United States there are some who want their governments and courts to do more to control the 'offensive internet'. For example, the legal philosopher Brian Leiter has argued that Google should be held responsible in the United States for grossly intrusive or demeaning material about individuals that shows up in its search results.[77] But to realise this approach with complete consistency, you would have to build a Great Firewall of America, France or Australia, and a large surveillance apparatus within it. The practical difficulties, as well as the chilling effects and the invasion of privacy (in the name of defending privacy), suggest that such national legal efforts should be focused on what are clearly harms and not the fuzzy and often subjective category of the offensive.

A second alternative is for the internet to remain relatively free, and therefore doubtless offensive, and for individuals and groups to go on taking offence left, right and centre. That is a recipe for a thoroughly bad-tempered world—and in some places for violent conflict. Recall that violent protests occurred in several countries where the 'Innocence of Muslims' YouTube video was already blocked. Protesters were reacting to the rumour-embroidered fact of its continued availability online in America and Europe. To that extent, the option of national firewalls has already proved ineffective.

The third alternative is for us to recognise that we shall have to live with somewhat higher levels of offence, but to manage it as best we can through norms of many kinds, upheld in diverse ways. If we are unavoidably confronted with what we find offensive, in public spaces or on the bus, we can either ignore it or speak up against it—though always stopping short of violent intimidation. Rather than institutionalise thin skins we can encourage everyone, starting with ourselves, to grow thicker skins. The seventeenth-century poet George Herbert includes in his list of English proverbs this one: 'there were no ill language if it were not ill taken'.[78] We can keep a sense of proportion and, most valuable of all, a sense of humour. This may sound demanding, but it is what most so-called ordinary people—who are, of course, far from ordinary—do online and on city streets every day of the week.

It will by now be abundantly clear which path I think we should take. The unprecedented conditions of cosmopolis only strengthen the case for a modernised version of a classic liberal position. We should use criminal law and the coercive power of the state to combat real harms. Given the sheer volume of speech now whizzing around the globe, states have their work cut out even to do that. However, we should take positive steps of many different kinds, whether in education, journalism, local communities or our own personal conduct, not merely to equip us to live with offence but to develop a culture of open debate and robust civility. These are twin tasks. The better we succeed in the latter, the less we will have need of the former.

Now, reasonable people can and do disagree on where a particular piece of 'speech', be it an article, a cartoon, a theatre performance, a burqa or a flag-burning, should be placed on the line between the most serious harm and the most trivial offence. They will also disagree about where, on the line from the hardest law to the softest norms, the appropriate response is to be found. These are separate judgements. I might agree with you on the characterisation of the harm and disagree about the appropriate remedy, or vice versa.

One way of thinking about this to envisage a personal judgement grid, with three axes marked Context (of the speech act), Justification (of the constraint) and Justified Constraint. We place each case within the three-dimensional grid to determine the most appropriate constraint. Context includes the time, manner and place of the speech, the audience(s), the medium or media involved, and the historical and cultural background. Was it an angry mob before an investment banker's unguarded mansion? Or a seminar of decrepit dons, barely able to lift a pencil in anger? A television programme that reached tens of millions through a widely respected broadcasting organisation, an individual tweet that reached just ten other twits, or an entirely private conversation in bed with your partner? What is the deep history of the images, music or words used in that particular place and time? Justification means the grounds for limiting freedom of expression. Justified Constraint refers to the many different ways in which that freedom can be limited.

We can argue about every case and its proper place, but the overall organising principle will be clear. The greater the harm, and the more conducive to that harm is the context, the firmer should be the constraint. The weaker the justification, and the more harmless the context, the softer the justified constraint. Thus, for example, those who advocated exterminating Tutsis 'like cockroaches' on Radio Télévision Libre des Mille Collines in Rwanda should have been stopped, arrested, tried, convicted and imprisoned.[79] Someone who tells a borderline racist joke at a private lunch deserves a cool reaction or a pointed rebuke. It is quite wrong to think that because a limit is not enforced by a policeman knocking on your door at 5 A.M., it is not a constraint. These are constraints, and of the most desirable kind. This is how we learn to navigate the high seas of free speech: by taking the boat out, encountering choppy water, adverse winds and other boats.

READING JOHN STUART MILL IN BEIJING

By this point, some readers will want to object: 'but in our culture . . .' Your whole argument, they will say, is built on purely Western intellectual foundations. How can that possibly be the basis for a transcultural debate? This challenge deserves a careful answer.

The first and easiest—too easy—part of that answer is to point out that the same judgement grid can be used to present propositions that a Western liberal would abhor. Ayatollah Khomeini's call for the execution of Salman Rushdie, the Chinese Communist Party's case for arresting the dissident Liu Xiaobo, a socially conservative father's argument for locking his daughter in her bedroom to prevent her from going out: all can in principle be presented in the form 'If someone says X, constraint Y is justified by Z'. All three propositions would be scorned by a liberal, but they can be represented in the same basic schema. We can argue about them. Yet to treat these purely as *propositional* differences is to ignore two deeper and more intractable levels of difference: the linguistic and what I will call the foundational.

Interestingly, linguistic frontiers endure on the internet even where interstate ones have virtually disappeared—or disappeared virtually. (I say more about this under principle 3.) In *The Hitchhiker's Guide to the Galaxy*, Douglas Adams imagined a creature called the Babel Fish. If you stick it in your ear, it will translate from any language into your own. In real life, the journey from Babel to Pentecost is not so easy. Even displaying many languages on the same website can be difficult, especially when, like Arabic, Farsi and Urdu, they run from right to left. On freespeechdebate.com, our web developers created a new open-source tool so that you can flip seamlessly between scripts. They called it Babble.[80] Machine translation technologies such as Google Translate—alongside one called Babelfish—have made remarkable progress. We use Google Translate and it often enables you to get the broad drift of a comment left in another language, especially if it is translating between two Western languages, as well as producing hilarious gobbledygook. With time, these tools will surely improve, but they don't begin to get at the deeper, conceptual difficulties.

Thus freespeechdebate.com's human translators—native speakers of the 13 languages in which it is presented—struggled to identify proper equivalents for key terms in our principles such as 'the believer'. Our native speakers of Arabic, Urdu and Turkish had difficulty finding a generic word for religious believers. The familiar *mu'min* (Arabic), *Mümin* (Turkish) and *mu'min* (Urdu) have strong connotations of 'believer in the one true faith of Islam'—rather as in mediaeval Europe 'the faithful' meant Christians, as opposed to believers in all other faiths, who were 'infidels'. But the broader, more generic words they essayed risked sounding so vague that they lost the clear connection to religious belief. The linguistic difficulty of finding a generic term for 'the believer', thus putting all faiths on an equal footing, revealed a deeper truth about these societies. Because we painstakingly stripped the principles down to their simplest, most universally comprehensible form, the remaining 'lost in translation' moments show up differences that are more than linguistic.

I use the rather colourless term *foundational* for these deepest differences because any alternative label—such as cultural, philosophical, moral, religious, epistemological or ideological—privileges one aspect of them. The nature of the foundational will vary from person to person. If I am a devout Christian, it will be religious; if I am a convinced Communist, it will be ideological; if I am Chinese, I may be persuaded that it is civilisational.

It is facile to imagine that such differences exist only between the West and the Rest. For a long time, practitioners of Anglo-Saxon analytic philosophy, in the style of A. J. Ayer and J. L. Austin, and those of continental European philosophy, in the style of Edmund Husserl and Martin Heidegger, would barely concede that what the other practiced was really philosophy. They still struggle (sometimes not very hard) to understand each other. The German writer and social democrat Heinrich Mann once described what it was like trying to negotiate an alliance against Nazism with the German communist Walter Ulbricht. 'You know', Mann told a friend, 'I can't sit down at the table with someone who suddenly declares that the table at which we are sitting is not a table but a duck pond, and who wants to compel me to agree'.[81]

In the twentieth century, those duck pond moments were most likely to be ideological. In the early twenty-first century, they have more often appeared to be religious or cultural. As we move further into the twenty-first-century, we face what may best be described as ideologies of civilisational difference. The communication problem remains the same: how do you move forward from the point when you are sure it's a table and the other guy insists it's a duck pond?

One proposal is a so-called dialogue between civilisations. But what does this mean? Can one reliably discern the 'essential' position of a given civilisation or religion on an issue like freedom of expression? Who speaks for Islam, or Confucianism, or Christian Orthodox civilisation? Yes, a study of original or sacred texts often reveals certain irreducible, core differences. No one can credibly maintain that Islam endorses multiple gods, as in Chinese folk religion, or that

Confucianism accepts the premise that there is only one God and Muhammad is his messenger.

Yet both across the centuries and across today's world—diachronically and synchronically—the interpretations of what those original teachings and sacred texts should mean for individual and communal life have varied enormously. As the political scientist Alfred Stepan puts it, all the great religious traditions are 'polyvocal'. Any claim to return to a pure, original version of the faith— Salafist for Islam, Puritan for Christianity—is itself a highly contestable historical interpretation, and Salafists and Puritans are no strangers to factional divisions. The idea, popularised by the work of Samuel Huntington, that one can simply identify 'the Islamic' or 'the Christian' position on an issue such as free speech is dangerous nonsense. By analogy with Vulgar Marxism, I call such an approach Vulgar Huntingtonism.

There never was a time when some absolutely pure Chinese, Hindu, Islamic or Christian cultures existed in neatly delineated blocks of primary colour, as in a painting by Piet Mondrian. 'Cultural purity', writes Kwame Anthony Appiah, 'is an oxymoron'.[82] Cultures have forever grown through mingling, and creativity thrives on the irritation of difference, the surprise of the new.

In particular, over the last 500 years all but the most isolated cultures— perhaps a tiny tribe deep in the Amazonian rain forest—have been heavily influenced by an at once colonising and modernising West. The colonial treatment of most of humankind as inferior, if not subhuman, has left deep, transgenerational scars that help to explain the resistance to Western ideas today. 'We may', Mill blithely observes in the first chapter of *On Liberty*, 'leave out of consideration those backward states of society in which the race itself may be considered as in its nonage'. (Nonage means being a minor, not having attained the maturity for voice and vote.)[83]

In 1860, just a year after *On Liberty* was published, British and French troops looted, ransacked and torched the exquisite buildings and gardens of the Summer Palace, originally laid out by the eighteenth-century Emperor Kangxi as a Chinese Versailles. Britain's noble cause was to persuade the current emperor to accept the import of opium from British India, thus filling British bank accounts at the cost of Chinese lives. A British Army chaplain who witnessed the scene wrote, 'a good work has been done'.[84] You can still walk around the beautiful triste ruins left behind by this act of European barbarism. It is now officially called a National Base for Patriotic Education. Obviously, the history of national humiliation is exploited for all its worth by China' s communist rulers, but they have some good material to work with. A Chinese student of mine, whose high school was in the middle of the old Summer Palace grounds, told me that when he first came to Britain he brought with him a stock of postcards of the ruins and would pointedly send them to British friends. So you can understand why a Westerner lecturing on John Stuart Mill and free speech to a Chinese university class in Beijing, as I once had the rare opportunity to do, might meet some initial resistance.

Yet the encounters between the intellectuals we call Western and Eastern—labels that are all themselves terms of art—have never been one-way. It is true that thinkers of the European Enlightenment projected fantasies of Oriental barbarism onto an imagined East that was as geographically close to them as Poland and Transylvania, let alone Persia, Barbary and Hind.[85] But writers such as Montesquieu and Leibniz were also intrigued by what they could learn of China. Montesquieu writes extensively about China in *The Spirit of the Laws*. Leibniz edited and introduced a book called *Novissima Sinica*—The Latest News from China—which mainly consisted of contributions from Jesuits based there. To one of them, Father Bouvet, Leibniz wrote excitedly about his own discovery that 'all numbers are formed by the combinations of 1 with 0, and that the 0 is sufficient to diversify them'. With the modesty characteristic of so many intellectuals, before and since, Leibniz suggested that this would 'in my opinion, carry great weight with the Chinese philosophers, and perhaps with the Emperor Kangxi himself, for he loves and understands the science of numbers'.[86] We may doubt whether the Emperor Kangxi ever leapt up from his bench in the Summer Palace gardens, electrified with excitement at this discovery—although the binary system that Leibniz identified is the basis of everything we now call digital, including the internet that so unsettles today's Chinese rulers. Nonetheless, we can note that even European Enlightenment philosophers were not indifferent to the possibilities of transcultural learning.

In the nineteenth and twentieth centuries, exchanges became more frequent and direct. For the most part, it was Eastern intellectuals trying to learn from the West—be it the Chinese scholar Yan Fu translating John Stuart Mill at the end of the nineteenth century, an Indian called Mohandas Gandhi studying law in London or the Egyptian Said Qutb visiting Colorado. This could end up in violent rejection of the West (as the disastrous example of the Islamist Qutb shows), or wholesale imitation of the West, or an attempt to find a fusion (thus at least implicitly accepting the substantive claims of universalism), or what the Iranian writer Daryush Shayegan called 'cultural schizophrenia'.[87] Many individual intellectuals went through or oscillated between several of these phases or psychological states in the course of a single lifetime.[88]

In the early twenty-first century, in cosmopolis, the scale of such exchanges has grown exponentially, as millions of students, scholars, writers and journalists have spent long periods living, studying and working in other countries. These experiences can be formative. I once asked a friend at Peking University why the politics of a Chinese mutual acquaintance, a New Left thinker who at that time enthusiastically supported Bo Xilai's so-called Chongqing model—'sing red, smash black'—were so different from his own. I expected a reply digging deep into Chinese history, politics and intellectual traditions. 'Well', said my friend, 'the thing is, you see, while we were both at the University of Chicago I was working with Edward Shils at the Committee on Social Thought but he was in Political Science'.

Not only are such intellectuals influenced—'infected', the retro-purists would say—by ideas from the West. They also adduce arguments of Western provenance to advance their own positions. Thus, for example, the reformist Iranian Shi'ite theologian Mohsen Kadivar uses Islamic theology and jurisprudence to reject the claim that apostasy from Islam is punishable by death—and, indeed, by any other this-worldly punishment. But he cites Article 20 of the Covenant to bolster his demand that 'insulting religious and atheist beliefs' should everywhere be punished by law, as a species of hate speech.[89]

While the simplistic, essentialising approach to civilisations and religions—Vulgar Huntingtonism—is mistaken, there is an opposite tendency which is also problematic. I call it liberal raisin-picking. You pick out a few striking quotations from thinkers in non-Western (or not originally Western) traditions, and exclaim 'you see, they think this too!' For every choice quotation from Confucius, Ibn Rashid or the Indian emperors Ashoka and Akbar, one has to ask: how typical is that of their thought as a whole? What did it mean in their time? What part has it played in the subsequent tradition? Take, for example, this observation by a modern Chinese political thinker:

> Correct and good things have often at first been looked upon not as fragrant flowers but as poisonous weeds; Copernicus's theory of the solar system and Darwin's theory of evolution were once dismissed as erroneous and had to win out over bitter opposition. Chinese history offers many similar examples . . .[90]

Purest Mill! Yet the speaker was Chairman Mao, and the speech (popularly known by the catchphrase 'Let a Hundred Flowers Bloom') was followed by the arrest of intellectuals who actually followed his encouragement to speak out, and the brutal suppression of free speech in the Cultural Revolution.

Translation can be misleading in the more optimistic direction (from a liberal viewpoint), as in the other. Take Confucius's striking admonition to the wise counsellor, which in the translation of the Analects by Simon Leys reads: 'Tell him [the ruler] the truth, even if it offends him'. But in a translator's endnote,

Leys observes that 'another interpretation is also possible: if you oppose him, do it loyally'.[91] Other translations of the same Analect render it as 'Never oppose him by subterfuges' (Arthur Waley), 'make sure that you are not being dishonest with him when you stand up to him' (D. C. Lau), or 'Never deceive him; oppose him openly' (Burton Watson).[92] We don't actually know what Confucius said, because his sayings were only written down many years later, or what he really meant, which can only be understood in the largely lost context of the 'knowledge community' of his time. Moreover, Confucianism as a more or less consistent system of thought, or ideology, traces many of its foundations back to a group of philosophical interpreters, now called Neo-Confucians, in the eleventh century C.E., a mere 1,600 years after the Master's death.[93]

Few sights are more ridiculous than that of a Western atheist, with only a superficial knowledge of Islam, brandishing his lightly thumbed Penguin translation of the Qur'an and proclaiming, 'You see, Islam says that apostasy is always punishable by death!' But up there with him would be the Western liberal, brandishing his lightly thumbed copy of the Analects and exclaiming, 'You see, Confucius endorses free speech!'

Transcultural interpretation is an issue of expertise *about* but also of authority to speak *for*. Here, the pope is the exception who proves the rule. Few if any other religions or life philosophies have such a clear central authority with a precisely specified body, a *magisterium*, of the Church's teaching. Islam, Taoism, Confucianism and Buddhism certainly do not; nor do other branches of Christianity. Even many Roman Catholics, including theologians and monks, did not accept the stipulations of Pope Benedict XVI—the Bavarian conservative Joseph Ratzinger—as the last word on their faith.

This is a problem that the most influential philosopher of modern English-language liberalism, John Rawls, touched on with his powerful notion of the 'overlapping consensus' on which a politically liberal society could be built. 'Such a consensus', he writes in *Political Liberalism*, the second of his two major works, 'consists of all the reasonable opposing religious, philosophical and moral doctrines likely to persist over generations and to gain a sizable body of adherents in a more or less just constitutional regime'.[94] In reply to a critique by Jürgen Habermas, Rawls dips his toe a little further into the muddy waters of real life:

> Consider the political sociology of a reasonable overlapping consensus: since there are far less doctrines than citizens, the latter may be grouped according to the doctrine they hold. More important than the simplification allowed by this numerical fact is that citizens are members of various associations into

which, in many cases, they are born, and from which they usually, though not always, acquire their comprehensive doctrines. The doctrines that different associations hold and propagate—as examples, think of religious associations of all kinds—play a basic social role in making public justification possible. This is how citizens may acquire their comprehensive doctrines. Moreover, these doctrines have their own life and history apart from their current members and endure from one generation to the next.[95]

This seems a rather old-fashioned, not to say illiberal, view of how people actually acquire comprehensive doctrines, inasmuch as they have them. How many Londoners or New Yorkers today would accept that they have acquired their comprehensive doctrines from associations into which they were born? The real-life political sociology of our twenty-first century cosmopolis is both more eclectic and more individualised than this passage implies. It is obviously true that there are fewer doctrines than there are people, but many of us are a kind of one-woman or one-man 'overlapping consensus' of doctrines drawn from various sources and developed in our interactions with other individuals.

Another way of trying to get at foundational differences is therefore to look at aggregated individual opinions, through opinion polls. The evidence here is not abundant, partly because authoritarian regimes seldom allow sensitive questions about free speech to be put to their citizens, but we do have some. The World Values Survey has asked the following question in a number of countries across three successive 'waves' of polling:

If you had to choose, which one of the things on this card would you say is most important?

- Maintaining order in the nation
- Giving people more say in important government decisions [or, in the two earlier waves, simply 'give people more say']
- Fighting rising prices
- Protecting freedom of speech

Perhaps unsurprisingly, a larger proportion of people in democracies tended to favour some combination of 'protecting freedom of speech' and 'giving people more say' over 'maintaining order in the nation' and 'fighting rising prices'. Taking the 2005–2009 polling, in France some 41 percent gave one of the two free speech answers; Britain, 56 percent; the Netherlands, 55 percent; Canada, 60 percent; United States, 45 percent. In China, by contrast, it was only 17 percent for the two free speech answers together, as against 38 percent for 'maintaining order in the nation'. In Turkey, it was 30 percent prioritising free speech against 52 percent for order; Russia, 16 percent against 53 percent; Indonesia, 16 percent against 60 percent; Jordan (this was before the Arab Spring) 14 percent against 56 percent. The 2010–2014 results for a few selected countries are shown in Figure 7, and the trend across the first years of the twenty-first-century in Figure 8.

These polling results are no more than suggestive. After all, people were being asked to rank four good things. India, where (in the 2005–2009 polling) only 19 percent opted for one of the two free speech answers, against 27 percent for maintaining order and 40 percent for fighting rising prices, is nonetheless one of the world's noisiest, most argumentative societies, with a raucously outspoken media. In Taiwan, a mere 14 percent chose free speech against 58

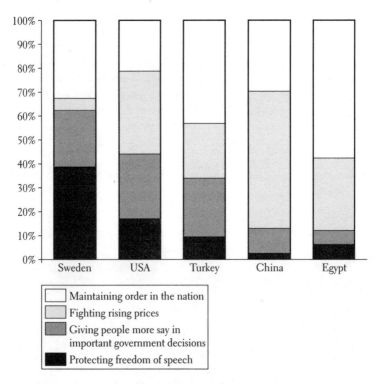

Figure 7. What priority for free speech?
Respondents were asked: 'If you had to choose, which one of the things on this card would you say is most important?'
Source: World Values Survey, 2010–2014.

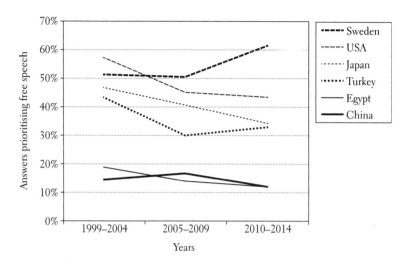

Figure 8. Support for free speech, 1999–2014
The percentage is formed by aggregating the two free speech answers of Figure 7:
'Protecting freedom of speech' and 'giving people more say'.
Source: World Values Survey, 1999–2014.

percent for 'maintaining order', which might suggest that a Chinese cultural preference trumps the contrast between democracy, as in Taiwan, and authoritarianism, as in mainland China. But another set of polling results, gathered in the same period for the East Asian Barometer, showed a significant difference between democratic Taiwan and authoritarian China on the question of whether the government should decide what ideas should be discussed in society (see Figure 9).[96]

I once worked with the Pew Global Attitudes Survey to include a question which essentially asked people to prioritise among Franklin D. Roosevelt's 'four freedoms' (of speech, of worship, from fear, from want), but this yielded no plausibly interpretable results.[97] Beside all the obvious reservations about polling techniques and the way people understand such questions in their own languages, there is a more fundamental point about the answers given in unfree countries. This is what I call the Catch-22 of debating free speech. One of the core arguments for freedom of speech is that you cannot properly make up your mind on a subject unless you have access to the relevant information, have been exposed to the arguments and alternatives and had a chance yourself freely to debate them. If that is true, then it must also apply to arguments for and

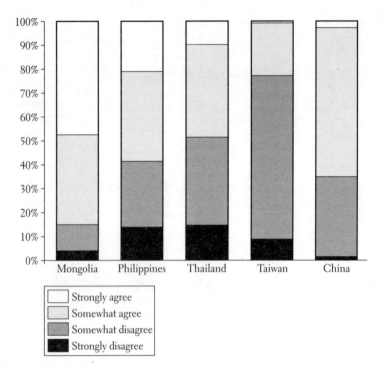

Figure 9. Should the government decide what people can discuss?
Respondents were asked if they agreed with the statement: 'The government should decide
whether certain ideas should be allowed to be discussed in society'.
Source: East Asian Barometer, 2005–2008.

against freedom of speech. But how can you hear and debate those arguments
unless you already have freedom of speech? Catch-22.

This is not just a theoretical observation. While writing this book, I talked to
many audiences outside the West, in places such as Egypt, China, India, Thailand and Burma. Speaking at universities, think tanks, literary festivals or café-
bookshops, I was hardly, as it were, plunging into the paddyfields, where the most
profound cultural differences and misunderstandings might be found. Yet even
among these urban, educated audiences, it seemed that many listeners were
confronted with some of these classic arguments for the first time. Maybe they
were just being polite and had heard it all before, but if so, they certainly made
a good pretence of being unfamiliar with the kind of reasoning reflected in our
ten draft principles. Sometimes they were stimulated to vigorous disagreement,

for example with the principle on religion: 'We respect the believer but not necessarily the content of the belief'. Before my eyes, in a lecture hall in Cairo, a café-bookshop in Beijing or a literary festival in Yangon, I saw a Millian moment unfold, as people reflected freshly on unfamiliar arguments.

That evidence is of course anecdotal. It is, by definition, very difficult to test the Catch-22 proposition. We do not know what people in unfree countries would end up thinking about free speech if they were able to speak freely about it, because they are not allowed to speak freely about it. But one small piece of more rigorous research is suggestive. The political scientist James Fishkin has pioneered a technique called deliberative polling, in which a representative sample of people in a given place are asked their views on a given theme, then presented with carefully balanced evidence and arguments for and against different approaches, and then polled again. Remarkably, he was able to work with Chinese partners to conduct such an exercise on the subject of press freedom in Macao, the former Portuguese colony which is now, like Hong Kong, a Special Administrative Region in the People's Republic of China. The results were unambiguous. After being presented with evidence and arguments, more people came out in favour of more media freedom.[98]

But this process of listening and learning cannot all be one-way. In San Francisco, Sydney, Toronto, Berlin and London we have the opposite need: not to hear, yet again, the classic Western case for free speech, and the familiar disagreements about subjects like hate speech, but to listen, perhaps for the first time, to Confucian, Buddhist, Islamic, Indian, Chinese and Burmese perspectives on the subject.

Next to a willingness to listen and not just to preach, there need to be platforms on which the exchange of information and the battle of ideas can take place. We must also provide adequate translation to overcome the linguistic frontiers that persist on the internet, even as it erodes—though it does not demolish—political frontiers. Both of these things freespeechdebate.com attempts to offer, as do websites like TED, with its impressive array of volunteer translators. But the challenge does not stop there. What about those foundational differences? Here we need what might be called a deep-water Babel Fish. We have to make the best attempt we can to enable a real conversation—not just a dialogue of the deaf—between those who are sure they are sitting at a table and those who insist it is a duck pond. To do that, we should make the most informed, imaginative effort of which we are capable to see the matter from the other person's point of view, and to understand the culturally embedded meanings of terms they use.

In doing so, I discern at least five possibilities: 1. We may use the same words for the same ideas and give them the same order of priority. 2. We may use the same words for the same ideas but give them a different order of priority. 3. We may use the same words for what are actually quite different ideas. 4. We may use different words for different ideas. 5. We may use different words for what turn out, on closer examination, to be quite similar ideas.

Even within the West, Variant 1 obviously does not exist across the piste. For example, Europeans and Canadians tend to place a higher priority than Americans do on social security as against individual liberty. Most of the differences between liberal left and liberal right are of this prioritising kind. Variant 2 thus opens many possibilities for productive conversation between political theorists, writers, netizens, experts in the academic discipline of International Relations and practitioners of international relations. For example, we can agree to give the same meaning to terms like sovereignty and self-determination, equality and liberty, peace and justice, but then argue about which should take priority in what circumstances. (Admittedly, to make things more complicated, this presupposes some version of Isaiah Berlin's value pluralism, in which there are held to be multiple, genuine values that are not all reconcilable with each other, in perfect monist harmony.)

Variant 3—same words, different meanings—comes in both superficial and profound versions. The superficial ones—such as a promiscuous use of the term 'democracy' by governments that are anything but democratic—may have more immediate political importance, but the profound ones are more interesting intellectually. For example, the Chinese intellectual historian Li Qiang has written searchingly about the difficulty of translating into Chinese the Western ideas of freedom and liberty (themselves not identical, even in Western languages).[99] Older Chinese terms carry different connotations, while newer ones can feel like Western imports. Liberty sometimes comes out sounding like licence.

This is something Yan Fu wrestled with in his influential translation of Mill's *On Liberty*. As both Li Qiang and the Taiwanese scholar Max Ko-wu Huang have shown, Yan Fu significantly changed Mill's meaning at many points, starting with the book's title, which in his Chinese version became *The Boundary between Self and Group*. He also shifted from Mill's neutral word 'opinion' to a bald notion of true or false.[100] Although the students in the class I taught on Mill at a Beijing university used a modern Chinese version, perhaps something of the same translation problem showed through in the way they nagged away at the very idea of truth. Or perhaps their semantic environment, polluted by both political and commercial lies, propaganda and advertising, had simply made them sceptical about the possibility of any truth. ('I don't think truth exists!' said one.)

Fourth, and most obviously, there are different terms for different ideas, be they Confucian, Taoist, Hindu, Marxist or Muslim. Here we require the skilled labour of dedicated scholars to understand as best we can what distant sages were on about, in the full context of the knowledge communities of their time. This is the kind of deep excavation done by the Cambridge school of intellectual history and the 'concept history' developed by German scholars such as Reinhart Koselleck. To do it well requires a lifetime of study, which is one reason we need universities. Last but not least, there are different terms which, carefully examined, reveal more similarities in the underlying thought than is apparent at first glance.

At the end of this conversation, we may still find mutual incomprehension or fundamental disagreement, but that should not be assumed in advance. After all, it might turn out that what the other person means by 'duck pond' is not so completely different from what I mean by 'table'. Or it might turn out that we do mean completely different things, or see the same object in profoundly different ways, but can nonetheless agree on some basic principles or norms for life around what I still insist is a table and you still call a duck pond.

Jürgen Habermas, in his critique of Rawls, describes a consciously idealised version of such a conversation:

> Under the pragmatic presuppositions of an inclusive and noncoercive rational discourse among free and equal participants, everyone is required to take the perspective of everyone else, and thus project herself into the understandings of self and world of all others; from this interlocking of perspectives there emerges an ideally extended we-perspective from which all can test in common whether they wish to make a controversial norm the basis of their shared practice; and this should include mutual criticism of the appropriateness of the languages in terms of which situations and needs are interpreted. In the course of successively undertaken abstractions, the core of generalizable interests can then emerge step by step.[101]

You may need to read that twice, if not thrice, but there's an important idea in there. Habermas doesn't claim that this is what such a conversation will look like in the messiness of real life; he says this is what it ideally should look like.

In a later text, reflecting on the specific conditions of contemporary Western Europe, where atheists and religious Muslims (or Christians) struggle to understand each other, Habermas admonishes:

> secular citizens . . . are expected not to exclude a fortiori that they may discover, even in religious utterances, semantic contents and perhaps even

hidden intuitions of their own that can be translated and introduced into a public argument.[102]

Given the essential 'separation of church and state', he posits what he calls a 'filter', which allows only 'translated', that is to say secular propositions to pass from the 'Babylonian babble' of public debate onto the agendas of state institutions. So to be acceptable as the basic for public policy in a secular state, these thoughts have to be translated into a language that we might call Secularese.

Since, however, we are not here concerned only with state policies and laws, our deep-water Babel Fish need not be confined to such austere, secular-state water filtering. It can enable the saltwater poetics of different faiths, ideologies and worldviews to be exposed to each other, in the quest for shared, or at least compatible, norms. It can also help us to clarify those ineradicable value differences with which we can nonetheless live. What we are talking about here is nothing less than the quest for a universalism fitted to the transformed circumstances of cosmopolis.

TOWARDS A MORE UNIVERSAL UNIVERSALISM

For most of its history, the practice of Western universalism was anything but universal. It excluded many people at home and almost everyone abroad. Women and those in 'lower' social classes were treated as second-class human beings. Thomas Jefferson kept slaves. From about 1500 on, Western universalism manifested itself to most of the world as colonialism.

In 1905, the British Viceroy of India, Lord Curzon, admonished a group of British colonial administrators

> to remember that the Almighty has placed your hand on the greatest of His ploughs . . . to drive the blade a little forward in your time, to feel that somewhere among those millions you have left a little justice or happiness or prosperity, a sense of manliness or moral dignity, a spring of patriotism, a dawn of intellectual enlightenment, or a stirring of duty, where it did not before exist. That is enough. That is the Englishman's justification in India.[103]

As if India, home to civilisation during long periods of European barbarism, had never known moral dignity or intellectual enlightenment until the Brits arrived. Small wonder that Gandhi, when asked by a reporter what he thought of Western civilisation, is supposed to have replied: 'I think it would be a good idea'. He probably never said that, but the popularity of the quotation testifies to the truth many feel it contains.

For some, this history of Western universalism manifesting itself as imperialism has continued into our own time. When, in the early twenty-first century, a Westerner goes around the world extolling the universal value of free speech, it is therefore not surprising that he encounters the suspicion, and sometimes the explicit charge, that this is just another variant of Western liberal imperialism. When I delivered a lecture with the same title as this section—Towards a More Universal Universalism—at the Stanford Centre at Peking University in 2014, I was not only addressing a subject that the Party's Document Number 9 had recently declared to be one of the seven Don't-Mentions ('universal values'), I was also speaking less than a mile from the ruins of the Summer Palace, destroyed in the name of Western civilisation. None of this is for a moment to endorse a Western cultural cringe, but it does help to explain a certain reticence.

One response to the charge of Western liberal imperialism is to point out that what are identified, by supporters and critics, as Western values are not, as a matter of historical fact, exclusively Western. This is the case made eloquently by authors such as Amartya Sen and Kwame Anthony Appiah, who point to the presence of comparable if not identical values in other cultures. Formulations of the so-called Golden Rule of reciprocity, for example, can be found not just in the Bible but also in Confucius's Analects and the ancient Indian epic called the *Mahabharata*.

In fact, the Confucian and Sanskrit versions of the Golden Rule are more liberal, in the classic 'negative liberty' sense of not imposing constraints on others, than the Christian one. In the King James Bible translation of the gospel according to Matthew, Jesus Christ preaches in his Sermon on the Mount: 'Therefore all things whatsoever ye would that men should do to you, do ye even so to them'. Colloquially, this is quoted as 'do unto others as you would have done unto you' or simply 'do as you would be done by'.[104] This Christian version of the Golden Rule earned a witty rebuke from the writer George Bernard Shaw: 'Do not do unto others as you would have done unto you; their tastes may not be the same'. Confucius and the *Mahabharata* avoid that danger by formulating the Golden Rule in a negative rather than a positive form. 'What you do not wish for yourself, do not do to others', says Confucius.[105] And in the *Mahabharata*: 'This is the sum of duty: do nothing to others that would cause you pain if done to you'.[106]

In other cultures, one encounters the notion that good rulers need counsellors who will speak truth to power. 'Decisions on important matters should not be made by one person alone', declares the Japanese Buddhist prince Shotoku's 'Constitution of 17 Articles', promulgated in 604 C.E. 'They should be discussed with many'.[107] In the extensive endnotes to his translation of the Analects of

Confucius, Leys makes exhilarating connections between, for example, the Confucian idea of the gentleman (who, famously, 'is not a pot') and Blaise Pascal's notion of the *honnête homme*. He compares the Confucian value of *de*, conventionally translated as virtue—Leys says 'moral power'—with the original primary meanings of the Latin *virtus*, Italian *virtù* and French *vertu*.[108]

Perhaps Leys, as an outsider, might still be accused of liberal raisin-picking. Yet every living intellectual tradition involves reinterpretation, as people read and reread the masters for the conditions and purposes of their own times. Thus, for example, a group of leading Chinese Confucians wrote to the highest authorities in Beijing to protest at the rewriting of the Southern Weekly's 2013 New Year editorial. Their letter, dated 'Confucius Calendar Year 2564 and January 7, 2013', dug deep into the history of Chinese political thought to make the case for free speech. It quoted the rebuke of the ninth-century-B.C.E. Duke Zhao to King Li of Zhou, as reported in the fourth-century-B.C.E. Discourses of the States: 'The repression indeed blocked the people from voicing their opinions. However, the consequences of muzzling them are more dangerous than damming the flow of a river. When an obstructed river bursts its banks, it will surely hurt a great number of people. People are like this, too. For this reason, those who regulate rivers dredge them and lead the flood; those who regulate people dredge [channels] and let them talk . . .'.

These contemporary Confucians went on to comment: 'The coercively-inserted opening paragraphs of the Southern Weekly's revised editorial claimed that "Yu the Great controlled the waters 2000 years ago". The ignorance of literature and history behind this writing is indeed laughable; more regrettably, the author forgot precisely the most important political ideal which Yu the Great has left the Chinese people: "Those who regulate rivers lead the flood; those who regulate people dredge [channels] and let them talk"'.[109] (The ignorance is 'laughable' because Yu the Great is a legendary figure, as well known to the Chinese reader as King Arthur is to the British, and is thought to have lived some 4,000 years ago, not 2,000.)

In his autobiography, Nelson Mandela recalls the almost Athenian practice of his African home village:

Everyone who wanted to speak did so. It was democracy in its purest form. There may have been a hierarchy of importance among the speakers, but everyone was heard: chief and subject, warrior and medicine man, shopkeeper and farmer, landowner and labourer. People spoke without interruption and the meetings lasted for many hours. The foundation of self-government was that all men were free to voice their opinions and were equal in their value as citizens. (Women, I am afraid, were deemed second-class citizens.)[110]

Here are powerful reminders that free speech is valued in both the theory and the practice of other cultures. When Aung San Suu Kyi received an honorary doctorate from Oxford University, she was presented by the university's public orator, in Latin, as an 'eastern star' (*praesento stellam orientalem*). But in her response, she said that universities, at their best, teach 'respect for the best in human civilisation, which comes from all parts of the world'.[111] We should think of civilisation in the singular, then, rather than civilisations that allegedly must clash, or nervously respect each other's spheres of influence.

Yet it is a huge and plainly indefensible intellectual leap from this to the suggestion that a liberal philosophy and practice of speech, as outlined in the first part of this chapter, is to be found equally in all cultures and places. There is no ducking this truth: as systematic, institutionalised legal, political, educational, journalistic and artistic practice, free speech—as we are interpreting the term here—is a speciality of the modern West. Figures like Mandela and Suu Kyi are such inspiring advocates for freedom of expression because of their courage in the face of long silencing, but also because they blend a large dose of Western influence and education with the non-Western traditions of their own countries. Rudyard Kipling, a poet who sometimes brilliantly captured the complexity of colonial encounters between the West and the rest, wrote that 'there is neither East nor West when two strong men stand face to face', but with Mandela and Suu Kyi it is rather 'there is *both* East and West'.[112] And in Mandela's case, both South and North.

At this point, it is important to distinguish between several different kinds of universalism. First, there is anthropological universalism. This aspires to identify certain universals that all human beings—Donald Brown's 'Universal People'—have in common. One such list, quoted by Brown, is:

Age-grading, athletic sports, bodily adornment, calendar, cleanliness training, community organisation, cooking, cooperative labour, cosmology, courtship, dancing, decorative art, divination, division of labour, dream interpretation, education, eschatology, ethics, ethnobotany, etiquette, faith healing, family, feasting, fire making, folklore, food taboos, funeral rites, games, gestures, gift giving, government, greetings, hair styles, hospitality, housing, hygiene, incest taboos, inheritance rules, joking, kin-groups, kinship nomenclature, language, law, luck, superstitions, magic, marriage, mealtimes, medicine, modesty concerning natural functions, mourning, music, mythology, numerals, obstetrics, penal sanctions, personal names, population policy, postnatal care, pregnancy usages, property rights, propitiation of supernatural beings, puberty customs, religious ritual, residence rules, sexual restrictions, soul concepts, status differentiation, surgery, tool making, trade, visiting, weaning, and weather control.[113]

It is good to see 'joking' up there as a human universal. Anthropologists can and will continue to argue about what belongs on the list, but one thing is clear: while language and other forms of communication take a prominent place in any anthropologist's catalogue, free speech, in the sense we are discussing it here, is not an anthropological universal. Most human societies have not enjoyed it for most of history.

Then we might talk of political-sociological universalism. Here we would find, for example, the claim often made in soaring speeches by American politicians that, given the choice, everyone will prefer freedom and democracy. I spent my formative adult years writing about countries in communist-ruled central and eastern Europe where people did yearn for more freedom and democracy—and seized the chance when it came. But it is hard to sustain the claim that all societies always share this aspiration. Even when people have overcome the Catch-22 of not being able to speak freely about free speech, they may end up embracing other priorities. Some would argue that this happened in a number of Middle Eastern countries after the liberating moment of the Arab Spring.[114] Even in postcommunist central Europe, many people revealed other preferences once they had achieved more political freedom—including that stubborn human preference for the thing you do not have over the thing you do. When Czechs and Hungarians had security, they longed for freedom; once they had freedom, they longed for security.

Another approach is to attempt a synthesis of the moral and ethical values to be found in the world's main cultures and religions. Thus, for example, a meeting of a so-called Parliament of the World's Religions in 1993 produced a 'Declaration Towards a Global Ethic'.[115] It was initially drafted by the German theologian Hans Küng and subsequently signed by an impressive array of religious leaders including, for 'Neo-Pagans', one 'Rev. Baroness Cara-Marguerite-Drusilla' and for 'Native Religions' one 'Burton Pretty on Top'. Beside the issues of authority and representation already discussed (who speaks for the Neo-Pagans?), and the highly questionable claim that a global ethic—no, 'an irrevocable, unconditional norm for all areas of life'—is to be sought only in religion (what about science or nonreligious philosophy?), the problem with this Global Ethic Declaration is the bloated vagueness of its catalogue of good intentions. Thus, in a section on media, information and education, the key quality appears to be 'truthfulness'. 'Young people', it says, 'must learn at home and in school to think, speak and act truthfully'. But truthfulness is nowhere defined. What if the Reverend Baroness Cara-Marguerite-Drusilla truthfully thinks that one of the practices of Burton Pretty on Top's religion should be banned in any civilised community, and Burton Pretty on Top truthfully disagrees? Such a blancmange of oecumenical waffle will not get us far.

At the opposite extreme is the pellucid justificatory universalism of the philosopher Ronald Dworkin. Political morality should allow for cultural differences, Dworkin acknowledges, but it must be based on principles which are universal because they are true. Liberalism, the version of political morality for which he argues, is ultimately derived from truth discovered by the use of reason. 'We must', he says, 'import liberalism from the realm of objective, universal truth'.[116] That truth is clearly defined and can then be tested by logic and scientific enquiry, against counterargument and evidence, in the Enlightenment tradition of Western thought. And liberalism is universal because it is true: 'if liberalism is true for anyone it is true for everyone'. If it were not true for everyone it would not be true for anyone.

Intellectually, I respect the clarity of Dworkin incomparably more than the waffle of Küng. But for our purposes, the component of 'discourse', in the Habermasian sense, and the search for a degree of normative consensus across countries and cultures, is more salient than it is for the individual philosopher who may proudly say: 'That is the truth. It remains true even if I am in a minority of one'.

As the international relations theorist Andrew Hurrell observes, when it comes to the search for global norms of any kind, 'the relationship between agreement and foundations will always be contested: Do we agree because it is right? Or is it right because we agree?'[117] Ideally, we should all agree on something because it is right. In practice, states and corporations often agree on, or at least tolerate, practices that are wrong—especially in rich and powerful places where they have interests to pursue. How far should we compromise our own sense of what is true and right in the interest of achieving wider agreement?

In the quest for global free speech norms, that is not just a theoretical question. As we have seen, a multiplicity of powers, public and private, interact and compete with each other to determine our effective freedom of expression in any given place and time. This may seem daunting, but it also offers us multiple openings to insert ourselves into the struggle. After reflecting critically on the historical myopia of European universalism, Immanuel Wallerstein exclaims:

It is not that there may not be global universal values. It is rather that we are far from yet knowing what these values are. Global universal values are not given to us; they are created by us. The human enterprise of creating such values is the great moral enterprise of humanity.[118]

That is a giant job description for us all, and an inspiring one. To advance this enterprise, we need to start with more than an empty online comment box. We require a better understanding of where other people are coming from, and the West has some catching up to do. Those we sweep together under the catch-all label 'Eastern' have spent centuries listening to and learning from the West, voluntarily and involuntarily. Westerners should repay the compliment, by translation, study and thought. Lacking the linguistic and cultural competence for all but a few Western cultures, my contribution in that respect is necessarily limited and derivative, and I make no larger claims for it. The other part of this enterprise of pursuing a more universal universalism consists in laying out our own principles, and explaining the grounds for them, in ways that enable a meaningful transcultural conversation. That was the point of reading John Stuart Mill in Beijing and that is the purpose of this book. Our governments may not speak for us but blank sheets do not speak at all.

The goal is not that we should agree on everything—perish the thought—but that we should agree on how we disagree. I nurture no childish illusions that we will achieve that any time soon. This is only a beginning; more modestly and accurately, it is to take forward work that others have already begun.[119] That work is more essential than ever in a connected world, replete with competing powers and burgeoning conflicts. The never-ending journey towards what Kant called a 'world civil society' has acquired a new urgency in our time.[120]

Part II

USER GUIDE

The ten principles that follow are distilled formulations of a modern liberal position on free speech, intended for cosmopolis. They are not exact prescriptions for laws. Rather, they lay out norms that we can promote, through any and all of the forces I have identified in Part I, including international bodies, nation states, private powers and networked individuals. The principles are meant to complement each other and form a coherent set. They have been drafted to make them as accessible as possible across languages, cultures and countries, an undertaking sharpened by the practical exercise of translating them into twelve other major world languages.

They have been extensively discussed with experts, and with anyone open to such a discussion, online and in person, from Oxford to Beijing and Cairo to Yangon, and then revised in the light of those debates. But the versions published here are not a 'lowest common multiple' representation of a supposed overlapping consensus, let alone a would-be UN treaty. These are not wordings with which I myself only partly agree or which, as the exhausted diplomat says at the end of a bruising negotiation, 'I can just about live with'.

I believe these precepts are as close to right as I can make them. It seems to me that if everyone everywhere followed them, everyone everywhere would be better off. Now, if you, dear reader, think you have a better set of principles, please put them on the table. Then we can talk about it. Maybe one of us will discover that the other has a point, and modify our proposals accordingly. If someone says, 'well, my universal principle is that every government should be free to do whatever it likes', I will reply: 'No! There are some universal principles which all should always respect—and, by the way, your state has signed up to them in international covenants'. If, however, someone says, 'well, your

more detailed formulation on religion, or civility, or privacy, has to be understood and applied differently in our context, and here's why . . .', then it would
be foolish and arrogant not to engage in that discussion. Since I have repeatedly
stressed that context is crucial in judging speech, it would be self-contradictory
not to apply the measure of context to my own speech. There are limits to the
degree of contextual difference that is compatible with the essentials of liberal
universalism, but those limits will be wider for specific recommendations than
for fundamentals.

The chapters then explain more of what is meant by the few plain words of
each principle. Even though some of my commentaries are quite detailed, they
still only scratch the tip of the iceberg, but links in the post-Gutenberg book allow you to dive down and explore each iceberg's underwater expanses. I also say
something about the means, ranging from penal servitude to unforced individual courtesy, by which each principle will best be implemented. Some—such
as the second principle, on violence—call for the full force of criminal law.
Others—such as the fifth, on living with diversity—emphasise positive action
by individuals and civil society rather than restrictions policed by the state. In
each chapter, I explore some revealing and challenging examples, drawn from
different times and places. Every week in cosmopolis throws up a new controversy and every case has to be judged—by you, never mind the titular judge in
solemn robes—on its own merits and circumstances.

Needless to say, there are countless topics and places that I do not cover. A
20-volume encyclopaedia would still leave much untreated. I say more about
some countries, less about others: partly for strategic reasons that I have explained, partly from my own lamentable ignorance. With some regret, I have
touched only in passing on issues such as dress (for example, the hijab), minarets, tattoos and dietary taboos ('what's your beef with my freedom to eat it?' as
one of our Indian students quipped in a discussion of Indian dietary controversies).[1] Any objection of the form 'why don't you discuss X or Y?' will be welcome
if it leads to a substantial argument for reformulating a principle or adding a
new one.

1

LIFEBLOOD

'We—all human beings—must be free and able to express
ourselves, and to seek, receive and impart information
and ideas, regardless of frontiers'.

This principle is first not just in order but in importance. It is the basic principle. Freedom of expression is not merely one among many freedoms. It is the one upon which all others depend.

The power of speech is what distinguishes us from other animals and from any machines yet invented. If we cannot express our thoughts and feelings, we can never realise our full humanity. If we cannot hear and see those other human beings, we will never understand what it means to be them. (Listen again to Nina Simone singing 'I wish I knew how it would feel to be free'.) The richer and more open our interactions with others, the better we will understand ourselves as well, for 'who knows one, knows none'.[1]

On any subject we care about, freedom of information helps us to find the facts, while freedom of expression allows us to hear the competing arguments. They therefore enable us to get as close as humanly possible to the truth on that subject. The more we know about any kind of power, the better we will be able to scrutinise that power; and power, whether public or private, always needs to be checked. The more freely a wide range of alternatives is aired for any decision, the better chance we have of choosing the best course of action since free speech is the lifeblood that 'enables opinion and fact to be carried round the body politic'.[2] Even if it turns out that we got it wrong, we will have done so together, by a process of frank debate. Ideally, we will all have a voice in decisions that affect us all. That is the purest form of self-government, known as democracy: equal voice, then equal vote.

Free speech helps us to live with the new intimacy of diversity. Only by peacefully expressing our human differences can we understand what matters to the ever more diverse women and men next to whom we are now likely to find ourselves living, as physical and virtual neighbours. If we can learn how to articulate openly all kinds of human difference—real or imagined—without coming to blows, we will be on the way to living as good neighbours in this world-as-city.

There are other arguments for free speech, but the four I have briefly reprised here—Self, Truth, Government, Diversity: STGD—are more than sufficient to justify the basic principle.

To the word 'We' I have added 'all human beings', to make it clear that this is a universal right for everyone. This right is not confined to the citizens of a state, nor should it be enjoyed by corporations. 'We' means we, all the people.

FREE AND ABLE

As we have seen, freedom of expression is recognised as a universal human right in Article 19 of the Universal Declaration of Human Rights and the same article of the subsequent International Covenant on Civil and Political Rights. Using language on which this first principle draws directly, Article 19 speaks of 'freedom to seek, receive and impart information and ideas of all kinds, regardless of frontiers'.[3] Most states in the world have subscribed to that Covenant—a word implying solemn, even sacred agreement.[4] That matters. You can say to your rulers, 'Hey, you've signed up to this!' But what if their answer is to ignore you? Or to silence, torture and imprison you, as many governments still do their free-speaking citizens? What if, for a host of other reasons, you are only theoretically free to express yourself, in the way that a poor woman is only theoretically free to dine at her country's most expensive hotel?

Recognising the force of these objections, this basic principle adds to the classic Article 19 formula one small but vital word: 'able'. We must be not just theoretically free but practically able to 'seek, receive and impart information and ideas'. This is a matter not merely of law and human rights but of power and human capabilities.[5] We all know that people's effective freedom of expression in much of the world is limited by restrictions that, when we judge them illegitimate, we call censorship. (Throughout, I use the word 'censorship' in this pejorative sense, although in earlier times it was often used positively.) Yet there are many other constraints that are less easily identified than the frontal act of a government declaring, 'If you say that, you will be locked up'.

Our early twenty-first-century world is replete with examples of an even older and cruder threat to free speech: 'If you say that, we will kill you'. Such threats occasionally come from governments but more often from terrorists, mafiosi of all stripes or religious and ideological fanatics. I discuss them in the next chapter. Our effective freedom of expression is constrained by private as well as public powers. If you live in a country where most of the mass media are controlled, openly or covertly, by just a handful of owners, your effective ability to reach and hear your fellow citizens is drastically circumscribed.

Many people, even in supposedly free countries, feel unfree to speak out in their workplaces, for fear of losing their jobs, especially in economic or personal circumstances where it might be difficult to get another one. After the end of communist rule in east central Europe it was fascinating and depressing to observe how the locus of unfreedom shifted from the state to the workplace. This goes beyond the civilised self-restraint necessary for good cooperation. Employees can be afraid to say things that they feel they really should say. It is well documented that whistleblowers get treated badly for doing what even the law of the land acknowledges to be the right thing.

In the United States, the most explicitly and consistently pro–free speech country in the world, money howls through political campaigns. This reality takes it far away from the ancient Athenian, seventeenth-century English and—in its most developed form—twentieth-century American ideal of 'equal voice, then equal vote'. The muffling of the voices of the less powerful is compounded by the promotion of distorted versions of reality and one-sided narratives. 'Spin' is the polite term used in English, but often these narratives deserve the plainer epithet 'lies'. As a Yiddish proverb observes, 'A half truth is a whole lie'.

Yet at least in most democratic countries there are two (or more) competing false narratives, and having two is more than twice as good as having only one. As you move across the spectrum of political systems, through hybrid regimes and outright authoritarian ones, you approach the totalitarian nightmare, in which the public sphere is not just partially occupied by a few competing half truths but totally occupied by the single big lie of an all-dominating power. For most of us, however, a single Big Brother is not the biggest threat to free speech in our time. Rather, we have to watch out for multiple, often hidden brothers— and a few sisters—who curb our freedom of expression in less obvious ways.

Then there are the basic entry conditions that are still denied to billions of human beings. My description of the transformed world of cosmopolis in the first part of this book applies to the approximately three out of every seven human beings who (at this writing) have regular access to the internet, in the broad sense in which I am using the term. What about those who don't? Tim Berners-Lee, the inventor of the World Wide Web, argues that internet access is a necessary condition for the effective exercise of the right to free speech.[6] He is not alone: four out of five people asked in a BBC World Service poll in 26 countries said internet access should be 'a fundamental right of all people'.[7] Equally vital are literacy, light by which to read and other basic conditions of human development.

IN YOUR OWN TONGUE

You should also be free to express yourself in your own language, and to hear others express themselves in theirs. Harold Pinter, the master playwright of menace, wrote a short play about this, inspired by the Turkish government's denial of language rights to the country's large Kurdish population. In *Mountain Language*, an old woman is visiting her son in prison:

> Elderly Woman: I have bread—
> *The Guard jabs her with a stick*
> Guard: Forbidden. Language forbidden.
> *She looks at him. He jabs her*
> It's forbidden. (*To the Prisoner*) Tell her to speak the language of the capital.
> Prisoner: She can't speak it.[8]

Things may have improved somewhat for the Kurds in Turkey since Pinter wrote, but the truth his scene captures is universal.

There is room for reasonable disagreement about how far states should be obliged to afford speakers of a minority language access to education, media and official services in their own tongue, and how far members of a linguistic minority may legitimately be obliged to learn and to function in the language of the majority. In 1982, a Canadian judge roundly declared that 'freedom of expression does not include the freedom to choose the language of expression'. But that judgement was overturned on appeal, and Canada went on to become one of the most systematically bilingual countries in the world.[9]

A manifesto for linguistic diversity promulgated by PEN International in 2011 made ambitious claims. For example: 'every linguistic community has the right for its language to be used as an official language in its territory' and 'school instruction must contribute to the prestige of the language spoken by the linguistic community of the territory'. But who decides what is a linguistic community and where are the boundaries of its territory? For reasons of 'prestige', should formal interpretation really be provided on all occasions between Serbian, Croatian, Bosnian and Montenegrin? (A writer who grew up as a speaker of a language then called Serbo-Croat quips: 'I never knew I was good at languages, but suddenly I speak four'.) Two liberal political theorists argue that while a liberal democratic state does not necessarily have a duty to keep all languages alive, it should respond positively if a non-negligible group of people clearly express the will to keep a particular language alive.[10]

Wherever we draw the lines, the principle of being free to use your own language — your own tongue — is an important one. So is the ability to communicate across those stubborn frontiers between wikinations that, as we have seen, persist online even where political borders have become more permeable. There may be no universal right to a decent translation, but that is what communication 'regardless of frontiers' ideally requires. It is no accident that the Universal Declaration of Human Rights is reportedly the most translated document in the world, with versions in at least 440 languages or (according to taste) dialects.[11]

The word 'language' is usually taken to refer to speech and writing, but the 'languages' of freedom of expression are so various that they cannot be captured in a simple formula. The Covenant version of Article 19 refers to 'information and ideas of all kinds' being sought, received and imparted 'either orally, in writing or in print, in the form of art, or through any other media . . .'. Theatre, film, YouTube videos, graffiti, styles of dress, Instagram photos, blogs, demonstrations, playing a national sport, flying a particular flag or burning it, architecture, leaking official or corporate documents online, displaying a religious symbol — all these are also forms of expression and the sharing of information.

The American scholar Elizabeth Daley has suggested that the 'multimedia language of the screen' may even supplant writing as the primary medium of mass communication online, as Latin was gradually overtaken by vernacular languages such as English, French and German after the spread of printing in the fifteenth and sixteenth centuries.[12] Emojis, GIFs and shared pictures are thrusting up beside text. Jimmy Wales, the founder of Wikipedia, told me that the most frequent and difficult controversies they had to deal with on Wikipedia related to images rather than words.[13]

When a Polish pole vaulter, Władysław Kozakiewicz, made a rude gesture to the mainly Russian crowd after winning a gold medal at the 1980 Moscow Olympic Games, that was clearly self-expression. Elegantly described in French as the *bras d'honneur*, this well-known gesture involves emphatically placing one hand in the crook of the other arm. The Soviet ambassador to Poland said Kozakiewicz should be stripped of his medal because he had 'insulted the Soviet people', but the Polish authorities explained that the athlete had suffered involuntary muscle spasm. The *bras d'honneur* is now widely known in Polish as 'Kozakiewicz's Gesture'. By the same token, almost everything we wear can be a form of expression or 'speech'. Restrictions on the Islamic hijab, niqab or burqa worn by Muslim women in Europe; Western clothing banned in Bhutan; women punished for wearing trousers in North Korea; men fined for sporting makeup at a fashion show in Sudan: these are also free speech issues.[14]

In some contexts, to be silent is to speak. The General Comment of the UN Human Rights Committee says, 'freedom to express one's opinion necessarily includes freedom not to express one's opinion'. This has practical and legal consequences. A British Supreme Court verdict found that a Zimbabwean asylum seeker could stay in Britain because if she returned to Robert Mugabe's dictatorship, 'she would be forced to lie in order to profess loyalty to the regime'.[15] The Belarussian dictatorship of Aleksander Lukashenko was so frustrated by electronically organised 'silent protests', in which people simply stood around quietly together, that it passed a law criminalising the 'joint mass presence of citizens for the purposes of . . . action *or inaction*' (my italics).[16] So in Belarus it became a crime just to hang about silently doing nothing.

In fact, many acres of jurisprudence are devoted to determining what is or is not 'speech', as we say in English, or 'expression', the term more often used in other languages. In addition, especially in the American tradition, there is a large literature on what qualifies as valuable speech, deserving a higher level of protected freedom under the law. The Arizona Supreme Court found, for example, that tattoos qualify as protected speech under the First Amendment.[17] The U.S. Supreme Court concluded that sleeping overnight in a protest camp tent in front of the White House was 'expressive conduct protected to some extent by the First Amendment'. However, a park regulation forbidding it was held to be a reasonable restriction on grounds of time, manner and place.[18] (But what if you shouted protests in your sleep?)

One of the most amusing American court judgements on the boundaries of speech concerned a talking cat called Blackie. Blackie had purred 'I love you' to the district judge, although, as the appeal court observed in a footnote, 'this affectionate encounter occurred before the Judge ruled against Blackie'. The cat's owners maintained that Blackie should enjoy First Amendment protection. The appeal court said it would not hear the claim that Blackie's free speech rights had been infringed, first because the pussy was not a 'person' enjoying protection under the Bill of Rights and second because 'even if Blackie had such a right, we see no need for appellants to assert his right jus tertii [i.e., by his owners on his behalf]. Blackie can clearly speak for himself'.[19]

'Information and ideas of all kinds' is also drastic shorthand. Feelings, identities, prejudices, sensibilities, desires, tastes, jokes, inanities—all these and more belong here. (Freedom must include the freedom to make a fool of yourself.) The distinction between information and ideas is not as sharp as that between fire and water, but there is a difference. Information includes facts about the physical and human world and data that governments, companies, churches and individuals often prefer to keep secret. Freedom of information is not the same as freedom of expression, but closely related to it. The authoritative interpretation of Article 19 by the UN Human Rights Committee says it embraces a general 'right of access to information held by public bodies'. What exactly does that mean? The German constitution declares that citizens must be free to inform themselves 'from generally accessible sources'.[20] What about generally inaccessible ones? How can I effectively question my government's case for going to war if the head of that government says, 'Our intelligence tells us that the enemy has battle-ready weapons of mass destruction', but we are not allowed to know what that intelligence is? Asymmetries of information are also asymmetries of power.

SEEK, RECEIVE AND IMPART

'Seek, receive and impart' covers three distinct though related activities. If your search engine systematically hides from you information and ideas that are out there, you may be theoretically free but will not practically be able to seek. Or you may know they are out there but be unable to receive them, because of censorship, public or private, or obstacles such as illiteracy, limited education, language barriers and poor internet access. Or you may be able to seek and receive, but not to impart back—at least, not in any effective way.

Even if, empowered by the internet, you are practically able to do all these three things, there can be a tension between the last two. There's the freedom of the woman, man or child who wants to impart something and that of the person who wants to receive. Some of the arguments for free speech concentrate on the former (for example, self-expression), some on the latter (for example, having access to the relevant facts and arguments). But what if I don't want to receive what you wish to impart? What if I don't want to see your sexually explicit drawing, cartoon of Muhammad or musings on the allegedly lower intelligence of certain races or nations?

So far as humanly possible, the guiding principle here must be that we are free to choose. But should there not be exceptions to that general rule? There is a growing literature on what has come to be called compelled listening.[21] Most of us accept, for example, that it is reasonable that we are obliged to listen to the safety advice at the beginning of an airline flight. But how about that irritating comedy video blasting in your face from the dropdown screen to lighten the time you spend in the plane during a long takeoff delay? Thirty years ago there were alluring designs on cigarette packets. A 1940s American advertising campaign declared, 'More Doctors Smoke Camels Than Any Other Cigarette'.[22] Now, in many countries, there are stark black-and-white health warnings: 'Smoking Kills', 'Smokers Die Younger', 'Smoking Seriously Harms You and Others around You' and 'Smoking Can Damage the Sperm and Decreases Fertility'.[23]

In South Dakota, a doctor is obliged by law to warn a woman seeking an abortion that she is terminating the life of 'a whole, separate, unique, living human being' and that abortion carries a significant risk of psychological trauma. Even if the claims contained in the compulsory wording were not themselves highly contestable, to put it no more strongly, should she be compelled to hear that (and the doctor to say it)?[24]

As we have seen, one advantage of the internet is that it makes it easier to give people the choice of not looking if they don't want to. On freespeechdebate.com, we have adopted the one-click-away principle. Where there is an image which we can reasonably assume a significant number of people might prefer not to pop up in front of them unasked, we give you the explicit choice of clicking through or not. So click here (in the post-Gutenberg book) to see animal rights campaign posters which a German court banned in Germany, because they show photographs of caged animals side-by-side with photos of Nazi concentration camp inmates.[25] Or not, if you'd rather not. Click here for the Wikipedia page showing the Danish cartoons of Muhammad.[26] Or don't, if your sensibilities will be offended. It's up to you.

Even on the internet, these are difficult judgements. They invariably invite the objection: if you choose to put this sort of thing one click away, then why not that sort of thing? Thus, the worldwide community of Wikipedians got itself into a tremendous tangle over a proposal for the free encyclopaedia to have an image filter, so that users (or their parents) could filter out images that they might not want themselves (or their children) to see. At this writing, no such filter has been introduced. The more Facebook has attempted to implement nuanced community standards for its nearly 1.5 billion users, the more millions of reports it has received asking for content to be reviewed.[27]

Such editorial decisions are even more testing in less intrinsically flexible media. I will never forget arriving in the Bosnian capital of Sarajevo in 1995, at the end of a brutal little European war, and finding displayed on a rack outside a shop, for anyone to see, a newsmagazine cover photograph of some charred hunks of human flesh left hanging from a fence, after another bombing of a marketplace. ('Again!' said the headline.) I nearly vomited on the pavement. Yet I thought: 'Why have I never seen such photos before?' Is it right that most media, even as their foreign correspondents do their utmost to evoke such horrors in words, spare us these powerful images? For the sake of humanity, shouldn't we be confronted with such evidence of inhumanity?

The same dilemmas arose with videos made by the Islamic State terrorist organisation of gruesome beheadings of Western hostages in Syria and Iraq. Did the public interest in seeing them outweigh the distress to the victims' families and friends? In this case, the judgement was further complicated by the fact that the beheading videos were deliberately made as propaganda: to deter those who would stand up to the terrorists and attract a perverted minority drawn precisely by revolutionary violence. Fortunately, these are still unusual circumstances. For the most part, this rule holds good: you should be free to receive what others wish to impart—or not, if you don't want to.

REGARDLESS OF FRONTIERS

Finally, there is 'regardless of frontiers'. When this visionary phrase was first used in the 1948 Universal Declaration of Human Rights, it expressed an ideal and a dream. The dream is now, thanks to the internet, a technical possibility—but one that many governments, and other forces, are acting to diminish and deny.

Does 'regardless of frontiers' mean that there should be no limits to the flow of information and ideas? Obviously not. It means that any limits on speech must be justified, proportionate, clear and open to challenge. The same international agreements that anchor this most explicitly global of human rights go on to spell out the grounds on which states may restrict freedom of expression. Such restrictions must be 'provided by law and . . . necessary', says the latter part of the International Covenant version of Article 19. Article 10 of the European Convention raises the bar, saying 'as are prescribed by law and are necessary *in a democratic society*' (my italics). As we have seen, both treaties then list a number of grounds on which such legal and necessary limits may be imposed. This is a long list in the European Convention, a mercifully short one in the International Covenant. But the latter's Article 20 then declares that 'any propaganda for war shall be prohibited by law', as shall 'any advocacy of national, racial or religious hatred that constitutes incitement to discrimination, hostility or violence'.[28]

Across the globe, free speech advocates start from the words of these international agreements and urge governments to abide by them. In doing so, they draw on documents such as the authoritative General Comment of the UN Human Rights Committee on Article 19, the judgements of various courts, and philosophical, political and psychological arguments of the kind I have explored.

Their work has traditionally been concentrated on states and international organisations, laws and the executive actions of governments. I have argued that in the cosmopolis created by mass migration and the internet, we must also look at other levels of the multidimensional struggle for word power, especially the role of private powers and that of self-shaping, networked communities, both online and offline. ('Offline' is a strange term, almost implying that 'online' is the richer, fuller human condition. 'Real world', on the other hand, falsely suggests that the online world is unreal.) I have also argued that we should only reach for the coercive power of the state when other means will not achieve the essential restraint. So the question we have to ask is not just 'what limit, with what justification?' but 'what kind of limit, to be achieved how, when, where and by whom?'

Since context is all, the answer will differ depending on the place, time, audience and medium, so we need a fine-grained judgement on each case. Although so much depends on the particular, we can nonetheless venture some generalisations. At one end, we can identify content and forms of expression that should be prevented—or, if that is not possible, subsequently punished—at all times and in all places by every legitimate means. At the other, there is stuff which should, at all times and in all places, be purely a matter for individual men and women to sort out for themselves, without any external constraint. Since this is the heartland of freedom, it should be as large as possible.

In between, there are areas which may best be constrained or promoted by national laws, by the technological, commercial and editorial practices of private powers, by the voluntary standards of self-regulating communities and by individual behaviour. So there are general arguments to be made about how, when and by whom free speech should or should not be limited in order to defend privacy, or reputation, or religious sensibilities, or national security, or intellectual property, or whatever the claimed good may be. Yet it is equally vital to think creatively about the ways in which we can promote the best uses of free expression—the great ship *Euagore* ('good speech')—while recognising that what is best will itself always be disputed. The question 'how should free speech be?' is as crucial as the more familiar 'how free should speech be?' and, ideally, the pair will be inseparable.

VIOLENCE

'We neither make threats of violence nor accept violent intimidation'.

'If you say that, we will kill you'. Here is the most extreme threat to freedom of expression. In Europe alone, thousands of people are living in hiding or in fear for their lives because of death threats from violent Islamist extremists, mafias of various kinds, powerful interests, abusive family members or oppressive regimes. In Africa, the Middle East and parts of Asia, the numbers are much higher.[1] And we are not just talking about threats. The names of Hrant Dink, the Turkish-Armenian editor, Chico Mendes, the Brazilian environmental activist, Anna Politkovskaya, the Russian reporter, Salman Taseer, the governor of Punjab, and all the murdered journalists of France's Charlie Hebdo magazine must stand here for those of many more who have paid with their lives for exercising and defending the universal right to freedom of expression.

There are two sides to the principle spelt out at the top of this chapter. Both are vital. The first is that we do not ourselves make threats of violence. This widely accepted norm is enshrined in the laws of the most pro–free speech countries in the world, although more needs to be said about what constitutes the kind of incitement to violence that should be banned by law. As important is the other side of the coin: do not accept violent intimidation. This may seem obvious, but yielding to a real or merely putative threat of violence has become a chronic weakness of free societies.

Such an attitude sometimes deserves the overused label 'appeasement', especially when it aims precisely to appease—that is, to keep or restore the peace. Yet like the policies of Britain and France towards Nazi Germany that gave the word a bad name, such appeasement can end up having the opposite effect. It tells men and women of violence that their threats are working and therefore encourages them to threaten some more. In this sense, to accept violent intimidation can itself become a kind of objective incitement to violence.

THE ASSASSIN'S VETO

An American free speech scholar coined the term 'heckler's veto' to describe the way loud, persistent hecklers at a public meeting can silence a speaker.[2] Adapting his eloquent phrase, I have called the deadlier challenge we now face 'the assassin's veto'.[3]

When we first presented these principles on freespeechdebate.com, this one was only in sixth place. The more I worked on the project and travelled around the world talking about it, the more I became convinced that it deserves a salience second only to the basic principle. The generic evil underlying so many illegitimate abuses of and curbs on free speech turns out to be the real or attributed threat of violence. Remove that, and even extreme expressions of intolerance can lose their chilling effect. Lift the fear of violence—except as legitimately exercised by a rule-of-law state—and all other limits on free speech, including those in the principles that follow, can themselves be freely debated.

There is a long-running argument about whether hate speech should be prohibited by law. Many Europeans, Canadians, Indians and Australians argue that it should be, and in varying degrees they do make it illegal, whereas Americans, true to the First Amendment tradition, generally don't. Yet wherever you stand on that issue, it is vital to distinguish between the extreme harm of violence and other sorts of harm, such as infringing human dignity and equality, that may be attributed to hateful speech.

While there is a grey zone, which includes psychological harms so serious as to be close to actual violence, it is an abuse of language to suggest that these are all the same harm. In an otherwise carefully argued commentary on the massacre of the cartoonists of Charlie Hebdo magazine in Paris in 2015, the British Muslim theologian Abdal Hakim Murad wrote: 'to laugh at the Prophet, the repository of all that Muslims revere and find precious, to reduce him to the level of the scabrous and comedic, is very different from "free speech" as usually understood. It is *a violent act* surely conscious of its capacity to cause distress, ratchet up prejudice and damage social cohesion' (my italics).[4] If the mere drawing of cartoons in a satirical magazine was itself 'a violent act', what words have we left to describe the assassination of the cartoonists? Every thing is what it is and not another thing.[5] The physical integrity of the human person is one thing. Psychological well-being is another. Dignity is dignity. Equality is equality. They are all good things, but they are not all the same thing. Violations of them may not all properly be called violence.

In confronting the assassin's veto, it is essential to keep the focus sharply on where the threat is coming from and not end up blaming the victim — or yourself. When Yale University decided that the American publisher of this book, Yale University Press, should not publish any images of Muhammad in a book about the Danish cartoon controversy written by the Danish scholar Jytte Klausen, the publisher included in the book a statement explaining that 'the overwhelming judgement' of a number of experts consulted by Yale was that 'the republication of the cartoons by Yale University Press ran a serious risk of instigating violence'.[6] In an interview, the director of the Press, John Donatich, expressed it even more vividly. He said that in the past he had 'never blinked' when it came to publishing controversial books, such as an unauthorised biography of Thailand's king, but 'when it came between that and blood on my hands, there was no question'.[7]

Whatever your view on the actual decision not to publish the illustrations — and, to be clear, I disagreed with it — this is to pin responsibility in the wrong place. Had any violence followed, the blood would have been on the hands of those who perpetrated it, not those of the publisher. According to the *Oxford English Dictionary*, to 'instigate' means 'to spur, urge on, to stir up, stimulate, incite, goad (mostly to something evil)'. The publisher would no more be 'instigating violence' than a young woman wearing a short skirt would be instigating rape.

The mistake of blaming and constraining the wrong person is one that has been made many times, and continues to be made, by the police in England. Far too often, they quietly advise people to stop the performance or action against which others are taking violent offence. This happened, for example, when a Sikh crowd angrily protested against a play called Behzti being staged in Birmingham, and again with the London showing of a work of performance art called Exhibit B, which was also cancelled following demonstrations.[8]

Fortunately, English courts have sometimes put the police to rights. In 1997 a policeman arrested a Christian fundamentalist called Alison Redmond-Bate who was preaching with two others from the steps of Wakefield Cathedral. A crowd had gathered, with people shouting 'bloody lock them up' and 'shut up'. She was subsequently convicted of obstructing a police officer in the execution of his duty. On appeal, the conviction was overturned. The appeal judge, Stephen Sedley, noted that 'nobody had to stop and listen'. 'Freedom only to speak inoffensively', he added, 'is not worth having'.[9] And he referred back to the 'classic authority' of an older English law case which makes the point clearly.

In 1882, the Salvation Army organised a raucous but lawful demonstration in the English seaside town of Weston-super-Mare. Its march was opposed and disrupted by a group calling itself the Skeleton Army, 'with shouting, uproar and noise, to the great terror, disturbance, annoyance and inconvenience of the peaceable inhabitants of the town'.[10] Leaders of the Salvation Army were arrested and convicted of a breach of the peace. But a higher court reversed this verdict, pointing out that 'the disturbances were caused by the other people antagonistic to' the Salvation Army leaders and that 'no acts of violence were committed by' the Salvationists. Take this as a general rule: wherever we are, we must confront the Skeleton Armies of our day—be they mafia, Al Qaeda or dictators' hoodlums—and not silence the Salvation Armies.

Those who threaten violence must be met with the full rigour of the law. They should not themselves be killed or wounded unless they are immediately engaged in perpetrating rather than inciting violence and cannot be stopped by any other means. We must be consistent: nothing ever justifies killing someone just because of something they say, even if that something is 'if you say that, we will kill you'. But the physical constraint of long imprisonment, following the due process of law, is entirely justified as a response. That being so, our first task is to work out what kinds of expression actually constitute a threat of violence in the transformed conditions of cosmopolis.

MODERNISING THE BRANDENBURG TEST

A classic modern starting point is the US Supreme Court case of Brandenburg v Ohio. Clarence Brandenburg was a leader of the racist Ku Klux Klan in rural Ohio. In 1964, he invited a local television channel to film him and his colleagues gathering around a burning cross, wearing their Ku Klux Klan gowns and pointed hoods. A hooded man, identified as Brandenburg, was filmed telling his fellow Klansmen, 'We're not a revengent organisation, but if our President, our Congress, our Supreme Court, continues to suppress the White, Caucasian race, it's possible that there might have to be some revengeance taken'. Another reel showed him saying, 'Personally, I believe the nigger should be returned to Africa, the Jew returned to Israel'. He was convicted under an Ohio state law. Overturning the conviction in 1969 and finding the Ohio law incompatible with the First Amendment, the Supreme Court declared that freedom of speech and the press 'do not permit a State to forbid or proscribe advocacy of the use of force or of law violation except where such advocacy is directed to inciting or producing imminent lawless action and is likely to incite or produce such action'.[11]

This led to what became known as the 'Brandenburg test'—thus incidentally immortalising a minor American racist. The Brandenburg test has three parts, each of them treated as essential. Violence must be intended *and* likely *and* imminent. Thus, in a subsequent judgement, the Supreme Court decided that a demonstrator who said, 'We'll take the fucking street later', was not intending to produce imminent disorder and overturned his conviction.[12]

The Brandenburg test remains the clearest and best starting point for thinking about what defines a threat of violence that should be banned by law. But since context is always crucial, we need to look more closely at what makes violence 'likely' or 'imminent'. As we have seen, the internet telescopes both space and time. What is expressed in Bradford is visible instantaneously in Lahore, and vice versa. What was expressed yesterday may still be up there, for billions of people to see, years later. It can be harmless for months before suddenly becoming the occasion for violent action, as happened with 'Innocence of Muslims'. What, then, is 'imminent' when everything online is, so to speak, immanent?

This is only the beginning of the complications. There is good historical evidence that a constant drip-drip of dehumanising abuse of a particular group of human beings can eventually incline people to violence against that group.[13] Contemplating the atrocities committed by soldiers and paramilitaries of Slobodan Milošević's Serbia against Bosnians, Kosovo Albanians and other ethnic groups in former Yugoslavia, the historian Noel Malcolm highlighted the role of television. Imagine how Americans would have behaved, he said, if all three major US television news channels had been taken over for five years by the Ku Klux Klan.[14] To be sure, the Yugoslav atrocities occurred in the 1990s, when there were still just a few dominant terrestrial television channels and the internet was in its infancy. The internet gives people the capacity to counterbalance systematic distortions by state-controlled or private near-monopoly media. With two clicks of your mouse, you can seek out contrary facts and alternative views. But how many people actually do?

The American scholar Cass Sunstein was among the first to suggest that in practice the internet can contribute to what he calls group polarisation.[15] Far from being confronted with a diversity of opposing views, as in an ideal liberal public sphere, people seek out and commune online with a like-minded minority. Jihadists read only jihadi websites, which link to each other; far-right extremists listen only to far-right extremists, atheists to atheists, flat-earthers to flat-earthers. A 15-year-old British schoolgirl who flew to join the Islamic State terrorist organisation in Syria had, it turned out, been following 74 radical and fundamentalist Islamist Twitter accounts.[16] Unlike in the physical world, the internet makes it easy for the conspiracy theorist to find the 957 other people across the planet who share his or her particular poisoned fantasy. The increasingly personalised nature of internet searches on Google and other search engines can exacerbate the problem, with everyone disappearing into his or her own 'filter bubble'.[17]

This is a much broader problem, to which we will return, but it clearly affects the analysis of speech and violence. Thus, for example, the Norwegian mass murderer Anders Behring Breivik was reinforced in his paranoid views by obsessive reading of anti-Islamic and anti-multiculturalist websites such as Pamela Geller's 'Atlas Shrugs' and Robert Spencer's 'Gates of Vienna', from which he quoted in his online 'crusader' manifesto.[18] Does that mean such sites should be blocked and their content censored? Surely not. The yardstick for what speech is allowed by law cannot be its potential impact on a single unbalanced mind anywhere in the world.

The difficulties of judgement are not confined to the online world. As a contemporary example of violent intimidation, I have mentioned the threats against the 'Danish cartoons' and their republication. Every one of the twelve Danish cartoonists subsequently had to live with a higher level of personal insecurity, including those whose cartoons had actually poked fun at the newspaper's idea of inviting people to draw such cartoons. Kurt Westergaard, who did the one of Muhammad with a bomb in his turban, was confronted by an axe-wielding assassin hacking at the door of the panic room at his home in Aarhus. Westergaard had not had time to scoop up his five-year-old granddaughter, Stephanie, who was left alone with the attacker. (She survived.)[19]

But what about those who protested against the publication of the cartoons by making generalised threats of violence? In February 2006, a group of publicity-seeking British-based Islamists organised a protest march from the Regent's Park mosque to the Danish embassy in London. They carried placards with slogans including 'Freedom of Expression Go to Hell', 'Massacre Those Who Insult Islam', 'Behead the One Who Insults Islam' and 'Slay the Enemies of Islam'. Their leaders led the crowd in rhythmic chants such as 'Denmark will pay! 7/7 on its way!' and 'Europe, you must pay! With your blood, with your blood!' Four of these leaders were sent to jail for terms ranging from four to six years, on charges of soliciting to murder and inciting racial hatred. The court found that those slogans were intended to be understood by others as solicitation or encouragement to murder.[20] So one part of the Brandenburg test ('intended') was met. But what about the other two? Was violence also likely and imminent?

An appeal court noted that the demonstration was not itself violent and reduced the prison terms on the grounds that 'this case falls at the lower end of
the range of conduct that is capable of amounting to soliciting to murder'.[21]
Should those British judges have gone further, sticking closer to the principles
embodied in America's Brandenburg test? Or does a generalised threat of violence which we know may later be converted into real acts of murder—at an
unknown time and by perpetrators as yet unknown—justify a more generalised
kind of deterrence?

DANGEROUS SPEECH

The American analyst Susan Benesch has developed a set of five guidelines
for determining when hate speech becomes dangerous speech.[22] Her first three
guidelines, which build on Aristotle's analysis of the three dimensions of rhetoric, are 'a powerful speaker with a high degree of influence over the audience', 'a vulnerable, impressionable audience, with grievances and fear that
the speaker can cultivate' and 'a speech act that is clearly understood as a call
to violence'. She adds two more: 'a social or historical context that is propi-
tious for violence' and 'a means of dissemination that is influential in itself, for
example because it is the sole or primary source of news for the relevant audience'. The last element—the means of dissemination—is the one that has been
transformed in our time. Aristotle did not have to worry about the worldwide
impact of a YouTube video.

Sometimes the causal connection between hateful things expressed and
atrocities committed seems relatively clear. For example, one study of the mass
murder of Tutsis (and of some moderate Hutus) by Hutus in Rwanda in 1994
argued that there were 65 to 77 percent more killings in villages which received
the signal of Radio Télévision Libre des Mille Collines (RTLM), a popular
radio station that broadcast repeated calls for a 'final war' to 'exterminate the
cockroaches'. Even those analysts who question whether hate radio made such
a decisive contribution to the genocide do not doubt that it played a part.[23]

In every case, we have to ask: was that speech (artwork, demo, performance,
tweet) dangerous in that context? In January 2010, a young man called Paul
Chambers was unable to fly to meet a woman whom he had first encountered
on Twitter because Robin Hood airport in Doncaster, South Yorkshire, was
closed by snow. Frustrated, he tweeted to his roughly 600 followers on Twitter:
'Crap! Robin Hood airport is closed. You've got a week and a bit to get your shit
together, otherwise I'm blowing the airport sky high!'[24] He was convicted in the

local Magistrates' Court of sending a 'menacing' electronic message, was fined, and reportedly lost his job as a result. The Crown Court upheld the conviction on the grounds that Chambers was 'at the very least aware that his message was of a menacing character'. Only more than two years after the original trial, and after prominent free speech advocates such as the actor Stephen Fry had ridden to his defence, did the High Court overthrow the conviction.[25] Was a legal sanction justified in such a case? Absolutely not. Violence was neither likely nor intended, let alone imminent. This was a silly joke. At the very most, it deserved a verbal caution from the police, and a warning snort from Chambers's friends would have sufficed.

But now consider the former leader of the ANC Youth League in South Africa, Julius Malema. At his 29th birthday party in March 2010, he sang a song from the period of armed struggle against apartheid, with the refrain *dubul' ibhunu* (translated into English as 'Shoot the Boer'), cocking his right thumb and pointing his finger like a pistol. When he struck up the song again a few days later at the University of Johannesburg, this was shown on television, with the words translated into Afrikaans. An Afrikaaner civil rights group, Afriforum, presented a protest petition to the ANC's head office in Johannesburg, along with a list of 1,000 recent victims of attacks on white farmers. Members of the Youth League responded by throwing the list into the gutter and trampling on it. Afriforum subsequently took Malema to court in a civil case, and his words were declared to constitute hate speech. But minutes later, a group of his supporters belted out the refrain of 'Shoot the Boer' in front of the courthouse, under the noses of the police.[26]

When U2's Bono was asked about this as he toured South Africa, he compared it to the Irish Republican Army (IRA) songs he had sung with his uncles as a child. 'It's about where and when you sing these songs', said Bono. Exactly so. The story of Malema and 'Shoot the Boer' is particularly instructive because his revival of an old struggle song became so controversial only after it was broadcast on television in Afrikaans, made the subject of Afrikaner protests and brought to court. When it went beyond the internal rituals of a particular group, like Bono privately singing IRA songs with his Irish Republican uncles, its meaning and implications changed irrevocably. As the judge noted, it 'would never be innocuous again'.[27] But was that Malema's intention? Was violence intended and likely?

Even more challenging is the story of Simon Bikindi, a Rwandan singer and musician whose songs were widely played before and during Rwandan genocide, especially on the notorious RTLM. The International Criminal Tribunal for Rwanda indicted him for incitement to genocide, singling out three songs.

The tribunal concluded that 'in 1994 in Rwanda, Bikindi's three songs were indisputably used to fan the flames of ethnic hatred, resentment and fear of the Tutsi. Given Rwanda's oral tradition and the popularity of RTLM at the time, the Chamber finds that these broadcasts of Bikindi's songs had an amplifying effect on the genocide'. But it did not convict him for incitement on this count. Instead, it found him guilty on a much clearer ground. Driving along a road in June 1994, he had declared through a public address system on the car he was riding in: 'the majority population, it's you, the Hutu, I am talking to. You know the minority population is the Tutsi. Exterminate quickly the remaining ones'.[28] That would obviously pass the Brandenburg test. But the verdict leaves open the much more difficult question of how firmly established a causal connection must be in order to justify criminal sanctions. In not going slightly further back up the chain of causality, even in such an explosive setting, are we putting the balancing point between free speech and the prevention of violence in the right place?

What about video games which encourage the user to practice simulated violence? Take RapeLay, released by a Japanese company called Illusion Soft in 2006.[29] The object of the game was to rape, repeatedly, a mother and her two young daughters and force them to have an abortion if they became pregnant. Illusion Soft indeed. RapeLay was in circulation in Japan for some three years and had spread across frontiers on the internet before protests by women's rights campaigners and international media attention got it taken off the shelves in Japan.

To what extent the more 'normal' types of simulated violence in video games contribute to violent conduct in real life remains fiercely disputed. In 2014, an article in the journal European Psychologist reviewed the evidence from 25 years of research, provoking a lively debate.[30] Its conclusions were anything but conclusive. Nonetheless, classifications and warnings, of the kind we are used to in cinemas and on television, are surely a wise precaution and hardly an infringement of free speech.

I could multiply examples of such grey zones from around the world. Context is all and the devil lurks in the detail. As a general rule we should be guided in our civic judgements by a modernised version of the Brandenburg test. Our core question remains: is violence intended, likely and imminent? We recognise that the same content can be harmless in one context and deadly in another. (If I rail against Uzbeks as I sit alone at my desk it will be stupid but not dangerous.) Yet in assessing what is likely and imminent in a given context we take account of the transformed circumstances of cosmopolis, in which all forms of expression can potentially reach farther and last longer than they did

even 20 years ago, let alone in the era of John Stuart Mill. We therefore sometimes need to go further up the food chain of violence than has been usual in
the modern First Amendment tradition in the United States.

We do not, however, confuse the specific problem of dangerous speech with
the much broader category of hate speech. This has happened too often in
Europe and in countries such as Canada. I argue in chapter 5 that hate speech
is generally better controlled by nonlegal means. There are many reasons for
this, but one practical one is the sheer scale of the challenge of dangerous
speech in cosmopolis. There are now so many opportunities for the dissemination and amplification of genuinely dangerous speech that just tackling them
will stretch the law enforcement resources of any state. If you spread the fishing
net too widely, you waste your time catching sardines while sharks swim free.
The fragmentary, inconsistent application of such laws not only is wrong in
itself but may also bring those laws into disrepute.

JUST WAR?

There is, however, a difficulty here which must be frankly acknowledged. I
argue for a distinction between dangerous speech and hate speech. As a liberal
internationalist, I also set great store by international human rights agreements.
I have emphasised earlier the solemn commitment made by most of the world's
governments to honour Article 19 of the Covenant. Yet Article 20 of that same
Covenant blurs precisely the distinction I wish to sharpen. As we have seen, its
second paragraph says, 'Any advocacy of national, racial, or religious hatred that
constitutes incitement to discrimination, hostility or violence shall be prohibited by law'. The crucial word here is 'or'. It's not 'discrimination, hostility and
violence' but incitement to discrimination *or* hostility *or* violence.

In the ordinary meaning of these words, that is very broadly drawn—so much
so that, when ratifying the Covenant, the United States entered the mother of
all reservations. It specified 'that Article 20 does not authorise or require legislation or other action by the United States that would restrict the right to free
speech and association protected by the Constitution and laws of the United
States'. Reflecting the United States' idiosyncratic attitude to sovereignty, this
reservation effectively said, 'we will respect this except when we won't'. Unfortunately, there is good reason to have reservations about Article 20, since
oppressive regimes of all stripes use it as a fig leaf for extensive restrictions on
what should be legitimate free speech. (Britain also entered a reservation, albeit
more in the spirit of Admiral Nelson when he put a telescope to his blind eye
and said: 'I see no signal'.)[31]

Another approach, often adopted by professional free speech advocates, is to interpret Article 20 as narrowly as possible, fleshing out the UN Human Rights Committee's contention that its provisions 'are fully compatible with the right of freedom of expression as contained in Article 19'.[32] Thus, for example, Article 19, the global campaign for free expression that takes its name from that same article, has interpreted 'hostility' as 'a manifested action' and what is manifested in that action as 'intense and irrational emotions of opprobrium, enmity and detestation towards the target group'.[33] Sympathetic though I am to their attempt at liberal ijtihad, this stretches the ordinary meaning of 'hostility' to breaking point. It may be more honest to accept that while Article 19 is a charter for free speech, Article 20.2 can be used as a licence by the enemies of free speech.

Article 20 also contains another paragraph that cannot be ignored when talking about threats of violence. With a plainness sadly lacking in Article 20.2, its first clause says, 'Any propaganda for war shall be prohibited by law'. Basta. So what were George W. Bush and Tony Blair doing when they mustered their vivid and factually inaccurate arguments for the invasion of Iraq in 2003? When is propaganda for war not propaganda for war? When it's *your* war?

Finding a better answer than that is important not just for the future of war and peace but also for holding the line between free speech and violence. Murderous Islamist jihadis and murderous anti-Islam fanatics such as Anders Behring Breivik agree on one thing: they themselves are not criminals but warriors. They are fighting a 'war' which, though it may not be legal according to the rules of the UN, is legitimate by some other code of morals, chivalry or religious law. Hence, their propaganda for war is as legitimate, nay as noble, as was Winston Churchill's propaganda for war against Adolf Hitler.

This is obviously wrong, but we need to spell out why. If our principle is 'we make no threats of violence', why is it sometimes legitimate for states to make threats of violence? One answer lies in the second part of our principle: to face down violent intimidation. As with the Salvation and Skeleton Armies, you have to work out where the threat originates. If your counterthreat is genuinely defensive, it can be legitimate. 'If you want peace, prepare for war', said the ancient Romans. Nuclear deterrence in the Cold War involved states making threats of violence on such a scale—mutually assured destruction, or MAD for short—that neither side would dare to use its nuclear weapons. President Barack Obama devoted part of his 2009 Nobel Peace Prize acceptance speech to explaining why it could be appropriate for the commander in chief of a nation engaged in two wars to accept a prize for services to peace.[34]

Without going into all the intricacies of 'just war' theory, as applied to our time, let us simply agree that a legitimate, UN-sanctioned use or threat of force by states must be distinguished from the generality of 'threats of violence' we seek to prevent, prohibit and counter.[35] Yet it would be naïve in the extreme to believe that states habitually abide by these fine criteria when they make propaganda for war, in chronic violation of Article 20.1. Moreover, distinguishing between sheep and wolves is made more difficult by the fact that the wolves almost invariably wear sheep's clothing. States' justifications of their wars would fill many chapters in a history of humbug.

'Rabbi, will the Third World War break out?' asked a Soviet joke. 'No, my son, but the struggle for world peace may become so fierce that no house will be left standing'. The Old Testament scholar Matthias Köckert tells us that a catechism for front-line German soldiers in the First World War annotated the commandment 'Thou shalt not kill' with the lapidary commentary '*Gilt nicht für den Kriegsfall*' (Does not apply in case of war).[36] In modern civil wars, hybrid warfare and 'wars against terrorism', including the use of undercover special forces, unmanned drones and targeted killings, the lines are even more blurred. For many Israelis, the rockets that 'collaterally' kill Palestinian civilians in the Gaza Strip are moral missiles, while the Palestinian rockets that kill Israeli civilians are immoral missiles. For many Palestinians, it is the other way round.

What matters most here is what people do, not what they say. Nonetheless, how states and political leaders speak about the use of force and formulate deterrent threats at home or abroad has implications for the distinction between legitimate free speech and illegitimate threats of violence. Fanatics will not be persuaded to desist by a careful, rational justification of the state's use of force, but some of their potential sympathisers might be. The more morally questionable a state's uses and threats of force and the more mendacious, euphemistic or hypocritical its justification of them, the more likely terrorists are to find responsive audiences for their own threats of violence.

CONFRONTING THE ASSASSIN'S VETO

Properly enforced law is a necessary instrument in such cases but not a sufficient one. Throughout history, the survival of free speech has depended on the courage of exceptional individuals who refuse to bow down or recant in the face of imprisonment, torture and death threats. This is so important that I have devoted the final principle to it. Yet for such individuals' resistance to be effective while they are still alive requires both the firmness of the state and the solidarity of society.

The state must use what Max Weber called its 'monopoly of the legitimate use of physical force' to protect such individuals and hunt down those who threaten to kill them.[37] Since round-the-clock protection is expensive, that means a serious commitment by a democratic government to put its money where its mouth is, even when some taxpaying voters are not happy about it.

This of course assumes that the state is not itself the open or covert source of violent intimidation and is prepared to do what it can to combat it. That cannot be taken for granted in a country such as Pakistan. In 1995, a Pakistani judge, Justice Arif Iqbal Batti, struck down charges of blasphemy against two Christians. A third Christian, charged with the others, had been murdered while leaving court under police protection. Justice Batti was himself shot dead in his office two years later.[38] (More on this when we come to religion in chapter 6.)

Yet even when the state is doing all it can to protect threatened individuals, their personal experience will be traumatic. In a memoir, Salman Rushdie describes how his life was turned upside down after Ayatollah Khomeini issued his fatwa on all involved in the publication of *The Satanic Verses*. Rushdie quotes from a journal he kept at the time: 'I am gagged and imprisoned. I can't even speak. I want to kick a football in a park with my son. Ordinary, banal life: my impossible dream'.[39] When the fanatical Islamist assassin of the Dutch film director Theo van Gogh left a message threatening Ayaan Hirsi Ali, she was catapulted into a similar limbo of shifting locations, curtained rooms and dependency on the orders of armed guards. Both authors describe how, to defend the individual liberty of others, they had to surrender their own.[40] In Hirsi Ali's case, there was an added irony: this credible threat of violence was in response to her own exposé of the violent oppression of women in many Islamic families and societies.

The Italian journalist Roberto Saviano wrote a powerful book called *Gomorrah*, exposing the Sicilian mafia, also known as Cosa Nostra. While speaking at a ceremony to inaugurate the new school year in the town of Casal di Principe he publicly singled out the local Camorra bosses and, with extraordinary bravery, asked them to leave the hall. He described the consequences in a memorable essay: 'for the last eight years, I have travelled everywhere with seven trained bodyguards in two bullet-proof cars. I live in police barracks or anonymous hotel rooms, and rarely spend more than a few nights in the same place'. 'This life is shit', he wrote; 'it's hard to describe how bad it is. I exist inside four walls, and the only alternative is making public appearances. I'm either at the Nobel Academy having a debate on freedom of the press, or I'm inside a windowless room at a police barracks'. He had realised the dream of every writer, with a huge audience for his international bestseller, 'but everything else is gone: the chance of a normal life, the chance of a normal relationship. My life has been poisoned'.

And then he offered a deeply sobering reflection: 'I'm often asked if I regret writing *Gomorrah*. Usually, I try to say the right thing. I say, "as a man, yes, as a writer, no". But that's not the real answer. For most of my waking hours I hate *Gomorrah*. I loathe it. At the beginning, when I told interviewers that if I had known what was coming, I would never have written the book, their faces would fall. If it was the last question in the interview, I'd go away with a bad taste in my mouth, feeling like I hadn't come up to scratch'.[41]

How many of us would be prepared to pay such a price? When popular outrage at the massacre of the Charlie Hebdo journalists crystallised around the slogan '*Je suis Charlie*', a British journalist, Robert Shrimsley, wrote, 'I am not Charlie, I am not brave enough'.[42] Yet the assassin's veto will prevail unless there is social solidarity as well as protection by the state. This requirement applies particularly to publishers, producers and journalists, for the assassins go after all those involved in publication or broadcasting of the work. While Rushdie survived unscathed, his Japanese translator was stabbed to death. His Italian translator and Norwegian publisher were both wounded by would-be assassins.

Such solidarity does not require or imply agreement with the threatened person, or endorsement of the cartoon, performance or novel that put her or him in harm's way. Voltaire never actually said, 'I disapprove of what you say but I will defend to the death your right to say it', yet that summary of his attitude by an early-twentieth-century author (one S. G. Tallentrye) perfectly captures the spirit we should aspire to.[43]

There can be a tension between this essential solidarity and the need to go on articulating substantive disagreement. If you criticise the views of an imprisoned, threatened or exiled writer or activist, an Alexander Solzhenitsyn, Aung San Suu Kyi or Ayaan Hirsi Ali, critics will say you are giving succour to the enemy. But to accept that is to yield indirectly to the assassin's veto. It must be possible to maintain Voltairean solidarity with a Solzhenitsyn and yet continue to reject his views on, say, the role of Jews in modern Russian history. I got into trouble some years ago for a critical review I wrote of one of Hirsi Ali's books.[44] My essay contained a couple of provocative formulations ('Enlightenment fundamentalist') that I subsequently concluded were wrong, and disowned, but there is nothing wrong in principle with giving an embattled hero or heroine a bad review. Upholding someone's freedom of expression does not mean you have to treat him or her as an angelic genius. We must retain the freedom to criticise the views, art or writing of those targeted by violent intimidation while defending to the utmost their right to 'say it'. Self-censorship is not a good way to uphold free speech.

CARTOONS AND THE REPUBLICATION DILEMMA

Among the many difficult issues that arise is whether and, if so, how to re-publish material against which someone has chosen to take violent offence. As I have noted, this was a dilemma faced by the American publisher of this book, Yale University Press, when Jytte Klausen wrote a scholarly book about the worldwide controversy that followed the publication in 2005 of the 'Danish cartoons'. A sheaf of illustrations was planned and supported by the Press's publication committee. It included the original full page of Jyllands-Posten, to show the context, and some earlier depictions of Muhammad in Islamic and Western art. Shortly before the book was to be printed, the author was told that the illustrations were being pulled, on the orders of the university that owns and controls the University Press.[45] Thus, in a scholarly work titled *The Cartoons That Shook the World*, the one thing that readers could not see was . . . the cartoons that shook the world.

The director of Yale University Press, John Donatich, subsequently explained in a contribution to freespeechdebate.com that concerns the cartoons were grotesque, insulting and, in his view, 'meant to hurt and provoke' would not in themselves have dissuaded him from publishing the illustrations. It was fears for the safety of staff and students that were decisive. He took the issue to the university, which 'consulted a number of senior academics, diplomats and national security experts. The overwhelming judgement of the experts with the most insight about the threats of violence was that there existed an appreciable chance of violence occurring if either the cartoons or other depictions of the Prophet Muhammad were printed in a book about the cartoons published by Yale University Press'.[46]

Now such concerns cannot simply be dismissed. They must be weighed by any responsible employer or institution. In a further twist, the board of Index on Censorship—a magazine dedicated to chronicling and combatting censorship—subsequently decided that it would not reproduce the cartoons to illustrate an interview with Klausen about Yale's decision not to publish the cartoons. Index, too, cited fears for the safety of its employees.[47]

Although she reluctantly went along with Yale's decision, Klausen thought that it was wrong. She noted: 'there has not been a single angry email, fax, phone call from anybody Muslim. Yale University has not produced any threatening letters, I have not received any threatening letters, the press has not received any'. She argues that if Yale had not made an issue of the illustrations, they would probably never have become one.[48]

The republication question came snorting back after the journalists of Charlie Hebdo were massacred in Paris in early 2015. Was there an editor who did not ask, in the hours after the news came in: shouldn't we republish (or broadcast, or post online) some of the Charlie Hebdo covers? I became involved in this discussion, launching an appeal for a week of solidarity in which a wide range of newspapers in many countries would simultaneously publish a carefully presented selection of the Charlie Hebdo cartoons, with an explanation of why they were doing so. This appeal was published in a range of papers, from El País to The Hindu, and there followed days of intense public and private debate, including personal exchanges with several editors.[49]

The week of solidarity did not happen. Danish, Dutch and Belgian papers said that they had already republished, as had many in France. East European papers, such as Gazeta Wyborcza in Poland, printed both my appeal and a range of cartoons, as did La Repubblica in Italy. Most British papers did not republish the original cartoons, although the Guardian and the Independent reprinted the cover of the memorial issue of Charlie Hebdo published the next week. It showed a mournful Muhammad holding a sign saying '*Je suis Charlie*', and above him the words 'all is forgiven'.

More was published online than was printed or broadcast. Quite a few newspapers posted images on their own websites that they did not print in the paper. The BBC reproduced the Charlie Hebdo memorial cover in a story on its website, citing its 'editorial judgement that the images are central to reporting the story'. It then told television viewers that they could find the image on its website. In the United States, purely online publications and platforms, such as Slate, the Huffington Post and BuzzFeed, published the cartoons much more quickly and fully than those with one foot still in print or broadcasting. So did Index on Censorship, on its website, consciously learning from what its current editor considered to be its earlier mistake over the Danish cartoons. Here was 'media pluralism' in action. This is what independent, competitive publications, broadcasters and platforms do: under the time pressure of a breaking news story, they make their own judgements, in line with their editorial values, tastes and styles.

I offered three main arguments for coordinated republication. First, we must demonstrate that the assassin's veto would not prevail. Second, there was now a genuine public interest—in journalistic terms, news value—in seeing what all the fuss was about. Had the Charlie Hebdo journalists not been murdered, there would have been no reason for others to republish their lewd, outrageous satirical cartoons, which blended the legacies of Rabelais, Marat and Dada in a heady post-'68 brew. These would have been seen only by readers of a small-circulation satirical journal, who knew exactly what to expect. It was the assassins who created a public interest in wider dissemination of cartoons of the Prophet whose image they claimed to be protecting. It was their actions that resulted in far more people around the world seeing the offensive images.

The third reason for coordinated republication was that earlier experience had exposed a collective action problem: every individual editor, left to decide alone, might reach a different decision from the one he or she would make if confident of being among many. More editors would publish if they knew that others were doing the same. I believe this analysis proved correct. For example, the editor of the Independent said that he was torn between his instinct to publish the Charlie Hebdo cartoons and fears for the safety of his staff, 'and I think it would have been too much of a risk to unilaterally decide in Britain to be the only newspaper that went ahead and published'. The keyword there is 'unilaterally'. That such fears were well founded was shown by the firebombing of the offices of the Hamburger Morgenpost the day after it republished some of the cartoons.

The atmosphere of violent intimidation extended to distributors and news-agents. I spoke to a newsagent in Oxford who, at the request of his customers, had ordered copies of the Charlie Hebdo memorial issue. He told me that he had received phone calls 'from Birmingham' threatening to burn down his shop. Himself a Kurdish Muslim, he had instructed the anonymous callers that they knew nothing of Islam which—he argued—insists that you abide by the law of the country in which you live. But then he cancelled his order for Char-lie Hebdo. What is more, while the police gave his shop protection for a few days, they also quietly encouraged him to cancel that order—another instance of the English police going after the Salvation Army rather than the Skeleton Army. Once again, violent intimidation worked and people could not buy cop-ies of Charlie Hebdo from a newsagent in a British university town.

Most striking was the case of Jyllands-Posten, the paper that published the original 'Danish cartoons'. Whereas many Danish papers republished the Charlie Hebdo ones, Jyllands-Posten did not, citing its 'unique position' and concerns for employees' safety. Flemming Rose, the man who commissioned the original cartoons and was now the paper's foreign editor, told the BBC frankly, 'We caved in'. 'Violence works', he added, and 'sometimes the sword is mightier than the pen'.

Accusations of cowardice whizzed around the internet, but I would like to meet the person—perhaps an anonymous blogger, personally risking noth-ing—who charged Flemming Rose with cowardice. Whatever one thinks of the wisdom of his commissioning the original cartoons in 2005, cowardly that was not. It is easy for someone who is only responsible for a personal Facebook page and Twitter account to toss around such charges. If you have a duty of care for the staff of an organisation, you face a more demanding moral choice.

Moreover, talking to the editors of publications that decided against republishing the Charlie Hebdo cartoons, it was clear that this was not their only consideration. For example, in the course of a lively debate at the Guardian, its editor-in-chief, Alan Rusbridger, argued that Britain's leading liberal daily should not change its own values under terrorist pressure or the moral blackmail of the Twittersphere. Among the Charlie Hebdo cartoons were some very offensive ones that the Guardian 'would never in the normal run of events publish', and it would not reprint them. The Guardian would not be blackmailed into departing from its own standards of liberal civility.

The New York Times did not republish the images. Its executive editor, Dean Baquet, told Politico that an important consideration for him was 'the Muslim family in Brooklyn'. Yet the New York Times had occasionally published images of anti-Semitic cartoons when they were directly relevant to a news story—relying on the Jewish family in Brooklyn to understand why the paper was doing so. It had also published a photo of Chris Ofili's painting The Holy Virgin Mary, showing a black Madonna 'with a clump of elephant dung on one breast and cutouts of genitalia from pornographic magazines in the background'—relying on the Christian family in Brooklyn to appreciate that this was Art.

The Associated Press said it would not republish the Charlie Hebdo cartoons of Muhammad because 'it's been our policy for years that we refrain from moving deliberately provocative images', but Twitterati swiftly pointed out that the AP had been selling images of Andres Serrano's Piss Christ, a well-known artistic photograph that shows a crucifix—that is, for Christians, a representation of the son of God in the moment of his martyrdom—immersed in urine. (The AP subsequently withdrew that image too.)[50] The argument for 'respect' is so uncomfortably intertwined with fear of the assassin's veto. If we are not careful, the conclusion drawn by anyone who wants to impose any taboo will be 'go and get a gun'.

But how can the assassin's veto be effectively, not just rhetorically, faced down? A major problem with the path of coordinated republication that I advocated is that it unintentionally shifts the focus of public debate from murders which most European Muslims could wholeheartedly condemn to a broader discussion about the publication of images of their Prophet, which most of them would abhor. Thus, in a poll conducted for the BBC soon after the Charlie Hebdo murders, 78 percent of the British Muslims interviewed said it was 'deeply offensive to me personally' when images of Muhammad were published, but 85 percent disagreed with the statement that 'organisations which publish images of the Prophet Muhammad deserve to be attacked'. That still left 11 percent maintaining that such organisations should be attacked. No less than 24 percent disagreed with the statement that 'acts of violence against those who publish images of the prophet Muhammad can never be justified'. Twenty-four percent of an estimated 2.7 million Muslims in Britain is more than 650,000 people.[51]

Clearly, we have our work cut out just persuading people that violence is never justified as a response to free expression. Moreover, the debate about republication sows confusion and leads to mudslinging among people who are all, in their different styles, friends of free speech, and hence gives comfort to its enemies. So here is the dilemma. Even if we were to achieve the collective action that I called for, which this experience suggests is unlikely, it risks swivelling the spotlight from the issue of violence, on which most can agree, to that of taste or offensiveness, on which there is chronic disagreement. But if we don't publish anything, the assassin's veto has prevailed.

What is to be done? The least-worst answer I can come up with, for what must remain exceptional cases, is the one-click-away principle. Let the offending material be posted one click away on the internet. The internet, which makes us all neighbours, is partly the cause of this problem, but it can also offer part of the solution. It has three great advantages: speed, distance and personal choice. The material can be published almost instantaneously, as soon as there is an issue of public interest. It is then more easily accessible to people everywhere, including those in less free countries. Thus, for example, virtually all media in Muslim majority countries did not dare, even if some of them privately wished, to show their readers a representative sample of the Charlie Hebdo cartoons. When one Turkish newspaper, Cumhurriyet, did publish several pages of cartoons and articles from the memorial issue of Charlie Hebdo, it faced protests and legal proceedings. Even under authoritarian censorship, many more readers in majority Muslim countries would in practice be able to visit foreign sites where such material could be reliably presented.

As important: readers and viewers can then choose for themselves whether they want to view images that they might find offensive. When an image is printed on the front page of every paper, it is difficult not to see it if you're walking past a newsstand. If it flashes up on the evening television news, the same applies. Online, you can be warned and the choice is yours.

This is not the same as simply saying, 'We don't need to publish this because it's on the internet anyway'. That is a cop-out. As we have seen, the internet is not some detached universal space, run by untouchable Olympians. What that sentence actually means is: 'We don't need to do it because someone else has taken the risk'. Wikipedia, for example, is a repository for many controversial images, but Wikipedia has volunteer editors and the full-time staff of the Wikimedia foundation, who could be targeted as much as any journalists. Moreover, the internet is full of hysterical misrepresentation and misinformation. It is not, in itself, a reliable source. What I suggest is, rather, that responsible media organisations and information platforms should actively place such material online, carefully presented in context and just one click away. (If you are reading this as a post-Gutenberg book, one click from our report on freespeechdebate. com will take you to a wide range of presentations of the cartoons.[52])

There is, I freely admit, a significant risk. Such a precedent could lead other groups to try to get images they find objectionable removed to the one-click-away space. The result could be another instance of the taboo ratchet. At worst, it would reward the demonstrative taking of offence, undergirded with an implicit threat of violence, and thus encourage precisely what we are striving to deter. But what is the alternative? A purely rhetorical insistence that 'everyone should publish' may be accompanied by acts of individual publishing courage, but what matters more for our effective freedom of expression is what mass media and information organisations do, as they confront all the concerns I have described. If they will not, in practice, agree to the collective action of coordinated republication, perhaps we, the netizens, should concentrate on promoting the norm that all such platforms should publish such material one click away, carefully presented online?

Note that what we are discussing here is the broad collective action of republication. Individual publications must remain free to make their own choices, however provocative. Faced with violent intimidation, magazines such as Charlie Hebdo must enjoy the full protection of the state and the Voltairean solidarity of society.

PRACTISING PEACEFUL CONFLICT

Thus far, I have described the need to ban, prosecute and defy violent intimidation. But there are also ways in which we can use the possibilities of free speech to channel potentially violence-inducing exchanges into peaceful conflict. This has been central to the strategies of civil resistance that have been developed over the last hundred years, since Gandhi identified nonviolent action as 'a force which is more positive than electricity and more powerful than even ether'. It is no accident that one of the most celebrated texts on modern civil resistance, Gene Sharp's list of 198 methods of nonviolent action, is also an anthology of forms of human expression, from 'slogans, caricatures and symbols (written, painted, drawn, printed, gestures, spoken or mimicked)', through 'mock elections', 'displays of flags and symbolic colours', 'protest disrobings', 'symbolic sounds' and 'rude gestures', all the way to 'sit-in', 'stand-in', 'ride-in', 'wade-in' and 'pray-in'.

Civil resistance does not always succeed. A research project led by the International Relations scholar Adam Roberts has explored in detail the reasons why civil resistance has been more or less successful in a number of historical cases, from British India to the Arab Spring. For all the failures, there is a cumulatively impressive record of movements channelling what might easily have become violent protest into nonviolent channels, and defeating, sooner or later, the violence of an oppressive power with the expressive instruments of Gandhi's 'force more powerful'.[53]

More recently, we have seen a number of initiatives to combat dangerous speech and online extremism with counterspeech. This has been tried mainly in two contexts: where there has been acute interethnic and political violence in developing countries, and to combat the online radicalisation of residents of mature democracies, a small minority of whom end up as perpetrators of terrorist acts. Thus, for example, a popular radio soap opera in Rwanda was used to undermine hostile stereotypes of Hutu and Tutsi. When there was widespread violence in Kenya during and after the 2007 election, a group of friends joined together to map where the violence was, who seemed to be committing it and who the victims were. This crowdsourced initiative, known as Ushahidi ('testimony'), was soon being used in other disasters and emergencies. Four episodes of a Kiswahili-language television show, 'Drama in the Courtroom', were specially written to expose the inflammatory rhetoric of interethnic incitement. A campaign called 'Give Me Truth', also in Kiswahili, countered false and inflammatory rumours using social media. These and many other efforts contributed to the 2013 Kenyan elections being notably more peaceful than those in 2007. In Ambon, Indonesia, where Muslim-Christian violence had been sparked by false rumours of attacks by one group on the other, which spread rapidly through text messages, a group called 'Peace Provocateurs' tried fighting text with text. Where a girl was said to have been seriously injured, they texted a photograph showing that she was fine.[54]

Faced with violent extremism at home, mature democracies have poured a good deal of money into projects aimed at countering extremist narratives and promoting alternative ones. For example, the Against Violent Extremism project brought together former violent extremists with experts on social media marketing to try to create effective countermessages. A campaign called

MyJihad aspired to reclaim the concept of jihad from both Muslim and anti-Muslim extremists. In one ingenious experiment, white power T-shirts were distributed at a German neo-Nazi music festival. The first time your 'Trojan T-shirt' was washed, the white power logo changed to 'what your T-shirt can do, so can you—we'll help you break with right-wing extremism' and displayed the EXIT Deutschland logo. (This optimistically assumes that neo-Nazis wash their T-shirts.)[55]

All these initiatives were well intentioned, but how many were effective? Here we again encounter the bane of so many disputes about free speech: the mismatch between a wishful plethora of claims for causality and a dearth of hard evidence. If it is difficult, even in the extreme conditions of impending genocide, to establish a firm causal connection between hateful speech and specific acts of violence—that is, between something said and something done—it is even more difficult to prove a causal link between counterspeech and the absence of violence, that is, between something said and something not done.

Nonetheless, attempts have been made to test claims for such strategies, and the results are suggestive. Those specially crafted 'Drama in the Courtroom' episodes were shown to a focus group of Kenyans, while four regular episodes of the same soap opera were shown to another. It seemed that the first group had become more sceptical of inflammatory language.[56] More systematically, a field experiment was designed to test the impact of a campaign against political violence in Nigeria's 2007 national and state-level elections. As the researchers note, these 'proved to be an all-too-suitable context for our purposes, as during the two days of these elections over 300 people were killed'. In selected areas, the experiment used T-shirts, caps, hijabs for Muslim women, leaflets, posters and stickers carrying the message 'No to election violence! Vote against violent politicians!' The message was driven home by town meetings and popular theatre performances—at least one of each in every 'treatment location'. In the 'treated' areas, the researchers found less political violence and a reduced vote for politicians who had resorted to violent intimidation.[57]

Another potentially significant finding came from a survey of hate speech on the internet in Kenya. In a dataset containing thousands of examples of hateful speech, more than 80 percent were on Facebook while less than 5 percent were on Twitter. This strongly suggested that people were more ready to say inflammatory things when they thought they were speaking only to like-minded 'friends'. On Twitter, they knew the communication was public and anyone could respond to it. In fact, some people had been criticising inflammatory tweets, using the hashtag #KOT (Kenyans on Twitter). One who had previously posted that he would be okay with the disappearance of another ethnic group, and was criticised for it, then tweeted, 'sorry, guys, what I said wasn't right and I take it back'. We have to interrogate this evidence, which is fragmentary, and beware of wishful thinking, but it does offer some support for the view that the best answer to bad speech is more and better speech.[58]

We can use speech to stir each other up and cooperate more effectively to kill each other, or we can use it to negotiate our differences without coming to blows. As Winston Churchill put it, we have the choice between war-war and jaw-jaw. In a sense, everything that follows is about defending the line drawn in this second principle while we exercise the right spelt out in the first.

Knowledge

*'We allow no taboos against and seize every chance for
the spread of knowledge'.*

One of the strongest arguments for freedom of expression is that it helps us seek the truth. Along the many paths of that search, there must be as few obstacles and as many open vehicles as possible. Everything that enables us to create, acquire and spread knowledge has a special claim to be protected and promoted.

SCIENTIFICALLY SPEAKING

Natural science is a good place to start, since its story is littered with illegitimate curbs. One of the oldest consists in putting the claims of truth with a capital *T*, as supposedly revealed by religious faith, before those of truth with a small *t*, approached by testing hypotheses against evidence. Thus, most famously, in 1633 the Roman Catholic Church forced the Italian scientist Galileo Galilei to recant his assertion that the earth orbits around the sun. In our own time, a British scientist and imam, Usama Hasan, received death threats for defending the theory of evolution in a talk delivered in his own mosque. You should not, quipped one of his critics, shout 'Evolution!' in a crowded mosque.[1] In many Muslim majority countries, the science of evolution is still taboo.

In a world where private powers can be as potent as public ones, corporations and professional associations have also blocked or obfuscated lines of inquiry they find threatening. Thus, for example, the giant pharmaceutical company Merck brushed aside scientific indications that a drug it marketed as Vioxx led to an increased risk of heart attack or stroke. Instead, it funded numerous events and publications, including papers placed in peer-reviewed journals by Merck employees and their consultants, to show the opposite. By the time the drug was withdrawn, because it did in fact increase the risk of stroke or heart attack, annual sales had topped $2.5 billion and more than 80 million people had been prescribed the medication.[2]

Or take Tamiflu, a drug manufactured by another pharmaceutical giant, Roche, on which the British government alone spent £424 million of taxpayers' money in preparation for a threatened flu pandemic. The Cochrane Collaboration, a group of respected independent academics, subsequently tried to test the evidence that Tamiflu did what Roche said it did. They struggled for years to obtain the unpublished trials on which these bold claims were based, either from the company or from the authorities supposed to be regulating it. When they finally succeeded, with the aid of a journalistic campaign led by the British Medical Journal, it turned out that Roche's claims about cutting down serious illness and reducing the burden on hospitals were unfounded. They were mainly based on a single research paper, using company statisticians. Out of such experiences emerged a movement, animated by the science writer Ben Goldacre, calling for all past and present clinical trials to be registered and their methods and results reported.[3]

Another British science writer, Simon Singh, was sued for libel by the British Chiropractic Association because he wrote that the organisation 'happily promotes bogus treatments' based on 'not a jot of evidence'.[4] Although Singh eventually won his case on appeal, he had to persevere through years of expensive and stressful litigation. Outrage at the chiropractors' manipulation of Britain's libel law contributed to its subsequent reform.

There are legitimate limits to the dissemination of scientific knowledge. If, for example, a research scientist discovered that a simple combination of two widely available substances would produce an undetectable bomb capable of killing thousands of people, a responsible journal would have good reason not to publicise the discovery. But the harm that would result from publication must be clear, significant and probable. This kind of balancing issue arose when the US National Science Advisory Board for Biosecurity asked two well-known scientific journals, Science and Nature, to redact the details of a study about an easily transmitted form of the H5N1 virus, or bird flu, arguing that the information could be misused by terrorists. The journals' editors resisted the pressure, insisting that the information it contained could be important in the development of treatments for this lethal form of flu. In the end, the government advisory board agreed.[5]

A constraint of a different kind is seen in the tale of a scholar who got into hot water by undiplomatically thinking aloud. In 2005, the famously acerbic economist Larry Summers, at that time president of Harvard University, spoke at a conference on 'diversifying the science and engineering workforce'. Stressing that he was advancing hypotheses subject to falsification, in a manner intended to provoke debate, Summers suggested that the low proportion of women in senior positions in science and engineering might result from innate differences of ability and inclination, as well as the pressures of family life and other factors. The resulting storm of protest subsided only with his resignation from the presidency of Harvard. But what if his offensive analysis were right? Or more likely—to recall Mill's argument in *On Liberty*—what if his analysis, while not sound overall, nonetheless contained grains of truth that could advance knowledge?[6]

Should concerns for civility, social harmony and equality override empirical enquiry into a deeply uncomfortable hypothesis? Our guiding principle cannot be the one formulated by the German comic poet Christian Morgenstern in the immortal words *weil nicht sein kann, was nicht sein darf* (since what may not be, cannot be). There is, to be sure, a special need for care, delicacy and civility when we talk about all forms of human difference, and especially innate and perhaps immutable differences. (Much more on this in chapter 5.) But the kinds of people who make bold, original guesses at the frontiers of science may not always be the careful, sensitive, emotionally intelligent types we need in intercommunity relations.

Intent is crucial. Was Summers setting out to insult or demean women? Or was he, however provocatively, genuinely trying to advance scientific understanding? Looking at the evidence, I judge that it was the latter. While other elements obviously fed into the pressures for him to resign, that was not a proportionate response to what he said.

ON CAMPUS

This brings us naturally to the subject of free speech in universities. Academic freedom is about more than free speech. It includes claims for the institutional autonomy of universities and the self-government of scholars within them. But it has an important free speech dimension. This involves both what is expressed on campus, which I shall concentrate on here, and what academics say in wider public debate, perhaps far outside their own disciplines. (Noam Chomsky on US foreign policy comes to mind.) The US Supreme Court has described academic freedom as a 'special concern of the First Amendment'.[7]

Universities should be the embodiments of this draft principle: places where ideas are debated without taboos. If not here, where? Universities aspire to create an environment in which all competing claims and controversial opinions can be heard, and no one feels threatened or intimidated. This is a balancing act, and there never was a golden age when universities always got it right. (Books by Milton and Hobbes were publicly burned in the quadrangle of the Bodleian library at Oxford in 1683.) Nor is academic freedom the contemporary global norm. In many countries, universities are anything but free. Despite my best efforts, I could not, for example, get a lecture at a Chinese university announced with the words 'free speech' in the title.[8] I had to find some other title—and then work in what I wanted to say about free speech. But there have been growing concerns that freedom of speech is being eroded in more subtle, incremental ways even in Western universities.[9]

In the 1980s and 1990s, controversy raged around speech codes, which American universities developed to avoid harassment, distress or simply offence to members of their increasingly diverse student bodies. More recently, attention has turned to 'trigger warnings', which university teachers are asked to attach to any material which might trigger a traumatic memory (for example, of a sexual assault) or cause distress to any group. It has also concerned protests that resulted in prominent speakers being disinvited from official university or student-organised events.[10]

Now it is right that universities should set themselves high standards of civility, and reasonable that warnings should be given when something could genuinely trigger trauma. After all, quality television news programmes quite often warn that some viewers may find images in the next item disturbing. Moreover, a university without student protests against visiting speakers would be like a forest without birds. But in their more extreme forms, these have become the campus versions of the subjective, individual 'I'm offended' veto and the heckler's veto.

An article in a Columbia University student paper, the Columbia Spectator, reported a student who had previously suffered sexual assault being deeply upset by an assigned reading of the myths of Persephone and Daphne in Ovid's *Metamorphoses,* and by the fact that 'her professor focused on the beauty of the language and the splendour of the imagery when lecturing on the text'. As a result, she 'completely disengaged' and 'did not feel safe in the class'. The article went on to observe that the *Metamorphoses* contain 'triggering and offensive material that marginalises student identities in the classroom. These texts, wrought with histories and narratives of exclusion or oppression, can be difficult to read and discuss as a survivor, a person of colour, or a student from a low-income background'.[11]

That was just one article in a student paper, but a draft guide for faculty at Oberlin College in Ohio suggested an even more extensive trigger canon: 'be aware of racism, classism, sexism, heterosexism, cissexism, ableism and other issues of privilege and oppression', it admonished, going on to observe that while Chinua Achebe's *Things Fall Apart* is a 'triumph of literature that everyone in the world should read', it could 'trigger readers who have experienced racism, colonialism, religious persecution, violence, suicide and more'. Other candidates for trigger warnings have included Shakespeare's *Merchant of Venice* (anti-Semitism) and Virginia Woolf's *Mrs. Dalloway* (suicide), while African American students objected to a professor of literature teaching Joseph Conrad's *Heart of Darkness* (portrayal of black people). Jonathan Haidt assigned a magazine article describing the dilemmas faced by a doctor whose patient was dying of cancer, and a student complained that Professor Haidt should have included a trigger warning.[12]

Some of these examples are so silly it is almost too easy to pick them off, and if students couldn't write wild articles in student papers what would the world be coming to? Moreover, that Oberlin draft guide was withdrawn after objections from faculty members. Yet from many conversations with academic colleagues, especially in North America, I fear that these small individual icicles do cumulatively have a chilling effect. One should not overstate it, but university teachers are just that little bit more nervous about stretching their students' minds with testing material that reflects the attitudes of other times and places, and sometimes end up not assigning it. As Randall Kennedy, a Harvard Law School professor, points out in his book *Nigger: The Strange Career of a Troublesome Word*, if any material containing the word 'nigger' were to be considered out-of-bounds, then students could not be invited to read Martin Luther King's 'Letter from a Birmingham Jail'.[13] There may occasionally be the need for a cautionary note, but the new normal cannot be that you have to put a warning on—let alone not teach at all—anything that might possibly offend any single student.

Even more concerning is the habit of disinvitation. I first came across this when the controversial German historian Ernst Nolte was disinvited by a college at Oxford. Other colleagues made up for it by inviting him to speak to the whole university, and a Jewish scholar who had narrowly escaped the Holocaust as a child quoted John Stuart Mill before Nolte addressed a large audience. The bioethicist Peter Singer has had similar difficulties, especially in the German-speaking world, because of his views on euthanasia. More recent examples include Ayaan Hirsi Ali being disinvited by Brandeis University and obstacles placed in the way of the American neoconservative Ann Coulter speaking at some Canadian universities.[14] Condoleezza Rice, the former US secretary of state, and Christine Lagarde, the managing director of the IMF, both felt impelled to withdraw from delivering lectures at leading American universities after substantial protests against their scheduled appearances.[15]

This practice is now sometimes called 'no-platforming', but it is precisely in universities that the widest possible range of influential and controversial views should be given a platform—and then met with civil, robust, well-informed criticism. Demonstrations against the speakers must be allowed. The angry chants of protesters may be audible through the windows of the lecture hall, theatre or art gallery, but inside, the voices of the speakers must be heard, the play or artworks visible. A campus, like the chamber of a democratic parliament, should be distinguished by civilised self-regulation of speech to enable the highest quality of debate. But a university is the last place on earth where the individual, subjective 'I'm offended' veto, the assassin's veto or the heckler's veto should ever be allowed to prevail.

LEGISLATING HISTORY

One area where this principle is both vital and widely violated is knowledge of the past. States, groups, churches and other institutions try to ban, limit or dominate discussion of past events which they believe are still capable of shaping the present and future. The same goes for figures from the past who are, so to speak, dead but still alive. At the extreme, this approaches the Orwellian dystopia of *1984*, with its 'memory hole' down which the true record of past events disappears.

The most notorious examples involve totalitarian regimes systematically occluding or misrepresenting embarrassing episodes from their own histories. For decades, the Soviet Union denied the very existence of a secret protocol to the 1939 Nazi-Soviet nonaggression pact, providing for the partition of Poland between the Soviet Union and Nazi Germany. (In 1979, a Soviet historian who would later be in the avant-garde of scholarly glasnost told me, 'This document does not exist in our archives'.[16]) For decades, it also claimed that Polish officers murdered by Soviet security forces at Katyn in 1940 had in fact been murdered by the Nazis in 1941. People were imprisoned for suggesting otherwise: that is, for telling the truth.

In today's China you may not freely discuss or disseminate knowledge about what happened on and around Tiananmen Square in 1989. A search for 'Tiananmen massacre' on the Baidu search engine in China is likely to meet this message: 'In compliance with relevant laws, regulations and policies, some search results are not displayed'.[17] In the Islamic Republic of Iran, you may not publish a critical biography of the state's founder, Ayatollah Khomeini. Such measures are not confined to totalitarian and authoritarian governments. In Turkey, journalists have been prosecuted for making critical claims about or satirical representations of the country's founder, Kemal Atatürk, something forbidden by Turkish law. A serious biography of Gandhi by a former editor of the New York Times was banned in the Indian state of Gujarat, because it allegedly suggested that Gandhi may have been bisexual.[18]

Significant legal restrictions on historical debate exist in some of Europe's most liberal, law-abiding democracies, where you can be sent to prison for denying that the Nazis murdered millions of European Jews during World War II. One could argue that there was a justification for criminalising Holocaust denial in the years after 1945 when there could still be serious fears of a Nazi revival in Germany or Austria. In fact, such laws only began to spread in the 1990s, when the danger of a Nazi revival was vanishingly small. France's so-called Gayssot law, passed in 1990, set off a wave of 'memory laws' across the continent. Germany only introduced an explicit ban on Holocaust denial in 1994, although denial had previously been punished under a more general provision of the penal code. At this writing, Holocaust denial has been criminalised, often in the form of broader prohibition of denying genocide or crimes against humanity, in at least 14 European countries, with penalties ranging from one to ten years' imprisonment.[19]

Let me be clear: as someone whose formative experiences were in central Europe in the long shadow of that horror, the memory of the Holocaust has been central to my life's work. For me, what we have done in Europe since 1945, and the whole project of constructing liberal international order is, at the deepest level, about trying to ensure that something like that never happens again. But banning people by law from denying that the Holocaust happened is entirely the wrong way to go about it.

There is an overwhelming body of historical evidence to disprove the claim that the mass murder of Europe's Jews did not happen. If someone does not believe all that evidence, he or she is not going to be convinced just because there is a law saying so. At best, they will be frightened to say in public what they think in private. A classic example of the inefficacy of such laws, and the greater efficacy of the free speech alternative, is provided by the story of the historian David Irving. An American scholar, Deborah Lipstadt, described him, on the basis of a careful reading of his published words, as having been a Holocaust denier. Irving sued for libel in the British courts. After a widely publicised trial, with extensive testimony by professional historians, he lost. The judge concluded that he was 'an active Holocaust denier'. Irving was now publicly and authoritatively discredited. But when, some years later, Austria imprisoned him for Holocaust denial, that jail term enabled him to pose as a martyr for free speech. A prestigious student society at Oxford subsequently invited him to speak in a debate about free speech. Which was the better way to counter his lies?[20]

There is also the taboo ratchet. Other groups say, 'If the martyrdom of European Jews is to be elevated to a legally enforced taboo, ours should be too'. This has happened in Europe. As I mentioned at the beginning of this book, in 1995, Bernard Lewis, an eminent historian of the Ottoman Empire, was convicted by a French court for arguing that the terrible suffering inflicted on Armenians in the last years of Ottoman rule might not correctly be described as 'genocide'.[21] In 2007, a Turkish politician and journalist called Doğu Perinçek was sentenced in Switzerland, which has a law forbidding you to deny that what happened to the Armenians was genocide.[22] Meanwhile, in Turkey the Nobel Prize–winning writer Orhan Pamuk was prosecuted for suggesting, in an interview with a Swiss magazine, that it was genocide.[23] What was state-ordained truth in the Alps was state-ordained falsehood in Anatolia.

In 2008, a well-intentioned German justice minister, Brigitte Zypries, pushed through a EU Framework Decision stipulating that all member states should criminalise the 'public condoning, denying or grossly trivialising of crimes of genocide, crimes against humanity and war crimes' as defined by the International Criminal Court and the post-1945 Nuremberg tribunal, which tried leading Nazis.[24] A European Commission memorandum noted that these changes were 'largely inspired by the German law'.[25]

Zypries argued that 'historical experience puts Germany under a permanent obligation to combat systematically every form of racism, anti-Semitism and xenophobia. And we should not wait until it comes to deeds. We must act already against the intellectual pathbreakers of the crime'.[26] As with the elision between hate speech and dangerous speech, that word 'pathbreakers' smuggles in an unproven claim of causality. At that time, the list of European countries with Holocaust denial laws included some of those with the strongest right-wing xenophobic parties on the continent, from France's National Front and the Vlaams Belang in Belgium to the Greater Romania party. Self-evidently those parties didn't exist as a result of Holocaust denial laws, but the laws had not prevented their vigorous and dangerous growth. If anything, the bans and resulting court cases gave their leaders the nimbus of persecution that far-right populists love to exploit.

Moreover, the advocates of this Europe-wide extension of German practice were soon confronted by central and east European states suggesting that denying the horrors of communist totalitarianism should be criminalised too. The

Hungarian parliament passed a law criminalising Holocaust denial in 2010. Later that year, a new right-wing nationalist majority in that parliament changed the formulation of the law to: 'punish those who deny the genocides committed by national socialist or communist systems'. Poland has a law prohibiting the denial of both Nazi and communist 'crimes against the Polish nation'.[27]

Such laws also lay European countries open to a broader charge of double standards. Some Muslims say, 'So you—Europeans, Christians, Jews, Enlightenment liberals—protect by law what is most sacred to you, the memory of the Holocaust, but insist that we Muslims must allow what is most sacred to us, the memory and image of the prophet Muhammad, to be subject to caricature and abuse. There's one rule for you and another for us'. Historical facts and religious beliefs are not entirely comparable, but these critics nonetheless have a point. In this mixed-up world, we must be consistent, in one direction or the other. If we put together all the taboos in the world, there won't be much left that we can talk about.

The position I have outlined here is supported by the authoritative UN Human Rights Committee interpretation of Article 19, which says plainly, 'Laws that penalise the expression of opinions about historical facts are incompatible with the obligations that the International Covenant on Civil and Political Rights imposes on states'.[28] None of this is to suggest for a moment that falsifications of history, or any other branch of knowledge, should be accepted. On the contrary: they must be openly and vigorously contested. Historical knowledge advances precisely by testing hypotheses and interpretations, however extreme, against challenges based on evidence.

A different question is what the state does in its expressive rather than its coercive role. Here, public powers necessarily make historical judgements. Which historical events, groups or figures merit a commemorative day or monument? An Independence or Republic Day? An Armistice Day, marking the end of World War I? Holocaust Memorial Day? Columbus Day? (Or, as they say in Berkeley, Native Americans Day.) Which historical figures get statues in your main public squares? Which historical museums merit public subsidy? Should the Polish president Lech Kaczyński have been buried with Polish kings and heroes in the royal castle in Kraków? Should Margaret Thatcher have received such a grandiose funeral? Should Lenin still lie in honoured state on Moscow's Red Square and Chairman Mao still smile down onto Tiananmen Square from the gates of the Forbidden City?

These 'politics of memory' are inevitably contested. The state is bound to make choices when it 'speaks' through such symbolic acts. The free speech condition is that these choices should be open to public debate, without intimidation or taboos—and that private individuals and associations should be free to set different historical accents of their own.

More challenging is the issue of school textbooks, curricula and teaching methods, which may have an enduring influence on impressionable minds. There are several dangers here. The most obvious is that the state feeds pupils only a partisan, nationalist, selective version of history. In 2001, for example, Japan's ministry of education approved for use in junior high schools a so-called New History Textbook, which gave a highly sanitised account of the conduct of Japanese forces in World War II.[29]

Where two countries have a past of violent conflict, like Poland and Germany, there have been attempts to produce joint textbooks. Admirable though these are, they risk another kind of sanitisation: gliding over all the difficult subjects. The more that historical writing attempts not to offend anybody, the blander it becomes: witness the 'from Charlemagne to the euro' school of writing European history. Ideally, students will be presented with a solid core of established, significant facts and evidence, shown competing interpretations that lead them to think critically for themselves, and pointed to the galaxy of places beyond the classroom—most of them easily accessible online—where the knowledge-enhancing contestation continues without taboos.

Yet the principle of 'no taboos' cannot prevail inside the schoolroom to quite the extent that it does outside. A teacher who fills his young pupils' minds with a wild, distorted, hate-filled account of the crimes allegedly perpetrated since time immemorial by Sikhs, Jews, Muslims, Turks, Greeks, homosexuals, women or socialists should not be allowed to continue in that function— whereas, provided he does not incite to violence, he should be free to do so as a ranting blogger, and there, in the blogosphere, we should treat him with the contempt he deserves. The argument for freedom of expression that flows through this book is based on the Enlightenment premise that grown men and women should not be treated like children. In the classroom, children should be educated to become sovereign adults, but not treated as if they already are.

EVERYTHING OPEN TO EVERYONE?

Thus far I have talked about limits and taboos. What of the second, positive half of this principle? What does it mean to 'seize every chance' for the dissemination of knowledge?

In 1938, H. G. Wells published a book called *World Brain*, in which he envisaged a permanent world encyclopaedia as 'the material beginning of a real World Brain'. It would, he suggested, 'have the form of network' between physical records and those working on them. Greatly daring, he added that its printed materials 'might to a large extent be duplicated'. By this, he presumably meant keeping multiple copies in different places, perhaps with the aid of a mimeograph or spirit duplicator, and he mentions the very latest new technology: microfilm.[30]

Wells was not the first to envisage bringing it all together. The ancient Great Library of Alexandria already had something of this aspiration, and Wells himself refers to the French Enlightenment scholar Denis Diderot's *Encyclopédie*. You can still view in Mons, Belgium, giant wooden filing cabinets holding the 12 million index cards of the *Mundaneum*, a project founded by two Belgian lawyers to collect all the world's knowledge. In the early twenty-first century we have come closer to this dream than ever before.

As I sit at my computer, I am surrounded by printed reference books. To check a quotation, however, I will start by googling it on screen, rather than reaching just an arm's length for my faded blue *Oxford Dictionary of Quotations*. I will usually find the source more quickly and discover some intriguing detail along the way. I then need to check the quotation, scrutinising the source to ensure its reliability, but many of those original sources are available online. There is a project called Electronic Enlightenment which makes available, in easily searchable form, the correspondence of the leading thinkers of the seventeenth- and eighteenth-century Enlightenment, including Diderot and his fellow *Encyclopédistes*.[31] The chance we have in the twenty-first century may be described as Electronic Enlightenment in a broader sense. But it is only that: a chance, not a certainty.

Viktor Mayer-Schönberger and Kenneth Cukier estimate that had all the data stored in the world in 2013 been printed in books, they would have covered the entire surface of the United States to a height of some 52 volumes, from shore to dusty shore. Had it been placed on CDs, they would have stretched to the moon in a galactic bridge five CDs thick.[32] Yet data is not knowledge, let alone wisdom. A famous image, credited to the systems theorist Russell Ackoff, has a pyramid reaching upwards from the broad base of Data, through Information and Knowledge to the narrow apex of Wisdom — the DIKW pyramid. (See Figure 10. Ackoff originally had Understanding between Knowledge and Wisdom, but that is now usually dropped in the interests of, well, understanding.)

This pyramid image is questionable in at least two ways. The dividing lines between data, information and knowledge are far from clear, and the more definitions of 'information' and 'knowledge' you read, the fuzzier the lines become. Moreover, the pyramid image suggests that knowledge and wisdom are achieved by an upward filtering of data and information. Often they are, especially in

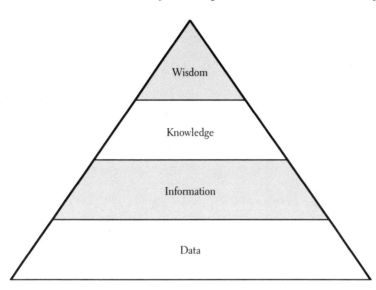

Figure 10. The DIKW pyramid

science; but sometimes knowledge and wisdom may be attained just by living alertly with other human beings, or by thinking hard, or by meditation.[33]

Nonetheless, something important has changed. There is an unprecedented and rapidly growing ocean of data, information and digitally reproduced materials from the past, available to anyone who has the requisite time, education and internet access. It has taken much human skill to enable us to navigate rapidly online from a superabundance of raw data and information towards knowledge and understanding, and the means chosen will inevitably highlight some things and obscure others. Those determinants of what we find when we seek online are seldom apparent at first glance. We do not see what we do not see. Moreover, this giant leap forward in the availability of data, information and knowledge (draw the dividing lines where you will) poses large questions about what should be made accessible when, how, to whom, and at what cost.

What are the limits on our free access to knowledge? What should they be? When does our right to know collide with other rights? There is also, in some limited circumstances, a right not to know. For example, if you may have an inherited genetic predisposition to a serious disease, you should have the choice whether to learn that or not. And certainly you should not be compelled to share the information with others, including health insurance and pension providers. (In subsequent chapters, I explore the balancing acts between official secrecy, privacy and free speech.)

One of the biggest clashes in our time is between the movement towards open access and the defence of intellectual property, including copyright. Once a boring if profitable byway for lawyers, at the beginning of the twenty-first century this suddenly became one of the most dramatic battlefields in the struggle for word power.[34] Even more than hate speech, privacy or pornography, intellectual property rights mobilised a new generation of internet users—online, on the streets and through organised politics. As we have seen, the self-styled ACTAvists triumphed over the Anti-Counterfeiting Trade Agreement (ACTA) in Europe, while those two ugly sisters SOPA and PIPA—the Stop Online Piracy Act and Protect Intellectual Property Act—were defeated in the United States.[35]

Meanwhile, the academic world was stirred by a dramatic shift towards open access to scientific journals and research results. Thousands of academics boycotted the academic publisher Elsevier to protest against its extortionate journal prices. The richest university in the world, Harvard, called on its scholars to make their work available in open-access journals, saying that its library could no longer afford the $3.5 million annual bill payable to the likes of Elsevier.[36] The British government demanded that the results of any publicly funded research should be made freely available to the public and commissioned a report on the best way to cover the editorial, peer-review and production costs of academic publications.[37]

Tragically, this battle over intellectual property claimed the life of a brilliant young man. Aaron Swartz, an American computing prodigy, co-developed Reddit, an online bulletin board which by 2015 clocked more than 150 million unique monthly visitors viewing more than six billion pages. He was involved in pioneering the widely used RSS web feed, worked with Tim Berners-Lee to improve data sharing through the Semantic Web and with cyberlaw guru Lawrence Lessig on the Creative Commons licences. All this by age 26.[38]

Swartz believed passionately that data, information and knowledge should be freely accessible to all. So he obtained the book-cataloguing data kept by the Library of Congress, for which it usually charged, and posted it on something called the Open Library. He found his way into 19.9 million pages of electronic records of US court proceedings and uploaded them for all to see on theinfo .org.[39] Using his computer skills and his Massachusetts Institute of Technology (MIT) guest access to the JSTOR online library of journal articles, for which most universities pay a hefty fee, he started downloading articles to a laptop hidden in a wiring cupboard at MIT. By January 2011, he had downloaded—liberated, he would have said—nearly 5 million documents.

Then he was caught, and US prosecutors decided to make an example of him. JSTOR declined to support their case, but MIT allowed it to go forward. Bringing charges under the vaguely worded Computer Fraud and Abuse Act, US Attorney Carmen Ortiz declared that Swartz faced 'up to 35 years in prison, to be followed by three years of supervised release, restitution, forfeiture and a fine of up to $1 million'. Though it would probably not have come to that, Swartz, worn down by the strain, committed suicide on 11 January 2013.[40]

He left behind a manifesto which is a good place to start addressing the question that concerns us here: In what direction should we, as citizens and netizens, attempt to push the commercial, technical, legal and political forces that will decide the outcome of this struggle? Unless we believe that absolutely everything should be freely available to everyone all the time, where should the line be drawn?

Swartz's Guerilla Open Access Manifesto starts with the familiar statement that 'information is power' and goes on to assert that much of it 'is increasingly being digitized and locked up by a handful of private corporations'. (It's interesting, and characteristic of his generation in the West, that he sees the face of Big Brother in the corporation, not the state.) In practice, he says, people work around this, 'trading passwords with colleagues' and 'liberating the information locked up by the publishers'. Then comes his central claim. Such hidden, covert action, he writes, is 'called stealing or piracy, as if sharing a wealth of knowledge were the moral equivalent of plundering a ship and murdering its crew. But sharing isn't immoral—it's a moral imperative. Only those blinded by greed would refuse to let a friend make a copy'.[41]

There is the twenty-first-century cyberleveller's radical vision. It echoes the internet founders' cyberlibertarian thinking, and I have a lot of sympathy with it. Electronic Enlightenment should indeed mean that the 'wealth of knowledge' is freely available to all. Two further observations support this claim. First, open access has the potential to reduce a drastic global inequality in the spread of knowledge. In principle, so long as she has an affordable fast internet connection and sufficient education, the impoverished farmer's daughter in Eritrea would have access to exactly the same common trove of human learning as a Harvard professor. Well-designed online educational resources could help her find her way around Aladdin's cave. The carefully crafted and widely used Creative Commons licences, pioneered by Lawrence Lessig, give a clear set of rules, allowing several variants of free reproduction.[42] Freespeechdebate.com uses one of them, a Creative Commons Attribution-NonCommercial-ShareAlike licence, which means that you are free to copy, distribute, display and perform the content of the site, and to make derivative works from it, provided you give credit to the original author of the content, do not use the content for commercial purposes and distribute any derivative work under the same kind of Creative Commons licence.[43] Freely available digital library resources, such as the Digital Public Library of America, Europeana and the Internet Archive—to name but three—support this purpose.[44] So does the scientific preprint site arXiv, which reportedly includes half of all the world's physics papers.[45]

Second, open access can enhance not merely the dissemination but the production of knowledge. On occasion, crowdsourcing has generated scientific results that could not have been found by a single researcher, or only at vast expense of time and money. Two researchers sitting in an English pub had the crazy idea of asking the general public to help them scan tens of thousands of photos of galaxies. With mass participation, this Galaxy Zoo not only classified numerous previously unclassified galaxies but also identified a new kind of galaxy.[46] A Cambridge mathematician put an open invitation on his blog for people to help him solve a difficult mathematical problem. He called this experiment the Polymath Project. Six weeks later, he announced that they had solved not just the original problem but also a harder one that included the original as a special case.[47]

When it comes to discussions not of what is but of what should be, of values and norms, the dialogue across frontiers, cultures, faiths and political camps is itself part of the research. To find out what other people think, where they agree and where they disagree, is in itself to generate knowledge. The medium is not the message, but the discussion is the research.

Yet there are also objections we must take seriously. One concerns the definition of what is to be covered by this special dispensation. In a 2007 interview, the founder of Pirate Bay, Gottfrid Svartholm-Warg, defended the appearance of paedophile content in his bay: 'I think paedophiles and terrorists are horrible . . . but I believe they have the right to voice their opinions'.[48] Opinions? Can the music, movies and pornography which constitute a large part of what is shared on a site like Pirate Bay really all be wrapped in the noble flag of 'knowledge'?

Then we have to ask: who pays, who profits and who decides? The cyberlawyer Andrew Murray pithily unpacks the touchy-feely word 'share': 'By sharing we mean copy. By copy we mean take without paying the person who created it'.[49] But the production of knowledge is not cost-free. Ideally, universities, foundations, companies and governments can between them fund the original research, workshops, collaborations, expert editing, peer review and so on needed to produce and present knowledge that will then be freely available to any user. But those funding models have to be developed, and each of them will inevitably have gatekeepers, biases and constraints. What if your university decides not to pay the 'article processing charges' for your learned article on seventeenth-century Portuguese mandolins to be published under Britain's proposed open-access journal scheme?[50]

Last but not least, what about the lone, hungry poet, composer or painter, shivering in his garret? It is no accident that when, in 1710, the English parliament passed the first copyright law to place rights firmly with the author—and not just, as previously, with the printer or publisher—it was called An Act for the Encouragement of Learning. I am fortunate enough to be at a stage in my professional life when I could afford to publish this book, on which I have laboured for many years, without receiving a penny for any copies sold. But suppose I were a young freelance author, with two children and a mortgage?

So this is not a simple battle between the global, emancipatory spread of knowledge, on the one hand, and antiquated, reactionary property rights on the other. The maximisation (in quality as well as quantity) and spread of knowledge itself requires a carefully redrawn, strictly limited but then also effectively enforced protection of intellectual property.

PUBLIC GOOD VIA PRIVATE POWER

Knowledge is a public good that is often supplied by private powers. That is, in itself, nothing new. What is new, however, is the scale, global reach and small number of the dominant private powers now performing this function. As we have seen, they create 'privately owned public spaces' (POPS).

That being so, we need to scrutinise the rapidly evolving practice of each private superpower. Here, I shall look at two of the biggest global knowledge and information giants to illustrate the issues that arise. In many Western languages the most frequent first call people make in the search for knowledge is via a Google search to a Wikipedia article. Over the years, Google has become such a vast for-profit company, with so many products and futuristic research enterprises, that in 2015 it announced a change in the name of the overall company to Alphabet. But the verb 'google' means to search, and search remained its core business. Since that is what I am considering here, I will continue to refer to the superpower as Google. Google's official statement of its company mission is 'to organize the world's information and make it universally accessible and useful'. Wikipedia wants us to imagine, in the words of its founder, Jimmy Wales, 'a world in which every single person is given access to the sum of all human knowledge'. Those are aspirations, not achieved realities—but in 2015 there were well over 3 billion individual searches on Google in some language every day, while an estimated half a billion people consulted Wikipedia or one of its connected free knowledge projects every month.[51]

Google Search, and especially the US mother site, google.com, is a consciously pro–free speech space. Its American executives and lawyers are usually disciples of the Church of the First Amendment. When Google takes down content to comply with a legal request, it generally puts a notice of that takedown on an independently operated website called lumendatabase.org (previously chillingeffects.org).[52] It publishes a transparency report, which enumerates requests from governments and copyright owners for content to be removed, those from governments and courts for user data, and identifies countries where its own services are being disrupted.[53]

Almost entirely untransparent, by contrast, is the way in which the search engine itself determines which results come up in the top ten—the ones most of us look at. We are told that the ranking is determined by Google's 'algorithms', a word that evokes images of pure scientific neutrality. In fact, those algorithms are both written and adjusted by computer engineers, the Brahmins of Silicon Valley, and they make many value judgements along the way. (I say more about this in chapter 9.)

Google actively looks for, removes and helps law enforcement authorities to find the producers of child pornography. Very few people in the world would disapprove of that. Like other information superpowers, it has come under growing pressure from governments to give similar treatment to material putatively contributing to terrorism. But what if, some years hence, perhaps responding to pressures from government, powerful lobbies or normative shifts in society, this gateway to the world's knowledge chose to remove some other category of information or expression? Suppose it decided that anti-Semitism, or homophobia, or racism, or anti-Americanism, were an evil comparable to paedophilia?

'Ridiculous!' you may exclaim. 'Trust us!' cries Google. But here's one small example of how Google does occasionally slide into editorial judgement, even on google.com. If you search in English for 'the Jew', then at the bottom or right-hand side of the page you find an 'ad' from Google itself titled Offensive Search Results, with the explanatory line 'We're disturbed about these results as well. Please read our note here'. Click through and a hand-wringing note says that 'you may have seen results that were very disturbing', that Google does not endorse them, that 'the beliefs and preferences of those who work at Google, as well as the opinions of the general public, do not determine or impact our search results'—a statement both parts of which are clearly untrue. It concludes, 'We apologise for the upsetting nature of the experience you had using Google', and a postscript refers to some additional information from the Anti-Defamation League.[54]

Search for 'was Christ a criminal?' or 'Muhammad + paedophile' or 'find girls to fuck in the ass' and no such delicate warning comes up, although reasonable persons could clearly find these results 'disturbing' and 'upsetting'. Instead, when I first searched for 'find girls to fuck in the ass' — perhaps triggering alarms somewhere in the ethical depths of a university computing service — three ads appeared at the top of the page, linking to sites purportedly helping you to do just that: page-top ads from which Google earned money.[55]

Another problem is the personalisation of search results which Google first introduced in 2009. Many people still operate on the vague assumption that if you google it and I google it, we will find more or less the same results. That is ever less true. Try it with a few friends scattered around the world and see what comes up. If you are logged in as a Google user, your results will be customised not just on the basis of your location and previous search history but also on information Google has collected from your Gmail accounts, your use of its social networks and any other online source to which it has access. The most alarming aspect of this is the threat to our privacy, which I discuss more in chapter 7, but it can also impair our pursuit of knowledge. If the effect of search personalisation is to give a higher ranking to sites we and our online contacts have previously viewed, then we are in danger of being hived off into 'filter bubbles' of the like-minded. Google will reply that it is just giving people what they want — a more personalised, customised service. But that is only half the story. The other half is that Google is giving advertisers what they want: the capacity to target individual consumers ever more precisely. If information is power, personalised information is also money.

Google Search is a fantastic, transformative tool in the quest for knowledge. I have used it to find material to support this critique of Google. But at least three distinct causes for concern emerge as we consider the world's largest example of public good delivered by private power. The first is that, to a greater extent than the wizard-weasel word 'algorithms' implies, Google Search reflects the underlying values of those who run it. The second is that one private power has such a dominant position as the information gatekeeper in so much of the world. (Where it isn't dominant, that position is held by another gatekeeper, such as Baidu, which is deeply entangled with censorship by the Chinese party-state.) The third is that this giant corporation's desire to maximise profit from advertising increasingly shapes what we find when we 'google it'.

So long as disciples of the First Amendment continue to run Google, the influence of their personal values is probably the smallest of these concerns. More systematic transparency about its own editorial value judgements, rather than explanations buried away in Google blog posts, would go a long way to address it.[56] The second is more serious, and requires strong regulatory authorities defending fair competition against monopoly or near-monopoly players. An internal memorandum from a 'case team' inside the US Federal Trade Commission suggested in 2012 that the search company had 'unlawfully maintained its monopoly over general search, search advertising and search syndication'.[57] At the very least, as Tim Wu argues, such giants should be *insecure* monopolies.[58] The third concern is potentially the biggest of all. For it may well be that 'what gives you the best access to knowledge' and 'what makes Google the most money from selling you to advertisers' will increasingly diverge. If we want to protect the pure knowledge-seeking beauty of googling from the commercial temptations for Google, we need to raise our voices and vote with our mice.

Wikipedia, one of the most popular websites in the world, is a very different animal. First and foremost, it is not for profit. This makes it unique among the big cats. In the most widely used ranking of the world's hundred most popular websites, Wikipedia came in at number 7 in 2015. The only other not-for-profit on the list was the BBC, which sneaked in at number 86.[59]

How did this come about? In 2001, Jimmy 'Jimbo' Wales, an entrepreneurial libertarian, and Larry Sanger, a recent philosophy graduate, had the crazy idea of starting a free online encyclopaedia, to which anyone could contribute articles which anyone else could then edit at will. To their own and everyone else's surprise, it took off like a rocket. Fourteen years later, there were editions in more than 290 different languages with a grand total of some 35 million articles. The largest was English-language Wikipedia, with nearly 5 million entries, followed by the German, French, Spanish, Italian, Polish, Russian, and Swedish ones, all of which contained over 1 million.[60]

In 2003, Jimbo had an even crazier idea: he would vest ownership of the whole thing in a not-for-profit Wikimedia Foundation. There are few if any examples in recent history of an individual, apparently in full possession of his faculties, voluntarily surrendering such a vast potential fortune. To enter the modest headquarters of the Wikimedia Foundation in San Francisco is a quite different experience from that of visiting any other Silicon Valley giant. In the stylish reception areas of Google, Twitter and Facebook, the first thing the hip receptionist has you do is to sign (electronically, of course) a confidentiality agreement. When I first visited the Wikimedia Foundation, I was amazed to discover that it did not even have its own reception. I had to tap hard on the closed ground-floor doors of the office building to attract the attention of a sleepy porter. The foundation feels like what it is: a medium-sized NGO, funded by individual donations and philanthropic grants. Wikipedia does not sell you to any advertiser. It has ambitious plans to increase its traffic, especially in the non-Western world, but not for commercial reasons.

How good is it? The answer varies considerably between what the founda-tion calls the 'mature' encyclopedias, especially those in the major Western languages, and the scrappier small ones. Quality also varies among entries. Its co-founder, Larry Sanger, makes a nice distinction between useful and reli-able knowledge.[61] The Wikipedia entry generally gives you a useful first bite at a topic, but to be sure of having reliable information you need to check elsewhere. The problem of reliability is especially sensitive in the case of en-tries on living individuals. Although one of Wikipedia's explicit guiding prin-ciples is 'respect for living people', prominent individuals often complain about inaccuracies in its entries on them. Thus, for example, a British member of parliament exploded in an email to me: 'I am a Zionist, secret Jew, criminal expenses fiddler—allegations perhaps as well as lies . . . Most MPs just give up on Wikiliepedia as it is called. It takes a lot of effort and know how to get this stuff off and then a day later they can pop up again'.[62]

Yet, given the free-for-all way in which they are created, many of the substan-tive entries in the best of the mature Wikipedias are remarkably good. Their verifiability has been improved by the programmatic addition of electronic link footnotes, so you can check the source for yourself. Several studies have found that Wikipedia could stand comparison with renowned reference works such as the Encyclopedia Britannica in English and Brockhaus in German.[63] It is also faster, including rapidly updated, crowdsourced chronicles of major events such as the Arab Spring.

Lawrence Lessig dedicates *Code 2.0*, the second edition of his seminal book, to 'Wikipedia, the one surprise that teaches more than everything here'. But what exactly does it teach? Those who study and oversee Wikipedia agree that the key to its success has been that early on it found the 'right crowd', a commu-nity of dedicated, idealistic, more or less like-minded volunteers. In 2015, fewer than 5,000 people regularly made more than 100 edits a month on the English-language Wikipedia. In earlier years, it had been a few thousand more. Although anyone can write or edit a Wikipedia entry, in practice this community of just a few thousand 'power editors' has been instrumental in creating and maintaining an online English-language encyclopaedia that can boast more than 8 billion page views a month.[64] An internal study revealed that these core Wikipedians were overwhelmingly male, aged between 18 and 30, well educated and single.

This volunteer community—roughly the size of an assembly in ancient Athens—went to enormous lengths to build an unprecedented knowledge re-source. They and the small foundation staff had to defend it against a mounting problem of vandalism. As Figure 11 illustrates, the more Wikipedia grew, the greater this challenge became.[65]

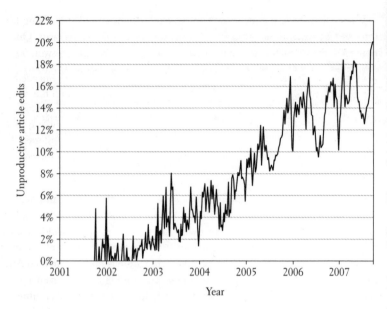

Figure 11. Fighting vandalism on Wikipedia
Source: Broughton 2008.

Meeting it required extraordinary commitment. By 2015, the core group of 'power editors' was shrinking and the foundation was exploring automated methods of data processing and translation to sustain the encyclopaedia's growth.[66]

Second, Wikipedia has a balance of democracy and authority. Huge emphasis is placed on open, deliberative democracy, and all editorial policy choices are the subject of exhaustive online debate. Unlike most of the commercial private powers, Wikipedia has a high level of transparency about itself. You can see the whole editing history of every article online, including some 'edit wars' that make Europe's Thirty Years' War look like a coffee break. (One of the most ridiculous was a battle on the English-language Wikipedia about the correct spelling of the Voßstrasse in Berlin. Should it be Voßstrasse, Vossstrasse, Voss strasse or Voss-strasse?)[67] You can also follow almost all the broader policy debates, on issues such as what to do about controversial content, or whether to introduce an image filter for parents who do not want their children to stumble upon sexually explicit images and Muslims who do not want to see images of Muhammad.[68]

Wikipedians have a characteristically geeky joke about this, parodying the time-consuming complexity of their own quests for editorial consensus. Question: How many Wikipedians does it take to change a lightbulb? Answer: 69.

1 to propose change; 5 to support; 1 to dispute whether the change is a needed process; 7 more to pile on from IRC [Internet Relay Chat] and join the dispute; 2 to open a request for comment; 37 to vote at the straw poll; 5 to say votes are evil; 1 to MFD it [propose it as "Miscellany for Deletion"]; 9 to object until the MFD gets speedily closed; 1 to mark the proposal historical. Afterward on AN [Administrators' Noticeboard], all opposers claim the consensus favoured darkness [i.e., no lightbulb!].[69]

One of the longest-running arguments has been about what should qualify for inclusion. So-called deletionists want a higher admission standard of significance, while 'inclusionists' think that even the most trivial entry should have its chance, provided it meets some minimum editorial standards. After all, no one is obliged to read it. These battles have been fought daily on lists marked AfD (Articles for Deletion) and PROD (Proposed Deletion). There was even a project called the Article Rescue Squadron.[70] The writer Nicholson Baker, himself a professed Wikiholic, once suggested in the New York Review of Books that there should be a 'Wikimorgue' for all these deleted articles.[71] A reader wrote in to point out that it already existed: the Wikipedia Knowledge Dump.[72] Beyond that, there is an Uncyclopedia, a 'content-free encyclopedia' which parodies Wikipedia and is amusing if you like that kind of thing.[73]

Yet beside all this open democracy there is authority. Experienced editors are given more extensive editing rights than novices. Hovering over them are a few thousand Administrators, with the power to delete articles for good and to ban vandalous contributors. Above them are super-administrators called Bureaucrats, armed with still greater powers. There is an Arbitration Committee, to arbitrate major disputes, and the board of the Foundation. If a volunteer-driven Wikipedia in any language were to go really wild, the Foundation could take it down. And then there is the founding father, Jimmy Wales, who still enjoys unique personal authority. Rejecting the description of him as a benevolent dictator—'I wasn't a dictator', he told me, 'and certainly not benevolent'—he prefers to characterise himself as a British-style constitutional monarch.[74]

Beside these structures of authority, there is a vast online codex of self-regulatory principles and rules, most of them translated into many languages and given their own acronyms. Among the most important are the requirement to keep a neutral point of view (NPOV) and the imperative of verification, as well as a host of more specific guidelines. Thus, for example, more than seventy detailed pages are devoted to standardising naming conventions for everything from ancient Egyptian to ice hockey, and from games to the thorny nomenclature of Macedonia.[75] And, sobered by experience: 'all biographies of living people created after March 18, 2010, must have references'. What it takes to be a successful Wikipedia editor is described by a veteran of the craft, John Broughton, across 476 detailed pages of *Wikipedia: The Missing Manual*.[76]

Crucial to the whole enterprise are the guidelines for interactions between Wikipedians, including the injunction to assume good faith (AGF) on the part of other contributors and a strong insistence on civility—which comes out in French as *savoir-vivre communautaire*. The desired courtesy of interaction, combining honesty and politeness, is described as Wikiquette or even Wikilove (in German, *Wikiliebe*) and modestly defined as 'a general spirit of collegiality and mutual understanding'. In other words, this is an online community aspiring to live by a set of shared norms.

An optimist for transcultural convergence through debate would point to this extraordinary self-governing community of Wikipedians. A sceptic would highlight the very specific, relatively homogenous, mainly Western character of that community. She could also point to the unique nature of an encyclopaedia, where arguments are mainly about facts, and its failures on subjects where views are strongly polarised (e.g., 'George W. Bush'). Efforts to 'wiki' opinions rather than facts have not been successful. The Los Angeles Times tried running a user-edited Wikitorial. The experiment was stopped after it descended into farce, with the whole text being replaced by the words 'Fuck USA' and pornographic images.[77]

FROM BABEL TO BABBLE

Wikipedia is divided up by languages, not states. Here, all the English speakers in the world are reunited in one vast English-language wikination. The Spanish wikination embraces all Spanish speakers, the Portuguese wikination includes Portuguese speakers in Portugal and Brazil, as well as in Angola or Mozambique, although Brazilians and Portuguese quarrel over which version of their language should be used.

Wikipedia has a language committee to adjudicate disputes and decide which languages qualify for a Wikipedia.[78] Wikipedia thus creates a knowledge community in which the significance of political frontiers is reduced, though not abolished, but the frontiers between languages remain stubbornly persistent. For those who do have uncensored, affordable internet access, and the education to use it, language barriers are among the highest left standing in an otherwise joined-up world. One study published in 2010 found a remarkable lack of overlap between the content of even the two largest Western Wikipedias, those in English and German.[79] Imagine what it's like between the Chinese and Urdu ones.

Figure 12 shows the top ten languages on the internet, with Chinese and English outstripping the rest. We are still closer to the tower of Babel, where everyone babbles on in mutually incomprehensible languages, than we are to Pentecost, when all comprehend each other as they 'speak in tongues'. Indeed, this biblical imagery of Babel and Pentecost would itself be alien to much of humankind. If we believe that free speech for a connected world requires us to 'seize every chance for the spread of knowledge', as this principle suggests, then to overcome language barriers remains one of our biggest practical challenges. We may be virtual neighbours, but what use is that if I literally can't understand what my neighbour is saying?

Attempts to advance down the road from Babel to Pentecost range from conventional, professional translation to the automated machine translation of

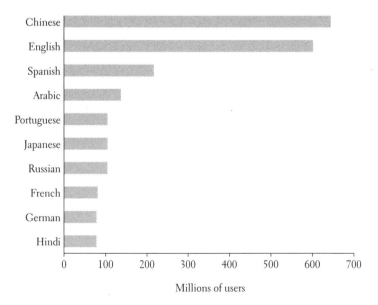

Figure 12. Wikinations: Top 10 languages on the internet
Chinese includes simplified, traditional and Wu Chinese.
Source: Adapted from Liao 2013.

Google Translate, which machine-analyses a word hoard larger than that contained in all the books in the Library of Congress.[80] Between these extremes, there are promising experiments in volunteer translation. Thus, for example, talks on the TED website have been subtitled in several languages, in a well-organised Open Translation Project, along with transcripts.[81] One of the most ingenious and ambitious schemes is Duolingo, which allows people to learn a language by translating content already online. Implausible though it sounds, by graduating volunteer translators from simpler to more complex text, and by having people compare, correct and consolidate multiple versions, Duolingo claims to produce translations of high quality. Its inventor, Luis von Ahn, calls this 'massive online cooperation'.[82]

On freespeechdebate.com, our web developers faced the challenge of getting everything displayed properly in 13 languages, some of them running from right to left. In the end, they developed a new open-source tool, available for any of the roughly 75 million websites built on WordPress. They called it Babble: still many leagues from Pentecost, but a step forward from Babel.[83]

Thus far, I've been writing about words. But what of images, which, along with music, make up a growing part of online content? Remember Elizabeth Daley's argument that images may even be supplanting writing as the primary medium of mass communication online, as Latin was supplanted by vernacular languages such as English, French and Spanish after the spread of printing. 'A picture is worth a thousand words', says the cliché, and clearly some images, such as the famous 1972 photo of a naked, terrified little girl running down a road in Vietnam, screaming with the pain of burns from napalm dropped by US forces, can achieve a universality beyond the power of words.[84] Yet many symbols and hand gestures mean different things in different countries. The swastika adorns old editions of the work of Rudyard Kipling, but as a Hindu symbol, not a Nazi one. This is before you get to Chinese internet memes, such as the Grass Mud Horse, intended to dance around the censors. The transcultural translation of images is at least as challenging as that of words.

Attempts to map 'geographies of the world's knowledge' remind us of another stubborn divide: that between the global north and south.[85] If we use measures such as the Thompson Reuters Web of Knowledge Journal Citation Reports, the predominance of the economic North and cultural West seems overwhelming, although projections show China catching up in some fields.[86] On block maps, which convert publications and citations per country into the size and shade of a rectangular block representing that country, most of the South does not exist. Even within the North, the English-speaking countries and classic European homelands of the cultural West appear as hyperpowers.[87] The same has been true of the distribution of Wikipedia articles, although the Wikimedia foundation is trying to correct that imbalance. One argument for open-access publications is that they help to address both sides of this problem: offering people in poorer countries the chance not just to learn but also to publish their own findings and arguments.

We must beware a possible distortion: these maps show the distribution of knowledge according to criteria that the North/West has established for the definition and measurement of knowledge. Unsurprisingly, the North/West seems to win at its own game. A Buddhist abbot in northern India might respond that this is not knowledge at all, only the stuff of futile transient human striving. Those economically rich but spiritually poor creatures who live by sales figures and Journal Citation Reports are still bound to the wheel. True knowledge, and true freedom, is to be found elsewhere.

Plainly we should steer clear of an equal and opposite danger: Orientalist romanticising of the exotic, accompanied by boundless epistemological relativism. For there is, without question, hard scientific knowledge that is both desperately needed by the poor in the global south and cruelly denied to them. Is there a mother alive who does not want to know how to stop her child dying from a tropical disease? A subsistence farmer who does not yearn to help his undernourished family by increasing his crop yield?

Yet there is a serious point here. One of those foundational differences that I have discussed is precisely about what constitutes knowledge. Perhaps there are other kinds of knowledge, more cultivated in the intellectual, cultural and spiritual traditions of other countries, which are not yet adequately represented in these online knowledge networks. In the West, too, the philosopher, novelist and painter need solitude for cogitation, meditation and creativity. You cannot reproduce the depth of meditative silence through the breadth of deliberative noise.

HOMO ZAPPIENS

Recall that the apex of the DIKW pyramid is not knowledge but wisdom. So is what we have gained from the digital revolution truly a great leap forward for the spread of knowledge, let alone of wisdom? As T. S. Eliot wrote,

Where is the wisdom we have lost in knowledge?
Where is the knowledge we have lost in information?[88]

Most trivially, this self-interrogation may start with the observation that computers are still a long way from being able to do what humans can do. As I was researching this subject, I found a website called WolframAlpha which at that time claimed to make 'the world's knowledge computable' and to bring 'broad, deep, expert-level knowledge to everyone . . . anytime, anywhere'. So I typed in: 'how free should speech be?' Response: 'WolframAlpha doesn't understand your query'.[89]

We still have some time to go before artificial intelligence may get close to our own. More fundamentally, we need to ask not what computers could do but what we should want them to do. Joseph Weizenbaum, the computer scientist who developed the early talking computer programme called Eliza, was shocked by the exaggerated expectations that others raised for his creation. He went on to write a book called *Computer Power and Human Reason* which argued that the limits to what we expect of computers should be ethical rather than technological or mathematical: 'since we do not now have any ways of making computers wise, we ought not now to give computers tasks that demand wisdom'.[90]

In the meantime, there has emerged a small school of cybersceptics, reacting against the cyberutopianism of Silicon Valley and the technological determinism that often underpins it. There is, they point out, a vast ocean of rubbish, nonsense and lies online. (A similar complaint was made after the spread of printing in sixteenth-century Europe.) Nicholas Carr and Andrew Keen deplore the online 'cult of the amateur', which inordinately privileges mass participation over authority, openness over expertise, Wikipedia over Britannica.[91] And the former, they argue, is eroding the latter. Jaron Lanier writes caustically of colleagues who believe that 'a million, or perhaps a billion, fragmentary insults will eventually yield wisdom'.[92]

As we are tempted into what Nicholas Carr calls 'the shallows' of the online world, so we might all succumb to attention deficit disorder. 'Homo Zappiens' is the nice coinage of two Dutch scholars for the generations that have grown up since the 1990s 'zapping' between multiple channels and devices.[93] Just as social intercourse may be diminished by people's endless darts to tap or check something on their äppäräti, so the quest for knowledge is subverted by multiple distractions. Why, our very brains are being changed. One study found that habitual googlers showed intense activity in the dorsolateral prefrontal cortex when online, while those who had rarely used the internet before displayed minimal activity there. With time, these neurological changes will become hardwired, because 'cells that fire together, wire together'—and the change, we are warned, may be for the worse.[94] Homo sapiens becomes homo zappiens, splashing childishly in the shallows.

These Cassandra cries are useful as warnings. In writing this book, I have repeatedly succumbed to the temptations of online distraction. Wwilfing around the web is so much easier than the hard work of trying to put the best words in the best order. ('Wwilf' = 'what was I looking for?') And there's always that email or text message to answer.

In the Acknowledgements to her novel NW, Zadie Smith offers special thanks to a piece of software called Freedom. Freedom enables you to turn off your internet access for a specified period, allowing you to get on with writing, or whatever else you want to do on your computer, undistracted by email or wwilfing. I have used it to finish this book. There is an obvious irony in the ultimate 'Freedom' on the internet being freedom from the internet. Yet one can also read this story differently. The same human intelligence that has produced this ocean of information gives us the means to save ourselves from drowning in it. Gradually we learn how to navigate these new high seas, with all the attendant risks. We learn by sailing.

4

JOURNALISM

'We require uncensored, diverse, trustworthy media so we can make well-informed decisions and participate fully in political life'.

Before the press there was the pnyx. On a hillside in ancient Athens, some 6,000 citizens gathered to debate matters of public interest. A chairman announced the agenda of the day. A herald asked, 'Who will address the assembly?' Then any adult male citizen could stand on the speaker's platform, hewn from rock, and speak his mind to fellow citizens gathered around him. Special attention would probably be accorded to better-known speakers, including those who had distinguished themselves during their service on the city-state's governing council, but everyone had an equal right to speak freely. After the allotted time for debate, there was often a vote. It was thus, for example, that Athenians took the fateful decision to fight the invading Persian forces at sea, in what became the naval victory of Salamis, rather than mustering their forces on land or abandoning the city. Democratic deliberation produced a decision that saved the world's first democracy.

The architectural layout of the pnyx gradually developed so that as many citizens as possible could hear and see each other. In its fourth-century-B.C.E. form, the speaker would look up from his rock to a massed audience sitting or standing on a stepped theatre-like construction, perhaps giving it something of the acoustic qualities of the great theatre at Epidaurus. To this day, you can view in Athens the timeworn speaker's platform at the heart of this original version of a 'public sphere'.[1]

In town hall, village or workplace meetings, we can still occasionally reproduce that ur-experience of speaking freely and directly to each other. And today, unlike in ancient Athens, women and noncitizens sometimes have a voice. It is striking how the popularity of live events such as literary festivals and debates has grown in pace with, and perhaps partly because of, the spread of the virtual. Thus, for example, the New York Times's strategy, announced in 2013, was to do more online content and more live events—with that old printed-paper thing, the newspaper, being squeezed between the post- and the pre-Gutenberg.[2] Yet most of today's communities, states and nations, let alone transnational networks, are obviously far too big for everyone to get together in a hall or on a hillside.

Even in the ancient pnyx, you needed a strong voice. The rhetorician Isocrates, to whose *Areopagiticus* Milton pays explicit tribute in the title and text of his *Areopagitica*, complained that he could not command the live audience because he had a weak voice. So instead, he had his 'orations' written out by hand, on papyrus scrolls. Copied by slaves, these 'reading speeches' were circulated by admiring citizens and perhaps even available for purchase at a kind of bookstore—as were the disquisitions of Isocrates's rival, Plato.[3]

The media scholar Michael Schudson is probably right to say that 'there was no journalism in ancient Greece'—for there were no journals and no journalists.[4] Yet these two public intellectuals, Plato and Isocrates, plainly did encourage the circulation of written versions of their competing views, to reach beyond the physical range of their voices in a citizens' assembly on the pnyx. Here we glimpse the very first shoots of those mediated political, civic and intellectual exchanges that, revived in the inns and coffee shops of Europe some two thousand years later, would become the stuff of journalism, the press and what we now call media.[5]

MEDIA

What does that word mean? In his illuminating book *The Creation of the Media*, Paul Starr distinguishes between 'media', meaning various modern channels of communication, and 'the media', meaning a set of powerful institutions controlling those channels and our access to them.[6] Four main forces shape the media we have in any particular place and time: technology, culture, money and politics. It is revealing that 'the press' is at once the name of a technology (Gutenberg's invention), a term for the printed newspapers and journals that emerged in a complex process from the late sixteenth century onward, and a collective noun for the women and men who work for them, known since the eighteenth century as journalists.[7]

To this day, individual countries have very different media landscapes, each of which reflects a unique combination of markets, politics, cultures and technological preferences. An influential modern study of 18 Western European and North American democracies distinguishes three main patterns of 'media system': Polarised Pluralist, as in much of southern Europe; Democratic Corporatist, as in Scandinavia; and Liberal, as in the United States, Britain and Canada. The range is vastly greater if you look at the more than 170 other countries in the world.[8]

In the first decades of the twenty-first century the media are going through one of the most dramatic transformations since they came into existence. For a couple of centuries, reading a daily paper was what the philosopher Hegel called our '*realistic* morning prayer' (my italics). Hegel contrasted it with the other possible morning prayer: 'One orients one's attitude toward the world either by God or by what the world is'.[9] In the twentieth century, we added a few radio channels, then a few television ones, with large audiences and equally large pretensions to authority. The veteran American TV news anchor Walter Cronkite used to end his evening news programmes with the words 'and that's the way it is'.[10]

In the early twenty-first century, two apparently contradictory things are happening simultaneously: divergence and convergence. There is an extraordinary fragmentation of the ways in which we transmit and receive news and views. At the same time, all traditionally distinct mediums, such as newspapers, television and radio, are converging on single platforms, where they both combine and compete with live video streaming, podcasts, social media, tweets, and other user-generated content, such as footage of dramatic events taken by passersby on their mobile phones.

Since our concern is free speech, the essential question we have to ask remains the same: what do we want from our media? Only then follows the instrumental supplementary: how do we get it? These days we can get it by demanding, as consumers, activists and voters, that others provide the media we need, but also by contributing to those media and creating new ones ourselves.

Obviously everyone wants several things from the media, and people have different priorities. Most of us wish to be entertained. Many also want to learn things—and not just stuff that's immediately useful. A managing editor of the Washington Post newsroom in the 1970s referred to SMERSH, explaining that he meant not the name of Stalin's dreaded agency for bringing 'death to spies' but 'Science, Medicine, Education, Religion and all that Shit'.[11] Online, there is a large appetite for amusing, weird and celebrity news. There is a major overlap, if not a continuum, between the dissemination of knowledge and information discussed in the last chapter and what we are considering here. The classicist and political scientist Josiah Ober analyses the public debates on the ancient Athenian pnyx as an experiment in the aggregation of knowledge, while the contemporary media scholar Stephen Coleman says news is 'a form of public knowledge'. Next to articles on Cairo's ancient Egyptian pyramids, Wikipedia has user-generated chronicles of current events, such as the 2011 protests on Cairo's Tahrir Square that toppled the country's longtime dictator, Hosni Mubarak.[12]

Nonetheless, there is a difference of emphasis. Recall our four central arguments for free speech (STGD). Where the first concern for universities, scientific research and encyclopaedias must be the T for truth, the reason we need good media is more especially the G for good government. Obviously, they can also help us to choose the best shoes, movie or budget flight, but their vital function is to enable us to make well-informed choices on issues of public policy and participate fully in political life. Media, old and new, are the primary means we have to create a public sphere and to practise self-government. They are our electronic pnyx.

This fourth principle attempts to summarise the qualities we need from our media in three words: uncensored, diverse and trustworthy. Each needs to be unpacked.

UNCENSORED – BUT NOT WITHOUT LIMITS

If you say 'free speech', two associations that will immediately come to many minds are 'a free press in a free country' and journalists battling state censorship in unfree countries. From the seventeenth century to our own, this has been one of the central struggles for freedom of expression. In a letter penned in 1787, Thomas Jefferson declared: 'were it left to me to decide whether we should have a government without newspapers, or newspapers without a government, I should not hesitate for a moment to prefer the latter'.[13] Put most simply: a free press is a defining feature of a free country while censorship is a defining feature of a dictatorship. A democracy cannot long survive without the former, a dictatorship without the latter.

I spent the first decade of my working life travelling behind what was then called the iron curtain, in communist-ruled central and eastern Europe. In Warsaw, Prague and Budapest, I saw people battling daily with censorship. Friends sat up all night in their cramped apartments to type *samizdat* copies of works by George Orwell or Václav Havel on ancient manual typewriters, and were sent to prison when caught. This also had its lighter moments: because the Czechoslovak official press was not allowed even to mention the name of the tennis player Martina Navratilova, who had incomprehensibly abandoned the socialist fatherland, a newspaper reported that 'in the semi-finals at Wimbledon tomorrow, the following will be playing . . .' and then printed three names. Everyone knew Martina must be the fourth. I still possess a Polish censor's verdict from April 1989 recording in all due form that a Polish magazine must excise 'fragments' of an essay of mine concerning the 'total bankruptcy' of socialism, and specifically the passage from 'incompetence of the rulers' to 'party apparatus'. Five months later, the country had its first noncommunist prime minister for more than forty years and the system was . . . totally bankrupt.[14]

Yet that detailed censor's verdict was itself a sign that censorship was weakening. The most effective and insidious censorship, as in contemporary China and Iran, has no explicit written rules, relying instead on the arbitrary, unappealable decisions of state and party officials. The barbed-wire frontiers of the permissible move daily, even hourly. This is why, in the mid-1980s, a feisty, independent-minded Hungarian writer called István Eörsi launched a plangently ironic appeal to the authorities. 'Give us censorship!' he cried, arguing that explicit, publicly defined limits would be a great advance.[15] When the Chinese author Yu Hua reflected on the contrast between China's notoriously lax standards of food safety and its tight media censorship, one Chinese netizen commented: 'Let's have those in charge of film, newspaper and book censorship take over food safety, and have those responsible for food safety censor films, papers and books. That way we'll have food safety—and freedom of expression as well!'[16]

While 'censorship' generally refers to something done by a state—and, in lawyerly definitions, often more narrowly to 'prior restraint' on publication—it's important to remember that it is also exercised by religious organisations, corporations, media owners, criminal gangs, political parties and other organised groups. Between 1559 and 1966, the Roman Catholic Church had an 'Index' of prohibited books, a blacklist to which the title of the journal Index on Censorship, which documents, analyses and fights censorship worldwide, makes ironic reference.[17] The difference, at least traditionally and in the pre-internet age, is that such censorship does not cover the whole territory of the country and all media in it, and is not directly enforced by the state. If you are censored in one paper, church, corporation or party, you can go to another. In practice, however, if your newspaper proprietor is threatening to sack you, a drug company to litigate you into bankruptcy or the mafia to assassinate you, that difference can feel rather theoretical.

There is a whole book to be written about the endlessly brave and inventive ways in which people fight, subvert and circumvent censorship. Aung San Suu Kyi's late husband, Michael Aris, once showed me the *longyis*—traditional Burmese wrap-around cotton dresses—on which she had written what became her *Letters from Burma*, while under strict house arrest. A housekeeper would arrive at the heavily guarded gate of Suu Kyi's run-down villa on University Avenue in Yangon wearing a yellow *longyi*. That same housekeeper would walk out a few hours later, past the guards, still wearing a yellow *longyi*. But it was a different *longyi*—and on the inside of this one was penned, in Suu Kyi's own careful, elegant hand, her latest letter from Burma. When she was released from house arrest in 2010, a popular football magazine called First Eleven ran a strange headline: 'SUNDERLAND FREEZE CHELSEA UNITED STUNNED BY VILLA & ARSENAL ADVANCE TO GRAB THEIR HOPE'. First Eleven submitted this to the censors in black and white but published it in multiple colours. The letters in bright red spelled out 'SU . . . FREE . . . UNITE . . . & . . . ADVANCE TO GRAB THE HOPE'.[18] When a biography of the shah by the exiled Iranian historian Abbas Milani was banned from publication inside Iran, he posted it online, free to download for anyone with an Iranian IP address. It was downloaded well over 100,000 times, becoming a best-seller in spite of—doubtless also because of—being banned.[19] The Chinese bloggers who invent ingenious new internet memes and make jpeg files of critical texts to avoid automated online censorship are just the latest in a great tradition.

Tempting though it is to continue these inspiring stories of good triumphing over evil, the more difficult question we have to address here is: when is 'censorship' not censorship? We could also formulate that more provocatively: when is censorship justified? This wording would not have seemed as odd to people in the past as it does today, for historically the word 'censor' had positive connotations.

The original censors in ancient Rome—so called because they also kept the register or 'census' of citizens—were, one seventeenth-century English author wrote, 'the guardians of the discipline and manners of the city'.[20] In the same letter in which Thomas Jefferson says that, forced to choose, he would rather have newspapers than a government, he writes 'the people are the only censors of their governors'.[21] The historian Robert Darnton notes that eighteenth-century French royal censors were men of literary taste and discrimination who identified themselves, with pride, as '*censeur du roi*'. (One censor graciously approved an anthology he himself had edited.)[22]

What we now know as the British Board of Film Classification was called, from its foundation in 1912 until a delicate name change in the Orwellian

year of 1984, the British Board of Film Censors. During its first year of operation, it rejected more than 22 films in their entirety on grounds that included
indecent dancing, cruelty to animals, excessive drunkenness, 'native customs
in foreign lands abhorrent to British ideas' and 'materialisation of Christ or
the Almighty'.[23] In the United States, film classification is done by a 'board
of parents' working for the Motion Picture Association of America, a private
body. In 2008, 'Wendy and Lucy', a fine, spare melancholy film about a young
woman and her dog travelling through the poorer parts of American life was
rated R, meaning that no one under 17 should be allowed to see it without an
accompanying adult, although it contained no nudity, sex or violence. As the
film critic A. O. Scott dryly commented: 'The rating seems to reflect, above
all, an impulse to protect children from learning that people are lonely and
that life can be hard'.[24]

The consistently negative usage of the term is more recent than many imagine. When I say 'censorship', however, I am always referring to what I maintain
is an illegitimate curb on freedom of expression, by contrast with terms such as
'regulation', meaning a legitimate limitation of media freedom. Keeping that
distinction sharp is as difficult as it is important, since so many try to blur it. As
we have seen, authoritarian regimes hide censorship behind the euphemisms
of regulation, as practised in free countries.

At the other extreme, newspaper editors in free countries sometimes refuse
even a smidgen of external regulation, decrying it as censorship. When British
tabloid newspapers, also known as 'red-tops', were caught red-handed hacking
into the mobile phones of thousands of British citizens, from the deputy prime
minister and members of the royal family to a teenage girl called Milly Dowler,
who had been abducted and subsequently murdered, an inquiry led by a judge,
Lord Justice Leveson, suggested a stronger structure of press self-regulation,
with a minimal statutory underpinning.[25] At once, the tabloids cried 'censorship!' To defend their right to invade and expose the private lives of anyone
whose goings-on might possibly interest the public, and hence help them to
sell more papers, they wrapped themselves in the garments of Milton and Mill,
denouncing 'a mortal threat to the British people's historic right to know' and
'the end of more than 300 years of press freedom'.[26]

In fact, many countries with robust traditions of free expression have also
had, and continue to have, external regulation of their media. Even in the
United States, with its First Amendment forbidding Congress to make any law
abridging the freedom of the press, the Federal Communications Commission
(FCC) for decades enforced a Fairness Doctrine on radio and television. This
required each broadcaster to provide coverage of 'controversial issues of public

importance' and 'to present opposing viewpoints as a condition of retaining its license'. It was abolished in 1987, under the deregulatory free market administration of Ronald Reagan. Reagan's head of the FCC described television as 'just another appliance . . . a toaster with pictures'.[27] Since then, American radio and television have become ever more ideologically polarised and partisan, so a listener to one station often only gets one point of view.

Most of these twentieth-century regulatory structures treated each medium—radio, television, newspapers, etc.—separately. But what is to be done in a world where all the different media are converging and getting mixed up together, both across platforms and across frontiers? An American magazine, a Brazilian TV channel, a German radio station—all are accessible on your box. It is ever more anachronistic for each medium to be subject to different rules and regulators.[28] How, if at all, should we set limits in such a mixed-up media world? One expert in this field, Stewart Purvis, who spent years working for the British broadcasting regulator Ofcom, edges close to a radical conclusion. Perhaps regulators like Ofcom should work towards their own extinction: 'leave quality to the market and protection to the law of the land'.[29]

This approach chimes with one that runs through this book: maintain strict, consistent legal enforcement for clear harms, but mobilise the republic of norms for the rest. To do that, however, we should be in a position to know the kind of product we are dealing with and what its editorial standards are. Individual judgement calls will need to be made every day within any guidelines: Do I write, photograph, publish or broadcast that horror, provocation or intimate detail? If yes, how, in what context, with what headline or explanation? But the principles underlying those specific judgements should be explicit and freely available. Transparency is the best path to accountability in this billion-media universe, and legally mandated transparency may be the acceptable face of state regulation. As the philosopher Onora O'Neill puts it, our media should be not just accessible but *assessable*.[30]

You can read online the immensely detailed editorial guidelines of the BBC and the New York Times.[31] In 2015, Facebook produced a new, more explicit set of community standards, although their wording still left a wide margin of interpretation. YouTube's community standards are vaguely worded and have been inconsistently applied—as we saw in the case of 'Innocence of Muslims'—not least because they, like Facebook, depend on users flagging 'bad stuff'. The editorial principles that underlie Google Search or the Facebook News Feed can only very partially and with considerable effort be deduced from conversations with insiders, corporate blog posts and leaked documents such as the Google Search Quality Rating Guidelines.[32]

There are other ways of increasing the transparency of journalism which, after all, spends much of its time trying to shed light on the practices of others. Papers such as the New York Times and the Guardian have a readers' editor or public editor who responds to readers' queries and explains the background to their treatment of controversial issues. BBC radio has a programme called 'Feedback' which invites listeners' criticisms and then asks those who created the programmes to respond.

The London-based Media Standards Trust developed a microformat tag called hNews which was to be like a food content label for online news. As your supermarket food packet is supposed to tell you what's in it, so the metadata tag should tell you who originated, first published and subsequently changed the story you're reading online, and the journalistic code of practice (if any) the originating or republishing platform adheres to. In 2012, the New York Times introduced rNews, a new standard for embedding machine-readable publishing metadata into HTML documents', and similar schema.org tags have been developed with the backing of major internet companies.[33]

Then there is the idea of a more general sort of kitemarking, so that you know what kind of speech store you are visiting. Is it an organic foods delicatessen, a supermarket, a corner store or an unauthorised street vendor's stall? Lara Fielden suggests four tiers: 'Premium standard'—formally regulated, public service broadcasting, where 'broadcasting' is presumably understood to mean on all platforms; 'Ethical private media'—adhering to a rigorous but voluntary code and procedures of self-regulation; 'Baseline private media'—such as privately posted videos, which would claim only to adhere to minimal standards set out in, for example, EU law and regulations; and 'Totally unregulated'—that is, in my analogy, the street vendor, whose meatballs or kebab you ingest at your peril.[34]

A variant of Fielden's 'ethical private media', already practiced in Ireland, has the state providing incentives for private media to join those more demanding codes and structures of self-regulation. The state can, for example, establish an arbitration procedure for dealing with complaints from readers, viewers and users that would be much cheaper than going to court—but make it available only to those media that sign up to the self-regulation process. Or it can offer tax advantages. But the balance will always be tricky. Where, for example, would that leave satirical journals like the British Private Eye, the American The Onion, and France's Charlie Hebdo and Le Canard Enchaîné, which live by transgressing such sober norms?

The more the state is involved in media regulation, the greater the temptation for political powerholders to abuse it. A perfect example was provided by the conservative-nationalist FIDESZ government in Hungary, which in 2010 introduced a so-called Public Service Foundation and Media Council to 'regulate' the country's media. It aped the language and forms of Western European democratic regulation of the media, but its effect was to privilege the position of one party (guess which) and hence erode freedom of expression in that still fragile postcommunist democracy.[35]

Yet if any interference by the state has to be watched carefully, so that legitimate regulation does not slide into censorship, it is an illusion to believe that media of the kind we need for good government will automatically be generated by the free-for-all of a commercial and political marketplace. Patterns of media ownership, the imperative of making a profit, the influence of corporations with their PR armies, special-interest lobbies and political parties—all produce powerful distortions of their own. The marketplace of proprietors and parties is a necessary but not a sufficient condition for securing Oliver Wendell Holmes's 'marketplace of ideas'.

DIVERSE: MEDIA PLURALISM BETWEEN MONEY AND POLITICS

The starting point of this book is that the digital revolution has given unprecedented opportunities for billions of people to publish their views—and in that sense to speak directly to everyone who has a box, like an ancient Athenian addressing his fellow citizens. Yet if you ask what voices and views actually get *heard*, then you realise how far we still are from an ideal of fully represented diversity.

The technical term specialists use for the quality this principle summarises in the word 'diverse' is 'media pluralism'. A useful European study identifies five dimensions of media pluralism: ownership and control, media types and genres, political viewpoints, cultural expressions (an awkward phrase, embracing religious, linguistic, ethnic and sexual groups and orientations) and local and regional interests. It goes on to offer a tool with which we can measure the extent of media pluralism in a given country.[36] Those fourth and fifth dimensions should not be neglected: the languages, cultures, voices and faces of minorities and regions—Kurds in Turkey, Catalan or Basque in Spain, Tamil in Sri Lanka, native peoples in Australia, Muslims in Germany, Tibetan and Uighur in China—have often been drastically underrepresented, confined to folkloristic tokenism or totally excluded from the mainstream media of a country. I say more about this in the next chapter, on diversity.

Probably the biggest distortion of media pluralism remains ownership. I have already quoted the famous bon mot of A. J. Liebling that 'freedom of the press is guaranteed only to those who own one'. This comment was actually a parenthetic aside in a passage about the trend towards monopoly in newspapers published in individual American cities. That trend was dramatic: whereas in 1880 more than 60 percent of US cities had competing daily newspapers, by 1960, the year in which Liebling published his essay in the New Yorker, it was little more than 4 percent. Local newspaper monopoly had become the norm. 'What you have in a one-paper town', wrote Liebling, 'is a privately owned public utility that is constitutionally exempt from public regulation, which would be a violation of the freedom of the press'.[37]

What we might call Liebling's Law has a much wider application. Often these owners not only have strong personal views but are closely connected to political forces. Thus, for example, a television documentary called 'Beyond Citizen Kane' suggested that at the high point of Brazil's presidential election in 1989 the country's leading television channel, Rede Globo, broadcast a montage of the final televised debate between the two run-off candidates that was clearly slanted in favour of the eventual winner, Fernando Collor—and that Rede Globo did this on the explicit instructions of its owner.[38]

While Turkish police brutally crushed a large popular protest in Istanbul's Taksim Square in summer 2013, CNN Türk broadcast a documentary about . . . penguins. The political scientist Kerem Öktem, who was there at the time, argues that the downplaying of the protests on CNN Türk and several other leading Turkish broadcasters resulted, at least in part, from the fact that these channels were owned by business conglomerates concerned to keep good relations with the government of Recep Tayyip Erdoğan. That government was in a position to give or withhold major contracts to other parts of those conglomerates.[39]

By contrast, a story singled out by the development economist Paul Collier in his book *The Bottom Billion* highlights the positive potential of diverse ownership. The corrupt government of president Alberto Fujimori in Peru bought influence over nine of the country's ten national television channels, but it chose not to bother with the tenth, a small financial news satellite service with only ten thousand subscribers. That was its undoing. Someone leaked a video of a government official bribing a congressman and it was broadcast on that one channel. The spark lit a wildfire. Mass protests spread, the government fell and Fujimori ended up in prison.[40]

The facts and interpretation of any single case can be disputed, but there is hardly a country in the world where we cannot point to examples of distortion due to the patterns of ownership and practices of owners. The last remaining totalitarian regimes such as North Korea might be viewed as exceptions, but in fact they have a single monopoly owner—the party-state. Clear and crass instances can be found in all post-totalitarian and authoritarian countries, but also in classic homelands of democracy.

Here, as elsewhere, one of the greatest threats to the effective enabling of freedom of expression is P^2, the nexus of public and private power. In introducing the shorthand P^2, I cited the example of Italy under the premiership of Silvio Berlusconi, where that sleazy tycoon controlled most of the public and private television channels from which Italians got their political news. If Italy had been a small country applying to join the European Union, it would have been roundly rebuked by Brussels and probably not admitted to the EU until it had achieved the required level of media pluralism. (Once inside, you can tear up the rulebook, as Viktor Orbán's Hungary would demonstrate.)

In Britain, it was the overweening power of a few newspaper proprietors (and one long-serving editor, Paul Dacre of the Mail group) which in the 1990s and 2000s produced the worst distortion of that ideal English public sphere imagined by Milton and Mill—one in which truth and falsehood, argument and counterargument, would grapple in free and fair exchange. As far back as the 1930s, the Conservative prime minister Stanley Baldwin attacked Britain's press proprietors for 'aiming at . . . power without responsibility, the privilege of the harlot down the ages'. Baldwin borrowed the phrase from his cousin, the writer Rudyard Kipling, who, according to Kipling's son, coined it after hearing the owner of the Daily Express—Max Aitken, later Lord Beaverbrook— say, 'What I want is power. Kiss 'em one day and kick 'em the next'.[41] Eighty years on, those harlots were still with us and, despite the digital revolution and a large public service broadcasting sector, politicians now courted them as if they were kings.

It would be entirely plausible to suggest that from the mid-1990s until some time around 2011, Rupert Murdoch, the late twentieth century's quintessential harlot-king, was the second most powerful man in Britain. Opposition leaders and prime ministers from Tony Blair to David Cameron abased themselves to curry favour with him. Cameron employed a former editor of Murdoch's News of the World, Andy Coulson, as his communications director, first in opposition and then in No. 10 Downing Street, even though Coulson had resigned as editor of the sensationalist tabloid following allegations that he was complicit in illegal phone hacking by his journalists. (Those allegations subsequently turned out to be true, and Coulson was sent to prison.) Echoing Baldwin, a member of the British cabinet told the journalist and writer John Lloyd that Paul Dacre, the long-serving editor-in-chief of the Daily Mail and the Mail on Sunday, 'has absolute and unaccountable power'.[42]

How much these papers really swayed public opinion is another question. 'It's The Sun Wot Won It', the claim made by a famous headline in Murdoch's The Sun following a surprise election result in 1992, has long been debated.[43] What matters is that British politicians collectively believed that they could not win elections against these papers and individually feared personal attacks in their pages, including exposure of real or alleged shenanigans in their private lives.[44] This was a very British version of 'The Godfather'—without the machine guns, to be sure, but even Don Corleone did not murder his tame politicians. These press proprietors claim, rightly, that a politically and financially independent press is a classic check on political power, but they themselves wield power that needs to be checked.

Even after the exposure of large-scale, routine, illegal phone hacking by the Murdoch tabloids—an exposure led not by the police, who sat on the evidence for years, but by other parts of Britain's fortunately still diverse media—and the jailing of Coulson, the press barons continued to exercise enormous power in at least two ways. First, they shaped the public debate around press regulation so that most British readers were simply not informed about alternative proposals and were actively misinformed about what Leveson was proposing. A legendary former editor of the Sunday Times, Harold Evans, called this misrepresentation 'staggering'. Second, they privately lobbied politicians at the highest level so as to preserve their own unaccountable power. In the first two months of 2013 alone, the prime minister and the two other ministers most directly involved had more than 30 meetings with senior executives and editors from the press. We may assume they were not talking about the weather.[45]

Powerful proprietors advancing their own business interests and political views through the media they own, and the politicians they lean on, are a particularly clear example of the distortions that occur at the high-voltage junction box where money, media and politics meet. They are not the only ones. All corporations, professions and interest groups try to push their causes through the media. While the number of professional journalists has dwindled, as the traditional business models of newspapers have been undermined in the online age, the number of lobbyists and PR people has grown exponentially. According to US Bureau of Labour statistics, in 2014 there were more than 264,000 'public relations specialists' and 'public relations and fundraising managers' in the US, against less than 47,000 'news analysts, reporters and correspondents'.[46]

These twin developments have exacerbated the phenomenon of 'churnalism'. Instead of actively going out to gather news, journalists are reduced to what the veteran investigative reporter Nick Davies describes as 'passive processors of whatever material comes their way, churning out stories, whether real event or

PR artifice, important or trivial, true or false'.[47] A 2006 Cardiff University study found that 54 percent of British news articles had some form of PR in them.[48] In India, there is a chronic problem of 'paid news', with companies, parties and individuals paying newspapers to place favourable reports, presented as if they were just regular journalistic work.

In its Citizens United verdict in 2010, the US Supreme Court held that corporations and unions have a constitutional right to spend as much as they wish on television election commercials supporting or targeting particular candidates.[49] The case revolved around a derogatory movie about Hillary Clinton produced by a small corporation called Citizens United. According to the legal philosopher Ronald Dworkin, the clear implication was that corporations should enjoy the same free speech rights as individuals under the First Amendment.[50] 'Corporations are people, my friend', as Republican presidential candidate Mitt Romney responded to a heckler at the Iowa State fair in 2011.[51] In the end, corporate support did not win the election for Romney, but there is no doubt that the Citizens United verdict further increased the potential for monied interests to shape the American debate. The old saying 'money speaks' is now truer than ever. (More on this in chapter 9.)

Corporations, and to a lesser extent other lobbies and interest groups, also influence media by the promise of advertising and the threat of withholding it. Since most media must make a profit to survive, they have to attract some combination of paying readers (users/viewers/listeners) and paying advertisers. As we have seen, Liebling's observation that 'the function of the press in society is to inform, but its role is to make money' is as true of early-twenty-first-century for-profit online platforms as it was of early-nineteenth-century newspapers.[52]

'If we can sell it, we tell it' therefore becomes the motto of profit-pressured editors, alongside 'If it bleeds, it leads'. This influences the selection of subjects covered and the space given to them. When we posted an earlier draft of these principles on freespeechdebate.com, one of the first responses, from a contributor calling himself acellidiaz, contrasted the fate of two new websites in his home country, Venezuela. He suggested that one, lapatilla.com, had powerful business backing and specialised in 'sometimes vain and superficial articles about sex, celebrities or astrology, together with the usual portion of politics', while the other, redigital.tv, with less powerful business backing and more serious content, lagged far behind.[53]

In their book on India's very unequal social and economic development, *An Uncertain Glory*, Jean Drèze and Amartya Sen argue that the fact that India's hugely vigorous and diverse media—some 86,000 newspapers and periodicals, with a circulation of more than 370 million, and nearly 900 television channels—pay so little attention to issues such as health, nutrition, sanitation and education is among the main reasons why those crucial social problems are not more actively addressed by the country's rulers. By contrast, the Indian media offer endless coverage of Bollywood, cricket, food and fashion. Drèze and Sen quote a leading editor speaking to a group of children's rights advocates in Delhi: 'don't have any illusions, you will never be able to compete for attention with the wardrobe malfunction of a model on the ramp'.[54]

Now a cynic might say: 'Indian readers have only themselves to blame. People get the media they deserve'. Yet no one could seriously suggest that India's hundreds of millions of rural poor are not interested in seeing their children survive until adulthood without life-threatening disease and achieve a better quality of life. But most of them can't afford to buy a newspaper, even if they have the literacy to read it. It would be more accurate to say that people get the news that they can afford, and that advertisers will wish their advertisements to appear beside. That does not only apply to India.

A similar problem arises with foreign news. In an increasingly connected world, we should obviously know more about developments in other countries. In practice, however, the professional foreign correspondent is a dying breed, as most for-profit media have closed foreign bureaus and slashed travel expenses. Thus, while there is a crying need for more news of the world, what most readers are getting is more News of the World—meaning the kind of celebrity, sex and crime titillation for which Murdoch's now-defunct tabloid became a by-word. An analysis of three leading English-language newspapers in India found that the space devoted to foreign news declined, from 21 to 24 percent in 1979 to 5 to 6 percent in 2012.[55] This at a time when India was becoming one of the world's most important emerging powers.

To some extent, this is counterbalanced by the unprecedented amount of live video coverage, blogs, tweets and 'citizen journalism' available on platforms such as YouTube. But these platforms are themselves an extreme example of simultaneous fragmentation and concentration. On the one hand, a platform like Facebook allows 1.5 billion people to speak directly to each other and in that sense can be described as radically open. On the other hand, near-monopoly concentration of ownership power is an extreme example of a power-law curve. Arguably, this is a double power-law curve, first of the platforms themselves, then of voices on those platforms, with the result that a very few reach very many, and very many reach very few.

Recall Liebling's description of a monopoly paper in a one-paper city: 'a privately owned public utility'. That applies to Facebook, YouTube and Twitter today, with one small difference — their city is the world. They set editorial standards for cosmopolis. Wherever you are, full frontal nudity, if reported to Facebook, will be taken down. Some gruesome videos of beheadings in Syria will be taken down from Facebook but probably left up on YouTube, if YouTube's 'Deciders' consider them to be of news value. When you talk to those responsible at YouTube and Facebook, you find that a lot of thought goes into these decisions, yet they remain the untransparent editorial choices of unaccountable American private superpowers. These choices reflect the cultural norms of those who own and work in these private superpowers (other cultures are less fazed by nudity but more worried by hate speech), but also their commercial concerns, including fear that advertisers will be put off by appearing beside certain kinds of content.

One student of YouTube, Alexandra Juhasz, draws this conclusion:

> The result of my analysis of the site is simple: what they want you to do is move as quickly and unpredictably as possible from one thing to another, because that is how they are going to get your eyeballs to ads. It's a perfectly viable model to make money, but it's not a viable model for moving expression and art through a culture. You can see in YouTube the profound constraints that are written into the system because it is organised first to make money, not democracy, culture, community — and certainly not revolution.[56]

Achieving a genuine, deep and broad media diversity takes more than the technical ability of individuals to 'speak' online. It requires conscious pressure from users to demand more transparency from these private powers. It also requires close attention to competition policy, so that market dominance does not turn into monopoly or cartel. Much will depend on for-profit news organisations finding business models that allow them to give us the facts we need to make informed decisions. Digging up those facts, getting them right and putting them in context does not come cheap, especially in inaccessible, difficult and dangerous places. The great Manchester Guardian editor C. P. Scott's famous statement that 'comment is free but facts are sacred' has been ironically rephrased as 'comment is free but facts are expensive'. For-profit media will not alone deliver the full spectrum of this public good. That requires at least two other funding models. A small but potentially vital one consists in not-for-profit foundations, such as the Pro Publica organisation, which describes itself as 'an independent, non-profit newsroom that produces investigative journalism in the public interest'.[57] Pro Publica helps fund the kind of serious, time-consuming investigative journalism that only a few newspapers and broadcasters are currently able and willing to support.

Then there are public service media such as the BBC. The BBC has many limitations and faults. Its own longtime business editor, Robert Peston, reflects that, because of its dedication to impartiality, scrupulous editorial principles and—not least—chronic nervousness about criticism from politicians (upon whom it depends for the renewal of the licence fee that delivers its funding), it is not as daring as the rambunctious and sometimes irresponsible privately owned British newspapers, with their 'cat-may-look-at-a-king arrogance'.[58] It also suffers from what the American media analyst Brooke Gladstone slyly describes as 'fairness bias'. As she explains it: 'journalists will bend over backward to appear balanced by offering equal time to opposing viewpoints, even when they aren't equal'.[59] The BBC would not give equal time to those who claim the earth is flat and those who boldly assert that it is round, but when it comes to climate change, there is more bending over backwards than is justified by well-established science.

And the BBC is about as good as it gets. Even in other mature European democracies, public service broadcasting seldom achieves this degree of independence and balance. If I go to Spain, or Italy or Poland, let alone to Ukraine or Thailand, I find that most people simply assume that public service television news will be slanted to suit the political party or parties in power, whether nationally or regionally. In Austria, political parties have direct influence over programme content.

So it is worth considering an alternative model which starts from the premiss that a Social Democrat does not see her country or the world in the same way as a Conservative, a Liberal or a Green. Why not make that explicit? In Scandinavia, for example, most newspapers have historically been linked to political parties. Around 1970, party dailies represented 92 percent of all the press in Denmark and 87 percent in Norway.[60] Those ties have subsequently weakened and journalists have become more independent. Yet in Oslo, a journalist sitting down to interview me could still say flatly, 'we are the Social Democratic paper'. Even where there is not a direct link with a party, a newspaper or channel is often clearly associated with a particular political orientation, and its readers or viewers tend to identify with that orientation. A study of the 2008 parliamentary elections in Italy found that more than 50 percent of those who watched Canale 5, Berlusconi's most popular channel, voted for his political party and only 10 percent of them for the main left-wing party, whereas 44 percent of those who watched Rai3, the traditionally left-leaning public service broadcasting channel, voted for the main left-wing party and only 9 percent for Berlusconi's party.[61] Cause and effect are hard to disentangle here: do I vote for that party because I watch that channel or do I watch that channel because I support that party?

The media scholar Paolo Mancini calls this 'external pluralism' rather than the 'internal pluralism' to which the liberal model of Anglo-American quality journalism aspires. Thus, instead of the classic BBC-style attempt to offer impartiality—that is, multiple relevant viewpoints given a fair hearing in the same place—you have multiple partialities.[62] Even in the United States, the trend is clearly towards multiple partialities: partisan Fox News for Republicans, partisan MSNBC for Democrats.

What's wrong with that? One obvious concern is that new political forces will find it more difficult to break through to a wider public and therefore the electorate: you don't get voters unless you have access to media and you don't have media access unless you have voters. Catch-22. This objection is weakened by the power and variety of new media, so that, for example, the Italian comedian Beppe Grillo began his insurgent Five Star Movement, which went on to win 25 percent of the vote in the 2013 Italian parliamentary elections, with a blog. The Pirate parties in Sweden and Germany also broke through (albeit transiently) using new media—unsurprisingly, perhaps since defending internet freedom was one of their great causes.

FROM DAILY ME TO DAILY KIOSK

A bigger question is whether people will actually seek that 'external pluralism' of political views—for if they seek, they can certainly find. We know from bitter experience that you can have too little media diversity, but can you also have too much? Is hyperdiversity as much of a threat to a well-informed public sphere as political or commercial monopoly? Here we again note the danger of people going off into their own little echo chambers, their 'Daily Me', where they only encounter opinions that reinforce their own prejudices, with facts—or factoids—to match. As the comedian John Oliver put it on the American satirical TV news programme 'The Daily Show': what people really want on the internet is 'to have their own views pushed back at them for free'.[63] A rather pretentious word for this echo-chamber effect is 'homophily', although that makes it sound vaguely like a sexual preference.[64]

Cass Sunstein, the American scholar who has warned most influentially about this danger, acknowledges that the evidence that people actually lust for homophily is far from conclusive.[65] In a survey conducted for Oxford University's Reuters Institute for the Study of Journalism in a number of developed countries in 2013 some two thirds of those asked said they preferred news that has 'no particular point of view', while the other third was divided between 11 percent seeking news that 'challenges your view' and 23 percent who wanted

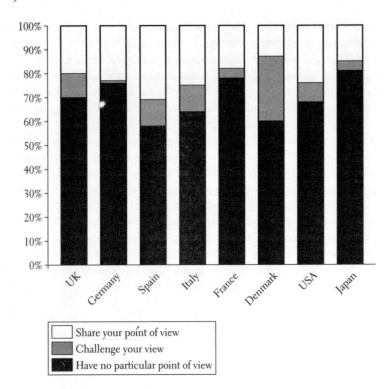

Figure 13. Preference for media being impartial
Respondents were asked 'Thinking about the different kinds of news available to you,
do you prefer if they . . . ?' and given the three choices shown in the figure.
Source: Adapted from Newman et al. 2013.

news that 'shares your point of view' (see Figure 13). So nearly four out of five
of those asked expressed a preference for hearing views other than their own.

The finding was reinforced a year later, when the proportion of respondents
preferring reporters to give 'a range of views' stretched from a low of 69 percent
(in Italy, the motherland of Mancini's multiple partialities) to 87 percent in
Germany and 88 percent in France.[66] Whether what they actually watched and
read—their 'revealed preferences'—reflected their ideal of what they thought
they should be looking for is, of course, another question.

The 'Daily Me' can also be seen as an opportunity. The term 'Daily Me'
was originally popularised by Nicholas Negroponte to imagine an individually
customised online newspaper.[67] In the meantime, something called the Daily
Me came into existence twice, as a local online newspaper for Maine and as an

entrepreneurial attempt to do something like what Negroponte envisaged. But it is the idea that concerns us here.

Why should I confine myself to one newspaper when I can sample 50? That is what people already do online. There is a rapidly evolving ecosystem of RSS feeds, aggregation, curation and, not least, verification. This enables us to sample, select and assess a range of news and views far wider than anything available to our parents or grandparents. I have some 20 bookmarks on my browser, several of which lead with one click to aggregation sites offering another 20. You can follow 2,000 accounts on Twitter or Weibo, each of which takes you to more sources, images and voices. Twitter has become one of the main news sources for professional journalists. A site called Storify enables you to put together your own 'story' from material gathered across the whole internet.[68] The particular instruments will develop between this writing and your reading of these words, but the point remains the same: beyond the Daily Me, you can make your own Daily Kiosk.

You can assess and verify what you have in it. Robert Cottrell, who spends many hours a day reading on the internet in order to choose pieces for a curation site called thebrowser.com, says that 1 percent of what he finds is of value to the intelligent general reader and another 4 percent counts as 'entertaining rubbish', while the remaining 95 percent has no redeeming features. But, he insists, even the 1 percent is 'an embarrassment of riches, a horn of plenty, a garden of delights'.[69]

Beyond that, you can use fact-checking sites to see if an alleged fact is fact or factoid. In Britain, you can copy and paste a passage from an online article into the search box in churnalism.com to get to get a rough idea how much of the piece comes directly from some PR release. Increasingly sophisticated methods have been developed for verifying footage of alleged horrors uploaded to YouTube or submitted in other ways.[70] If a user-friendly metadata tag were to become a well-understood norm, we would have food labelling for journalism.

Obviously, if you are not curious in the first place to learn what others think, you won't go looking for it. Even if you are, you need 'media literacy'. Once again, the idea is an old one. Thomas Jefferson explains but also qualifies his claim to put the value of newspapers above that of government with this crucial sentence: 'But I should mean that every man should receive those papers and be capable of reading them'.[71] Schools should do more to educate people to navigate their way through the new media kaleidoscope. The journalism scholar Stephen Coleman has suggested 'newsgroups', rather like reading clubs, to discuss what the media is offering up.[72]

Yet the term 'media literacy' seems to suggest a passive relationship, like a child being taught to read, whereas the reality is already way beyond that. One of the many traditional frontiers that has broken down is that between the journalist and the reader. There are countless ways in which people who are not professional career journalists already contribute actively to what has traditionally been called journalism. Whole sites such as Global Voices and Demotix are devoted to encouraging and showcasing citizen journalism.[73] The Reuters Institute Digital News Report lists twelve ways of online and offline participation around news, including sharing a news story on a social network, rating or Facebook 'liking' news stories, reposting a video and voting in an online poll.[74] As Figure 14 shows, a large proportion of respondents in many countries say that they 'participate' in, share or comment on news coverage every week. In cosmopolis, it is not just journalists who do journalism.

TRUSTWORTHY: WHO IS A JOURNALIST? WHAT IS GOOD JOURNALISM?

I have spent nearly 40 years working as a journalist as well as in academia. Over this period, the answer to the question 'Who is a journalist?' has changed dramatically, but the answer to the question 'What is good journalism?' has changed not at all. Whether or not others see you as a journalist, you can still do good journalism.

The *Oxford English Dictionary*'s first definition of a journalist—'one who earns his living by editing or writing for a journal or journals'—looks gloriously old-fashioned today. 'Earn a living!' the struggling young freelancer and the recently sacked middle-aged correspondent will exclaim. Yes, some people still make a good living working for news organisations. And the catchy book title claim 'We're All Journalists Now' remains hyperbole.[75] Most people aren't. But there is a whole spectrum from the national TV anchor to the occasional blogger and tweeter. The criteria specified for receiving accreditation to cover the US Senate are even more quaint than the Oxford dictionary definition. Admission to those hallowed benches is reserved for 'bona fide correspondents of repute in their profession' whose 'income is obtained from news correspondence intended for publication in newspapers entitled to second-class mailing privileges'.[76] Pass the quill, Obadiah.

Moreover, if we distinguish between journalism as a business, a profession and an activity, it is not obvious that the journalism that best serves the public good described in this principle is always best provided by professional journalists working for media businesses. The profit imperative, and the heavy hands

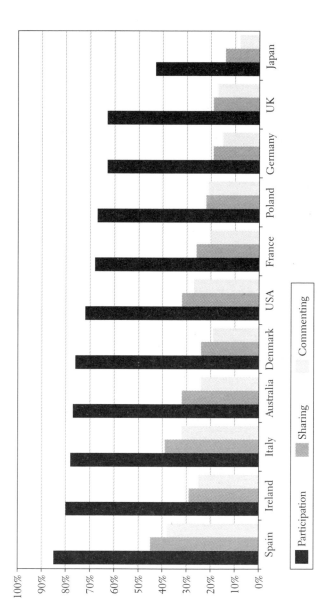

Figure 14. Your news: Participation, sharing and commenting

Respondents were asked: 'During an average week in which, if any, of the following ways do you share or participate in news coverage?'

Source: Adapted from Newman et al. 2015.

of owners, advertisers, PR, lobbyists and political forces, may outweigh the employees' advantages of time and resource. The activity of journalism needs the businesses and full-time professionals, but cannot be confined to them.

So what are the qualities of good journalism? Good journalism tries to get at the truth, or at least at some important part of it. It goes after all possible sources, including ones that are hard and dangerous to reach. It checks its facts and makes explicit judgements about the quality of its evidence. One of its purest forms is that of the eyewitness to important events. Then good journalism attempts to tell the story, to describe, show, explain and analyse, as clearly and vividly as possible, making the subject accessible to audiences that would not otherwise learn about it.

'Journalism's first obligation is to the truth'—thus the very first of the 'Elements of Journalism' listed by Bill Kovach and Tom Rosenstiel.[77] 'There can be no higher law in journalism than to speak the truth and shame the devil', writes Walter Lippmann.[78] Among 'modes of truth-telling', Hannah Arendt includes 'the solitude of the philosopher, the isolation of the scientist and the artist, the impartiality of the historian and the judge, and the independence of the fact-finder, the witness and the reporter'.[79] Michael Schudson interprets Arendt as making the reporter the culmination of her list: 'the reporter holds a special place among those who commit themselves to seeking the truths that self-governing people depend on'.[80]

This is heady stuff: the reporter up there with Plato, Newton, Macaulay and Michelangelo. Such a high-flown description will make anyone who has had much to do with journalists, let alone worked as one, feel a little uneasy. Why? First, because the word 'journalist' covers an incredibly wide range of professional (and unprofessional) activities. There are corrupt judges, incompetent surgeons and sexually predatory teachers, but when we say 'judge', 'surgeon' or 'teacher' we have a reasonably well-based expectation of the normal range of activity associated with that profession. But the tabloid reporter who rifles through dustbins, hacks into mobile phones and fraudulently obtains ('blags') personal medical information in order to expose the private life of a footballer—purely to titillate readers, sell more papers and please his or her boss, with no genuine public interest served by the disclosure—is as much a journalist by profession as the finest war correspondent risking her or his life to bring home a vital hidden truth. A contemptible journalist doing contemptible journalism, but still a journalist. Is there another job description in the world which covers such a gamut of activities, from the criminal to the heroic?

Second, and to make things more complicated, even journalists dedicated to the mission of truth-telling in the public interest often pride themselves on being, well, not entirely respectable: chancers, ornery stirrers-up, no vicars we. A useful corrective to the high-flown rhetoric comes in a well-known piece by a British journalist called Nicholas Tomalin, who was subsequently killed by a Syrian missile while reporting from the Golan Heights during the Yom Kippur war. 'The only qualities essential for real success in journalism', Tomalin writes, 'are ratlike cunning, a plausible manner, and a little literary ability'. He goes on to say that the 'ratlike cunning'—a phrase that became proverbial among British journalists—is needed 'to ferret out and publish things that people don't want to be known (which is—and always will be—the best definition of News)'. In another account of the reporter's trade, he asserts that 'the gathering of newspaper information almost invariably involves guile, subterfuge, humiliation, lying, cheating, and a healthy amount of straightforward criminality'.[81]

There is an element of boyish bravado in this, but also some truth. Reporting from dictatorships, I have routinely lied and used subterfuge to avoid unwelcome attention from the secret police and protect my sources. I still have the visiting cards for a purely fictitious trading company called Edward Marston Ltd. which I 'established' to get a visa to visit Aung San Suu Kyi in Burma, when she was still a dissident leader. At times, I acted like a spy, but—at least in my own understanding—I was a spy for the truth.

Yet the third reason for unease is that to say we are tellers of truth, even without a capital *T*, is such a big claim. I prefer the more modest assertion—elaborated in the introduction to my book *Facts Are Subversive*—that we get at facts. Tomalin, in full debunking mode, will not even allow that. 'The idea of a "fact" is so simplistic it is a lie', he writes. 'Facts are not sacred; the moment any reporter begins to write his story he has selected some and not others, and has distorted the situation. The moment he composes the "facts" into a narrative form he has commented on the situation'. This, discounting for roguish hyperbole, is right, but it calls into question the larger claims for journalists attaining truth, impartiality or objectivity, not the fact that there are facts. However much you select or build a narrative around it, it remains a fact that Nazi Germany attacked Poland on 1 September 1939. It is also a fact that Tomalin wrote an article dismissing the idea of a fact.[82]

Given all these reservations, anyone familiar with the journalist's workaday trade may prefer slightly more modest formulations of what good journalism should do: for example, the former foreign correspondent and director general of the BBC Hugh Greene's motto, 'sail as close to the wind as you can and get it right'.[83] Trust in the *intention* of the writer, blogger or broadcaster is crucial. It makes all the difference in the world whether you believe she or he is trying to 'tell it as it is' and 'get it right' or not. I have called this quality 'veracity', but the investigative reporter Nick Davies puts it even more simply: 'for journalists, the defining value is honesty—the attempt to tell the truth. That is our primary purpose'.[84]

Here is the key feature of what I mean by 'trustworthy', the third dimension of the media we need. BBC-style 'impartiality', let alone the actually unattainable goal of 'objectivity', is only one way of earning that trust. Aspiring to be impartial and fair in your reporting is an excellent discipline, but pretending to be strictly objective can simply conceal hidden biases—perhaps even conceal them from your own liberal or conservative self. As Jay Rosen insists: '"Grounded in reporting" is far more important than "cured of opinion"'.[85] Sometimes, making your own standpoint clear to the reader, what we might call transparent partiality, can be more honest than pretended impartiality. The classic example of this is George Orwell's *Homage to Catalonia*, one of the greatest works of modern political reporting. In his last chapter, Orwell writes, 'In case I have not said this somewhere earlier in the book I will say it now: beware of my partisanship, my mistakes of fact and the distortion inevitably caused by my having seen only one corner of events'.[86] In effect, he says 'Don't believe me!'—and so we believe him.

Attempted impartiality and transparent partiality do not begin to exhaust the options for good journalism. For example, a good many people have ingested much of their political news from satirists such as Jon Stewart on 'The Daily Show' (until he retired), his Egyptian counterpart Bassam Youssef (until his programme was driven off air) and Britain's Ian Hislop (editor of the satirical magazine Private Eye) on the TV programme 'Have I Got News for You'.[87] On these satirical news shows, wild comic exaggeration and sometimes manipulated photomontages mix with sharp political analysis and commentary. A whole different set of conventions applies—one that would have those old spinster ladies, the New York Times and BBC News, fainting on the chaise longue—yet there is no question that, as well as entertaining us, they are trying to get at some truth.

In this kaleidoscopic world of simultaneously converged and fragmented media there are multiple, diverse contracts with the reader, viewer or user. The essential point is that there is some such contract, on which trust is built. Trust is lost when that contract is violated by the writer, blogger, broadcaster or social media self-publisher.

A painful example is the brilliant Polish writer Ryszard Kapuściński. When one of his journalistic disciples became his biographer, he tracked down and talked to some of the original sources for Kapuściński's famous account of the fall of Haile Selassie and his reportage from Bolivia. They complained that the Polish writer had distorted, exaggerated and frankly fabulated what they told him. On at least one occasion, he had even recounted as happening to him dramatic things that actually happened to other people. In short, he had wittingly blurred the frontier between fact and fiction.

There is an interesting twist to this story, which shows how that contract will differ with time and place. When Poles read Kapuściński's original reportage from Africa in communist-ruled Poland in the 1970s, most were not much bothered about factual, detailed accuracy on places most of them would be unable to visit anyway. They loved what they perfectly understood to be a strong element of subversive allegory, smuggling a critique of authoritarian power past the communist censors. But when these same texts were translated into English, they were read as factual reportage, as that craft is understood in the Anglo-American journalistic tradition. Kapuściński was celebrated for having witnessed these horrors and survived to tell the tale. As even his friends began to question his factual veracity, Kapuściński himself never quite came clean. In my view, he broke his contract with his readers.[88]

You do not need to be a professional journalist employed by a news business to have such a contract with the reader (listener/user/viewer) and to maintain a discipline, ethos and standard of fact-finding, truth-telling, investigative or satirical exposure, explicitly partisan commentary—or whatever other way of doing it you choose. It helps to learn from people who have done it professionally for some time, whether by attending journalism school or on the job. It is a great advantage to have a good editor, and a blessing beyond price to work with a great one. But there are other ways of learning by doing.

In short, the very transformation of communications technology which has plunged the business and profession of journalism into economic crisis has opened vast opportunities for the activity of journalism. You don't have to be a journalist to do good journalism.

TOWARDS A NETWORKED PNYX

Does this mean that we can achieve a global virtual pnyx, ancient Athens for more than 7 billion citizens of the world? Not so far ahead as I can see. The largest currently achievable pnyx is probably a worldwide single-language community, such as the Spanish-speaking, Polish-speaking or German-speaking wikinations on Wikipedia, or people following and debating with each other on Twitter or in Chinese on Weibo. With our own very modest attempt to create a genuinely interlingual pnyx on freespeechdebate.com, we discovered how difficult it is to sustain debate across the language barriers. For media, as for online scholarship, language is the new if not the last frontier of cyberspace.

The largest substantive, deliberative conversations about politics, in the broadest sense, remain national ones—such as that enabled by the 'Today' programme on BBC radio, with a regular audience of close to 7 million in a country of 63 million.[89] Tellingly, despite decades of efforts and the emergence of a highly integrated European Union there are still no genuinely European mass media, and therefore no true European public sphere beyond a narrow segment of elite or special interest media. Except, of course, when it comes to talking football, which is the common language of all Europeans.

The familiar dialectic of concentration and fragmentation, convergence and divergence, is seen in this respect too. We have the possibility of listening and speaking online to billions, but in practice more and more people are making their own individual versions of the Daily Kiosk. The space of shared deliberative discourse is at once theoretically larger and practically often smaller, but those smaller spaces are themselves more diverse and cosmopolitan.

This should be no cause for fatalism. We can realistically hope for what Yochai Benkler has called a 'networked public sphere' and one that, for the first time ever, stretches across most of the planet.[90] There will not be a single global pnyx, but there can be multiple, overlapping ones, which those of us who enjoy the preconditions for internet use can visit as we please, both listening and speaking as we go. Despite the formidable political and commercial forces in play, we can shape this networked public sphere. We can ourselves work to create the uncensored, diverse and trustworthy media we need to make informed choices and participate fully in political life. As with the previous principle, on knowledge, of which this is a close first cousin, the new opportunities far outweigh the dangers.

DIVERSITY

*'We express ourselves openly and with robust civility
about all kinds of human difference'.*

In cosmopolis, more people encounter more human diversity than ever be-fore. Every second inhabitant of Toronto is foreign-born.[1] At least 300 languages are spoken in London.[2] According to an official forecast, non-Hispanic whites will be a minority of the US population by 2042.[3] ('In 2042, there'll be more of us than of you', chanted the chorus at a Chicago cabaret.[4]) Even if you are not physically rubbing shoulders with people of every colour, nationality and faith on the London tube, you meet them on YouTube. You don't have to live in a global city to be in the global city.

There is both a new intimacy of diversity and a proliferation of shades of dif-ference. When president-elect Barack Obama was telling an expectant world that his daughters would get a pet dog from a shelter, he memorably added that a lot of shelter dogs are 'mutts like me'.[5] The fastest-growing ethnic category in the British census is 'mixed ethnicity', which almost doubled between the 2001 and 2011 surveys.[6] Where 50 years ago people spoke of 'homosexuality', I recently received an application from a student wishing to research European Union policies towards 'LGBTIQ (Lesbian, Gay, Bisexual, Transgender, In-tersex, Questioning/Queer)' activists in the Western Balkans. The people who used to speak a language called Serbo-Croat now speak supposedly separate languages called Serbian, Croatian, Bosnian and Montenegrin.

Diversity is both a product and an enrichment of liberty. If there were no diversity, there would be no alternatives for us to choose between. But living with such an intimate plenitude of difference is also difficult, and many people might prefer to live more among 'their own'. This difficulty is hardly new. It is something that those inhabiting the territories we now call India and Pakistan have wrestled with for millennia. The emperors Ashoka and Akbar were promoting peaceful coexistence between communities and sects long before Europeans discovered the virtue of 'toleration'. Yet the combination of mass migration and the internet has produced a staggering growth in visible diversity on the physical streets of a global city and the online pages of the virtual one.

Unsurprisingly, some of the most intense free speech controversies of our time have concerned how people express themselves about such differences. Across the quarter century since the Rushdie affair exploded in 1989, many of those controversies have involved religion. For that reason, and because many believers consider—or at least, believe they should consider—their faith to be the most important thing in their lives, I have devoted a separate principle to it. The next chapter does, however, follow from and expand the argument of this one. In the vast library of literature on this area, the largest stack is occupied by arguments for or against what are loosely called hate speech laws. I will come to them, but that is not the right place to start. First we have to work out what we are trying to achieve.

OPENNESS AND ROBUST CIVILITY

What we need is a mixture of openness and robust civility. Civility is a rich concept.[7] In English, and in many Latin languages, its roots connect with the words for city, citizen, civic, civil, civilised and civilisation. Civility is needed in a city, because the city is where different kinds of people live together. Reflecting in his *Politics* on the nature of the city-state, or polis, Aristotle wrote that a city-state 'is not made up only of so many men, but of different kinds of men; for similars do not constitute a state'.[8] Machiavelli uses the term *civiltà* to mean the civil order you have in a well-ordered Italian city-state.[9] A city-state is sustained by its citizens, and Edward Shils calls civility 'the virtue of the citizen'.[10]

Civility is more than just politeness, etiquette or good manners narrowly conceived. Thomas Hobbes speaks of Manners, but insists that 'by Manners, I mean not here, Decency of behaviour; as how one man should salute another, or how a man should wash his mouth, or pick his teeth before company, and such other points of the *Small Moralls*; but those qualities of man-kind, that concern their living together in Peace, and Unity'.[11] There are people who know the right dinner fork to use and never to speak with their mouths full but, when they do open their mouths, emit a torrent of snobbish and racist prejudice. Montesquieu distinguishes between manners, which he says are about 'external' conduct, and mores, which concern 'internal' conduct. Having praised the Chinese for their habits of civility, he writes, 'civility is preferable, in this regard, to politeness. Politeness flatters the vices of others, and civility keeps us from displaying our own'.[12]

Civility is therefore something deeper than manners in the conventional sense. It is an attribute of civil society, which Shils describes as 'a society of civility in the conduct of the members of the society towards each other'.[13] Among the many meanings of 'civility' listed in the *Oxford English Dictionary*, the ones that come closest to that intended here are 'behaviour or speech appropriate to civil interactions' and 'the minimum degree of courtesy required in a social situation'. The word 'minimum' is important. Civility is a cool virtue. It does not demand warmth or friendship. It just asks that you stay in the same space and, as wartime negotiators say, keep talking.

Civil is also counterposed to military, or violent. Civility, as used by Erasmus and others, was what Europeans were meant to practice instead of killing each other in wars of dynastic, aristocratic and sectarian rivalry. Wise burghers should know better. It therefore also connects to what we now call civil disobedience or civil resistance.

In another formulation, Shils says that civility is 'respect for the dignity and desire for dignity of other persons'.[14] That brings in two other vital concepts—respect and dignity—which we will have to examine more closely. These in turn take us to the Israeli philosopher Avishai Margalit's argument that a decent society is one in which people are not humiliated.[15] They also connect to claims for equality and hence against discrimination.

Insofar as civility concerns the beliefs and views of other people, it is also closely related to the ideas of tolerance or toleration. 'Toleration makes difference possible, difference makes toleration necessary', writes Michael Walzer.[16] But an attitude of tolerance, underpinning a policy of toleration, is always a difficult balancing act. As Thomas Scanlon observes, tolerance asks us to position ourselves somewhere between 'wholehearted acceptance and unrestrained opposition'.[17] For the sake of living together peacefully in cosmopolis, we accept the free expression of beliefs, values and lifestyles that we find profoundly wrong. So we accept them but don't accept them. 'To tolerate is to insult', Goethe mused in one of his notebooks.[18] Yet if we go too far in tolerating those who are themselves programmatically intolerant, we will end up destroying the foundations of tolerance. Karl Popper calls this the paradox of tolerance: 'unlimited tolerance must lead to the disappearance of tolerance'.[19]

Exploring the idea of civility thus takes us to the heart of an unending debate about the internal balances of a liberal, pluralist, open society. Experts on each thinker that I have quoted may object that Montesquieu, Machiavelli or Goethe meant something more complex when using the term, which obviously they did. Moreover, ideas of civility vary considerably between countries and cultures, even within the historic West. Thus, for example, James Whitman shows how French and German notions of civility and respect differ from American ones.[20] The former consist, he argues, in a kind of generalisation of aristocratic codes of honour inherited from the age of chivalry, while the latter aim at their wholesale abolition. In effect, France says, 'everyone should be treated like an aristocrat', while America says, 'nobody should be treated like an aristocrat'. There is 'levelling up' on one side of the Atlantic and 'levelling down' on the other. Whitman suggests that this helps explain the contrast between European and American approaches to defamation and hate speech.

And that is just within the West. When we tried to translate this principle into 12 other languages on freespeechdebate.com, we encountered predictable difficulties.[21] Interestingly, our Chinese, Hindi, Farsi and Urdu translators felt that they had found good equivalents in their tongues, although some of their compatriots might disagree. The French have the exact word, *civilité*, but, as Whitman shows, may understand something different by it. Russian seems to have no obvious word for civility, while our Turkish and Japanese translators settled for politeness. Our German team preferred 'politeness and respect' over what they considered the depressingly scholastic *Zivilität*, while our Arabic translators plumped for 'in a civilised manner'. The former chief rabbi of Britain, Jonathan Sacks, celebrates the value of civility but tells us there is no Hebrew word that precisely captures its meaning.[22]

Such difficulties are inevitable if we seek shared principles that extend across cultures and countries. This is the coalface work of seeking a more universal universalism: we lay out what we think is right, trying to make it understandable across language frontiers, but are open to what comes back in terms that are probably unfamiliar to us. For example, the Buddhist philosophy of 'right speech' prescribes an elaborated code of voluntary personal conduct for avoiding what we now call hate speech. The legal philosopher Leslie Green has made a pioneering attempt to translate that philosophy into terms usable in a Western society.[23]

This challenge is new in scale and complexity, because of the conditions of cosmopolis, but not in its essential character, because what today's liberal, pluralist and secular societies have been striving to achieve, in a long, painful process from the seventeenth to the twenty-first century, is a public sphere regulated by norms that are not those of any particular culture or community. As Robert Post writes, the idea is that there should be not just a 'marketplace of ideas' but a 'marketplace of communities'. The standards of civility will, so to speak, hover above and enable a contest which is, amongst other things, about the right standards of civility. This is a paradoxical position: Post calls it the 'paradox of public discourse'.[24] That means it is also demanding. In practice, when it comes to issues like obscenity, public bodies still resort to notions such as 'contemporary community standards', even though it is increasingly unclear which community is being referred to. The British media regulator Ofcom refers, in the section of its broadcasting code on harm and offence, to 'generally accepted standards'.[25] Generally accepted by whom?

If this is difficult inside one established democracy, how much more demanding must it be across the whole city planet. Yet as ideas, information and images flow across frontiers, and if we want them to do so, this is the conversation we must have. Theoretically, there are two extreme positions, which we might call Westphalian and Wilsonian. The first says, 'We do it our way here, and you do it your way over there'; the second says, 'Everyone should do it the same way everywhere'. Since 'here' and 'there' are increasingly mixed up, but people are still very attached to doing things their own way, we are almost certainly going to end up somewhere in between. That may not be the worst place to be. In fact, humankind would be doing remarkably well if we achieved a world in which one overarching code of minimal civility allowed multiple communities to practice (within those outer limits) their own different civility norms—whether in France, on Facebook or on fuckyou.com. (I just made that last one up, but then googled it and of course it already exists. Don't even go there.)

So we should aspire, without illusions, to civility as a norm of a world civil society or, to put it another way, a civil world society. But this argument for civility must immediately be qualified in at least three ways. First, there are some very old and important transgressions of the normal rules of civility, including art and humour. Second, there is a case for incivility as the weapon of the weak, the marginalised and the oppressed, and that needs to be addressed. Third, and most important, the norm that I propose is not civility alone but a combination of robust civility and openness. Openness without civility may lead to anarchy, but civility without openness is a recipe for unfreedom.

Thus, at first glance, it seems good that Sina Weibo urges its users to 'tweet with civility', but if the limits of civility are decided by that morning's Party line then this is not civic virtue but censorship. If, in more free countries, the veto statement 'I am offended' is held to be sufficient for public authorities or private powers to tell another person to shut up, then the notion of 'respect' has been inflated in a way that dangerously curbs liberty.

This kind of respect-inflation is nicely satirised by Salman Rushdie in his fable *Luka and the Fire of Life*. What Rushdie calls the Respectorate of I. is ruled by rats, with a capital R. 'That you say you are offended, insults me mortally', cries the Border Rat. 'And if you insult one Rat mortally, you offend all Rats gravely'. When the hero asks why everything in the Respectorate is grey, he is told that there had been a 'colour problem' there:

> the Rats who hated the colour yellow because of its, well, cheesiness were confronted by the Rats who disliked the colour red because of its similarity to blood. In the end all colours, being offensive to someone or other, were banned by the Rathouse . . .[26]

I shall have more to say in the next chapter about the different meanings of 'respect' and how to distinguish between them.

Openness about all kinds of human difference is as vital as civility. I cannot fully express myself—that is, my self—unless I identify my differences with others. This is Nina Simone's 'I wish you could know / what it means to be me'. We all notice differences and respond to them both consciously and unconsciously. Unless we explore these responses and feelings, we have no chance of digging down to the hidden biases of which we are not aware. If we 'speak what we feel / not what we ought to say', as Shakespeare puts it at the end of *King Lear*, we can learn from experience what is hurtful to others, and hence discover for ourselves what it takes to live together as neighbours. Rather than brushing our perceptions of human difference under the carpet, where they fester like rotting banana skins, we speak about them openly but civilly—as well as in such special registers as art and humour.

What we need is therefore not just civility but robust civility. The word *robust* should be understood here in two senses. First, robust as in frank and open *parrhesia*, not mincing words, pussyfooting or self-censoring. We must be able to accommodate frank and even offensive description and articulation of difference within a broader framework of civil disagreement. But second, I mean robustness as a quality of civility itself. We build a frame that is robust enough to withstand gales blowing through it.

The danger of not allowing the free public expression of thoughts and fears that are present anyway is illustrated by a controversy that exploded in Germany in 2010.[27] Germany, like other Western European countries, had experienced a significant level of immigration over the previous half century, much of it comprising people of Muslim faith, or at least Muslim heritage. Some 4 to 5 percent of Germany's population now identified themselves as Muslims, and they were especially noticeable in some quarters of large cities.[28] Many Germans worried about this, as did their British, French and Italian counterparts. Because of Germany's pre-1945 record of persecuting minorities, there was intense nervousness among journalists, intellectuals and politicians about bringing such worries into public debate: *So was sagt man nicht!* (One doesn't say things like that.) But the more people didn't say it publicly, the more they thought it—and probably said it privately, in the corner pub and at home.

So the pressure of the publicly unspoken built up, like steam in a pressure cooker, until, in summer 2010, a board member of the Bundesbank called Thilo Sarrazin published a hysterical book titled *Germany Abolishes Itself*. Sarrazin combined the cultural pessimism of a reach-me-down Oswald Spengler with sweeping generalisations about Muslims and his own amateur eugenics. Intelligence is 50 to 80 percent inherited, he insisted, Jews are 15 percent more intelligent than Germans, and one chapter was subtitled 'more children of the clever, before it is too late'. This seriously bad book became the biggest political best-seller in Germany since unification, selling some 1.2 million copies in six months. While Chancellor Angela Merkel was holding an 'integration summit' in the Federal Chancellery in Berlin, the mass-market tabloid Bild was printing extracts from what it described as 'thousands' of fan letters to Sarrazin. So instead of starting with an open, civilised, well-informed discussion about an issue of real concern to many Germans, the debate was dished up in a stinking bouillabaisse of eugenics and cultural pessimism.

If you therefore accept, as a statement of principle, that we should aim to achieve a combination of openness and robust civility, the question becomes: how? Each of the four major forces that I have identified as determining your effective freedom of speech in a given place and time—international bodies, nation states, private powers and networked individuals—has an influence in this respect. Within the boundaries of a particular country, however, international institutions and treaties are given effect mainly through national governments and courts, while private powers and networked individuals can be viewed as part of civil society. Thus the legal scholars Arthur Jacobson and Bernhard Schlink (the latter also a well-known German novelist) argue that the difference between the United States and continental European countries is not, as is sometimes loosely suggested, that 'America doesn't stop hate speech while Europe does' but that European countries try to stop it by using the restraining power of the state while America relies on the self-restraint of civil society.[29] As examples of civil society restraints, Jacobson and Schlink cite US workplace rules, broadcasting standards and campus speech codes.

This illuminating dichotomy turns the spotlight from common ends—a combination of openness and civility—to contrasting means. It is important to stress again that the coercive or deterrent power of the law is not the only instrument available to the state. A state can also 'speak', in what Corey Brettschneider calls its expressive rather than its coercive function, through monuments, museums, the public statements and gestures of its leaders, high-profile events such as the opening ceremony for an Olympic Games and, not least, education.

Yet over the last half century the most visible way in which states in Europe and the English-speaking world, apart from the United States, have addressed the issue of free speech about burgeoning diversity is through hate speech laws. This has generated one of the longest-running disagreements about free speech within the liberal democratic world, with contrasting American and Euro-Canadian-Antipodean positions so well worn that they resemble nothing so much as schoolboys' highly polished prize conkers (horse chestnuts threaded on string and hit against each other in a traditional British schoolyard game.) So we must bite the chestnut and turn to hate speech laws.

ENFORCING CIVILITY?

Hate speech laws are needed, writes the French scholar-judge Roger Errera, 'to defend the basic civility of our society'. 'Which form of civility?' he asks. 'That which forbids us to attack an individual or a group of persons on the grounds of what they are, that is, for their identity'.[30] Errera offers two propositions: that the existence of hate speech laws contributes significantly to the preservation of civility and that without them it would not be preserved (otherwise they would not be 'needed'). Given that we have had such laws on the statute books for decades in dozens of countries, including many mature democracies, we must surely be in a position to ask whether the first proposition is borne out by the evidence, before looking at alternative, nonlegal ways of sustaining a civil society. In short: have these laws worked? Are they working better or worse given the explosion of expression of all sorts in the transnational virtual world, including a daily ocean of often anonymous abuse?

Before addressing those apparently simple questions, we have to recognise that almost every aspect of hate speech laws is contested and often elusive. This starts with the very notion of hate. 'Incitement to [fill in the box] hatred' is sometimes talked about as if the emotion of hatred must be bad itself—hence the related idea of 'hate crimes'. As the British actor Rowan Atkinson observes, incitement to 'intense dislike' would not sound so bad.[31] Yet I hate injustice, oppression, racism and sexism, and these are good hatreds. 'They will never love where they ought to love', wrote Edmund Burke, 'who do not hate where they ought to hate'.[32] Everything depends on what it is you are hating.

Hate speech, as Errera says, generally denotes attacking, insulting or abusing an individual or a group on the basis of some generic or group characteristic, such as the colour of your skin, your religion (or atheism), gender, sexual orientation or a disability. But the definition and range of characteristics to be protected is constantly disputed, with the list getting longer and more complicated as groups compete for recognition by the law. If race, why not religion? If religion, why not homosexuality? If sexuality, why not disability, age, obesity? If Christianity (protected under traditional European blasphemy laws), why not Islam? If Islam, why not Scientology? If homosexuality, why not bisexual, transgender and intersex? If fat, why not thin? If old, why not young?[33]

The pivotal word or phrase also varies significantly. Is it speech 'by which a group of people is threatened, insulted or degraded', as in Denmark, or 'provocation' to discrimination, hate or violence against groups, as in Spain? Is it intended or likely to 'stir up' hatred, as in England, or, as in the Netherlands, a statement which someone 'knows or should reasonably suspect to be offensive to a group of persons on the grounds of their race, religion, or personal beliefs, or their hetero- or homosexual orientation'?[34] Beneath each formulation lies a slightly different idea of the harm, offence or moral wrong caused or embodied by the words, images or gestures at issue — or several different ideas, not clearly distinguished from each other. Eric Heinze has identified no fewer than 19 varieties of justification for hate speech laws.[35]

Many of these ideas are supported by claims about the consequences for the women, men and children who are attacked, insulted, threatened or 'stirred up' against. These claims are difficult to test empirically, partly because there are so many elements in play and the harm may result from the cumulative impact of a thousand tiny cuts. Jeremy Waldron argues that the effect is analogous to air pollution.[36] Moreover, the question 'Where's the evidence?' is sometimes treated as niggling, given the obvious nastiness of what is being expressed. Yet if we are to be serious, we must distinguish between the different kinds of harm, offence or moral wrong that hate speech legislation is supposed to punish, deter or at least stigmatise.

As I argued in chapter 2, any form of expression that is both intended and likely to lead to physical violence should meet with the force of the law. Working out what is 'dangerous speech' in the age of mass migration and the internet is not easy, and the Brandenburg criterion of 'imminence' should be modified accordingly. Then there is verbal aggression, intimidation and harassment directed at an individual or individuals: speech directly *to*, not simply *about*. Even if the result is not physical injury, bullying with threatening words and abusive gestures clearly can do psychological harm to its victims. You can't take a photograph of the inner cuts and bruises, but who would doubt that in many cases serious damage is done? Our ordinary life experience, and a library of memoirs and novels, tell us this is so.

Even the American First Amendment jurisprudence, which does not criminalise hate speech, outlaws 'fighting words'. The definition has been traditionally confined to those delivered 'face-to-face', but what exactly is face-to-face in the age of Facebook? Suppose someone uses the access afforded by social media to thrust crude threats of violence ('I'm coming to kill you, you kike', 'You deserve to be raped, you whore') into my virtual personal space. This may not be as intimidating as a drunken thug looming over me in a dark street, especially since we know that anonymous rudeness is ubiquitous online, but there comes a point when it will meet the same test. Twitter, which is essentially a public forum, struggles most with the use of the @ tag, because this brings the use of tweets closer to personal intimidation. Bullying trolls are using their freedom of expression to curb yours. A 15-year-old Canadian girl called Amanda Todd committed suicide after suffering years of cyberbullying.[37]

As we cross the line between physical and mental harm, we need to reflect again on the relation between words and deeds. Generations of schoolchildren have read Aesop's fable about an army trumpeter who is put to death by the enemy for stirring up his side's troops to fight, and its resonant moral: 'Words are deeds'.[38] Actually, Aesop never wrote that—at least, it is not in the earliest texts we have. But whether or not Ludwig Wittgenstein was influenced by a childhood reading of Aesop, that is exactly what the philosopher did write in a notebook around 1945: *Worte sind Taten* (words are deeds).[39] Philosophers have subsequently developed a whole typology of 'speech acts', with a professional jargon as dense as the thickest gorse bush ('illocutionary' and 'perlocutionary', 'verdictive' and 'exercitive'). If you can get through the gorse bush, what emerges is important.

There are words that are just words. There are words that lead directly to deeds. ('Shoot her', says the Hutu militia commander, and the Tutsi woman is killed.) There are words that are themselves deeds, in the sense that what we say *is* what we do. ('I apologise'. 'I promise'. 'I do', in a traditional wedding ceremony.) And, as poets and novelists know, there are multiple gradations in between. What we have to assess in every case is a particular speech act in a particular context, with its time, manner and place, the position of the speaker and the nature of the audience. 'Shoot her', spoken by the Hutu militia commander, is not the same as 'I think Jones should be shot', spoken over tea by my elderly mother. Although the correlation is not exact, as we move across the spectrum of evils attributed to hate speech, we tend to move from words that demonstrably cause physical deeds, through words that are deeds, to words that are just words.

Thus, for example, another harm attributed to hate speech is that of discrimination, a violation of the principle of equal treatment. Once again, the difficulty lies in establishing to what extent that definite, individual harm may be said to result from the propagation of negative stereotypes about a particular group (Jews, women, Rohingya in Myanmar, homosexuals, Muslims). An even broader claim is that the way certain groups are persistently characterised in public itself amounts to discrimination.

One of the most far-reaching and vaguest international treaties prescribing curbs to free expression on these grounds is the International Convention on the Elimination of All Forms of Racial Discrimination. Adopted in 1965, it says in Article 4 that 'States Parties condemn all propaganda and all organisations which are based on ideas or theories of superiority of one race or group of persons of one colour or ethnic origin, or which attempt to justify or promote racial hatred and discrimination in any form'.[40] States are instructed to make the dissemination of such ideas 'punishable by law'. On this basis, the UN Committee on the Elimination of Racial Discrimination, which monitors implementation of the Convention, found that the German government should have taken legal steps against Thilo Sarrazin, who did, after all, suggest that Jews are superior to Germans, and both groups to Muslims.[41] (The German government replied that the federal government was 'currently examining the German legislation concerning criminal liability for racist statements in light of the committee's views'.[42])

Then there is a whole set of attributed harms that cluster around the notion of human dignity, also involving ideas of respect, recognition and reputation. Even if there is no physical violence, direct intimidation or actual discrimination, the argument goes, the persistent visibility of hate speech means that individual members of the pilloried group are not given public assurance of their equal dignity as members of a well-ordered society. In Avishai Margalit's terms, they are publicly humiliated. They are not afforded the full collective recognition and individual respect enjoyed by members of more established or powerful groups. According to some interpreters, they suffer 'group defamation'—the collective equivalent of what happens to an individual when she or he is libelled. (This approach is sometimes connected to the continental European idea of enforcing civility and respect by 'levelling up'. Everyone should be treated like a Grand Seigneur.)

But who should decide when someone has suffered this kind of 'dignitary harm'? Avishai Margalit argues that 'there must be a presumption in a decent society in favour of the interpretation given by vulnerable minorities as to the humiliating nature of the gestures directed at them'.[43] Listen to the victims. They know best. As a prescription for psychological understanding and human decency, this is surely right. As a criterion for legal prosecution it carries us over the line between some external (though never, of course, objective) recognition of equal dignity and the internal, subjective condition of taking offence. This risks encouraging the 'I'm offended' form of heckler's veto. When British schools were asked by the government to keep a log of all racist incidents among their pupils, the question arose: who decides what is racist? One head teacher had a simple answer: 'If the child feels the incident is racist, it is'. The five-year-old should decide.[44]

If you want to avoid this danger, you face an equal and opposite one—that of paternalism, or treating adults as if they are children. An odd but illuminating example was that of an uncommonly small Frenchman called Manuel Wackenheim who earned money by participating in 'dwarf-throwing' events, in which people would pay to throw him a short distance onto an airbed. French courts ruled that this violated his dignity. He objected that the court was violating his dignity by not allowing him to make his living in the way he chose. The UN Human Rights Committee sided with the French courts, but it seems to me that Monsieur Wackenheim had a strong point. Unlike the five-year-old defining racism, an adult in full possession of his faculties should surely be the best judge of his own dignity.[45]

If you describe the harms of hate speech in this way, you are condemned to steer a tricky course between the cliffs of paternalism and the rocks of a purely subjective 'I'm offended' veto. It may be possible to chart such a course in theory, but it seems more important to ask whether courts and police have successfully done so in practice.

Beyond paternalism there is moralism. The old moralism of 50 years ago—separate beds for couples in Hollywood movies—has been laughed out of court. But a new paternalistic (or maternalistic) moralism has crept back almost unnoticed by those who invoke it, which tends to be the way with moralism. Explaining why an extreme Islamist publicity seeker should not be interviewed on the BBC, a British Home Secretary said he had 'disgusting views', as if having 'disgusting views' were in itself sufficient grounds to exclude someone from public debate.[46]

This brings us to a final idea, which is that these laws are justified simply as an expression of certain core moral standards of the given state and society. Never mind if those laws are seldom used and we cannot show that they deter hate speakers. They nonetheless send a signal, especially to members of vulnerable minorities. They are like a school motto or a company slogan: 'No hate speech here!' That is the kind of country we want to be.

WHY MATURE DEMOCRACIES SHOULD MOVE BEYOND HATE SPEECH LAWS

Even this whistlestop tour around the main arguments for hate speech laws demonstrates why it is impossible to reach any conclusive verdict on their efficacy. Quite apart from the many variations between jurisdictions, it depends which of these multiple purposes we are assessing them against. If it is the last-mentioned—simply to make a statement of shared values—then these laws must by definition be a success. The message is the message.

Moreover, so much depends on the context. Harmless hate speech in Reykjavik is dangerous speech in Rwanda. In the argument that follows, I shall confine myself to mature democracies, having the rule of law, diverse media and a developed civil society. Here there is a compelling case that the advantages of hate speech laws, as they have actually worked over the last half century, are outweighed by the disadvantages, including their unintended consequences.

There is scant evidence that mature democracies with extensive hate speech laws manifest any less racism, sexism or other kinds of prejudice than those with few or no such laws. Take France, which has a relatively high level of hate speech prosecutions. There were about 100 convictions per year in the five-year period from 1997 to 2001, and an annual average of 208 in 2005 to 2007. French courts have convicted Brigitte Bardot five times for incitement to racial hatred, on account of her fulminating attacks on Muslims in France, starting with the way they slaughter animals. The distinguished intellectual Edgar Morin was found guilty for a fierce attack on Israel's treatment of the Palestinians, and a member of parliament, Christian Vanneste, for expressing 'homophobic views', although both convictions were overturned on appeal. Yet France has endemic discrimination in its labour market against people of migrant origin and especially Muslims, racist monkey chants in its football stadiums and a xenophobic party, the Front National, which gains the support of a large number of French voters.[47]

Similarly, the British writer Kenan Malik has pointed out, recalling his own personal experience of racist attacks, that the decade after Britain passed legislation against incitement to racial hatred in 1965 was probably the country's worst for racism.[48] Plainly we can't argue that the persistence of prejudice is a result of the laws, and some will say that, on the contrary, it shows how necessary they are. Indeed, the apparent ineffectiveness of Britain's 1965 law was one reason it was strengthened in 1976, so that you did not even have to intend to stir up racial hatred; your words or actions just had to be 'likely to' stir it up.

A causal connection cannot be proven either way. What is clear is that there is no correlation between the presence of extensive hate speech laws on the statute books and lower levels of abusively expressed prejudice about human difference. If, as Errera argues, the main purpose of such laws is to enforce civility, they have not succeeded. Interestingly, even two of the most outspoken American critics of racist hate speech, from the perspective of what they call 'critical race theory', Jean Stefancic and Richard Delgado, found the efficacy of such laws to be 'an open question'.[49]

The application of good laws is clear, predictable and proportionate. That of hate speech laws has been unpredictable and often disproportionate. In Canada, the uncertainty has been even greater because findings on hate speech have in part been delegated to Human Rights Commissions in each individual province. As a result, the Canadian Human Rights Tribunal found in 2009 that section 13 of the Human Rights Act, which mandated controls over hate speech on the internet, violated the free speech clause of the country's own Charter of Rights and Freedoms. Section 13 was repealed in 2013.What is more, laws intended to afford protection to 'vulnerable minorities' have often ended up being used against members of those minorities. There is a reason for this. Members of a secure majority, where it still exists, are less likely to express themselves in extreme terms. They don't feel the need to scream to make themselves heard.

The internet has brought an explosion of offensive, extreme expression, exacerbated by the online norm of anonymity. Reacting instantly, behind the mask of a pseudonym, people jerk out things online that they would never say when using their real name in a face-to-face encounter or public meeting. If we believe in openness and robust civility, we must address this challenge, and I shall say more about how this can be done by civil society, online communities and private powers. However, this new reality weakens rather than strengthens the case for hate speech laws. Given this explosion, the law struggles to identify and prosecute even those cases of online abuse which plainly do constitute incitement to violence against particular people, harassment and the online equivalent of 'fighting words'. It does not catch many of them.

If, beyond that, the state attempts to prosecute more general forms of rude and offensive speech, it will be bound to catch only a tiny fraction of what is out there. As the Hungarian scholar Péter Molnár notes, trying to stop extreme speech on the internet is 'like jumping on a shadow'.[50] The result will be even more legal uncertainty. Again and again, people will ask: 'why me but not him—and him, and her, and him?' The very principle of equality—specifically a claim for equal treatment by the state—which is one of the justifications for such laws will be undermined by their arbitrary application.

Then there is the question of which group characteristics should be protected. A distinction is often made between so-called immutable characteristics, which should enjoy strong protection, and mutable ones, which should enjoy less or no protection. 'You can't change your race', the saying goes, 'but you can change your religion'. Thus, for example, when English hate speech laws were being extended to people on grounds of homosexuality, and sexual orientation more broadly, the English free speech lawyer Anthony Lester observed: 'the question is whether you think that homophobic hate speech is more like race hate speech or religious hate speech. Does homophobic hate speech attack people for the way they are born, for their common humanity, unlike religious hate speech, which attacks people because of their beliefs or their chosen practices?' His conclusion was that homosexuality should be treated like race, not religion.[51]

Yet what is most immutable about me may not be what is most important to me. I may indeed be able to change my religion, in a way that I cannot change my skin colour, but that does not mean I regard my skin colour as more important than my religion. Most believers would say the opposite, and it is often converts who are the most fervent defenders of their faith—hence the proverbial 'zeal of the convert'. I have yet to meet someone who believes that their prospect of being saved from everlasting torment depends on their skin colour or gender. Moreover, the distinction between immutable and mutable becomes less sharp on closer examination.

It is true that, unless I am as rich and eccentric as Michael Jackson, I cannot significantly change my skin colour. But the colour of our skins is never actually a Photoshop white or black. Brazil's census takers once asked a sample of Brazilians to describe their own skin colours. They came up with 134 terms, including *alva-rosada* (white with pink highlights), *branca-sardenta* (white with brown spots), *café-com-leite* (coffee with milk), *morena-canelada* (cinnamon–light brunette), *polaca* (Polish—apparently meaning very white), *quase-negra* (almost black) and *tostada* (toasted).[52] (I'm *alva-rosada* myself.) As societies become more mixed, so do skin colours, facial types and other inherited physical features. More and more of us are, in Obama's memorable phrase, 'mutts like me'. Strictly speaking we all are, since studies of mitochondrial DNA show that we are all descended from a group of perhaps 5,000 women who lived some 200,000 years ago—our mitochondrial Eves.[53] Not to mention all the subsequent licit and illicit couplings that Daniel Defoe captured in his portrait of the True Born Englishman:

Thus from a mixture of all kinds began,
That het'rogeneous thing, an Englishman:
In eager rapes, and furious lust begot . . .[54]

Race, by contrast, is not immutable. It is a social and political construct that varies from place to place. Under the notorious 'one drop of blood' rule, people with quite light skins were long classified in the United States as 'black'. In Brazil, the opposite happened: a few drops of white made you 'white', or at least not 'black'. The attribution of colour also changed with social and economic status. Money whitened. A Brazilian sociologist once told me about an encounter with a millionaire who came from a very poor background in the favelas. Leaning back in his rocking chair, puffing on his cigar, the millionaire reminisced, 'When I was black . . .'.[55]

By now, some readers will be screaming: 'But this academic pin-dancing entirely misses the point, which is that every day thousands of people are being taunted and abused because of the colour of their skin, or other aspects of their appearance'. Indeed they are. There is a huge amount of racism about, some of it exploiting freedom of expression. 'Racism is real, but races are not', writes the American scholar David Hollinger—and that is exactly right.[56] All human beings possess inherited characteristics; indeed recent medical research emphasises the sometimes decisive impact of specific genes. But unless you take Heinrich Himmler as your scientific authority, there are no immutable characteristics of whole 'races' such as 'the Jews'. (The discussion is complicated by the fact that 'race' in the United States means something different again, centrally involving the legacy of slavery.)

The trouble is that defining people by such group characteristics as 'race', and then trying to prevent insults to them on the basis of it, inevitably highlights that attributed group characteristic. Thus the logging of racist incidents in British schools had the perverse effect of racialising children's perception of each other. (Remember that head teacher's remark: 'If the child feels the incident is racist, it is'.) This is the very opposite of what we need if we are to live together in increasingly diverse societies. To do that well, we need to appreciate, on the one hand, the things that we all share as human beings, our common humanity, and on the other, the billionfold variety of individual human difference.

In cosmopolis, where people increasingly have multiple ethnic and national identities, often being 'transnational', or, to adapt a wonderful German word, *hinternational*, they cannot be reduced to 'tick only one box' categorisation. What 'race', for example, is the golfer Tiger Woods? He describes himself as 'Cablinasian' (Caucasian, Black, American Indian and Asian).[57]

Reflecting on the ethnic cleansing of central and eastern Europe in the mid-twentieth century, the anthropologist Ernest Gellner observed that a painting by Oskar Kokoschka (all shades, stippling and mixes) had become a Piet Mondrian (sharply separated, neat blocks of solid colour). The last half century, however, has seen most developed societies move in the opposite direction, from Mondrian to Kokoschka. This is a result of mass migration and its longer-term consequences, but also of freedom. People have used their freedom in increasingly liberal societies to define ever more subtle and fluid variations of identity. A good example is the multiplication of categories of sexual orientation: LGBTIQ.

One of the assumptions underlying hate speech laws is that there are vulnerable minorities that need to be protected in ways not required by a secure majority. The sociological basis of that assumption looks increasingly old-fashioned. It is not yet true to say that 'we are all minorities now', but in many mature democracies, there are cities where the national majority is a local minority— so-called majority minority places. If those US census projections are right, then in 2042 there will be no ethnic majority in the United States as a whole, only a plurality.

In short, one of the problems with hate speech laws is not, as some old-fashioned curmudgeons imply, that they are too respectful of diversity, but that they are insufficiently respectful of the true plenitude of our diversity. The principle that heads this chapter says, with deliberate emphasis, '*all* kinds of human difference'—not just the few simplistic categories of what Seyla Benhabib witheringly calls 'poor man's sociology'.[58]

A further weakness that emerges from the history of hate speech laws is that they tend to encourage people to take offence rather than learn to live with it, ignore it or deal with it by speaking back. A lot is written about what is offensive, but the novelist J. M. Coetzee, writing out of his experience of censorship in apartheid South Africa, takes it from the other end and looks at the psychological and moral condition of being-offended. 'The punitive gesture of censoring', he writes, 'finds its origin in the reaction of being offended. The strength of being-offended, as a state of mind, lies in not doubting itself; its weakness lies in not being able to afford to doubt itself'. Urging us to mark and resist the 'stirrings of being-offended' within ourselves, he points to Dostoevsky's 'mordant analysis [which] identifies taking offence as the blustering move of the soldier-bully and the last resort of the threadbare clerk'.[59] Is this the example we want to give our children?

Rather than encouraging people to be thin-skinned, what we need in a world of increasing and increasingly intimate diversity is to learn how to be a little more thick-skinned, to live and cope with difference. It has become almost a commonplace of liberal discourse that, as Ronald Dworkin put it, no one has a right not to be offended. The British-Canadian scholar Simon Barrow takes this a step further and argues that 'we have a duty not to take offence too readily'.[60] It seems questionable whether one can really posit a *duty* not to take offence— after all, my freedom of expression must include my freedom to express a sense of being offended—but it is certainly wise advice for living together well in freedom.

The habit of taking offence does not only spread among individuals. Since hate speech laws proceed by the definition of group characteristics, they also encourage groups, or at least their chosen or merely self-anointed leaders, to compete for recognition by the state on the generic grounds of 'If you protect X, why not Y'. The result is what Kenan Malik has called 'an auction of victimhood'.[61] By securing a new protection under the law, or a prosecution under an existing one, those group or community leaders mobilise constituencies, translating real or simulated indignation into publicity, supporters and votes.

An at once classic and extreme example of this is India, the world's largest democracy, one of the most historically multicultural societies on earth and a swing state for the future of free speech. India's penal code has some of the most capacious hate speech restrictions you can find anywhere. Section 153A, for example, threatens up to three years in prison for anyone who 'by words, either spoken or written, or by signs or by visible representations or otherwise, promotes or attempts to promote, on grounds of religion, race, place of birth, residence, language, caste or community *or any other ground whatsoever*, disharmony or feelings of enmity, hatred or ill-will between different religious, racial, language or regional groups or castes or communities . . .' (my italics).[62]

On the face of it, that may look like the ultimate contemporary multiculturalist recipe. In fact, it goes back to the days of the British empire, since a penal code originally drafted by the historian Thomas Babington Macaulay was taken over wholesale by postcolonial, independent India.[63] Yet Macaulay was no admirer of native customs and described his goal as 'firm and impartial despotism'.[64] The logic of his section 153A was thus one of colonial oppression: keep the lid on those restless natives, by having the power to lock up anybody for saying anything offensive to anyone else. In a strange transmogrification, democratic India has imaginatively connected this legislation back to more benign and ancient Indian traditions of promoting intercommunity harmony. Moreover, the historian Neeti Nair has shown how the wording of another section of the penal code, 295A, which forbids outrage to 'religious feelings' and insult to the religious beliefs of any 'class', was actively shaped by Indian politicians and intellectuals in the 1920s, while still under colonial rule.[65]

Yet the results are often perverse. Section 295A has been used to go after one of India's most famous artists, M. F. Husain, for his abstract paintings of Hindu gods and goddesses, and to ban books on important Indian historical themes. Community leaders now routinely make political capital out of demanding the prosecution of someone who has allegedly offended their community. I witnessed a textbook case of this at the Jaipur literary festival in 2013. An outspoken sociologist called Ashis Nandy made a provocative remark about how 'most of the corrupt' in India come from the poorest parts of society, curiously known as the OBC (Other Backward Classes), Scheduled Castes and Scheduled Tribes. (Scheduled Castes include the Dalit, formerly known as the 'Untouchables'.) All hell broke loose. A video clip of his remarks, taken out of context, was endlessly replayed on television, and protesters marched on the festival site. Nandy was charged under a Prevention of Atrocities Act and festival organisers were charged with lesser offences.[66]

Observers noted that the state of Rajasthan, to which Jaipur belongs, would hold elections later that year and, yes, those people whom Nandy allegedly insulted were looking for votes. Community leaders and politicians therefore compete to use hate speech legislation, especially at local and state levels, for their own political ends. Far from encouraging harmony, these laws create a perverse incentive to stir up discord. As the political scientist Pratap Bhanu Mehta observes, 'If you can incite violence, or show that you are deeply offended, you will have your way. Indian laws are not protecting us against offensive speech; they are inciting us to produce it, and in turn provoking bans'.[67]

Something similar has happened in several European democracies. Muslim lobbyists say: if Jews are protected by racial hatred or Holocaust denial laws, and Christians by blasphemy laws, we should be protected too. If incitement to racial and religious hatred is criminalised, insists the LGBTIQ lobby, so should incitement on grounds of sexual orientation. And so on. Sometimes, these groups win legal bans not through the strength of their arguments but through the argument of their strength. At the extreme, this is not normal interest group lobbying but something close to the heckler's veto.

Reflecting on the situation in Britain, the conservative and Roman Catholic commentator Charles Moore notes, not without quiet indignation, that

an odd coalition has grown up of those who must not be offended. This consists on the one hand of Muslims and those ethnic groups who are furthest in background from traditional British culture and — on the other — the most progressive opinions (often not widely held among those groups) of educated whites. Thus, you must not offend Mohammed (who wasn't massively into the gay rights agenda) nor must you say anything even remotely "homophobic".[68]

The crucial question is: what follows from this? That you should not be allowed to insult Christians in Britain? Or that you should be free to insult Muslims, Jews and homosexuals just as you can Christians, Old Etonians and estate agents?

Identity lobbyists feed on the strong claim for equality in modern democracies but themselves often display double standards. In 2006, the then secretary general of the Muslim Council of Britain, Sir Iqbal Sacranie (who once said death was perhaps too good for Salman Rushdie) denounced the publication of the Danish cartoons of Muhammad, but scarcely a month later he publicly declared that gays are 'harmful' and 'spread disease'.[69] Abraham Foxman and Christopher Wolf of the Anti-Defamation League in the United States argue that YouTube was right to leave up the 'Innocence of Muslims' video (which they mildly describe as 'mean-spirited') but insist that Facebook should take down Holocaust denial because it is hate speech.[70]

If we are to be free of such double standards and take seriously the claim for equal treatment under the law, we stand at a crossroads. Call it the crossroads of cosmopolis. In one direction lies the path down which many mature democracies have been treading for several decades. In what I have called the taboo ratchet, ever more characteristics must be added to the list of those protected from hate speech: race, religion, ethnicity, gender, sexual orientation, disability. But how can we justify stopping there? What about 'idiot', 'moron', 'paranoid', 'fatso', 'dwarf', 'midget', 'fat slob'?

As a bearded person, I have sometimes encountered prejudice against beards. If I could establish a well-funded and organised Anti-Pogonophobia League, or Bearded Council of Britain, and mobilise sufficient voices and votes, why should I not get the law changed to forbid hateful insult to my facial hair? That is a frivolous example, but the case of overweight people is not. Well over a quarter of the population of several developed countries, including Britain, Canada and the United States, are classified as obese.[71] A survey published in the American Journal for Public Health in 2010 found that 'Negative attitudes toward obese persons are pervasive in North American society. Numerous studies have documented harmful weight-based stereotypes that overweight and obese individuals are lazy, weak-willed, unsuccessful, unintelligent, lack self-discipline, have poor willpower, and are noncompliant with weight-loss treatment'.[72] No reasonable person will doubt that fat people may suffer real hurt and serious loss of self-esteem from constant, derisory comments on their weight. This can be just as bad for the person concerned as being called 'queer' or 'Yid' or 'chocolate bar' (one of the racist insults logged by a British school).

By the same token, why should not the myths, symbols and taboos of all minorities represented in a given jurisdiction, be they Inuit, Goth, Druid or Scientologist, not enjoy the same protection as those of larger and more widely acknowledged minorities—and, indeed, majorities? But since, in cosmopolis, you have people from everywhere, with every variety of self-identification, this produces a formidable array of no-go areas. If we were to put together all the characteristics on the basis of which people may feel themselves to be insulted, and all the taboos of all the cultures in the world, and then rule them all off-limits, there would be precious little left that we could talk about.

If we believe in the value of freedom, we must therefore take the other path. Instead of levelling up the legally enforced taboos, we should level them down. There should indeed be equal treatment under the law, but it should be equality that permits the widest possible articulation of human difference. This will involve carefully pruning back even laws that are quite widely accepted, such as those forbidding incitement to racial hatred. Interestingly, some British human rights activists deeply committed to free speech privately acknowledge the need to amend if not repeal Britain's law on incitement to racial hatred, on precisely these grounds of equal treatment, but few will say this publicly. Liberals, too, have their taboos.

Here, as in everything else to do with free speech, we must always be sensitive to local circumstances. What is entirely harmless in Sao Paolo may be lethal in Saudi Arabia. Yet sensitivity to time and place also entails recognising how laws that may arguably have prevented dangerous speech at one time may not be needed now. For example, one could argue that a ban on Holocaust denial might have contributed to preventing the real danger of a neo-Nazi revival in Germany in the 1950s and 1960s, yet recognise that danger is much smaller now.

Or take India. A former Indian attorney general, Soli Sorabjee, has observed:

Experience shows that criminal laws prohibiting hate speech and expression will encourage intolerance, divisiveness and unreasonable interference with freedom of expression. Fundamentalist Christians, religious Muslims and devout Hindus would then seek to invoke the criminal machinery against each other's religion, tenets or practice. That is what is increasingly happening today in India. We need not more repressive laws but more free speech to combat bigotry and promote tolerance.[73]

Few have made the case against hate speech laws more eloquently. Yet it does not follow that India should overnight abolish restrictions that it has lived with for so long. One could plausibly argue that this would result in an upsurge in intercommunity violence. Of course, what the world's largest democracy does must be entirely up to its citizens and their representatives, but there would clearly be a case for moving gradually towards widening the legal boundaries of freedom of expression—explaining, testing and monitoring along the way. A good starting point would be how India treats the words and images that flow across its frontiers on the internet. As we have seen, Germany makes a strong symbolic point about Holocaust denial and Nazi symbols but does not in practice deny its citizens access to foreign sites where these can be found.

To be clear: many instances of what is colloquially described as hate speech should be combatted by law on the grounds that they do demonstrable harm. These include dangerous speech, 'fighting words', direct harassment, intimidation and bullying, both online and offline. The advocacy of discrimination should be allowed by law—and then heavily criticised in free debate—but actual discrimination should definitely not be. Sometimes the police and the courts do have to intervene to protect public order, although in Britain the 1986 Public Order Act has too often been misused to punish the merely offensive. Thus, for example, an elderly evangelical Christian street preacher called Harry Hammond was convicted for brandishing a handmade sign which, with the words 'Jesus is Lord' in each corner, declared 'Stop Immorality, Stop Homosexuality, Stop Lesbianism'.[74] A student was arrested and spent a night in jail for saying to a policeman, 'Excuse me, do you realise your horse is gay?' (A police spokesman said 'he made homophobic comments that were deemed offensive to people passing by'.)[75] A 16-year-old schoolboy was issued a court summons for holding up a placard outside the Church of Scientology's London headquarters saying 'Scientology is not a religion, it is a dangerous cult'.[76] All were locked up on the grounds that their words were 'threatening, abusive or insulting', under section 5 of the Public Order Act, which allows a constable to arrest someone without warrant if 'he engages in offensive conduct which a constable warns him to stop'. After widespread criticism and a campaign for reform, the word 'insulting' was removed in 2013, but the rest remained—as did the provision that the offending words had only to be uttered within sight or hearing of a person 'likely to be caused harassment, alarm or distress'.[77]

Along the way, there are fine judgement calls. Is it really OK for activists of the Westboro Baptist Church of Topeka, Kansas, who believe that America's military casualties are God's punishment for 'the fag lifestyle of soul-damning, nation-destroying filth', to hold up signs at the funerals of American soldiers saying 'Thank God for Maimed Soldiers'?[78] Imagine the feelings of a dead soldier's mother on her way to that funeral. Is it legitimate freedom of expression for shouting crowds to confront young women visiting an abortion clinic with shocking photos of aborted foetuses? But what if the protesters are just quietly praying for their immortal souls? At this writing, New Hampshire allows a 25-foot area to be provided around its abortion clinics, in which anti-abortion protesters are not allowed to demonstrate, but the US Supreme Court struck down a Massachusetts law providing for a 35-foot buffer zone.[79] Yet all these borderline cases are not a mere 10 feet but 100 miles away from a generalised attempt to enforce civility.

If, however, we conclude that the disadvantages of trying to enforce civility by legal ban outweigh the advantages, this does not mean we give up on civility. On the contrary, it means redoubling our efforts to achieve robust civility where it belongs, in civil society. An essential and defining feature of a mature, liberal democracy is that, so far as humanly possible, it replaces external constraint with self-restraint.

CREATING A CIVIL SOCIETY

Let us start by acknowledging that this is not easy. The internet is also history's largest sewer. Vast shit-tides of abuse are waiting to flow out of your box, if you only open the wrong gate. Fuckyou.com is the least of it. On you go to 'Fuck niggers and kikes white power', a YouTube video, or Kill a Jew Day and 'Join if you hate homosexuals', both formerly on Facebook. No sooner is one head of the cyberhydra cut off than three more appear. Some people despair. Declaring that he would abandon Twitter, the Indian film star Shah Rukh Khan wrote, 'Sad, i read so much judgements, jingoism, religious intolerance on the net & i use to think this platform wl change narrowmindedness, but no!'[80]

The classic liberal answer is 'we should respond to bad speech with more and better speech' — or counterspeech for short. Counterspeech online is made more difficult by the 'echo chamber' effect, where people seek out the company of those who share and reinforce their particular prejudice. These reinforced prejudices can then appear on the streets of multicultural cities as discrimination, harassment or murder.

Online anonymity further encourages the expression of naked prejudice and faecal rudeness. A piquant example is the official YouTube campaign video of the No Hate Speech Movement, an admirable counterspeech initiative with a logo showing a loving heart. This came up second when I entered the search term 'hate speech' on YouTube in February 2013, despite its having just

4,909 views in 10 months. Yet among the 'top comments' on the YouTube page were DemilichFan saying,

> about 100 white women in the US are raped every day by black men . . . Do you suppose the No Hate Speech Movement gives a shit about these crimes? This is just anti-White cultural marxism.

And varashnikov observing,

> Niggers are less intelligent than white Aryans. Hitler did nothing wrong!

'No Hate Speech' indeed. Anyone familiar with online commentary will recognise the tone.

A couple of virtual bowel movements further down we have foxtailedcritter, who observes:

> Look it doesn't matter if you're a Nigger, Fag, Chink, Americunt, Greasy Italian, Jap, Cracker, Germball German, Towel Head, Transgender-faggot, Hoe, Shit stabber, Dyke, Fence Jumper Mexican, Failure Nazi, White Burning Ghost (KKK), Spick, Spook, Juan or anything else you're still going to have a hate word against you. So instead of bawwing man the fuck up and get on with it or go an hero yourself.

At first glance, this may look like more of the same, but then foxtailedcritter adds an almost charming postscript:

> Oh shit i forgot to say Ausfailure (Where I'm from.) Point is quit your bitching like a baby and man up or drink bleach either one will do.

This may not be exactly what Montaigne or Adam Ferguson would have recognised as civility, yet our Australian friend is not expressing prejudice but rather urging us to ignore it. And ignoring the sewage is what most of us do online most of the time. Any practical prescription for dealing with hate speech in cosmopolis must include a large element of that everyday common sense.

Yet plainly we cannot leave it at that. Who else can do what else to uphold robust civility, without resorting to hate speech laws? First of all, there is much that a liberal state can do in its expressive rather than its coercive role. In 2004, an interesting revision was made to the 190-year-old Norwegian constitution. After a detailed affirmation of the constitutional right to freedom of expression and information, Article 100 says: 'It is the responsibility of the authorities of the State to create conditions that facilitate open and enlightened public discourse'.[81]

How? All political leaders can set an example in the way they talk about minorities and human difference of all kinds in their own societies. Most leaders of mature democracies speak out after a particularly shocking crime: the stabbing of a black youth or a white soldier, for instance, or an extremist group setting fire to a house lived in by Turkish Gastarbeiter. Far fewer politicians are prepared to go against the prejudices of their voters on a regular basis. Chancellor Angela Merkel, for example, initially reacted to Thilo Sarrazin's reported views by saying, 'Such simplistically sweeping judgements are stupid and don't get us any further'. Yet when his simplistically sweeping judgements turned out to be popular among her own conservative electorate, she temporised. She told her Christian Democrat party conference that she 'takes seriously . . . the broad discussion about migrants of the Muslim faith', and 'it is after all not the case that we have too much Islam, but rather that we have too little Christianity'.[82]

Often, the cry of 'something must be done' moves governments another notch down the taboo ratchet. Thus, outrage at brutal attacks on individual French and British soldiers by Islamist extremists led politicians in both countries to call for the blocking of extremist websites and a sharpening of hate speech laws. For the democratic politician, it is so much easier to pass the task of combatting hate speech to officials or judges, rather than risk losing electoral support by doing it yourself.

It is not just politicians whose voices count. Film and sports stars often have wider influence. Just as politicians should not pass the buck of moral leadership to the courts, so leaders and role models in civil society should not leave it to the state. One word from the Indian film idol Shah Rukh Khan is worth ten thousand from an Indian politician.

To say that schools have a vital role in forming members of a civil society should be a statement of the obvious. Yet the political debate about education in mature democracies has tended to emphasise the economic function of education (teaching job skills and making the country more competitive) at the expense of this civic one. Less obvious is how schools should do it. One mistake is to wallow in benign platitudes, hoping social harmony can be achieved merely by proclaiming it, with the aid of bland history textbooks and bowdlerised literary classics. Another is the artificial accentuation of a limited palette of human differences, based on ascribed group characteristics such as race, religion, ethnicity or nationality. Worst of all is a combination of the two.

Instead, schools should prepare people for living with diversity by talking about it. Some English schools have developed a technique they call 'constructive controversy'. Tackling sensitive subjects such as race, religion or the death penalty, they invite pupils to make the case, with reasons and evidence, for what they considered to be right. Then they have to swap sides and make the best case they can for an opposing view. I watched this in the classroom of a school where more than half the pupils come from an ethnic minority background. As they debated the legalisation of drugs and the place of women in sport (a sensitive issue for Muslim parents), the effect was remarkable. I could almost see a lightbulb of mutual understanding being switched on.[83]

Young people are thus equipped to think critically about prejudices they may well have inherited from their parents and to understand where other people are 'coming from'. They are led to think for themselves. But they are also asked to step inside someone's skin, to have that imaginative sympathy which is a vital complement to the critical use of reason and which can be learned from studying literature, theatre and art. Teachers at a more advanced stage can dig down to explore what have been called the 'hidden biases of good people'—the 'mindbugs' of which we ourselves are not aware, revealed by techniques such as implicit association tests.[84] Teachers can also show, with the aid of research in social psychology, how vulnerable the human spirit is to the expression of prejudice. Experiments suggest, for example, that if women are emphatically warned that they are unlikely to be good at a test in mathematics or science, they do less well than those who have not been so warned. Not least, teachers can explicitly discuss both sides of the question of freedom of expression: not just 'how free should speech be?' but also 'how should free speech be?'

As I stressed in discussing the dissemination of knowledge, the principle of 'no taboos' has to be qualified in the case of young minds faced with an older person in a position of authority. One of the landmark hate speech cases in Canada concerned a teacher, James Keegstra, who told his pupils that Jews were 'child killers' who had 'created the Holocaust to gain sympathy'. He also marked students down if they did not reproduce these views in exams. Corey Brettschneider argues that it was wrong to subject Keegstra to criminal prosecution, but he should certainly not have been left to propagate anti-Semitic falsehoods in the classroom. Today, a bright future would have awaited him as a pseudonymous ranter on the No Hate Speech YouTube thread.[85]

The danger of trying to brush over prejudices that exist, supported by a legal backstop of criminalisation, rather than developing a pedagogy of open debate, is well illustrated in the story of a former French schoolmaster, Marc-Antoine Dilhac, who went on to be a professor of ethics and political philosophy at the University of Montréal. While teaching a class of 18-year-olds in a small town in southern France, Dilhac had occasion to show a picture of the gas ovens at Auschwitz. 'At that very moment', he recalls, 'I heard from behind someone telling an awful joke and his friends laughing out loud: "they used the oven to get tanned, you know . . . '". Dilhac angrily confronted them and got nowhere.

The next day, having reflected on his own response, he invited his pupils to a frank discussion of their views. 'At first, my proposal was roughly dismissed: "no sir, we cannot talk about that. For one thing, we're not on the same side, you know it, we know it. And if we told you what we thought of Jews, we would break the law, you would have to make a report to the head, and we would be in big trouble . . . So please let's move on"'. But he managed to convince them that whatever they said would not go beyond the four walls of that classroom.

Then the teenagers opened up. 'Basically', Dilhac writes, 'they thought in good faith that because of the Shoah, we do not pay attention to other massacres such as genocide in Rwanda; they claimed that because of the past suffering of Jews, we shut our eyes to the suffering of Palestinians. It is worth mentioning that there was no Arab, no North African in my class'. These were native-born, rural French lads. At the end of an intense, frank discussion 'they told me that they were grateful that I let them talk freely, that they understood the mistakes and why it was morally wrong to support and spread anti-Semitic views'. In a thoughtful conclusion, Dilhac acknowledges that such a change would be more difficult to achieve in the wider public sphere.[86] But one can turn that thought around: it is easier to change young minds in a direct encounter with the authority of the teacher than to change more settled older ones in a more diffuse public sphere, especially when struggling against an echo chamber effect on the internet. So don't delay the open debate. Start young.

Once minds are older and more rigid, opening them is more difficult. But there are still powerful influences at work, all of which can cut both ways. Four of the most important are advertising, media, online platforms and, last but not least, everyday personal interactions. Advertising is a huge business which produces some of the most widely visible, artfully produced and striking images around us. These images often appeal not to our reason and conscious sense of ourselves, but to hidden desires and biases. That makes them all the more powerful. The faces we see in advertisements may always be beautiful, but what we see if we honestly look at ourselves in the mirror of advertising is a lot less pretty. One advertisement for BMW showed a handsome young male model in bed on top of, and presumably penetrating, a largely naked young woman. Entirely covering her face is a large photograph of a BMW car. Across the advertisement runs this slogan: 'the ultimate attraction'.[87] So a BMW is an even better sex machine than a woman—*and* it does not answer back. There are several ways in which we, as members of a would-be civil society, can counter such advertising images. We can make ourselves critically alert to what they are up to, starting with a lesson in advertising literacy at school. We can dismiss them with contempt and ridicule them with satire. Not least, we can protest to the companies concerned (and head off to sleep with a Saab instead).

There are, to be sure, some aspects of advertising which involve core goods of free speech: informed choice, even if the information presented is partial and one-sided, not to mention human creativity and humour. Moreover, advertising regulation can be abused by intrusive public powers. A magnificent example, worthy of Gogol, was found by a Russian student on our freespeechdebate. com team, Sergey Fadeev. A taxi company in the Russian city of Kostroma was fined 4,000 roubles for an advertisement saying, 'If you make five typos in the word "bread" you get "taxi"'. The local Council of Veterans had complained that the ad 'besmirches the Slavic people and insults the world's revered bread'. The authority responsible for enforcing the Russian advertising law found that the taxi company's slogan was 'offensive for products such as bread'. As Sergey observed: 'if you can be fined for offending bread, what next?'[88]

Yet within reasonable limits, it is hard to maintain that some regulation of advertising restricts what is valuable in free speech, in the way that curbs on political expression, scientific research or news reporting plainly do. For the most part, the purpose of 'commercial speech' is to sell us things we might not otherwise buy—appealing to, magnifying and even manufacturing our desires. If an advertising regulator tries to protect children from highly sexualised images on billboards near schools, must we really protest on grounds of free speech? Or if an ad for Marlboro cigarettes implies that they will make you a healthy, sexy cowboy? The harm of limiting free speech is in this case outweighed by the harm of smoking.

When it comes to ethnic or religious differences, the negative influence of biased, stereotyping and sometimes outright inflammatory media coverage is probably greater than that of advertising. It would take just a few hours to compile a whole international anthology of such coverage. Much of it is quite unvarnished: 'A Jew to represent Turkey in Eurovision?' asked one Turkish headline.[89] More is revealed by content analysis. Figure 15 gives one example, from British press coverage of Muslims.

Among the groups subject to the most persistently negative coverage across Europe are the Roma, arguably the continent's most discriminated-against minority. In the Turkish media, it is Armenians and Kurds who generally come off worst. Media across the Middle East either do not report on homosexuality or do so in relentlessly hostile ways, using words that in English might come out as 'pervert' or 'faggot'.[90]

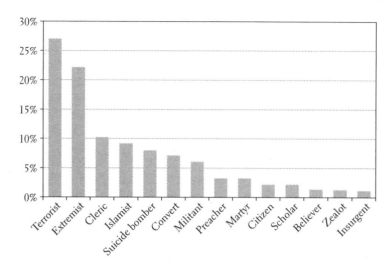

Figure 15. Muslims in the British press
The most common nouns used in conjunction with Muslims, based on a search
of UK national newspapers in the Nexis database, 2000–2008.
Source: Petley et al. 2011.

How can this be countered without illegitimate curbs on free speech? In general terms, we need uncensored, diverse and trustworthy media, as discussed in the previous chapter. Specifically, we need a dual representation of diversity: in the media and by the media. If there is a significant minority in a given society, we need to see some of their faces on television, hear their voices on radio, read their bylines in print and online. This should not be achieved by giving jobs to people not competent to do them, nor should the two kinds of representation be confused. Precisely because the suspicion will be that 'she's only there because she's black/Muslim/female/whatever . . .', we should not ask Muslim journalists only to report on Muslims, any more than we expect Christians only to report on Christian matters, or women only on women. At the height of the Eurozone crisis, I got my daily update from the economics correspondent of Britain's Channel 4 News. His name was Faisal Islam, but I was not turning to him for news about Islam.

As for the representation of diversity by the media, this is a vital component of media pluralism. Part of the state's expressive function can be to support public service media in minority languages, or covering minority communities.

Admittedly this, like hate speech laws, carries the risk of stimulating successive self-identified minorities to lobby for state recognition. As our diversity becomes ever more diverse, including majority-minority communities, it becomes increasingly difficult to decide who deserves special treatment. Unlike hate speech laws, however, public subsidy of media pluralism increases the range of available ideas, images and ways of seeing and feeling, rather than decreasing it.

Even less problematic is support for minority media by NGOs or individual donors. Thus, to give just one example, the Budapest-based Romedia Foundation, supported by George Soros, has produced sympathetic television documentaries on many aspects of Roma life in Europe. It would be an exaggeration to say, as does its director, Katalin Barsony, that Romedia does 'objective journalism'.[91] Its social impact may also be doubted, given that these documentaries are generally taken up by relatively small-audience channels. Nonetheless, this is a desperately needed corrective to overwhelmingly negative media coverage.

The editorial standards of public service and quality private media also spell out the mixture of openness, journalistic care and sensitivity with which such issues should be treated. Some broadcasters and newspapers have complaints procedures, and some countries mandate a right of reply for those who reasonably feel they have been misrepresented. We, the citizens, can also take our own steps to scrutinise how media represent us. For example, a foundation established in memory of the assassinated Turkish-Armenian journalist Hrant Dink carefully monitors what it calls hate speech in the Turkish media, especially about Armenians, Kurds and other minorities.[92] I might quarrel with its expansive definition of hate speech, but since this is not enforced by coercive state power, it cannot remotely be considered a barrier to free speech. Again, we may wonder about its impact, but it is a resource. Many journalistic prejudice-pedlars are named; a few might even feel shamed.

Equally important is the way writers and intellectuals from minority communities write and speak about problems that arise in those communities. Following Orwell's advice, we should be especially critical of our own side—precisely because it is our side. When mainstream British media were tiptoeing gingerly around the fact that an appalling child sex ring uncovered in Oxford consisted largely of British Asian and at least culturally Muslim men exploiting young white girls, a local Muslim intellectual, Dr. Taj Hargey, bravely wrote: 'apart from its sheer depravity, what also depresses me about this case is a widespread refusal to face up to its hard realities. The fact is that the vicious activities of the Oxford ring are bound up with religion and race: religion, because all the perpetrators, though they had different nationalities, were Muslim; and race, because they deliberately targeted vulnerable white girls, whom they appeared to regard as "easy meat", to use one of their revealing, racist phrases'.[93]

By rights, the most effective constraint on media should be us, the readers, viewers and users. Recalling Albert Hirschman's famous triad of exit, voice or loyalty, either our voice or our exit should have an impact. Unfortunately, there are few positive examples. When we cross the increasingly blurred line between media and online platforms (the dichotomy of 'old' and 'new' media is itself hopelessly old), this is even more true. As we have seen, user-generated content is, amongst other things, a vast anthology of rudeness and prejudice. Users, especially when speaking anonymously, often turn out to be less civil even than the most cynical, whisky-soaked hack. Witness those comments on the No Hate Speech video.

What is to be done about this sewage-ocean of online hate? When faced with demands for external regulation, whether of hate speech, defamation or intrusions into privacy, the big American online platforms typically have two responses. Most of the time they say, 'We should not be held responsible as a newspaper or publisher. We do not have "intermediary liability". We are more like what in American legal usage is called a "common carrier" (such as a telephone network) or a "public square". To ask us to block or filter content is to infringe "net neutrality" and "internet freedom" (unless the content is illegal in the US)'. But sometimes they call on, or at least imply, a quite different argument: 'You are infringing our First Amendment right to free speech'. The American legal scholar Eugene Volokh has made this argument explicitly even for Google Search.[94]

Logically, these positions are incompatible but in the messiness of real life there is an awkward mixture of the two. As we have seen, even the supposedly neutral Google Search makes editorial and value judgements. Many of these are hidden in its algorithms, but a few are made explicit. On 7 February 2014, the opening day of the Winter Olympics in Vladimir Putin's Russia, which had been much criticised for its anti-gay legislation, the famously minimalist Google Search home page carried not just colourful, stylised images of winter sports athletes but also, under the search box, a quotation from the Olympic Charter: 'The practice of sport is a human right. Every individual must have the possibility of practising sport, without discrimination of any kind and in the Olympic spirit, which requires mutual understanding with a spirit of friendship, solidarity and fair play'. The words 'without discrimination of any kind' were not actually put in bold, but this was nonetheless an American liberal editorial.[95]

On the other hand, a global search engine or a social media site with more than 1 billion users plainly cannot be responsible for everything that appears on it, as I and the publishers are responsible for every word that appears in this book. So these online platforms struggle between their own desire to maintain certain basic standards; the fear of being held legally responsible as publishers or being denounced for 'censorship'; the pressure from states, lobbyists and civil society to do more in areas such as hate speech; and, above all, the sheer mass of user-generated content appearing on their pages every day.

I shall concentrate on Facebook and YouTube, not only because they are two of the biggest platforms but also because, aspiring to host 'global communities', they both face the problem that millions of people across the world post both words and images that others find offensive, hateful and sometimes harmful (but applying widely varying notions of harm). In 2015, an estimated 300 hours of video were uploaded to YouTube every minute, while some 1.8 billion photographs were shared on Facebook, WhatsApp, Flickr and Instagram every day.[96] Facebook received more than 10 million reports of offensive material every week, and that was only for stuff that others noticed and were moved to complain about.[97] There might be far worse things up there that people did not notice, or did not flag because they agreed with it: the 'Kalar Beheading Gang' and other anti-Rohingya incitement in Burmese, for example, or anti-Roma agitation in Europe.

How should Facebook or YouTube manage this unprecedented challenge? Automated filtering designed by clever engineers can detect nudity and block much spam. But even the world's most sophisticated algorithm cannot make the individual judgement of time, place, manner and context which determines what is hate speech, as opposed to merely rude speech, and when hate speech becomes dangerous speech. A trivial but amusing example arose when Facebook's automated system refused to allow someone to identify his or her hometown as Effin. But there is a real town called Effin, in County Limerick in the Irish Republic. Ann Marie Kennedy, who started an online Facebook group to secure recognition, explained, 'I'm a proud Effin woman and I always will be an Effin woman'.[98]

Facebook and YouTube would need an army of private censors bigger than that of the Chinese party-state to enforce their own proclaimed community standards consistently, without waiting for user reports, across all the pages of perhaps 2 billion users, in all languages. Both platforms try to combine active top-down and 'community-led' bottom-up approaches. They have teams of what the legal commentator Jeffrey Rosen has dubbed the Deciders, sitting at screens in Mountain View and a few other places, deciding what their community standards should be, how they should be interpreted and which controversial items should be taken down.[99] This is not the judgement of Paris but the judgement of Mountain View. Google, writes Tim Wu, exaggerating to make the point, 'is trying to create a free speech jurisprudence, a project that the Supreme Court spent much of the 20th century working on'.[100] Yet there is no democratically elected parliament to make their laws, no legal process and scant right of appeal.

These Deciders, however, are only responding to user reports. Facebook and YouTube are coy about the number of full-time Deciders they have. In 2014 both told me 'hundreds', but by 2015 it was over 1,000 each. YouTube developed a 'smart queue' of flaggers, prioritising takedown requests by such criteria as the nature of the complaint, whether the item had been flagged already and the track record of the flagger. Partly in response to lobbying by interest groups and governments, it created a group of privileged flaggers whose alerts were given top priority. They included the British Home Office. According to a senior figure at YouTube, reports from these privileged sources had a 90 percent removal rate, as against around 30 percent for all flagging.[101] Amusingly, YouTube initially called these privileged flaggers 'Deputies'. YouTube was like Gary Cooper in 'High Noon', handing out Deputies' stars (except with more takers). So now, as well as competing for special recognition by the state, identity lobbies can compete for special recognition by the private superpowers. Facebook, for its part, developed a layered system of social reporting. One of its public policy leaders, Richard Allan, explained this to me in the form of the pyramid shown in Figure 16.[102]

All this will obviously continue to develop, but the basic free speech issues are clear. The American online platforms say they defend freedom against state censorship; their critics accuse them of practising censorship. They insist they are upholding a single, free, worldwide internet against Balkanisation and authoritarian interference; China, Russia and Iran denounce them for creating cybercolonies of the United States. The Deciders of Silicon Valley implement standards of American universalism as well as commercial self-interest; bottom-up community reporting will naturally favour cultural particularism. Burmese users will not report things that Californians would report, and vice versa. How do you navigate between the opposing cliffs of unilateral universalism and moral relativism?

There have been small but promising experiments in promoting counter-speech. A Facebook page known as WHOF — originally 'Wipeout Homophobia on Facebook' — acquired more than 400,000 'likes'. It became not just a place to flag, report and share concerns about homophobic Facebook pages but a community resource for all those touched by hostility to homosexuality.[103] And remember Syed Mahmood's YouTube response to the 'Innocence of Muslims',

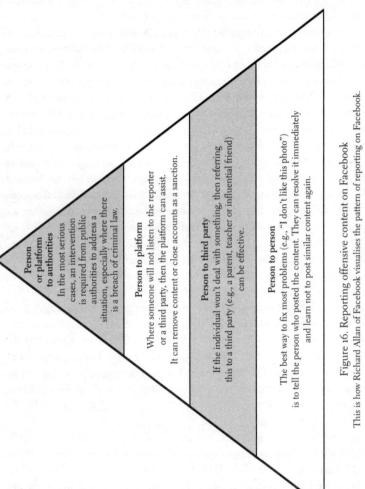

Person or platform to authorities
In the most serious cases, an intervention is required from public authorities to address a situation, especially where there is a breach of criminal law.

Person to platform
Where someone will not listen to the reporter or a third party, then the platform can assist. It can remove content or close accounts as a sanction.

Person to third party
If the individual won't deal with something, then referring this to a third party (e.g., a parent, teacher or influential friend) can be effective.

Person to person
The best way to fix most problems (e.g., "I don't like this photo") is to tell the person who posted the content. They can resolve it immediately and learn not to post similar content again.

Figure 16. Reporting offensive content on Facebook
This is how Richard Allan of Facebook visualises the pattern of reporting on Facebook.
Source: Richard Allan, personal communication.

with its nearly half a million viewings. It is hard to predict exactly what will catch on, but there is every reason for users, platforms, NGOs and governments to explore what works best. The devil should not always have the best tunes.

Finally, there is everyday life. We may say of a teenager who spends his days in front of a computer screen that he 'lives online', but most people don't live on-line. Nor do they live entirely offline. They live in a combination of the virtual and physical worlds. Direct, personal, human interaction is still the most important thing for most of us, in love as in hate. If you ask people with a migrant background what has helped them feel at home in the country or city where they live, or hindered them from integrating, they almost invariably mention everyday interactions at school, at work and in the street. Small slights alienate; small courtesies integrate. The quality of civility therefore remains most vital in its original sphere: that of real people meeting real people. Amongst the qualities that take civility beyond Hobbes's 'Small Moralls'—although one could argue that this all belongs to good manners, properly understood—is what is now called cultural competence. As in those bank advertisements plastered along the walls of airport boarding ramps, you have to know which hand gesture is a sign of greeting in one culture but an insult in another.

It is one thing to argue that an ever-longer list of epithets, symbols and gestures should be banned by law. It is quite another to suggest that we voluntarily refrain from using them in contexts where we judge that people might be hurt or just offended by them. Here, unlike in law, a concern about mere offensiveness is perfectly appropriate. A right to offend does not mean a duty to offend. Yet the rich grammar of real-life interactions allows for much more than a simple binary choice between civil and offensive. What are apparently the most outrageous ethnic slurs can have a completely different meaning when delivered humorously. This brings us to two of our most important assets for achieving freedom in diversity.

ART AND HUMOUR

'What are the three most important questions for a Basque?' Answer: 'Who are we? Where do we come from? Where shall we go for dinner?' (The Basques are famous for their cuisine and their devotion to it.) 'What's the difference between an introvert Finn and an extrovert Finn?' 'When you're introduced to him, the extrovert looks down at *your* shoes'. 'What's the difference between the Slovak National Uprising and the film about the Slovak National Uprising?' 'The film is half an hour longer'. 'I'm the only Iranian comedian in the world', says Omid Djalili, 'and that's three more than Germany'. Another Djalili joke:

Two Indian men are in bed together, and one says to the other, 'I tell you, this wife-swapping is a terrible waste of time'. Half the jokes told by humankind draw upon national, ethnic, religious, social or sexual slurs.

For at least 2,500 years, comedy and satire have enjoyed special licence to transgress the frontiers of civility, decency and decorum. In the fifth century B.C.E., the Athenian tyrant Cleon tried to shut up the playwright Aristophanes but failed under the pressure of public opinion.[104] For just as long, the powerful have been trying to suffocate the spirit of satire. In 2012, the South African president Jacob Zuma went to court to have removed from a gallery and website a picture titled The Spear, which showed him fully clothed in a smart suit, but with a giant penis sticking out.[105]

Humour is a deflater, a safety valve, a way of talking about things that we don't otherwise discuss—and a priceless antidote to all fanaticisms. In the early 1990s, on the burnt-out shell of the post office in Sarajevo, destroyed in bitter fighting as Bosniak Bosnians defended themselves against Bosnian Serbs, a Serb had scrawled the familiar red graffito 'This is Serbia!' That was crossed out by a Bosniak, who declared, 'This is Bosnia!' Underneath, a third graffitist wrote: 'No, you idiots, this is a post office'.[106]

Now, more than ever, we need the spirit of the third graffitist. The Israeli novelist and political writer Amos Oz observes, 'I have never once in my life seen a fanatic with a sense of humour, nor have I ever seen a person with a sense of humour becoming a fanatic, unless he or she has lost that sense of humour'. If only, Oz reflects, he could compress a sense of humour into capsules 'and persuade entire populations to swallow my humour pills, thus immunising everybody against fanaticism'.[107]

Interestingly, in its landmark judgement on 'fighting words', the US Supreme Court defined them as those 'said without a disarming smile'.[108] The 'disarming' capacity of humour is not merely metaphorical. While living in London, Voltaire was set upon by a mob, who berated him as a 'French dog'. He averted a beating by standing on a nearby boundary stone and saying, 'My fine Englishmen, am I not already wretched enough that I was not born one of ye?'[109]

Humour consistently transgresses conventional norms of civility but also enables and strengthens civility. While this is unprovable, I would posit a strong correlation between humour and tolerance in any society. At best, humour consciously subverts prejudice. A Jew goes into a Belfast pub and is immediately asked, 'Are you a Catholic or Protestant?' 'I'm a Jew', he says. 'But are you a Catholic Jew or a Protestant Jew?' Or again: A Jew and a black man are sitting next to one another in the New York subway. To his astonishment, the Jew sees that his black neighbour is reading a newspaper in Yiddish. He asks, 'Are you *Jewish*?' 'Hey man', comes the reply, 'give me a break'.[110]

A remarkable illustration of this positive effect comes from Senegal, which has a well-established custom of what the political scientist Alfred Stepan describes as 'bantering games and pretend insults which deliberately involve unfavourable stereotypes of the other person's ethnic group'. One anthropological survey found that 40 percent of Senegalese respondents said they practised such joking exchanges 'everyday' or 'often'. Asked why relations between ethnic communities in Senegal were good, one in four mentioned 'joking'.[111]

But hateful and arguably harmful prejudice can also be smuggled in under the guise of art and humour. 'I was only joking', says the racist or sexist. 'Have you no sense of humour?' Was that portrayal of Zuma a legitimate satire on 'political power and patriarchy', as the artist argued, or racial stereotype? And how about these lines from the rapper Eminem's track 'White America':

All I hear is: lyrics, lyrics, constant controversy, sponsors working round the clock, to try to stop my concerts early
surely hip hop was never a problem in Harlem only in Boston, after it bothered the fathers of daughters starting to blossom
so now I'm catching the flak from these activists when they raggin', actin' like I'm the first rapper to smack a bitch, or say faggot
shit, just look at me like I'm your closest pal, the poster child, the motherfuckin' spokesman now for—White America! . . .

and his supremely civil conclusion:

Fuck you, Ms. Cheney! Fuck you, Tipper Gore!
Fuck you with the free-est of speech this divided states of embarrassment will allow me to have, Fuck you!

You might not want your little daughter to listen to it, but nor would Eminem let his daughter Hailie: 'I don't blame you, I wouldn't let Hailie listen to me neither'.[112]

But now consider the Cameroonian-French comedian Dieudonné, who used his comic licence to say of the French-Jewish radio anchor Patrick Cohen: 'Me, you see, when I hear Patrick Cohen speak, I think to myself—"gas chambers . . . too bad"'.[113] Just a joke? The French president was perhaps ill advised to suggest that local authorities deny Dieudonné performance venues on the grounds of 'public order', thus giving the provocateur free publicity from the highest level. But neither should that remark be accepted as legitimate humour.

Even comedy has its limits, which must be determined by artistic and social judgement. Everything depends on who is expressing what, when, how and where. While making a vigorous defence of the right to offend, the British cartoonist Martin Rowson says he follows the American satirist H. L. Mencken in defining his role as to 'comfort the afflicted and afflict the comfortable'. In consequence, Rowson reflects that he would not have commissioned a page of cartoons of Muhammad, as Jyllands-Posten did, 'because they targeted people less powerful than themselves' and therefore failed his 'Mencken test'.[114]

Sometimes the difference between a Jewish joke and an anti-Semitic one is who is telling it, for many classic Jewish jokes are jokes against Jews. The American TV comedy show 'Seinfeld' captured this perfectly in a skit about a dentist who converted to Judaism and immediately started telling Jewish jokes. Visiting a priest to complain about the dentist's conversion, the Jewish comedian character Jerry complains that the dentist converted 'just for the jokes'. 'And this offends you as a Jewish person?' asks the priest, solicitously. 'No', replies Jerry, 'as a comedian'.[115]

What is true of humour can also be said of literature, and art more broadly. According to the Czech novelist Milan Kundera, the two are closely connected. Accepting the Jerusalem prize in 1985, Kundera quoted a Jewish proverb: 'Man thinks, God laughs'. 'Inspired by that adage', he went on, 'I like to think that François Rabelais heard God's laughter one day, and thus was born the idea of the first great European novel. It pleases me to think that the art of the novel came into the world as an echo of God's laughter'.[116] What God is laughing at, according to Kundera's creative interpretation of Jewish tradition, is the fact that the more people think, the more they differ. We are back to diversity again.

Zadie Smith's rambunctious novel of multicultural London, *White Teeth*, begins with the leading character, Archie Jones, trying to kill himself by feeding the exhaust fumes through a tube into the driver's window of his car, which is stopped outside the Hussein-Ishmael, a halal butcher's shop. But the butcher, Mo Hussein-Ishmael, foils his attempt, forcing open the driver's window and saying, 'we're not licensed for suicides around here. This place halal. Kosher, understand? If you're going to die round here, my friend, I'm afraid you've got to be thoroughly bled first'.[117] Grossly offensive to both Muslims and Jews. Prosecute the author at once.

Literature, theatre, film, painting, sculpture and many other arts enable us to understand the experience of others in countless ways, with what Martha Nussbaum has called the 'inner eye' of imaginative sympathy.[118] They allow us to get inside the skin of other human beings who live in utterly different circumstances from our own, and to discover common humanity beneath the alien garb. The benefit of such empathy is not just that I see myself in the Ecuadorean campesino or the Japanese gangster. The ultimate prize of the liberal imagination is to see oneself as another—*soi-même comme une autre*—in the memorable phrase of the French philosopher Paul Ricoeur.[119]

The distance we can traverse through art is not just geographical and cultural; it is also historical. Travelling across centuries, we find the same duality of deep cultural difference and shared humanity. 'The past is a foreign country: they do things differently there', as the famous opening line of an English novel has it.[120] It is obviously right that children should not be casually exposed to a jingle like 'eenie, meenie, minie, moe, catch a nigger by his toe', as I was in my early childhood. It is wrong that children should not be taught one of the great works of American literature, *The Adventures of Huckleberry Finn*, because its author uses the word 'nigger'.[121] Lesser writers can be useful for a history lesson, since they exemplify the attitudes of another time. Great writers teach an even more important lesson, since they simultaneously reflect and transcend the attitudes of their time.

Censorship touches many areas of speech—politics, journalism, science—but it is no accident that so many celebrated cases of censorship have concerned works of art, for art, like humour, transgresses. In a fine book called *Transgressions: The Offences of Art*, Anthony Julius offers eight possible interpretations of Theodor Adorno's famous epigram: 'Every work of art is an uncommitted crime'.[122] Artists are to speech what explorers are to travel. The histories of art and censorship are two different ways of mapping the same territory.

Many of these cases appear ridiculous today. We laugh about the 1960 English court case against the publication ban on D. H. Lawrence's novel *Lady Chatterley's Lover*, with its explicit and erotic scenes of lovemaking between the lady of the house and the gamekeeper. 'Is it a book that you would even wish your wife or your servants to read?' a prosecution lawyer asked the jury.[123] Even after the book was allowed to be published in England, the Lord Chamberlain's office—the official censor of English theatre until 1968—insisted that a 1961 stage production show the lady and the gamekeeper decently clothed as they ascended to orgasm.[124]

We may find less hilarious some of the 1960s ideas of limitless sexual liberation that contributed to the sweeping away of those prudish censorial sensibilities. In the 1970s and early 1980s, a British group called the Paedophile Information Exchange promoted sex between adults and children in the name of sexual liberation. The group was widely criticised at the time but also received some support. For some years, it was affiliated with the National Council for Civil Liberties. In 1977 the Campaign for Homosexual Equality passed by a large majority a resolution condemning 'the harassment of the Paedophile Information Exchange by the press'.[125] A half century later, England saw a wave of prosecutions of elderly pop stars and disc jockeys for sexually harassing underage girls in the 1960s and 1970s. Norms change over the decades. (What habits and taboos of our own time will our grandchildren look back on as either horrendous or fatuous? Our treatment of animals? Our insouciance about the ecological destruction of our planet?)

None of this is to suggest that there is another country called Art where anything and everything may be expressed, with no limits at all. Take the alleged anti-Semitism of the poet T. S. Eliot. Critics argue furiously over whether lines like 'the Jew is underneath the lot' are anti-Semitic.[126] It seems to me that they probably are, although we should not view pre-Holocaust language through a post-Holocaust lens. We can sigh: 'look how even the greatest writer can share the prejudices of his time'. But Eliot should not get a free pass just because this is Literature. Otherwise, you risk introducing a kind of class system in insults. The famous poet's anti-Semitism is quietly ignored, as if the king had farted at a banquet, but the street-level anti-Semitism of an impoverished immigrant brings the police to his door. Arguably, the reverse should be the case. The writer, 'accustomed to responsibility by language', as Thomas Mann once put it, should be held to a higher standard, not by the law but by a civil and civilised society.[127]

Moreover, the frontiers of art, like those of humour, will always be contested. There is no internationally recognised border with a sign saying, 'You are now entering the Kingdom of Art' or 'Welcome to the Republic of Humour'. As the example of Dieudonné shows, the claims of artistic and comic license can be abused. The frontier is especially elusive in the case of contemporary visual arts, where the definition of art sometimes seems to be 'what is shown in a gallery'. This applies also to the more or less 'artistic' depiction of naked women, men, children and sexual acts.

PORNOGRAPHY

In 2013, the British Museum organised an exhibition called 'Shunga: Sex and Pleasure in Japanese Art'. The paintings and prints from a tradition of erotic art going back centuries were, as the journalist Katie Englehart describes them,

> replete with pubic hair and sex toys and gravitationally implausible scenes of coitus. One shows a nun with a shaved head having sex with a priest who is hidden in a large bag. Another shows a group of men engaged in a 'phallic competition': their gigantic, exaggerated penises resting on tables and kickstands. A third shows a woman being pleasured by two octopuses.

The exhibition curator said Shunga 'celebrates the pleasures of lovemaking, in beautiful pictures that present mutual attraction and sexual desire as natural and unaffected'. And he reflected, 'in the West, we have created a state of affairs where there has to be a firewall between art and pornography, but Shunga is both sexually explicit and demonstrably art'.[128]

More intense controversy has been generated by well-known artists and photographers using images of children. An exhibition in Cincinnati showed a photograph by Robert Mapplethorpe of a four-year-old girl sitting on a garden bench, wearing a skirt that clearly revealed her genitals. The museum director was charged with obscenity and the misuse of a minor in pornography. Australian police raided a gallery in Sydney and removed photographs by the well-known artist Bill Henson, including one of a naked teenage girl. After Finnish police closed down an exhibition titled 'The Virgin-Whore Church', which featured hundreds of images of child pornography in an attempt to provoke discussion about how easily available they are, the European Court of Human Rights found that this display had indeed been an exercise of freedom of expression. However, since it showed child pornography, the police action was legitimately and proportionately enforcing a limit that was, in the familiar wording of the European Convention, 'necessary in a democratic society'.[129]

Pornography is one of the most debated subjects in the Western literature on free speech over the last half century, and among the most contentious. What is pornography? Is it art? Is it 'masturbation material', as the feminist writer Catharine MacKinnon declared? Is it speech? Is it hate speech? If we take the definition of pornography offered by Ogi Ogas, 'anything that stimulates the sexual regions of your brain', then it probably covers much of men's everyday life, and a fair amount of art history.[130] By contrast, Catharine MacKinnon and Andrea Dworkin more narrowly defined it as 'the graphic sexually explicit subordination of women through pictures and/or words'.[131]

The range of evils attributed to pornography range from some of the most terrible harms anywhere—such as the sexual abuse of children—through the gamut of justifications for hate speech bans, with phrases such as 'cultural harm' being used to describe its effect on wider social attitudes.[132] Arguments against it are made on grounds of harm, offence, paternalism (or maternalism) and moralism, to recall Joel Feinberg's categorisation.

Jo Fidgen, a journalist who describes herself as 'a feminist and liberal', has looked carefully into the academic research on the subject and finds it satiated with ideology.[133] Take, for example, the claims for a causal connection between pornography and sexual violence. Quoting the case of a man who committed a particularly horrible sexual murder of a little girl after reading an issue of Penthouse showing women tied up and hung, Catharine MacKinnon asserts that 'such linear causality, an obsession of pornography's defenders, is not all that rare or difficult to prove'.[134] But a US presidential commission and the British committee on obscenity chaired by the philosopher Bernard Williams both concluded that a general causal connection was not firmly established.[135] Other studies argued that the overall incidence of sex crimes actually declined as pornography became more widely available in Japan and Denmark. So does fantasy lead to reality or substitute for it?[136] Neil Malamuth, who has spent years researching the evidence, summarises his conclusions: 'exposure to pornography does not have negative effects on attitudes supporting violence against women, sexually aggressive tendencies, for the majority of men. However, such exposure to pornography—particularly . . . violent pornography—does have a negative effect on an important sub-set of men, namely those who have other risk factors for committing sexual aggression'. But even if the latter group is small, the effect must be dangerous, increasing the likelihood of particularly brutal rapes.[137]

Yet all this is furiously disputed. For this is not simply a literature on pornography and free speech, in the way that, say, the discipline of military history produces articles on war. This literature is part of a war. And rather than being just writing *on* free speech, it exemplifies the power *of* free speech to change minds. The assault on pornography is one of the ways in which feminist writers have contributed to shifting men's attitudes to women, at least in Western societies.

Catharine MacKinnon's *Only Words*, for example, is an extraordinary piece of rhetoric. It beats men around the head, with hammer blow after hammer blow, so we wake up to the way women have been treated. MacKinnon's are Only Words, perhaps, but what words! Yes, she makes sweeping overstatements which do not hold up to nuanced empirical scrutiny, but that's rhetoric for you. Her work advances a claim for equality for women, characterising pornography as discrimination, but also pushes, with the power of those words, towards the attainment of that equality. And who would doubt that the progress (however incomplete) towards more equality and respect for women has been one of the great normative shifts in Western societies over the last half century?[138]

Yet this forceful feminist use of word power now faces two problems. First, the fact that the scholarly literature has been one of the main fields of battle leaves us with a more than usually acute difficulty of distinguishing analysis from rhetoric, evidence from assertion. Second, and more importantly, the digital revolution means that the spread of these more civilised norms in real-world interactions has coincided with a nuclear explosion of pornography online. Estimates vary widely, but two computer scientists reckon that roughly 13 percent of the 400 million online searches they analysed were for some kind of erotic content. As another indicator, they calculate that in 1997 there were about

900 pornography sites on the web but by 2010 the American filtering software CYBERsitter alone was blocking 2.5 million 'adult' websites.[139] That number has doubtless multiplied since, and this is before we even get to the 'dark net', where the vilest, most violent pornography hides.

When writers conclude that we need 'more research' on a subject, it usually feels at once self-serving and feeble, but in this case, that is my reluctant conclusion. To be more precise, I think we need something like a new Williams committee, calling on the best available expertise from all disciplines and scrupulously weighing the evidence, but one with a wider remit and international composition. While norms do vary between cultures, this is a subject on which considerable international consensus seems possible and, given the way online pornographers skulk between jurisdictions, international cooperation is indispensable.

In some respects, more should be done by law: for example, to protect people who are harmed in the making of pornography and to penalise threats of sexual violence. 'Revenge porn', in which people post online naked pictures of former sexual partners, with malicious intent, has rightly become a criminal offence in Britain.[140] Whatever is done in a field vital to every parent should be overseen by an accountable public authority, under law and with a right of appeal. While parents should obviously be able to put filters on their children's computers, a proposal to make the default setting on all computers 'opt-in', so that you would have to contact your service provider and say, 'I want to be able to see porn', would set a dangerous precedent. We already see the taboo ratchet at work, with the suggestion that the blocking now applied to extreme and child pornography should be extended not just to terrorist content but even to nonviolent extremism. Imagine having to contact your service provider to say, 'I want to be able to view extremist content'. You might as well 'bcc' your message to the security services yourself. But I do want to view extremist content, because I need to see what the enemies of freedom are saying, the better to combat them.

When all reasonable legal restrictions have been imposed, there will remain an ocean of pornography into which millions of people will wish to dip. The content will range from hard-core porn, with no artistic merit, to erotic art displayed at the British Museum. Within limits set by the law, individuals should be free to view this material if they want to—and not be confronted with it if they don't want to. Traditionally, the 'not if you don't want to' has involved placing porn magazines on the top shelf at the newsagent, but when I drop into my local newsagent in Oxford, I see on the bottom shelf, at child's-eye level, tabloid newspapers with titles like Star and Sport that routinely run front-page pictures of half-naked women as objects of sexual titillation. One I recall showed a photograph of a young woman taken from behind, with her head down, legs astride and her cleft covered only by skimpy panties. If that is not 'objectification' of women, I don't know what is.[141] It should be on the top shelf, until active citizens have dissuaded these rags from running such front pages, just as they eventually got The Sun to abandon its daily page 3 pictures of topless girls. On the internet, what one might call ordinary indecent porn should be one click away.

But then people must be free to choose. The late-twentieth-century feminist portrayal of pornography as being only about men slavering and masturbating over images of sexually dominated women is, at the very least, drastically incomplete. I once heard the founder of Mumsnet, a very popular website for mothers, say almost casually in a panel discussion: 'a lot of people are very keen on porn on Mumsnet . . . you should see our Friday nights'. There was a massive revolt of Indian women when the Indian authorities blocked access to Savita Bhabhi, an online comic strip featuring a promiscuous housewife with an insatiable appetite for sex.[142] Each of the LGBTIQ sexual orientations must have a pornography, or erotica, which does not simply consist in men dominating women.

These are, however, just a few tentative observations on a large and important subject. My reluctant conclusion stands: We need that new, international Williams report, to understand what really is before deciding what should be done about it.

CIVILITY AND POWER

About six months into our freespeechdebate.com experiment, one of our students said (very civilly) that he did not accept all this civility stuff. He felt that our principles took insufficient account of the drastically unequal power relations in most societies. Civility would only amplify the voice of the powerful, who held the microphone. 'Those who do well in society', Sebastian Huempfer argued, 'cannot feel genuine offence and have no need for violent speech, or shouting, or swearing, or for writing disturbing lyrics and music videos. And they like civility because they define its very meaning'.[143]

As we have already seen, this identifies a real danger. The president and the pope do not have to shout to make themselves heard. The downtrodden and marginalised are more likely to feel the need to scream and use extreme language. This is one reason why they are often the ones to get prosecuted for hate speech, which only strengthens the case against hate speech laws. But the objection does not have the same force if we understand robust civility as a norm, not a universal, legally binding standard, with potential criminal sanctions. We can then recognise that there will be exceptional circumstances in which there is a case for incivility. Or, even if that case is not persuasive, the fact that a particular group or individual feels repeatedly impelled to resort to such extreme, uncivil language can be seen as a warning signal on the instrument panel of an open society. It could be that this group or individual is just intemperate, extreme or unbalanced, but there may be good reasons why they feel the need to scream, because their voices are not being given a fair hearing in the public sphere.

Another member of our team, Jeff Howard, responded to Sebastian, suggesting that he had not taken sufficient account of the words 'and able', which distinguish our first principle from the Covenant's Article 19.[144] Throughout this book I have emphasised that the weak, the few and the persecuted, not just the powerful and the many, must have an effective capacity to make themselves heard. The freedom of which I speak is not the purely notional freedom of the beggar to dine at the Ritz. A society that guarantees free speech on paper but does not give its less powerful members equal and effective voice is only halfway to what free speech should be.

In real life, of course, no society lives up to that ideal, and there are always inequalities of power. At the extreme, in the face of tyranny, these justify not merely incivility but armed resistance. Even Gandhi thought that cowardice in the face of evil was worse than violence in opposing evil.[145] Friedrich Schiller describes such moments of last resort magnificently in his play about the Swiss freedom fighter Wilhelm Tell:

> No, there are limits to the tyrants' power.
> When a man finds that justice is denied him,
> When he can bear no more, then he will look
> To Heaven at the last with bold assurance
> And claim from Heaven his eternal rights,
> Which hang there like the very stars themselves,
> Inalienable, indestructible.[146]

Yet armed rising and violent revolution bring their own dangers. Even then, the path of civility may still be best in the long run, for the road you take determines where you arrive. Your chosen means define your end. As the historian Judith Brown summarises Gandhi's view: the right means produce moral ends, while bad means inevitably produce immoral ones.[147] 'Taught by history', wrote the Polish dissident Adam Michnik, 'we suspect that by using force to storm the existing Bastilles we shall unwittingly build new ones'.[148]

Here is the case for the most exceptional and heroic form of civility: civil resistance. I will start as I mean to go on, even if it costs me my life. I know nonviolent struggle will probably take longer than armed struggle, but in the end my people will end up in a better place. 'We are not like Them', as the crowds chanted during the velvet revolution in Prague in 1989, exhorting each other to nonviolence. As we have seen, one of the most characteristic features and weapons of civil resistance is an outpouring of creative free expression in slogans, images, chants and gestures: civic theatre, the crowd as artist and the artist as politician. Free speech is also a means to make yourself free.

But this chapter is not mainly concerned with such extreme circumstances. We are thinking about societies where there are undoubtedly unequal power relations but also chances to even them up using the word power of free speech, as African Americans did in the 1960s, as feminists did in the late twentieth century, as Muslims are doing in the Western Europe of today—and, let us hope, as Roma may do in the Eastern Europe of tomorrow. A combination of openness and robust civility emphatically allows for the provocative, the transgressive in art and humour, and the offensive. In my argument, the quality of robustness refers not just to the individual speech act but to the entire framework in which we speak. If we get it right, that framework will be robust enough to accommodate and respond to the shrieks of the disempowered. This is the best way to sustain freedom in diversity.

RELIGION

*'We respect the believer but not necessarily the content
of the belief'.*

When I presented an earlier version of these ten principles to a diverse
group of Indian MPs, they at once united in singling this one out for noisy
disapproval. Hindu, Sikh, Muslim and secularist politicians alike insisted that
in India such a distinction was impossible to maintain. When I pressed them
to explain why, two objections emerged. One was that to allow questioning
of each other's beliefs would result in violent mayhem between multiple offended communities. Such freedom to question might be desirable in principle, but you could not risk it in India, and certainly not yet. The other objection was more fundamental: this distinction, they said, simply made no sense.
You cannot distinguish between the believer and his or her belief. Respect
me, respect my belief.

These two arguments take us to very different places. The first can be addressed by drawing the line between hate speech and dangerous speech,
which always depends on context. Speech that is safe in Philadelphia may be
dynamite in Punjab, but we can work, over time, to make it less dangerous
in Punjab. That will be complicated by the intimacy of cosmopolis—Pastor
Terry Jones burns a Qur'an in Florida and there are riots in Afghanistan—but
no new distinction of principle needs to be made. If we accept the second
argument, by contrast, then religion will always, by its very nature, require
special treatment.

THE ARGUMENT FOR SPECIAL TREATMENT

What, if anything, qualifies religion for special treatment? Is it, as Ronald Dworkin once asked, 'because people killed each other over it in the 17th century?'[1] Is it because people are still killing each other over it in the twenty-first? For most of human history, people have felt a tension between religion and freedom of expression, and most of humankind still does. The struggles for free speech in seventeenth- and eighteenth-century Europe and North America were crucially about the freedom to preach and practice different religions.

Astonishingly, many European countries still have blasphemy offences in their penal codes, although people are rarely prosecuted for them.[2] Russia and Poland have, however, convicted people under laws against 'offending religious feelings'. Ireland reintroduced an offence of blasphemous libel in 2009. Moreover, the decline of religious practice and belief in many European societies remains exceptional. Jürgen Habermas shared the Western European assumptions of his time when, in the early 1960s, he developed his model of the public sphere with almost no reference to religion.[3] China may have no traditionally dominant monotheistic religion and a potent legacy of communist atheism, yet alongside enduring folk religion there is a notable growth of popular interest in Buddhism, Confucianism and Christianity, as well as Falun Gong, Feng Shui and other forms of spirituality.[4] When this takes people beyond the permitted bounds of the five officially recognised and controlled national faiths— as, for example, in unofficial Christian 'house churches', or the Falun Gong movement—the problem in China is not the freedom to criticise religion without fear but the freedom to *embrace* religion without fear.

In India, with its kaleidoscope of faiths, section 295A of the penal code, inherited from the British colonial period, says that 'whoever, with deliberate and malicious intention of outraging the religious feelings of any class of citizens of India, by words, either spoken or written, or by signs or by visible representations or otherwise, insults or attempts to insult the religion or the religious beliefs of that class' shall be punished with up to three years imprisonment.[5] In Pakistan, that same section of the British imperial penal code was modified and extended under the military dictatorship of General Muhammad Zia-ul-Haq, so its section 295C now reads 'whoever by words, either spoken or written, or by visible representation or by any imputation, innuendo, or insinuation, directly or indirectly, defiles the sacred name of the Holy Prophet Muhammad (peace be upon him) shall be punished with death, or imprisonment for life, and shall also be liable to fine'.[6]

In many other Muslim-majority countries, both blasphemy and apostasy carry fierce punishments in law. This is before we come to religious judgements such as the fatwa, which can be issued by any qualified Islamic jurist. Beyond that, we see offended believers taking the law into their own hands. Thus, beside the heckler's veto and the assassin's veto we have the fanatic's veto, and it reaches across frontiers.

A practical reason for offering religion special treatment might therefore be that a large part of humankind apparently believes that it deserves it. But is this a good reason? What, if any, is the substantive justification for constraining freedom of expression more tightly for religion than for other kinds of human difference, sentiment or opinion? And what should qualify as religion?

I have already rehearsed one argument why religion should enjoy less protection than an immutable characteristic such as colour or gender. There is no rational argument against having skin that is black, brown or white, and you cannot change your skin. By contrast, there are plenty of rational arguments against the propositions of any religion—and you can change your religion.

Against this, however, we have to recognise that religion cannot be reduced to a set of propositions. Most religions include some propositions, but none are confined to them. Embracing ritual, dress, music, architecture, rules of conduct and diet, special observances and community practice, they are better described as comprehensive forms of life. Religion, writes the philosopher Leszek Kołakowski, 'is not a set of propositions but a way of life in which understanding, believing and commitment emerge together in a single act'. Religious truth, he argues, is 'preserved and handed over in the continuity of collective experience', and he quotes a twentieth-century chief rabbi of Geneva who insisted that the Torah can only be understood through partaking in the life of the Jewish people. 'Meaning', adds Kołakowski, 'is formed by acts of communication, and has to be recreated in those acts time and time again'.[7]

Moreover, religion sits uncomfortably with secular liberal arguments for freedom of speech because it generally has a different relation to both freedom and speech. True freedom, it typically claims, is to be found not in the absence of external constraint but in voluntary submission to a higher cause. The seventeenth-century English *Book of Common Prayer* describes God as one in 'whose service is perfect freedom'. This is what the theologian Oliver O'Donovan calls 'the Christian paradox of freedom perfected in service'.[8] The word 'Islam' means 'submission'. One plausible Latin derivation of the word 'religion' is 're+ligare': that which ties the believer to God. (An alternative etymology, traceable back to Cicero, is 're+legere', 'to read and read over again'.)[9] Even religions that do not acknowledge a deity have this idea of a voluntary binding of one's own instincts, desires and free will.

The same is true of speech. Religious speech soon takes off into places where pedestrian empiricists may find it hard to follow. Thus a former Master of the Dominican Order, Timothy Radcliffe, writes, 'there is no universal language of pure communion except Christ, and we do not yet know fully how to speak the Word that he is'. And again: 'Christianity stands or falls on the truth of its claims, but complex issues are raised in trying to understand the sense in which they are true . . . They are not just bald statements of fact. Our faith reaches through and beyond the propositions to the mystery of God which is beyond words'.[10] Even for someone who was steeped in Christianity throughout his childhood, it requires a considerable exertion of the sympathetic imagination to follow him.

Or take this, translated from one of humankind's earliest surviving religious texts, the Upanishads:

> That which cannot be expressed by speech,
> By which speech itself is uttered,
> That is Brahman—know thou this—
> Not that which is honoured here as such.

> That which thinks not by the mind,
> By which, they say, the mind is thought,
> That is Brahman—know thou this—
> Not that which is honoured here as such.[11]

To speak of religion is to speak of the unspeakable. Taboos about the naming of gods, or 'taking His name in vain', reflect this special relationship to words. This is done, writes the modern Christian theologian Paul Tillich, 'because, within the name, that which bears the name is present'.[12] The great linguistic philosopher Ludwig Wittgenstein recognised this distinct character of religious language.[13] Even if the dividing line is not quite as hard and bright as was once believed, the Truth with a capital *T* that believers reach towards by faith is clearly different from the kinds of truth that we have been discussing when looking at the dissemination of knowledge or the media we need for informed choice and good government.

This has led the evolutionary biologist Stephen Jay Gould to talk of religion and science as nonoverlapping magisteria—NOMA—where 'magisterium' is to be understood as 'sphere of authority' or 'domain of competence'. But the theologian Alister McGrath seems closer to the mark when he talks of them as POMA—partially overlapping magisteria.[14] For there are religious propositions, including moral precepts and historical claims, that can be subjected to the same kind of scrutiny as scientific and philosophical ones. We can argue scientifically about when and how human life on earth developed. As Eric Barendt points out, a claim such as 'the fundamental right is the right to be treated with equal concern and respect' and a religious one such as 'we are all equal in the sight of God' both draw on contested philosophical concepts that are not subject to empirical verification.[15] Immanuel Kant's insistence that human beings must be treated as ends, not means, cannot be disproven.

Think of it as a Venn diagram with two intersecting circles. There is a significant area of overlap where adherents of all religions and of no religion can contest each other's claims, rationally and with mutual comprehension, and there is an area where they cannot. I can no more argue with your mystical experience of revelation or transcendence than you can argue with the colour of my skin. Our guidelines for free speech and religion have somehow to take account of both these areas, with their very different epistemologies, logics and varieties of human experience.

That is what this principle does with its distinction between the believer and the content of the belief. I am well aware that religion is not coterminous with belief. You do not even need to believe in God in order to qualify as a devout religious Jew, so long as you faithfully observe Judaism's rules and rituals. Stephen Prothero goes so far as to say that 'faith and belief don't matter much in most religions. Often ritual is far more important, as in Confucianism. Or story, as in Yoruba religion'.[16] But 'the content of the belief' describes that area which is rationally contestable by speech, as that word is usually understood in the phrase 'free speech'.

BUT WHAT IS RELIGION?

If we accept that religion is peculiar—not necessarily deserving greater protection, but having a special relationship to both speech and freedom—then we need to decide what qualifies as religion. For many people throughout history, and not a few in our own time, there has been only one true religion: their own. Everyone else's is heresy or superstition.

Then there is limited mutual recognition, as, for example, between Christianity, Judaism and Islam. When Cairo's historic Al-Azhar University was attempting to regain credibility after the overthrow of president Hosni Mubarak in 2011, it issued a Statement on Basic Freedoms. This went a long way to endorse freedom of expression but qualified it by a 'need to respect the divine beliefs and rituals of the three Abrahamic faiths'.[17] Never mind the rest—and to hell with the Baha'i. In 2003, the Islamic Research Centre of that same university

Part II

had issued a fatwa declaring Baha'i to be apostates and urging the state to 'an-
nihilate' their community.[18]

A more pragmatic, secular understanding recognises all those with a significant following who define themselves as a religious group or in relation to religion. Figure 17 provides the most reliable overview of the main ones. Note
that its category of 'unaffiliated' embraces more than 1 billion people, of whom
many would certainly identify themselves as atheists, secular humanists or agnostics. In British law, a 'religious group' is now a 'group of persons defined by
reference to religious belief or a lack of religious belief'[19]. Yet that truly catholic
definition does not absolve us from the hard work of deciding who qualifies.

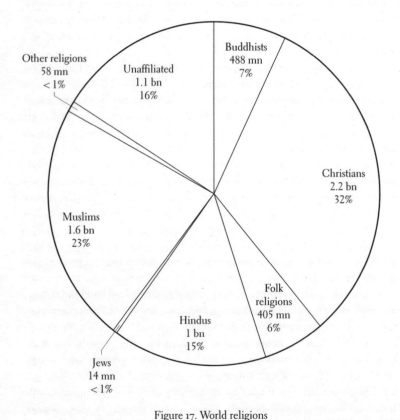

Figure 17. World religions
'Unaffiliated' includes atheists, agnostics and those who do not identify with a particular religion.
Source: Pew-Templeton Global Religious Futures Project, 2010.

What about a tiny group following one visionary leader, who makes what seem to his contemporaries eccentric and shocking claims? The problem is nicely captured in this limerick:

> There was an old man of Moravia
> Who refused to believe in our Saviour
> So he set up instead
> With himself as its head
> The Church of Decorous Behaviour

Yet there is a much more serious, real-life example: Jesus Christ. As John Stuart Mill observes in a magnificent passage, 'the man who left on the memory of those who witnessed his life and conversation, such an impression of his moral grandeur, that eighteen subsequent centuries have done homage to him as the Almighty in person, was ignominiously put to death, as what? As a blasphemer'.[20] (Strictly speaking, Mill was wrong, since Jewish leaders in the Sanhedrin changed their charge to treason in order to secure the death penalty under Roman law, but we take the point.)

In our time, the question has arisen in relation to such groups as Mormons and Scientologists. The religion of 2012 US presidential candidate Mitt Romney teaches that the angel Moroni appeared in the 1820s to a young American called Joseph Smith and led him to some golden plates buried on a hillside near his home in western New York. Written in an otherwise unknown language called Reformed Egyptian, and deciphered with the aid of two stones called Urim and Thummim, these texts became the Book of Mormon. This is regarded by Mormons as divine revelation, alongside a supposedly earlier version of the Bible. 'Mormon', Smith explained in a letter to a newspaper, derives from the Reformed Egyptian word '*mon*', meaning 'good', 'hence with the addition of more, or the contraction mor, we have the word Mormon; which means, literally, more good'.

In this holy book, North America was described as 'a land which is choice above all other lands' (II Nephi 1:5), and nineteenth-century Americans were assured, in a kind of retrospective prophecy, that 'it shall be a land of liberty' (II Nephi 1:7). What is more, if Native Americans converted to the true faith, they would have the chance to become 'a white and a delightsome people' (II Nephi 30:6). The official online version has corrected this to 'a pure and a delightsome people'. But then, thanks to its doctrine of Continuous Revelation, this Church of Jesus Christ of Latter-day Saints can obtain advice from on high to revise its doctrines with the times—renouncing polygamy, for example, when that was a condition for Utah to join the United States, and allowing black people to become leaders of a congregation in 1978. Moreover, according to the teachings of Smith, Mormons can, by their own strenuous efforts and good works, themselves aspire to become gods.[21]

The United States, with its generous recognition of most competitors in the marketplace of religions, also accepts the Church of Scientology as a religious organisation—an acceptance officially sealed by a ruling of the Internal Revenue Service. But several European countries do not, and Germany has put Scientology under security service surveillance as a cult that potentially threatens the country's liberal democratic order. In 1997, a US federal immigration judge granted asylum to a German member of the Church of Scientology on the grounds that she had a justified fear of religious persecution in Germany.[22]

In 2013, Britain's Supreme Court ruled that a couple could have an officially recognised wedding in a Scientology church, now legally acknowledged to be a 'place of meeting for religious worship'. This learned judgement wrestled at length with the problem of definition, describing religion as a 'spiritual or non-secular belief system, held by a group of adherents, which claims to explain mankind's place in the universe and relationship with the infinite, and teach its adherents how they are to live their lives in conformity with the spiritual understanding associated with the belief system. By spiritual or non-secular', wrote the main author of the judgement, 'I mean a belief system which goes beyond that which can be perceived by the senses or ascertained by the application of science'.[23]

But what exactly are Scientologists such as the actors Tom Cruise and John Travolta supposed to believe? It is not easy to find out, because lawyers for the Church of Scientology aggressively pursue anyone who attempts to put its more esoteric sacred texts online, charging them with copyright violation. It is an interesting question whether an organisation that enjoys the special recognition and tax privileges of a religion should have the right to protect its revelations like commercial secrets—or, on the contrary, a duty to make them freely available to all. But if you go to the website Operation Clambake, you can see some of the original handwritten texts of the founder of Scientology, L. Ron Hubbard. Here, for example, is an extract from the entry-level Operating Thetan I:

1. Walk around and count bodies until you have a cognition. Make report saying how many you counted and your cognition.
2. Note several large and several small female bodies until you have a cognition. Note it down.[24]

Are we really supposed to take such infantile poppycock seriously? To treat it with respect?

TWO KINDS OF RESPECT

Respect is one of the most heavily used and abused terms in the debate around free speech and religion. 'Don't be so damned polite and respectful!' I heard the (very polite) atheist Richard Dawkins exhort an audience in California. Karen Armstrong, the well-known writer on comparative religion, takes an entirely contrary view: 'the principle of free speech implies respect for the opinions of others'.[25] In 2007, BBC radio reported 'a call for schools to respect some Muslims' belief in creationism'.[26] Christopher Hitchens insisted that all too often 'the believable threat of violence undergirds the Muslim demand for "respect"'.[27] Faced with actual violence, in protest at the 'Innocence of Muslims' video, the EU's high representative for foreign policy, Catherine Ashton, co-signed a statement with (among others) the secretary general of the Organisation of Islamic Cooperation. 'While fully recognising freedom of expression', it averred, 'we believe in the importance of respecting all prophets, regardless of which religion they belong to'.[28] (Really? Including Joseph Smith and L. Ron Hubbard?) The Dalai Lama rejects any exclusive claim for one Truth but suggests that 'secularism means respect for all religions, and for non-believers as well'.[29]

Faced with this cacophony, it is tempting to step around a term of such uncertain meaning. Yet the very fact that 'respect' comes up so often suggests it touches on something important to believers and nonbelievers alike. So instead of ignoring the concept, let us clarify it. The philosopher Stephen Darwall distinguishes between two kinds of respect. He calls them recognition respect and appraisal respect.[30] In nontechnical language, the former is the unconditional respect that I owe you simply because you are a human being, endowed with the same basic humanity and inherent dignity as me. Appraisal respect, by contrast, has to be earned, whether by the persuasiveness of your argument, the beauty of your musical performance, your skill as a footballer, your dedication as a nurse, your generosity to the poor or your fortitude in adversity. Here is the crucial distinction our principle draws upon. We respect the believer, in the sense of recognition respect, but not necessarily the content of the belief, in the sense of appraisal respect.

Indian MPs are not the only people who resist this distinction. Even liberal Christians can be reluctant to accept it. At the very least, one leading Catholic intellectual suggested to me, you should be prepared to listen carefully and engage seriously with my belief, otherwise you are not really respecting me as a person. Yet some version of this separation of respects is essential if we are to have both religious freedom and freedom of expression. Religions have such a large influence over both individual lives and the ordering of whole societies that if we were not free to challenge their claims and commandments, vast tracts of human life would be removed from free debate. The more religions there are in a given society, the more no-go areas there would be—and in cosmopolis, all religions are present, either physically or virtually.

This matters not just to those who wish to challenge faith in the name of reason, but also to those who challenge one faith in the name of another. The freedom to proselytise and to be converted is itself a vital part of the freedom of religion, as guaranteed in Article 18 of the Covenant—'this right shall include the freedom to have *or to adopt* a religion or belief of his choice' (my italics)—and Article 9 of the European Convention on Human Rights, which refers to the 'freedom to change' religion or belief.[31] If I believe that eternal punishment is in store for you on account of your mistaken belief, it may feel even more urgent for me to convert you to my version of revealed truth than it will seem for me, as an atheist, to persuade you of scientific rationalist truths. Leszek Kołakowski once developed a satirical fantasy about a Conversion Agency which would convert customers from any belief system to any other. The fee, he suggested, should depend on the difficulty of the conversion: pricey to get you to Albanian Communism or Khomeini's version of Islam, a modest charge for reaching relatively undemanding faiths such as Anglicanism or liberal reform Judaism. The agency could be called Veritas, or Happy Certitude.[32]

The question then becomes not 'to respect or not to respect?' but a more subtle one: what belongs in the realm of recognition respect, which is unconditional, and what in the conditional realm of appraisal respect? A now-familiar supplementary follows: what, if anything, should be enforced by law, and what is better promoted by (and if so, by which) nonlegal means?

At a minimum, recognition respect must include the believer's basic right to freedom of religion and conscience. That is helpfully spelt out in Article 9 of the European Convention as freedom 'either alone or in community with others and in public or private, to manifest his religion or belief, in worship, teaching, practice and observance'. So this is more than just a matter of private conviction, in your own head and home. Since religions usually prescribe comprehensive ways of life for self-defined communities, this right can be held to embrace everything from prayer times and dietary restrictions to segregation of the sexes, punishments for children, architectural features (such as the mosque minarets banned after a referendum in Switzerland), calls to prayer and items of dress—the Sikh dagger, the hijab, the Christian cross round a nurse's neck.

It therefore can and does come into conflict with another basic demand that can be justified by recognition respect: that all human beings should enjoy the same human and civil rights and be equal before the law. What if the law—or merely lore—of your religion says that women should not be treated as the equals of men, and infidels should be afforded less rights than the faithful? The wording of the second part of Article 9 of the European Convention allows limitations on the freedom to manifest one's religion 'as are prescribed by law and are necessary in a democratic society in the interests of public safety, for the protection of public order, health or morals, or for the protection of the rights and freedoms of others'. That list is very much of its time. Who, for example, would now confidently say 'morals'? By reference to what ethical code should judges decide what 'morals' trump others? Nonetheless, in a quietly modernised form, and especially in its last phrase ('the rights and freedoms of others'), it captures the difficult balancing act between these two core demands of recognition respect.[33]

Everything I said in the previous chapter about robust civility applies here. The question is whether recognition respect for those things believers hold most sacred makes desirable a higher standard of civility, or even something more active than civility. That is what the third-century-B.C.E. Indian emperor Ashoka advised. In front of the National Museum in Delhi you can admire, on a giant boulder, a metallic reproduction of the 'rock edicts' which he commanded to be displayed across his empire, in several languages.[34] The 12th edict begins:

> King Priyadarsi honours men of all faiths, members of religious orders and laymen alike, with gifts and various marks of esteem. Yet he does not value either gifts or honours as much as growth in the qualities essential to men of all faiths. This growth could take many forms, but its root is in guarding one's speech to avoid extolling one's own faith and disparaging the faith of others improperly or, when the occasion is appropriate, immoderately.
>
> The faiths of others all deserve to be honoured for one reason or another. By honouring them, one exalts one's own faith and at the same time performs a service to the faith of others. By acting otherwise, one injures one's own faith and also does disservice to that of others. For if a man extols his own faith and disparages another because of devotion to his own because he wants to glorify it, he seriously injures his own faith.[35]

This is not just an appeal for voluntary self-restraint. Ashoka has an idea of communication and debate that puts the focus as much on the listener as on the speaker. As Rajeev Bhargava summarises Ashoka's thinking, if the adherents of all the different sects can get together and hear each other out, 'they may then become *bahushruta*, i.e., one who listens to all, the perfect listener, and open-minded'. This is remarkably close to what that Catholic intellectual said to me 2,300 years later. What matters is not just how we speak, but how we listen.[36]

Yet clearly we cannot prescribe such an attitude as a minimum social norm for all to follow. The Anglo-Dutch liberal writer Ian Buruma makes a more modest suggestion, closer to the ideas of religious toleration developed in both his native lands between the seventeenth and twentieth centuries. 'If one truly believes in the separation of church and state', he writes, 'which all democrats should, a certain discretion about the religious beliefs of others is in order'. After all, 'there is not much point in using rational arguments against the belief in God, for it is a belief, not an opinion'. We should leave theology to the theologians.

One can add two further points to support this suggestion. First, there is a growing body of evidence from science, and especially from evolutionary psychology, to indicate that some kind of religious impulse or inclination is quite deep in our brains. Possessing what has been called 'the faith instinct' seems to be part of what distinguishes humans from other animals. We can speculate that it gave us an evolutionary advantage.[37]

This does not mean that we are all bound to cherish religious beliefs today, any more than we are bound to leap on the nearest fecund female or male stud so as to ensure the survival of the species. It does, however, suggest that there is likely to be a lot of religion in a lot of minds for some time to come. A solid body of evidence demonstrates how much of human behaviour is not determined by conscious, rational thought. Science itself therefore suggests a limit to the persuasive power of science—which is, of course, no reason to abandon the attempt to persuade.

Second, while most religions aspire to permeate everything an individual does, those for whom this is the case are a small minority among the multitude who say they subscribe to a religion. In modern societies, religion has not been eradicated or fully privatised, but it is increasingly compartmentalised. Moreover, everyday experience suggests that the fact that people believe, in some corner of their beings, things that appear to us profoundly untrue, need not make them any less trustworthy as accountants, car mechanics or life partners. An alarmingly large proportion of Western Europeans apparently say they believe in astrology.[38] Obviously, the more irrational and wrong someone's belief system seems to us, and the more it intrudes on wider areas of life, the more problematic it becomes. You may be happy enough to have a creationist as your dentist but not to have him teach your son biology. Employing a High Fiver (a believer that 2 + 2 = 5) as a company accountant might create some difficulties. Yet there are vast tracts of life where, in practice, such beliefs do not create problems.

There is also one important kind of appraisal respect which can be divorced from the content of the belief. I can find your beliefs to be utterly misguided and yet still admire your personal conduct. What is more, I can recognise that, by your own account, your admirable conduct is largely or wholly motivated by those beliefs—and why should I be a better judge of your motives than you? You do things that I regard as good, brave or noble, on grounds that make no sense to me. Suppose it were the case that all members of the small but select congregation of High Fivers performed extraordinary, selfless service to the weak and suffering in their societies, always insisting that they did this because it was a commandment of their faith. Would we not be moved to express a genuine appraisal respect for their behaviour, even while continuing to maintain that the central tenet of their faith was arrant nonsense?

In a less parodic form, this is the attitude that a secularised post-Christian may take to the example of Jesus Christ. It is anticipated in a letter written by the historian Jacob Burckhardt in 1844: 'As God, Christ means nothing to me—what can one do with him in the Trinity? As a human being he goes ringing through my soul, because he is the most *beautiful* apparition in world history. If someone wants to call this religion, so be it—I don't know what to do with *that* concept'.[39] The English radical Thomas Paine put it rather more cautiously in his *The Age of Reason*: 'nothing that is here said can apply, even with the most distant disrespect, to the *real* character of Jesus Christ. He was a virtuous and an amiable man. The morality that he preached and practised was one of the most benevolent kind; and though similar systems of morality had been preached by Confucius, and by some of the Greek philosophers, many years before, by the Quakers since, and by many good men in all ages, it has not been exceeded by any'.[40]

Yet if such appraisal respect for the conduct of the believer has always to be earned, so does respect for the content of the belief. However much we might admire the good works of a High Fiver, it would never follow that 2 + 2 = 5. In that large area of overlap on the Venn diagram, we must be entirely free to challenge the claims of religion with all the available instruments of free expression. While it is usually both courteous and prudent to preface our objections with the words 'with respect', and to express them accordingly, it cannot be that proponents of secular humanism are condemned to argue with one hand tied behind their backs. Religions draw powerfully on the appeal of art, including music, painting, sculpture, architecture and costume, not to mention 'bells and

smells', and their competitors must be free to do the same—even if the resulting art or satire is offensive to the believer. What is sauce for the religious goose
must be sauce for the atheist gander.

If the Hindu, Christian, Sikh, Muslim or Mormon claims the right to propagate his or her faith, then by the same token—and according to the same international human rights conventions—he or she must allow others an equal
right to do the same. This is what still spectacularly fails to happen across much
of the planet. The worst examples are in majority Muslim countries, especially
those in the Arab world, but in practice, even if not in constitutional theory, the
inequality extends even to mature secular, liberal democracies. After opening
in 2011, a satirical musical called 'The Book of Mormon' was staged with great
success in America and Britain. A performance was attended by US Secretary
of State Hillary Clinton. The Church of Jesus Christ of Latter-Day Saints responded calmly with this statement: 'the production may attempt to entertain
audiences for an evening but the Book of Mormon as a volume of scripture
will change people's lives forever, by bringing them closer to Christ'. Can we
imagine an equally calm reaction to the staging of a satirical musical called
'The Book of Muhammad'?[41]

A few years earlier, BBC television did broadcast a satirical musical called
'Jerry Springer: The Opera', in which a Jesus Christ figure appears as a flabby
grown-up dressed only in a baby's nappy. There were angry protests from Christian fundamentalist groups, one of which unsuccessfully attempted to bring a
prosecution against the BBC and its director-general, Mark Thompson, under
the then still existing English blasphemy law. I put it to Thompson that 'the
BBC wouldn't dream of broadcasting something comparably satirical if it had
been the Prophet Muhammad rather than Jesus'. He replied, 'I think essentially
the answer to that question is yes'—in other words, the BBC would not dream
of doing so.[42] When the Daily Mail picked this up in an article, one D. Acres of
Balls Cross, West Sussex, commented on the widely read MailOnline website:
'this man [Thompson] is disgusting. He should be taken out and put up on a
cross. That would teach him not to disrespect this country and its Christian
faith'.[43]

Intolerance is not a Muslim monopoly. But there is an asymmetry of treatment which to a significant degree results, as Christopher Hitchens rightly observed, from the demand for 'respect' being undergirded by a credible threat
of violence. The headline to an article on the Spectator magazine's website
captured the point sharply. It read, 'Should Christians kill Mark Thompson?'[44]
Here again, our second principle, on violence, describes an essential precondition for the realisation of all the others.

I have so far explored attitudes we might individually adopt as we pick our way through the minefield of free speech and religion. Another way to think about this is in terms of the character and organisation of the public sphere. I cannot begin to summarise the vast and subtle literature on secularism, but let us here draw a simple distinction between freedom *in* religion, freedom *from* religion and freedom *for* religion.[45] Most religions claim that true freedom is to be found only in religion. ('For freedom he has set us free', says St. Paul.)[46] The atheist argues for freedom from religion. The liberal pluralist proposes freedom for religion—including for those who argue against all religion. Each of these approaches can be translated into an ideal type of the public sphere. In the first, only one god (or extended family of gods) is allowed in the public square. In the second, no god is allowed in the public square. In the third, all gods are equally welcome in the public square. Some majority Muslim countries come close to the first ideal type, North Korea implements the second and the United States approximates to the third.

It should be obvious that the only one of these compatible with freedom of expression is the last: a public sphere organised on the principle of freedom *for* religion. Not only must people be legally free to practice and promote their competing visions of freedom in and freedom from religion, they must also feel free to do so. That feeling of freedom is a product not just of law and state policy but of social, cultural and media practice—starting with the freedom from fear of violent intimidation. Most countries in the world are still far from this ideal. Even in the United States, atheists feel themselves not to be a fully accepted minority. (How many American politicians will dare to admit that they have no faith?)

In several Western European countries, including France and Britain, Christians sometimes make the same complaint. Even as the spiritual leader of an established church, Rowan Williams, then the Archbishop of Canterbury, worried about 'a coarsening of the style of public debate and a lack of imagination about the experience and self-perception of others . . . the arrogant assumption of the absolute "naturalness" of one's own position', especially when that assumption was associated with 'uninterrupted access to the dominant discourse and means of communication in one's society'.[47] He clearly did not think that Christianity enjoyed a dominant position in Britain's public sphere. And this is long before we get to the extremes of the Middle East or China.

BY LAW OR CUSTOM?

The original idea of blasphemy law was to protect God, or at least, the respect due to God.[48] From an atheist perspective this makes no sense: since God does not exist, blasphemy is a victimless crime. Even for a sincere believer, it is an odd idea. Does the Almighty really have need of human laws to protect him? Isn't he big enough to look after himself? 'God doth not need / either man's work or his own gifts', wrote Milton. And in his poem 'Allahu Akbar', the Muslim intellectual K. H. Mustofa Bisri declared, 'if all of the 6 billion human inhabitants of this earth, which is no greater than a speck of dust, were blasphemous . . . or pious . . . it would not have the slightest effect upon His greatness'.[49]

As the jurisprudence of blasphemy developed in the Christian and post-Christian West from the eighteenth to the twentieth century, it became generally accepted that it was not God being protected but rather the feelings and convictions of religious groups—which, if scandalised, could contribute to public disorder. Thus, to give just one example, the relevant clause in the Danish penal code was transferred in the early twentieth century from a section titled 'crimes with regard to religion' to one called 'violations of public order and peace'.[50] This is also the main justification of India's still frequently invoked section 295A.

The more one compares both the laws and the record of actual prosecutions across countries, the more comprehensively incoherent they appear. In many mature democracies, bans persist only on paper. Norway, despite the explicit and carefully modernised free speech clause in its constitution, had the offence of blasphemy in its penal code until 2015. But there had been no prosecution since the 1930s, and no successful one since 1912, when a blasphemer was fined 10 Norwegian crowns (about two days' wages for a worker at that time).[51]

Elsewhere, there have been occasional prosecutions, whether under old blasphemy laws or new ones variously formulated. In Poland, a pop singer known as Doda was convicted of 'offending religious feelings' and fined the modest sum of 5,000 zlotys for saying in a 2009 newspaper interview that she believed more in dinosaurs than in the creation story as presented in the Bible. 'It is', she commented, 'hard to believe in something written by people who drank too much wine and smoked herbal cigarettes'.[52] The idea that Polish Christian believers could seriously have been offended by that piece of feather-headed silliness is itself offensive to those believers' intelligence.

Some might hope that the European Court of Human Rights would bring more consistency into the flounderings of 47 European countries' national courts, as they sporadically apply vague and archaic laws. Unfortunately, it has not. For example, the Strasbourg court held that the Austrian authorities were not violating the right to freedom of expression enshrined in Article 10 of the European Convention when they prevented the showing, in a private cinema club called the Otto Preminger Institut, of a film which portrayed Christ as an idiot and mocked the Virgin Mary and the Eucharist. The court noted, with the Austrian courts, that the film was seized to prevent 'an abusive attack on the Roman Catholic religion according to the conception of the Tyrolean public' and to avoid Tyroleans feeling themselves to be 'the object of attacks on their religious beliefs in an unwarranted and offensive manner'.[53] The court also upheld the British Board of Film Classification's refusal to allow the showing of a video called Visions of Ecstasy, on similar grounds.[54]

In both cases, the Strasbourg court relied heavily on the 'margin of appreciation' doctrine, which makes generous allowance for differences between national legal cultures and traditions. In subsequent cases, the court tilted towards more protection of free expression, but Europeans have been left with no clear guidelines—in relation not merely to believers but also to beliefs. One reason is precisely that, although the distinction I have drawn between the two kinds of respect is important, it is fiendishly difficult to apply with the instruments of secular law.

Another difficulty is illustrated by the prosecution in the Netherlands of the politician Geert Wilders. Wilders had made a successful political career for himself and his Freedom Party, winning nearly a sixth of the seats in parliament in the 2010 elections on the back of extreme and undoubtedly offensive criticism of the scale and character of Muslim immigration to the Netherlands, and of Islam itself. He compared the Qur'an to Hitler's *Mein Kampf* and called for it to be banned. He produced a film called 'Fitna' (the Qur'anic term for 'discord') which conflated Islam, terrorism and immigration and ended with statements such as 'Islam seeks to destroy our Western civilisation'. He also said, 'there is no such thing as a moderate Islam'—although, in a speech delivered in a room in the British House of Lords, he did add that 'there are many moderate Muslims'.[55]

Wilders was prosecuted for having crossed the line from legitimate criticism of Islam to group defamation of Muslims, which is forbidden by the Netherlands' hate speech laws, even though the prosecutor's office had initially decided that the evidence did not justify taking the case to court—not least, on the grounds that Wilders was a politician active in public debate. Predictably enough, the trial gave him massive free publicity, allowing him to pose as a heroic defender of free speech. 'This trial is not about me', he told the court. 'It is about something much greater. Freedom of speech is not the property of those who happen to belong to the elites of a country. It is an inalienable right, the birthright of our people'.[56] Equally predictably, the trial ended with an acquittal, which Wilders hailed as 'a victory for freedom of expression in the Netherlands'.[57] His demagogic, inflammatory views should have been and were countered by politicians, commentators, intellectuals and adherents of other religions, but using the law against him did more harm than good.

In a highly competitive field, Britain takes the gold medal for confusion. In 2007, the country saw the blasphemy case I have already mentioned, brought by a group of Christian fundamentalists against the BBC for broadcasting 'Jerry Springer: The Opera'. It was only the second prosecution for blasphemy since 1922, the other being against the editor and publisher of Gay News, who were convicted in 1977 for printing a poem describing homosexual acts performed on a dead Jesus after his crucifixion.[58] The ancient offence of blasphemy was abolished after the failure of the BBC case, but meanwhile, in 2006, the country had introduced a new offence: 'incitement to religious hatred'. This legislation had been promised by the Labour Party in the 2005 election, at least partly as an attempt to woo back Muslim voters alienated by Britain's participation in the Iraq war under the leadership of Tony Blair.[59]

However, following a major mobilisation of free speech supporters, the veteran liberal legislator Anthony Lester managed to have inserted into the law a clause—sometimes known as the English PEN clause—which provides that this legislation is not to be

> given effect in a way which prohibits or restricts discussion, criticism or expressions of antipathy, dislike, ridicule, insult or abuse of particular religions or the beliefs or practices of their adherents, or any other belief system or the beliefs or practices of its adherents, or proselytising or urging adherents of a different religion or belief system to cease practising their religion or belief system.[60]

So magnificently comprehensive is that exclusion that nearly a decade after the bill became law there has been only a tiny number of convictions under it—although it is frustratingly difficult to establish exactly how many. One of those very few convictions was of a young British Pakistani Muslim for writing angrily about a college in India on a website called Islamicawakenings.com. Thus, having finally got rid of an ancient and anachronistic law, under which there had been only one prosecution in 40 years, Britain replaced it with a modern and empty one, under which almost nobody was prosecuted.[61]

I could go on multiplying examples of bad, anachronistic, inconsistent, vacuous and counterproductive applications of laws attempting to curb freedom of expression in the name of respect for religion and the religious. We could add to these an even longer list of administrative measures, sometimes then challenged in the courts, such as preventing an air stewardess or nurse from wearing a Christian cross around her neck in the workplace, or students being ordered to take off their Jesus and Mo T-shirts at a London School of Economics student welcoming event.[62] (Jesus and Mo is a cartoon strip. The cartoonist wisely remains anonymous, for otherwise he would have to fear for his life.)

So we stand again at the crossroads of cosmopolis. Either we level up the legally enforced taboos or we level them down. There was a powerful move in the years 2009 to 2011, led by the 57 states (if one includes Palestine) belonging to the Organisation of the Islamic Conference, to persuade the United Nations to enshrine a prohibition of 'defamation of religions'. This was ultimately seen off by a coalition of more liberal states, but the impulse behind that initiative is still there. Drawing on the expansive wording of Article 20 of the Covenant, even the courageous and open-minded Iranian Shi'ite theologian Mohsen Kadivar argues that while people should be free to 'criticise' religion, they should not be free to 'insult' it.[63] Yet that line is impossible to draw clearly in law. One man's criticism is another man's insult.

Hence there is an overwhelming case for taking the other path. This is not at all because religion is less important than other forms of human difference: on the contrary, for the true believer it is the most important thing. Rather it is because, in laws applying specifically to religion, even more than in the case of skin colour, national origin or sexual orientation, it is impossible to distinguish clearly and consistently between that which it is vital to keep within the realm of entirely free discussion and that which is to be criminalised on the grounds of insulting, offending or demeaning the individual or group. If you have your clause explicitly protecting free speech, the law will rarely if ever be used; if you don't, the law will spasmodically and inconsistently curb free speech.

Individuals and groups defined by religious affiliation will and should be protected by laws covering incitement to violence, interpreted contextually to include dangerous speech, along with those on harassment, bullying and actual discrimination. Beyond that, it is up to us. Just because so little, in such a sensitive area, can be done well by law, a great deal more needs to be done by civil society—and by the state in its expressive function. Thus, for example, in a society where many faiths are present, early education at school about the beliefs of others is essential. Religious education, which many schoolchildren have traditionally treated as a chance to catch up on lost sleep, is actually vital if we are to live together well in cosmopolis. Needless to say, this is no longer education into one particular religion but education about all religions and the alternatives to religion. If my neighbour knows what it means to wish me 'Happy Christmas', I should know what it means to wish her 'Happy Eid'. That remains true even if we both retreat to the saccharine 'Happy Holidays'.

Similarly, the representation of religious groups in and by the media requires the media diversity, careful thought and mixture of openness and robust civility that I have explored in earlier chapters. On any realistic assessment, the way Hindus, Jews, atheists, Muslims or Sikhs are presented in the media has a hundred times more influence on mutual perceptions than anything written in the black letter of all the laws we have been examining. So do everyday human interactions in the workplace, the shop and the street. Having a right to offend does not imply a duty to offend. Quite the contrary: it brings a duty to be offensive only when there is good reason to be so.

THE TROUBLE WITH ISLAM

Has there been, over the last decades, a special problem with free speech and Islam? Yes, there has. We can point to many cases in which other belief systems and religiously identified groups have been implicated in the violent curbing of freedom of expression: Buddhists in Burma, Hindus in India, Christian militias in the Central African Republic, communist atheism in North Korea. In several of these cases, Muslims have been among the victims. The trouble with Islam has, however, been distinguished by four things: its scale, its impact on liberal democratic societies that particularly value freedom of expression, its association with terrorism, and the degree of intolerance shown by both governments and societies in majority Muslim states to adherents of other religions and of none.

The simple fact of scale must not be underestimated. Islam is the world's second-largest religion, with some 1.6 billion adherents—a number projected by the Pew Research Center to grow to more than 2.7 billion by 2050. If a similar proportion of the world's currently 2.2 billion Christians, and of majority Christian states, were equally intolerant, then we would have an even bigger problem.[64] In fact, the Christian world did have that problem for hundreds of years. Diarmaid MacCullough, a distinguished and sympathetic historian of Christianity, has written that 'Western Christianity before 1500 must rank as one of the most intolerant religions in world history: its record in comparison with mediaeval Islamic civilisation is embarrassingly poor'.[65] According to one estimate, the Spanish Inquisition may have been responsible for as many as 350,000 deaths.[66] Moreover, taboos and ways of thinking that contemporary Europeans sometimes qualify as 'mediaeval' persisted in the Christian world until quite recently. Remember that when it was established in 1912, the British Board of Film Censors prohibited 'materialisation of Christ or the Almighty'. Film buffs will recall that in the 1925 silent version of 'Ben-Hur', all we are allowed to see of Jesus is his disembodied forearm. Even in the 1959 version, which shows us all too much of Charlton Heston, we are barely permitted a glimpse of the saviour's face. Yet the taboo on portraying Muhammad is sometimes treated as uniquely archaic. In 1864, the Roman Catholic Church put liberalism on its Syllabus of Errors and fought it tooth and nail for a century.[67] Only following the Second Vatican Council in the early 1960s did it accept what most Western Europeans now regard as the basic terms of liberal secularism.

Indeed, this partly explains the vehemence of Western European reactions to the versions of Islam that mass migration has brought to many of their societies. Europeans shaped by the cultural revolution of the 1960s felt they had finally freed themselves from the shackles of one socially conservative religion, only to have an even more conservative one come knocking at the back door. Shortly before he was murdered, the gay, socially liberal and fiercely anti-Islamic Dutch politician Pim Fortuyn was asked by a reporter why he felt so strongly about Islam. 'I have no desire', he replied, 'to have to go through the emancipation of women and homosexuals all over again'. He might have added the emancipation of the tongue. On the plinth of his statue in Rotterdam are engraved the words *loquendi libertatem custodiamus*—let us guard freedom of speech.[68]

Fortuyn was not, in the event, murdered by a Muslim fanatic, but one of his admirers was: the Dutch filmmaker Theo van Gogh. A young man called Mohammed Bouyeri shot van Gogh and then, according to an eyewitness, cut his throat with a machete 'as though slashing a tyre'. Bouyeri was convinced that he was acting in defence of Islam. Like the original 'assassins', who gave us the word, he was a Muslim religious fanatic.[69]

Even if all Muslims in and around Europe had remained entirely nonviolent, liberal and atheist Europeans would still have had a problem with their socially conservative religiosity. Conservative, devout Christian Americans might not have. The neoconservative Christian Dinesh D'Souza even argued that the social liberalism of the United States' 'cultural left' was partly to blame for the 9/11 terrorist attacks.[70] But atheist Europeans and Christian Americans have been united in their opposition to the violence.

This book has identified many threats to freedom of expression in the twenty-first century, but the biggest single chilling effect in Western Europe over the 25 years following the fatwa declared on Salman Rushdie in February 1989 was the result of threats of violence from people identifying themselves as Muslims. Whereas that same quarter century saw a dramatic expansion of free speech in the eastern half of the continent following 1989, it witnessed a narrowing of the boundaries of free speech in the western half.[71] The extent of this new constriction obviously cannot be equated with that in a dictatorship, let alone with a totalitarian semantic occupation of the entire public sphere, but the personal threat is often sharper.

Not only have individuals such as Theo van Gogh and the cartoonists of Charlie Hebdo been murdered. A useful publication titled 'Victims of Intimidation' offers short biographies of 27 European politicians, writers, academics, journalists, artists and activists, mostly of Muslim background, who have been compelled to go into hiding, take police protection or otherwise walk in fear of their lives.[72] That list is far from exhaustive. Equally long is the catalogue of publications, art exhibitions, theatre productions and television programmes that either have not been made at all out of fear, or have been pulled at the last minute, or have faced violent protests. Looming in the background are the terror attacks on New York, London and Madrid. Once again: Muslims are not the only ones who have resorted to violence in the name of their faith (and been disavowed by the majority of their co-religionists). In South Asia, we can point to large-scale violent actions against Muslims by Hindus and Buddhists, and in Britain, to the Sikh protests that caused the play Behzti to be taken off the stage.[73] But for Western societies, Muslim violent intimidation has been in a class of its own.

One notable feature of this intimidation is the extent to which its fire has been concentrated on two groups: ex-Muslims, whether they have converted to another faith or turned to atheism, and those whom, for want of a better label, I will call reformist Muslims—women and men who wish to develop, enrich and reform their faith from within. Recall that the British imam Usama Hasan received death threats for suggesting in a lecture in his mosque that there was a scientific case for the theory of evolution ('you should not shout "Evolution!" in a crowded mosque'). And the threats worked. The British police advised him no longer to go to his own mosque, so he was silenced where it mattered most that he should be heard.[74] Irshad Manji, the outspoken Canadian liberal feminist Muslim writer, refused to be intimidated, dropping the security guard offered to her and even encouraging people to repost the death threats. (She did, however, see the case for insisting that people use real names online: '"Anonymous" is the one who's constantly threatening me with death'.)[75] So while those who perpetrate these atrocities, or make credible threats of murder, present themselves as defenders of Islam, this is as much an argument *inside* the world of Islam as it is between Islam and atheism, Christianity, Judaism or other faiths.

In cosmopolis, what happens in multicultural Western liberal democracies cannot be neatly separated from conditions in the majority-Muslim countries from which many of those democracies' inhabitants come and to which they still have close connections. I have illustrated this already with the story of the

'Innocence of Muslims' video. A small but revealing example was the British award of a knighthood to Salman Rushdie in 2007. Noteworthy in Britain itself was the relative moderation of British Muslim responses, compared with the hysterical reaction to the publication of *The Satanic Verses* in 1989. It is true that the British Muslim politician Lord (Nazir) Ahmed puffed himself up to object to 'honouring the man who has blood on his hands—sort of, because of what he did—honouring him I think is going a bit too far'.[76] But in general, the objections were almost Anglican in their mildness. More than that, the British Muslim commentator Inayat Bunglawala, who confessed to having been 'truly elated' at news of the fatwa in 1989, now declared: 'in the intervening years I have managed to travel to Egypt, Sudan, Pakistan, Malaysia, Indonesia, Turkey and elsewhere and it is always with a sense of warmth that I return to the UK. Our detractors had been right. The freedom to offend is a necessary freedom'.[77]

That was not, however, the reaction in some of those countries that Bungla-wala had visited. In Pakistan, the religious affairs minister, Muhammad Ejaz-ul-Haq, told his parliament, 'if somebody commits suicide bombing to protect the honour of the Prophet Muhammad, his act is justified'.[78] (He later returned to the National Assembly to clarify that he had not meant what he had said. The speaker had his comments expunged from the record of parliamentary proceedings, citing 'the national interest'.[79]) This ul-Haq was the son of the former Pakistani dictator Zia-ul-Haq, under whose swagger stick Pakistan's version of section 295 had been revised to prescribe the death penalty for disrespecting the Prophet.

Pakistan has a literally fatal mixture of highly repressive blasphemy law and extrajudicial violence. If the court does not get you, the mob will. A notorious case is that of Asia Bibi, a Christian woman who was accused by Muslim fellow villagers of blasphemy after an altercation over taking a drink of water from a well. Her family had to go into hiding, for fear of the lynch mob. Incredibly, she was sentenced under section 295 to death by hanging for blasphemy (and at this writing has been on death row for five years).[80] Salman Taseer, the governor of Punjab, bravely criticised these blasphemy laws and visited Asia Bibi in prison. His reward was to be shot dead by one of his own security guards. Two months later, Pakistan's minister for minorities Shazbaz Bhatti, another outspoken critic of the blasphemy laws, was assassinated in his car on his way to work.[81] Since the largest single group of British Muslims comes from Pakistan, the chilling effects are not confined to that country. In January 2014, a 70-year-old British citizen from Edinburgh, Mohammed Asghar, was sentenced to death for blasphemy by a court in Rawalpindi, even though he reportedly suffered from paranoid schizophrenia.[82]

Pakistan is an extreme example of a majority-Muslim country manifesting grotesque intolerance, but not the only one. The US State Department's International Religious Freedom Report for 2009 noted that in Washington's great ally Saudi Arabia, 'mosque speakers prayed for the death of Christians and Jews, including at the [state-sponsored] Grand Mosque in Mecca and the Prophet's Mosque in Medina'.[83] Dangerous speech could hardly get closer to the historic heart of Islam. In Saudi Arabia, as in several other majority-Muslim countries, some of the most extreme repression is concentrated on practitioners of other variants of Islam, or minority belief systems derived from Islam, such as the Ismaili, Ahmadiyya and Baha'i. In 2014, Saudi authorities introduced new anti-terrorism regulations which appeared to equate 'calling for atheist thought in any form, or calling into question the fundamentals of the Islamic religion on which this country is based' with terrorism.[84]

Christians are an embattled minority across the region where their faith was born. According to one estimate, Christians comprised 14 percent of the population of the Middle East in 1910 but only 4 percent by 2010. In 2014, it was projected that, if current trends continued, the numbers of Christians in the region would be reduced from around 12 million to just 6 million by 2020, and their persecution by Islamist extremists has only intensified since.[85] Almost amusingly, when, in the wake of the Danish cartoons affair, the initiative to create a UN-recognised international offence of defamation of religion came before the Saudi Consultative Council, it rejected the idea on the grounds that this would 'make it obligatory to recognise some religions and will facilitate establishing places of worship for them in Muslim countries'.[86] God forbid.

One angry Western reaction to this has been 'if they don't give freedom to our religion over there, why should we give freedom to theirs over here?' But two wrongs don't make a right. Those who believe in secular, tolerant, open societies should live up to their own standards, not down to those of others. A more serious debate concerns the relationship of this empirically undeniable intolerance to the doctrinal core of Islam. On this there are two extreme positions. One, articulated by such learned scholars of Islamic jurisprudence as George W. Bush, is that Islam is a 'religion of peace'. The terror and violent intimidation is all misunderstanding or conscious distortion. The other, represented by anti-Islamic bloggers such as Pamela Geller, is that intolerance, violence and jihadi terror are of the essence of Islam. Each can find quotations from the Qur'an and hadiths to prove the point. ('There shall be no compulsion in religion . . . ', Qur'an, II.256; 'if they desert you seize them and put them to death wherever you find them', Qur'an, IV.89.[87])

Both these extreme views fall into the same epistemological trap, which is to speak as if there were a single, unchangeable essence of Islam, which can be extracted to reveal the one true Islamic position on free speech. While a revealed Truth may exist, in an important sense, for each individual Muslim believer, the only indisputable truth detectable by a non-Muslim observer is that Muslims have throughout history interpreted and applied their faith in widely differing ways — many of them incompatible with the principle I am proposing here, but not all. As Edward Mortimer concludes at the end of his book on the politics of Islam, written in response to the Islamic revolution in Iran that led a decade later to the fatwa on Salman Rushdie: 'For me . . . there is no Islam, in the sense of an abstract, unchangeable entity, existing independently of the men and women who profess it. There is only what I hear Muslims say, and see them do'.[88] And what Muslims say and do in the name of Islam continues to vary enormously.

For example, the ex-Muslim author who writes under the name Ibn Warraq asserts, with extensive quotations from the Qur'an and Islamic jurisprudence, 'it is quite clear that under Islamic law an apostate must be put to death'.[89] Equally confidently, the reformist Shi'ite theologian Mohsen Kadivar insists that in an 'Islam that is based on the principles of the Qur'an and the authentic tradition of the Prophet and his family' it is clear that 'no one is to be punished for changing religions or leaving a faith such as Islam. Placing any sort of worldly punishments, such as execution, for apostasy is against Islamic principles'.[90]

Since precedent matters in most religious traditions, it is not just historically tactful but potentially helpful to point out, as Diarmaid MacCullough and others have done, that the Islamic rule seen in the Mughal empire in India, in the Muslim-occupied region of Spain known as El Andalus and in large parts of the Ottoman Empire was somewhat more tolerant of other religions than Western Christianity — tolerant, of course, by the standards of that time, not of our own. More relevant is to observe the range of practice prevailing today among the 57 member states (including Palestine) of the Organisation of the Islamic Conference. The political scientist Alfred Stepan points out that more than 300 million Muslims live in non-Arab Muslim-majority countries that are now democracies: Indonesia, Turkey, Senegal and Albania. Upwards of 170 million also live as a large and growing minority in the world's largest democracy, India. Stepan argues that Indonesia and Senegal, like India, have developed their own versions of what he calls 'religiously friendly' religion-state-society relations. These may not resemble the American version of what Stepan has dubbed the 'twin tolerations' — toleration of an elected government by religious groups, and of religious groups by an elected government—but they are, he argues, still recognisably variants of secularism.[91] Indonesia has practised what its own former president calls 'mild secularism' in a multireligious society, under the umbrella of a state philosophy called *panasila* ('five principles'). This has been severely challenged by religious extremism more recently but is still far removed from the fundamental intolerance of Saudi Arabia.[92]

Turkey since the time of Kemal Atatürk has had a version of secularism closer to the French model of *laïcité*, although it became significantly less secular in the early twenty-first century under the influence of the Islamist governments of Recep Tayyip Erdoğan and his AK party. Thus, for example, the internationally known Turkish pianist and composer Fazil Say was prosecuted in a Turkish court for a couple of humorous tweets, such as 'What if there is raki in paradise but not in hell, while there is Chivas Regal [whisky] in hell and not in paradise? What will happen then? This is the most important question!!'[93] He received a 10-month suspended prison sentence.[94] Yet, as we found when we took the freespeechdebate.com project to Istanbul, Turkey is a country where freedom of expression around religion can still be vigorously and publicly debated.[95] If China, Brazil and India are swing states for the future of free speech on the internet, then countries like Turkey, Indonesia and Malaysia are swing states for free speech and Islam.

The Arab Spring brought hopes of a new opening near the heart of historic Islamic civilisation. I was able to present the freespeechdebate.com project in a lively panel discussion just off Tahrir square in Cairo in 2012. I also visited scholars at Al-Azhar University, which had just issued its relatively liberal Statement of Basic Freedoms.[96] But between the intolerant impatience of the Muslim Brotherhood and violent oppression by the military, those hopes were soon crushed. Only in Tunisia, where the Arab Spring began, did there still seem some prospect of political Islam allowing freedom of expression for those of other religions and of none.[97]

As an entry-level metaphor it may make sense to talk of the need for a Muslim or Islamic Reformation, although historians will remind us that Christianity's wars of religion actually intensified after the reform movement begun by Martin Luther. But there is no central authority, no pope in Rome, against whom a Muslim Reformation could be conducted. Only the pope can issue an encyclical, but any qualified Islamic jurist can pronounce a fatwa (and some who are not qualified do so anyway). The Islamic 'reformation', if and when it comes, will therefore be more multicentred, not to say chaotic, than the Eurocentric metaphor of Reformation suggests. Those swing states in today's Islamic world would have to lead the way, while in the most reactionary Islamic states, such as Saudi Arabia and Pakistan, the process will take decades. Not just different countries but different theological schools and tendencies will have their own trajectories.

More than that: so will millions of individual Muslims, especially those living in countries that enjoy more freedom of expression. Olivier Roy, one of the finest analysts of contemporary Islam, makes a subtle observation. Referring to the Islamic 'neofundamentalism' that, he argues, appeals especially to second- and third-generation European Muslims of migrant origin, he observes that 'neofundamentalism is a paradoxical agent of secularisation, as Protestantism was in its time . . . because it individualises and desocialises religious observance'.[98] Thus, for example, Lamya Kaddor, who describes herself as a 'German of Muslim faith with Syrian roots', goes on to insist: 'it's not up to others to tell me what Islam is or should be: I want to decide for myself how I live my Islam'.[99] This individualised version of Islam has, in a sense, already taken on board that core message of the Enlightenment: think for yourself. She chooses to believe in her own way.

So this is also a contest for individual hearts and minds. Extensive research on the radicalisation of young European Muslims suggests that the most potent recruiting mechanism is a combination of online extremist propaganda and personal contact with a persuasive individual. This physical-virtual mix is, as we have seen, characteristic of cosmopolis. It seems plausible to suggest that a similar combination may contribute to the opening of hearts and minds. Online platforms, civil society groups and governments have devoted considerable resources to looking at ways of promoting positive messages both online and on the street. Broadly speaking, four different kinds of potential influence are competing for the attention of the people who could go either way: traditional authority figures (including self-appointed community leaders and imams imported from the country of origin), radical Islamists (sometimes quite expert in using modern techniques of communication), Muslim reformers and ex-Muslims.

When I first started writing about this subject, I argued that Muslim reformers were more likely to sway more Muslims towards accepting the basic terms of coexistence in a liberal society and secular state than were ex-Muslims. My argument was a pragmatic one. It was already a big stretch from the interpretation of Islam taught by your local Algerian, Mirpuri or Somali imam, and by your parents, to the minimum degree of mutual toleration required in a free society. To ask people to abandon the faith of their fathers and mothers, in effect to choose between being European and being Muslim, would be a stretch too far.[100] And there is testimony to the influence that the modernising yet still devout voices of reformers have on those who might otherwise have ended up as terrorists. The former Islamist Ed Husain writes movingly of the impact that the American convert Sheikh Hamza Yusuf Hanson had on him: 'a powerful yet soft voice coming over the loudspeakers broke my deep sleep. I listened enthralled to its Californian accent filled with well-pronounced Arabic references to poetry and the Qur'an'.[101] Husain himself subsequently became a leading figure in the struggle against Islamist radicalisation.

One critic objected that we simply could not know who in the end would have greater impact, the Islamic modernisers speaking from inside the faith or the deeply challenging ex-Muslims such as Ayaan Hirsi Ali and Ibn Warraq. As many Muslims as possible should be exposed to both kinds of voice, indeed to as many different voices as possible, and then make up their own minds. That is, of course, absolutely right. The voices of ex-Muslim atheists must never be silenced by violent intimidation and censorship, nor marginalised by media and academic self-censorship.

Nonetheless, there is an interesting and difficult issue of prioritisation. Suppose you are, as I am, both an atheist and a liberal secularist. As an atheist, you are bound to say that there is no God, and therefore Muhammad obviously cannot have been his messenger. To pretend otherwise is to say something that you believe to be untrue. Yet to make that simple assertion is frontally to deny the *shahada*, the core statement of belief which makes anyone a Muslim and without which you cannot be a Muslim. No 'reformation' can revise this contradiction away. There is therefore no appraisal respect for the content of the belief—although, as we have seen, there might still be for the conduct of the believers.

At the same time, denial of that core belief clearly cannot be a condition for having equal rights and possibilities to participate in the public sphere, to speak and be listened to with the respect due to anyone and everyone. A public sphere which allowed full rights only for atheists would be as profoundly illiberal as the public sphere in Pakistan or Saudi Arabia, which allows those rights and possibilities only to Muslims.

TOLERANCE

There is, of course, no contradiction between being an atheist, when it comes to disputing the nature of truth, reality and morality, and a liberal pluralist, when debating the political and legal arrangements for the public sphere. But there is a question about the priority that you give to the two. Is it more important to you personally to challenge the content of the belief or to promote the conditions in which all believers (including nonbelievers) can freely and peacefully compete?

This is complicated by the fact that the global spectrum of secularisms is very wide, ranging from Stepan's 'religiously friendly' ones in Malaysia, where it is at the very least uncomfortable to be an atheist, all the way to France's *laïcité*, tartly described by Martha Nussbaum as 'the establishment of nonreligion'.[102] Unsurprisingly, even if all participants in the debate are in principle liberal secularists, atheists tend to favour the French end of the spectrum while religious believers prefer something between England (with its established church of lukewarm Christianity) and, say, Malaysia or Indonesia.

There is also an analytical disagreement about the relative importance of theological interpretation and doctrinal revision. The Second Vatican Council was a turning point in the Roman Catholic Church's acceptance of a liberal secular public sphere, although that position remains contested inside even that highly centralised organisation. Equally, in a much more decentralised way, the spread of reformist, modernist interpretations of Islam—*ijtihad* redefining the nature of *jihad*—will be helpful for millions of Muslims who earnestly want to be both good believers and good citizens of states for which freedom of expression is constitutive. But without the happy Mormon gift of Continuous Revelation, there are limits to such a process of explicit doctrinal revision.

By contrast, there are almost no limits to the human capacity to divorce theory from practice—to chant one thing in your place of worship and do another in your place of work or pleasure. Call it hypocrisy if you will. Call it human weakness. Or call it the strength of our common humanity. Polish Catholics treated Pope John Paul II as a saint long before he was formally made one, but many of them lustily ignored his stern injunctions on sexual life. At the end of the Bosnian war, in 1995, a professor in Sarajevo was explaining to me how the Bosniaks were good Muslims. There was a knock at the door and a waiter came in bearing a large tray with glasses of rakia, a strong alcoholic drink. Pausing only to take a glass and knock it back in one go, he went on extolling his people's devotion to Islam.

Personally, I put the practical achievement of peaceful coexistence in freedom before doctrinal confrontation. Like the singer Iris DeMent, I'm inclined to say, 'let the mystery be'. The Lord moves in mysterious ways his wonders to perform. Accommodations that would require Olympic feats of exegetical acrobatics to justify doctrinally happen quietly every day. If evolutionary psychologists are right to argue that some element of religious belief is quite deep in our brains, and if religious identification is an important aspect of that sense of group belonging which is vital to most human beings, then persuading people to abandon it explicitly will be an uphill struggle. For me, ensuring that they respect the freedom of others takes priority over attempting to convince them of the wrongheadedness of their religious beliefs. But this is a personal choice, not a prescription for anyone else. Others must be entirely free to engage in frontal criticism of the content of religious belief, just as the Christian, Muslim or Sikh must be free to regard propagating religion as the most important thing in his or her life.

The philosopher Thomas Scanlon suggests that instead of 'In God We Trust', Americans might inscribe on their coins the words 'In Tolerance We Trust'.[103] (As he also points out, one would have to be careful not to speak the first two words too fast, making it 'intolerance we trust . . .'.) 'In Tolerance We Trust' seems to me the best motto for the Bitcoin of cosmopolis.

We should have no illusions. Religion will continue to be one of the most difficult areas for free speech. Tolerance is difficult. Even for someone who does not feel impelled to challenge frontally the religious beliefs of others, finding the right mix of tact and honesty, imaginative sympathy and steadfastness is a daily challenge. Even the nuanced principle and commentary I have offered here will face this ultimate objection: are you not, in fact, asking us to place one belief above all others—the belief, that is, that everyone should learn to rub along together in this way, giving and receiving the same freedom? For the liberal virtue of tolerance makes the remarkable demand that we should accept others continuing to hold and (within the limits of the harm principle) act upon convictions that we think both intellectually mistaken and morally wrong.

How can it be right to accept what is wrong? Because, we argue, there is a higher good, which is that people should be free to choose how to live their own lives, so long as this does not prevent others from doing the same. Our claim is that the path of tolerance is not merely another 'one true way'. It is the only one whose purpose is to enable human beings to live out a multiplicity of other true ways. This requires a difficult balance between an unconditional recognition respect for the believer and what may be a total lack of appraisal respect for the content of the belief. If that is a compromise, it is a compromise in the defence of which we must be uncompromising.

PRIVACY

*'We must be able to protect our privacy and to counter
slurs on our reputations, but not prevent scrutiny that is
in the public interest'.*

On the internet, it is much easier to make things public and more difficult to keep things private. It follows, as the night the day, that while the greatest opportunity of cosmopolis lies in the public sharing of knowledge, opinions, images and sounds, its largest danger is the loss of privacy.

This would be true even if the internet were entirely run by choirs of angels, since the surveillance possibilities afforded by today's information and communication technologies are beyond a Stasi general's wildest dream. Most of us voluntarily carry around with us electronic tracking devices. They are called mobile phones. Put together all the data and so-called metadata from our emails, mobile phone calls, online searches, other data-sending equipment such as your smart fridge and central heating meter, as well as tiny radio frequency indicator chips in things we use, not to mention facial recognition analysis of footage from CCTV cameras and photos posted online, and an observer can know far more about us than does an ornithologist following a flock of electronically tagged birds. We are all tagged pigeons now.

Yet this technology does not design itself. The terrifyingly detailed personal information it collects is so easy to 'data-mine' and collate because it has been designed that way. Angels, solicitous for our individual privacy rather than company profits or government interests, would have designed it differently. But the internet is not in the gentle arms of angels. It is run and exploited by companies and, to a varying but always significant degree, controlled and accessed by governments. Each of those two forms of power, private and public, constitutes a threat to privacy; the combination of the two, P^2, is the biggest threat of all. This is the lesson that people rightly drew from Edward Snowden's revelations that US and British authorities had both legally compelled telecommunications and internet companies to share data with them and illegally tapped into their cables. (More on this in the next chapter.)

ARE YOU EVER ALONE?

'Surveillance is the business model of the internet', says security expert Bruce Schneier. 'We build systems that spy on people in exchange for services. Corporations call it marketing'.[1] He compares us to tenant farmers on the great estates of Google or Facebook. The rent we pay is our personal data, which they use for targeted advertising.[2] The more the technical capacity to collect 'big data' grows, the more what Jaron Lanier calls 'spying/advertising empires' will know about us and, in that elementary sense, the less privacy we will have.

A lot then depends on the approach taken by these big cats. 'Privacy is dead— get over it': as with so many famous quotations, it seems that Scott McNealy, then chief executive of Sun Microsystems, did not say exactly this when asked about privacy at the end of the last century. According to the best source we have, he said, 'You have zero privacy anyway. Get over it'.[3] But there are reasons that some quotations become proverbial, often in a slightly snappier form than the original. McNealy's remark perfectly sums up both an empirical claim and an attitude. Privacy is dead: there is nothing that you, little mouse, can do about it. And 'get over it': man up, you have nothing to fear but your fears. The further we go into the twenty-first century, the more people question both that claim and that attitude. As I write, there is a political and civic mobilisation to 'get our privacy back'. The mice are on the march.

Companies like Google are deeply conflicted about these issues. Google's longtime chief legal counsel, David Drummond, distinguishes between value to Google and value for Google. Free speech, he argues, is both of value to Google (i.e., helps its business) and a value for Google—what he calls a 'core Google value'.[4] The same cannot be said of privacy. As we have seen, Google makes most of its money by collecting private information about us and then selling us on to others as potential consumers, supposedly anonymised. 'We need to fight for our privacy', writes Eric Schmidt in his co-authored book *The New Digital Age*, seemingly unaware that to many this will seem like the devil declaring that we must fight for salvation.[5] To help launch our Oxford research project, I spoke at a 'speakers' corner' kind of event organised by Google at the

Brandenburg Gate in Berlin.[6] When I had finished, someone piped up from the crowd: 'But the biggest threat to free speech is Google!'

Was he right? Is Google a threat to free speech or only to privacy? Or is it free speech itself that threatens privacy? What is the relationship between the two? In much of the legal literature, this is analysed as a balancing act: how much free speech, about what individuals and in what circumstances, is weighed against how much privacy for them. This is done formally in European court cases, where judges balance individual citizens' free speech rights under Article 10 of the European Convention on Human Rights against their privacy rights under Article 8. And we ourselves may choose to say, 'Yes, in this or that circumstance I subordinate my free speech rights to the demands of privacy'.[7]

However, privacy is also a condition of free speech. To be more precise: the ability to choose what you wish to keep private, and then to have confidence that this choice will be respected, is such a condition. As anyone who has lived in a police state knows, when you fear that someone else might be listening in all the time, you curb your tongue. You no longer speak your mind. I think back to eastern European dissident friends in their kitchens, writing down cryptic messages on scraps of paper to avoid the listening microphones of the secret police. On one occasion, someone asked me to memorise a message she had scribbled on a roll-up cigarette paper and then swallowed the paper. She ate her words. The Russian journalist Vladimir Pozner saltily observes that the only place you can enjoy complete freedom of speech is 'on the toilet'.[8] But under a Saddam Hussein, a Kim Il-Sung, Jong-Il or Jong-Un, people fear to speak their true thoughts even there, on what in English used to be called 'the privy'.

In free countries, the way in which privacy can be a precondition for free speech is exemplified by the prisoner's dilemma—not the well-known one from game theory, but a real-life dilemma. Can you trust your jailers when they say that your letters home will not be opened? As Eric Barendt points out, the confidentiality of prisoners' mail has been defended in European courts under the European Convention's Article 8, on privacy, but it could equally be considered to fall under its Article 10, on freedom of expression.[9]

Yet worries about the privacy of our communications also affect those of us who are not prisoners in a detention facility or a totalitarian state. We all speak differently to different audiences: more freely to some, less to others. 'Off the record . . .' says the politician, and what he crypto-confidentially tells the journalist over a drink at the bar is still not what he confides to his aides, let alone to his wife—and perhaps, in yet another redaction, to his mistress. The poet W. H. Auden once observed that if men knew what women said to each other about them, the human race would die out.[10] (We might ask how exactly he, a man, knew that, but we take the poetic truth.) The varied tones and registers we use in different contexts, those infinite shades of irony, parody, understatement and overstatement, of the half spoken and the delicately implied, are the stuff of novels and poetry. They are the multiple keyboards, pedals and stops of the greatest organ the world has ever seen. 'There are truths', wrote the nineteenth-century Polish poet Adam Mickiewicz, 'that the wise man proclaims to all the world; there are those that he whispers to his own nation; there are those that he confides to close friends; there are those that he may not reveal to anyone'.[11]

Whatever free speech rightly means, it does not mean that what you thought you were whispering only to the man or woman who shares your bed is revealed the next day, against your will, for the titillation of millions of tabloid newspaper readers. So the historically unprecedented erosion of privacy, enabled by the technologies and commercially shaped norms of the virtual world, is also a threat to freedom of expression.

PRIVACY, REPUTATION AND THE PUBLIC INTEREST

Our guiding principle therefore has to take into account both aspects: privacy balanced against free speech and privacy as a condition for free speech. Unoriginally, it proposes a test of 'the public interest' to determine when violations of privacy, and casting aspersions on someone's reputation, are justified. At first glance, this looks relatively simple, but the deeper you dig, the more elusive the notions of privacy, reputation and the public interest all appear.

In one of the most influential American law review articles ever written, privacy was defined by Samuel Warren and Louis Brandeis in 1890 as a 'right to be let alone'. But they also saw it as 'a part of a more general right to the immunity of the person—the right to one's personality'.[12] Alan F. Westin, a powerful voice in the late-twentieth-century American debate on privacy, identified four 'states' of privacy: solitude, intimacy, reserve and anonymity.[13] Each of these takes you in a slightly different direction. In time, the American lawyers who followed Warren and Brandeis separated out four distinct branches of privacy violation: unreasonable intrusion upon the seclusion of another, unreasonable publicity given to another's private life, appropriation of another's name or likeness, and publicity that unreasonably places another in a false light before the public.[14] And that is only the beginning, in a single legal tradition.

In the continental European tradition, the 'right of personality' is central and often defined more expansively. In 1970, a French court ruled that a privacy article recently included in France's civil code protected 'the right to one's name, one's image, one's intimacy, one's honour and reputation, one's own biography, and the right to have one's past transgressions forgotten'.[15] Many Europeans see privacy as a 'European value', upon which they place more weight than Americans do.

Privacy is deeply contextual.[16] What people regard as properly private varies enormously over time, between countries and cultures, generations and social groups, workplace, school and home and from individual to individual. From the evidence of excavated latrines, it appears that the good citizens of the ancient Roman city of Ephesus sat sociably to defecate, cheek by cheek.[17] I found the same mildly disconcerting arrangement when I visited the public lavatory in a hutong in contemporary Beijing. As Norbert Elias points out in his classic work *The Civilising Process*, early modern manuals of civility contain detailed instructions on how two strangers should behave when sharing a bed. The bedroom, he notes, was not a private space as we think of it now.[18]

For some writers, privacy is closely associated with the advance of civilisation itself. In 1928, Louis Brandeis, by then a Supreme Court justice, called it 'the right most valued by civilised man'.[19] In his influential essay 'Two Concepts of Liberty', Isaiah Berlin acknowledges the relative historical novelty of a 'sense of privacy'—'scarcely older, in its developed state, than the Renaissance or the Reformation'—but then insists that 'its decline would mark the death of a civilisation, of an entire moral outlook'.[20] The philosopher Thomas Nagel has written of 'concealment as a condition of civilisation'. 'There is much more going on inside of us all the time than we are willing to express', he observes, 'and civilisation would be impossible if we could all read each other's minds'.[21]

Nonetheless, privacy standards continue to vary widely, even among Western liberal societies. Germans are very resistant to CCTV cameras but much less bothered by people sunning themselves in the nude in public parks, while Brits appear much more relaxed about CCTV cameras, of which Britain was estimated in 2013 to have nearly 6 million, but you would be ill-advised to try German 'free body culture'—that is, going naked—in Hyde Park. (You can find online a map of the officially designated areas for such un-English behaviour in Munich's Englischer Garten.)[22]

And these privacy standards continue to evolve. It has become a commonplace for middle-aged people across the Western world to say that 'the young' have very different notions of privacy, exemplified by the sharing of intimate photos on social media.[23] But Danah Boyd, a researcher who has spent a lot of time talking to young people about how they navigate the internetworked world, shows that the truth is far more complicated. (Her book is called *It's Complicated*.) A geeky 17-year-old who goes by 'Waffles' tells her, with exasperation, 'Every teenager wants privacy. Every single last one of them, whether they tell you or not, wants privacy'. And one kind of privacy they particularly value is privacy from their parents.[24] Moreover, that younger person's norm may shift when fined by university authorities on the basis of a Facebook photo or when refused a job on the basis of something shared online years before.[25] The American blogger and internet guru Jeff Jarvis wants us to establish a new norm of what he calls 'publicness'. He leads the way by sharing intimate details of his treatment for prostate cancer and its impact on the behaviour of his penis.[26]

Violations of privacy may involve intrusion without public exposure (as practiced by the NSA before Snowden spilled their beans) or both intrusion and exposure. The former involves only what others know about you; the latter adds what they say about you. At that point, the matter of privacy slides into the business of reputation. Defamation, also known as libel and slander, has its own richly variegated cultural and legal history, connecting to notions of honour (which is explicitly referred to in the German constitution), dignity, property and social order.[27]

Max Mosley, the son of the British fascist Oswald Mosley and longtime president of the governing body of Formula One racing, sued Rupert Murdoch's News of the World after it alleged on its front page that he had indulged in a 'Nazi Orgy with Five Hookers'—and won, because the Nazi charge was entirely unfounded.[28] Reflecting on the experience, and on his long, expensive campaign to have references to his 'Nazi orgy' removed from search engines around the world, Mosley says he sees a clear difference between privacy and reputation. Your reputation can be restored by a prominently placed correction and public retraction by the defamer, plus a court verdict of libel if need be, but your privacy cannot be restored, any more than an ancient oak cut down by vandals can be brought to life again. I call this the Mosley Rule. It would not have helped, Mosley told me, with the hint of a naughty smile, if the News of the World had the next day printed a front page story saying, 'Sorry, it was a private orgy'. Nonetheless, privacy and reputation are closely enough related to treat them together.[29]

This is one of the most universal concerns of our time. When I presented freespeechdebate.com in Poland, I expected the discussion to dance around traditional themes such as the Catholic Church, national history, anti-Semitism and Russia. To my surprise, we rapidly moved on to privacy and anonymous online abuse, about which the veteran dissident Adam Michnik was almost as indignant as he had once been about communist lies. Everywhere I travel, this crops up as a major worry.

For all the complexities of definition and context, you can get a long way by thinking of privacy as a matter of individual control and choice. Privacy

International says on its website: 'privacy is the right to control who knows what about you, and under what conditions'.[30] That may not take us to the deepest psychological, emotional and cultural questions about the value of solitude or the nature of the self, but it is a solid starting point for discussing the relationship of privacy and free speech. With the precision that is a salient virtue of the best legal scholarship, Eugene Volokh defines 'information privacy' as 'my right to control your communication of personally identifiable information about me'.[31] In the 1980s, the German constitutional court pioneered the concept of 'informational self-determination', and when we say 'data protection' what we mainly mean is 'protection of identifiable personal information'.[32]

So I decide what I want to share with you, and you decide what you want to share with me. If you want to offer an in-depth report on the performance of your penis, believing this will be helpful to others suffering from similar medical conditions, go right ahead. If you don't, don't. No one should be in a position to compel you either way.

Moreover, though privacy may be hard to define, you know it when you lose it. And the harms caused by violations of privacy are very serious. In 2002, a chubby Canadian 14-year-old called Ghyslain Raza filmed himself in his school's video studio, practising some rather comical 'Star Wars' Jedi moves, using a golf ball retriever as his light sabre. A schoolmate discovered the clip and posted it online. It went viral, becoming known around the world as 'the Star Wars Kid video', and according to one estimate was watched 900 million times.[33] Raza recalled a decade later, when he decided to speak out in order to help others who were experiencing cyberbullying, how horrible the results had been: 'In the common room, students climbed onto tabletops to insult me'. He had to change schools. 'No matter how hard I tried to ignore people telling me to commit suicide, I couldn't help but feel worthless, like my life wasn't worth living'.[34]

When Google launched a social network called Buzz in 2010, a woman known by the alias of 'Harriet Jacobs', who was living in hiding from a physically abusive ex-husband and parental home, found that all the personal contacts on her Gmail account had been involuntarily shared with all the others. 'My privacy concerns are not trite', she wrote in her pseudonymous blog. 'They are linked to my actual physical safety'.[35] In the same year, an 18-year-old student at Rutgers University, Tyler Clementi, was covertly filmed by his roommate as he became intimate with another man. The roommate streamed the video online from his computer's webcam, for all the world to see. Distraught, Tyler jumped off the George Washington Bridge into the Hudson River and killed himself. His farewell message on Facebook read: 'Jumping off the gw bridge sorry'.[36]

As we have seen, the problem is compounded by the fact that the internet concertinas both space and time. What happens 1,000 miles away can be immediately visible on your handheld screen. What you did 30 years ago can be up there forever. Like the proverbial elephant, the internet never forgets. 'Anything you share online is a tattoo', warns the founder of one social networking site.[37] In 2006, a Canadian psychotherapist called Andrew Feldmar tried to cross the border into the United States, as he had hundreds of times before. A border guard did an internet search and found a journal article in which Feldmar mentioned that he had taken LSD in the 1960s. He was detained for four hours, fingerprinted and barred from entering the United States.[38]

The harms of exposure have to be weighed against the harms of nonexposure, and the test is 'the public interest'. But what does that mean? As with privacy and reputation, there is no simple definition of the public interest. The BBC's editorial guidelines say 'it includes but is not confined to: exposing or detecting crime, exposing significantly anti-social behaviour . . . preventing people from being misled by some statement or action of an individual or organisation . . . Disclosing information that allows people to make a significantly more informed decision about matters of public importance'. Different British authorities offer multiple, overlapping, always noncomprehensive lists of what the public interest entails.[39]

In the United States, the privacy tort is tested against the notion of 'legitimate public concern'. 'In determining what comprises a matter of legitimate public interest', says the guiding Second Restatement of Torts, 'account must be taken of the customs and conventions of the community; and in the last analysis what is proper becomes a matter of the community mores'.[40] But what if people living in the same space, and on the same internet, have very different customs and conventions? What are the 'community mores' of cosmopolis? As Robert Post observed long before these dilemmas of cosmopolis became acute, the exercise of drawing these lines is about shaping community standards as well as reflecting existing ones.[41] Our privacy standards evolve in response to social, cultural and technological changes, but also through debating what those standards should be.

In the 1950s, the fact that Prime Minister Winston Churchill had suffered a serious stroke was entirely concealed from the British public. A member of his government noted in his diary: 'Churchill is now often speechless in Cabinet; alternatively, he rambles about nothing'.[42] Today, it seems to us obvious that we should know whether our political leaders are thus seriously incapacitated. News bulletins inform us about the findings of medical checkups on US presidents. Nonetheless, both a Canadian candidate for prime minister, Jack Layton, and an Irish finance minister, Brian Lenihan, felt that the public interest did not oblige them to share the details of their terminal cancers.[43]

Once again, context is all. There is no substitute for a detailed balancing of privacy and reputation against the public interest in every individual case. At the borderlines, this balancing is done by courts of law, but in the vast inland territories of speech it needs to be done every minute, not just by editors and publishers but by every one of us who has become a potential publisher simply by virtue of having internet access.

The judicial balancing acts are often delicate. German courts found that popular magazines should not have published photographs of Princess Caroline of Monaco in the company of an actor in a garden restaurant in the south of France but that, since she was a public figure, it was all right to reproduce pictures of her in public places. The European Court of Human Rights ruled that those photos too should have been covered by her right to a private life.[44]

Our personal judgements can be equally complex. Take, for example, the so-called human flesh searches in which Chinese netizens crowdsource and then expose the identities of people who are accused of having done something those netizens object to. In one case, a woman committed suicide and her sister then published the dead woman's diary online, revealing that her husband had a mistress. The husband and mistress were hunted down, receiving threatening phone calls and death threats. Both eventually left their jobs at the advertising agency where they worked. Justified or unjustified? In another well-known flesh search, netizens identified and hounded a nurse called Wang Jue, who had been privately filmed by a friend crushing a kitten with her high heels. Wang lost her job as a result. Justified or unjustified?[45]

A young woman called Chen Yi posted a message on a popular online bulletin board, saying that her mother was dying of liver disease and needed a transplant. Donations poured in. Then, in what was hailed as the first independent investigation on the Chinese internet, two netizens flew to her home city to check out her story. After nosing around, they claimed her sob story was bogus. In the subsequent outpouring of moralistic fury, a netizen hacked into her personal email account and discovered that her story was largely true: her mother did indeed have serious liver disease and subsequently died during surgery. Chen Yi then posted a detailed statement of how the RMB 114,550 she had received in contributions had been spent—some RMB 40,000 for her mother's surgery, the rest to a charity for children with leukaemia. Chen Yi was the one who had initially 'gone public', and since the public had given money there was in some sense a public interest in knowing that it had been properly spent. The irony is that it took a clear violation of her privacy to correct the 'false light' cast by the original citizen-journalist enquiry.[46]

Now consider the hounding of an apparatchik called Zhou Jiugeng, the head of the real estate department in the Jiangning district of the city of Nanjing. In December 2008, he warned that developers selling properties at a price below the actual cost would be prosecuted. A day later, a post titled 'Eight Questions to Property Bureau Chief Zhou' started a flesh search. Within three days, netizens had posted pictures of Zhou smoking expensive cigarettes and wearing a Vacheron-Constantin watch reportedly worth some RMB 100,000; another three days, and someone revealed that Zhou's brother was a property developer. A year later, Zhou had been dismissed, tried and sentenced to 11 years imprisonment for taking more than RMB 1 million in bribes. Whatever the motives of those who initially went after him, and of the far-from-independent Chinese court which gave him that long sentence, it is hard to argue that the public interest was not served.[47] So there you have it: four 'human flesh searches', four different judgement calls.

BATTLEFIELDS OF THE POWERFUL

Free speech, like law, should be a bulwark for the weak against the strong. At its best, it gives power to the powerless. But the rich and powerful always try to bend it to their own purposes. They exploit and abuse claims for privacy or reputation, and those for publication in the public interest. Lenin famously formulated the power question as 'who whom?' Here, this translates as: who is in a position to get away with saying what about whom? And: who is in a position to stop other people saying what about whom?

The earliest English libel laws were written to protect the 'great men of the realm' against what a statute of 1275 called *scandalum magnatum*. Truth was no defence. 'The greater the truth the greater the libel' is a saying attributed to an eighteenth-century English judge.[48] We have moved on a little from those days, but well into the twenty-first century it was the rich and powerful—the magnates of our day—who exploited Britain's libel laws to stifle legitimate criticism. As we saw in the case of Rachel Ehrenfeld's book, neither the litigants nor the publication needed to be based in Britain for someone to indulge in 'libel tourism'. In a libel action against Vanity Fair magazine in 2003, the film director Roman Polanski was even allowed to testify by video link from Paris, since he feared that if he came to London in person he might be extradited to the United States to serve his sentence for a sexual assault he had perpetrated on a 13-year-old girl in 1978. So, as the media lawyer Geoffrey Robertson acerbically notes, 'the Oscar-winning director, fully made-up, directed his own performance, and wowed the jury'. The British jurors awarded Polanski £50,000 for damage to his reputation and costs reportedly amounting to £1.8 million.[49] Not for nothing did London become known as 'a town named Sue'. Most ordinary people, by contrast, felt they could not afford the financial risk of going to court to defend their reputations. Even after the reform of English libel law, and some timid attempts to give cheaper, faster forms of redress through improved media regulation, the cost remained a powerful deterrent.

The most extreme example of socially unequal protection is the ancient offence of lèse-majesté, which, like blasphemy, remains on the law books of several European countries, including Belgium, the Netherlands and Spain. The Norwegian constitution still declares, 'the King's person is sacred; he cannot be censured or accused'.[50] In practice, you can say almost anything you like about most reigning European monarchs, not to mention the heir to the British throne, Prince Charles, who is the butt of ceaseless satire.

In Thailand, however, draconian lèse-majesté laws were extended in 1976 to prescribe a penalty of between 3 and 15 years imprisonment. They have been used to defend not just the monarchy but one side in a fierce political struggle between the so-called yellow shirts and red shirts. There were 765 court actions for lèse-majesté between 2006 and 2009. In 2011, an American blogger called Joe Gordon was arrested, tried and condemned to two and a half years in prison for posting on his blog extracts translated into Thai from an unauthorised biography of King Bhumibol Adulyadej. (He was released after seven months, ironically enough by royal pardon.)[51] When I visited Bangkok in 2013 to speak at a conference organised by the EU to highlight this issue, an editor and red shirt activist called Somyot Pruksakasemsuk had just been condemned to 10 years in prison for lèse-majesté.[52] In 2015, two Thai students were sentenced to two and a half years in prison for staging a play about a fictional monarch.[53]

Next to monarchs, there are billionaires. A publication about privacy by something called the Private Wealth Council, based in Liechtenstein, culminates in an interview with Hereditary Prince Alois of Liechtenstein. His Highness describes privacy as a unique selling point of the mini-principate: 'in our country, we have a strong culture of privacy protection—well above and beyond finance and tax issues—that is commonly associated with Liechtenstein'.[54] The privacy of billionaires' Liechtenstein bank accounts is not what we have in mind with the wording of our principle.

There is a growing problem of powerful corporations exploiting the law to defend their brands and hide their secrets. This is not to suggest that there should be no laws protecting trademarks, patents, industrial secrets or commercial speech. It is, however, to insist again that—contrary to that famous remark by Mitt Romney ('Corporations are people, my friend')—the rights of corporations must not be elided with those of human beings. Corporations should neither enjoy the same free speech rights as individuals nor be allowed to claim the same rights to privacy and reputation.

The counterbalancing idea of the public interest has also been abused by those possessing wealth and power, and especially by parts of the media. Take, for example, that News of the World front-page story about Max Mosley's 'Nazi orgy'. When Mosley sued for violation of his privacy, it emerged during the trial that the paper's chief reporter had offered £25,000 to one of the women involved, equipped her with a hidden video camera and (as recorded on that camera while he was showing her how to use it) instructed her: 'When you want to get him doing the Sieg Heil [the camera] is about 2.5 to 3 metres away from him and then you'll get him in'. In short, this was a salacious setup. Yet the paper's legal representatives had the cheek to claim in court that there was a 'legitimate public interest' because Mosley's behaviour was 'so debased, so depraved that the law will not offer it protection from disclosure' and that his activities had mocked the Holocaust. This was humbug to make even one of Charles Dickens's arch-hypocrites blush. A former assistant news editor on the same paper was more accurate when he told a colleague some years earlier: 'This is what we do . . . We go out and destroy other people's lives'.[55]

In 2011, the popular Gawker group of online gossip, scandal and sex story websites paid a young man for pictures of his one-night stand with Christine O'Donnell, a candidate for the US Senate who had taken a strongly moralistic stand on sexual behaviour, even advocating abstinence from masturbation. Responding to criticism, the founder of Gawker, a British journalist called Nick Denton, initially offered the public interest defence. But he subsequently told the American journalist James Fallows that he had been wrong to do so: 'It's helpful when someone is a hypocrite, but we should just have said that our interest is voyeuristic. "We did this story because we thought you would like it. We thought it was funny, so we thought you'd think it was funny too". And there was a tidal wave of traffic and attention'. This at least has the virtue of frankness.[56] (Amusingly, Gawker's online Content Guidelines said, 'respect the privacy of others'.)[57]

There is undoubtedly a game, played out over our heads, in which politicians, pop stars, footballers and other celebrities at once seek publicity and attempt to control it. They do this with the aid of a multimillion-dollar PR and 'reputation management' business that has an increasingly powerful influence over media struggling to find a post-Gutenberg business model. Do we really think that some precious privacy was lost because Hello! magazine published unauthorised photographs of the wedding of the movie stars Michael Douglas and Catherine Zeta-Jones, when the happy couple had given exclusive rights to OK! magazine?[58] But there was a genuine violation of privacy when a British newspaper, the Daily Mirror, published photographs of the fashion model Naomi Campbell leaving a meeting of Narcotics Anonymous. As one of the appeal judges observed, 'It is not enough to deprive Miss Campbell of her right to privacy that she is a celebrity and that her private life is newsworthy'.[59] The public interest is not just 'what interests the public'.

One leading British blogger, who uses the pseudonym Guido Fawkes, says, 'My view can be summed up as essentially believing that public figures implicitly consent to public scrutiny. If you want privacy, stay a private person'.[60] But one effect of this is to deter able people from running for public office. 'Is it worth it?' they ask. 'Why put your family through that agony?' In the world of Gawker and the News of the World, the United States would probably never have had a President John F. Kennedy, since his promiscuous sex life was at odds with the public morality of his time. In 2010, the leader of Turkey's main secular opposition party, Deniz Baykal, resigned after the release of a video online purporting to show him and a woman in a bedroom. Fair game, according to the Fawkes principle? And what about the sex life of Guido Fawkes—real name, Paul Staines—who is surely himself a public figure?

Plainly the harms done by unjustified, gross privacy violations and defamation can be so serious, ruining lives and driving vulnerable people like Tyler Clementi to suicide, that the law must attempt to combat them. However, our principle says not merely that we should have a right but that we must be *able* to protect our privacy and to counter slurs on our reputations. In practice, there are serious difficulties for individuals trying to achieve this through the courts, even in the minority of countries where independent courts adjudicate carefully worded privacy and defamation laws passed by democratic parliaments.

So far as privacy is concerned, the Mosley Rule applies even to the richest and most powerful: once you've lost it, you've lost it. In 2012, a French magazine called Closer published paparazzi photographs of Kate Middleton, the Duchess of Cambridge, sunbathing topless while on holiday in the south of France. An Irish newspaper and an Italian magazine immediately followed. The royal couple secured an injunction in the French courts, but a Danish and a Swedish magazine blithely republished the snaps.[61] What is more, I just googled 'Kate Middleton topless' and was able to find them with two clicks. This is lèse-majesté sans frontières: the paparazzi were laughing all the way to the bank and the wife of a future king had, in practice, no effective redress.

There is also what has become known as the Streisand effect. In 2003, the American singer-songwriter Barbra Streisand tried to suppress an online photograph documenting coastal erosion, which happened to show her seaside mansion in Malibu, California. The result of her unsuccessful suit for violation of privacy was to give vastly wider publicity to the very image she was trying to suppress. Before she filed her lawsuit, the photograph—one in a series of thousands showing coastal erosion—had only been downloaded from the photographer's website six times, and two of those downloads were by her lawyers. When the case became known, more than 420,000 people visited the site in one month. The fame of the 'Streisand effect' has doubtless brought many more visitors since.[62]

In cases of defamation, rather than privacy violation, there is somewhat more chance that court proceedings will restore what you want restored—your reputation. But this will happen only after considerable time, stress and expense, and litigation carries the risk that not just the original slur but any other item of dirty linen that the defence lawyers can plausibly bring into the case will be hung out on a very public clothesline.

The costs can be enormous. Max Mosley, being a very rich and determined man, launched an extraordinary campaign not only to secure damages but also to have the false story about his 'Nazi orgy' removed from numerous websites in several countries. I wrote to ask him how much it had cost. He wrote back, mentioning 'a feeling (since realised!) that I would be rather shocked by the figures when I finally had them'. Which indeed he might, for the total legal costs he had incurred in the more than six years since the original publication in the News of the World amounted to nearly £3.5 million. That was without his personal travel and accommodation expenses, and 'about £1.5 million on lobbying and security plus advice and help with the media'. Against that, he had won what he called 'modest damages' from a number of websites.[63] His was an exceptional campaign, to be sure, but it gives some idea of the sums involved. And still I have only to google 'Max Mosley + Nazi orgy' to find all the facts of the case and commentary on it.

Difficult though it is, legislators and courts do have to take on the challenge of making and administering good laws that address the jurisdiction-defying publicity of cosmopolis and keep up with the dizzying development of the technologies of intrusion and exposure. Yet the desired end cannot be achieved by law alone. Whether we are able, and not just theoretically entitled, to defend our privacy and reputations depends at least as much on the practices and standards of the big cats (media, internet platforms, social media sites) and of individual mice (citizens and netizens) as it does on those of the big dogs (governments, courts, Europe's intercanine league). Obviously, I cannot explore all the ramifications of these transnational dog, cat and mouse games, but here are five battlefields to watch.

TRIAL BY TWITTER

One thing the law must try to protect is the fair administration of the law. Freedom of speech is the foundational freedom, but the right to a fair trial runs it close, in both antiquity and importance. To a large extent the two are complementary. The idea of 'open justice, openly arrived at' can also be seen as a free speech ideal. The witness in the courtroom, like the ancient Athenian parrhesiast at the pnyx, should speak the truth in all frankness. It is no accident that there are so many great trial scenes in literature, theatre and film. The proverbial saying that everyone should have his or her 'day in court' conjures an image of someone speaking freely and publicly.

Yet these two lodestars of liberty—free speech and fair trial—are not always perfectly aligned. Some compromise then has to be made. In this as in other areas, the United States has historically privileged free speech more than most European countries, including Britain. For example, the American press has usually been free to report prior convictions of the accused when the British press has been barred from doing so on the grounds that this could prejudice the jury.[64] Yet on both sides of the Atlantic, provision has been made for rape victims, children and those who have reason to fear violent reprisals to testify anonymously. For good reasons, there may be closed hearings in family courts. More problematically, there are the secret judgements of the now notorious Foreign Intelligence Surveillance Act (FISA) courts in the United States, which I will return to in the next chapter.

Television, the internet and social media have both magnified and drama- tised the tensions between free speech and fair trial. Occasionally, they have helpfully revealed jurors' prejudices that undoubtedly existed in earlier times but were only expressed over the kitchen table at home, or in the men's locker room. (For any reader of American literature and history, white juries trying black men in the American South spring immediately to mind.) For example, a British man called Kasim Davey was empanelled as a juror in a trial involving an allegation of sexual activity with a child. He posted this update on his Face- book page: 'Woooow I wasn't expecting to be in a jury Deciding a paedophile's fate, I've always wanted to Fuck up a paedophile & now I'm within the law!' He was found guilty of contempt of court.[65]

The main question, though, is whether the tropical storms of publicity around cases involving well-known people and sensational circumstances make it more difficult to achieve a fair trial. Even if the judicial process is not prejudiced, can that publicity nonetheless do unjustified damage to the reputations of those involved? Plausibly, the answers to these questions are yes and yes. It is, for example, hard to believe that the massive publicity surrounding the televised murder trial of O. J. Simpson did not affect the jury, and hence the verdicts, in the criminal and subsequent civil proceedings against him. An estimated 100 million people across the world watched the televised delivery of the verdict in his criminal trial.[66]

An illuminating episode occurred in Britain in 2013. The country's Law Commission, which recommends changes to the law and legal procedure, had just published a scrupulous report about 'contempt of court', wrestling with the problem of how jurors might be protected from information (true or false) and commentary that they could access with two taps of a fingertip on their smartphones. Should 'internet-enabled devices' be barred from the courtroom or the jury room? Should there be a new offence of searching for extraneous material?[67] The attorney general, a minister in the government headed by David Cameron, had just issued a new warning to people to be careful what they said about ongoing court cases on social media, otherwise they might be liable to prosecution for contempt of court.[68]

Meanwhile, a high-profile case was rollicking the tabloids and social media as the celebrity food writer and TV personality Nigella Lawson, who had just spectacularly split up with her also well-known husband, Charles Saatchi, appeared in court as a prosecution witness against two of their former staff, the Grillo sisters, accused of fraud. Speaking under oath, Nigella admitted that she had occasionally used cannabis and cocaine—most recently to alleviate the unhappiness of her marriage to Saatchi. Tabloid frenzy! Facebook fizzling! Trending on Twitter! At which point, the prime minister, no less, was asked by the editor of the Spectator magazine, 'Are you on Team Nigella?' (#TeamNigella was a Twitter hashtag used by her supporters.) Cameron replied: 'I am. I'm a massive fan, I've had the great pleasure of meeting her a couple of times and she always strikes me as a very funny and warm person. Nancy [Cameron's then nine-year-old daughter] and I sometimes watch a bit of Nigella on telly. Not in court, I hasten to add'.[69] He hastened a little slowly.

Counsel for the defence immediately applied to have the trial halted, on the grounds that the most important prosecution witness had received 'endorsement from the highest possible level'. The judge declared, 'It is of regret when people in public office comment about a person who is involved in a trial which is in progress', and admonished jurors, 'You will realise that what public figures may feel about this case or a witness in this case can have no bearing on your own views'.[70] But following the attorney general's stern warning, should not the prime minister have been prosecuted for contempt of court?

When the trial was over, with the Grillo sisters cleared, Lawson issued a statement criticising the way the judicial process, combined with the media coverage, had almost turned her into the accused: 'I did my civic duty, only to be maliciously vilified without the right to respond. . . . Even more harrowing was seeing my children subjected to extreme allegations in court without any real protection or representation. For this I cannot forgive the court process'.[71] Her protest was reported by the Daily Mirror, which took the opportunity to repeat the malicious vilification in classic tabloidese: 'Nigella's reputation lay in tatters tonight after being forced to admit in court to snorting coke through rolled up £50 notes with her late husband John Diamond and even being driven to drugs through her loveless marriage to Saatchi. During two days of impassioned evidence in the witness box, the bestselling author was forced to admit to smoking cannabis with her children'.[72]

But what was the ultimate effect on most people's attitude towards Nigella Lawson? One columnist claimed that 'however scandalous the headlines, the British public showed time and again that they were not interested in a woman such as Lawson being bullied, belittled, smeared and taken down. We are not so easily manipulated'.[73] Such claims are impossible to prove, but it is a reasonable guess that many people sympathised with her (even while taking a voyeuristic interest in every last detail) and that, whatever happened in the court of law, her reputation was not greatly damaged in the court of public opinion.

DEFENDING YOUR REPUTATION

Probably the most influential judgement in modern First Amendment jurisprudence, the 1964 Supreme Court verdict in New York Times v Sullivan, was about an alleged libel. The New York Times had published a fund-raising appeal that attacked 'Southern violators of the Constitution'—clearly including, though not actually naming, L. P. Sullivan, the police commissioner of the city of Montgomery, Alabama—for their harassment of Martin Luther King and other civil rights activists. Sullivan sued for libel. An Alabama court, presided over by a judge who made no secret of his sympathies with the Confederate side in the American Civil War, awarded punitive damages of $500,000 against the northern, liberal New York Times. Overturning that verdict, the Supreme Court ruled that even though the fund-raising advertisement contained some inaccuracies, it was legitimate political speech covered by the First Amendment, for the United States had 'a profound national commitment to the principle that debate on public issues should be uninhibited, robust and wide-open, and that it may well include vehement, caustic, and sometimes unpleasantly sharp attacks on government and public officials'.[74]

The case is justly celebrated and remains a kind of international gold standard for allowing vigorous criticism of public officials in the cause of good government. In China, 40 years later, a provincial Communist Party leader sued the authors of a book that exposed his corrupt treatment of local peasant farmers. A courageous human rights lawyer, Pu Zhiqiang, took up the case and cited New York Times v Sullivan in his closing statement to the provincial court. Unlike in the United States, however, there was no decisive verdict—let alone a Supreme Court one—establishing a precedent for robust criticism of public officials. Instead, a decade later the crackdown on free speech under President Xi Jinping saw the lawyer himself arrested, tried and convicted for critical remarks he had posted on Sina Weibo.[75]

Yet the scrutiny of how officials do their day jobs, and whether they serve the public as they should, is very much at the easy end of defining 'the public interest'. Beyond that the waters become murkier. Even one of the great proponents of First Amendment jurisprudence, Anthony Lewis, wondered aloud whether the Supreme Court had been right to expand the notion of 'public figures' to include celebrities: 'If a supermarket tabloid prints a sensational story about a movie actress, why should she have to meet the same test as a politician if she sues for libel?'[76] The British free speech legislator Anthony Lester thinks this has gone altogether too far in the United States, pointing out that under New York state law the status of public figure 'has been extended to: a dolphin trainer; a belly dancer; a woman who billed herself as a 'stripper for God'; and a restaurant with a drag queen cabaret where female impersonators are both waiters and performers . . .'[77]

Where should libel law draw the line? The UN Human Rights Committee's 'general comment' on Article 19 says defamation laws 'should include such defences as the defence of truth and they should not be applied with regard to those forms of expression that are not, of their nature, subject to verification. At least with regard to comments about public figures, consideration should be given to avoiding penalising or otherwise rendering unlawful untrue statements that have been published in error but without malice'. 'In any event, a public interest in the subject matter of the criticism should be recognised as a defence'.[78]

Every country has its own defamation law, reflecting its own legal tradition, and it is impossible to discuss them all. Britain is, however, an interesting example. Having for years had one of the worst encrustations of defamation law of any mature liberal democracy—a standing invitation to libel tourism and bullying—it finally acquired a new Defamation Act in 2013, following a campaign by free speech advocates and a high-quality parliamentary debate. This new law attempted to strike the right balance between freedom of expression and the protection of reputation, as well as addressing the new circumstances of cosmopolis.

A statement could be defamatory only if it caused 'serious harm' to the reputation of the claimant. It would not be defamatory if it was 'substantially true', expressed an 'honest opinion' or was on a matter of public interest. In some specified circumstances, if the defendant 'reasonably believed' that the publication was in the public interest then the court should disregard 'any omission of the defendant to take steps to verify the truth of the imputation conveyed by it'.[79] Anthony Lester, who was one of the law's chief architects, made clear that the spirit of the Sullivan judgement marched through these words.[80] Moreover, bearing in mind what we saw in chapter 3 about the way drug companies and professional lobbies have used libel actions to curb scientific debate, it made special provision for peer-reviewed publication in a scientific or academic journal. Recognising the vital contribution of free speech to good government, it gave a blanket exemption for summaries of any information produced by 'a legislature or government anywhere in the world; an authority anywhere in the world performing a governmental function; an international organisation or international conference', as well as the documents produced by a court of law anywhere in the world. Moreover, 'serious harm' to the reputation of 'a body that trades for profit' should mean only 'serious financial loss': corporations are not, after all, people.

Addressing the transformed conditions of cyberspace, the new law introduced a 'single publication rule': action could be taken only on the basis of, and within a reasonable time after, the first publication. Heading off the monster of libel tourism, it specified that people domiciled outside Europe could have an action heard only if 'of all the places in which the statement complained of has been published, England and Wales is clearly the most appropriate place in which to bring an action'. By that criterion, the Saudi businessman could not have sued the American author Rachel Ehrenfeld simply because 23 copies of her book were imported to the UK, and lawmakers in the United States would therefore not have needed to pass 'Rachel's law' and subsequently the federal SPEECH Act. Moreover, 'operators of websites' would not be held liable for stuff posted on those sites, unless the operators failed to respond to complaints in ways to be specified by regulations.

The proof of the pudding would be in the eating, but Britain's new Defamation Act both illustrated the difficulties of legislating for cyberspace and made a decent stab at framing in law the balance proposed in our seventh principle. Yet what came shouting through the public debate around it is that the last thing most people want is to have to pursue a libel case to defend their reputations. One politician summarised what his constituents had told him: 'I don't want any money. I just want them to say sorry'.[81] Thus, for example, many would be happy with a mediation procedure—also known as 'alternative dispute resolution'—resulting in a published correction or apology.[82]

In Germany, a right of reply was first introduced in the state of Baden in 1831. Today's federal states often have in their press laws a stipulation that an individual, association, company or public body can insist on the publication of a correction, free of charge, in the next possible issue of the publication, in the same section and in the same type size as the original statement. Thus you can even get your correction in headline type on the front page of a tabloid. If the publication refuses your request, you may have it enforced by judicial order in a civil court.[83] This seems a quick, simple and fair way of restoring your reputation, although not—remember the Mosley Rule—your privacy.

Yet this is also a remedy from the Gutenberg age, when you would typically expect people to be reading the same newspaper or magazine with their daily coffee or tea—Hegel's 'realistic morning prayer'. The post-Gutenberg world works differently. I talked to someone employed in the burgeoning 'reputation management' business, which specialises in the reputations of the rich. (The office was located round the back of the Ritz hotel in London.) She told me that while they looked at mainstream and social media, the golden key to reputation management is the top ten results that come up when you google the name of some individual or corporate body. The service for which the magnates of our day will pay a lot of money is to nudge the undesirable story (a past scandal, an inconvenient affair) out of the top ten, and a desirable story up in its place. The euphemistically named business of 'search engine optimisation' is a constant catfight over those top results.

As we have seen, Google and other US-based search engines toggle between two incompatible legal postures: one day, they are mere intermediaries, common carriers, their disembodied algorithms automatically producing neutral, clean results; the next, they are themselves exercising the right of free speech, and their decisions should therefore enjoy First Amendment protection.[84] The truth rests somewhere awkwardly in between. Those algorithms are sets of instructions, executed by machines in millions of automated repetitions, but the instructions, and constant tests to improve them, are given by humans who make both broad editorial judgements and some quite specific tweaks.

One senior Google Search engineer told me the following story. In most US states the police are obliged to make available to any member of the public, on demand, the images of anyone they have arrested and photographed in those instantly recognisable full-face and side-of-head mugshots. Some unscrupulous characters saw an opportunity, obtained these en masse, posted them online, and then discreetly invited people to pay to have their own mugshots removed. So now the Google engineers had spent considerable time and ingenuity enabling their computers to identify that particular kind of site, with its characteristic and therefore machine-recognisable sequence of front-and-sides mugshots, and to push the links way down in the search results. Google was thus acting responsibly to protect individual reputation. But should there not be some transparency and accountability about editorial decisions that have such an effect on people's public images (literally images, in this case)? Ah, say the Googlefolk, sharing that information would enable the bad guys to game our system: an argument almost identical to that advanced by intelligence agencies for not revealing their surveillance methods. They have a point, but they also have a commercial motive for secrecy.

Or take the 'autocomplete' suggestions that come up when you start typing a name into the Google Search box. These suggestions are generated by an algorithm based on the search terms most frequently entered by other users in connection with that name. Bettina Wulff, the wife of the then German president Christian Wulff, found that when people typed in her name, autocomplete suggested terms including 'escort' and 'prostitute', reflecting scabrous rumours that she had once worked as 'Lady Viktoria' in a certain Chateau Osnabrück. In 2012, shortly after her husband had resigned as president over corruption charges, she sued Google for defamation, arguing that her 'right of personality' was infringed by the suggestive algorithm.[85]

Predictably, the Streisand effect kicked in. One public opinion poll found that 81 percent of Germans had not heard the rumours before she started her campaign to stop them. But now most people knew about them.[86] German courts eventually ruled that a number of suggestive prompts should be removed from google.de.[87] Yet when I just searched for her name on google.co.uk and google.com, those items still came up, especially if you type in 'Bettina Wulff pr . . .'. (the first two suggestions are 'PR', then 'prostitute'). However, these searches also take you to her refutation of the claims, not least in a memoir whose sales, cynics noted, were probably helped by the whole furore. Ironically enough, after separating from her husband, Wulff returned to her old profession: not pr . . . but . . . PR.

Actually being *able*, not just morally and legally entitled, to defend your reputation is thus a complex business. As the legal commentator Jeffrey Rosen observes, the indelible memory of the internet could mean that 'there are no second chances—no opportunities to escape a scarlet letter in your digital past. Now the worst thing you've done is often the first thing everyone knows about you'.[88] You may not even have done it, but when you try to put the record straight the Streisand effect will result in far more people learning about the allegation. This has led to demands, especially in Europe, for a 'right to be forgotten', to be enforced by an intercanine league of European regulators and courts.

A 'RIGHT TO BE FORGOTTEN'?

There is something odd about the fact that it was the institutions of post-1945 European integration, such as the European Commission, Parliament and Court of Justice, which were in the forefront of demanding a 'right to be forgotten'. For the leitmotif of post-1945 Europe was 'never forget!' Never forget the horrors of the Holocaust, Gulag, multiple wars, occupations and dictatorships. I have lost count of the times I have heard European and especially German politicians repeat George Santayana's line that those who forget the past are condemned to repeat it.[89]

This 'never forget!' was itself a departure from a centuries-old European tradition of dealing with a difficult past by consigning it to oblivion. Just two days after the murder of Caesar, Cicero declared in the Roman Senate that all memory of the murderous discord should be consigned to eternal oblivion: *oblivione sempiterna delendam*. European peace treaties from one between the heirs of Charlemagne in 851 to the Lausanne Treaty of 1923 called specifically for an act of forgetting, as did the French constitutions of 1814 and 1830. The English Civil War ended with an Act of Indemnity and Oblivion. In practice, selective forgetting continued in much of post-1945 Europe, be it Austria revarnishing its past to make itself 'Hitler's first victim', de Gaulle's France suppressing the memory of Vichy collaboration or Spain after 1975, embracing what the writer Jorgé Semprun called 'a collective and willed amnesia'.[90] Nonetheless, the default setting was to the importance of remembering.

You may counter that there is a difference between the collective and the individual, but that is not persuasive. The fact that the former UN secretary-general and Austrian president Kurt Waldheim conveniently 'forgot' his wartime role in Nazi-occupied Yugoslavia exemplified something about his country, but it was also an issue of individual responsibility. To be sure, there was an evident public interest in that case, since Waldheim was a major public figure. Yet few would argue that even the most junior camp guard at Auschwitz has a right to be forgotten. In 2015, a German court convicted a 94-year-old former Auschwitz bookkeeper and sentenced him to four years in prison.[91]

So what was actually being demanded here? In large part, it was the restoration of conditions that prevailed before the digital age, when individuals had more possibilities of 'moving on', 'making a new start', putting painful and embarrassing passages of their past behind them. This reaches down to the deepest levels of what it is to be a person. Psychologically, the condition of remembering everything would be almost unbearable. Viktor Mayer-Schönberger reminds us of the young man Ireno Funes in Jorge Luis Borges' short story 'Funes, the Memorious' who, after a riding accident, has lost his ability to forget. 'To think', Borges writes, 'is to ignore (or forget) differences, to generalise, to abstract. Since his accident, Funes is condemned to see only the trees and never the forest'. Mayer-Schönberger points to the real case of a patient known as AJ, a woman in California, who actually has this condition and finds it crippling.[92]

'Forgetting' does not entirely capture what we human creatures usually do.[93] To function well, we do have to forget a lot: as Sherlock Holmes once put it, we must clear the junk into the attics of our minds. But we also *re-remember* our own pasts, in ways that make them more comfortable for our present selves.[94] This effect sets in very quickly: if two friends give you separate accounts of an argument they had just an hour ago, it seems that they both won.

The indelible memory of the internet threatens both the forgetting that enables us to function and this constant reconstruction of the self. Referring to the collective memory of nations, I have argued that they should steer a course between the unhealthy extremes of amnesia and hypermnesia. I call this psychologically and morally desirable middle way, neither shamelessly forgetting nor obsessively remembering, the path of *mesomnesia*.[95] Individuals need something similar.

Closely related is the possibility of making a new start in the eyes of others. In the North American tradition, this was associated with 'going West'. But in the age of the internet it is almost impossible to 'go West', because the digital scarlet letter travels with you. Truth should indeed be a sufficient defence against a charge of defamation, but this does not mean that publicising a truth is always morally justified. There is such a thing as malicious truth. Writing in the dim and distant 1980s, Joel Feinberg offered the following imaginary example:

A New York girl supports her drug addiction by working as a prostitute in a seedy environment of crime and corruption. After a brief jail sentence, she decides to reform and travels to the far West to begin her life anew. She marries a respectable young man, becomes a leader in civic and church affairs, and raises a large and happy family. Then, twenty years after her arrival in town, her neurotically jealous neighbour learns of her past, and publishes a lurid but accurate account for the eyes of the whole community. As a consequence, her "friends" and associates snub her; she is asked to resign her post as church leader; gossipmongers prattle ceaselessly about her; and obscene inscriptions appear on her property and in her mail.[96]

Such things could happen even before Facebook. Many admirable organisations now exist to defend our 'digital rights', but it is the circumstances that have changed, not the underlying rights. Those rights are not digital but human.[97]

Similarly, most jurisdictions recognise a right for people not to be obliged forevermore to declare their previous convictions. At its most trivial, this is the speeding points disappearing from your driving licence after some years have elapsed. In Britain, this principle of rehabilitation was codified in the 1974 Rehabilitation of Offenders Act. But countries differ as to how far this should go, creating more of the clashes between different national jurisdictions characteristic of cosmopolis. Thus, for example, the German Constitutional Court ruled in 1973 that, in the interests of rehabilitation, and more broadly on grounds of 'the right of personality', citizens should generally not have their earlier criminal convictions referred to in media reports years later.[98] On this basis, two German murderers tried to have their names removed from the English- as well as the German-language Wikipedia article about their victim. Predictably enough, they failed in the United States. German courts also refused the murderers' demand, finding that the interests of press freedom outweighed those of rehabilitation.[99]

That was an old and serious crime being recalled by a new medium. More typically, there is a host of less serious things that people, often children or students, have at some point posted online, especially in the first fine careless rapture of direct publishing and social media. There are at least three distinct though connected concerns here: first, that they did not fully understand how widely these pictures and words would be shared; second, that they did not appreciate the serious consequences that might follow years later (for example, being turned down for a job); and third, that they were not of an age to make mature choices about what they self-publicised.

Europe, with the high value it places on privacy and reputation, drawing on much older, chivalric, courtly and aristocratic traditions of honour, as well as post-Holocaust concerns about human dignity, has been especially alert to these dangers. Given the scale of its single market and the degree of its political and legal integration, the European Union has also had both the power and the will to take on the American internet giants—and what many Europeans regard as their cavalier and commercially self-interested attitude to privacy. The proverbial 'privacy is dead, get over it' was now joined by a remark of Google's Eric Schmidt, who jokingly suggested that young people should change their names and start again at age 21. This was often quoted against him. 'Death by Twitter', Schmidt called it, protesting to a sympathetic author: 'It was a joke. It is a joke. It will remain a joke'.[100] Less sympathetic observers might feel that, since Google Search itself has the effect of globally perpetuating real or alleged remarks, Schmidt was hoist with his own petard.

Wherever the balance between my right to privacy and other people's right to know should be struck, it clearly should not require me to change my name at age 21. 'Data protection' was the characteristically dull concept around which this European debate crystallised, as prescribed by an EU directive of 1995 and implemented—with considerable national variations—by data protection agencies of individual member states. It was then in the long-running debate about a new version of that EU directive, now to take the stronger form of a regulation having direct legal effect in all member states, that a putative 'right to be forgotten' acquired prominence.[101]

Even before that proposed regulation came into force, however, the issue erupted with a judgement of the European Court of Justice against Google in spring 2014. In 2010, a Spaniard called Mario Costeja González applied to Spain's data protection agency to have a news item that had been published in 1998 in a Spanish newspaper, La Vanguardia, removed from both the newspaper's website and Google Search. The 36-word news item reported that González's house had been repossessed because of unpaid debts. The data protection agency decided that the newspaper did not have to remove the original item, since that had been lawfully published, but Google must take down the search links to it. Google appealed to Spain's highest national court; that court referred it to the European Court of Justice (the ECJ, not to be confused with the Strasbourg-based European Court of Human Rights); and the ECJ ruled that, in line with the 1995 EU Data Protection Directive, Google must remove the link from all searches on its EU-localised search engines (google.es, google .de, google.pl, google.co.uk, etc.).[102]

The first effect of this was entirely predictable: Mario Costeja González Streisanded himself. With massive international coverage of the case—the Guardian counted 840 articles in the world's largest media outlets on a single day—his name was now indelibly associated across the globe with the very incident that he wished to erase.[103] I just put 'Mario Costeja González' into my google.co.uk search box, and all the top 10 results refer to this case.[104] In trying to restore his privacy, González made himself not merely a public figure but a historic one. He would forever be remembered as the man who wished to be forgotten.

But that was only the beginning. Google was faced with a deluge of requests for links to be 'delisted'. By the next summer, Google had received more than 300,000 such requests, evaluated more than 1.1 million URLs as a result and delisted some 40 percent of those.[105] Whereas previously it had removed links to what its chief legal officer, David Drummond, called 'a very short list' of categories of content—including child sexual abuse imagery, personal information such as bank details, and defamation and intellectual property violation, when properly notified—it now swam into a vast ocean of what Drummond acknowledged were 'difficult value judgements'.[106] Where Googlefolk had once preached the one true faith of the Church of the First Amendment, they now articulated a special respect for European concerns. 'We're trying now to be more European and think about it maybe more from the European context', said Google founder Larry Page. 'A very significant amount of time is going to be spent in Europe talking'.[107] An advisory council of 'external experts' was set up and public hearings held across Europe before that council produced a final report, with several dissenting views.[108] In short, legal action by one of the world's biggest dogs had prompted one of the world's biggest cats to issue an open invitation to all European mice.

This story raises four big, closely related questions: what should be removed, where, how and by whom? These questions are pertinent far beyond the specifics of Google Search and Europe. The 'what' question involves those complex, contextual judgements that are the meat and vegetables of this book. The 'where' reveals again the dilemmas of cosmopolis. If Google decided a search link should be removed to comply with European concerns, it would usually do so only for the search engines localised in member states of the European Union. Any searcher, simply by entering 'google.com/ncr', could find the delisted information on the American mother ship. So European privacy proponents suggested that the delisting should also happen on google.com. Instead of American First Amendment norms being imposed on Europe, European privacy norms should be imposed on the United States.

That takes us to the 'how'. For years, Google's practice had been to indicate with an italicised line at the bottom of the first page of search results when a link to something had been removed, be it a Holocaust denial site on the Germany-based google.de or Señor González's now unforgettable wish to be forgotten. But that notice itself invites the curious to go looking for the missing piece. Not to do this, however, would risk turning Google into Orwell's Ministry of Truth, consigning historical records to the memory hole. Mayer-Schönberger suggests there should be an internet-wide norm of 'expiration dates', so that we can ourselves decide how long we want personal information we post online to remain visible.[109] The Harvard internet scholar Jonathan Zittrain, by contrast, argues that the *removal* of links to information from a search engine should be only for a limited time.[110] The technical feasibility of entirely removing any piece of information across the whole of the internet must surely be doubted—but that does not free us from the obligation to seek a reasonable principle and apply it as effectively as possible.

Perhaps the most interesting question is the fourth: 'by whom?' Is it better to leave these decisions in the hands of private powers, with all the dangers of arbitrariness, nontransparency and commercial self-interest that brings? Or is it better to hand them over to public powers, potentially with more legal consistency, democratic accountability and transparency, but also with significant risks of political manipulation, overstrengthening state power and excessive official secrecy? Explaining Google's European charm offensive, Larry Page made this curiously muddled observation: 'In general, having the data present in companies like Google is better than having it in the government with no due process to get that data, because we obviously care about our reputation. I'm not sure the government cares about that as much'.[111] But what 'due process' do we have for finding out what Google knows about us? Indeed, the phrase evokes precisely the legitimate, effective control over public powers that the rule of law should give citizens in a well-ordered liberal democracy.

Then again, as we will examine more closely in the next chapter, when it comes to controlling and exploiting our personal information there is a large gulf between 'should' and 'is'. The right answer in theory (hand such decisions to transparent, legally and democratically accountable public powers) may not be right in practice. What is certain is that the best, but also the worst outcomes will result from P². Benign, transparent collaboration between the big cats and dogs offers the best chance we have of restoring privacy and defending reputation in this transformed world; uncontrolled, hidden collaboration between them leads to a nightmare of total surveillance.

In sum, the notion of a generalised 'right to be forgotten' is indefensible in a society that believes in freedom of expression. As the Oxford internet scholar William Dutton punchily observed, 'Forget about the right to be forgotten!'[112] We do, however, need more control over our personal information. A basic principle must be that my data remains mine—and not yours to data-mine. Citizens and netizens should have what the Germans call 'informational self-determination'. This right is trumped only when there is a genuine public interest in that information being known and the public interest outweighs the harm done to the individual by publication. Although simply stated, this principle is fiendishly difficult to implement, for once the genie is out of the bottle, the cat out of the bag, the rat out of the sack, it is very hard to put them back again. So if we value our privacy and reputation, we should take more care about the personal information we share in the first place.

DON'T BE ZUCKERED

In 2010, the Electronic Frontier Foundation tweeted an appeal for 'a new word that means "deliberately confusing jargon and user-interfaces which trick users into sharing more info than they want to"'. @heisenthought responded: 'how about "zuck"? As in: "that user interface totally zuckered me into sharing 50 wedding photos. That kinda zucks'. Other suggestions included 'Zucker-mining', 'Infozuckering' and alternative variations on the name of Facebook founder Mark Zuckerberg.[113] By this time, Facebook had become notorious for, well, zuckering you. A New York Times technology blogger had tweeted 'Off record chat w/ Facebook employee. Me: how does Zuck feel about privacy? Response: [laughter] He doesn't believe in it'.[114] Although, as we have seen, popular protest had forced Facebook to withdraw its Beacon service, an online graphic vividly showed how Facebook's default privacy settings had evolved between 2005 and 2010 to lead users to share more and more.[115]

Max Schrems, an undergraduate law student at the University of Vienna, used a provision of Irish law—Facebook's European operation being tax-advantageously located in Ireland, and therefore coming under Irish jurisdiction for EU data protection purposes—to obtain a copy of all the information the company had collected and kept on him. Although Schrems was not a heavy user of the social network, Facebook sent him a computer disc containing 1,222 pages of information. He then filed a complaint with the Irish Data Protection Commissioner, alleging 22 violations of European privacy law. To assist in his campaign, he set up a website called Europe versus Facebook (europe-v-facebook.org).[116]

These concerns were not confined to Europe. The US Federal Trade Commission found in 2011 that Facebook had 'deceived consumers by telling them they could keep their information on Facebook private, and then repeatedly allowing it to be shared and made public'.[117] Moreover, even American teenagers started migrating to other platforms, such as Snapchat, WhatsApp, Secret and Whisper, doubtless partly because those were snappier on a smartphone, but perhaps also because—as the names Secret and Whisper might suggest— they were seen as more attentive to privacy. (Facebook responded by buying WhatsApp.)

Under such sustained criticism from both dogs and mice, but probably above all because it feared the loss of customers, Facebook introduced new privacy settings in 2014. These were still very complicated. For example, in answer to its own question 'What data is stored by Facebook?', it recommended that users read its data policy, with further study needed if you wanted permanently to delete rather than just 'deactivate' your account.[118]

Moreover, in the very week that it announced this new privacy policy, Facebook unveiled a new feature on its smartphone app. Eerily, this could activate the microphone on your smartphone by remote control and listen in to what was happening around you, identifying music being played and what you were watching on television. As one commentator, Kashmir Hill, observed: 'The payoff for users in allowing Facebook to microphone-lurk is that the social giant will be able to add a little tag to their status update that says they're watching an episode of Game of Thrones as they sound off on their happiness (or despair) about the rise in background sex on TV these days'. Initially, Hill used the word 'eavesdropping' but then revised her wording online, since, as she scrupulously observed, Facebook wasn't secretly listening in 'but rather doing so with the permission of users'.[119]

Facebook is actually at the more visible end of zuckering: everyone knows that its whole idea is to share things. But when more than 1 billion people downloaded a free video game called Angry Birds, how many knew that it was sharing their personal information wittingly with online advertising services and unwittingly with the security services of the United States and Britain?[120] In 2009, a British filmmaker called David Bond made an intriguing documentary called Erasing David, in which he attempted to disappear without trace. He was tracked down in 18 days by two private detectives, who started only with his name. Near the end of the film, when he has been 'caught', we see him shocked to enter a room filled with all the information they had managed to find on him, some of it extracted from his dustbin or blagged on the phone, but much of it discovered online.[121] These days, one room would not be large enough.

How can we avoid being zuckered? In 1980, making an influential early attempt to shape a discussion about privacy, the Organisation for Economic Co-operation and Development listed seven desiderata for the protection of personal information: notice, purpose, consent, security, disclosure, access and accountability.[122] In theory, the first three are covered by the legal small print of privacy policies; in practice, these provisions are almost useless. If we want to use an app or service, we click the 'I agree' button. Ian Brown of the Oxford Internet Institute quotes an estimate that it would take about 20 hours to read all the privacy policies we agree to in a year.[123] Even if we did read them, most of us would not understand the legalese.

This does not mean we are powerless. First of all, following the principle of disclosure used so effectively by Max Schrems, we need to understand what is being done with our (notionally 'informed') consent. Teachers at a local school I work with in Oxford leapt at the opportunity to raise their pupils' understanding of online privacy. Tools like Collusion enable you to see just how much information is being shared, via cookies, about the websites you visit.[124]

Legally enforceable regulation has an important role to play here, including the practical implementation of the access principle. This says not only that we should be allowed to access our data but that we should be able to correct inaccurate information held on us. If we are citizens of democracies, we can influence that regulation through our parliaments and diverse media, although we should never underestimate the monied power of the lobbies we will be up against. As consumers, we can influence the big cats directly, both by raising our voices and even more, by exiting to other providers. If you have the patience and skill, there are also relatively simple technological steps you can take to enhance your individual privacy. Bringing together these different kinds of power, we can start trying to shift the technological and commercial norm to what are called privacy-enhancing technologies, or PETs for short. These industry-wide shifts do sometimes occur, as for example towards low CO_2 emission cars, and when they do, they are more powerful than any individual battles. Solitary Davids must fight Goliath; networked Davids can change him.

Yet computer scientists rightly warn us that technological privacy protection is only as strong as its weakest link: the human being. The PET is no better than its owner. In 2007, sensitive personal information about nearly half the population of Britain was lost because someone at HM Revenue and Customs sent the computer discs by post to the National Audit Office. They did not even use registered delivery. In autumn 2015, hacking, revenge by a disgruntled employee and programming error resulted in personal information on hundreds of thousands of customers of, respectively, Talk Talk, a mobile phone operator, and two popular retailers, Morrisons and Marks & Spencer, being compromised. And those were just the reported data breaches in one country in one autumn.[125] Few if any technological safeguards will withstand the combined forces of human stupidity, corruption and voyeurism, especially when these are resourcefully exploited by private investigator, journalist, hacker and spy.

If we believe that varying levels of privacy and publicness are essential to the richness of free speech, we will therefore, when everything possible has been done by law, regulation, technology and industry standards, still have to consider how, in these dramatically changed conditions, we choose to speak. And what do we express where? A radical suggestion comes from Randi Zuckerberg, the sister of Facebook's founder. In a children's book, she portrays a little girl called Dot, who starts out spending all her time with various digital devices, on which she knows how to tap, touch, tweet, tag, surf, swipe, search and talk, talk, talk. Then her mum says, 'Go outside, Dot!' There, happy little Dot discovers how to tap plants, touch flowers, tweet with the birds, share with a dog and talk, talk, talk with real people in the sunshine. The book concludes: 'This is Dot. Dot's learned a lot'.[126]

Even if we don't adopt Randi Zuckerberg's advice to abandon her brother's virtual empire in favour of the local park, we can reflect on how we use Facebook and other online platforms. If we master the privacy settings sufficiently to limit who we share with, and are able to take stuff down afterwards—perhaps with the aid of something like Mayer-Schönberger's built-in default expiration dates—we can start to restore the traditional limitations of time and space that the internet has blown apart. That leaves us free to use the internet's time- and space-transcending potential when we really do want, as that nineteenth-century Polish poet put it, to share our truths with everyone.

Moreover, as people get wise to what's going on, they adapt their forms of self-expression in ingenious ways. Danah Boyd, the researcher who has studied how young people use the internetworked world, gives interesting examples. For example, a 17-year-old called Shamikah deployed a technique called 'whitewalling', making sure that as often as possible her front Facebook page—originally called the wall—is blank. She knew perfectly well that people could bring a post or photo back onto it, but she was sending a message about how she wanted things to be. Then there is all that playing around you can do with name and profile. On MySpace, a high school pupil called Allie listed her age as 95, her place of origin as Christmas Island and her income as \$250,000+ per year.[127] This brings us to a fifth and final battlefield.

JANUS ANONYMOUS

'On the internet, nobody knows you're a dog': the now proverbial phrase was originally the caption of a 1993 New Yorker cartoon.[128] It showed a dog sitting in front of a desktop computer, talking to another dog. What this has come to mean is: on the internet nobody knows whether you are who you say you are, and you usually don't have to say anyway.

If we have a right to be forgotten, perhaps we also have a right to be somebody else? It is very widely accepted that you should not impersonate somebody who actually exists. Recall that one of the four privacy violations in US law is the appropriation of another person's name or likeness. You must not pretend to be me and I must not pretend to be you. But what about being somebody who does not exist? Why shouldn't we have a pseudonymous identity, a virtual self—or several of them?

Anonymity is among the most double-edged affordances of the internet. It has contributed to some of the largest evils of online communication. Remember the comment of the Canadian Islamist feminist Irshad Manji: '"Anonymous" is the one who's constantly threatening me with death'.[129] Online, middle-aged male paedophiles pretend to be young girls in order to groom their victims. As anyone who has spent more than 10 minutes reading comment threads knows, anonymity can encourage stream-of-consciousness ranting, hateful remarks, obscenities and abuse. It also lends itself to other kinds of deception. During the Arab Spring, many readers (including journalists) were captivated by the 'Gay Girl in Damascus' blog, describing the dramatic experiences of an American-born lesbian called Amina Abdallah Arraf. When reports of her abduction from the streets of Damascus triggered a US State Department enquiry, it finally emerged that she was actually Tom MacMaster, a middle-aged American man studying in Scotland.[130]

The assumption underpinning most civilised person-to-person conversation is that we should know who we are talking to. So we start by introducing ourselves. At its best, this expresses a presumption of equality between all speakers and listeners—*isegoria*, as the ancient Athenians called it. The secret police interrogator barking questions at you from behind a blinding lamp personifies, precisely in his unidentifiability and impersonality, an unequal power relationship. He is anonymous.

Yet Janus Anonymous also has another face, one that can support privacy and enable self-expression. Facebook insists people use their real names yet stakes its own claim to protect your privacy on the anonymisation of your personal data. Yes, says Facebook, we may share your data with a company called Datalogix, to establish what percentage of those who view an ad actually go on to buy a product from that advertiser—but you will always be anonymous to them.[131]

If only such claims were plausible. I often behave online as if I believed them, but on the evidence I should not. Most of us have had the disconcerting experience that, minutes after searching for, buying online or just emailing about, say, sandals, advertisements for sandals start popping up on our screens. I choose a deliberately innocuous example. The companies may say that only the computer knows your most secret desires (sandals?), but some fallible, corruptible human being runs that computer. The more data that is held on us, the more unlikely privacy-serving anonymity becomes. This is the curse of 'big data'.[132]

In the mid-1990s the Massachusetts health insurance scheme released anonymised data on the health records of state employees. The governor of Massachusetts, William Weld, assured the public that patient privacy was well protected. A graduate student in computer science, Latanya Sweeney, set out to prove him wrong. Using publicly available sources such as electoral rolls, she identified the health records of the governor himself, including diagnoses and prescriptions, and sent them to his office. This celebrated incident has become known as the 'Weld re-identification'. Sweeney went on to argue that 87 percent of all Americans could be uniquely identified using only three bits of information: ZIP code, birthdate and sex.[133]

In 2006, AOL released a dataset of 20 million search queries. It too cited the interests of research and insisted that the data had been anonymised. Within days, the New York Times had identified user number 4417749 as Thelma Arnold, a 62-year-old widow living in Lilburn, Georgia. 'My goodness', she told a reporter, 'it's my whole personal life'.[134] Then Netflix released an anonymised dataset of its users. Two young researchers found a way of correlating the data with people who posted reviews on the Internet Movie Database to reveal their identities.[135] Each time this happens, there is an outcry and rules are supposedly tightened, but the sheer quantity of 'big data' makes identification ever easier.

Sometimes, it is not just privacy that is protected by anonymity but someone's personal safety. In fact, millions of people across the world would be in danger if they used their real names or were otherwise readily identifiable. This is self-evidently true in authoritarian regimes. Middle Eastern security services have confronted activists with material from their Facebook pages and Twitter accounts. Wael Ghonim set up the 'We are all Khaled Said' Facebook page, which helped to animate the popular demonstrations that overthrew Egyptian president Hosni Mubarak in 2011. Ghonim recalls how essential it was that he and other administrators of such pages remained anonymous—and how terrified he was when he once accidentally revealed his own identity.[136] The page was also temporarily taken down by Facebook—not Mubarak—when the administrator was reported for using a pseudonym, but the social network then bent its own rules to restore it. It is no accident that the Chinese party-state has demanded that people reveal their real names to the country's internet service providers—and hence to the party-state itself.[137]

This consideration does not apply only to life under authoritarian regimes. Even in a free country, if you live in an abusive relationship or oppressive family, you may feel able to speak freely only if you do not use your real name. The same is true of those whose sexual orientation, religious belief or political view is persecuted, criminalised or simply frowned upon in their society, community or extended family. People can also feel unfree at the workplace. Many fear, sometimes rightly, that they may be denied advancement or even lose their jobs if their views become known to their employers.

Here, the interests of personal safety and privacy shade into those of free speech. If privacy is a condition for free speech, then we have to acknowledge that, for many people in many circumstances, anonymity (or pseudonymity) is in practice a precondition for expressing yourself freely. In Myanmar, as it emerged from the long darkness of military rule, I met a poet who writes under the name Pandora. A spirited, decisive young woman, electronic box always to hand, she gave me her card, which had no postal address or landline but listed her blog, Facebook page, Twitter account, mobile phone number and Gmail address. She had started blogging in the bad old days of 2007 and found artistic and personal freedom online. 'Facebook for me is another country', she told me. 'I have another life in another country'.[138]

This liberating potential of virtual identities and online worlds takes us to a broader point. All of us present outward images of ourselves that are often different from what we feel inside. Erving Goffman famously analysed 'the presentation of self in everyday life'.[139] It is not only teenagers who experiment with different images and delight in role-playing. We have an idea of mature personal integrity that consists in knowing exactly who you are and letting others know it too—Martin Luther's 'here I stand, I cannot do otherwise'—but our inner realities are more complicated. What you express through a digital persona, or even an avatar in the game Second Life, may be as true, in some sense, as the real-life 'you' who relates to your mother or workmates. At the very least, it may express another part of your self and your personal truth. A contributor to freespeechdebate.com, who identified himself only as Bob, posted on our thread about privacy a quotation he attributed to Oscar Wilde: 'Man is least himself when he talks in his own person. Give him a mask, and he will tell you the truth'.[140] Yes, even the mask of Bob.

On freespeechdebate.com we suggest that contributors use their real names. We argue that this should be a norm of civilised debate in a free country. It is better—more honest, more dignified—if you and I both know who we are talking to. But we acknowledge that people often have good reasons to choose a pseudonym and should be free to do so.

The variations on this theme of online identities are endless: some of them deadly serious, some less so. For example, it emerged in 2010 that Orlando Figes, a distinguished historian of Russia, had been posting reviews on Amazon book pages under the pseudonym 'Historian'. He lamented the award to another author of a prize for which one of his own books had been in contention: 'Oh dear, what on earth were the judges thinking . . .' He denounced the work of fellow historians of Russia as 'rubbish', 'dense' and 'pretentious', while praising as 'beautiful and necessary' the latest from his own masterly pen. In a feat of denial that would surely have interested Sigmund Freud, he initially sued his fellow historians for daring to suggest that he might be 'Historian', then claimed his wife had written the offending posts, before collapsing in a heap with contorted apologies and the payment of damages.[141]

Gogolesque in a different way was an application called Lives On which promised to enable you to go on tweeting after your death. Not Second Life but After-Life. Its advertising slogan was 'When your heart stops beating, you'll keep tweeting'. The early results were dire, splicing together in unintentionally Dadaist fashion parts of earlier, real-life tweets. For example: 'also it sounds like absolute turd, we'll write you a nice monologue when you get down to london in a buddhist temple'.[142] But if the algorithm were to get better, interesting questions would arise. Who would be the 'speaker' here? Would it be the dead man talking or a living machine? Many liberal legal systems hold that you cannot libel the dead, but could the dead libel the living?

More seriously, there is a qualitative difference between a pseudonym consistently used by one person over a longer period and the pure, covert anonymous. Unlike Janus Anonymous, Janus Pseudonymous can himself or herself be the bearer of a good reputation, even if according to the legal register there is no one of that name. 'George Orwell' was, after all, a pseudonym. Other examples are Mark Twain, John Le Carré and George Eliot—the male pseudonym of Mary Ann Evans, a great female novelist. (Ban this impostor from Facebook!) But the more persistent and clearly identified with a real person the pseudonym is, the less it protects his or her privacy, safety and freedom from fear of the consequences of speaking freely. Moreover, even persistent pseudonyms can be abused.

Anonymous is generally at the harder edge. On the one hand, it is the hallmark of the torturer, the paedophile and your bog-standard online scatologist.

On the other, it is a mark of protest against established powers. An influential group of hacker activists, or 'hacktivists', uses the Twitter account @AnonymousWiki. Their motto is:

We are Anonymous
We are Legion
We do not forgive
We do not forget
Expect us.

Parmy Olson, in her book *We Are Anonymous*, points out that 'we are Legion' derives from a passage in the King James translation of the Bible where Jesus approaches a man possessed by demons and asks his name, to which the man replies: 'My name is Legion: for we are many'.[143] Anonymous, in this incarnation, hacks into the accounts and websites of companies and organisations (including even the FBI), makes public their internal communications and posts messages of protest.

But maybe the combined secret power of the state and companies, P^2, is sometimes such that you need these extraordinary measures to combat it? It was not just hacktivists who covered their faces with the stylised Guy Fawkes mask of Anonymous, inspired by the film 'V for Vendetta', when they joined real-life protests at what they saw as the abuse of anonymous state and corporate power revealed by Julian Assange and Edward Snowden.[144] After all, police or secret services would photograph you as you marched, and enter your digital image ineradicably into a searchable database. Perhaps it takes anonymous to restrain the power of anonymous?

SECRECY

> 'We must be empowered to challenge all limits to freedom
> of information justified on such grounds as national
> security'.

S: You can't say that.
C: Why not?
S: We can't tell you.
C: Why can't you tell me?
S: It would endanger your security.
C: Why?
S: We can't tell you why it would endanger your security because to tell you that would endanger your security.
C: So I may not know what I may not know and I may not know why I may not know it?
S: Next caller please.

Harold Pinter did not actually write this dialogue, but he might have. Such is the sense of overwhelming impotence that a citizen feels when faced with a state that flatly refuses, on grounds of national security, your right to speak and to know.

My Pinteresque dialogue is not plucked from thin air. In 2006, defending a programme in which the National Security Agency (NSA) conducted large-scale surveillance of communications inside the United States without a warrant, the country's then attorney general, Alberto Gonzales, told CNN that this operation had 'been extremely helpful in protecting America' from terrorist attacks, but 'because the programme is highly classified . . . he could not make public examples of how terrorist attacks were actually disrupted by the eaves-dropping'.[1] Interviewed on BBC radio, a former head of Britain's domestic security service said that newspapers that published material leaked by Edward Snowden about mass surveillance by Britain's Government Communications Headquarters (GCHQ) could never know what terrorist plots 'will not now be detected and not now be thwarted . . . the damage which I don't think anybody outside the intelligence community can readily detect or judge'. Therefore the newspapers should not publish.[2]

One response to such assertions was suggested by a former editor of the Independent, Chris Blackhurst. 'If the security services insist something is contrary to the public interest', he wrote, 'and might harm their operations, who am I . . . to disbelieve them?'[3] What we might call the Blackhurst Principle places extraordinary confidence in the judgement and integrity of members of the security services. But why should just that group of men and women, unlike any other—priests, politicians, judges, soldiers, businesspeople or architects—be granted this exceptional trust? Why, in this area alone, should the boundary of what may be expressed and known about be set unilaterally by officials and members of the executive?

SECURITY AND THE CHALLENGE PRINCIPLE

It is a condition for the survival of free speech that any limits to free speech, on whatever grounds, must be open to public challenge. Such limits can be tested by brave individuals saying what they are forbidden to say and facing the consequences. They can also be challenged more generically along the lines of 'We should be free to say that kind of thing; explain to us, oh powers that be, why we are not . . .'

When we first formulated a version of this principle for freespeechdebate.com, we included other grounds for setting limits, such as public order and morality. Recall that Article 19 of the Covenant includes among its justifications for legitimate restrictions 'the protection of national security or of public order (*ordre public*), or of public health or morals'. That thought remains here in the words 'on such grounds as' national security, and the challenge principle applies to those other grounds too. Yet they are generally easier to interrogate because the facts and the justifications are in plainer view. We can disagree with a restriction based on morality, religion, privacy or personal honour, but at least we know what it is and why it's there.

'Public order' is already more slippery. Even in recent times, public order has sometimes been taken to include not merely the absence of public disorder but also elements of social and moral order, propriety and decorum.[4] As we saw in chapter 5, Britain's capacious and often misused Public Order Act illustrates how a public order justification can give the police quite arbitrary powers to curb free speech. ('Your horse is gay' said that tipsy student to the mounted policeman, and the student was locked up for the night under the Public Order Act.) In less free countries, variations on 'public order' are used to detain people for months or even years without any due process.

National security is, however, the most extreme and genuinely challenging case. It is traditionally argued that the first duty of the state is to protect the security of its people. That obviously includes defence against invasion from abroad and armed uprising at home. Yet in an age when terrorists both fly across frontiers and emerge from the back rooms of ordinary houses in the country where they live, there is an elision, or at least a sliding scale, between national security—that of the country as a whole—and the personal security of individual citizens. Thus when the United States created a Department of Homeland Security after the 11 September 2001 terrorist attacks, it institutionalised an idea—'homeland security'—wider than national security classically conceived.[5] Elsewhere, security is even more broadly defined. In 2012, Russia's penal code was amended to criminalise 'financial, material or technical assistance, consultancy or any other assistance to a foreign state, international or foreign organisation' directed against 'the security of the Russian Federation', and what had previously been 'external security' was changed to just 'security'.[6] In China and North Korea, the party-state has a ministry of 'public security'. In such cases, it is not just the security of the public that is being protected but that of the current state powerholders against their own publics.

Often we talk of a balancing act between security and liberty, and sometimes there is a real trade-off between the two. But a group charged by President Obama with reviewing the United States' electronic surveillance arrangements, following the Snowden revelations, started its report—subsequently published as *The NSA Report*—by pointing out that this can also be viewed as a balance between two different kinds of security, national and personal. After all, the Fourth Amendment to the US Constitution provides for 'the right of the people to be *secure* in their persons, houses, papers and effects, against unreasonable searches and seizures . . .'[7] (Emphasis added in the report.) Security in this second sense is closely related to privacy, so the tension is also between national security and privacy.

Not all aspects of this problem directly concern freedom of expression but, as I have repeatedly emphasised, privacy is a necessary condition for free speech. A survey of more than 520 American writers conducted by American PEN in autumn 2013 suggested that their realisation of the extent of NSA surveillance had a chilling effect. Roughly a quarter of the writers interviewed said that, as a result, they had curtailed or avoided social media activity and deliberately avoided certain topics in phone or email conversations. This chilling effect extended even to web searches relating to terrorism, Islamist extremism and the Middle East.[8] Thus, the infringement of privacy in the name of security also carries a cost to speech. To put it in American constitutional terms, riding an electronic coach and horses through the Fourth Amendment ends up denting the First Amendment too.

It was on these grounds that Wikipedia filed a lawsuit against the NSA on the grounds of violating both the Fourth Amendment and the First. Noting that the head of Egypt's main spy agency had boasted that he was 'in constant contact' with the CIA, Jimmy Wales and the executive director of the Wikimedia foundation invited readers of the New York Times to imagine a Wikipedia editor in Egypt who wanted to edit a page about opposition to the Egyptian military regime, or discuss it with fellow editors: 'If that user knows the NSA is routinely combing through her contributions to Wikipedia, and possibly sharing information with her government, she will surely be less likely to add her knowledge or have that conversation, for fear of reprisal. And then imagine this decision playing out in the minds of thousands of would-be contributors in other countries'.[9]

Security is also the field in which the imbalance of power between an effective modern state and the citizen is greatest. (This obviously does not apply to the many places in today's world where warlords, gangs, businesses or local cabals are stronger than a weak or failed state.) The sociologist and historian Charles Tilly famously observed that 'war made the state and the state made war'.[10] It is in times of war that the state is most likely to invoke both the necessity and its own strongest powers to curb free speech. The First Amendment scholar Geoffrey Stone argues that across more than 200 years, 'virtually every instance in which the United States has directly punished political dissent has occurred during wartime. In peace time, and in times of relative tranquillity— which, by my definition, make up roughly 80% of our history—the United States has *never* punished political dissent' (his italics).[11] In his book *Perilous Times*, Stone identifies six periods in which United States saw itself as being at war: in the late 1790s (against the French), the American Civil War, the First World War, the Second World War, the Cold War (the era of McCarthyism in particular) and the Vietnam War.

Then there was the War on Terror after the 9/11 attacks. Or was that just 'war'? Another vital question is precisely in what conditions you are at war, justifying unusual limits on freedom of expression and information. This in turn has a vital corollary: who gets to decide that? What the administration of George W. Bush and the government of Tony Blair called the War on Terror, other democratic governments, including many in Europe, treated as combatting a particularly dangerous form of international crime. The military historian Michael Howard immediately and wisely warned against the grave implications of calling this a 'war'.[12] On the other hand, there are instances, such as the aerial attacks on Pakistan and Syria ordered by President Barack Obama, where some would argue his administration went to war while insisting it was not.[13]

Even if the state does not declare war, it may proclaim a 'state of emergency'. The German philosopher Carl Schmitt argued that the power to declare what he called the *Ausnahmezustand*—an exceptional state or condition—is the defining feature of state sovereignty. In suspending the existing legal order which supposedly constitutes it, the state shows that it is at once part of and above that order. It does this by pronouncing one word: 'war'. Or 'emergency'. Or *Ausnahmezustand*. What I have called word power is not just the power of words in themselves but their impact when combined with other forms of power.

The Italian philosopher Giorgio Agamben shows how what in the English version of his work is translated as a 'state of exception'—a seductive but potentially confusing conflation of two meanings of 'state'—has a long history. He argues that the United States did it again after 9/11.[14] Elsewhere, the exception becomes the rule, and state of exception secures the current powerholders' rule over the state. Egypt maintained a 'state of emergency' from 1981 until 2012. Swaziland has, at this writing, been in a 'state of emergency' for more than 40 years. In Orwell's *1984*, the rulers of Oceania justify permanent repression at home by being permanently at war abroad. Western democracies are clearly a long way from that, and it is hyperbole to suggest otherwise. Yet people in countries such as Britain and the United States have lived since 2001 in what has been called, with reference to the colour-coding of national security risk levels, 'a perpetual state of yellow'.[15] For some of them, especially for noncitizens suspected of terrorist connections, this has meant long-term deprivation of human rights and civil liberties.

Another reason for the imbalance of power between state and citizen is the development of those very technologies that have given us an unprecedented increase in our ability to communicate with others. Peter Swire, a member of the panel charged by President Obama with preparing what became *The NSA Report*, argues that the early twenty-first century is a 'golden age of surveillance' for security services. He ascribes this to three technological developments in particular: the minutely detailed location data provided by mobile phones, the 'social graph' of contacts that we all produce, even if we are not active on social media, and the array of 'big data' that has created digital dossiers on us all.[16] We should add to Swire's list of technologies the phenomenon of P^2, since private companies actually collect most of the information into which states tap, licitly or illicitly. Commercial surveillance, for the twin purposes of better customer service and maximising profit, feeds state surveillance, justified in the name of security. When I wrote a book about reading my own Stasi file in the mid-1990s, I used the image of the 'glass person', a famous exhibit at the Dresden Hygiene Museum, which shows through its glass body various brightly coloured internal organs, veins and muscles. Today, even the citizens of traditionally free countries are increasingly becoming glass people.

Two things came together to produce the growth of state surveillance in the United States and Britain after 9/11. First, there was a sense that security services must do everything possible to prevent something like that ever happening again, a sentiment heartily shared by their political masters, who did not want 'another 9/11' to recur on their watch. Second, and coincidentally, there were the technological developments that produced Swire's 'golden age of surveillance' for the state even as they produced a golden age of communication for the individual. The answer to the question 'Why did you collect all that personal data?' was in part 'Because we had to do everything possible' and in part 'Because we could'. The result was what has been called the preemptive state: one that tries to preempt all possible threats, not least by collecting all possible information.[17]

THE PRICE OF SECRECY

The other side of this state power is official secrecy. Secrecy has always been a powerful weapon in the hands of rulers, who jealously guard what the ancient Roman historian Tacitus called the *arcana imperii*. As US Senator Daniel Patrick Moynihan once observed, 'Secrecy is the ultimate form of regulation because the people don't even know they are being regulated'.[18] This weapon is doubly powerful when the state secretly knows so much about its citizens. One could express the character of a regime as a ratio between two variables: what the state knows about the citizen (S) and what the citizen knows about the state (C). The higher the ratio of C to S, the better the state you're in. The best case is a state that combines the greatest possible privacy for the citizen and transparency of the rulers. The worst is one where the citizen is transparent to the state, like the glass person in the Dresden Hygiene Museum, but the state is entirely opaque to the citizen.

This eighth principle focuses specifically on freedom of information. That is deliberate. There are, to be sure, many occasions when national security is invoked by powerholders to shut people up simply for expressing opinions that the rulers find unsettling or likely to destabilise their rule. When they respond with accusations of 'sedition', as the offence has historically been called in the common law world, no new or hidden information is necessarily involved. Thus, for example, India has repeatedly seen section 124A of its penal code used to prosecute as 'sedition' what in most liberal democracies would be regarded as merely dissent, criticism or satire. The cartoonist Aseem Trevidi was arrested and initially charged with sedition on the basis of his cartoons. (The charges were dropped after protests.) A philosophy student in Kerala faced the same charge for allegedly 'sitting and hooting' when the national anthem was played in a theatre.[19] In some famous cases in the United States, people were charged with sedition during the First World War merely for campaigning against military service. No secret information there. Similarly, the offence of 'glorifying' terrorism, introduced in a 2006 change to British antiterrorism legislation, does not involve discovering or disseminating any new information.

Very often, however, there is some element of new or previously hidden information involved. While people have been prosecuted merely for possessing materials classified as official secrets, it is generally the combination of obtaining and publishing—information and expression—that brings down the full wrath of the state. This was famously the case with the so-called Pentagon Papers, published by the New York Times and the Washington Post in the early 1970s to which I will return. An extreme example is that of the Chinese historian Xu Zerong. He was sentenced to 13 years imprisonment, of which he served 10, for allegedly leaking state secrets. All he had done was to share with a South Korean scholar copies of some Chinese documents about the long-distant Korean War. These materials were classified as 'top secret' only after the Chinese court had delivered its verdict.[20]

It would, however, be too easy simply to offer a long list of instances in which state secrecy has been abused, usually in the name of national security. We must acknowledge a genuine dilemma here. One of the key arguments for freedom of expression is its instrumental value for enabling good government, but good government can also be served by secrecy. Even behind closed doors, politicians and officials will not freely debate all the alternatives—which may include reversals of their own current policies—if they fear that those confidential discussions will become known to the world a few hours later. A friend who worked in the US State Department during the second term of President George W. Bush told me that he had once suggested writing a memo posing fundamental, highly critical questions about US policy in Iraq. 'Don't even think of it', he was warned, because it would be sure to appear in the next day's New York Times.[21]

Fighting crime and terrorism, not to mention prosecuting an outright interstate war, self-evidently requires secrecy and outright deceit. I would not be here to write this book if the Western allies had not successfully concealed from Hitler's Germany the intended location and time of the D-Day landings in the Second World War. If the German high command had been forewarned, the young soldier who subsequently became my father would probably have been gunned down as he landed on that Normandy beach with the first assault wave in 1944.[22] Will anyone seriously claim that the Obama administration should have briefed the American public and the world in advance about its planned operation to capture or kill Osama bin Laden? Online, violent criminals, drug gangs and foreign armies exploit the so-called dark net, using all the tricks of hacking, malware, denial-of-service attacks and cyberwar. Spies risk their own necks to infiltrate dangerous groups, foiling plots that could cost thousands of innocent lives.[23] Secrecy and openness are semantic opposites, but some secrecy is needed to defend an open society. Yet how can secrecy be reconciled with the transparency and accountability that are essential for the rule of law and representative government? As three legal scholars pithily observe: 'Constitutional democracies cannot live with secrecy, but cannot live without it either'.[24]

Official secrecy has too often been used to conceal things that should not have been concealed—and sometimes to 'reveal' things that did not exist, such as weapons of mass destruction in Saddam Hussein's Iraq. Thus, for example, in the early 2000s a senior NSA official, Thomas Drake, repeatedly went to his superiors, to the inspectors general of the NSA and the Pentagon and to the relevant congressional committees to express his concerns about a surveillance programme called Trailblazer. In his view, this violated the Fourth Amendment and would waste billions of American taxpayers' dollars when a better, cheaper, more privacy-protective alternative was available. It was only when he got nowhere through all these proper channels that he leaked a small part of what he was concerned about to a reporter at the Baltimore Sun. For Drake, there followed a personal nightmare of investigation, interrogation and eventually prosecution under the 1917 Espionage Act, with charges that could have meant up to 35 years in prison. In the end, while sentencing him to one year's probation and community service, a federal judge said that Drake had been through 'four years of hell' and that the manner in which he was treated had been 'unconscionable'. With what we know now, it seems clear that claims for official secrecy were used to silence discussion of Drake's legitimate concerns.[25]

When a much more famous NSA whistleblower, Edward Snowden, was creating shock waves in Washington, the head of the NSA, General Keith Alexander, initially claimed that the mass collection of communications data inside the United States had contributed to preventing 54 terrorist plots. His deputy subsequently revealed, under questioning, that only about a dozen of these plots had any connection to the American homeland and just one of them might have been disrupted as a result of the mass surveillance.[26] A report by the United States' official Privacy and Civil Liberties Oversight Board into the collection of the telephone records of millions of Americans concluded—based on information 'including classified briefings and documentation'—that 'we have not identified a single instance involving a threat to the United States in which the program made a concrete difference in the outcome of a counterterrorism investigation'.[27]

The authorities claimed that they were only collecting 'metadata' rather than 'data', such as the content of telephone calls or emails, but this distinction was worthless. In the conditions of 'big data', metadata is data—and of a kind that is deeply corrosive of privacy. As the NSA's own general counsel, Stewart Baker, observed: 'Metadata absolutely tell you everything about somebody's life. If you have enough metadata, you don't really need content'. A former director of both the NSA and the CIA, General Michael Hayden, subsequently endorsed that view, memorably adding, 'We kill people based on metadata'.[28]

While there is sometimes a trade-off between security and liberty, here was a case where privacy was violated on a massive scale, for no gain in security. As happens so often, that secrecy went hand-in-hand with mendacity, each hand hiding the other. In a hearing before the US Senate Intelligence Committee in March 2013, the director of national intelligence, General James Clapper, was asked by Senator Ron Wyden, 'Does the NSA collect any type of data at all on millions or hundreds of millions of Americans?' Clapper responded, 'No, sir'. Wyden: 'It does not?' Clapper: 'Not wittingly. There are cases where they could inadvertently perhaps collect, but not wittingly'.[29] Those two words 'not wittingly', for which he subsequently apologised, are probably the only ones for which General Clapper will be remembered. They cry out for a new verb: to *clapper*.

Such a sacrifice of liberty with no commensurate gain in security is still not the worst case, which is when you sacrifice liberty and end up less secure as a result. In Egypt, for example, freedom of expression has been drastically curbed in the name of national security, and the Egyptian military—dominant, almost untouchable for decades, except for a brief window in 2011–2013—unilaterally decides what is necessary for security. The scale of the Egyptian military's economic activities is not even known, let alone subject to parliamentary and public scrutiny. When I presented our project in Cairo, during that brief window of fragile freedom in the Arab Spring, the historian Khaled Fahmy argued that more freedom of information would actually enhance Egypt's national security. Since there was no access at all to the Egyptian military records of the 1967 and 1973 wars against Israel, which Egypt disastrously lost, there was no way to learn from the country's mistakes. Summing up his argument, Fahmy said, 'National security in Egypt threatens national security'.[30]

Egypt is not the only country where we find examples of the Fahmy paradox. In 2003, the United States and Britain, together with a 'coalition of the willing', invaded Iraq, claiming that Saddam Hussein possessed weapons of mass destruction that would imperil both his neighbours and the wider world. That claim was based on a misrepresentation of secret intelligence, not merely highlighting erroneous information but also suppressing important counterindications. According to an account by the American reporter Ron Suskind, these included separate indications from Saddam's own intelligence chief and foreign minister of what turned out subsequently to be the truth: that Saddam no longer had any weapons of mass destruction worthy of the name, but wished his neighbours, especially Iran, to believe that he did.[31]

The details will be disputed by historians for years to come, but the basic fact is plain: Britain and America went to war on a false prospectus. It seems likely that the United States under the Bush administration would have gone to war anyway, but that is not true of Britain. Such was the opposition to following President Bush down this path, both in parliament and in the country at large, that Prime Minister Tony Blair felt impelled to take the decision to the House of Commons. In a dramatic debate, he secured a parliamentary vote for war.[32] So here was deliberative democracy in action. Like the ancient Athenians confronted with Persian invasion in the fifth century B.C.E., the representatives of the people gathered on the pnyx, freely debated all the alternatives and reached a fateful decision. But where the Athenian decision was based on the facts being made publicly available, to the best of everyone's ability, and then on *parrhesia*—truth-seeking, fearless speech for the public good—the British decision was based on the concealment and misrepresentation of secret intelligence, and then on spin. Where ancient Athens had the *parrhesiast*, modern Britain had the spin doctor.

The citizens of ancient Athens reached a strategic decision—to fight at sea—which saved their democracy from the tyranny of Persia. The elected representatives of modern Britain reached a strategic decision which, among its many disastrous consequences, greatly strengthened the regional position of the current tyranny in Persia (now more usually known as Iran). Saddam Hussein's regime was a brutal dictatorship, but it did not have weapons of mass destruction nor was it a base for Al Qaeda. After the invasion and the disastrously mishandled occupation, Al Qaeda emerged in Iraq. In 2006, the United States' own National Intelligence Estimate reported that 'the Iraq conflict has become the "cause celebre" for jihadists'.[33] Iraq was torn apart in a disastrous civil war, with at least one hundred thousand people killed and millions made homeless. Across the Middle East, the ancient rift between Sunni and Shia was bloodily reopened. The heavy hand of the Islamic Republic of Iran was strengthened. As a bitter joke went: 'The Iraq war is over. Iran won'. Sober estimates put the long-term, overall cost to the United States alone at more than $2 trillion.[34] And in 2014, President Obama went on television to warn the American people that a ruthless terrorist organisation called ISIL, or Islamic State, directly threatened the security of the American homeland. ISIL was, he explained, 'formerly Al Qaeda's affiliate in Iraq' which had gone on to exploit the chaos created by the civil war in neighbouring Syria.[35] The danger to countries like Britain, more of whose own young Muslims had gone to wage jihad with ISIL and other groups in Iraq and Syria, was even more direct.

Obviously, all these horrors cannot be attributed solely to the original invasion. Subsequent blunders of Western policy, the accumulated poisons of postcolonial autocracies across the Middle East and the unintended consequences of the Arab Spring in countries like Syria must all be given their due weight. But you would need to be a spectacularly blinkered person to suggest that the original decision to invade Iraq had ended up enhancing the national security of Britain and the United States. Yet the original justification was precisely national security, based on claims about secret intelligence, unverifiable for the citizens or their elected representatives.

And so we come back to the Fahmy paradox. In this case, freedom (specifically, of information) was not traded for a net gain in security, as it may be in some circumstances. It was not even, as with the NSA and GCHQ mass surveillance programmmes, that freedom (specifically privacy, an important aspect of individual liberty) was eroded for no significant gain in security. No, in this case, freedom (specifically, that of properly informed public debate) was sacrificed in the name of security, and the result was not merely a loss of liberty but also a loss of security.

HERE WE NEED LAWS

In this principle, and in no other, I use the word 'empowered'. Obviously, we should also be empowered to have access to knowledge, protect our privacy and resist violent intimidation. But I use the word here because no other area manifests such a large imbalance of power between state and citizen. Empowerment has two main senses: to invest with a formal power or authority to do something and, more broadly, to give the strength to do something. We need both. The representative institutions of a liberal democracy, conscious of the dangers I have outlined, should themselves create formal checks and balances. These will not suffice or endure, however, unless we, as citizens and netizens, are ready to resort to less formal means, up to and including civil disobedience, to make sure the 'proper channels' protect our liberties.

An important starting point is that even the most secret services and operations, including those that block, filter or eavesdrop on the internet, should be based on publicly available laws. By contrast with other areas of expression, such as hate speech, where I argue that law has been used too much, here we cannot have too much of it: explicit, detailed and clear.

In this respect, it is interesting to dive into the thickets of a report issued by a group of telecommunications companies, including Vodafone and Telenor, to document the legal frameworks under which they must operate, country by country. Whereas the entry for Germany has many pages of detailed legal provisions, that for Egypt is brief and full of wording such as 'the instrument may be a direct order from an authorised member of the armed forces or security agencies. There are no explicit regulations regarding the latter'. Or again: 'generally, the armed forces and national security agencies are largely exempt from any control or oversight by the communications regulator'.[36] Understanding the central importance of freedom of information, as described by Khaled Fahmy, Egyptian activists spent several years following the overthrow of President Hosni Mubarak trying to get a proper freedom of information law, but the military and security apparatus frustrated their attempts. Here is the perfect model of unaccountability. If there is no law, you can't accuse anyone of breaking it.

The telecommunications report also reveals another variant of the Pinteresque, encountered in one of the world's most democratic, rule-of-law states: carefully drafted laws that prohibit the disclosure even of the mere fact that a company or other body has disclosed information to the government under that law. Thanks to Snowden, the politically informed public would become familiar with such secret FISA court orders and National Security Letters. But a few years earlier, when I heard about them for the first time, I asked senior figures at both Facebook and Twitter whether they could at least give me some idea of the number of such orders they had received and complied with. Tens? Hundreds? Thousands? Shifting in their seats and looking deeply uncomfortable, these faithful sons of the Church of the First Amendment said they would be breaking the law if they did that. They dared not even say what they could not say.[37]

A third problem is laws that are drawn up in such broad and impenetrable language that it is extremely difficult to mount a defence against them. Just try reading Britain's Regulation of Investigatory Powers Act (RIPA), a law under which 514,608 authorisations for accessing people's communications data were issued in 2013.[38] The British government's own independent reviewer of terrorism legislation, David Anderson, says of it:

> RIPA, obscure since its inception, has been patched up so many times as to make it incomprehensible to all but a tiny band of initiates. A multitude of alternative powers, some of them without statutory safeguards, confuse the picture further. This state of affairs is undemocratic, unnecessary and — in the long run — intolerable.[39]

For all these dangers — in fact, precisely because of them — the struggle for publicly available, clearly worded national laws, specifying what may and may not be done in the name of (national, homeland, public, state) security, is a vital part of civic self-empowerment. The relevant laws are of two kinds: those that affect only freedom of expression and those that concern freedom of information, together with the right to pass some of that information on.

So far as pure expressions of opinion are concerned, the First Amendment scholar Harry Kalven once observed that the existence of an offence of seditious libel is the hallmark of an unfree society. Writing in the early 2000s, Eric Barendt dryly commented: 'If this is the case, there are remarkably few free countries' — for many liberal democracies still retained the ancient offence on their statute books.[40] Yet plainly Kalven had a point. What used to be considered seditious libel (an offence abolished in Britain only in 2008) is what a modern liberal democracy should treat merely as the vehement expression of political dissent. The narrower the circle of 'sedition' in a country, the wider the circle of political freedom of expression, and vice versa.

The only legitimate restriction here is on words or images that are intended and likely to lead to violence. In short, we are back to the modernised version of the Brandenburg test for which I argued in chapter 2. As we have seen, the causal connections, and therefore how dangerous that speech is, are difficult to determine. But the quest for security in an age of cross-border terrorism has led established democracies to err in the wrong direction, proposing to block websites, ban organisations and prosecute speakers for propagating even non-violent 'extremism'.[41]

Some who propose such restrictive measures were young adults in the late 1960s or early 1970s. Contemporaries of these old 1968ers, and perhaps they themselves, were involved in, or at least sympathised with, groups on the far left. Whether Marxist-Leninist, Trotskyist or Maoist, these groups idealised tyrannies which were even then imposing horrendous suffering on their own peoples. The human suffering inflicted by the Cultural Revolution in China, for example, can stand comparison with that under Islamist regimes today. In short, these youthful enthusiasts glorified terror.

There were calls at that time not just for those who had actually turned to terrorism (the Red Brigades in Italy, the Baader-Meinhof gang in Germany) to be prosecuted, but for those who sympathised with them—*Sympathisanten* was the German word—to be excluded from employment in the public sector and otherwise discriminated against. While there was some hysterical overreaction, European democracies facing a genuine but limited terrorist threat resisted the temptation to declare a long-term 'state of exception', let alone a state of war. Within a few years, most of these verbal extremists had turned away from the advocacy or support of political violence, to pursue lives as journalists, academics, lawyers, civil society activists or politicians. Scratch a leading figure in the Western Europe of today and you will probably find a youthful Maoist, Trotskyist, Marxist-Leninist, anarchist or firebrand of another extremist grouping some 40 years ago. They were reintegrated into, and became pillars of, a free society precisely because their verbal extremism was not confused with genuinely dangerous speech. Why should the same not be true of angry young Western European Muslims in our time? Do we have so little trust in tolerance and faith in freedom? Or are we thinking (perhaps without fully acknowledging the thought to ourselves) that what worked for offspring of the white Western middle class will not work for people of darker skin colour and different cultural backgrounds?

So far as freedom of information is concerned, the legal balancing act is mainly between our right of access to information and secrecy justified in the name of national security. Since the fall of the Berlin Wall, there has been a massive spread of laws providing for freedom of information. By 2014, more than 5 billion people in nearly 100 countries had some such law on their statute books. However, all these laws spelt out an exception for national security, and many countries also have official secrecy acts. The authoritative General Comment on Article 19 warns against using the article's national security justification 'to suppress or withhold from the public information of legitimate public interest'.[42] Over the last 20 years, there has been a remarkable effort, led by free speech advocacy organisations, to thrash out some detailed international norms for striking this balance, and then to scrutinise national laws or proposed laws in light of them.

A set of principles drawn up in 1995 by a group convened by the campaigning organisation Article 19 attempted to distinguish between legitimate and illegitimate national security interest. A restriction justified on grounds of national security, these Johannesburg Principles suggested, is not legitimate 'unless its genuine purpose and demonstrable effect is to protect a country's existence or its territorial integrity against the use or threat of force, or its capacity to respond to the use or threat of force, whether from an external source, such as a military threat, or an internal source, such as incitement to violent overthrow of the government'. The Johannesburg Principles then gave some examples of illegitimate invocation of national security, such as 'to protect the government from embarrassment or exposure of wrongdoing, or to conceal information about the functioning of its public institutions, or to entrench a particular ideology, or to suppress industrial unrest'.[43]

In a process led by the Open Society Justice Initiative, a more detailed set of 'global principles on national security and the right to information' was drafted by a group of experts from more than 70 countries, in consultation with the relevant special rapporteurs of the UN, the OSCE, the Organisation of American States and the African Commission on Human and Peoples' Rights. These were finalised in the South African town of Tshwane, near Pretoria, in 2013, and therefore called the Tshwane Principles. They not only spell out in great detail what kinds of information (defence plans, weapon systems, etc.) may legitimately be kept secret on grounds of national security, but also identify what they carefully call 'categories of information with a high presumption or overriding interest in favour of disclosure'. These include violations of human rights or international humanitarian law, information about torture and the death of people in custody, military and security budgets and matters affecting public health or the environment. They further propose a set of rules for determining what should be classified as secret, as well as procedures for challenging the classification, handling requests for information and so on.[44]

Now the self-styled realist may dismiss all this as *bien pensant* liberal internationalist pie in the sky, having little connection to the real world of power politics. But in countries where there is a genuine public debate, such international standards and international comparisons ('You are proposing that, but in countries X, Y and Z they do it like this') can have traction, especially when amplified through free, diverse media. Thus, for example, in South Africa, the country where both of these sets of principles were finalised, a very bad official secrecy bill—formally known as the Protection of State Information Bill—was proposed in 2010. This would have imposed draconian penalties on whistle-blowers and journalists for disclosing a wide range of state information. A wave of domestic and international criticism, led by a bevy of Nobel Prize winners, delayed the passage of the bill, and five years later the President had still not signed it into law.[45] When Japan rushed through an Act on the Protection of Specially Designated Secrets in 2013, critics were able to point not just to inter-national standards but also to other national laws, suggesting that 'Japan could look to the laws of Chile, Colombia, the Czech Republic, Germany, Mexico, Moldova, the Netherlands, Norway, Paraguay, Romania, Spain and Sweden for provisions in law prohibiting the classification of information concerning cor-ruption, crimes against humanity or human rights violations'.[46]

Yet clearly the soft pressure of public reason alone will not suffice when hard interests of the state and individual powerholders are at stake. Even if publicly available laws on freedom of information and official secrecy live up to the highest standards of clarity, precision and self-limitation, the question remains how hidden violations of these laws can be exposed.

WHO WILL GUARD THE GUARDIANS?

Who will guard the guardians? One possible answer is: the guardians them-selves. As in Plato's Republic, they will be men (and today also women) of such exquisite virtue that they will resist all temptations. Their lies to the public will always be noble lies. Now it is not foolish to suggest that those entrusted with special powers and secrets should be imbued with a particular ethos of public service and self-restraint, and almost certainly some of them are.[47] There may be a particular heroism in the dangerous and courageous life's work of men and women whose stories can never be told. But no one can seriously believe that all our spies, soldiers and security officials embody the virtues of Platonic guard-ians. Whether or not you follow Karl Popper's specific critique of Plato, there is a superabundance of history to demonstrate how inadequate this Platonic answer is.

The truth is that there is no single key, but rather an awkward, uncomfort-able, shifting combination of checks and balances. The executive, the legisla-ture and the judiciary (in British terms: government, parliament and the courts) all have a part to play, as does the media. But as we saw in chapter 4, in the internet age nobody quite knows where the media begin and end. For example, is WikiLeaks part of the media? Or is it, as the title of a film about it suggested, the fifth estate? What about networks of bloggers, citizen journalists, civil society activists and NGOs? Are they a sixth estate? Where do we fit into this picture the use of information and communications technologies, such as encryption and Tor, to counter the repressive potential of those same technologies?

I shall touch only briefly on the roles that can be played by executive, judiciary and legislature, say a few words about the media and then argue that all these constraints will be inadequate without the contribution of two particular kinds of free speech: leaking and whistleblowing.

The executive branch of government can do more than just cultivate virtue in its servants. It can, for example, install a privacy advocate inside the machinery of confidential decision making. It can also create more effective internal procedures for scrutinising what its own agencies do. Several years before the Snowden revelations, a formidably well-documented report prepared for the US National Research Council, *Protecting Individual Privacy in the Struggle against Terrorists*, proposed precisely that. It argued that privacy is an American value, that scientific evidence strongly suggested pattern-based data mining would be ineffective against terrorists and that every information-based counterterrorist programme should therefore be systematically and regularly reviewed for efficacy, lawfulness and 'consistency with US values'.[48] Note that the existence and process of such regular, internal review could be made public without compromising any operational secrets.

A good parliament will pass and constantly review clear laws covering the activities of every arm of the state. By the same token, it will try to control those shadowy networks that are described in countries such as Egypt and Turkey as the 'deep state'. One obvious problem here is that the laws have lagged far behind the development of surveillance technologies.

An effective legislature should also ensure that it is involved in major decisions concerning war and peace, and the various 'states of exception' in between, even if this involvement cannot always be made public. The same Themistocles who argued publicly on the Athenian pnyx for fighting the Persians at sea once came up with a plan for a covert operation against Sparta. Since it was to be covert, he could not go shouting it from the rock platform in the pnyx. So he offered to share the operational details with two men chosen by the assembly. According to the historian Diodorus Siculus, the assembly chose Aristides and Xanthipus, because they were 'upright characters' but also because they were in 'active rivalry' with Themistocles 'for glory and leadership'.[49] This is one of the earliest documented examples of the kind of 'across the aisle' confidential consultation on key national security decisions that is practised in mature democracies to this day. Again, we accept that we may not be apprised of all the details, but we can and should know that such parliamentary procedures exist and are being used.

Another thing parliaments can do is oversight by special committees. These committees exist in almost all liberal democracies, and almost all of them have so far proved inadequate to the task. When the New York Times finally revealed the existence of that programme for warrantless telephone eavesdropping, members of the Senate intelligence committee found out about it from the press. As one committee member, Senator Ron Wyden, commented: 'What do I know? I'm only on the Intelligence Committee'.[50] The equivalent British parliamentary committee did even worse. The reasons for the weakness of parliamentary oversight are complex, but they certainly include a lack of expertise in general and technological know-how in particular. The generally middle-aged or elderly parliamentarians on the committees were anything but digital natives. A veteran CIA officer nicely summarised the agency professionals' attitude to such committees. You deal with them, he said, as you grow mushrooms: 'keep them in the dark and feed them shit'.[51] If these committees were to be more effective, they would need more technical advice—the US Congress used to have an Office of Technology Assessment, but it was closed in 1995—so at least they would know what questions to ask; a privacy advocate, to put that side of the argument; and some influence over the purse strings. Even the former head of the NSA, Michael Hayden, argues that while intelligence services can never be transparent, they should make more efforts to be 'translucent'.[52] After 'Snowden', this view could be widely heard among those involved in overseeing security services.[53]

Then there are the courts, which should adjudicate whether those laws—where they exist—are being properly applied, to whom they apply (for example, what about noncitizens and people living in other countries?), how they relate to other laws and precedents and when individuals' rights are being violated. In some legal systems, they can also rule on the compatibility of the laws themselves with either a national constitution or a binding international legal agreement, such as the European Convention on Human Rights. But how can 'open justice, openly arrived at' be reconciled with the secrecy required for security? In trials, such as the one in which Nigella Lawson was an unhappy witness, we saw a tension between the two ancient liberties of free speech and fair trial. Here, by contrast, the interests of free speech and fair trial are usually aligned, against secrecy justified by security. The compromises necessarily proposed— secret courts, anonymity for some witnesses (such as members of the security services), 'sworn counsel' given special access to secret evidence—may end up imperilling both free speech and fair trial. I have neither the space nor the legal competence to go further into this, but the challenge principle applies here too. Whatever else, we must be free and empowered to ask: Is this restriction on open justice justified? And even if it was justified a year ago, is it still necessary now?

In general, the experts agree that there is a tendency for judicial deference towards the executive on matters of national security. An example is the Indian Supreme Court which, following the wording of an Official Secrets Act originally passed under British colonial rule in 1923, almost invariably seems to leave it to the government to decide what should or should not be an official secret.[54] By contrast, Israel's Supreme Court is often cited as a model of how judges can openly scrutinise state actions justified by national security. The Israeli Supreme Court's judgements on issues such as targeted killings and preventive detentions have on occasion exemplified careful ethical as well as legal weighing of extraordinarily difficult issues. In one famous case, it declared it illegal for people to be detained as 'bargaining chips' to be traded for the release of Israeli captives. Yet a careful study shows that over a 10-year period the court did not actually order the release of any of the 322 people 'preventively detained', although some were set free through a process the author describes as 'bargaining in the shadow of the court'.[55]

Although I have only touched the surface of what can be done by executive, legislature and judiciary, and we should always be looking for things they can do better, experience suggests that these checks alone will not suffice. Traditionally, writers then turn to the 'fourth estate'. They point to a free press as the single most important control on secret abuses of state power justified in the name of national security. Some of journalism's finest hours have come when performing that role.

Many Americans will think of the publication of the Pentagon Papers by the New York Times and Washington Post in the early 1970s: leaked copies of internal US government reports showing just how unsuccessfully and mendaciously the United States was prosecuting the Vietnam War. More recently, we think of the publication by the Guardian and other leading newspapers and magazines—including Der Spiegel, Le Monde and The Hindu—of carefully redacted versions of secret US State Department communications leaked by Private Bradley (subsequently Chelsea) Manning via Julian Assange's WikiLeaks, and then a selection of the NSA and GCHQ documents passed to them by Snowden. When he first met the journalists involved, in a hotel in Hong Kong, Snowden specifically explained that he wanted experienced news media to decide what it would be in the public interest to publish.[56]

One can always argue about this or that specific editorial decision, but in general, these newspapers exercised an important controlling function in the public interest; one which government, parliament and the courts had failed to perform. In Britain—unlike in the United States, with its First Amendment explicitly protecting the freedom of the press—the authorities not only attempted to stanch the flow of revelations ('You have had your debate', the country's top civil servant told the Guardian) but even threatened the newspaper and its editor-in-chief, Alan Rusbridger, with prosecution ('You are in possession of stolen property').[57] It took courage for Rusbridger and his colleagues to proceed as they did, especially given the lack of support from many other parts of the British media.

The ecosystem of information challenge is obviously far more diverse than just a newspaper publishing a whistleblower's revelations. One of the greatest campaigning journalists of the twentieth century, I. F. Stone, collected his information mainly by dredging through little-used but publicly available sources. A lot can still be done by academics, think tanks and NGOs as well as journalists. There exists in the United States another NSA: the National Security Archive. Despite its official-sounding title, this is a not-for-profit organisation which has done extraordinary work using the country's Freedom of Information Act to secure the release of official documents.

Then there are measures taken by people expert in information and communication technologies. Technical advice is now readily available about how to protect your privacy online, making it at the very least more difficult for security agencies (and information businesses) to track your every move. These include encryption and surveillance-evasion software, such as Tor, which was developed with the support of the US government. To cries of indignation from securocrats, Apple announced in 2014 that its latest iPhone would have a high level of encryption fitted as standard. So encryption is used against encryption, secrecy against secrecy.

Beyond individual self-defence, internet specialists working at leading research centres such as the Citizen Lab in Toronto, the Berkman Centre at Harvard and the Oxford Internet Institute have sometimes been able to turn the tables on states' secret watchers. Using sophisticated techniques, they can identify where and how state surveillance (and censorship) is taking place.[58] Since surveillance literally means watching from above, this has been called sousveillance, or watching from below.

Valuable as all these methods are, it remains doubtful whether all of them together can be effective unless information is passed by individual human beings with access to official secrets. Most of the great counterblows to hidden abuses of state power have involved some element of whistleblowing or leaking.

WHISTLEBLOWERS AND LEAKERS:
AN ESSENTIAL BACKSTOP

The words 'whistleblower' and 'leaking', in the sense I am using them here, date only from the late 1960s. To be sure, we can find examples of what might now be described as whistleblowing and leaking throughout history. In 1777, a group of sailors on the good ship *Warren*, fighting for American independence against the British, wrote a letter to the Continental Congress enumerating the misdeeds of their well-connected commander. He was fired as a result.[59] But the elaboration of the specific roles of the whistleblower and the leaker is a phenomenon of the last half century.

What is the difference between the two? 'Whistleblower' has a more unambiguously positive valence. A whistleblower is someone who, seeing something that he or she regards as wrong happening inside an organisation, passes on that information to others in the hope of exposing the wrongdoing.[60] Many laws around the world now encourage and supposedly protect whistleblowers. Someone who blows the whistle on malpractice in a pharmaceutical company, bank, hospital, prison or government department is held to have done something good. The US Securities and Exchange Commission, which regulates US financial markets, actually has an Office of the Whistleblower.[61] Whistleblowing International Network, a consortium of NGOs working to support and protect workplace whistleblowing around the world, writes on its blog that 'whistleblowing—speaking up in the public interest about wrongdoing or risk—is at its core an act of loyalty and concern for the greater good'.[62] An influential book about whistleblowers characterised them as 'ethical resisters'.[63]

Leakers and leaking, by contrast, are generally viewed either neutrally or more negatively. The means used by leakers—passing on information that those who control it want to keep confidential—are indistinguishable from those of the anonymous whistleblower, but the intentions are often found to be less high-minded. Whether the leak is from a part of government, a political party or a company, the leakers are as likely as not doing it to promote either the organisation's interests or those of a faction within it. Although leaking is ubiquitous in early-twenty-first-century politics and business, and many journalists would be lost without it, few impute noble motives to the leakers. Phrases like 'the dark arts' are applied to the party-political use of leaks, and sometimes leaking is the hallmark of outright villainy.

An illustration of the difference is provided by the story of one of the most famous American whistleblowers in the field of national security, Daniel Ellsberg. Ellsberg was a brilliant, patriotic American who initially supported the war in Vietnam but, after firsthand experience, came to deplore both the terrible suffering of the Vietnamese civilian population and the fact that the American public was being misinformed about the conduct of the war. This is why he passed to an acquaintance at the New York Times a copy of the Pentagon's internal history of US policy in Vietnam from 1945 to 1967, later to become known as the Pentagon Papers, which revealed those casualties and lies. Ellsberg himself held back the parts which he thought might endanger national security.

Most revealing for the distinction I am teasing out here is the reaction of President Richard Nixon. While his administration decided to prosecute both Ellsberg and the newspapers that published the Pentagon Papers, Nixon also felt that, since this internal history of the Vietnam War only went up to 1967, it was helpfully damaging to his Democrat predecessors. He concluded that his administration should do even more leaking of material damaging to his political opponents. 'If we do this correctly', he said, the Democratic Party 'will be gone without a trace'. While he identified Ellsberg as a perfect target for public crucifixion—'You know what's going to charge up an audience. Jesus Christ, they'll be hanging from the rafters . . . Going after all these Jews'—his conclusion was not that leaks should be stopped but that they should be managed better.[64] 'We have', he told his aides, 'to develop . . . a program for leaking information'. So there you have it: Ellsberg the archetypical whistleblower, Nixon, the arch-leaker.

Plainly we need more noble whistleblowers and fewer nefarious leakers. But here's the problem: the track record so far suggests that, for all the encouraging laws and promised protections, whistleblowers almost invariably end up having a terrible time. Those on whom they blew the whistle somehow find a way to identify them and take revenge. Their health, finances and families suffer. A former special counsel to the US Merit Systems Protection Board advised officials not to blow the whistle 'unless you're in a position to retire or are independently wealthy'. 'Don't put your head up', he said, 'because it will get blown off'.[65] A careful study by C. Fred Alford, based on in-depth conversations with many whistleblowers, reports that 'almost all say they wouldn't do it again'. He quotes one John Brown: 'If I had to do it over again, I wouldn't blow the whistle for a million dollars. It ruined my life. . . . I didn't just lose my job. I lost my house, and then I lost my family. I don't even see my kids any more'.[66]

The price exacted is very high for almost all whistleblowers, but especially for those concerned with national security. The American soldier who first exposed the abuse of Iraqi detainees in Abu Ghraib prison was publicly commended by the US Defence Secretary, but he received death threats, had his property vandalised and was called a traitor by neighbours back home. He and his wife had to change jobs, move to a different town and do 'everything but change their identities'.[67] While the Supreme Court struck its famous blow for free speech by deciding that the New York Times and Washington Post could go on publishing the Pentagon Papers, Daniel Ellsberg was prosecuted under the 1917 Espionage Act, with charges that could theoretically have led to a 117-year sentence. The case did not come to trial because people acting under orders from the White House broke into his psychiatrist's office to collect material they could leak to discredit him. The judge then dismissed all charges because this 'unprecedented' government misconduct had 'incurably infected the prosecution of this case'. But no court ever found that Ellsberg had acted in the public interest, or according to the letter or the spirit of the First Amendment.[68]

Edward Snowden was stranded in Putin's Moscow, certainly not where he wished to be. The Obama administration said that the debate catalysed by his revelations was an important one, in the public interest, but that Snowden himself should be prosecuted, probably under the 1917 Espionage Act. The Obama administration had already brought more prosecutions under that act than all other presidencies combined.[69] Former president Jimmy Carter told USA Today, 'I think it's good for Americans to know the kind of things that have been revealed by [Snowden] and others'. Nonetheless, said Carter, Snowden should be prosecuted, although 'I don't think he ought to be executed as a traitor or any kind of extreme punishment like that'.[70] Very reassuring. So whereas a Christian approach is usually summarised as 'Love the sinner, hate the sin', here the guiding principle seems to be 'Love the sin, crucify the sinner'.

THE TROUBLE WITH 'WELL-PLACED SOURCES'

Can we, should we, really expect individual men and women to pay such a price? And will there be enough of them if the price is known to be so high? Such individual courage is, after all, very rare. Rahul Sagar argues that the alternative to the courage of the publicly identified whistleblower is anonymity, the hallmark of the leaker.[71] Certainly, more should be done to provide channels for anonymous whistleblowing without such retribution. The US financial regulator's Office of the Whistleblower, for example, provides for whistleblowers to be represented by a lawyer, with a form signed 'under penalty of perjury' when you make your anonymous submission. But the office cautiously acknowledges that it cannot guarantee to protect your identity, especially if court proceedings result.[72] The NSA Report recommended that intelligence community whistleblowers should be able to go directly to a Civil Liberties and Privacy Protection

Board, a newly constituted 'independent agency in the Executive Branch', but the Obama administration did not implement this recommendation.[73]

Ideally, channels should be created through which people inside the security services can blow the whistle internally, be listened to seriously and protected. Yet decades of experience suggest that the odds are stacked against such protection being effective. Those on whom the whistle has been blown will find a way to identify and punish the person they regard as a traitor. (This happened even with perhaps the earliest American whistleblowers, those sailors on the *Warren* in the 1770s. Two of them were sued for criminal libel by their former commanding officer, arrested and imprisoned, before finally being cleared by a court.[74]) Moreover, even if these internal channels for anonymous whistleblowing were secured, experience suggests this alone would not be sufficient. As Justice Hugo Black wrote, concurring with the majority in the Supreme Court decision on the Pentagon Papers: 'only a free and unrestrained press can effectively expose deception in government'.[75] But to do that, journalists must be able to protect their sources.

It is a curious fact that while journalists' right to protect the identity of their sources is written firmly into national law in several European countries, in the land of the First Amendment it is not. While there are 'shield laws' in a number of states, the veteran First Amendment advocate Floyd Abrams has argued that there should be a 'federal shield law' to make this protection ironclad.[76] In effect, this would pit the anonymity of journalistic sources against the secrecy of a state security apparatus. There are several issues here. One we have already explored: Who is a journalist? Would a shield law protect a freelance blogger? Or WikiLeaks? Even if the journalist is a reporter for New York Times or the BBC, this deposits a particular trust in his or her judgement and integrity. There is an interesting passage in a sworn affidavit in which James Risen, a New York Times reporter who wrote about warrantless phone tapping by the Bush administration, explained why he would not acknowledge the identity of one of his sources (who faced a much more serious prosecution). Describing his journalistic methods, Risen wrote:

> I take very seriously my obligations as a journalist when reporting about matters that may be classified or may implicate national security concerns. I do not always publish all information that I have, even if it is newsworthy and true. If I believe that the publication of the information would cause real harm to our national security, I will not publish a piece. I have found, however, that all too frequently, the government claims that publication of certain information will harm national security, when in reality, the government's real concern is about covering up its own wrongdoing or avoiding embarrassment.[77]

To me, that rings true. But the key phrase here is 'if I believe that' national security would be harmed. In effect: trust me. So the spies say, 'Trust us; we judge that our secret sources show that this covert surveillance is essential for your security', while the journalists say, 'Trust us; in our judgement the information from our anonymous sources shows that this publication is essential for your liberty'. The symmetry is not perfect: although top spy chiefs do now sometimes testify (and *clapper*) to parliamentary committees, normally it is politicians who represent or misrepresent claims about secret intelligence. While for obvious reasons the general public cannot form a view on the credibility of an individual spy, they can on that of a journalist. Someone like Risen has a track record, and we can judge him on it.

Yet even Risen's own colleagues on the New York Times disagreed with his personal judgement about the balance of benefit and harm in publishing that story and held it back for some time. And here we are talking about the very top end of quality journalism. As we have seen, the words 'journalism' and 'journalist' cover some virtues but also a multitude of sins. It is an interesting question who was responsible for more damaging invasions of privacy in Britain in the 2000s: GCHQ's mass data-gulping spooks or Rupert Murdoch's phone-hacking hacks. The former certainly collected far more data, but they did not publish it. The latter collected less, but ravaged lives by publishing it. If politicians and security chiefs have a motive for keeping more information secret than is truly in the public interest, commercial media also have a motive for publishing more than is truly in the public interest: the profit motive. With both newspapers and online media searching for a business model, there is a powerful temptation to confuse the public interest with what interests the public, thus selling more copies and bringing advertisement-ready eyeballs to your site or app. If it is naïve to think that security officials will all be Platonic guardians armed with invincible virtue, why should we believe that of journalists? So, taken on its own, the journalist's 'trust me' is as inadequate as the spy's.

The responsible use of anonymous sources will remain essential to good journalism. A public interest was served by the publication in leading newspapers of carefully selected and redacted documents from among those that Bradley (subsequently Chelsea) Manning passed to WikiLeaks. To give just one instance, I will never forget the emotional impact of a routine military report from Afghanistan reproduced in the New York Times. Summarising a raid targeting an Al Qaeda commander, it included this sentence: 'GFC passed initial assessment of 7 x NC KIA (children)'.[78] NC KIA stands for noncombatants killed in action. It is the simple word 'children', coming after those conscience-freezing bureaucratic acronyms, that is so powerful.

Morally indefensible, by contrast, was Assange's subsequent decision to publish a whole trove of documents, unredacted, revealing the identities of low-level informants of the Western powers, in places such as Iraq and Afghanistan, whose lives and families were thereby potentially endangered.[79] This was one of the reasons a key member of his WikiLeaks team, an idealistic young German called Daniel Domscheit-Berg, broke with Assange and announced his intention to set up a rival site called Open Leaks. Giving the same promise of anonymity, and using similar techniques of encryption, Open Leaks would invite whistleblowers to specify which news organisation, NGO or other group they wished to make the editorial selection from the material they leaked.[80] In the event, his idea was not realised, but many mainstream news organisations set up their own online leak-boxes.

For the quality of public debate, however, anonymous sources are always second-best, since we cannot judge for ourselves the quality and character of the source. We have to take it on trust, and sometimes, even with the most prestigious publications, that trust is misplaced. A fine illustration of the pitfalls of using anonymous sources is provided by the case of the former New York Times reporter Judith Miller. Miller was responsible for a number of news stories in the New York Times in 2002 and 2003, citing anonymous sources to support claims that Saddam Hussein had weapons of mass destruction. These stories were in turn used by senior Bush administration officials to bolster their case for going to war.

A subsequent, scrupulous investigation by the New York Times itself, as well as by other journalists, revealed that Miller's sources had often been highly unreliable associates of the Iraqi exile Ahmed Chalabi, who was pushing his own agenda of war for regime change in Iraq.[81] Standard American journalistic practice and internal Times procedures ask for corroboration from at least one other source, but Miller was easily able to get that from officials in the Bush administration who were themselves being (mis)informed by Chalabi, and shared his regime change agenda. The result was a poisonous circle. Her official and unofficial anonymous sources neatly corroborated each other. Unreliable exiles fed intelligence agencies, politicians and journalists; security and intelligence sources helped feed the politicians, who fed journalists like Miller, whose work in turn gave support to the politicians' campaign for war. The key ingredients of the poison were the anonymity of journalistic sources and the secrecy of intelligence ones. Whereas anonymity (of whistleblowers, leakers, journalistic sources) is supposed to provide a vital counterbalance to official secrecy, in this case anonymity and secrecy reinforced each other—combining to produce one of the greatest strategic blunders of modern times.

Ironically, while all this was being exposed, Miller herself was going to jail to protect one of her sources. But who was that source, and what had he been leaking through her? The source was I. Lewis 'Scooter' Libby, a senior adviser to Vice President Dick Cheney, and the subject of their conversation was a retired American ambassador called Joseph Wilson, who was challenging a claim made by President Bush—in his State of the Union address, no less—that Iraq was obtaining uranium from an African country (identified in briefings as Niger). Wilson knew that this claim was false, because he had been sent by the CIA to investigate it at firsthand, and he went on to say as much roundly and publicly.

What Libby told Miller was that Wilson had been put up for the mission by his wife, a CIA operative called Valerie Plame. Libby, who was subsequently convicted for lying about his part in this affair, had claimed explicit authority from the vice president to reveal some of the secret information. Although it was not actually Miller who broke the story of Valerie Plame, this was the source and this the story for which Miller was now heroically going to jail. A brave action certainly, but just consider the merits of the case. What was Miller protecting? Answer: an underhand attempt, worthy of Richard Nixon, to discredit a public-spirited whistleblower by secretly leaking the fact that his wife was a CIA operative, so as to shore up secret intelligence claims in support of a war that ended up damaging the United States' national security. Here was another dark face of our old friend Janus Anonymous.[82]

While we cannot do without anonymity as a counterbalance to the abuse of official secrecy, it is also double-edged. If secrecy is both essential to and incompatible with constitutional democracy, anonymity is both essential to and corrosive of the kind of public debate that we must aspire to if we believe in free speech as a means to good government.

THE IMPORTANCE OF NOT BEING ANONYMOUS

There is, I conclude, no substitute for the courage of the publicly self-identified whistleblower, the woman or man who puts face, name, reputation, savings, family and even life on the line to expose hidden wrongdoing. It is no accident that a single surname—'Snowden'—came to be used around the world as shorthand for a whole complex of concerns about mass surveillance justified in the name of security. It was not just what he leaked. It was the fact that he put his name, his face, his biography and character in the public scales. He did this consciously from the outset. Interviewed in his Hong Kong hotel room by the journalists who would break the story, he said that he wished to be named because 'I think it is powerful to come out and be, like . . . I'm not afraid'.[83]

We can thus make informed personal judgements on individual whistleblowers — who are, as I hope is now clear, a particular and rare breed of public speaker, or parrhesiast. I, for example, find Snowden, Drake and Ellsberg not just convincing but impressive; Assange I do not. While some of the material published by WikiLeaks was valuable, Assange's own approach, character and ideology seem to me deeply problematic. But we can make these judgements and disagree about them precisely because he is not Anonymous.

'Anonymous whistleblowing happens', Fred Alford writes in a powerful passage, 'when ethical discourse becomes impossible, when acting ethically is tantamount to becoming a scapegoat. . . . Whistleblowing without whistleblowers is not a future we should aspire to, any more than individuality without individuals or citizenship without citizens. If everyone has to hide in order to say anything of ethical consequence (as opposed to "mere" political opinion), then we will all end our days as drivers on a vast freeway: darkened windshields, darkened license plate holders, dark glasses, speeding aggressively to God knows where'. (Alford is surely conscious of the irony that to make his own investigation he had to promise anonymity to almost all his whistleblower sources, changing most of their names, including the 'John Brown' I quoted earlier, and details of the organisations in which they worked — so that anonymity was necessary to make his case against anonymity.)[84]

To take such an extreme step, you have to be an unusual individual. Some dismissively described Snowden as a narcissist. Exploring the motivation of the whistleblowers he studied, Alford detects what he calls 'narcissism moralised'. But Alford insists that he is using the word 'narcissism' in a neutral, not a pejorative sense, and memorably adds: 'As far as I can tell, narcissism moralised is the leading motive of Socrates, Saint Augustine and Gandhi'.[85] I have had the good fortune to know several great political dissidents, from Lech Wałęsa to Aung San Suu Kyi, and to study many more, ever since I started researching the German resistance to Hitler as a student some 40 years ago. It is not hard to detect in many of them an element of what might loosely be called narcissism. You must have an unusual sense of yourself and your role in the moral universe to stand out so strongly, at such a personal cost, against the received wisdom of your time. Most of us don't. Studies in behavioural psychology famously show that while on our own we can see perfectly clearly that one black line on the page is slightly longer than another, when surrounded by a group of people who (prepped to lie by the researcher) insist the longer line is shorter, most of us change our minds. Group lie prevails over individual truth.[86]

So don't expect people who are doing such an extraordinary thing to be, well, entirely normal. Yet, in a further paradox, sustaining good general norms requires individuals to step outside the comfort zone of the normal, to question those norms and challenge them—which is, of course, part of the argument for free speech. Nowhere is this more true than with limits justified in the name of security, that political ace of trumps, especially when those limits are not merely defended but made invisible by secrecy. We don't know what we don't know. Even with all the other checks and balances I have discussed in this chapter, our freedom—and our security, for it cuts both ways—will not be durably secured without the occasional exceptional actions of public, self-identified whistleblowers. The best of them are exemplars of our final principle: 'we decide for ourselves and face the consequences'.

ICEBERGS

'We defend the internet and other systems of communication against illegitimate encroachments by both public and private powers'.

I treasure a photograph that shows the wonderment on my 88-year-old mother's face as her grandson in Beijing pops up on the screen of a silver-coloured magic box. Then he smiles and speaks to her: 'Hello, Granny. Happy Christmas!' Even to those more accustomed to it, the way we can communicate from box to box seems almost magical. So direct. So easy. As if we were sitting face-to-face at the kitchen table, able verbally and visually (though not yet by touch) to express whatever we like to each other. But this was not magic and our communication is not as free as it appears.

Enabling but also limiting these apparently direct exchanges are fearsomely intricate systems of communication, with many layers and choke points at which multiple powers can intervene. My comments here will be mainly about the internet, defined in the broad sense which I have used throughout this book, but the same fundamental considerations would apply if we were discussing fax machines, or carrier pigeons, or sandal-clad ancient Greeks carrying parchment scrolls. Without being experts, we need to understand the system of communication sufficiently to see how and by whom it is being manipulated or constrained. Then, measuring that information against our own principles, we must decide what are legitimate and what are illegitimate encroachments.

ICEBERGS

To capture something of the complexity of the internet's architecture, Ian Brown and Christopher Marsden use the image of an iceberg shown in Figure 18.[1]

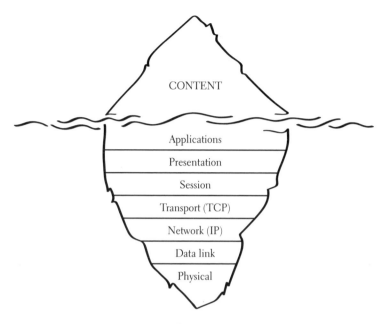

CONTENT

Applications

Presentation

Session

Transport (TCP)

Network (IP)

Data link

Physical

Figure 18. The internet iceberg
Source: Brown et al. 2013.

Most of us only see the tip of that iceberg. Note that the bottom layer is marked 'physical'. For all the wonders of wireless, at some point our communications, broken down into individual 'packets' of digital data—that is, strings of the numbers o and 1, as commended to the Chinese emperor by Leibniz in the seventeenth century—are transmitted through physical, usually fibre-optic cables, laid under the oceans and snaking across continents. (Some of the main submarine cables can be seen in Map 8.)

In 2011, a 75-year-old granny called Hayastan Shakarian was scavenging for firewood and scrap metal near a railway line that runs past her village in rural Georgia. She cut into a cable—and the internet went down in most of neighbouring Armenia for about 12 hours. ('I have no idea what the internet is', said granny Shakarian.)[2] Almost all this infrastructure is privately owned, but it is legally and sometimes illegally accessed by public powers. Britain's telecommunications spies tapped directly into transatlantic cables that make landfall among hardy holidaymakers in Bude, Cornwall.

Most internet traffic is then routed through major internet exchanges known as IXPs, of which there are just a few hundred across the world. When he was

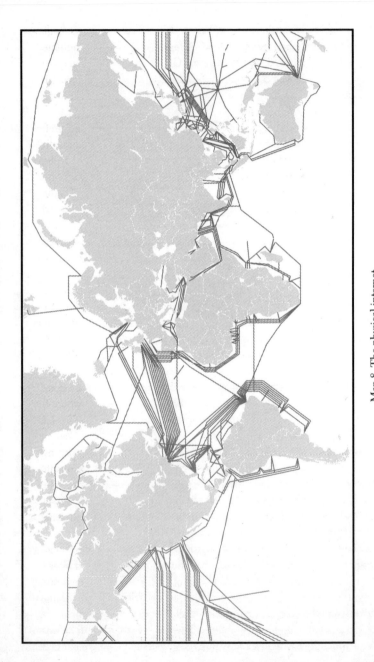

Map 8. The physical internet
This map shows major submarine internet cable systems.
Source: TeleGeography, 2015.

being shown round one of these in Toronto in the early 2000s, the Canadian cyberexpert Ronald Deibert noticed some red tags attached to the equipment down one corridor. He asked what they were. 'Oh, those are the wiretaps', replied his guide, and moved on.[3] One of the largest, the London Internet Exchange, is located in London's Docklands. Unsurprisingly, these facilities are not widely publicised. We must hope they are well secured.

At every level of the iceberg, there are forms of access, control and preference setting: physical, technical, commercial, diplomatic, legal, administrative, editorial, cybersecurity and cybercriminal. Moreover, our sketch of the iceberg only shows part of the whole. The struggle for power in and through these systems also involves financial institutions, such as banks, credit card companies and payment services (such as those that were denied to WikiLeaks under US government pressure), and intermediaries of many other kinds. Laura DeNardis identifies nine layers on which the free flow of information through the internet can be intentionally or unintentionally disrupted, and more than 100 'levers of control'.[4]

What I call (forgive the pun) internet-ional relations is one of the most complex fields on the planet. It involves domestic and international actors of every kind, not just states and companies but also international organisations, informal task forces, NGOs, independent commissions, user networks, law enforcement agencies, national and international courts, and multiple overlapping fora. One point of contention is precisely which forum or body should be responsible for what. If a state, company or group does not get satisfaction in one forum, it may go 'forum shopping' for another. So this is a sport where the players don't even agree on the location and boundaries of the playing field, let alone the rules of the game.

Figure 19 is a representation of some of the relevant actors, norms, institutions and procedures, drawn up by Joseph Nye, a leading scholar of international relations. Nye emphasises that his diagram is a simplification, which leaves one wondering what complicated would look like. He describes this state of affairs as a 'regime complex', somewhere between 'a single legal instrument at one end and fragmented arrangements at the other'.[5]

Although I have read quite a few books on the subject (some of them lucid), I shall not attempt to summarise the universe of what is usually called internet governance, which itself is only one large subset of our systems of communication. You would drown in a sea of acronyms before I was halfway through. Moreover, the situation keeps changing. So I shall only direct a spotlight at a few segments of the iceberg, to give some sense of how we might distinguish between illegitimate and legitimate encroachments by both public and private powers.

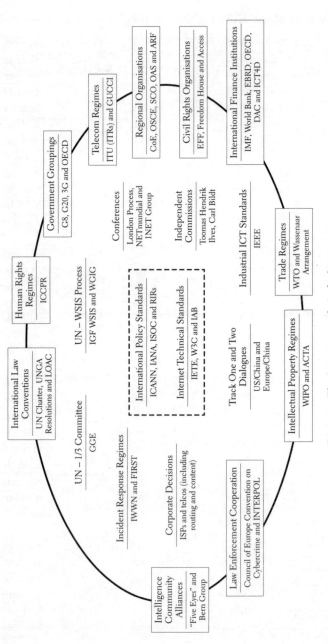

Figure 19. The 'regime complex' of cybergovernance
Source: Nye 2014

ONE INTERNET, UNDER WHOM?

At the end of the twentieth century, there was an extraordinary moment. As we have seen, most people with internet access around the world could emigrate online to a virtual United States, where they enjoyed all the free speech possibilities created by the 'legal firewall' of the modern First Amendment tradition. The global allocation of top-level domain names and IP addresses was controlled by a Californian not-for-profit corporation called ICANN. The internet's deliberately libertarian architecture was sustained by an informal group called the Internet Engineering Task Force. There was only one .gov, and that was the US government. If this was a high point of American power in international relations altogether—remember 'the hyperpower' and 'Prometheus unbound'?—that was nowhere more true than on the internet. What I have characterised as the United States' unilateral universalism seemed at that moment to be triumphant.

Fifteen years later, things looked very different. As in other areas of international politics, so also in the struggle for wordpower there had been a massive pushback against American unilateral universalism. This happened in several different ways. First, states reasserted their control over the internet in their own territories. Against the Clintons, the Chinese Communist Party said, 'Okay, just watch us nail Jell-O to the wall'. China was not alone in asserting its old-fashioned territorial sovereignty over cyberspace. Other authoritarian countries such as Russia shared this aspiration, but so did more democratic rising powers, including Brazil, India and South Africa. The governments of the so-called BRICS countries (Brazil, Russia, India, China, South Africa) united around a notion of 'information sovereignty'.[6] Although this came in many national variants, it was in general closer to the Chinese approach that I have characterised as universal unilateralism. Universal unilateralism suggested that the twenty-first century should, in this respect, be more like the late sixteenth than the late twentieth century. Where the 1555 Treaty of Augsburg had proclaimed the principle *cuius regio, eius religio* (whose realm, his religion), these old-new powers said *cuius regio, eius interrete*: who rules you determines what kind of internet you get.[7]

This mattered because of the shift in political and economic power generally with China being already the world's second largest economy. It mattered specifically because the current and prospective growth in internet use, particularly on mobile and smartphone, came very largely in these countries. The norm of net neutrality was already weaker on the mobile internet than on the fixed, and ever more people were using wireless devices. As we have seen,

China had become a major exporter of information and communication technologies, especially to Africa and Latin America, as well as a powerful player in the media of those regions. To some extent, its 'information sovereignty' norms could be built into the equipment and platforms it sold or heavily influenced.

This struggle was reflected in negotiations over the international framework for internet governance. Simplifying greatly, we can say that the emerging powers attempted to shift the locus of control from ICANN, that Californian not-for-profit corporation, to a United Nations agency called the International Telecommunication Union. In a dramatic moment at an international meeting in Dubai, colourfully described by one commentator as an 'internet Yalta', non-Western powers pushed the issue to a rare vote, which went 89 states to 55 against the United States and its liberal democratic allies. The 89 included not just obvious rivals such as China and Russia but also Brazil, Indonesia, Mexico, South Korea and South Africa.[8]

The United States, with some support from NGOs and other nongovernmental actors, tried to defend what it called a 'multistakeholder' model. ICANN now had an Affirmation of Commitments, with lots of waffle about 'a multi-stakeholder, private sector led, bottom-up policy development model' and 'a private coordinating process, the outcomes of which reflect the public interest'.[9] Like the private internet giants, ICANN invoked a never-defined 'community' to justify its approach.[10] An open though not entirely transparent application process was introduced for the registration of new top-level domain names on payment of a hefty fee ($185,000 in 2015).[11] As one specialist pointed out, applications for '.god' and '.satan' did not seem likely to get far, but there were plenty of other candidates to spark controversy.[12] A meeting of ICANN's governmental advisory committee, which as the word 'advisory' suggests does not have voting rights, saw a heated argument about whether .wine and .vin should be allowed as top-level domain names. The French were furious about this attempted Anglo-Saxon abrogation of their national patrimony.[13]

Given the 'hourglass' architecture, illustrated in Figure 20, the allocation of numerical IP addresses is the master key to the whole worldwide internet. That process of address allocation, formally exercised by something called the Internet Assigned Numbers Authority, was for many years covered by a contract between ICANN and the National Telecommunications and Information Administration (no prizes for guessing which Nation), with renewal options extending to 2019. But in 2014, the US government announced its intention to transfer these crucial functions to 'the global multi-stakeholder community'.[14] Nonetheless, most of the so-called root zone servers, containing the authoritative registry of top-level domain names and corresponding IP addresses, remained

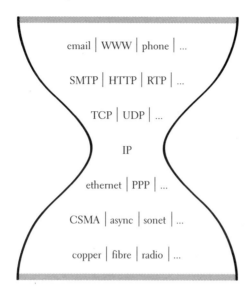

email | WWW | phone | ...

SMTP | HTTP | RTP | ...

TCP | UDP | ...

IP

ethernet | PPP | ...

CSMA | async | sonet | ...

copper | fibre | radio | ...

Figure 20. The hourglass architecture of the internet
Source: Zittrain 2008.

in American hands.[15] An American corporation, Verisign, retained exclusive and lucrative rights to the management of all .com and .net addresses, and there was still only one .gov. In internet-ional as in other areas of international relations, the United States was fighting to defend a unique position, but history was not going its way.

Among the consequences of the Snowden revelations was a further push for enhanced 'information sovereignty'. Since much of the personal information about people in other countries had been hoovered up as it passed through cables and data centres in the United States or Britain, or from American 'cloud' servers, there were demands for such data to be kept only in the country where those people lived. Russia passed a law to this effect in 2014, but the blowback was not confined to authoritarian states.[16] Brazil and Germany, both particularly indignant about the tapping of their leaders' telephones, also considered such moves. In unison, the American government and the American internet giants warned that this could lead to a 'Balkanisation' of the internet.

One might say that the American government had only itself to blame: it was responsible for allowing such massive intrusion by its security agencies into the privacy of people all over the world and then for letting top-secret information about this mass surveillance to leak. A former head of the NSA acknowledged to me that Snowden's best argument was Snowden himself. If our data was 'safe with them', how come it wasn't?[17] But American private powers also played a part in eroding the original American libertarian vision of open, free cyberspace. Increasingly, these companies stored our words, images and data in separate silos—whether in Apple Apps, an Amazon account or on the Facebook platform—where it could not freely be exchanged with other places on the internet. The matter is complicated by the fact that these closed systems were sometimes more secure, efficient and attractive than the open-source alternatives. The internet heretic Jaron Lanier suggests that closed systems can also be more innovative. 'Why', he rumbles, 'did the adored iPhone come out of what many regard as the most closed, tyrannically managed software-development shop on Earth?'[18]

This is only the briefest, most impressionistic sketch of a developing struggle, waged simultaneously on multiple fronts. Yet the fundamental questions have become clear. What architecture, organisation and governance should we want for the internet, and other systems of communication, to maximise our freedom of expression? How, if at all, can we ensure that along the way we do not lose the privacy which is a necessary condition for free speech? Having worked out what our goals are, how can we use the power of the mouse to promote them?

What we need, as Tim Berners-Lee observed on the 25th anniversary of his invention of the World Wide Web, is an open, neutral internet, 'without worrying about what's happening at the back door'.[19] The shadowy figures sneaking in through the back door work for both governments and companies. There is certainly no reason to assume that our interests are always best served by what the US government or large US companies want. Transparent, democratically accountable regulation by legitimate public powers is in principle preferable to untransparent, unaccountable control by a half-hidden combination of public and private power. Europe is the single most credible alternative source of public regulation. There is even, in principle, a respectable argument that an association of sovereign states, under United Nations auspices, is a more legitimate way to oversee a global digital public space than the very peculiar ICANN model.

In practice, however, that theoretically desirable equality of states would almost certainly be achieved at the cost of effective freedom of expression and information for many of their citizens. With more 'information sovereignty' for their governments, individual Chinese and Russians, and perhaps even Brazilians and Indians, would end up with less access to what is thought and said in other parts of the world. Messy and opaque though the 'multistakeholder' structures are, more theoretically consistent arrangements could produce a worse result. But this will only remain true if those structures are subjected to constant scrutiny by networked citizens. Moreover, the United States cannot credibly preach what it does not itself practice.

NET NEUTRALITY

The most important effects that free countries have on other countries derive from what they do at home, not abroad. The single most effective thing the West did during the Cold War was to make its own societies dynamic, open and attractive. That mattered because, to an extent previously unknown in international relations, people living in unfree countries could learn — whether from individual travels, the stories of friends and relatives, or Western radio broadcasts reaching them in their own homes — how the other half lived. If that was true back then, when cyberspace was just a science fiction word, how much more is it true in the age of mass migration and the internet. One of the things that people can see through the internet is what the United States and other liberal democracies do about the internet, and they can compare what we say with what we do. Visible double standards are the most rapid deflaters of soft power.

This, taken together with the still-leading position of American information platforms and telecommunication companies, is why the battle over net neutrality inside the United States has had an importance far beyond its frontiers. Net neutrality (more formally, 'network neutrality') is a term coined by the American scholar Tim Wu.[20] It generalises ideas that underpinned the original libertarian architecture of the American-built internet, with its end-to-end principle, its vision of 'dumb pipes' along which you would deliver my packets and I would deliver yours, with all the intelligence concentrated at the ends.[21] The technical and legal ramifications of net neutrality are immense, including several competing definitions of what it is, but the basic idea is straightforward. This is a nondiscrimination principle. Put most simply, it is 'the idea that broadband providers should treat all internet traffic the same'.[22] Those who transport the packets should not discriminate between them on the grounds of their content, the application or service being used, the sender or the recipient. Internet service providers, including cable and phone companies, should not speed up delivery because one partner pays more, slow it down for another who pays less, let alone block delivery altogether — except in certain narrowly and transparently defined conditions, specified by law and appealable through the courts. Like the old-fashioned postman, they should just deliver your mail, whether it be a supermarket circular, a bank statement or a perfumed letter from a lover.[23]

This has an important corollary. If you are to discriminate between different kinds of mail, you have to know what is in the different envelopes or boxes. The more you want to discriminate, the more you need to know. So then it is not just a case of the postman deciding to hold back your copy of, say, a men's magazine while hastening to deliver the bank statement. To make more detailed judgements, he will have to read your letters as well. Yet a well-established American principle, anchored in the Fourth Amendment, protects the privacy of the mails.[24] In this sense, net neutrality is also a defence of privacy. Since, due to the development of what is known as 'deep packet inspection', it has become technically much easier for internet service providers to steam open your letters, strong legal and social constraints are needed to counterbalance the intrusive affordances of this technology.

Unlike the larger field of internet governance, net neutrality mainly concerns the so-called last mile of delivery to your box, whether by cable, stationary Wi-Fi, or wireless signal to a mobile device. For most of us, this is normally done by one or two companies, and regulated by one country.[25] Thus, it is also something that individual nations can address: Chile in 2010 and the Netherlands in 2011 also were among the first countries to enact laws prescribing net neutrality in their own territory.[26]

Even the most passionate advocates of net neutrality recognise the need for 'reasonable traffic management' so that if, for example, everyone is wanting to watch a video of the World Cup or some popular soap opera, that gets through but does not crowd out everything else. Experts also acknowledge that the challenges of traffic management are greater on wireless networks, although that still does not require discriminating between senders, content and applications at the higher levels of the wireless iceberg.[27]

Moreover, in developing countries where poor people are accessing the internet mainly from mobile phones, some procedural violations of net neutrality might arguably have the practical effect of increasing those users' effective freedom of information and expression. For example, mobile providers will sometimes 'zero rate' (make no additional or metered charge for) use of Google, Twitter, WhatsApp or WeChat. Wikipedia experimented with using this possibility in its WikiZero project, giving free access to Wikipedia on mobile phones in poorer countries. In such circumstances, there is at least an argument that the interests of free speech can be served by this kind of positive discrimination.[28]

But this was not the issue in the titanic battle over net neutrality in the United States, one that saw President Barack Obama making a personal video appeal for the Federal Communications Commission (FCC), an independent governmental agency, to implement net neutrality by classifying internet service providers as 'common carriers'. More than four million people sent individual messages to the FCC, and it was not Russia or China that the president and the netizens were up against. Nor was it anyone wanting to help poor people in developing countries get free access to information. Rather it was the private power of a handful of big cable and phone companies, including Comcast, Verizon and AT&T, which had spent hundreds of millions of dollars in lobbying, so that they could make hundreds of millions more dollars by charging other big companies, such as Netflix, for speeding their content down a fast lane.[29]

These companies, their lobbyists and their supporters in the US Congress argued that the profits made would help companies provide better internet access for all Americans. They also invoked the freedom of the market against some leftist, egalitarian version of free speech. (Republican senator Ted Cruz called net neutrality 'Obamacare for the internet'.[30]) But this was not persuasive. The whole history of information and communications businesses, especially in the United States, suggested a tendency towards monopoly, or at least oligopoly, with a concentration of economic power in the paws of a few big cats. What was needed was actually more effective freedom of the market: that is, a well-regulated level playing field, so that new, agile entrants could sharpen the competition. Interestingly, Britain, though legally and administratively more restrictive of free speech than the US, had been more successful in securing competition in the telecommunications and internet marketplace—helped in this respect by EU competition law. In short, the free speech interest in net neutrality and the free market interest in competition were not contradictory but complementary. The marketplace of ideas would be enhanced by a wider marketplace of providers, and vice versa.[31]

In February 2015, the FCC came out with a decisive, closely argued ruling in favour of net neutrality. As common carriers, broadband providers would not be allowed to block access or speed up connections for a fee. The US Telecommunications Industry Association said it would take immediate legal action to challenge the ruling, and such litigation could drag on. Nonetheless, the ruling was an important moment for an open, free internet, at least so far as it was still based in the United States.[32]

People still sometimes spoke as if net neutrality were a default position for the worldwide internet. That is what people who believe in it think it should be. The Electronic Frontier Foundation, an NGO rooted in the libertarian and free speech traditions of the American internet founders, assembled a global coalition to further the cause, with participating groups from more than 70 countries.[33] But in the second decade of the twenty-first century, net neutrality was not the reality for a growing proportion of the world's internet users, especially those on mobile devices in unfree or semifree countries. A careful 'Web Index' survey commissioned by Tim Berners-Lee's World Wide Web Foundation found that, in 2014, three quarters of the countries surveyed either lacked clear and effective net neutrality rules and/or showed evidence of traffic discrimination.[34] If anything, this made what happened in the United States not less but more significant. If even America were to abandon it, what hope would there be for net neutrality anywhere else?

PRIVATISING AND EXPORTING CENSORSHIP

Net neutrality obviously does not mean that no intermediary ever blocks anything anywhere along the path from end to end. We want to stop malware, spam, criminal hackers and cyberattackers. As we have seen, trying to prevent the spread of paedophile child pornography, recognising the appalling harm to which it directly contributes, is one of the few things on which almost everyone in the world agrees. We also recognise that intermediaries should comply with a legal request in a jurisdiction where independent courts administer laws promulgated by a democratically elected legislature. That leaves large questions about the clash of jurisdictions (should Europe's privacy norms be enforced on the US mother site google.com?) and whether the laws of North Korea should be respected to the same degree as those of France. But if we are using the word censorship to mean an illegitimate restriction, then most of this cannot properly be called censorship.

However, there are at least three ways in which some combination of private and public power produces what are arguably illegitimate restrictions that— and here's the rub—we will find it hard to identify because they result from hidden, untransparent, nonaccountable interventions somewhere lower down an iceberg. First, there are things information and communication companies do for their own commercial, experimental or design reasons, or sometimes just because they think it's the right thing to do, in line with their founders' preferences.

Second, there is the way in which democratic governments try to get intermediaries to do for them what they regard as desirable blocking and filtering. In Britain, for example, decisions about which sites internet service providers should block have been delegated to a nongovernmental body called the Internet Watch Foundation. This is largely funded by information and communication companies, which voluntarily undertake to follow its recommendations. If the site to be blocked is based in Britain, the foundation approaches the host with a request to take it down. If it is based abroad, the foundation adds the address to a confidential blacklist distributed to British internet service providers. Now 95 percent of the time, perhaps 99 percent, if we saw what was being blocked we would probably agree with the decision—especially since the foundation has mainly been concerned to stop child pornography. But now and then a case comes to light, either by chance or as a result of journalistic or NGO investigation, where the intervention has been mistaken and disproportionate. A famous example is the blocking of a Wikipedia page showing the provocative LP cover for the Scorpions' album *Virgin Killer*. This had the unintended consequence of preventing UK-based Wikipedians from editing the online encyclopaedia at all when using those internet service providers.[35]

Why should this job not be done by a properly constituted public authority, accountable to parliament, with decisions appealable at law? In a report on the internet published in 2011, the UN's Special Rapporteur on freedom of expression, Frank la Rue, stated emphatically that 'censorship measures should never be delegated to private entities'.[36] The pragmatic arguments for sticking with the 'multistakeholder' model of international internet governance do not apply here, because there is every reason to believe the result would be better in terms of transparency and accountability. In fact, these informal arrangements, however well intentioned, enable both governments and companies to avoid the full glare of public scrutiny, in a murky instance of P^2.

What is more, democratic governments have increasingly been asking internet service providers to demonstrate their 'social responsibility' by either passing on to government, or themselves blocking and filtering, 'extreme' content of various kinds. Thus, partly in response to pressure from government, most British internet service providers were already filtering what came into most British homes, with services such as BT's Cleanfeed.[37] The government of David Cameron responded to a parliamentary report critical of the intelligence and security services' failure to pick up two Islamist assassins, who had brutally butchered a British soldier on a street in Woolwich, London, by turning the spotlight on Facebook, because one of the assassins had proclaimed his intention to murder a British soldier in an earlier post on his Facebook page.[38] It would be consistent with our second principle to suggest that Facebook employees should have alerted the government to such an explicit threat of violence, if they had managed to pick it up among the millions of items being posted daily on Facebook. But, leaving aside the government's questionable attempt to divert popular attention from the failings of its own security services, the question is how this should be done. That question becomes critical when governments start calling on private platforms to block more vaguely defined nonviolent 'extremism'.

In fairness, we must acknowledge that both public and private powers are wrestling with a genuinely difficult problem—a new and not fully understood nexus between the virtual and real worlds which, at the extreme, can contribute to the death or horrible abuse of innocent people.[39] But this way of addressing that problem is itself problematic. For governments, it shifts the censorial and surveillance responsibility onto the companies, without the hard, democratic work of transparent legislation and regulation. For the companies, this kind of informal collaboration with the executive can be more comfortable than facing hard-edged legal responsibility. Moreover, motives are always mixed and companies have multiple interests in their relations with governments. For example, they might think that being especially 'cooperative' with governments in such areas could help to spare them more rigorous regulation of their anti-competitive practices. The public interest in privacy and free speech could get squeezed between a government's interest in being seen to do everything to protect its citizens' security and the companies' interest in maximising profit. And the more that censorship is delegated to private intermediaries in a non-transparent process, the easier it is for the Russian and Chinese authorities to say: 'Well, we are only doing what you do. We just have a slightly different definition of "extreme" and "obscene"'.

This brings us to a third way in which P^2 has threatened freedom of expression: Western companies selling to oppressive regimes. We may not be surprised that Chinese, Russian or Saudi information businesses help their governments to monitor and censor the communications of their own citizens, but there are numerous examples of leading Western information companies supplying such governments, in the pursuit of profit.[40]

The roll of dishonour is long. A company called SiemensNokia sold mobile network surveillance technology to the Islamic Republic of Iran and other repressive regimes. IBM did the same for China Mobile, the biggest Chinese mobile phone operator. The Great Firewall of China (formally the Golden Shield) uses equipment supplied by the American information giant Cisco. A leaked internal Cisco presentation from 2002 noted the Chinese authorities' wish to use their 'golden shield' to 'combat Falun Gong evil religion and other hostiles'.[41] An investigation by the Citizen Lab in Toronto traced the worldwide export by just one California-based provider, Blue Coat Systems, of sophisticated technologies that can be used for filtering, censorship and surveillance. This generated a map of 'Planet Blue Coat', showing all the countries where Blue Coat products were almost certainly being used for such purposes. Investigators from Privacy International managed to attend marketing exhibitions for international surveillance equipment, and the range of repressive technologies being promoted by Western companies took their breath away.[42]

Lenin is apocryphally reported to have said that 'the capitalists will sell us the rope with which we will hang them'. Here, capitalists sell dictators the rope with which they hang their own citizens. All these companies have legal and PR departments which will send you long emails or letters (as SiemensNokia did to me on one occasion) explaining how the story was not exactly as reported and the products are no different from those they supply to Western networks.[43] But while these often are 'dual use' technologies, deployed for less oppressive purposes in democracies, the companies know perfectly well the kind of regimes they are dealing with. Selling a sharp knife to a fisherman is not the same as selling a sharp knife to a murderer.

After the first popular rising of the Arab Spring took place in Tunisia, the head of the country's Internet Agency revealed that, under the ancien régime of Zine el Abidine Ben Ali, several Western companies had used the agency as a testing ground for internet censorship technologies which they might then sell to other friendly dictators.[44] When the Arab Spring came to Egypt, protesters found documents showing how the British-based Gamma Group had offered to sell a spyware programme called FinFisher to the military security state of Hosni Mubarak. But three years later, when spring had turned to fall in Cairo, an Egyptian newspaper leaked a fresh document from the Ministry of the Interior. This was a call for tenders to support a new cybermonitoring system, targeted at 'destructive ideas' being spread on the internet, and it helpfully listed examples. 'Destructive ideas' included blasphemy and scepticism in religion, spreading rumours, sarcasm, using inappropriate words, lack of morality, 'inviting demonstrations' and 'taking statements out of context'.[45]

By now, there were probably Chinese and Russian companies that might bid for such an attractive authoritarian tender. But how could companies based in democracies be prevented from doing so, wrapped in the cloak of secrecy and sporting the crimson scarf of hypocrisy? 'Only with great difficulty' is the realistic answer, since companies could find many ways round restrictions, while early-twenty-first-century democratic governments and legislatures were themselves both legitimately interested in exporters' contribution to economic growth and chronically susceptible to corporate lobbying. It would take a combination of national and international regulation (for example, modernising and tightening up the so-called Wassenaar Arrangement on dual-use exports), NGO scrutiny, media exposure and consumer pressure to check this kind of corporate prostitution.[46]

ETHICAL ALGORITHMS?

Some of the most high-profile editorial or (if you find them illegitimate) censorial decisions made by private powers are the personal judgements of individual employees. If there is significant popular response or media attention, that
judgement is rapidly reviewed and either confirmed or reversed by a higher-
placed person. Richard Allan, Facebook's European director of public policy,
has noted from his own experience how rapidly such decisions went up to the
very top of his organisation.[47]

In 2007, Verizon Wireless stopped an American pro-choice advocacy group
(supporting women's right to choose whether to have an abortion) from getting the text messaging short code that would enable it to send messages to its
supporters. After a story appeared about this in the New York Times, the decision was reversed. During the 2012 London Olympics, the Twitter account
of a US-based British journalist called Guy Adams was suspended. Adams
had tweeted complaints about the time delay on NBC broadcasts from the
Olympics, for the duration of which Twitter had a cross-promotional business
partnership with NBC. After protests, Adams's account was restored. Twitter's general counsel then acknowledged that it was actually a Twitter employee who had identified the offending tweet and encouraged NBC to file
a complaint.[48] I could list other cases that came to light, but how many more
never did?

That said, most of the decisions— choices? switches?—determining what we
do or do not see on our boxes are made by computers, following instructions
contained in algorithms. An algorithm is, in the most general terms, 'a precisely
defined set of mathematical or logical operations for the performance of a particular task'.[49] So in principle I could have an algorithm for doing my weekly
laundry. These days, however, the word is mainly used to mean a sequence
of instructions for a task to be carried out by a computer. Such algorithms
determine the top ten results to pop up in your search box and the items on
your Facebook News Feed.[50]

Their potential influence is enormous. This is why companies and wealthy
individuals spend millions on search engine optimisation. If, due to some small
change in the algorithm, 'Bates Motel + Fairvale' disappears from the top 10
results, that could be the commercial kiss of death for that delightful hostelry.
The internet scholar Zeynep Tufekci argues that Facebook's News Feed algorithm unintentionally buried news of the first days of protests against the killing of a black youth by a white policeman in the town of Ferguson, Missouri,
in summer 2014.[51] The psychologist Robert Epstein, an outspoken critic of

Google, goes further, talking of a search engine manipulation effect. In a study conducted with 1,800 undecided voters in India's 2014 parliamentary election, he claimed to have shifted votes by an average of 12.5 percent to particular candidates simply by improving their placings in search results found by the individual voter.[52]

An extreme example of algorithmic choice could be provided by Google's computer-driven car. An old chestnut for students of ethics is the 'trolley problem': you control the railway points and have to decide whether the trolley will turn left and run over one person or turn right and kill five. Now suppose this automated Google car, steered by computer, faces a similar choice. It cannot stop in time. It has to run over either that grey-haired old woman on the left or that funky young man on the right. Which way will the computer turn the steering wheel? Who would an ethical algorithm decide to kill? When we came up with this dilemma in a workshop at Stanford, one participant quipped: 'Oh, that's easy: the one who contributed least to Google's advertising dollars'. Even the Google employee in our group joined in the laughter.[53]

The time may come, perhaps sooner rather than later, when the question about the ethics of algorithms will need to be posed in respect of an evolving artificial intelligence, or even addressed to that machine-mind.[54] At the moment, it is still essentially a question to the human beings who write the algorithms. Only after carving my way through front-of-house PR folderol to proper conversations with senior executives and engineers did I realise just how much these algorithms embed quite specific human value judgements. To be sure, these are immensely complex, multifactored coding formulas, and many of those factors are themselves automated inputs. But then a senior search engineer would tell me, 'Oh yes, we had to tweak the algorithm on that'—and 'that' was an issue I had raised concerning science, morality, privacy or free speech.

One of the two legal positions between which search engines toggle—the First Amendment one rather than the neutral intermediary one—explicitly acknowledges this. In his influential white paper on First Amendment protection for search engine search results, commissioned by Google, the legal scholar Eugene Volokh writes, 'This selection and sorting is a mix of science and art: it uses sophisticated computerised algorithms, but those algorithms themselves inherently incorporate the search engine company engineers' judgements about what material users are most likely to find responsive to their queries. In this respect, each search engine's editorial judgement is much like many other familiar editorial judgements'. Volokh's examples included newspapers' judgements about which stories to run and guidebooks' judgements about which attractions to highlight.[55] Sue Halpern puts it vividly: 'The algorithm is, in essence, an editor, pulling up what it deems important, based on someone else's understanding of what is important'.[56] For now, the human 'someone else' still has the whip hand.

These humans constantly attempt to improve those algorithms. Their definition of 'improve' includes notions of giving optimal service to the user, quality control (for example, privileging some scientific sources over others), maximising user-eyeball-hours and increasing the company's advertising revenue. Among the techniques for improvement, the most generically salient is testing them, internally and externally. Typically, this takes the form of an A/B test, when two algorithmic alternatives are tried out simultaneously on a split sample group. These experiments are being made on us all the time, usually with our formal legal consent (that 'I Agree' button again) but without our being aware of it.

An experiment conducted by Facebook's Core Data Science Team in 2012, but only made public in a scientific paper that appeared in 2014, 'manipulated the extent to which people ($N = 689,003$) were exposed to emotional expressions in their News Feed'. One group among those 689,003 users had their News Feeds manipulated to select more positive emotional content coming from their Facebook friends, while another got more negative emotional content. Result: the recipients of gloom became gloomier in their own Facebook posts, while those of cheerfulness became cheerier. The scientific paper, co-authored by scholars from Cornell University, found this to be significant evidence of 'emotional contagion'. I cannot help wondering what would have happened if an already depressed person had been tipped over the edge into suicide by this manipulated stream of emotional negativity. Or perhaps one of them was? (The scientific paper on the Facebook mood experiment blithely asserted that 'it was consistent with Facebook's Data Use Policy, to which all users agreed prior to creating an account on Facebook, constituting informed consent for this research'. If that was *informed* consent, I am a crocodile.)[57]

Given the power of these algorithms to shape what we see, hear, know and feel, shouldn't they be made more transparent and accountable? The companies will reply that they are too complex to be understood by outsiders, that if they are understood they can be 'gamed', and that anyway these are commercial secrets. But we cannot rest content with a situation in which secret, unaccountably determined algorithms have such a potentially distorting influence over our effective freedom of information and expression. As with the security services of the state, which draw heavily on the data collected by these companies, we have to find a middle way between unachievable transparency and unacceptable secrecy. Could there be some secure, confidential public regulation of the ethics of algorithms? Might there be a process of self-regulation in which, as suggested already for media, platforms are kitemarked as meeting certain minimal standards of editorial responsibility? How can we achieve algorithmic accountability?

MONEY SPEAKS (TOO LOUDLY)

Aryeh Neier has a secure place in the history of twentieth-century American struggles for free speech. Born to a Jewish family in Berlin in 1937, and having barely escaped the Holocaust, he nonetheless famously went on to defend the free speech right of a group of American neo-Nazis to march through the small town of Skokie, Illinois, which was home to a number of Holocaust survivors. In the book he wrote about the Skokie case, *Defending My Enemy*, he explained why: 'Because we Jews are uniquely vulnerable, I believe we can win only brief respite from persecution in a society in which encounters are settled by power. As a Jew, therefore, . . . I want restraints placed on power. The restraints that matter most to me are those which ensure that I cannot be squashed by power, unnoticed by the rest of the world'.[58]

Thirty-five years later, when he emailed me about our original draft principles, it was another kind of squashing power that preoccupied him. In addition to our ten, he proposed an eleventh on nonverbal communication (which I have tried to address by using throughout this book a broad definition of 'speech') and then two more: 'we believe that commercial speech may be regulated in the public interest' and 'we believe that equitable restrictions on financial contributions to political campaigns do not violate freedom of speech'.[59]

He was not the only major American free speech advocate to turn his attention to the impact of money. As we have seen, Lawrence Lessig was a pioneer both of thinking about the relationship between law and cyberspace and of how to create a legal framework for information and knowledge to be shared freely online. But Lessig then directed his powerful searchlight at the corrupting influence of money on American politics. In the Preface to his book *Republic, Lost*, he recalls how he became 'convinced that the questions I was addressing in the fields of copyright in internet policy depended upon resolving the policy questions—the corruption—that I address here'. And he shows how the US Supreme Court's Citizens United verdict of 2010 was followed by an explosion in independent campaign spending, 460 percent up on the last off-year congressional election. Even when there was not a direct quid pro quo, he suggests, the US Congress had become systemically dependent on financial contributors, whereas it was meant to be dependent only on the will of the voters.[60] Figure 21

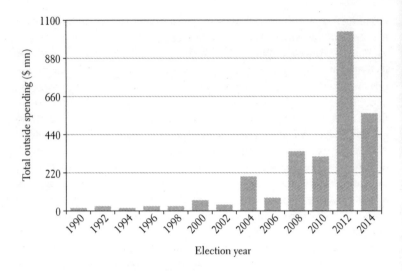

Figure 21. Money speaks in US politics
Total outside spending refers to the money spent by politically active nonprofits, such as
Super PACs, that are not subject to regulations limiting candidates' campaign finances.
Source: Center for Responsive Politics, 2015.

gives some sense of this development, although it does not capture all sources of campaign funding.

Another American lawyer posed a further striking challenge to the early-twenty-first-century United States. 'Who is a person?' asked Eric L. Lewis. 'As a corporate litigator who has also spent more than a decade defending Guantá-namo detainees, I have been trying to figure out why corporations are worthy of court protection and Muslims held in indefinite detention without trial by the United States at a naval base in Cuba are not'. How could the US treat the former as persons, but not the latter?[61]

Again and again, through successive chapters of this book, we have bumped up against this power of money: from corporate lobbyists in Washington and Brussels, media ownership almost everywhere, only the rich being able to afford the lawyers to defend their reputations in court, wealthy individuals and corporations using that disparity of financial-legal power to deter critical comment that is in the public interest, all the way to the profit motive of information giants determining algorithmically what we see online. The problem is by no means confined to the United States, but it is especially salient there, not least because other constraints still painfully apparent in much of the world play a lesser role in the United States.

While the American constitutional and legal tradition has been superb when it comes to restraining public power, it has been much less good at restraining private power. Yet on the internet, private powers are as important as public ones. In the land of the First Amendment, in the second decade of the twenty-first century, the limiting, distorting and corrupting power of money is the biggest single cause for concern around free speech. Money speaks, too loudly.

To be sure, the role of money is by no means only negative: a free market of purveyors enhances the free marketplace of ideas. The pursuit of profit is a turbo-driver of innovation, and many of those innovations are good for freedom of expression and information. The fact that some of the commanding heights of the Chinese internet are in private hands is, in the longer term, a cause for hope about free speech in China. Like the power of the state, that of an information giant can be used for good as well as evil. But, like the power of the state, it always has to be checked and balanced. Inasmuch as the United States fails to do that, it will not just directly constrain freedom of expression across the world, given the reach of its leading platforms. It will also be setting a bad example.

Courage

'We decide for ourselves and face the consequences'.

Think for yourself: that central enlightenment principle of free speech applies also to determining its limits. You, the individual are sovereign, and individual self-determination makes for a more sovereign country. To be sure, there are meaningful senses in which an authoritarian state may be said to have territorial, political and 'informational' sovereignty, but the truly sovereign state will build its own sovereignty on that of each and every citizen.

Such countries we call free. If you are fortunate enough to live in a state sufficiently approximating to that ideal, you can articulate your views about the proper norms, limits and conditions of free speech through diverse, uncensored media and through the political process. Whether directly or indirectly, you will influence a parliament: that is, etymologically, a place of speaking. You can combine voice and vote, those two things for which several languages use one and the same word: *Stimme* and *Stimme*, *głos* and *głos*, *sawt* and *sawt*. You can also affect the policies of companies and other private powers. If the corporation doesn't change its ways, you should be able to change providers. And you can participate, through NGOs and networks of netizens, in shaping international rules.

With luck, you will achieve an outcome which, though it will not be entirely what you want, protects what you regard as the essentials—and you can go on arguing about the rest. If these methods of changing law or policy do not achieve what you believe to be an essential minimum, you can resort to peaceful protest, extraparliamentary action and civil resistance. If your liberal state functions as it should, some time in prison may be the price, but not persecution, torture or death.

Yet even in a law-abiding liberal democracy, the risks are often higher and more unpredictable than this. Challenge the taboos of a religious group whose more extreme members believe in violence, and you may end up being butchered one morning on a quiet city street. Expose the corruption of the rich and powerful, whether individual or corporate, and you may end up losing job, home and family. Blow the whistle on deep state wrongdoing, committed under the cloak of official secrecy, and you may lose your country as well. Beside the speech-restricting state, there is the oppressive community, company, tribe or family.

Since words and images, information and ideas, have great power, they will always be contested. Freedom of speech, like the rule of law, strengthens the arm of the weak against the strong. Remember the Russian proverb quoted by Solzhenitsyn and quoted on Sina Weibo by the Chinese actress Yao Chen: 'One word of truth shall outweigh the whole world'. We should therefore not be surprised that the strong take extreme measures to withhold this weapon from the weak. An authoritarian or totalitarian regime typically sees restricting and manipulating speech as an essential foundation of its power.

Many 'habits of the heart'—to adopt a resonant phrase from Alexis de Tocqueville—are helpful in resisting such pressures, but two seem to me essential: courage and tolerance. Very occasionally we find these qualities combined in one great heart. Most often we do not. Usually, the mixture is uneven: this person exhibits more courage, less tolerance, that one, great tolerance, little courage. Yet securing the future of free speech requires both.

COURAGE

'Nothing is more difficult', wrote the German political writer Kurt Tucholsky, 'and nothing requires more character, than to find yourself in open contradiction to your time and loudly to say: No'.[1] First of all, it is intellectually and psychologically difficult to step outside the received wisdom of your time and place. What has been called 'the normative power of the given' persuades us that what we see all around us, what everyone else seems to regard as normal, is in some sense also an ethical norm. Numerous studies in behavioural psychology show how our individual conviction of what is true or right quails before the massed pressure of our peers. We are, as Mark Twain observed, 'discreet sheep'.[2] This is what John Stuart Mill picked up when he wrote that the same causes which make someone a Churchman in London would have made him a Buddhist or a Confucian in Beijing.[3] The same truth is gloriously captured in a humorous song by Michael Flanders and Donald Swann, in which a young cannibal revolts against the settled wisdom of his elders and declares that 'eating people is wrong'. At the end of the song, one of the wise elders exclaims, to huge belly laughs all round, 'why, you might just as well go around saying "don't fight people!"' Then he and his colleagues cry in unison: 'Ridiculous!'[4]

Yet norms change even within a single lifetime, especially as we live longer. So as octogenarian disc jockeys are arrested for having sexually harassed or abused young women in the 1960s, we should be uncomfortably aware that some other activity people regard as fairly normal now may be viewed as aberrant and abhorrent 50 years hence.

To step outside the established wisdom of your time and place is difficult enough; openly to stand against it is more demanding still. In his fine book on the First Amendment tradition in the United States, Anthony Lewis quotes a 1927 opinion by Supreme Court Justice Louis Brandeis, which Lewis says 'many regard as the greatest judicial statement of the case for freedom of speech'. The passage he quotes begins, 'Those who won our independence . . . believed liberty to be the secret of happiness and courage to be the secret of liberty'.[5] This is magnificent, although it also illustrates the somewhat self-referential, even self-reverential, character of the modern First Amendment tradition. Lewis cites Brandeis, who credits this thought to the eighteenth-century founders of the United States. But those founders would have been well aware that they got it straight from Pericles's funeral oration during the fifth-century-B.C.E. Peloponnesian War, as reported—if not invented, or at least much improved upon—by Thucydides. 'For you now', Thucydides's Pericles admonishes his ancient Athenian audience, after praising the heroic dead, 'it remains to rival what they have done and, knowing the secret of happiness to be freedom and the secret of freedom a brave heart, not idly to stand aside from the enemy's onset'.[6]

More directly, the American tradition of courage in the defence of free speech draws on the heritage of the seventeenth-century English. People like John Lilburne, for example. In 1638, while still in his early twenties, Lilburne was found guilty by the Star Chamber court of helping smuggle into England a tract against bishops, which had been printed in the Low Countries. He was tied to the back of a cart on a hot summer's day and unremittingly whipped as he walked with a bare back all the way from the eastern end of Fleet Street to Westminster Palace Yard. One bystander reckoned that he received some 500 blows which, since the executioner wielded a three-thronged whip, made 1500 stripes.

His untreated shoulders 'swelled almost as big as a penny loafe with the bruses of the knotted Cords', and he was then made to stand for two hours in the pillory in Palace Yard. Here, in spite of his wounds and the burning sunshine, he began loudly to tell his story and to rail against bishops. The crowd was reportedly delighted. After half an hour there came 'a fat lawyer'—ah, plus ça change—who bid him stop. The man whom the people of London had already dubbed 'Free-Born John' refused to shut up. He was then gagged so roughly that blood spurted from his mouth. Undeterred, he thrust his hands into his pockets and scattered dissident pamphlets to the crowd. No other means of expression being left to him, Free-Born John then stamped his feet until the two hours were up.[7]

As an Englishman, I find particular inspiration in the example of Free-Born John, and those of all our other free-born Johns: John Milton, John Wilkes, John Stuart Mill (and George Orwell, a free-born John in all but name). More broadly, there is no reason to understate, let alone to deny, a specifically Western tradition of courage in the advancement of free speech, one that can be traced from ancient Athens, through England, France and a host of other European countries, to the United States, Canada and all the liberal democracies of today's wider West. But it would be quite wrong to suggest that this habit of the heart is confined to the West. In fact, there have been rather few examples of such sturdy defiance in England in recent times, while we find them in other countries and cultures.

Consider, for instance, the Chinese dissident Liu Xiaobo. Liu was sentenced to 11 years imprisonment in 2009 for 'subverting state power'. Both his written response to the charges against him and his final speech in court are, like many of his earlier writings, lucid and courageous affirmations of the central importance of free speech. He definitely does not draw only on Western traditions. For example, he quotes a traditional Chinese 24-character injunction: 'Say all you know, in every detail; a speaker is blameless, because listeners can think; if the words are true, make your corrections; if they are not, just take note'. After paying a moving tribute to his wife ('Armed with your love, dear one, I can face the sentence that I'm about to receive with peace in my heart'), he looks forward to the day 'when our country will be a land of free expression: a country where the words of each citizen will get equal respect, a country where different values, ideas, beliefs and political views can compete with one another even as they peacefully coexist'. The judge cut him short in court before he had finished speaking, but free-born Xiaobo, like free-born John, still got his message out. In his planned peroration, Liu wrote: 'I hope that I will be the last victim in China's long record of treating words as crimes. Free expression is the base of human rights, the root of human nature and the mother of truth. To kill free speech is to insult human rights, to stifle human nature and to suppress truth'.[8]

Liu was by this time famous, and that great speech made him more so. He was awarded the Nobel Peace Prize in 2010. But perhaps the most inspiring examples of all come from people who are not famous at all: so-called ordinary people doing extraordinary things. People like the Hamburg shipyard worker who, at the launch of a naval training vessel in 1935, refused to join all those around him in making the Hitler salute. The photograph only achieved wide circulation on the internet more than 60 years later. There he stands amidst a forest of outstretched arms, with both his own firmly folded across his chest, a portrait of stubborn worker's pride. His name was August Landmesser. He had been a Nazi party member but was later expelled from the party for marrying a Jewish woman and then imprisoned for 'dishonouring the race'. After his release, he was drafted to fight in the Second World War and never returned.[9]

Again, such moments are emphatically not confined to the West. During the Arab Spring of 2011, a 'day of rage' was proclaimed by dissidents in Saudi Arabia. Faced with a massive police presence at the appointed location in the country's capital, Riyadh, almost nobody showed up. But one man, a strongly built, black-haired teacher called Khaled al-Johani, suddenly approached a group of foreign reporters. 'We need to speak freely', he cried, with an explosion of pent-up passion. 'No one must curb our freedom of expression'. A BBC Arabic service film clip, which you can watch on YouTube, shows a tall secret policeman, in white robes, headdress and dark glasses, looming in the background as he snoops on al-Johani's speech. A little further away, armed police mutter into their walkie-talkies. 'What will happen to you now?' asks one of the reporters, as they escort the teacher back to his car. 'They will send me to prison', al-Johani says, adding ironically: 'and I will be happy'. He was subsequently condemned to one and a half years imprisonment.[10]

In many places, we can find monuments to the Unknown Soldier, but we should also erect them to the Unknown Speaker.

TWO SPIRITS OF LIBERTY

Shortly after Isaiah Berlin died, Christopher Hitchens launched an almost Lilburnesque attack on him in the London Review of Books. The celebrated liberal philosopher, argued the celebrated polemicist, had been cowardly, weak, inconsistent, an apologist for the Vietnam war, a toady of the powerful. Berlin, wrote Hitchens, was 'simultaneously pompous and dishonest in the face of a long moral crisis where his views and his connections could have made a difference'. And he deplored the fact that Berlin's reputation stood 'like a lion in your path' if you 'chafe at the present complacently "liberal" consensus'.[11]

Berlin's most famous essay is 'Two Concepts of Liberty', but it seems to me that Hitchens and Berlin personified two spirits of liberty. The distinction between these two spirits is not a philosophical one, like that between two concepts. Rather, it is a matter of temperament, character, habits of the heart. Put most simply, Hitchens exemplified courage, Berlin tolerance. Hitchens was outspoken, outrageous, never afraid to offend, impressively undeterred by Islamist death threats. He was also almost never prepared to admit that he had been wrong, nimbly shifting his ground to defend, with equal vehemence, whatever contrarian position he chose to adopt at a particular moment. But he was brave, and utterly consistent in his defence of free speech.

Berlin was not notable for his courage. This was a weakness he struggled with. In a letter to a close friend, written when he was already a highly respected, middle-aged man, he wrote, 'I wish I had not inherited my father's timorous, rabbity nature! I can be brave, but oh what appallingly superhuman struggles with cowardice!'[12] And in an essay on his beloved Turgenev, he evokes 'the small, hesitant, self-critical, not always very brave, band of men who occupy a position somewhere to the left of centre, and are morally repelled both by the hard faces to their right and the hysteria and mindless violence and demagoguery on their left . . . '.[13]

Yet Berlin was one of the most eloquent, consistent defenders of a liberalism which creates and defends the spaces in which people subscribing to different values, holding incompatible views, pursuing irreconcilable political projects—in short, the Hitchens(es) and the anti-Hitchens(es)—can battle it out in freedom, without violence. Berlin personified not merely tolerance but also an extraordinary gift for empathy, that ability to get inside very different heads and hearts which is a distinguishing mark of the liberal imagination.

In a speech delivered in 1944, explaining what the United States was fighting for in the Second World War, to an audience that included many newly created American citizens, Justice Learned Hand declared: 'What then is the spirit of liberty? I cannot define it; I can only tell you my own faith. The spirit of liberty is the spirit which is not too sure that it is right; the spirit of liberty is the spirit which seeks to understand the minds of other men and women; the spirit of liberty is the spirit which weighs their interests alongside its own without bias'.[14] Who can doubt that Berlin was filled with that spirit of liberty? But Hitchens was filled with a spirit of liberty too.

Though they tend to distrust, even to despise each other, both these spirits are indispensable. Each has its characteristic fault. A world composed entirely of Hitchenses would tend to intolerance. It would be a permanent, if often amusing, shouting match, one in which there would be neither time nor space to understand—in the deepest sense of understanding, involving profound study, calm reflection and imaginative sympathy—where the other person was coming from. A world composed entirely of Berlins would tend to relativism and excessive tolerance for the sworn enemies of tolerance.[15]

Plainly this tension does not begin with those two late-twentieth-century writers. Towards the end of his life, the German-British liberal thinker Ralf Dahrendorf wrote a book about a line of political intellectuals he called Erasmians, among whom he included Isaiah Berlin. And the argument between these two spirits of liberty is already there in the sixteenth-century relationship between Erasmus of Rotterdam and Martin Luther. Erasmus, the most celebrated scholar of his day, prepared the way for the Reformation. So close was his intellectual affinity with Luther in earlier years that the joke went *aut Erasmus Lutherat, aut Erasmissat Lutherus*—now Erasmus Luthers, now Luther Erasmusses.[16] But when Luther made his break with the Roman Church, Erasmus would not follow. Men of goodwill, he insisted, must be able to conduct these arguments with civility and reason, within the body of the church. In his commentary on the Latin adage 'So many men, so many opinions' (*Quot homines, tot sententiae*), he attributes to Saint Paul the view that 'for the putting aside of strife, we should allow every man to have his own convictions'. (This was, one might add, adventurous ijtihad of St Paul).[17] In 1517, the very year that Luther nailed his protestant theses to a church door, Erasmus wrote an essay titled 'The Complaint of Peace', lamenting the 'word-warriors' who 'attack each other with poison pens, ripping each other up with the keen phrases of satire and hurling lethal darts of insinuation'.[18]

Dahrendorf recalls a scene when the mortally ill 35-year-old Ulrich von Hutten, a reformer who was in some ways even bolder than Luther, actually knocked on the door of Erasmus's house in Basel to seek help, 'but Erasmus, himself sick, and fearful both of physical and of spiritual infection, did not admit him. All Basel saw it . . .' Hutten had just enough strength left to pen an 'Expostulation' against Erasmus, including this stinging rebuke: 'Your own books will have to fight out the battle between them'.[19] For several years, Erasmus resisted pressure from church leaders to confront the reformers and when he finally did so, it was in the form of a learned dialogue disputing Luther's views on free will.[20] Hutten's barb was an early version of the twentieth-century jibe that a liberal is someone who can't take his own side in an argument.[21] It connects to a recurrent critique of liberalism as pale, bloodless, sickly, unable to stand up for itself in a fight.

People can possess these two qualities in different measures at different times. Dahrendorf himself was an Erasmian in his old age, but as a 15-year-old schoolboy in Nazi Berlin he had formed a resistance group and been incarcerated in a Gestapo camp.[22] There is the courage of youth and the tolerance born of experience. The mix in any one person is never entirely simple. Hitchens could be witheringly, contemptuously intolerant in print and on the public stage, yet in private he had a gift for good fellowship with a remarkably wide range of people. One of his characteristic and, for the recipient, mildly irritating rhetorical tropes was to say, 'X is a friend of mine, but . . .' followed by a fulminating attack on something said or written by X.

Erasmians also have their own brand of courage or, perhaps more precisely, of fortitude. It takes a certain quiet fortitude to maintain your intellectual independence when all about you are becoming partisan. 'On no other account do I congratulate myself more', Erasmus wrote towards the end of his life, 'than on the fact that I have never attached myself to any party'.[23] 'I love freedom', he responded to Luther's axe attack, 'and I will not and can not serve any party'.[24] It takes perseverance to keep calmly advocating an independent, liberal position—balanced, fair, respectful of complexity, more concerned to get at the truth than to be entertaining—when what Jacob Burckhardt called the *terribles simplificateurs* are harvesting youthful enthusiasm and collective emotion.

'So we must weigh and measure, bargain, compromise, and prevent the crushing of one form of life by its rivals', wrote Berlin, three years before he died, in a text subsequently published by the New York Review of Books as a 'message to the 21st century'. 'I know only too well that this is not a flag under which idealistic and enthusiastic young men and women may wish to march— it seems too tame, too reasonable, too bourgeois, it does not engage the generous emotions. But you must believe me, one cannot have everything one wants—not only in practice, but even in theory'.[25]

Raymond Aron was another such Erasmian, and his last hours are a perfect example of this cooler virtue. Convinced that his friend Bertrand de Jouvenel had been travestied in a book by an Israeli historian, Aron agreed to testify in a libel case de Jouvenel had launched against the author and publisher. Emphasising to the court that de Jouvenel had been wrong in his early assessment of Hitler, while Aron himself 'at once saw the devil in Hitler'—and, as his audience knew, had gone on to serve Charles de Gaulle's exile government in London—he nonetheless deplored the book as ahistorical: 'the author never put things into context. The definition he gives of fascism is so vague and imprecise that it could include anything'. It therefore represented 'the worst kind of libel—the result of a procedure which I deplore and condemn: guilt by association'. Having thus spoken up for intellectual clarity, historical understanding and elementary fairness, the frail old philosopher stepped out of the courtroom and into a car, where he suffered a massive heart attack and died. Just before he disappeared, he remarked to the journalist Marc Ullman: '*Je crois avoir dit l'essentiel*'. (Roughly translatable as: 'I believe I said what needed saying'.)[26] What finer death could there be for an Erasmian?

It is quite rare that these two spirits of liberty, with their distinctive qualities of courage and of tolerance, come combined in equal parts in one individual. The nearest I have seen to this was Václav Havel. Havel was a brave dissident, in the footsteps of his fourteenth-century compatriot Jan Hus. He proved that courage through four years in prison and multiple subsequent arrests. His solidarity with dissidents in other parts of the world was unwavering. One of his last public actions, when already a very sick man, was to stand outside the Chinese embassy in Prague to protest against the imprisonment of Liu Xiaobo—an exceptional, undiplomatic act for a former president. Yet Havel was also the epitome of Erasmian tolerance, not just unfailingly courteous but genuinely open to a wide range of philosophies and ways of life, wanting them all to be heard and seen. Usually, however, the two spirits of liberty are found unevenly distributed between individuals: the one more Lutheran, the other more Erasmian. Freedom needs both.

Most of the exemplars in this chapter have been drawn from the history of the modern West. Several are people I knew and loved. It is for others to say whether we can identify a similar dichotomy in other cultures and traditions. My own superficial impression from countries I know much less well, such as China, Myanmar and Egypt, is that we can. On my journeys for this book I have met deeply admirable people who seem to me to embody each of these two spirits of liberty. And was Gandhi perhaps, like Havel, an exception to prove the rule, combining both courage and tolerance? What is certain is that those who stand up for free speech in these countries, against the armed and booted orthodoxy of their time, make harder decisions, and face graver consequences, than most of us in the West ever will.

CHALLENGE

We need realistic idealism and idealistic realism. As an idealist, I hope that many readers will agree with these principles and promote them using the power of the mouse. As a realist, I know that many others, including powerful public and private forces, will disagree and try to stop us. But some of them may at least recognise that we need to talk about it because we are neighbours in a connected world.

A minimal consensus would consist in endorsing the first two principles but diverging from the third onwards. You might even say, if you are a strong believer in state sovereignty, that all the rest should be decided by your state. Since most countries in the world are signatories to the Covenant, to endorse the first two principles is simply to support what your government has already signed up to, adding to this only the vital imperative of neither threatening violence nor yielding to violent intimidation. That in turn requires a distinction between illegitimate uses of violence and legitimate ones, such as national defence and preventing crime. Implementing just these two principles would open the door to peaceful conflict over all the others. Ongoing debate about the limits to and positive conditions for free speech is itself a vital ingredient of free speech.

A more negative response would be to reject the liberal universalist framework yet still join in the debate. Some might want to do this while upholding their state's adherence to the Covenant, drawing on a tendentious interpretation of Article 19 and the woolly wording of Article 20. This seems to me implausible. Whatever reasonable differences of interpretation there may be, Article 19 is a liberal universalist statement. But whether or not you retained lip service to the Covenant, you would be laying out an argument based on very different philosophical, religious or cultural foundations.

As I explored in the first part of this book, the question then becomes how far such profoundly diverging positions are susceptible to rational debate. Even if we reach the point of articulating competing propositions, we will struggle with those deeper levels of linguistic and foundational difference. If I say we are sitting at a table and you say we are standing in a duck pond, where do we go from there? Nonetheless, the exercise will still have value in helping us to understand where the other person is coming from. Women and men of goodwill should wish to attempt it, even if they believe their positions are irreconcilable. We may yet surprise ourselves by arriving at practically compatible conclusions, although we get there by different routes from distant points of departure.

Others again might wish to turn away from the cold rigour of any set of principles, but instead propose some altogether different way of thinking about free speech, or feeling about it, evoking and depicting it, by poetry, music, dance, a joke or visual image. The house of free speech has many apartments.

Finally, there are those (and they are legion) who will reject the very idea of engaging not just with a liberal universalist argument but with any argument. 'You believe *that*, I believe *this*, there's no point in wasting any more breath on it', says the closed mind. 'You are wrong, I am right, so let us fight to the death', cries the violent fanatic. 'You do it your way over there, we do it our way over here, there's nothing more to discuss', insists the Chinese or Russian sovereigntist. Realistically, there is a limit to what a Western liberal internationalist can do to reach them. We may, however, nourish a cautious hope that individuals in those societies who are ready to debate with us may in turn be able to engage, in their own languages and contexts, with more intransigent compatriots or coreligionists.

The quest for a more universal universalism is one of the great challenges of our time. Over the last half century, human enterprise and innovation, from the jet plane to the smartphone, have created a world in which we are all becoming neighbours, but nowhere is it written, least of all in the book of history, that we will be good neighbours. That requires a transcultural effort of reason and imagination. Central to this endeavour is free speech. Only with freedom of expression can I understand what it is to be you. Only with freedom of information can we control both public and private powers. Only by articulating our differences can we see clearly what they are, and why they are what they are.

While we can only speculate about this, it seems a reasonable guess that when our remotest ancestors first acquired the gift of speech, they used it in two contrasting ways: to cooperate more effectively in combating other groups of human beings, consolidating their own language-based in-group, but also to negotiate their differences with other individuals and groups, without coming to blows. Fundamentally, the same opportunities exist today. This is no naive utopian attempt to abolish conflict. That will never happen and if it ever did, the result would be a sterile, faded world. But our inevitable, indispensable, creative human conflicts can be conducted peacefully, by making jaw-jaw rather than war-war.

We will never all agree, nor should we. But we must strive to create conditions in which we agree on how we disagree. At scale, in cosmopolis, that work has barely begun.

NOTES

Beside a few necessary caveats and amusing curiosities, these notes mainly give references to sources. They include those that can also be accessed by clicking on words highlighted in the main text of the e-book, when read on a connected device—the 'post-Gutenberg book'. Wherever possible, links are given in the perma.cc form, which has been developed to avert the familiar frustration of being electronically transported to gobbledygook. This has not been done for publications behind a paywall, since the perma link might then simply take you to the wall. Links to freespeechdebate.com are left as such, since clicking them will also bring you closer to related material on the website. Where digital online identifier (doi) references are available for scholarly articles, they are added in the Bibliography. References and links were checked in the period July to October 2015. Note that print and online titles of newspaper and magazine articles may vary slightly.

POST-GUTENBERG

1. in the age of the 'mobile internet', increasingly accessed from smartphones, it is difficult to say precisely how many people have internet access. The International Telecommunication Union (ITU) gave an estimate of 3.2 billion for 2015; see 'ICT Facts and Figures—The World in 2015', ITU, http://perma.cc/K5QM-T3PC . Mary Meeker, in her influential annual Internet Trends presentation, gave a figure of 2.8 billion in May 2015; see Mary Meeker, 'Internet Trends 2015—Code Conference', KPCB, 27 May 2015, http://perma.cc/GB7E-NQMX . For a mesmerising although obviously not precise live counter see 'Internet users in the world', internet live stats, http://www .internetlivestats.com/watch/internet-users/

2. in the second quarter of 2015, Facebook reported 1.49 billion active users (those who logged in at least once a month), while the population of China was estimated at 1.3 billion. Vindu Goel, 'Facebook Posts Solid Gains, a Feat Eluding Rivals', New

York Times, 29 July 2015, http://www.nytimes.com/2015/07/30/technology/facebook
-earnings-q2.html . For Chinese population data, see 'The World Factbook: China',
Central Intelligence Agency, http://perma.cc/ZN7B-W6GW

3. see Hobbes 2012, vol. 1, where Noel Malcolm also tells the story of the frontispiece in
meticulous detail. An online close-up of the frontispiece can be seen at http://perma
.cc/T7G6-WCG7

4. this comes in the preface to his *History of the World*. A facsimile of the 1614 first edition
can be viewed online at http://perma.cc/DP4M-5BL3

5. this description—*das Werk der Bücher*—actually comes in the document of a court
case in which Gutenberg was being pursued by a business partner; see Kapr 1996,
173–79

6. see 'Our Languages', Free Speech Debate, http://freespeechdebate.com/en/our-
languages/ , and Figure 12 in this book

7. the evolution of the site is being digitally archived by the Bodleian Library at Oxford,
https://archive-it.org/home/bodleian?q=free+speech+debate

8. see Timothy Garton Ash, 'Knowledge', Free Speech Debate, http://freespeech
debate.com/en/principle/p-3/info/ and then the original French court verdict of 21
June 1995, 'Condamnation judiciaire de Bernard Lewis', at http://perma.cc/27XW
-U5SD. In the crucial passage of his interview with Le Monde, 16 November 1993,
Lewis was reported as saying 'mais si l'on parle de génocide, cela implique qu'il y ait
eu politique délibérée, une décision d'anéantir systématiquement la nation arméni-
enne. Cela est fort douteux. Des documents Turcs prouvent une volonté de déporta-
tion, pas d'extermination'. The case also turned on a subsequent, clarificatory article
that Lewis had contributed to Le Monde

9. Foucault 2001, 109–10

10. Berlin 1998, 119. Steven Lukes recalls that the conversation was recorded in 1991, and
first published in Italian in 1992. Email to the author, 4 August 2014

COSMOPOLIS

1. of course this is to simplify a complex, contested and necessarily speculative story.
Estimates range from 1.8 million years ago to 50,000 years ago. I here follow the analysis of Robin Dunbar, although taking the most cautious view of his conclusion. He
himself says speech developed 'at the latest' by 100,000 years ago. Email to the author,
7 September 2015. See Dunbar 2014, esp. 234–44 and Dunbar 1996. For other views,
see Diamond 1993, 54–56 and 141–47 and Lieberman 2007

2. see, for example, IowaPrimate, 'Kanzi and Novel Sentences', 9 January 2009, https://
www.youtube.com/watch?v=2Dhc2zePJFE&noredirect=1 . Kanzi's level of linguistic
competence is the result of dedicated work by Sue Savage-Rambaugh

3. quoted in Sarah Knapton, 'Which Creature Makes Sir David Attenborough's Jaw
Drop? It's Not What You'd Expect', Daily Telegraph, 27 January 2015, http://perma
.cc/4H5R-F6HW

4. Dunbar 1996, 3

5. I quote from a personal conversation with him. See also Judt 2010, chapter 17

6. Brown 1991, 130–34

7. on cave paintings and musical instruments, see Werner Herzog's fine film 'Cave of Forgotten Dreams'. Shells and beads with holes pierced through them, presumably so they could be worn as a necklace or bracelet, found on the slopes of Mount Carmel in Israel, have been dated to 100,000 years ago; see Wilkins et al. 2012

8. Milton 1909 [1644], 27

9. the word being clue to the thing, this usage of 'virtual' dates from the early history of computing, in the 1950s

10. this obviously means a smaller number of people, many of whom would take multiple flights in a year

11. see United Nations, 'International Migrant Stock: Total', http://perma.cc/NC6W -MMV4 . See also the maps by Migration Policy Institute, 'Maps of Immigrants and Emigrants around the World', http://perma.cc/SD2T-3T7D

12. Pontifical Council for the Pastoral Care of Migrants and Itinerant People, 'Erga Migrantes Caritas Christi (The Love of Christ towards Migrants)', http://perma.cc/ Y4GV-2J7T

13. see UN Department of Economic and Social Affairs, 'World Urbanization Prospects', http://perma.cc/9QFX-WDFL

14. see Migration Policy Institute, 'Counting Immigrants in Cities across the Globe', http://perma.cc/9LTB-8LZE . For Toronto, see Garton Ash et al. 2013, 12

15. for 'postmigrants' see Timothy Garton Ash, 'Freedom & Diversity: A Liberal Pentagram for Living Together', New York Review of Books, 22 November 2012, http://www .nybooks.com/articles/archives/2012/nov/22/freedom-diversity-liberal-pentagram/

16. see Darnton 2009, 21–23

17. see Zittrain 2008, 27 and his online source available at http://perma.cc/RN6R-4JS2

18. see Post 2009, 30

19. the *Oxford English Dictionary* attributes it to Vint Cerf et al., 'Request for Comments' (1974). See also Internet Society, 'Brief History of the Internet', http://perma .cc/SNY8-TYAE

20. Mueller 2004, 86

21. Berners-Lee 1999, chapters 2–4; see also the original website at http://perma.cc/ MWR3-VASS

22. see 'The End of Moore's Law', The Economist, 19 April 2015, http://www.econo mist.com/blogs/economist-explains/2015/04/economist-explains-17 and John Markoff, 'Smaller, Faster, Cheaper, Over', New York Times, 27 September 2015, http:// www.nytimes.com/2015/09/27/technology/smaller-faster-cheaper-over-the-future-of -computer-chips.html . Note that Moore's Law is variously cited as predicting that the number of transistors on a microchip will double every two years, or every 18 months, while he originally predicted that it would happen every year. The basic point stands

23. this is according to the decimal scale. Confusingly, there is also a binary scale, with different multiples and prefixes: from kibi and mebi (1024^2) to zebi and yobi

24. see Maryam Omidi, 'Moving towards the Zettabyte Era', Free Speech Debate, http://freespeechdebate.com/en/2012/06/moving-towards-the-zettabyte-era/. The Cisco video estimate is for 2016

25. see note 1 to Post-Gutenberg

26. data and projections on smartphones from 'The Truly Personal Computer', The Economist, 28 February 2015, http://www.economist.com/news/briefing/21645131-smartphone-defining-technology-age-truly-personal-computer

27. Lev Grossman, 'The Man Who Wired the World', Time, 15 December 2014, http://time.com/magazine/us/3617654/december-15th-2014-vol-184-no-23-u-s/

28. see United Nations Educational, Scientific and Cultural Organization, 'The Next Generation of Literacy Statistics', http://perma.cc/W4FM-ZWGH, UNESCO, 'Statistics on Literacy', http://perma.cc/J3TJ-P786 and Dominic Burbidge, 'Free but Not Able?', Free Speech Debate, http://freespeechdebate.com/en/2012/12/free-but-not-able/. The minimal definition of literacy was established in 1958. Note that the UN estimate includes some 775 million adults and 122 million illiterate youth

29. Shteyngart 2010

30. Kurzweil 2005

31. Weizenbaum 1984 and Carr 2010, 201–8

32. Ian Sample and Alex Hern, 'Scientists Dispute Whether Computer 'Eugene Goostman' Passed Turing Test', The Guardian, 9 June 2014, http://perma.cc/9YMC-LJW7

33. John Markoff et al., 'For Sympathetic Ear, More Chinese Turn to Smartphone Program', New York Times, 31 July 2015, http://www.nytimes.com/2015/08/04/science/for-sympathetic-ear-more-chinese-turn-to-smartphone-program.html

34. see Future of Life Institute, 'Research Priorities for Robust and Beneficial Artificial Intelligence: An Open Letter', http://perma.cc/ZD2A-DP7E , and Martin Rees, 'Cheer Up, the Post-Human Era Is Dawning', Financial Times, 10 July 2015, http://www.ft.com/cms/s/0/4fe10870-20c2-11e5-ab0f-6bb9974f25d0.html#axzz3qv6zRoSp

35. this is essentially also the conclusion of Wu 2013

36. on the often neglected subject of touch, see Linden 2015

37. McLuhan 1962, 31

38. quoted in Jacobs 1993, 311

39. for Bouyeri quotation, see Buruma 2006, 157. For sentences typed on keyboards, see Hobsbawm 1994, 63

40. for 'global cities' see Sassen 2001

41. this was the American CEO of Penguin, Peter Mayer, quoted in Malik 2009, 10

42. Klausen 2009, 107

43. see Danyal Kazim, '"Innocence of Muslims" and the Manufacture of Outrage', Free Speech Debate, http://freespeechdebate.com/en/discuss/innocence-of-muslims-and-the-manufacture-of-outrage/

44. quoted in Eisenstein 1979, 304

45. quoted in Standage 2007, 162

46. Wohlstetter 1990–1991, 679–85

47. my attention was drawn to this term by Evgeny Morozov. Morozov 2011, 196–97

48. a notable exception was Tim Berners-Lee, who invented the World Wide Web while working at CERN, the European Organisation for Nuclear Research, on the

French-Swiss border. But his World Wide Web Consortium, or W3C, established in 1994, was based at MIT

49. ARPA, hence the original ARPAnet. It changed its name to Defense Advanced Research Projects Agency (DARPA) in 1971, back to ARPA in 1993, then back to DARPA in 1996. See Internet Society, 'Brief History of the Internet', http://perma.cc/SNY8-TYAE

50. David Clark, quoted in Paulina Borsook, 'How Anarchy Works', Wired, http://perma.cc/9XXM-PKKX

51. Mueller 2004, 74–75

52. the British scientist was Donald Davies; see Hafner et al. 2006, 67. For TCP/IP see the discussion in Mueller 2004, 5–7

53. this was certainly the case with Paul Baran at the Rand Corporation; see Hafner et al. 2006, 54–64

54. see Zittrain 2008, 31–33, and Wu 2010, 201–2. The cyberlaw expert Tim Wu is credited with coining the term; see Wu 2003. Listen to his discussion of it on 'Wu on His Phrase "Net Neutrality"', Free Speech Debate, http://freespeechdebate.com/en/media/net-neutrality-by-the-man-who-coined-the-phrase/ , and see the introduction on his website at http://perma.cc/4Z5P-RP4C

55. dated 8 February 1996; John Perry Barlow, 'A Declaration of the Independence of Cyberspace', http://perma.cc/V8VS-XHZD

56. full detail in Mueller 2004 and Mueller 2012

57. a useful account of the history is given on Wikipedia: http://perma.cc/Q36Q-366E

58. see several contributions to Levmore et al., eds. 2010 and Sunstein 2009, 83

59. Mike Godwin, conversation with the author, Wikimedia Foundation, San Francisco, 7 September 2010

60. Kurt Wagner, 'Kara Swisher Interviews President Barack Obama on Cyber Security, Privacy and His Relationship With Silicon Valley', re/code, 13 February 2015, http://perma.cc/D8K6-Z2KM?type=live

61. I owe this illuminating phrase to Ikenberry 2011

62. on this recurring pattern, see Spar 2001 and Wu 2010

63. some might argue that that apogee came in the years immediately after 1945. But while the United States then had a larger share of world GDP, it also had a global ideological, military and diplomatic rival in the Soviet Union. It had no comparable rival in the 1990s

64. see Castells 2013

65. see Nye 2011, esp. 5–14, 127–32; Lukes 2005, esp. 103 (Foucault quote) and his new Chapter 3 on 'Three-Dimensional Power'

66. Serres 2012, 13; and Bacon 1996

67. Castells 2013, 42–46, 417–21

68. see the summary of the 3 May 2005 judgement by Mr Justice Eady, http://perma.cc/T63H-9AAK . The book is Ehrenfeld 2005. This is the second, expanded edition, with a new preface explaining the beginning of the libel case

69. passed in 2008, it was formally called the Libel Terrorism Protection Act, http://perma.cc/R85M-JBV9. See the summary in Bollinger 2010, 96–97

70. Lessig 2006, 5, 123; Lawrence Lessig, 'Code Is Law', http://perma.cc/9QL7-NNMS

71. I first came across this helpful analogy in Zittrain 2008, 197

72. see Bollinger 2010, 137–42. See Brown et al. 2014 for an important argument that states should apply international human rights conventions when the effects of their actions are outside their territories but arguably within the exercise of their jurisdiction. They quote (page 247) the Advisory Opinion of the International Court of Justice on the Israeli wall in the occupied territories: 'the Court considers that the International Covenant on Civil and Political Rights is applicable in respect of acts done by a State in the exercise of its jurisdiction outside its own territory'. They also note that the United States and Israel do not accept any extraterritorial effect of their international human rights treaty obligations

73. for example, there is the International Covenant on Economic, Social, and Cultural Rights, also of 1966

74. although it is not a member of the UN, the Vatican City State is a party to a number of other international treaties and UN conventions

75. see the analysis by Jeff Howard, 'Article 19: Freedom of Expression Anchored in International Law', Free Speech Debate, http://freespeechdebate.com/en/discuss/article-19-freedom-of-expression-anchored-in-international-law/

76. see Human Rights Committee, 2011, http://perma.cc/4M9K-HTGM . For the committee membership, see http://www2.ohchr.org/english/bodies/hrc/elections30th .html . The committee had produced an earlier General Comment on Article 19 in 1983

77. see United Nations Treaty Collection, 'Chapter IV Human Rights—5. Optional Protocol to the International Covenant on Civil and Political Rights', http://perma .cc/48W4-DC9H . The figure of 115 was correct in 2015

78. for more detail, see the analysis by Jeff Howard at Jeff Howard, 'Article 19: Freedom of Expression Anchored in International Law', Free Speech Debate, http://freespeech debate.com/en/discuss/article-19-freedom-of-expression-anchored-in-international-law/

79. see James Fenton, 'Blood and Lead', The Poetry Archive, http://perma.cc/R384-5XR4 and Fenton 2012, 80

80. see Mead 2002

81. Bollinger 2010, 6

82. Hillary Rodham Clinton, 'Remarks on Internet Freedom Delivered at the Newseum, Washington DC', 21 January 2010, http://perma.cc/F3W6-5V8A

83. Victoria Nuland, 'State Department Daily Press Briefing, Washington DC, 21 August 2012', http://perma.cc/5WNU-XD9N . See also NDTV, 'Respect Internet Freedom, US Tells India', http://perma.cc/T3PZ-6ASH

84. I owe this term to colleagues working at Stanford University's Centre on Democracy, Development and the Rule of Law, especially Larry Diamond; see Diamond 2010

85. I believe I first heard this formulation from the French analyst of international relations Pierre Hassner

86. see the account by Jeff Howard, 'Article 19: Freedom of Expression Anchored in International Law', Free Speech Debate, http://freespeechdebate.com/en/discuss/article-19-freedom-of-expression-anchored-in-international-law/

87. see Victoria Nuland, 'State Department Daily Press Briefing, Washington DC, 21 August 2012', http://perma.cc/M7ME-K25U

88. LSE Media Policy Project Blog, 'Freedom Abroad, Repression at Home: The Clinton Paradox', http://perma.cc/BCG2-MAKZ

89. of the 1948 UN Declaration of Human Rights. Note, though, that the European Convention predates by 13 years and to some extent anticipates the more detailed Article 19 of the 1966 International Covenant

90. this has been true only since 1998; see Lester et al. 2009

91. see European Union, 'Charter of Fundamental Rights of the European Union', http://perma.cc/3B4K-ZKSG , with explicit mention of media pluralism in Article 11.2

92. see The Electronic Commerce (EC Directive) Regulations 2002, 'Regulation 19', http://perma.cc/8G82-GFLT . US-based websites, too, must take down what is illegal in the United States, as soon as they receive notice of its presence, for example under the Digital Millennium Copyright Act. But because of the First Amendment tradition, in its late-twentieth-century form, there is simply less that is illegal

93. the analysis in this paragraph closely follows Goldsmith et al. 2008, 173–77

94. Goldsmith et al. 2008, 174

95. Baldwin 2014, 378–440

96. for the French original, see Assemblée Nationale, 'Le Temps de l'Invention (1789–1799)', http://perma.cc/7E2C-KKYV

97. Lester et al. 2009, 7

98. Goldsmith et al. 2008, 90 citing Remarks by President Bill Clinton, Paul H. Nitze School of Advanced International Studies, Washington DC, March 8, 2000. See also 'China's Internet: A Giant Cage', The Economist, 6 April 2013, http://www.economist.com/news/special-report/21574628-internet-was-expected-help-democratise-china-instead-it-has-enabled

99. with the important exception of Hong Kong, which is outside the 'Great Firewall' and has much wider freedom of expression. I could, for example, freely demonstrate and discuss the Chinese version of our website, http://freespeechdebate.com/zh/, at Hong Kong University in 2012, whereas I could not in mainland China

100. see Agence France-Presse in Beijing, 'China Passes New National Security Law Extending Control Over Internet', The Guardian, 1 July 2015, http://perma.cc/6327-48L4 , and text at China Law Translate, 'National Security Law of the People's Republic of China', http://perma.cc/6TC5-U3WC . For the Xinhua expert: http://perma.cc/GH2X-XCTZ (in Chinese)

101. in MacKinnon 2012, xv. China's official media also highlighted the abuse of freedom of speech at the time of the Murdoch phone-hacking scandal; see Judith Bruhn, 'China and So-Called Freedom of Speech', Free Speech Debate, http://freespeechdebate.com/en/discuss/china-and-so-called-freedom-of-speech/ . Interestingly, the Beijing Daily also criticised 'commercial newspapers' inside China for being infected with the 'poison' of 'so-called freedom of speech'

102. Information Office of the State Council of the People's Republic of China, 'The Internet in China', http://perma.cc/R2XB-5MVY

103. 1.29 billion users as of February 2015; statista, http://perma.cc/U88W-YZ62

104. the nearest some middle-class Chinese get to it is channels such as Phoenix, broadcasting from Hong Kong

105. see useful accounts in Deibert et al., eds. 2010, esp. 449–87, and MacKinnon 2012, as well as the regular reporting on China Digital Times and the Hong Kong University China Media Project

106. for the Harvard studies, see King et al. 2013 and King et al. 2014. While the overall number of posts collected and analysed exceeded 11 million, more detailed study was made of a random sample of 127,283

107. see 'Guidance of Public Opinion', China Media Project, http://perma.cc/PXT7-6U3D

108. see Anne Henochowicz, 'Minitrue: Scrub Obama's Call for Open Internet', China Digital Times, 12 November 2014, http://perma.cc/5Q78-RQCM

109. see Sandra Fu, 'Directives from the Ministry of Truth: Wenzhou High-Speed Train Crash', China Digital Times, 25 July 2011, http://perma.cc/3LLC-6R2A

110. see the report, with amusing photograph of an award ceremony: Anne Henochowicz, 'Translation: Internet Clean-Up Awards', China Digital Times, 22 April 2015, http://perma.cc/C38E-ARYE

111. see the translation on ChinaFile.com: http://perma.cc/4NMA-UN8X

112. Qian Gang, 'China's Political Discourse in 2013', China Media Project, 1 June 2014, http://perma.cc/25EE-QNQ4

113. see our English translations of the original and the rewritten versions in Timothy Garton Ash, 'The Southern Weekly Affair: No Closer to the Chinese Dream?', Free Speech Debate, http://freespeechdebate.com/en/discuss/the-southern-weekly-affair-no-closer-to-the-chinese-dream/

114. see, with more interesting detail, Michael Rank, 'Orwell and China, Nineteen Eighty-Four in Chinese', http://perma.cc/7CAJ-9QSE , and Michael Rank, 'Orwell in China', The Orwell Society Newsletter, No. 5, December 2014

115. Amy Qin, 'The Grass Mud Horse Lexicon', Free Speech Debate, http://freespeech debate.com/en/case/the-grass-mud-horse-lexicon/

116. see 'Latest Directives From the Ministry of Truth, December 10, 2010', China Digital Times, 13 December 2010, http://perma.cc/YW4T-7KTX

117. see http://perma.cc/9ELM-C2P8

118. for the more than 100,000, see Yu Hua, 'The Censorship Pendulum', New York Times, 4 February 2014, http://www.nytimes.com/2014/02/05/opinion/yu-hua-chinas-censorship-pendulum.html

119. Murong Xuecun, 'Xuecun: Open Letter to a Nameless Censor', http://perma.cc/C5VL-HHVN . A note at the bottom says, 'This essay is translated by a nameless translator from the Chinese edition of the New York Times Chinese-language News site: http://cn.nytimes.com/culture/20130520/cc20murong/ '

120. Edward Wong, 'China Uses "Picking Quarrels" Charge to Cast a Wider Net Online', New York Times, 27 July 2015, http://www.nytimes.com/2015/07/27/world/asia/china-uses-picking-quarrels-charge-to-cast-a-wider-net-online.html

121. quoted in Brook Larmer, 'Where an Internet Joke Is Not Just a Joke', New York Times Magazine, 30 October 2011, http://www.nytimes.com/2011/10/30/magazine/the-dangerous-politics-of-internet-humor-in-china.html

122. Perry Link, 'China: The Anaconda in the Chandelier', New York Review of Books, 11 April 2001, http://www.nybooks.com/articles/archives/2002/apr/11/china-the-ana conda-in-the-chandelier/

123. in a conversation I had about this with Sheryl Sandberg at Facebook headquarters on 15 September 2011, it was clear that she felt a very strong commercial interest in going into China but was well aware of the potential reputational damage if, for example, someone were to be persecuted in China as a result of something they had posted on the Chinese version of Facebook. See also Evelyn Walls, 'Mark Zuckerberg's speech: a political statement about the future of Facebook?', http://freespeechdebate.com/en/ discuss/mark-zuckerbergs-speech-a-political-statement-about-the-future-of-facebook/

124. see Wekesa et al. 2014. I am most grateful to Markos Kounalakis for this reference and early sight of chapters of his forthcoming book. For a somewhat contrary view, see Iginio Gagliardone, 'Is China Actually Helping Free Media in Africa?', Free Speech Debate, http://freespeechdebate.com/en/discuss/is-china-actually-helping-free-media -in-africa/

125. quoted by Creemers, 'Virtual Lines in the Sand: China's Demands for Internet Sovereignty', http://perma.cc/U4WQ-FTGX

126. see Huntington 1998, 316. To be fair to Huntington, he also proposed 'the commonalities rule: peoples in all civilizations should search for and attempt to expand the values, institutions and practices they have in common with peoples of other civilizations' (320)

127. see Clifford Coonan, 'China Claims Victory as 19 Countries Spurn Nobel Ceremony', The Independent, 8 December 2010, http://perma.cc/KYA5-KSCM

128. I was already using this term before reading Maurer et al. 2014, but they make a very helpful attempt to identify swing states in the specific context of the debate about internet governance

129. see Laura Bernal-Bermudez, 'Is the Inter-American Court of Human Rights Setting Regional Standards?', Free Speech Debate, http://freespeechdebate.com/en/case/ iacthr-setting-standards/

130. Timothy Garton Ash, 'Freedom & Diversity: A Liberal Pentagram for Living Together', New York Review of Books, 22 November 2012, http://www.nybooks.com/ articles/archives/2012/nov/22/freedom-diversity-liberal-pentagram/

131. author's notes of meeting, Davos, 29 January 2010

132. MacKinnon 2012

133. 'Survival of the Biggest', The Economist, 29 November 2012, http://www.economist .com/news/leaders/21567355-concern-about-clout-internet-giants-growing-antitrust -watchdogs-should-tread

134. see for example Reynald Fléchaux, 'Google, Apple, Facebook, Amazon: 10 Choses à Savoir sur les Gafa', silicon, http://perma.cc/5G8F-Z35U , and Sylvie Kauffman, 'La Fin de l'Internet Américain', Le Monde, 18 November 2013

135. see Leo Mirani, 'Millions of Facebook Users Have No Idea They're using the Internet', Quartz, 9 February 2015, http://perma.cc/8S4E-ES5X . I am grateful to John Naughton for this reference. For the latest version of the 'leading social network' map, search online for Vincosblog, 'World Map of Social Networks'

136. see Felipe Correa, 'Rede Globo & the 1989 Brazilian Election', Free Speech Debate, http://freespeechdebate.com/en/case/rede-globo-and-the-brazilian-elections-of-1989/

137. Liebling 1975, 32. He was writing specifically about a 'one-paper town' where you have 'a privately owned public utility', but the witticism clearly has wider application

138. Liebling 1975, 6

139. for a typical example, see Vindu Goel, 'Facebook Posts Solid Gains, a Feat Eluding Rivals', New York Times, 29 July 2015, http://www.nytimes.com/2015/07/30/techno logy/facebook-earnings-q2.html. Goel notes that the company 'generates virtually all of its revenue from advertising' and in the second quarter of 2015 had an operating profit margin of 55 percent

140. see 'Vinton G. Cerf', ICANN, http://perma.cc/75GA-W3T2

141. posted by Andrew Lewis, under the alias blue_beetle on the website MetaFilter, 26 August 2010, and quoted with a slightly different wording in Pariser 2011, 21

142. Emily Steel, 'Datalogix Leads Path in Online Tracking', Financial Times, 23 September 2012, http://www.ft.com/cms/s/2/8b9faecc-0584-11e2-9ebd-00144feabdc0 .html#axzz3qv6zRoSp

143. Lanier 2011, 198

144. quoted in Pariser 2011, 147

145. see Feuz et al. 2011. Note that this was conducted before Google introduced default personalised search in December 2009

146. a term popularised by Pariser 2011

147. I take the term 'information cocoon' from the work of Cass Sunstein. For his definition, see Sunstein 2006, 9. More on the Daily Me under principle 4. On Breivik, see Borchgrevink 2013, 114–44, Seierstad 2015, 155–69, and Timothy Garton Ash, 'The Internet Nourished Norway's Killer, but Censorship Would Be Folly', The Guardian, 29 July 2011, http://perma.cc/R825-99LQ

148. Mill 1991 [1859], 58. The text of chapter 2 is available online at http://perma .cc/7G6A-8J9F

149. Zittrain 2008

150. see the article by Brad Stone, 'Amazon Erases Orwell Books from Kindle', New York Times, 17 July 2009, http://www.nytimes.com/2009/07/18/technology/ companies/18amazon.html

151. Laura McGann, 'Mark Fiore can win a Pulitzer Prize, but he can't get his iPhone cartoon app past Apple's satire police', NiemanLab, http://perma.cc/2LBB-CHDQ . For the end of the Amazon-Hachette affair, see Hannah Ellis-Petersen, 'Amazon and Publisher Hachette End Dispute over Online Book Sales', The Guardian, 13 November 2014, http://perma.cc/Y7L8-NREG

152. Wu 2010, 13, 121, 311

153. see Chilling Effects, https://chillingeffects.org/ . This was subsequently incorporated into the more comprehensive project called Lumen, https://www.lumendatabase.org/

154. Mancini 2011, 36

155. see Mayer-Schönberger et al. 2013

156. see Julia Angwin et al., 'AT&T Helped U.S. Spy on Internet on a Vast Scale', New York Times, 15 August 2015, http://www.nytimes.com/2015/08/16/us/politics/att-helped -nsa-spy-on-an-array-of-internet-traffic.html

157. quoted in New York Times, 'Microsoft and Russia', 15 September 2010, http://www
.nytimes.com/2010/09/15/opinion/15wed2.html

158. quoted in Goldsmith et al. 2008, 2

159. Adams, 'The Massachusetts Constitution', http://perma.cc/H4K6-E33Z , and Leys
1997, xxv

160. see Lumen Database, 'German Regulatory Body Reported Illegal Material', 14 December 2005, http://perma.cc/A4U5-HKSE

161. see Funda Ustek, 'YouTube in Turkey', Free Speech Debate, http://freespeechdebate
.com/en/case/17902/

162. see Timothy Garton Ash, 'Insult the King and . . . Go Directly to Jail', New York Review of Books. 23 May 2013, http://www.nybooks.com/articles/archives/2013/may/23/
insult-king-and-go-directly-jail/ and Maryam Omidi, 'Criticism of the Thai King',
Free Speech Debate, http://freespeechdebate.com/en/case/criticism-of-the-thai
-king/

163. see Judith Bruhn, 'Twitter's New Censorship Policy', Free Speech Debate, http://
freespeechdebate.com/en/discuss/twitters-new-censorship-policy/

164. quoted in Lovink 2008, ix

165. Solzhenitsyn 1972, 26, http://perma.cc/KY4G-ZACY

166. see Garton Ash 1999, 146

167. Kathrin Hille, 'Solzhenitsyn Quote adds to Clamour for Beijing Reform', Financial
Times, 8 January 2013, http://www.ft.com/cms/s/0/9aead3c0-58d6-11e2-bd9e-00144
feab49a.html#axzz3qv6zRoSp , and Yao Chen's comment dated 7 January 2013, http://
perma.cc/YVP5-FKNU

168. see the comment by Nobel Peace Prize winner Jody Williams quoted in Garton Ash
2005, 251. The (major) flaw is that a number of major powers, including the United
States, are not party to it. I am grateful to Adam Roberts for this point

169. see Roberts et al. 2009, Roberts et al. 2016, and http://www.avaaz.org/en/highlights
.php, as well as https://www.change.org/

170. see IFEX, 'The Global Network. Defending and Promoting Free Expression', http://
www.ifex.org/

171. see Graham Reynolds, 'ACTA: Open Agreement Secretly Arrived At?', Free Speech Debate, http://freespeechdebate.com/en/case/acta-open-agreement-secretly-arrived-at/

172. see 'Does ACTA Threaten Online Freedom of Expression & Privacy?', Free Speech Debate, http://freespeechdebate.com/en/media/acta-the-internet-freedom-of-expression
-privacy/ , and map of June 2012 at European Green Party, 'Europe-wide Demonstrations against ACTA', 8 June 2012, http://perma.cc/37XC-3Q4B

173. Jimmy Wales, the founder of Wikipedia, explained the reasons and the impact at
the Oxford launch of freespeechdebate.com, 'Free Speech Debate Launch with Jimmy
Wales', Free Speech Debate, http://freespeechdebate.com/en/media/free-speech
-debate-launch-with-jimmy-wales/

174. I first made this point at an 'Open Up?' conference organised by the Omidyar Network; see video here: http://vimeo.com/111748146. The variegated representatives of
NGOs did not seem all that keen to take it up

175. see, for example, the Twitris monitoring experiment: 'Twitris', http://perma.cc/
TP6X-CYVL

176. see Amy Qin, 'Wenzhou Train Collision', Free Speech Debate, http://freespeech debate.com/en/case/wenzhou-train-collision/

177. see Hirschman 1970

178. see Kirkpatrick 2010, 246–50

179. see the accounts in Markoff 2005, 47–57. Engelbart originally had the idea of a personal 'working station' in 1950. For a 1968 video with Engelbart demonstrating the workstation, see Stanford.edu, 'The Demo', http://perma.cc/66MU-Q4YW

180. see http://perma.cc/7JWT-LAJQ and http://perma.cc/9PG6-96XQ

181. quoted in Timothy Garton Ash, 'We Must Be Free and Able to Defend Private Lives against Tabloid Tyranny', The Guardian, 23 November 2011, http://perma .cc/48AD-X9ZT

182. as quoted by Sluiter et al., eds. 2004, 240

183. see Waldron 1995, and a critique in Cammack 2013

184. see 'Community Standards', Free Speech Debate, http://freespeechdebate.com/en/ community-standards/

185. Howe 2008, 282. The *Oxford English Dictionary* attributes the first use to an article by Howe published in Wired in 2006

186. see Hansen 1999; Ober 2008; Forsén et al., eds. 1996

187. Jim (T. J.) Reed, in a letter to the Oxford Magazine, Eighth Week, Michaelmas Term, 2010. His actual wording was 'the principle of thinking for yourself, which was Kant's plain and fundamental definition of Enlightenment'

188. see Miguel Marquez, 'Actor: Anti-Islam Filmmaker "Was Playing Us Along"', CNN, http://perma.cc/XZG2-M7WQ This article in Gawker quotes the original Craigslist advertisement: http://perma.cc/B3EE-M9VJ

189. see Crawley's own account at Myles Crawley, 'Actor Duped into Appearing in "Innocence of Muslims" Explains', Los Angeles Times, 18 September 2012, http://perma .cc/DUW7-L775 . When I emailed him, Crawley insisted on a $500 fee (payable via Paypal) for an interview (email of 4 January 2013). I did not pay up

190. see report in the International Herald Tribune, 15 September 2012

191. see http://www.myspace.com/media4christproductions . It gave its address as P.O. Box 1677 Duarte, CA 91009, so was presumably the same one. At least two other websites called 'Media for Christ' posted messages saying they had nothing to do with this disgusting film

192. see Sam Bacile, 2 July 2012, https://www.youtube.com/watch?v=qmodVun16Q4&bp ctr=1440735101 . Note that this now comes with the warning message 'The following content has been identified by the YouTube community'—ah, the 'community' again—'as being potentially offensive or graphic. Viewer discretion is advised'. But it did not carry that warning when I initially viewed it, although the one posted on 1 July did

193. with a first post on 5 September, online at http://perma.cc/XR27-P3BJ . Reported in Robert Mackey et al., 'Obscure Film Mocking Muslim Prophet Sparks Anti-U.S. Protests in Egypt and Libya', New York Times, 11 September 2012, http://the lede.blogs.nytimes.com/2012/09/11/obscure-film-mocking-muslim-prophet-sparks -anti-u-s-protests-in-egypt-and-libya/, but the link given to http://www.youtube.com/

watch?v=GsGPOTpU-dU&feature=youtu.be was subsequently marked by the up-loader as 'private'

194. 'From Film to Protests: The Publicization of "Innocence of Muslims" in Egypt', Daily Kos, 24 September 2012, http://perma.cc/AV2T-5Z7M

195. Erin Cunningham, 'Anti-US Protests: Was It All Politics?', Salon, http://perma.cc/SE6D-PBDS

196. this was the title of the reposted version (of 12 September 2012) that had the most views (more than 16.7 million by late October). The uploader subsequently changed the title to 'A Stupid Movie Not Worthy of Global Turmoil'; http://www.youtube.com/watch?v=MAiOEVov2RM . When checked in summer 2015, this link came up as 'unavailable', and it does not appear on Darth F3TT's public YouTube list (where his last post appears to be 'Return of the Jelly Infinite Scoring Glitch on Pinball FX2 Xbox 360'). He had presumably deleted it. Perhaps comments like 'You are a motherfucker JEW. Delete this Video other wise you will see that your Family Dead Bodies' (con-tributed by one Anmad Sarwar) may have had something to do with that decision; see https://www.youtube.com/user/DarthF3TT/discussion

197. David Kirkpatrick, 'A Deadly Mix in Benghazi', New York Times, 28 December 2013, http://www.nytimes.com/projects/2013/benghazi/#/?chapt=0 ,

198. our map is based on the interactive map prepared by John Hudson of The Wire, em-bedded in http://perma.cc/QVL3-YES9 and accessible directly at http://perma.cc/ATR9 -VJ8C . The daily evolving, crowdsourced Wikipedia pages documenting the affair once again demonstrated the online encyclopaedia's value as a crowdsourced aggregator of useful information on recent events. That information was not always reliable, but with more than 200 footnotes, many of them containing links, the reader could check it out

199. Raza S. Hassan, 'Two Cops Among 17 Killed in Karachi', Dawn, 22 September 2012, http://perma.cc/D6VP-TUDW

200. quoted in Washington Post, 17 September 2012; watch online at http://www.youtube .com/watch?v=zk2sNSbBVy8

201. David Kirkpatrick et al., 'Egypt's New Leader Spells Out Terms for U.S.-Arab Ties', New York Times, 22 September 2012, http://www.nytimes.com/2012/09/23/ world/middleeast/egyptian-leader-mohamed-morsi-spells-out-terms-for-us-arab-ties .html?pagewanted=all

202. as reported in Matt Bradley, 'Beyond Its Violent Core, Egypt's Protest Ebbs', Wall Street Journal, 14 September 2012, http://www.wsj.com/articles/SB1000087239639044 40237045776512227044454332

203. as reported in Pamela Constable, 'Egyptian Christian Activist in Virginia Promoted Video That Sparked Furor', Washington Post, 13 September 2012, http://perma .cc/6LTK-9LU7

204. as reported in David Nakamura, 'White House Asked YouTube to Review Anti-Muslim Film', Washington Post, 14 September 2012, http://perma.cc/P2AD-3X9L

205. see 'Community Guidelines', YouTube, http://perma.cc/K3T5-MTBA

206. see Robert C. Post, 'Free Speech in the Age of YouTube', Foreign Policy, 17 Septem-ber 2012, http://perma.cc/3VE4-TNTA

207. some of the repostings of the video were flagged with a warning, others not

208. see the account by Brian Pellot, 'Has Innocence of Muslims Ended the Innocence of YouTube?', Free Speech Debate, http://freespeechdebate.com/en/discuss/has-innocence-of-muslims-ended-the-innocence-of-youtube/

209. Danyal Kazim, '"Innocence of Muslims" and the Manufacture of Outrage', Free Speech Debate, http://freespeechdebate.com/en/discuss/innocence-of-muslims-and-the-manufacture-of-outrage/

210. I take (and extend) this metaphor from Post 2009, 185

211. see Sutter, 'YouTube Restricts Video Access over Libyan Violence', CNN, http://perma.cc/HA8C-TS2L

212. see 'President Obama's 2012 Address to U.N. General Assembly (Full Text)', Washington Post, 25 September 2012, http://perma.cc/GPP5-VEZY

213. see Permanent Mission of Egypt to the United Nations New York, 'Statement of H.E. Dr. Mohamed Morsy President of the Arab Republic of Egypt', http://perma.cc/ZAT7-BMES

214. see International Business Times, 'Pakistan President Zardari's Speech at UN General Assembly', http://perma.cc/8Z9X-LLEX

215. as reported on BBC News, 'Anti-Islam Film: Pakistan Minister Offers Bounty', http://perma.cc/CM52-X82H

216. on the BBC Radio 4's Today programme, 28 September 2012

217. see Asif Shahzad, 'Ghulam Ahmad Bilour, Pakistan Railway Minister, Taken off Taliban Hit List after Bounty Offer', Huffington Post, 26 September 2012, http://perma.cc/9UJY-VTUZ

218. the figure of 1.7 million comes from the 2011 UK census

219. see 'Judge Jails "Innocence of Muslims" Filmmaker', L.A. Now, 27 September 2012, http://perma.cc/M6SW-2HHU

220. see this account: http://www.huffingtonpost.com/edward-lee/youtube-save-cindy-lee_b_1926905.html; the February 2014 court order appears here: https://drive.google.com/file/d/0B_2Um__f9OiUUXA4dFd5NU5qaFU/edit; see also the court's opinion: https://drive.google.com/file/d/0B_2Um__f9OiUNXR0bkRjU1h3dzg/edit. In November 2014, the court agreed to reconsider its decision: http://www.nationaljournal.com/tech/court-agrees-to-reconsider-decision-over-benghazi-linked-anti-islam-video-20141112; in May 2015 it reversed it: http://www.theguardian.com/technology/2015/may/19/anti-muslim-film-youtube-innocence-of-muslims

221. this was http://www.youtube.com/user/DarthF3TT?feature=CAgQwRs= . The link is no longer available

222. see Susan Benesch et al., 'The Innocence of YouTube', Foreign Policy, 5 October 2012, http://perma.cc/HH9G-37SC and http://perma.cc/JY5N-SK9R

223. see http://www.youtube.com/watch?v=gg8Ynsr-5G4 . Absurdly, when I checked this link at Stanford University on 8 August 2015, it said 'this content is not available on this country domain due to a legal complaint. Sorry about that'. So the massive Google/YouTube automated machine was blocking a fine example of a devout Muslim's counterspeech. Sorry, indeed. See also my blog titled 'A Muslim Responds to the YouTube Movie—on YouTube', Free Speech Debate, http://freespeechdebate.com/en/2012/09/a-muslim-responds-to-the-youtube-movie-on-youtube/

224. see Shamsie 2009 for a critique of the Offended Muslim
225. conversation with Syed Mahmood, London, 29 April 2013

IDEALS

1. quoted in Motherwell, ed. 1989, 320
2. see 'A Muslim Responds to the YouTube movie—on YouTube', Free Speech Debate, http://freespeechdebate.com/en/2012/09/a-muslim-responds-to-the-youtube-movie -on-youtube/
3. see Kwadwo Gyasi Nkita-Mayala, 'Umuntu Ngumuntu Ngabantu: "A Person Is a Person Because of People"', http://perma.cc/F4LQ-GHKX
4. Waldron 1992, 778
5. Scanlon 2003, 15
6. Milton 1909 [1644], 51–52
7. Mill 1991 [1859], quotes on 34, 48, 49 and 59. The text of chapter 2 is available online at http://perma.cc/WAR7-4NN3
8. Williams, ed. 1981, 54
9. Abrams v United States, quoted in Lewis 2007, 32. For the full text of the Holmes judgement, see http://perma.cc/TE65-7D9U
10. Hayek 1945, https://perma.cc/6T9H-A86Q
11. Lewis 2007, 185
12. see the detailed account in Hansen 1999, 125–60. More on this under principle 4
13. Ryan Balot in Sluiter and Rosen, eds. 2004, 21
14. see Fishkin 2009
15. quoted in Garton Ash 2005, 15
16. Euripides quoted in Foucault 2001, 30
17. quoted in Sluiter and Rosen, eds. 2004, 30
18. Demosthenes quoted in Sluiter and Rosen, eds. 2004, 7
19. quoted in Sluiter and Rosen, eds. 2004, 218
20. quoted in Foucault 2001, 61
21. the argument is closely examined by Josiah Ober in chapter 2 of a forthcoming book, provisionally titled *Rational Cooperation in Greek Political Thought*. See also Ober 2008; Ober 2013; Herodotus 1998
22. Meiklejohn 1948, 6
23. Hare et al., eds. 2009, vii. Switzerland should also be mentioned, as perhaps the oldest continually practising deliberative democracy in the world
24. Lord Steyn, quoted in Sedley 2011, 234, referring to R v Home Secretary, ex parte Simms and O'Brien [1999] 3 WLR 328
25. Foucault 2001, 128
26. this comes from the Virginia Resolutions of 1798, quoted in Lewis 2007, 18
27. Sen 1999, 16, 180–82
28. Bollinger 2010, 48
29. in Hare et al., eds. 2009, 12

30. see Schell et al. 2013

31. Chafee 1946, viii–ix

32. Chafee 1946, 559

33. in Index on Censorship, vol. 41, no. 1, 2012, 28–29. Many asked whether Aung San Suu Kyi lived up to this prescription when she did not more forcefully condemn the appalling prosecution of the Muslim Rohingya population in Rakhine state in 2012–2015. By then, she was speaking not as a dissident 'antipolitician' but as a politician competing for the support of a majority Burman electorate seemingly infused with ethno-religious prejudice

34. Leslie Green, 'Right Speech', Free Speech Debate, http://freespeechdebate.com/en/media/right-speech/

35. Sluiter and Rosen, eds. 2004, 33

36. Mill 1991 [1859], 61

37. Samuel Johnson, lines added to Goldsmith's 'The Traveller', quoted in Garton Ash 2005, 247

38. BBC, 'Editorial Guidelines', 2015, http://perma.cc/TRX6-32G9

39. at a swimming pool in California I once heard a father admonish his young son not to use the word 'spastic', because 'we just don't say that and it's, you know, kind of British . . .'. Clearly a clinching argument

40. Pudd'nhead Wilson's New Calendar, quoted in Bollinger 1986, 7

41. Immanuel Kant, 'Beantwortung der Frage "Was Ist Aufklärung?"', reprinted in Bahr, ed. 1974, 9–17

42. see Weinreich 1945, 13. The original of this article is in Yiddish, and he attributed the saying to someone else

43. on expressive law, see Anderson et al. 2000

44. on soft law, see Thürer 2009, 159–78

45. Brettschneider 2012, main argument summarised in 1–23

46. Wu 2010, 120–21

47. for the full 1689 Bill of Rights, see http://perma.cc/H6LD-AH5C

48. Jack, ed. 2011

49. see Timothy Garton Ash, 'It Is Not Just Parliament's Buildings That Require Extensive Renovation', The Guardian, 27 March 2015, http://perma.cc/Z7N7-4NRV

50. Oxford University 'Code and Practice on Freedom of Speech', http://perma.cc/RWK4-L75N ; Stanford University, 'Student Matters', http://perma.cc/9U23-C5RH ; Yale College, 'Freedom of Expression', Yale University, http://perma.cc/J9YS-VXDT

51. see Chaos Computer Club, http://perma.cc/P2UJ-BSZ6 and http://perma.cc/KLE2-TVYR

52. Feinberg 1984

53. Feinberg 1984, 26–27

54. quoted in Williams 2005, 140

55. Mill 1991 [1859], 14

56. see Williams, ed. 1981, 102, 22–23

57. The Guardian, print edition, 11 January 2010. The online version only has its own headline; see Charlie Brooker, 'There Is No Hope Left for Labour—Apart, Perhaps, From Hopelessness Itself', The Guardian, 10 January 2010, http://perma.cc/FXJ3-BZQZ

58. as reported by Al Jazeera, 'No Let-Up in Gaddafi Offensive', http://perma.cc/ Q6RF-RTLT
59. Mill 1991 [1859], 62
60. Schauer 1982, 10
61. MacKinnon 1993, 17, 61
62. Delgado et al. 2004, 13
63. Waldron 2012, 105–8
64. Baldwin 1993 [1963], 83
65. Feinberg 1985, 10–13
66. Williams, ed. 1981, 122–23
67. Furedi 2011, 158
68. Shamsie 2009
69. Roth 2001, 6–10
70. see Lanre Bakare, 'Benedict Cumberbatch Apologises after Calling Black Actors "Coloured"', The Guardian, 26 January 2015, http://perma.cc/C9M4-ZSNH , and the measured account by Joseph Harker, 'Cumberbatch's 'Coloured' Gaffe Reveals Just How White the Film Industry Is', The Guardian, 27 January 2015, http://perma.cc/ SPX9-LNAP
71. Suzanne Moore, 'This Growing Culture of Outrage Doesn't Extend Free Speech—It Limits It', The Guardian, 18 January 2012, http://perma.cc/HG9H-F2HR
72. see Cat Macros, 'OMG I Have Been Offended', http://perma.cc/CLP9-SB2T . OMG is of course text message shorthand for 'Oh My God'
73. United Nations Treaty Collection, 'Chapter IV Human Rights—11. Convention on the Rights of the Child', http://perma.cc/GRX5-S5NG . The only state to have signed the convention but not ratified it is the United States
74. Council of Europe, 'Convention on Cybercrime CETS No.: 185', http://perma .cc/336S-MQPU
75. conversations with David Drummond and Gabriel Stricker, Google, Mountain View, 16 September 2010
76. on the dark net, see Bartlett 2015
77. in Levmore and Nussbaum, eds. 2010, 155–73
78. Herbert 1995, 266
79. the radio station repeatedly used the Kinyarwanda language word *inyenzi*. On 3 June 1994, a broadcast said 'the cruelty of the cockroaches can only be cured by their total extermination', quoted in Article 19, 'Broadcasting Genocide: Censorship, Propaganda and State-Sponsored Violence in Rwanda 1990–1994', http://perma.cc/6DYB-5EES
80. see Simon Dickson, 'From Babel to Babble', Free Speech Debate, http://freespeech debate.com/en/2013/11/from-babel-to-babble/
81. quoted in Kantorowicz 1959, 48
82. Appiah 2008, 113
83. Mill 1991 [1859], 14
84. quoted in Hevia 2003, 111
85. see Wolff 1994
86. see Mungello 1971, 19
87. Shayegan 1992

88. see Mishra 2013

89. Mohsen Kadivar, 'Islam between Free Speech and Hate Speech', Free Speech Debate, http://freespeechdebate.com/en/discuss/islam-between-free-speech-and-hate-speech/

90. quoted in De Bary et al. 1999, 462

91. Leys 1997, 70, 188

92. Waley 1938, 187; Lau 1979, 128; Watson 2007, 100

93. I am most grateful to Justin Winslett for clarifying my formulation of this point

94. Rawls 2006, 15. The particular sense in which Rawls uses the word 'reasonable' is discussed on pages 48–54

95. Rawls 2006, 389

96. World Values Survey, Wave 6, 2010–2014, http://perma.cc/Z2R6-Q3QC ; World Values Survey, Wave 5, 2005–2009, http://perma.cc/EG48-B7M9 ; World Values Survey, Wave 4, 1999–2004, http://perma.cc/TMJ5-5L4Y . In the fourth and fifth waves of the World Values Survey, the third option was 'Give people more say'. This was changed to 'Giving people more say in important government decisions' in the sixth wave. See Figure 7. East Asian Barometer Survey of Democracy, Governance and Development, data for China 2008, data for Taiwan, 2006: http://perma.cc/H9EW-HN6G

97. I worked with the late Andrew Kohut to formulate this question and review the responses

98. 'Macao Deliberative Polling on the "Amendment of the Press Law and the Audio-Visual Broadcasting Act"—Final Report', Macao Government Information Bureau, http://perma.cc/W9UA-KW2S

99. Li 1993 and Fischer 2004

100. Huang 2008, 130, 266 and the whole of his chapter 3. Mill's personal library, now preserved at Somerville College, Oxford, includes his copy of the earliest French translation of *On Liberty*. Unlike his father James, John Stuart was not a copious annotator of books, but he has covered many margins with corrections of the French translator's work, sometimes in important passages. Turning the pages, one can feel his irritation piping through the scribbles in his fluent hand. Now imagine him being able to read Yan Fu's translation. An inflammation of the pen would surely have resulted

101. Habermas 1995, 117–18

102. Habermas, 'Die Dialektik der Säkularisierung', Eurozine, 15 April 2008, http://perma.cc/KSA6-GHYR . My translation. An English version of this text can be found in Habermas 2009, 59–77

103. quoted in Wallerstein 2006, 11

104. George Bernard Shaw, quoted in Stace 1990, 136, and see his 'Maxims for Revolutionists', http://perma.cc/H56S-SYYT

105. Leys 1997, 77. Another version appears in Analects 12.2, 55, 'What you do not wish for yourself, do not impose upon others'

106. the *Mahabharata* 5:1517, quoted in Appiah 2008, 60

107. quoted in Sen 2006, 53

108. Leys 1997, Analects 2.12, 7.3 and 9.2, endnotes on 115–16, 150 and 158–59

109. I am most grateful to Daniel Bell of Tsinghua University for providing me with an English translation of this statement done by Yuhan Liu. The original was apparently published on Confucian websites but not in print

110. Mandela 1995, 24. My attention was originally drawn to this reminiscence by Sen 2006, 55

111. my notes of that ceremony, Oxford, 20 June 2012

112. Rudyard Kipling, 'The Ballad of East and West', http://perma.cc/2GGD-89XW

113. Brown 1991, 69–70. This 'partial list' was compiled by George Murdock and originally published in 1945

114. see Roberts et al. 2016. But the priority given to free speech in Egypt and Tunisia was still very high; see this polling by Pew over the period 2011–2014: 'Pew Global Attitudes and Trends Question Database', PewResearchCenter, http://perma.cc/S7M6-2X8U , and 'Global Attitudes and Trends', PewResearchCenter, http://perma.cc/Q9QU-FRJF

115. see Hans Küng, 'The Declaration of a Global Ethic', presented at the Parliament of the World's Religions, 1993, http://perma.cc/BT5H-WJG4

116. I quote from notes he sent me for his 2012 Ralf Dahrendorf Memorial Lecture at St Antony's College, Oxford, on 'How Universal Is Liberalism?' The full lecture can be watched at http://podcasts.ox.ac.uk/how-universal-liberalism

117. this fine formulation appeared in an earlier version of the argument made in Hurrell 2013. I quote it here with the author's permission

118. Wallerstein 2006, 28

119. see, for example, the sets of principles drafted by organisations such as PEN and Article 19, usually relating to specific areas. I refer to some of these at various points through this book. See also Ignatieff 2012, Rodin 2012 and the Carnegie Council for Ethics in International Affairs collaborative research project to which they both refer, which was due to publish its findings only after this book went to press

120. that is, *Weltbürgergesellschaft*. See Immanuel Kant, 'Beantwortung der Frage "Was Ist Aufklärung?"' reprinted in Bahr, ed. 1974, 9–17

USER GUIDE

1. Manav Bhuhshan, 'What's your beef with my freedom to eat it?', Free Speech Debate, http://freespeechdebate.com/en/case/whats-your-beef-with-my-freedom-to-eat-it/

1. LIFEBLOOD

1. observation by the German philologist and comparative religionist Max Müller, quoted in Prothero 2011, 16

2. Lord Steyn, quoted in Sedley 2011, 234, referring to R v Home Secretary, ex parte Simms and O'Brien [1999] 3 WLR 328

3. see Article 19 at Office of the High Commissioner for Human Rights, 'International Covenant on Civil and Political Rights', http://perma.cc/V4JK-N7XV

4. Jeff Howard, 'Article 19: Freedom of Expression Anchored in International Law', Free Speech Debate, http://freespeechdebate.com/en/discuss/article-19-freedom-of-expression-anchored-in-international-law/

5. on human capabilities, see Sen 1985 and Sen 1999

6. see 'Tim Berners-Lee on "Stretch Friends" & Open Data', Free Speech Debate, http://freespeechdebate.com/en/media/tim-berners-lee-on-stretch-friends-open-data/

7. the poll was conducted in 2009/10. See http://perma.cc/7XP7-VCSJ

8. Pinter 1988, 5

9. Green 1991, 219

10. for the Girona Manifesto, see PEN International, 'Girona Manifesto on Linguistic Rights', http://perma.cc/SS2B-QY7W . For the political theorists' argument, see the chapter by David Laitin and Rob in Kymlicka et al. 2003, 80–104

11. Office of the High Commissioner for Human Rights, 'Universal Declaration of Human Rights', http://perma.cc/D23U-TYYJ

12. see Elizabeth Daley, 'Expanding the Concept of Literacy', Educause Review, https://perma.cc/U54F-EVAZ and Christopher Caldwell, 'In the Unthinking Age, Seeing is Believing', Financial Times, 12 April 2013, http://www.ft.com/cms/s/0/79c6734a-9d3f-11e2-a8db-00144feabdc0.html#axzz3r7sgZpup

13. conversation with Jimmy Wales, Oxford, 19 January 2012

14. for Kozakiewicz, see Brian Pellot, 'The Greatest Olympic Free Speech Moments', Free Speech Debate, http://freespeechdebate.com/en/2012/07/the-olympics-greatest-free-speech-moments/ . On dress codes, see Maryam Omidi, 'What Not to Wear', Free Speech Debate, http://freespeechdebate.com/en/2012/06/what-not-to-wear/

15. RT (Zimbabwe) & Ors v Secretary of State for the Home Department [2012] UKSC 38, which also quotes the General Comment. I owe this point to Stephen Meili, and see his extensive discussion in Meili 2015

16. see Annabelle Chapman, 'When Doing Nothing Is Free Expression', Free Speech Debate, http://freespeechdebate.com/en/case/when-doing-nothing-is-free-expression/

17. Sam Favate, 'Arizona Supreme Court Says Tattoos Are Free Speech', Wall Street Journal Law Blog, 10 September 2012, http://blogs.wsj.com/law/2012/09/10/arizona-supreme-court-says-tattoos-are-free-speech/

18. Clark v Community for Creative Nonviolence [1998], 468 US 288

19. Miles v City Council of Augusta Georgia [1983] USCA11 929; 710 F.2d 1542

20. see Basic Law for the Federal Republic of Germany, 'Article 5', http://perma.cc/C43L-XMXE

21. see Corbin 2009

22. see Stanford Research into the Impact of Tobacco Advertising, 'More Doctors Smoke Camels', Stanford School of Medicine, http://perma.cc/7MV7-77RR

23. these are four actual warnings I photographed on an array of cigarette packets at Heathrow airport

24. see Post 2007

25. see Michele Finck, 'Can the Treatment of Animals Be Compared to Nazi Concentration Camps?', Free Speech Debate, http://freespeechdebate.com/en/2013/02/can-the-treatment-of-animals-be-compared-to-nazi-concentration-camps/ , and Gwen Sharp, 'PETA's "Holocaust on Your Plate" Campaign', Society Pages, 5 May 2008, http://perma.cc/2N2V-XH2R

26. see Wikipedia, 'Jyllands-Posten Muhammed Cartoons Controversy', http://perma.cc/C3SA-ZZ9Y

27. conversation with Monika Bickert, Facebook's head of Global Product Policy, Stanford University, 14 August 2015

28. Office of the High Commissioner for Human Rights, 'General Comment No. 11: Prohibition of Propaganda for War and Inciting National, Racial or Religious Hatred (Art. 20)', http://perma.cc/V8WP-ASU3

2. VIOLENCE

1. for a selection of victims of violent Islamist intimidation, most of them of Muslim background, see Murray et al. 2008. Roberto Saviano, 'My Life under Armed Guard', The Guardian, 14 January 2015, http://www.theguardian.com/world/2015/jan/14/-sp -roberto-saviano-my-life-under-armed-guard-gomorrah . Saviano noted that 585 people were living under state-provided armed guard in Italy alone

2. the term was coined by Harry Kalven Jr in his 1964 book *The Negro and the First Amendment.*

3. I believe I coined the term. See my 2012 text Timothy Garton Ash, 'Violence', Free Speech Debate, http://freespeechdebate.com/en/principle/p-2/info/ , and subsequently Timothy Garton Ash, 'Defying the Assassin's Veto', New York Review of Books, 19 February 2015, http://www.nybooks.com/articles/archives/2015/feb/19/defying -assassins-veto/

4. Abdal Hakim Murad, 'Scorning the Prophet Goes beyond Free Speech', Daily Telegraph, 17 January 2015, http://www.telegraph.co.uk/news/religion/11351280/Scorning -the-Prophet-goes-beyond-free-speech-its-an-act-of-violence.html

5. this is of course the famous formula of Bishop Joseph Butler

6. Klausen 2009, 'Publisher's Statement' on vi

7. Patricia Cohen, 'Yale Press Bans Images of Muhammad in New Book', New York Times, 12 August 2009, http://www.nytimes.com/2009/08/13/books/13book.html? _r=0 . For the biography of the Thai king, see Handley 2006

8. see Wikipedia, 'Behzti', http://perma.cc/2UWJ-N96Y and Doreen Carvajal, 'A Racially Charged Exhibition in London Is Canceled after Protests', New York Times, 24 September 2014, http://artsbeat.blogs.nytimes.com/2014/09/24/a-racially-charged -exhibition-in-london-is-canceled-after-protests/

9. Redmond-Bate v Director of Public Prosecutions [1999] EWHC Admin 732, http:// perma.cc/SG94-3G3N

10. Beatty v Gillbanks [1882] 9 QBD 308, https://perma.cc/Y4KP-CBJX?type=source

11. Brandenburg v Ohio, 395 US 444 1969, http://perma.cc/3ZWE-VC2R

12. Hess v Indiana 414 US 105 (1973), http://perma.cc/EFL3-VWKF

13. Leader Maynard et al. 2015; Semelin 2007

14. Noel Malcolm confirms that he said this, but cannot recall a reference in published form. Email to the author, 5 March 2015

15. Sunstein 2006; Sunstein 2009

16. see 'How a Schoolgirl Was Radicalised', The Economist, 28 February 2015, http:// www.economist.com/news/international/21645204-shamimas-list

17. see Pariser 2011

18. see Borchgrevink 2013, 122–41, Seierstad 2015, 154–69, and Timothy Garton Ash, 'The Internet Nourished Norway's Killer, but Censorship Would Be Folly', The Guardian, 29 July 2011, http://perma.cc/R825-99LQ

19. John F. Burns, 'Cartoonist in Denmark Calls Attack "Really Close"', New York Times, 2 January 2010, http://www.nytimes.com/2010/01/03/world/europe/03denmark.html , and Marie Louise Sjølie, 'The Danish Cartoonist Who Survived an Axe Attack', The Guardian, 4 January 2010, http://perma.cc/4H3Z-UVXY

20. Malik 2009, 186

21. R v Saleem [2007] EWCA Crim 2692, [2008] 2 Cr App R(S) 12 at [48]

22. see Susan Benesch, 'The Dangerous Speech Project', https://perma.cc/DEN4 -LKKG?type=source , and Leader Maynard et al. 2015

23. Yanagizawa-Drott 2014 and, for the more sceptical view, Straus 2007

24. 'Robin Hood Airport Tweet Bomb Joke Man Wins Case', BBC News, 27 July 2012, http://perma.cc/TG3C-BN35 , and Owen Bowcott, 'Twitter Joke Trial: Paul Chambers Wins High Court Appeal against Conviction', The Guardian, 27 July 2012, http:// perma.cc/DSR4-PNCW

25. Chambers v Director of Public Prosecutions [2012] EWHC 2157 (Admin), [2013] 1 WLR 1833 at [18]

26. see Benesch 2012, http://perma.cc/63VG-X8V2 and Nimi Hoffmann, 'Shoot the Boer: Hate Music?', Free Speech Debate, http://freespeechdebate.com/en/case/shoot-the -boer-hate-music/ . The case is Afri-Forum v Malema 2011 (6) SA 240 (EqC), [2011] 4 All SA 293 (EqC). The words were said to constitute hate speech at [108]. Later, a settlement was reached in which it was agreed that the song should not be sung

27. quotations in Benesch 2012

28. quoted in Benesch 2009

29. see Judith Bruhn, 'RapeLay: A Virtual Rape Game', Free Speech Debate, http:// freespeechdebate.com/en/case/rapelay-a-virtual-rape-game/

30. see Elson and Ferguson 2014, and commentaries on their article in the same issue. The article was accepted for publication in February 2013

31. see United Nations Treaty Collection, 'Chapter IV Human Rights—4. International Covenant on Civil and Political Rights', https://treaties.un.org/pages/ViewDetails .aspx?src=TREATY&mtdsg_no=IV-4&chapter=4&lang=en

32. Office of the High Commissioner for Human Rights, 'General Comment No. 11: Prohibition of Propaganda for War and Inciting National, Racial or Religious Hatred (Art. 20)', http://perma.cc/V8WP-ASU3

33. Agnès Callamard, 'Towards an Interpretation of Article 20 of the ICCPR: Thresholds for the Prohibition of Incitement to Hatred. Work in Progress', Article 19, http:// perma.cc/EN7A-JWZ5

34. for a written transcript, see The White House, 'Remarks by the President at the Acceptance of the Nobel Peace Prize', http://perma.cc/PUX3-B39E , and for a video, see http://www.nobelprize.org/mediaplayer/index.php?id=1221

35. see Biggar 2014

36. Köckert 2007, 76

37. see Weber's 1919 lecture 'Politics as a Vocation' as quoted in the Stanford Encyclopedia of Philosophy, http://perma.cc/83BT-BS9Y . The original wording is *das Monopol legitimer physischer Gewaltsamkeit*

38. see the blog by Madiha Sattar, 'Pakistan's Blasphemy Laws: A History of Violence', Foreign Policy, 2 March 2011, http://perma.cc/9E7N-82VC

39. Rushdie 2012, 170

40. Hirsi Ali 2007, 320–32

41. see Saviano 2007 and Roberto Saviano, 'Roberto Saviano: My Life under Armed Guard', The Guardian, 14 January 2015, http://perma.cc/F7XV-D4AL

42. Robert Shrimsley, 'Be Glad Someone Had the Courage to Be Charlie', Financial Times, 9 January 2015, http://www.ft.com/intl/cms/s/2/6ddff0c2-95c4-11e4-a390-00144feabdc0.html#axzz3r7sgZpup

43. Pearson 2005, 409 and 431

44. Timothy Garton Ash, 'Islam in Europe', New York Review of Books, 9 February 2006, http://www.nybooks.com/articles/archives/2006/oct/05/islam-in-europe/, reprinted in Garton Ash 2009

45. interview with Jytte Klausen, 'Jytte Klausen on Yale University and the Danish Cartoons', Free Speech Debate, http://freespeechdebate.com/en/media/jytte-klausen-on-yale-university-and-the-danish-cartoons/

46. see John Donatich, 'Why Yale UP Did Not Publish the Danish Cartoons', Free Speech Debate, http://freespeechdebate.com/en/discuss/why-yale-up-did-not-publish-the-danish-cartoons/

47. Jonathan Dimbleby, Index on Censorship, 18 December 2009, http://perma.cc/8XSR-Q524 . For a critical view from an Index board member, see Kenan Malik, Index on Censorship, 18 December 2009, http://perma.cc/A6DL-VKG8

48. see Klausen 2009 and Jytte Klausen, 'See No Evil', Eurozine, 25 January 2010, http://perma.cc/GJ3E-GPLD . See also http://perma.cc/ZYT4-4W9V

49. the following paragraphs draw very directly on my account in Timothy Garton Ash, 'Defying the Assassin's Veto', New York Review of Books, 19 February 2015, http://www.nybooks.com/articles/archives/2015/feb/19/defying-assassins-veto/

50. see Katie Engelhart, 'I Enjoyed the Book of Mormon Musical. Now for the Book of Islam?', Free Speech Debate, http://freespeechdebate.com/en/2013/05/i-enjoyed-the-book-of-mormon-musical-now-for-the-book-of-islam/

51. BBC ComRes poll, January-February 2015, 'Muslim Poll', http://perma.cc/R9PN-H7AX

52. Sarah Glatte, 'Charlie Hebdo Cartoons: To Republish or Not to Republish?', Free Speech Debate, http://freespeechdebate.com/en/discuss/charlie-hebdo-cartoons-to-republish-or-not-to-republish/

53. see Roberts et al. 2009 and Roberts et al. 2016. I was a participant in this project. See also Ackerman et al. 2003, Gandhi quote on 5, and Sharp 2005 (list of methods with his commentary on 51–65). The 198 methods list is online at A Force More Powerful, '198 Methods of Nonviolent Action', http://perma.cc/25WD-3H75

54. these examples are drawn from Benesch 2014 and and her 2014 talk 'Troll Wrestling for Beginners: Data-Driven Methods to Decrease Hatred Online', Berkman Center for Internet & Society, 25 March 2014, http://perma.cc/F9ZQ-5WDA . Katherine Bruce-Lockhart, 'From Incitement to Self-Censorship: The Media in the Kenyan

Elections of 2007 and 2013', Free Speech Debate, http://freespeechdebate.com/en/discuss/124451/ . On online counter-speech, see also Gagliardone et al. 2015

55. see Briggs et al. 2013, MyJihad on 14, Trojan T-shirts on 20
56. see Susan Benesch, 'Countering Dangerous Speech to Prevent Mass Violence during Kenya's 2013 Elections', Dangerous Speech Project, 2014, http://dangerousspeech.org/resources/countering-dangerous-speech-kenya-2013
57. see Collier et al. 2013
58. detail in Benesch, 'Countering Dangerous Speech', http://dangerousspeech.org/resources/countering-dangerous-speech-kenya-2013

3. KNOWLEDGE

1. see Usama Hasan, 'Is Nothing Sacred? Free Speech and Religion', Dahrendorf Lecture, 10 June 2011, http://media.podcasts.ox.ac.uk/sant/dahrendorf/2011-06-10_dahrendorf.mp4
2. Moynihan 2009. See British Medical Journal 2009, http://perma.cc/V6XC-AQND
3. on the Tamiflu saga, the best source are the papers gathered online by the British Medical Journal, 'Tamiflu Data: Who Saw What When', http://perma.cc/4SXW-4KT2 . See also Goldacre 2009, 82–91. The figure of £424 million comes from page 6 of the report of the House of Commons Committee of Public Accounts, 'Access to Clinical Trial Information and the Stockpiling of Tamiflu', http://perma.cc/H7YE-F38D . For the clinical trials movement, see Goldacre 2009, 220–21, Goldacre 2012 and http://perma.cc/TG7L-GPNL
4. Simon Singh, 'Beware the Spinal Trap', The Guardian, 19 April 2008, http://perma.cc/92RE-AGN4
5. see Roehr 2011 and Maryam Omidi, 'Bioterrorism and bird flu', Free Speech Debate, http://freespeechdebate.com/en/case/bioterrorism-and-bird-flu/
6. Lawrence H. Summers, 'Remarks at NBER Conference on Diversifying the Science & Engineering Workforce', http://perma.cc/9AK7-ZMQD
7. quoted in Post 2012, 61. The best guides to academic freedom with special reference to free speech are Post 2012 and, instructively comparing Britain, the United States and Germany, Barendt 2010
8. my talk to a class at Tsinghua University about John Stuart Mill and free speech was a rare exception, kindly but also informally organised by Daniel Bell
9. in the United States, a whole organisation, the Foundation for Individual Rights in Education (FIRE), has been dedicated to challenging such restrictions. Lukianoff 2012 is based on the work of FIRE
10. on trigger warnings, see Sarah Glatte, 'Whose Finger Should Be on the Trigger?', Free Speech Debate, http://freespeechdebate.com/en/discuss/whose-finger-should-be-on-the-trigger/
11. Kai Johnson, Tanika Lynch, Elizabeth Monroe, and Tracey Wang, 'Our Identities Matter in Core Classrooms', Columbia Spectator, 30 April 2015, http://perma.cc/8EX5-66VA

12. see Jennifer Medina, 'Warning: The Literary Canon Could Make Students Squirm', New York Times, 17 May 2014, http://www.nytimes.com/2014/05/18/us/warning-the -literary-canon-could-make-students-squirm.html?_r=0 and Greg Lukianoff and Jonathan Haidt, 'The Coddling of the American Mind', The Atlantic, September 2015, http://perma.cc/J94E-Z8JB . Joseph Conrad: personal communication

13. Kennedy 2003, 145

14. Nolte: Jürgen Krönig, 'Beifall für den Provokateur', Die Zeit, 24 February 1989, http:// perma.cc/C4JA-D7T3 . On the 'Singer Affair' in Germany, see Leist 1993. Coulter: Steven Chase, 'Ann Coulter's Speech in Ottawa Cancelled', Globe and Mail, 23 March 2010, http://perma.cc/A8ZV-BK49 . Hirsi Ali: Richard Pérez-Peña and Tanzina Vega, 'Brandeis Cancels Plan to Give Honorary Degree to Ayaan Hirsi Ali, a Critic of Islam', New York Times, 8 April 2014, http://www.nytimes.com/2014/04/09/ us/brandeis-cancels-plan-to-give-honorary-degree-to-ayaan-hirsi-ali-a-critic-of- islam.html

15. Douglas Belkin, 'IMF's Lagarde Won't Speak at Smith, Part of a Growing List', Wall Street Journal, 12 May 2014, http://perma.cc/6U33-6GTS

16. the historian was Vyacheslav Dashitschev

17. this was the wording as checked by someone in China in July 2015

18. see Irem Kok et al., 'The Private Life of a National Hero', Free Speech Debate, http:// freespeechdebate.com/en/case/the-private-life-of-a-national-hero/ . Vikas Bajaj and Julie Bosman, 'Book on Gandhi Stirs Passion in India', New York Times, 31 March 2011, http://www.nytimes.com/2011/04/01/books/gandhi-biography-by-joseph-lelyveld-roils -india.html?pagewanted=all&_r=0

19. see Hare et al. eds. 2009, part VI and detail on 543–45, 57–58

20. see Evans 2002, Lipstadt 2006 and Irving v Penguin Books Limited, Deborah E. Lipstadt [2000] EWHC QB 115, 11 April 2000, http://perma.cc/RSU2-HU3H . Oxford Union debate, 'This House Would Restrict the Free Speech of Extremists', 26 November 2007, http://www.youtube.com/watch?v=poSvZxUpYeI

21. see page 3 and see note 8 on page 384. Tribunal de Grande Instance de Paris, 'Condamnation judiciaire de Bernard Lewis', 21 June 1995, http://perma.cc/ J3Q4-VHP9

22. Tribunale federale, '6B_398/2007/rod', 12 December 2007, http://perma.cc/DVZ4 -HYXL . In 2015, the European Court of Human Rights overturned the main point of this conviction; see Perinçek v Switzerland, Application no. 27510/08, 15 October 2015, Grand Chamber

23. Reuters, 'Popular Turkish Novelist on Trial for Speaking of Armenian Genocide', New York Times, 16 December 2005, http://www.nytimes.com/2005/12/16/world/ europe/popular-turkish-novelist-on-trial-for-speaking-of-armenian-genocide.html, and Musa Kesler, 'Nobel laureate Orhan Pamuk gets fined', Hurriyet Daily News, 27 March 2011, http://www.hurriyetdailynews.com/default.aspx?pageid=438&n=orhan -pamuk-will-pay-compensation-for-his-words-court-decided-2011-03-27

24. Council of the European Union, '2908th Meeting of the Council', 27–28 November 2008, http://perma.cc/J4X6-YL7H , 37. For its story, and reactions to it until 2014,

see Luigi Cajani, 'EU versus Intellectual Freedom?', Free Speech Debate, http://freespeechdebate.com/en/discuss/eu-versus-intellectual-freedom/ . In 2014, the European Commission issued a report on implementation of the framework decision, noting that 13 member states had still not fully complied. European Commission, 'Report from the Commission to the European Parliament and the Council on the implementation of Council Framework Decision 2008/913/JHA on combating certain forms and expressions of racism and xenophobia by means of criminal law ', 27 January 2014, http://ec.europa.eu/justice/fundamental-rights/files/com_2014_27_en.pdf

25. European Commission, 'Proposal for a Council Framework Decision on Combating Racism and Xenophobia', 28 November 2001, http://perma.cc/7NKB-P5UP

26. quoted in Timothy Garton Ash, 'A Blanket Ban on Holocaust Denial Would Be a Serious Mistake', The Guardian, 17 January 2007, http://perma.cc/RQU4-H8PY

27. Freedom House, 'Freedom of the Press 2011', 23 September 2011, http://perma.cc/P3XW-7ZCP . The Polish law dates from 1998: The Institute of National Remembrance, 'The Act on the Institute of National Remembrance', http://perma.cc/VW82-SHSQ

28. Human Rights Committee, 2011, http://www.refworld.org/docid/4e38efb52.html

29. Ayako Komine et al., 'The Japanese New History Textbook controversy', Free Speech Debate, http://freespeechdebate.com/en/case/japanese-new-history-textbook-controversy/

30. Wells 1938, 70, 77

31. see electronic enlightenment, http://www.e-enlightenment.com/info/about/

32. Mayer-Schönberger et al. 2013, 9

33. for other suggestions on where to draw the line between information and knowledge, see Starr 2004 and Benkler 2006

34. on the history, see Baldwin 2014

35. see Amelia Andersdotter, 'Amelia Andersdotter on ACTA's Demise and the Internet's Future', Free Speech Debate, http://freespeechdebate.com/en/media/amelia-andersdotter-on-actas-demise-and-the-internets-future/ , Graham Reynolds, 'ACTA: Open Agreement Secretly Arrived At?', Free Speech Debate, http://freespeechdebate.com/en/case/acta-open-agreement-secretly-arrived-at/ , 'Does ACTA Threaten Online Freedom of Expression & Privacy?', Free Speech Debate, http://freespeechdebate.com/en/media/acta-the-internet-freedom-of-expression-privacy/ , and Brian Pellot, 'The Stop Online Piracy Act', Free Speech Debate, http://freespeechdebate.com/en/case/the-stop-online-piracy-act/ . See also 'Free Speech Debate launch with Jimmy Wales', Free Speech Debate, http://freespeechdebate.com/en/media/free-speech-debate-launch-with-jimmy-wales/

36. The Harvard Library, 'Faculty Advisory Council Memorandum on Journal Pricing', http://perma.cc/WJD2-Y7H4

37. Janet Finch, 'Accessibility, Sustainability, Excellence: How to Expand Access to Research Publications', Report of the Working Group on Expanding Access to Published Research Findings, June 2012, http://perma.cc/HQ4X-6Z2E

38. see David Amsden, 'The Brilliant Life and Tragic Death of Aaron Swartz', Rolling Stone, 15 February 2013, http://perma.cc/DZN2-GGUC . Latest Reddit figures at http://www.reddit.com/about/

39. see http://theinfo.org/ . At this writing, at least some of them are still viewable there, intriguingly displayed as rows of clickable dots

40. The US Attorney's Office Massachusetts, 'Alleged Hacker Charged with Stealing over Four Million Documents from MIT Network', 19 July 2011, http://perma.cc/ HL6U-99UX . MIT commissioned a report by a group led by computer scientist Hal Abelson, which gives a detailed account, and asks what lessons MIT should learn: 'Report to the President: MIT and the Prosecution of Aaron Swartz', http://perma.cc/ QL4D-PYPE

41. Aaron Swartz, 'Guerilla Open Access Manifesto', http://perma.cc/CHA9-PAL2

42. see http://creativecommons.org/choose/

43. 'Copyright & Attribution', Free Speech Debate, http://freespeechdebate.com/en/ copyright-attribution/

44. on the Digital Public Library, see Darnton, 'The National Digital Public Library Is Launched!', New York Review of Books, 25 April 2013, http://www.nybooks.com/arti cles/archives/2013/apr/25/national-digital-public-library-launched/. Europeana, http:// www.europeana.eu/portal/ and the Internet Archive, https://archive.org/index.php

45. see Nielsen 2012, 161–63

46. Galaxy Zoo, http://perma.cc/W5M4-PAHW

47. I take these examples from Nielsen 2012, 1–3, 133–42

48. see 'Gottfrid Svartholm-Warg on Freedom of Speech 2007', 20 May 2013, http://www .youtube.com/watch?v=FJiWuw7Qk5E

49. see Gabrielle Guillemin, 'Does ACTA Threaten Online Freedom of Expression & Privacy?', Free Speech Debate, http://freespeechdebate.com/en/media/ acta-the-internet-freedom-of-expression-privacy/

50. see, for example, University of Exeter, 'Green and Gold Open Access', http://perma .cc/A9VW-2VND

51. internet live stats, Google Search Statistics, http://www.internetlivestats.com/ google-search-statistics/ . Wikipedia: information to the author from Wikimedia foundation

52. launched in 2001, the Chilling Effects project's ambition was to 'map the copyright takedown landscape by tracking requests for content removal' and to serve as a research database. As the project had considerably expanded in scope by 2015, it was eventually renamed Lumen in order to make it more 'inclusive', 'accessible and comprehensible worldwide', and the chillingeffects.org page was changed to lumendatabase.org. See Lumen, 'Chilling Effects Announces New Name, International Partnerships', 2 November 2015, https://perma.cc/BC38-59PR

53. Google, 'Transparency Report', http://www.google.com/transparencyreport/

54. see http://www.google.com/explanation.html

55. when I mentioned this to Rachel Whetstone, Google's head of public policy, she said it had been fixed at her insistence. (Conversation, Google, Mountain View, 2 October 2014.) But a search on both google.com and google.co.uk on 21 March 2015 still produced an ad for 'Top 10 Sex Dating Sites' in the UK

56. when I first started enquiring into this, I kept being referred to a single blog post by Rachel Whetstone, 'Controversial Content and Free Expression on the Web: A Refresher', http://perma.cc/J7SN-8W79

57. Federal Trade Commission Staff Memorandum, 'Subject: Google Inc, file number 111–0163. Recommendation: "That the Commission Issue the Attached Complaint"', 8 August 2012. Half of the pages of this document were inadvertently released in an open-records request and published by the Wall Street Journal: 'The FTC Report on Google's Business Practices', Wall Street Journal, 24 March 2015, http://perma.cc/QYW6-JUWX . The Commission ultimately voted 5–0 not to bring charges against Google. Google argued that the document reflected the views of only one of two 'case teams' inside the FTC and that 'ultimately both case teams concluded that no action was needed on search display and ranking'. The FTC was again investigating Google in 2015, this time mainly for promoting its products through the Android mobile phone system, see Conor Dougherty, 'F.T.C. Is Said to Investigate Claims That Google Used Android to Promote Its Products', New York Times, 25 September 2015, http://www.nytimes.com/2015/09/26/technology/ftc-is-said-to-investigate-claims-that-google-used-android-to-promote-its-products.html

58. conversation with the author, New York, 30 June 2011

59. see http://perma.cc/3J2R-TE7K for the Alexa Internet ranking, last checked in September 2015

60. http://perma.cc/R67F-AQYX, last checked in September 2015

61. quoted in Stacy Schiff, 'Can Wikipedia Conquer Expertise?', New Yorker, 31 July 2006, http://perma.cc/F85A-55YR

62. Denis MacShane, email to the author

63. Giles 2005, 900–1. See also Imogen Casebourne et al., 'Assessing the Accuracy and Quality of Wikipedia Entries Compared to Popular Online Encyclopaedias', Wikimedia Foundation, http://perma.cc/FM7D-7JV2 ; 'Vergleichstest: Wikipedia Schlägt die Profis', Der Spiegel, 5 December 2007, http://perma.cc/2QBW-C6T7 ; Casebourne et al. 2012; Rachbauer 2011

64. these figures are for June 2015: http://perma.cc/M2B6-LQ3A . Note that Wikipedia does not record unique monthly users, so monthly page views is the best indicator available

65. Broughton 2008, 123

66. conversations with Lila Tretikov and Wikimedia Foundation staff, San Francisco, 12 and 30 September 2014

67. these are interestingly charted in a project called WikiWarMonitor; see http://wwm.phy.bme.hu. 'Talk: Vossstrasse / Archive 1', Wikipedia, http://perma.cc/5JFX-DRSD

68. see 'Why Wikipedia Needs an Image Filter', Free Speech Debate, http://freespeechdebate.com/en/media/the-proposed-image-filter/ , and Robert Harris et al., '2010 Wikimedia Study of Controversial Content', Wikimedia, http://perma.cc/PJ9R-HD8Y

69. Reagle 2010, 115

70. see Wikipedia, 'Article Rescue Squadron', http://perma.cc/4EYC-YQKR

71. Nicholson Baker, 'The Charms of Wikipedia', New York Review of Books, 20 March 2008, http://www.nybooks.com/articles/archives/2008/mar/20/the-charms-of-wikipedia/

72. Cliff Pickover, 'Is Your Entry about to Be Deleted from Wikipedia?', http://wikidumper.blogspot.co.uk

73. see http://en.uncyclopedia.co/wiki/Main_Page
74. Jimmy Wales, conversation with the author, Oxford, 19 January 2012
75. see 'Wikipedia Naming Conventions', Wikipedia, http://perma.cc/7ZHD-NMUL
76. Broughton 2008
77. Dan Glaister, 'LA Times "Wikitorial" Gives Editors Red Faces', The Guardian, 22 June 2005, http://perma.cc/SMT4-4864
78. 'Language Committee', Wikimedia, http://perma.cc/L774-PPAT
79. see Scott Hale, 'Online Language Bubbles: The Last Frontier?', Free Speech Debate, http://freespeechdebate.com/en/discuss/online-language-bubbles-the-last-frontier/ , drawing on Hecht et al. 2010
80. conversation with Google Translate inventor Franz Josef Och, Palo Alto, 9 October 2013. Wishing to suggest to Och that we split the cost of dinner, or 'go Dutch' as we say in British English, I tried out 'go Dutch' in Google Translate. The results were mixed, including 'Ga Nederlands' in Dutch, 'iru Nederlanda' in Esperanto and 'vade Dutch' in Latin
81. see 'TED Open Translation Project', TED, http://perma.cc/AN28-YBBG
82. TED Talks, 'Luis von Ahn: Massive-Scale Online Collaboration', http://www.ted.com/talks/luis_von_ahn_massive_scale_online_collaboration.html and 'Duolingo now translating BuzzFeed and CNN', duolingo, http://perma.cc/4MQA-B8B2 . Whether it has a sustainable business model is unclear. Ronald Barba, 'Duolingo Now Valued at Nearly Half a Billion Dollars', Tech.Go, 10 January 2015, http://tech.co/duolingo-raises-45-million-google-capital-2015-06
83. see our web developer's account: Simon Dickson, 'From Babel to Babble', Free Speech Debate, http://freespeechdebate.com/en/2013/11/from-babel-to-babble/
84. photo by Nick Ut, Washington Times, 8 June 1972, http://perma.cc/FV3Y-EAC9
85. Graham et al. 2011
86. see Thomson Reuters, http://wokinfo.com/products_tools/analytical/jcr/ . For Asian catch-up, see Mahbubani 2013, 29
87. see, for example, http://www.oii.ox.ac.uk/vis/images/?src=4e3c026c/journal_location.png
88. chorus from The Rock, quoted in Post 2012, 95
89. WolframAlpha, http://www.wolframalpha.com/ . More recently checked, WolframAlpha responds, less honestly, 'development of this topic is under investigation'
90. Weizenbaum 1984, 227
91. Keen 2007
92. Lanier 2011, 49
93. Veen et al. 2006. See also Wim Veen, 'Homo Zappiens: Learning and Knowledge: The Digital Mindset', http://perma.cc/2R7P-J7D5
94. Carr 2010, 27

4. JOURNALISM

1. on the pnyx and the institution of the assembly more broadly, see Hansen 1999, Ober 2008 and Sluiter et al., eds. 2004. I am most grateful to Josiah Ober and Carol

Atack for talking me through this fascinating topic. For a magnificently learned debate about the number of citizens who would have fitted into the physical space of the pnyx, an argument which revolves at one point around the difference in size between modern Western and ancient Greek buttocks, see Forsén et al., eds. 1996, esp. 18. For a photograph of the speaker's platform as it is today, taken by the author in summer 2015, see http://freespeechdebate.com/en/the-project/ . Since I am using the word pnyx in a broader sense, I have silently lowered its initial letter from the more conventional, historical Pnyx

2. Christine Haughney, 'A Leaner Times Aims for Global Growth', New York Times, 13 October 2013, http://www.nytimes.com/2013/10/14/business/media/a-leaner-times -aims-for-global-growth.html?_r=0, and conversations with New York Times journalists. The Guardian developed a comparable strategy

3. Ober 1998, 248, and Plato's Apology, 26 d–e, where reference is made to texts by Anaxagoras being available for sale for a drachma, see Plato 2003, 52 and 218. Note that Isocrates was actually making an argument almost the opposite of Milton's, arguing that authority should be put back in the hands of the counsel of supposedly wise elders who met on the hill called the Areo Pagos

4. Schudson 2008, 11

5. on that 'invention of news', see Pettegree 2014

6. Starr 2004, xi

7. Starr 2004, 30ff

8. Hallin et al. 2004 and, for a wider trawl, their own follow-up study Hallin et al., eds. 2012

9. the original can be found in Löwith 1998, 60. Hegel's remark is widely quoted from the reference to it in Anderson 1983, but Anderson does not emphasise the crucial word 'realistic'

10. quoted in Schudson 2008, 20

11. quoted in Schudson 2008, 203. He takes this story from the memoirs of Katharine Graham, then publisher of the Washington Post

12. see Ober 2008, esp. chapter 4, and Coleman et al. 2009, 9

13. Thomas Jefferson to Edward Carrington, 16 January 1787, in Boyd, ed. 1950 [1787], 48–49, http://perma.cc/N4NQ-Q8RG

14. censor's verdict dated 3 April 1989, addressed to the magazine Znak, http://freespeech debate.com/en/discuss/polish-censors-verdict/

15. see my account in Garton Ash 1989, 143–44

16. quoted in Yu Hua, 'Censorship's Many Faces', New York Times, 27 February 2013, http://www.nytimes.com/2013/02/28/opinion/yu-censorships-many-faces.html

17. Scammell 1983

18. I owe the details of this story to Aung San Suu Kyi's late husband, Michael Aris, who showed me some of these *longyis*. For more detail on Burmese censorship, see Timothy Garton Ash, 'Choices for an Uncrowned Queen', New York Review of Books, 6 June 2013, http://www.nybooks.com/articles/archives/2013/jun/06/burma -choices-uncrowned-queen/

19. for the dissemination of his biography of the shah, personal information from Abbas Milani

20. Conyers Middleton, 1742: *The History of the Life of Marcus Tullius Cicero, 3rd ed.*, quoted in the *Oxford English Dictionary* entry for 'censor', sense. Middleton writes that the election of censors was introduced at the same time to 'cure [the] corruption of morals, which had infected all orders . . . These censors were the guardians of the discipline and manners of the city, and had a power to punish vice and immorality . . . in all ranks of men, from the highest to the lowest . . . Their authority . . . was exercised with that severity which the libertinism of the times required: for they expelled above sixty-four from the senate, for . . . taking money for judging causes'

21. Thomas Jefferson to Edward Carrington, 16 January 1787, in Boyd, ed. 1950 [1787], 48–49, http://perma.cc/N4NQ-Q8RG

22. see Darnton 2014, 44 and Timothy Garton Ash, 'Censored!', New York Review of Books, 23 October 2014, http://www.nybooks.com/articles/archives/2014/oct/23/robert-darnton-censored/

23. see Rebecca Simpson, 'A Century of British Film Censorship', The National Archives, 31 December 2012, http://perma.cc/BD9P-KPG9

24. A. O. Scott, 'This (New) American Life', New York Times, 9 December 2008, http://www.nytimes.com/2008/12/10/movies/10wend.html?_r=0&pagewanted=print

25. see http://www.levesoninquiry.org.uk

26. Daily Mail editorial, 30 November 2012, and The Sun, 27 October 2013

27. see the excellent account in Bollinger 2010, 29–35, from which these quotations are taken

28. to give just one example, in 2011, the same BBC material was regulated differently when broadcast on a BBC television channel, when published on the BBC website and when sold commercially abroad by BBC Worldwide. See Fielden 2011, 3

29. see Stewart Purvis's 2010 Royal Television Society Fleming Memorial Lecture, https://perma.cc/GWE5-XGY2 , quote on 14

30. Onora O'Neill, 'The Rights of Journalism and the Needs of Audiences', Reuters Memorial Lecture, November 2011, http://perma.cc/6V5D-URF7

31. see BBC, 'Editorial Guidelines', http://www.bbc.co.uk/editorialguidelines/ , and New York Times, 'Standards and Ethics', http://www.nytco.com/who-we-are/culture/standards-and-ethics/

32. for the leaked one, found via Bing, not Google, see https://perma.cc/LXM7-ZNMZ?type=source . Google published a watered-down version of the document in 2012, after it was leaked; see http://perma.cc/K8XC-FEAD

33. see microformats, http://perma.cc/Z27Q-JR5Y ; Media Standards Trust, 'Transparency Initiative', http://perma.cc/VH4H-AFDH ; Evan Sandhaus, 'rNews Is Here. And This Is What It Means', New York Times, 16 February 2012, http://open.blogs.nytimes.com/2012/02/16/rnews-is-here-and-this-is-what-it-means/?_r=3%20and%20https://schema.org

34. Fielden 2011, 117–27

35. see Peter Bajomi-Lazar, 'Hungary's New Media Regulation', Free Speech Debate, http://freespeechdebate.com/en/case/hungarys-new-media-regulation/

36. Katolikie Universiteit 2009. For the tool, see K. U. Leuven—ICRI, 'Independent Study for Indicators on Media Pluralism', http://perma.cc/H9Q9-PZXQ

37. originally in the New Yorker, 14 May 1960, reprinted in Liebling 1975, 32. Figure for competing dailies from Hallin et al. 2004, 220

38. see Felipe Correa, 'Rede Globo & the 1989 Brazilian Election', Free Speech Debate, http://freespeechdebate.com/en/case/rede-globo-and-the-brazilian-elections-of-1989/

39. see Kerem Öktem, 'Why Turkey's Mainstream Media Preferred Penguins to Protest', Free Speech Debate, http://freespeechdebate.com/en/2013/06/why-turkeys-mainstream-media-preferred-penguins-to-protest/

40. Collier 2008, 147–49, and Hackett et al. 2005, 114

41. the full story is told on a delightful website, see 'Power without Responsibility—The Prerogative of the Harlot throughout the Ages', This Day in Quotes, http://perma.cc/D3FS-UBC6 . This links to the source for the story told by Kipling's son, an address to the members of the Kipling Society delivered in 1971

42. quoted in Lloyd 2004, 209

43. The Sun, 11 April 1992. See 'It's The Sun Wot Won It', Wikipedia article, http://perma.cc/82UG-LHAP , and J. Curtice, 'Was It The Sun Wot Won It Again? The Influence of Newspapers in the 1997 Election Campaign', a working paper for the Centre for Research into Elections and Social Trends, http://perma.cc/59JG-34LQ

44. a point strongly made by Onora O'Neill, 'The Rights of Journalism and the Needs of Audiences', Reuters Memorial Lecture, November 2011, http://perma.cc/6V5D-URF7

45. see the content analysis reported by Martin Moore, 'How the British Press Distorted Reporting of . . . the British Press', Free Speech Debate, http://freespeechdebate.com/en/discuss/how-the-british-press-distorted-reporting-of-the-british-press/

46. May 2014 National Occupational Employment and Wage Estimates, United States Bureau of Labor Statistics, http://perma.cc/JUQ4-CSXE . I am grateful to Rasmus Nielsen for drawing this source to my attention

47. Davies 2008, 59

48. see Cardiff School of Journalism, 'The UK "Quality" Press, Broadsheet Journalism and Public Relations', http://perma.cc/D4CY-PQKB

49. see Brian Pellot, 'Does Money Have the Right to Speak?', Free Speech Debate, http://freespeechdebate.com/en/case/does-money-have-the-right-to-speak/

50. Ronald Dworkin, 'The Decision That Threatens Democracy', New York Review of Books, 13 May 2010, http://www.nybooks.com/articles/archives/2010/may/13/decision-threatens-democracy/ , and the comprehensive discussion in Post 2914. Lawrence Lessig takes a slightly more sympathetic view in Lessig 2012, 238–45

51. Ashley Parker, '"Corporations Are People", Romney Tells Iowa Hecklers Angry over His Tax Policy', New York Times, 11 August 2011, http://www.nytimes.com/2011/08/12/us/politics/12romney.html

52. Liebling 1975, 6

53. this comment was actually posted under the draft principle about knowledge; see comment thread on Timothy Garton Ash, 'Knowledge', Free Speech Debate, http://freespeechdebate.com/en/principle/p-3/info/

54. Drèze et al. 2013, esp. 262–67

55. Painter 2013, 65–67

56. quoted in Moggridge 2010, 243

57. see Pro Publica, 'About Us', http://perma.cc/ZU9B-DAXV

58. see Robert Peston, 'Robert Peston's James Cameron Memorial Lecture—Full Text', *The Guardian*, 26 November 2013, http://perma.cc/ALU6-EXBZ

59. Gladstone 2011, 69–70

60. the figures are for 1968 for Denmark and 1973 for Norway, see Mancini 2012, 264

61. quoted in Mancini 2011, 41

62. Mancini 2011, 267–69

63. 'The Daily Show', author's notes from an episode in August 2013. Unfortunately, these episodes appear to be no longer available in full online, so we do not have an exact date

64. Sambrook 2012, 30

65. Sunstein 2007, 114–17

66. Newman et al., eds. 2013, 105, https://perma.cc/5499-5UAV . In the text, I follow their aggregate figures. Our Figure 13 excludes 'urban Brazil', which was included in the Reuters Institute survey, since this does not seem directly comparable with the percentages for whole countries. For the follow-up, see Newman et al., eds. 2014, 16, https://perma.cc/YMJ6-YCBY

67. Sunstein 2007, 4

68. see https://storify.com/

69. Robert Cottrell, 'My Life as a Screen Slave', *Financial Times*, 15 February 2013

70. fact-checking sites include factcheck.org, fullfact.org, politifact.com and washington-post.com/blogs/fact-checker/. For one account of verification, see Malachy Browne, 'Storyful: Verifying Citizen Journalism', Free Speech Debate, http://freespeech debate.com/en/discuss/verifying-citizen-journalism/

71. Jefferson 1787 in Boyd, ed. 1950 [1787], http://perma.cc/N4NQ-Q8RG

72. Coleman et al. 2009, 45

73. for an interesting discussion of citizen journalism, see Turi Munthe, 'Has Demotix Democratised Journalism?', Free Speech Debate, http://freespeechdebate.com/en/media/has-demotix-changed-the-internet/

74. Newman et al., eds. 2014, 66

75. Gant 2007

76. U.S. Senate, 'Senate Manual Containing the Standing Rules, Orders, Laws, and Resolutions Affecting the Business of the United States Senate', http://perma.cc/UCA2-M9PH

77. Kovach et al. 2007

78. quoted in Gladstone 2011, 101

79. Arendt 2006, 255

80. Schudson 2008, 10. One could also interpret Arendt's ordering another way, with the humble reporter bringing up the rear

81. Tomalin 1975, 77 and 93

82. Tomalin 1975, 83, and Garton Ash 2009
83. this was quoted to me by the veteran BBC correspondent Charles Wheeler
84. Davies 2008, 12
85. Jay Rosen, 'Objectivity as a Form of Persuasion: A Few Notes for Marcus Brauchli', 7 July 2010, http://perma.cc/N47X-SGVN
86. Orwell 1987 [1938], 186
87. on Youssef, see Max Gallien, 'Egypt: The Show Is Over', Free Speech Debate, http://freespeechdebate.com/en/discuss/127222/
88. see Domosławski 2012 and Timothy Garton Ash, 'Bearing Witness Is a Sacred Trust', The Guardian, 10 March 2010, http://perma.cc/RQ28-AZQ7
89. see 'About Today', BBC IPlayer Radio, http://perma.cc/95T4-EZMT, and 'The Reason Today Is Losing Listeners', The Guardian, 26 September 2014, http://perma.cc/Y3M3-2KNF
90. Benkler 2006, chapter 7

5. DIVERSITY

1. the 2011 Canadian census gave a figure of 51 percent foreign-born in Toronto; see Garton Ash et al. 2013, 12
2. see Baker et al. 2000
3. see Timothy Garton Ash, 'Freedom & Diversity: A Liberal Pentagram for Living Together', New York Review of Books, 22 November 2012, http://www.nybooks.com/articles/archives/2012/nov/22/freedom-diversity-liberal-pentagram/
4. reported to me by Stanford historian David Kennedy, with whose kind permission I quote it here
5. quoted in Jeff Zeleny, 'Obama, in His New Role as President-Elect, Calls for Stimulus Package', New York Times, 7 November 2008, http://www.nytimes.com/2008/11/08/us/politics/08obama.html?_r=0
6. 'Into the Melting Pot', The Economist, 8 February 2014, http://www.economist.com/news/britain/21595908-rapid-rise-mixed-race-britain-changing-neighbourhoodsand-perplexing
7. see, among others, Carter 1998, Sacks 2007, Shils 1997, Sennett 2012
8. Aristotle 1996, 31
9. see the extensive discussion in Benner 2009
10. Shils 1997, 49
11. Hobbes 2012 [1651], 150, part 1, chapter 11
12. Montesquieu 1989 [1748], 317
13. Shils 1997, 322
14. Shils 1997, 338
15. see Margalit 1998
16. Walzer 1997, xii
17. Scanlon 2003, 187
18. quoted in Schultze 1969, 11
19. Popper 1966 [1945], vol. 1, 265

20. Whitman 2000

21. see Maryam Omidi, 'Lost in Translation?', Free Speech Debate, http://freespeech debate.com/en/2012/02/lost-in-translation/

22. Sacks 2007, 184–86

23. see a first presentation of his argument at Leslie Green, 'Right Speech', Free Speech Debate, http://freespeechdebate.com/en/media/right-speech/

24. Post 1990, esp. 634 and 683

25. Ofcom, 'The Ofcom Broadcasting Code', http://perma.cc/Q89M-CJXW

26. Rushdie 2011, 71–72

27. for the next two paragraphs, see Timothy Garton Ash, 'Germans, More or Less', New York Review of Books, 24 February 2011, http://www.nybooks.com/articles/archives/2011/feb/24/germans-more-or-less/

28. for varying estimates, see Garton Ash et al. 2013, 14–15

29. in Herz et al. 2012, 217–41

30. in Coliver, ed. 1982, 156

31. in Appignanesi, ed. 2005, 60

32. quoted by Robert Post in Hare et al., eds. 2009, 124

33. the logic is well revealed by the 2014 report of Britain's Law Commission, 'Hate Crime: Should the Current Offences Be Extended?', http://perma.cc/S67U-VRPR

34. these wordings are taken from the relevant laws as quoted in an extremely useful summary: EU Network of Independent Experts on Fundamental Rights, 'Combating Racism and Xenophobia through Criminal Legislation: The Situation in the EU Member States', 28 November 2005, http://perma.cc/3FMZ-PCFB . There too you can find the variant formulations in the legislation of other EU member states. Wordings are correct as of October 2015

35. see Eric Heinze, 'Nineteen Arguments for Hate Speech Bans—and against Them', Free Speech Debate, http://freespeechdebate.com/en/discuss/nineteen-arguments-for-hate-speech-bans-and-against-them/ . A revised version of this was subsequently incorporated into his book *Hate Speech and Democratic Citizenship*, which I have included in the Bibliography (Heinze 2016) but not been able to use in its final form, although he kindly shared with me an earlier version

36. Waldron 2012, 96–97

37. see Judith Bruhn, 'Cyber-Bullying That Led to Suicide', Free Speech Debate, http://freespeechdebate.com/en/case/cyber-bullying-that-led-to-suicide/ , and on revenge porn, see Max Harris, 'Should "Revenge Porn" Be Illegal?', Free Speech Debate, http://freespeechdebate.com/en/discuss/privacy-free-speech-and-sexual-images-the-challenges-faced-by-legal-responses-to-revenge-porn/

38. quoted thus by Malik 2009, 190. But see Aesop 1998, 240

39. Wittgenstein 1980, 46

40. see Office of the High Commissioner for Human Rights, 'International Convention on the Elimination of All Forms of Racial Discrimination', http://perma.cc/9JRK-9MCF

41. see the amicus brief of the German Institute for Human Rights in support of the CERD's position, which contains a detailed discussion of Sarrazin's statements: German Institute for Human Rights, 'Amicus Curiae Brief', http://perma.cc/5PH2-94U8

42. see Permanent Mission of the Federal Republic of Germany to the Office of the United Nations and to Other International Organizations Geneva, 'Note Verbale Pol-10-504.14 SE TBB', http://perma.cc/7VJH-CFPN

43. Margalit 1998, 183

44. quoted in Hart 2009, 25

45. see Conseil d'Etat, 'Assemblée du 27 octobre 1995, 143578, inédit au recueil Lebon', http://perma.cc/M3FH-K8ZB , and the UN Human Rights Committee's response to Wackenheim's further appeal: UN Human Rights Committee, 'Manuel Wackenheim v France, Communication No 854/1999, U.N. Doc. CCPR/C/75/D/854/1999 (2002)', http://perma.cc/JA5G-N4S7 . I am most grateful to Jeremy Waldron for drawing my attention to this case. Rosen 2012, 63–69, gives a vivid and sensitive account of it, adding some interesting detail

46. Theresa May on the BBC 'Today' programme, 27 May 2013

47. Bleich 2011, 142. For Bardot, see Michèle Finck, 'Brigitte Bardot's Repeated Convictions for Inciting Racial Hatred', Free Speech Debate, http://freespeechdebate .com/en/case/brigitte-bardots-repeated-convictions-for-inciting-racial-hatred/, and Bruce Crumley, 'Is Brigitte Bardot Bashing Islam?', Time, 15 April 2008, http://perma .cc/M4E8-VP2X . On Morin, see Jon Henley, 'Le Monde Editor Defamed Jews', The Guardian, 3 June 2005, http://perma.cc/CUJ5-MN8L . On Vanneste, see Julia Ziemer, 'French Politician Vindicated over Homophobic Comments', PinkNews, http://perma.cc/MMB3-NGN3 . The general point is well made by Aryeh Neier, 'What's more important, human dignity or freedom of speech?' Columbia Journalism Review, 2012, and Neier 2014

48. Malik in Herz et al. 2012, 84

49. Stefancic et al. 1993, 745

50. quoted in Nicolas Kulish, 'Shift in Europe Seen in Debate on Immigrants', New York Times, 27 July 2011, http://www.nytimes.com/2011/07/28/world/europe/28europe .html?pagewanted=all&_r=0

51. House of Lords Debate, 18 May 2009, Lords Hansard, Column 1246, http://perma.cc/ F8PS-A5K5

52. see Timothy Garton Ash, 'In Brazil I Glimpsed a Possible Future in Which There Is Only One Race', The Guardian, 11 July 2007, http://perma.cc/QQJ3-M6VN

53. Dunbar 2014, 14

54. Daniel Defoe, 'The True Born Englishman', Poetry Foundation, http://perma.cc/ KMY4-TH2M

55. author's notes, Sao Paolo, 26 June 2007

56. Hollinger 2000, 39

57. see Thea Lim, '100% Cablinasian: Getting the Race Facts Right on Tiger Woods', Racialicious, http://perma.cc/4E4U-QP8Q

58. quoted in Lukes 2003, 34

59. Coetzee 1996, ix and 5

60. Barrow 2005, 266

61. Malik 2009, 184

62. World Intellectual Property Organisation, 'The Indian Penal Code (IPC) 1860 Act No. 45, 6 October 1960, https://perma.cc/L27B-QZ4D?type=source

63. Dean Nelson, 'Thomas Babington Macaulay: A Giant of the British Empire', Daily Telegraph, 27 October 2010, http://www.telegraph.co.uk/news/worldnews/asia/india/8090422/Thomas-Babington-Macaulay-a-giant-of-the-British-Empire.html

64. Masani 2013, 121

65. see Nair 2013. I am grateful to Pratap Bhanu Mehta for drawing my attention to this article. Current text of 295A. World Intellectual Property Organisation, 'The Indian Penal Code (IPC) 1860 Act No. 45, 6 October 1960, https://perma.cc/L27B-QZ4D?type=source

66. see my account in Timothy Garton Ash, 'India: Watch What You Say', New York Review of Books, 25 April 2013, http://www.nybooks.com/articles/archives/2013/apr/25/india-watch-what-you-say/

67. in Pratap Bhanu Mehta, 'Freedom's Our Defence', Indian Express, 4 March 2010, http://perma.cc/3GZJ-BR85

68. Charles Moore, 'Rage, Rather than Reason, Drives the Debate on Freedom of Speech', Daily Telegraph, 10 January 2014, http://www.telegraph.co.uk/news/uknews/law-and-order/10563744/Rage-rather-than-reason-drives-the-debate-on-freedom-of-speech.html

69. 'Muslim Head Says Gays "harmful"', BBC News, 3 January 2006, http://perma.cc/2TXT-A9YZ

70. Foxman et al. 2013, 45–46 and 107–8

71. data from CIA World Factbook, 'Obesity—Adult Prevalence', http://perma.cc/5EZK-U4YW : US: 33.0 percent, UK: 26.9 percent, Canada: 26.2 percent

72. see Puhl et al. 2010, 1019

73. quoted in the report of the House of Lords Select Committee on Religious Offences in England and Wales, HL, Paper 95-1, 10 April 2003, Para. 52

74. see Timothy Garton Ash, 'The Preacher against Homosexuality', Free Speech Debate, http://freespeechdebate.com/en/case/the-preacher-against-homosexuality , and Hare et al., eds. 2009, 30–40

75. see '"Gay" Police Horse Case Dropped', BBC News, 12 January 2006, http://perma.cc/7B2Q-UFVB , and Melissa Locker, 'You May Now Call a Police Horse "Gay" in the U.K.', Time, 16 January 2013, http://perma.cc/UQ7R-CK7V

76. see Anil Dawar, 'Schoolboy Avoids Prosecution for Branding Scientology a "Cult"', The Guardian, 23 May 2008, http://perma.cc/8YDA-S2HL , and 'Free Speech Victory as Charges against Teen Anti-Scientology Protestor Dropped', Liberty, 23 May 2008, http://perma.cc/M9EW-5BXW

77. see '"Insulting Words" Crime Ditched', BBC News, 14 January 2013, http://perma.cc/2TUJ-JTY3

78. see Casey Selwyn, 'Westboro Baptist Church: The Right to Free Speech?', Free Speech Debate, http://freespeechdebate.com/en/case/westboro-baptist-church-the-right-to-free-speech/

79. Kevin Landrigan, 'NH Senate Passes 25-Foot Buffer Zone around Abortion Clinics', The Telegraph, 20 February 2014, http://www.nashuatelegraph.com/news/statenewengl

and/1029349-469/nh-senate-passes-25-foot-buffer-zone-around.html . On the Supreme Court decision, see Max Harris, 'US Supreme Court Strikes Down Law Creating "Buffer Zone" around Abortion Clinics', Free Speech Debate, http://freespeechdebate.com/en/case/us-supreme-court-strikes-down-law-creating-buffer-zone-around-abortion-clinics/

80. Shah Rukh Khan, 'Sad, i read so much judgements, jingoism, religious intolerance on the net & i use to think, this platform wl change narrowmindedness, but no!', 9 January 2013, http://perma.cc/2C3U-9NXK . As of October 2015, Shah Rukh Khan was still active on Twitter, with more than 16 million followers

81. see the full text of the Norwegian constitution on the parliament's website at 'The Constitution', Stortinget, http://perma.cc/XE8X-UJ5E

82. see Timothy Garton Ash, 'Germans, More or Less', New York Review of Books, 24 February 2011, http://www.nybooks.com/articles/archives/2011/feb/24/germans-more-or-less/

83. the school was the Oxford Spires Academy, which is, despite its grand name, a formerly failing school in one of the poorer parts of Oxford, now turned into an academy, roughly equivalent to an American charter school. A first account of these techniques can be found in Alan Howe, 'Developing the Talking School: Action Research at Oxford Spires and St Mark's Church of England Academies', CfBT, http://perma.cc/73FL-2E9U

84. see Banaji et al. 2013

85. see Max Harris, 'A Landmark Canadian Hate Speech Case: Her Majesty the Queen v Keegstra', Free Speech Debate, http://freespeechdebate.com/en/case/a-landmark-canadian-hate-speech-case-her-majesty-the-queen-v-keegstra/ , and Brettschneider 2012, 102–3

86. see Marc-Antoine Dilhac, '"They Used the Oven to Get Tanned, You Know . . ."', Free Speech Debate, http://freespeechdebate.com/en/discuss/talking-about-the-holocaust-between-the-walls/

87. reproduced in Cortese 2008, 61. See the snippet on Instagram, https://perma.cc/2NRV-SAL5?type=source, and on the Visual Culture Blog at 'BMW AD', Visual Culture Blog, http://perma.cc/B5B4-WRQJ . Despite attempts by email, letter and Twitter, I and the Free Speech Debate team received no reply from BMW, confirming, denying or commenting upon this advertisement

88. see Sergey Fadeev, 'Is It a Crime to Offend Bread?', Free Speech Debate, http://freespeechdebate.com/en/2014/02/is-it-a-crime-to-insult-bread/

89. quoted in Hrant Dink Foundation, Media Watch on Hate Speech Periodical Report, January–April 2012, 38, https://perma.cc/WD32-6LPT?type=source

90. on Roma, see Garton Ash et al. 2013 and helpful 'explainer' at 'Explainers: The Roma and Open Society', Open Society Foundations, http://perma.cc/SRV6-UJSD . On reporting of homosexuality, see Brian Pellot, '(Not) Reporting Homosexuality in the Middle East', Free Speech Debate, http://freespeechdebate.com/en/case/not-reporting-homosexuality-in-the-middle-east/

91. see Katalin Barsony, 'Katalin Barsony on Empowering Roma with Technology', Free Speech Debate, http://freespeechdebate.com/en/media/katalin-barsony-on-empowering-roma-with-technology/

92. quoted in Hrant Dink Foundation, Media Watch on Hate Speech Periodical Report, January–April 2012, 38, https://perma.cc/WD32-6LPT?type=source

93. see Taj Hargey, 'The Oxford Sex Ring and the Preachers Who Teach Young Muslim Men That White Girls Are Cheap', Daily Mail, 15 May 2013, http://www.dailymail.co.uk/debate/article-2325185/The-Oxford-sex-ring-preachers-teach-young-Muslim-men-white-girls-cheap.html

94. see Eugene Volokh, 'First Amendment Protection for Search Engine Search Results', 20 April 2012, http://perma.cc/7YSD-9W6P

95. see Google, '2014 Winter Olympics', http://perma.cc/AXT8-UYE3

96. YouTube, 'Statistics', http://perma.cc/YB9N-88NE , and Naina Khedekar, 'We Now Upload and Share over 1.8 Billion Photos Each Day: Meeker Internet Report', Tech2, http://perma.cc/36UC-3RWW

97. conversation with Monika Bickert, Facebook's head of Global Product Policy, Stanford University, 14 August 2015

98. see Laura Bleakley, 'Effin in County Limerick Seen as "Offensive" on Facebook', BBC News, 2 December 2011, http://perma.cc/83S8-FAPC

99. Jeffrey Rosen, 'The Delete Squad', New Republic, 29 April 2013, http://perma.cc/768T-CLL7

100. see Tim Wu, 'When Censorship Makes Sense: How YouTube Should Police Hate Speech', 18 September 2012, New Republic, http://perma.cc/S7HC-V4ED

101. Victoria Grand, Head of Public Policy at YouTube, London, 5 November 2013

102. I am grateful to Richard Allan for supplying the draft on which my version of 'Allan's pyramid' is based

103. see Foxman et al. 2013, 133–37

104. see Sluiter et al., eds. 2004, 166–67

105. see Nimi Hoffmann and Maryam Omidi, 'Zuma and His Spear', Free Speech Debate, http://freespeechdebate.com/en/case/zuma-and-his-spear/

106. I owe this story to the Polish writer Konstanty Gebert

107. Oz 2012, 73–74

108. Chaplinsky v New Hampshire 315 (1942) 315 U.S. 568

109. Pearson 2005, 77

110. quoted in the wonderful anthology by Galnoor et al. 1985, 30, 36

111. Stepan 2012, 381–82 and see also De Jong 2005

112. quoted in Sluiter et al., eds. 2004, 410–12

113. the matter is complicated, but only slightly, by the fact that this was covertly recorded at a private performance. See Inti Landauro, 'France Faces Court Test over Free-Speech Case', Wall Street Journal, 8 January 2014, http://www.wsj.com/news/articles/SB10001424052702304347904579308710662277206 ; Hugh Carnegy, 'Paris Challenges Comedian Dieudonné over Anti-Semitism', Financial Times, 6 January 2014, http://www.ft.com/cms/s/0/461db31a-76d2-11e3-a253-00144feabdc0.html#axzz34QMAn4r2 and Christopher Caldwell, 'France Blurs the Line between Comedy and Crime', Financial Times, 10 January 2014, http://www.ft.com/cms/s/0/8cffeed0-7923-11e3-b381-00144feabdc0.html?siteedition=uk#axzz34QMAn4r2

114. Rowson 2009, 22–23, 54–55
115. Episode 145, 'The Tada Tada', 24 April 1997, quoted in Gould 2005, 16
116. his Jerusalem speech is reprinted in Kundera 2005, 157–65, this on 158. See also his reflections in Kundera 1995, 1–34
117. Smith 2001, 7
118. Nussbaum 2012, chapter 5
119. see Ricoeur 1992
120. this is the opening line of L. P. Hartley, *The Go-Between*, first published in 1953
121. for a sensitive and robust exploration of the history of the word 'nigger', see Kennedy 2003
122. Julius 2002, 222–35
123. Sutherland 1982, 23
124. see Sedley 2011, 398
125. see Tom de Castella et al., 'How Did the Pro-Paedophile Group PIE Exist Openly for 10 Years?', BBC News, 27 February 2014, http://perma.cc/9KHR-7A4T
126. see Julius 2003 and, for the opposing view, Raine 2006
127. Mann 1973, 103. This comes in his magnificent New Year 1937 response to a note informing him that he had been stripped of his honorary doctorate by the Philosophy Faculty of Bonn University, because he had been deprived of German citizenship by the Nazis
128. Katie Engelhart, 'Does a British Museum Exhibition Turn Porn into Art?', Free Speech Debate, http://freespeechdebate.com/en/discuss/does-a-british-museum-exhibition -turn-porn-into-art/
129. Warburton 2009, 74. Kim Wilkinson, 'Can Australia Distinguish between Art and Pornography?', Free Speech Debate, http://freespeechdebate.com/en/discuss/can -australia-distinguish-between-art-and-pornography/ ; Rónán Ó Fathaigh, 'Child Pornography and Freedom of Expression', Free Speech Debate, http://freespeech debate.com/en/discuss/child-pornography-and-freedom-of-expression/ . The Stras-bourg court judgement is Karttunen v Finland, Application no. 1685/10, 10 May 2011, admissibility decision
130. I quote Ogas from a transcript of a BBC Radio 4 Analysis programme: 'Pornogra-phy: What Do We Know?', presented by Jo Fidgen, first broadcast 24 June 2013. Mac-Kinnon describes it as 'masturbation material' in MacKinnon 1993, 17
131. quoted in Warburton 2009, 60
132. see Erika Rackley et al., 'The Cultural Harm of Rape Pornography', Free Speech De-bate, http://freespeechdebate.com/en/discuss/the-cultural-harm-of-rape-pornography/
133. see Jo Fidgen, 'Free to Fantasise? Pornography and Its Harms', Free Speech Debate, http://freespeechdebate.com/en/discuss/free-to-fantasise-pornography-and-its-harms/ , and the BBC Analysis programme mentioned in note 130. Trying to understand more about this subject, I organised a workshop on it in Oxford with my colleague Jeremy Waldron. It was a stimulating conversation of robust civility, but I must admit that I came away with the same conclusion. As Fidgen mentions, she was a participant in our workshop

134. MacKinnon 1993, 37
135. Barendt 2007, 373–74
136. for Japan, see Diamond et al. 1999 and for Denmark, Barendt 2007, 373–74
137. quoted in transcript of BBC Radio 4 Analysis: 'Pornography: What Do We Know?', presented by Jo Fidgen, first broadcast 24 June 2013. For the academic papers see, amongst others, Hald et al. 2010 and Kingston et al. 2009
138. a tiny semantic indicator is the care with which I have, in this book, used 'her or his' or 'his or her', 'he or she' or 'she or he', etc., once the exception, this is now the norm
139. see Ogas et al., 2012, 8 and 290, where they note that the 2.5 million figure dates from 30 August 2010
140. see Max Harris, 'Should "Revenge Porn" Be Illegal?', Free Speech Debate, http://freespeechdebate.com/en/discuss/privacy-free-speech-and-sexual-images-the-challenges-faced-by-legal-responses-to-revenge-porn/
141. on 'objectification', see the discussion in Langton 2009, 10–19 and chapters 10–12
142. Justine Roberts at a Google Big Tent, 18 May 2011. Quotation from author's notes. Maryam Omidi, 'India's Cartoon Porn Star', Free Speech Debate, http://freespeechdebate.com/en/case/indias-cartoon-porn-star
143. see Sebastian Huempfer, 'Free Speech in an Unfair World', Free Speech Debate, http://freespeechdebate.com/en/discuss/free-speech-in-an-unfair-world/
144. Jeff Howard, 'Fighting for Free Speech in an Unjust World', Free Speech Debate, http://freespeechdebate.com/en/discuss/fighting-for-free-speech-in-an-unjust-world/
145. in Roberts et al. 2009, 48–49
146. I quote from the translation of Schiller's *Wilhelm Tell* in Schiller 2005 [1804], 53
147. see Roberts and Garton Ash 2009, 388
148. see his 1985 'Letter from the Gdańsk Prison', quoted in Garton Ash 1999, 71

6. RELIGION

1. in Garton Ash, ed. 2009, 82
2. see the French scholar Alain Bouldoires's account of his research project on blasphemy laws in Europe: Alain Bouldoires, 'Should Europe Introduce a "Right to Blaspheme"?', Free Speech Debate, http://freespeechdebate.com/en/media/blasphemy-laws-in-europe/
3. see Calhoun 1992, esp. 35–36, 213–15, and Habermas's partial acknowledgement of the point in Calhoun 1992, 464–65
4. see Ian Johnson's extensive writings on the subject in the New York Review of Books and forthcoming book on the subject. Even according to official figures, there are more Christians in China than there are members of the Communist Party
5. World Intellectual Property Organisation, 'The Indian Penal Code (IPC) 1860 Act No. 45, 6 October 1960, https://perma.cc/L27B-QZ4D?type=source , section 295A, as amended. The wording was changed from 'Her Majesty's subjects' to 'citizens of India' in 1950, and the jail term increased from two years to three in 1961. For the origins of this section, see Nair 2013

6. section 295c of the Pakistan Penal Code (Act XLV of 1860) as amended, http://perma .cc/RJ8N-GJDS

7. Kołakowski 1982, 218 and 182

8. O'Donovan 1999, 275

9. *Oxford English Dictionary*, entry for 'religion'

10. Radcliffe 2005, 161 and 209

11. quoted in the translation by R. C. Zaehner in Kołakowski 1982, 165

12. quoted in Kołakowski 1982, 183

13. see Barrett 1991

14. McGrath 2007, 18–19

15. Sajó, ed. 2007, 32

16. Prothero 2011, 69

17. Ahmed El-Tayyeb, 'Al-Azhar's "Bill of Rights"', Free Speech Debate, http://freespeech debate.com/en/discuss/al-azhars-bill-of-rights/

18. Marshall et al. 2011, 63

19. section 29A of the amended Public Order Act 1986, quoted and discussed by Barendt 2011, 48

20. Mill 1991 [1859], 30

21. I here draw on Givens 2007 and my own summary in Timothy Garton Ash, 'Could You Vote for a Man Who Abides by Moronish Wisdom?', The Guardian, 27 December 2007, http://perma.cc/2PSW-8L36 . For black people in 1978, see Pinker 2011, 678

22. see report by Douglas Frantz, 'U.S. Immigration Court Grants Asylum to German Scientologist', New York Times, 8 November 1997, http://www.nytimes.com/1997/11/08/us/us-immigration-court-grants-asylum-to-german-scientologist.html

23. R (on the application of Hodkin and another) v Registrar General of Births, Deaths and Marriages [2013] UKSC 77, [2013] WLR (D) 492, http://perma.cc/E354-EE7C

24. 'Operation Thetan level I', xenu.net, http://perma.cc/H9Z9-HWWE

25. Karen Armstrong, 'An Inability to Tolerate Islam Contradicts Western Values', The Guardian, 21 July 2007, http://perma.cc/K4A7-YDNG

26. BBC Today programme, 6 October 2007

27. Christopher Hitchens, 'Why Are We So Scared of Offending Muslims?', Slate, 30 July 2007, http://perma.cc/VH9M-5FUK

28. European Delegation to the United Nations New York, 'Joint Statement on Peace and Tolerance by EU High Representative, OIC Secretary General, Arab League Secretary General, and AU Commissioner for Peace and Security', 20 September 2012, http://perma.cc/ZF6X-6F42

29. quoted in John Keane, 'Dalai Lama in Australia', The Conversation, http://perma .cc/2W26-45KH

30. see Darwall 1977. He develops the argument in Darwall 2013

31. Office of the High Commissioner for Human Rights. 'International Covenant on Civil and Political Rights', Article 18, http://perma.cc/V4JK-N7XV . European Court of Human Rights, 'Convention for the Protection of Human Rights and Fundamental Freedoms', Article 9, http://perma.cc/G3LD-N5JP

32. Kołakowski 1990, 120–28

33. on this, see the discussion of Article 9 in Lester et al. 2009, 453–74

34. see Timothy Garton Ash, 'India: Watch What You Say', New York Review of Books, 25 April 2013, http://www.nybooks.com/articles/archives/2013/apr/25/india-watch-what -you-say/

35. I here follow the translation preferred by Rajeev Bhargava in Stepan et al., eds. 2014, 198

36. for the emphasis on listening, see also Dominic Burbidge, 'Free Speech as Seen by a Believer in an Abrahamic Religion', Free Speech Debate, http://freespeechdebate .com/en/discuss/free-speech-as-seen-by-a-believer-in-an-abrahamic-religion/

37. see Dunbar 2004, Wade 2009

38. see Baldwin 2009, 174 and 305. Figures are from 1982 and 1986 for the US, and the source does not seem overwhelmingly rigorous, but even if one halved the reported figures—more than 60 percent in Britain and Germany, more than 50 percent in France—the proportions would still be alarmingly high

39. Burckhardt 1965, 115–16

40. Paine 2010 [1794], 26

41. see Bret Stephens, 'Muslims, Mormons and Liberals. Why Is It OK to Mock One Religion but Not Another?', Wall Street Journal, 19 September 2012, http://www .wsj.com/news/articles/SB10000872396390444450004578002010241044712 , and Katie Engelhart, 'I Enjoyed the Book of Mormon Musical. Now for the Book of Islam?', Free Speech Debate, http://freespeechdebate.com/en/2013/05/i-enjoyed-the-book-of -mormon-musical-now-for-the-book-of-islam/ . It is true that the 2010 comic film 'The Infidel' was relatively calmly received, but it did not directly satirise Islam, let alone the figure of Muhammad, in a way comparable with 'The Book of Mormon'

42. see Mark Thompson, 'Mark Thompson on the BBC and Religion', Free Speech Debate, http://freespeechdebate.com/en/media/mark-thompson-talks-religion/

43. see comment thread on Paul Revoir, 'Christianity Gets Less Sensitive Treatment than Other Religions Admits BBC Chief', Daily Mail, 27 February 2012, http://www .dailymail.co.uk/news/article-2106953/Christianity-gets-sensitive-treatment-religions -admits-BBC-chief.html . See also Timothy Garton Ash, 'One Rule for Jesus, Another for Muhammad?', The Guardian, 14 March 2012, http://perma.cc/X56V-BJF4

44. Nick Cohen, 'Should Christians Kill Mark Thompson?', Spectator, 27 February 2012, http://perma.cc/4KQ7-BSAN

45. on this, see, for example, Stepan et al., eds. 2014 and the monumental Taylor 2007

46. Galatians 5:1

47. Rowan Williams, 'Religious Hatred and Religious Offence', James Callaghan Memorial Lecture, 29 January 2008, http://perma.cc/W2M5-L228

48. see, for example, the chapter by Robert Post in Sajó, ed. 2007, 329–51, esp. 337ff

49. John Milton, 'On His Blindness', Sonnet XVI, https://perma.cc/S7UV -VC9Z?type=source quoted by Kyai Haji Abdurrahman Wahid, a former president of Indonesia, in his Foreword to Marshall et al. 2011, xvii

50. see Henning Koch, 'On Character and Caricature: Freedom of Speech or Freedom to Scorn?' in Koch et al. 2010, 317–50, this on 337

51. for the wages equivalent: data from the Norwegian central bank: Ola H. Grytten, 'Nominal Wages in Norway 1726–1940 by Occupation', Norges Bank Occasional Papers no. 38, http://perma.cc/9FVD-GMB6

52. see Annabelle Chapman, 'A Polish Pop Star Derides the Bible', Free Speech Debate, http://freespeechdebate.com/en/case/a-polish-pop-star-derides-the-bible/

53. Otto-Preminger-Institut v Austria (1994) 19 EHRR 34. See Michele Finck, 'Is the European Court of Human Rights Merely Defending the Uncontroversial?', Free Speech Debate, http://freespeechdebate.com/en/case/is-the-european-court-of-human-rights-merely-defending-the-uncontroversial/ , and accounts in Barendt 2011, Lester et al. 2009, and Hare et al., eds. 2009

54. Wingrove v UK (1997) 24 EHRR 1; see Barendt 2007, 192

55. on the Wilders case, see Rutger Kaput's case study: Rutger Kaput, 'Geert Wilders on Trial', Free Speech Debate, http://freespeechdebate.com/en/case/geert-wilders-on-trial/ , and his Dahrendorf essay, http://perma.cc/R2XM-NUBW . See also Timothy Garton Ash, 'Intimidation and Censorship Are No Answer to This Inflammatory Film', The Guardian, 9 April 2008, http://perma.cc/HP82-M2CH , and Timothy Garton Ash, 'To Fight the Xenophobic Populists, We Need More Free Speech, Not Less', The Guardian, 12 May 2011, http://perma.cc/FK9G-QCEC

56. Statement to the court, 7 February 2011, 'Geert Wilders: The Lights Are Going Out All Over Europe (english subs)', 8 February 2012, https://www.youtube.com/watch?v=opfEJaI2iS4

57. quoted in International Herald Tribune, 24 June 2011

58. the conviction was upheld by the House of Lords in 1979. See Nash 1999, 239–57; Barendt 2007, 186–92; and Anthony Lester in Sajó, ed. 2007, 158–61

59. Anthony Lester in Appignanesi, ed. 2005, 230–31

60. see Public Order Act 1986, s 29J, inserted by the Racial and Religious Hatred Act 2006, http://perma.cc/S4CX-FHCZ , and the account by Anthony Lester in Appignanesi, ed. 2005, 156–58. For the campaign, see Appignanesi, ed. 2005

61. a great deal of research, including questions kindly asked in the House of Lords by Anthony Lester and subsequent correspondence with the Ministry for Justice, has so far failed to establish the precise number. What we know is that from 2006 until 2007 there were two convictions under section 29B (the religious hate speech provision). There were no convictions in 2008 and then, from 2009 until 2012, there were seven convictions under religious or homophobic hate speech provisions. But there is no way to know from the records made available to us how many of these convictions related to religious as opposed to homophobic hate speech. Statistics are not yet available for the period since 2012. The case of the young British Muslim mentioned is R v Ahmad [2012] EWCA Crim 959, [2013] 1 Cr App R (S) 17. I am most grateful to Max Harris for his scrupulous work on this frustrating quest

62. see, for example, our case study by Dominic Burbidge, 'Can Christians Wear the Cross at Work?', Free Speech Debate, http://freespeechdebate.com/en/case/can-christians-wear-the-cross-at-work/ . For Jesus and Mo at the LSE, see this follow-up panel discussion at the LSE: 'Freedom to Offend?', Free Speech Debate, http://freespeechdebate.com/en/media/freedom-to-offend/ . For the Jesus and Mo website, see http://www.jesusandmo.net/

63. see Mohsen Kadivar, 'Islam between Free Speech and Hate Speech', Free Speech Debate, http://freespeechdebate.com/en/discuss/islam-between-free-speech-and-hate-speech/

64. numbers for 2010 from 'The Global Religious Landscape', Pew Research Center, http://perma.cc/WX95-TVBM , and see Figure 17. Projections made in 2015 at 'The Future of World Religions: Population Growth Projections, 2010–2050', Pew Research Center, http://perma.cc/F7X5-CL86

65. MacCulloch 2004, 676

66. Pinker 2011, 141. He includes in this figure victims who were remanded to secular authorities for execution or imprisonment (often a slow death sentence) together with the victims of branch offices in the New World. His source for the 350,000 figure is Rummel 2004, 70. The Vatican claims that only a few thousand died as a direct result of the Inquisition

67. Pope Pius IX, Syllabus of Errors (1864), http://perma.cc/Z7CG-W7JP

68. see the account in Buruma 2006, 31–59, quotations at 38 and 48

69. Buruma 2006, 2, 157

70. see his own summary of the argument of his book *The Enemy at Home: The Cultural Left and Its Responsibility for 9/11* at http://perma.cc/DP7F-LV2Z , his interview in Alex Koppelmann, 'How the Left Caused 9/11, by Dinesh D'Souza', Salon, 20 January 2007, http://perma.cc/62TY-ULND , and Alan Wolfe, 'None (but Me) Dare Call It Treason', New York Times, 21 January 2007, http://www.nytimes.com/2007/01/21/books/review/Wolfe.t.html?_r=1&

71. see my 2014 column, following an onstage conversation with Rushdie, Timothy Garton Ash, 'We Still Don't Know Who'll Win the Global Battle for Free Speech', 8 May 2014, http://perma.cc/26J2-E4QV , and the video of my conversation with him: 'Salman Rushdie: Free Speech, 25 Years On', Free Speech Debate, http://freespeechdebate.com/en/media/salman-rushdie-25-years-after-the-satanic-verses/

72. Murray et al. 2008

73. on this, and the intimidation of theatre, film and artistic representation more broadly, see the chapter by the playwright David Edgar in Hare et al., eds. 2009, 583–97

74. interview with Usama Hasan, London, 2 June 2011. See 'Is Nothing Sacred? Religion and Free Speech', Free Speech Debate, http://freespeechdebate.com/en/discuss/is-nothing-sacred-religion-and-free-speech-2/

75. Manji 2011, xix, and 'Irshad Manji on Allah, Liberty and Love', Free Speech Debate, http://freespeechdebate.com/en/media/irshad-manji-on-allah-liberty-and-love/. The quotation about 'Anonymous' comes from my notes of the subsequent discussion

76. Stephanie Kennedy, 'Rushdie Knighthood Evokes Anger from Muslim Groups', abc, http://perma.cc/XV25-HZHZ . This from a man honoured with a peerage, and subsequently reported to have made anti-Semitic remarks on a Pakistani TV channel in connection with his prison sentence for a fatal motorway crash: 'Muslim Peer Lord Ahmed Blames Jewish Conspiracy for Jailing Him', The Times, 14 March 2013, http://perma.cc/SYE2-F9GS

77. Inayat Bunglawala, 'I Used to Be a Book Burner', The Guardian, 19 June 2007, http://perma.cc/YGT3-MQTS

78. there are multiple, slightly different, versions of his remark in translations from the Urdu. I quote the translation by Reuters given in Duncan Campbell et al., 'UK "Deeply Concerned" over Rushdie Comments', The Guardian, 19 June 2007, http://

perma.cc/9BJ6-NW6H . For a slightly different version, see The Times, 18 June 2007. See also Timothy Garton Ash, 'No Ifs and No Buts', The Guardian, 22 June 2007, http://perma.cc/WCT7-JFTB

79. Reuters report, 21 June 2007

80. see report by Orla Guerin, 'Pakistani Christian Asia Bibi Has Price on Her Head', BBC News, 7 December 2010, http://perma.cc/S3SB-ZKSG , and the ghostwritten Bibi et al. 2012, which is, however, a problematic source because it is not even based on direct conversations with the 'author'

81. see Marshall et al. 2011, 99–100

82. see report by Jonathan Brown and Hussein Kesvani, 'Mohammad Asghar case', The Independent, 20 February 2014, http://perma.cc/RKT4-PZGJ

83. quoted in Marshall et al. 2011, 22

84. 'Saudi Arabia: New Terrorism Regulations Assault Rights', Human Rights Watch, 20 March 2014, http://perma.cc/3JP2-PVCP

85. estimate given in Eliza Griswold, 'Is This the End of Christianity in the Middle East?', New York Times Magazine, 22 July 2015, http://www.nytimes.com/2015/07/26/magazine/is-this-the-end-of-christianity-in-the-middle-east.html . A report in Time, 21 April 2014, gives a higher figure of 'one quarter' of the population in the last census conducted in the Ottoman Empire in 1914 and 5 percent 100 years later

86. quoted in Marshall et al. 2011, 23

87. I use the translation by N. J. Dawood in Koran 2003

88. Mortimer 1982, 396

89. Warraq, ed. 2003, 17

90. Mohsen Kadivar, 'Islam between Free Speech and Hate Speech', Free Speech Debate, http://freespeechdebate.com/en/discuss/islam-between-free-speech-and-hate-speech/

91. in Stepan et al., eds. 2014, 267–96

92. see Wahid 2001 but see also Elaine Pearson, 'Indonesia's Growing Religious Intolerance Has to Be Addressed', The Guardian, 5 February 2014, http://perma.cc/AD76-7NPX

93. Selcan Hacaoglu, 'Fazil Say, Turkish Pianist, Charged with Insulting Islam', Huffington Post, 1 June 2012, http://perma.cc/2ZN2-ZGXG

94. Suzan Fraser, 'Fazil Say Jailed: Turkish Pianist Receives Suspended Jail Term for Twitter Comments', Huffington Post, 15 April 2014, http://perma.cc/M7AH-HJ8H

95. 'Free Speech in Turkey & the World—Part One', Free Speech Debate, http://freespeechdebate.com/en/media/free-speech-in-turkey-the-world-part-one/ , and click through from the map on freespeechdebate.com for other material on Turkey

96. 'Free Speech at the Heart of the Arab Spring—Part One', Free Speech Debate, http://freespeechdebate.com/en/media/what-are-the-limits-to-freedom-of-expression-part-one/ , and Ahmed El-Tayyeb, 'Al-Azhar's "Bill of Rights"', Free Speech Debate, http://freespeechdebate.com/en/discuss/al-azhars-bill-of-rights/

97. see Roberts et al. eds. 2016 and, on Tunisia, Rory McCarthy, 'Who Is Threatening Free Speech in Post-Revolutionary Tunisia?', Free Speech Debate, http://freespeechdebate.com/en/discuss/who-is-threatening-free-speech-in-post-revolutionary-tunisia/ , and his longer Dahrendorf essay at http://perma.cc/7VD9-W3F4

98. Roy 2007, 76
99. in 'Blätter für Deutsche und Internationale Politik 10/2010', Eurozine, 2010, http://perma.cc/6L5Q-DGHS
100. see Timothy Garton Ash, 'Islam in Europe', New York Review of Books, 9 February 2006, http://www.nybooks.com/articles/archives/2006/oct/05/islam-in-europe/ , reprinted in Garton Ash 2009, 171–87
101. Husain 2007, 174
102. Nussbaum 2012, 95
103. Scanlon 2003, 197

7. PRIVACY

1. Fahmida Y. Rashid, 'Surveillance Is the Business Model of the Internet: Bruce Schneier', Security Week, http://perma.cc/S5AA-299Y
2. Lanier 2011, 198
3. quoted thus by Polly Sprenger, 'Sun on Privacy: "Get Over It"', Wired, 26 January 1999, http://perma.cc/FJY3-2DLM
4. conversation with the author, Google, Mountain View, 29 July 2010
5. Schmidt et al. 2013, 256
6. see Timothy Garton Ash, 'Timothy Garton Ash at the Brandenburg Gate', Free Speech Debate, http://freespeechdebate.com/en/media/timothy-garton-ash-at-the-brandenburg-gate/
7. see Eric Barendt, 'Freedom of Speech and Privacy', Free Speech Debate, http://freespeechdebate.com/en/discuss/freedom-of-speech-and-privacy/
8. see Vladimir Pozner, 'No Free Speech Please, We're Russian', Free Speech Debate, http://freespeechdebate.com/en/media/no-free-speech-please-were-russian/
9. Barendt 2007, 231. See also Lester et al. 2009, 448–542
10. Michael Newman, 'Interviews. W. H. Auden, The Art of Poetry, no. 17', The Paris Review, no. 57, Autumn 1972, http://perma.cc/SJ4S-AFYK
11. Mickiewicz, 'Stopnie Prawd': 'Są prawdy, które mędrzec wszystkim ludziom mówi; Są takie, które szepce swemu narodowi;
Są takie, które zwierza przyjaciołom domu;
Są takie, których odkryć nie może nikomu'. Online at http://perma.cc/6BB7-QKRD
12. Warren et al. 1890, 1, 4 — where the 'right to be let alone' is actually attributed to an earlier author, Judge Cooley. For 'the right to one's personality', see 207
13. in Private Wealth Council 2008, 22. See his pioneering account in Westin 1967
14. this is a common law tort; see Second Restatement of Torts 1977, as summarised by Post 1995, 51. The four-way distinction is often attributed to the work of William Prosser. At this writing, a Third Restatement of Torts is in preparation
15. quoted by Natasha Lerner in Index 2011, 58
16. see the argument of Nissenbaum 2010
17. see, for example, 'Roman Toilet, Ephesus, Turkey', Wikimedia, http://perma.cc/2VNA-48M8
18. Elias 2000, 136–42

19. Olmstead v United States (1928), quoted in Brown et al. 2013, 48
20. Berlin 2002, 176
21. Nagel 2002, 4
22. CCTV: 5.9 million, according to a report published by the British Security Industry Association in summer 2013; see '5.9 Million CCTV Cameras in UK', CBBC, 11 July 2013, http://perma.cc/U2AA-YSSH . For officially designated naked bathing or sunbathing areas in Munich, see this list: 'FKK und Nacktbaden in München', muenchen.de, http://perma.cc/47US-DJWC , with links to the official map
23. thus, to give just one example, Salman Rushdie in the course of an onstage conversation: 'Salman Rushdie: Free Speech, 25 Years On', Free Speech Debate, http://freespeechdebate.com/en/media/salman-rushdie-25-years-after-the-satanic-verses/
24. Boyd 2014, 55–56
25. as, for example, in the case of Stacy Snyder, who was refused certification to be a teacher because of one 'drunken pirate' photo the 25-year-old student had posted on MySpace. Mayer-Schönberger 2009, esp. 1–2, 109–10 and 197
26. Jarvis 2011, 33–38
27. for a superb analysis of the diverse meanings of reputation—as honour, property and dignity—see Post 1986. For Germany, see Barendt 2007, 213, and Casper 1971
28. see the useful summary in Petley, ed. 2013, 68–75
29. Max Mosley: 'The Difference between Privacy & Reputation', Free Speech Debate, http://freespeechdebate.com/en/media/privacy-v-reputation/
30. Privacy International, https://www.privacyinternational.org
31. Volokh 2000, 1050
32. I am grateful to David Erdos for helping me to clarify this meaning. The term 'data protection' was also pioneered in Germany
33. for a good account, see Solove 2007, esp. 44–48. When accessed in summer 2015, the version nearest the top on YouTube had more than 30 million views
34. see his interview in Macleans, 9 May 2013
35. MacKinnon 2012, 141–44. See also Charles Arthur, 'Google Buzz's Open Approach Leads to Stalking Threat', The Guardian, 12 February 2010, http://perma.cc/56CC-UYQF
36. Ed Pilkington, 'Tyler Clementi, Student Outed as Gay on Internet, Jumps to His Death', The Guardian, 30 September 2010, http://perma.cc/DPX2-X9EW
37. quoted in Jarvis 2011, 133
38. Mayer-Schönberger 2009, 3–4
39. see the extracts in Whittle et al. 2009, 74–75
40. quoted in Wacks 2010, 104
41. Post 1995, 67
42. Harold MacMillan, diary entry for 31 July 1954, quoted in Hennessy 2001, 197
43. see the chapter by Kevin Rafter in Petley, ed. 2013, 165–78
44. Barendt 2007, 242–44
45. Parker 2014, 85
46. see Yang 2009, 176–84, and Parker 2014, 82–86. Tan Renwei, 'The Girl Who Sold Herself to Save Her Mother: The Dilemma of Internet Charity in China', Southern

Metropolis Daily, 2 November 2005. Translated version available at http://perma.cc/
F6GX-T2T8

47. 'Official Outed by Netizens Gets 11 Years', China Daily, 12 October 2009, http://
perma.cc/U9EP-D6SW

48. Robertson et al. 2008, 95

49. Robertson et al. 2008, 117

50. Norwegian Constitution, 17 May 1814, Article 5, see https://perma.cc/NJX3-BV7U

51. see the comprehensive account in Streckfuss 2011, with the figure for court actions
on page 6. For Joe Gordon, see Maryam Omidi, 'Criticism of the Thai King', Free
Speech Debate, http://freespeechdebate.com/en/case/criticism-of-the-thai-king/

52. Timothy Garton Ash, 'Insult the King and . . . Go Directly to Jail', New York Review of Books, 23 May 2013, http://www.nybooks.com/articles/archives/2013/may/23/
insult-king-and-go-directly-jail/

53. see PEN International, 'Thai Student Activists Sentenced for Insulting the Monarchy
in a Play', ifex, https://perma.cc/EAW6-J5A6

54. Private Wealth Council 2008, 58

55. see the accounts in Petley, ed. 2013, 68–74, quotation on 71, and by Brian Cathcart in
Index 2011, 35–45, quotation on 44

56. see Lloyd 2011, 29–30

57. 'Content Guidelines', Kinja Legal, https://perma.cc/5D8F-95J8?type=source

58. Barendt 2007, 137

59. Barendt 2007, 239–41

60. Whittle et al. 2009, 16

61. see Judith Bruhn, 'The Topless Duchess', Free Speech Debate, http://freespeech
debate.com/en/case/the-topless-duchess/

62. Justin Parkinson, 'The Perils of the Streisand Effect', BBC News Magazine, 31 July
2014, http://perma.cc/3Y8A-M8KT , and 'Streisand Effect', Wikipedia, http://perma
.cc/WAV5-FS9M

63. emails to the author, 3 October 2014 and 15 July 2015

64. see Barendt 2007, 312–16, and generally his magisterial chapter IX on 'Free Speech
and the Judicial Process'

65. quoted in Law Commission 2013, 63, http://lawcommission.justice.gov.uk/docs/
lc340_contempt_of_court_juror_misconduct.pdf . The case is Attorney-General v
Davey [2013] EWHC 2317, http://perma.cc/7F3K-EBK9

66. Dershowitz 2004, 514–21. It is, however, clear that the jury for the civil trial was very
carefully vetted

67. Law Commission 2013, 117–21, 126–27, http://lawcommission.justice.gov.uk/docs/
lc340_contempt_of_court_juror_misconduct.pdf

68. see the Attorney General's (@AGO_UK) tweet on 4 December 2013, and Jo Joyce,
'Contempt of Court: Attorney General Warns Twitter Users on Legal Risks', http://
perma.cc/Y99T-7GKE . Previously, detailed 'advisories' had been sent to established
print and broadcasting media on a 'not for publication' basis

69. Fraser Nelson, 'David Cameron on Tax, Coalition, "Green Crap" and Team Nigella',
The Spectator, 14 December 2013, http://perma.cc/B7NT-NML4

70. see reports by Robert Booth, 'David Cameron's "Team Nigella" Quotes Could Have Sunk Saatchi PAs' Trial', The Guardian, 20 December 2013, http://perma.cc/MX7J -JM7X , and Jessica Best, 'Nigella Lawson Former PAs Trial: Jurors Warned to Ignore David Cameron's Comments about TV Chef', Daily Mirror, 12 December 2013, http://www.mirror.co.uk/news/uk-news/nigella-lawson-former-pas-trial-2918924

71. 'Nigella Lawson "Disturbed" by Court Process', BBC News, 20 December 2013, http://perma.cc/42W2-VYJA

72. Russell Myers, '"I've Been Maliciously Vilified": Nigella Lawson Launches Attack on Justice System after Ex-PAs Are Cleared of Fraud', Daily Mirror, 20 December 2013, http://perma.cc/XX3Y-JYT9

73. Barbara Ellen, 'In the Court of Public Opinion, There Has Been Justice for Nigella Lawson', The Guardian, 14 December 2013, http://perma.cc/2HMJ-ZMFE

74. see the detailed accounts in Lewis 2007, 47–58, and Bollinger 2010, 14–19, and Jeff Howard, 'A Right to Lie about Government?', Free Speech Debate, http://freespeech debate.com/en/case/a-right-to-lie-about-your-government/

75. for the original case, see Philip P. Pan, 'In China, Turning the Law into the People's Protector', Washington Post, 28 December 2004, http://perma.cc/Y6Y3-QV3T . So far as my Chinese-language researchers can establish, the provincial court case was actually never decided, but allowed to run into the sand; see http://perma.cc/K6KZ-PG98 . For Pu's subsequent detention, see Emma Graham-Harrison, 'Activist Lawyer Who Defended Ai Weiwei Charged with Provoking Trouble', The Guardian, 15 May 2015, http://perma.cc/W7K3-D8AS

76. Lewis 2007, 57

77. Lester 2014, 703

78. Human Rights Committee 2011, paragraph 47

79. 'Defamation Act 2013', http://perma.cc/7239-K7DV

80. Lester 2014, 707–12

81. Lord (Brian) Mawhinney in the House of Lords debate on the Second Reading, Hansard (House of Lords), Defamation Bill, Second Reading, 9 October 2012, Column 947, http://perma.cc/5C5S-3UP5 . Mawhinney had been an elected member of parliament from 1979 to 2005, so he was speaking from experience

82. see, for example the Alternative Libel Project, Robert Sharp, 'Alternative Libel Project—Final Report Launched', English PEN 16 March 2012, http://perma.cc/S8EY -QHAW . A cautious step further into the legal jungle is something known as 'early neutral evaluation' in which a judge gives a nonbinding opinion, on the basis of which the parties might agree to settle out of court

83. see Maximilian Ruhenstroth-Bauer, 'The Right of Reply in Germany', Free Speech Debate, http://freespeechdebate.com/en/case/the-right-of-reply-in-germany/

84. see Wu 2013, 1526–33

85. Hans Leyendecker, 'E wie "Escort", K wie "Kampf gegen Google"', Süddeutsche Zeitung, 10 September 2012, http://perma.cc/72AW-NY94

86. Nicholas Kulish, 'As Google Fills In Blank, a German Cries Foul', New York Times, 18 September 2012, http://www.nytimes.com/2012/09/19/world/europe/keystrokes-in -google-bare-shocking-rumors-about-bettina-wulff.html?_r=0

87. Mirjam Hauck, 'Googles Autocomplete verletzt Persönlichkeitsrechte', Süddeutsche Zeitung, 14 May 2013, http://perma.cc/G84Q-FUUS

88. Jeffrey Rosen, 'The Web Means the End of Forgetting', New York Times Magazine, 21 July 2010, http://www.nytimes.com/2010/07/25/magazine/25privacy-t2.html?pagewanted=all

89. Santayana 1980 [1905], 172

90. see my discussion of this in Garton Ash 1999, 258

91. '"Auschwitz Book-Keeper" Oskar Groening Sentenced to Four Years', BBC News, 15 July 2015, http://perma.cc/T9BV-KNAH

92. Mayer-Schönberger 2009, 12–13, 117

93. Lanier 2011, 200

94. Garton Ash 1997, 108–9, 249–50

95. Timothy Garton Ash, 'Bad Memories', Prospect, August 1997, http://perma.cc/R89M-ZCST

96. Feinberg 1990, 255

97. in Europe, European Digital Rights acts as an umbrella organisation for more than 30 privacy and civil rights organisations; see https://edri.org/about/. Similar organisations in Asia, Africa and the Americas include the Electronic Frontier Foundation (www .eff.org), Hiperderecho (www.hiperderecho.org) and Derechos Digitales (https:// www.derechosdigitales.org). The African Declaration on Internet Rights (http:// africaninternetrights.org) and RightsCon Manila (https://www.rightscon.org) bring together digital rights organisations from various parts of Africa and Asia

98. this is the so-called 'Lebach judgement' of 5 June 1973, http://perma.cc/2NHX-JBG6

99. Judith Bruhn, 'Does a Murderer Have the Right to Be Forgotten?', Free Speech Debate, http://freespeechdebate.com/en/case/does-a-murderer-have-the-right-to-be-for gotten/ , and John Schwartz, 'Two German Killers Demanding Anonymity Sue Wiki- pedia's Parent', New York Times, 12 November 2009, http://www.nytimes.com/2009 /11/13/us/13wiki.html?_r=0 . In the end, the German Constitutional Court decided against them

100. Jarvis 2011, 133

101. see, for example, Richard Falkenrath, 'Google Must Remember Our Right to Be For- gotten', Financial Times, 15 February 2012, http://www.ft.com/cms/s/0/476b9a08-572a -11e1-869b-00144feabdc0.html#axzz3rrQrPPYr

102. a useful summary is given in the official press release: Court of Justice of the Eu- ropean Union, 'Google Spain SL, Google Inc. v Agencia Española de Protección de Datos, Mario Costeja González', http://perma.cc/4FHG-SMGW . The full court ruling: 'Google Spain SL, Google Inc. v Agencia Española de Protección de Datos (AEPD), Mario Costeja González', InfoCuria, http://perma.cc/TR52-3AAC . See also Charles Arthur, 'Explaining the "Right to Be Forgotten"—the Newest Cultural Shib- boleth', The Guardian, 14 May 2014, http://perma.cc/KA38-N98L

103. James Ball, 'Costeja González and a Memorable Fight for the "Right to Be Forgot- ten"', The Guardian, 14 May 2014, http://perma.cc/DV2F-539Y

104. top 10 of some 113,000 results, accessed on 16 July 2014

105. see 'European Privacy Requests for Search Removals', Google, http://perma.cc/ G8QM-G63F . The figures I quote cover the period from the launch of the official request process on 29 May 2014 to early September 2015

106. David Drummond, 'We Need to Talk about the Right to Be Forgotten', The Guardian, 10 July 2014, http://perma.cc/6JJ7-NDSM

107. see Richard Waters, 'Google Bows to EU Privacy Ruling', Financial Times, 30 May 2014, http://www.ft.com/intl/cms/s/2/b827b658-e708-11e3-88be-00144feabdc0.html#axzz3rrQrPPYr

108. for its hearings and final report see 'Google Advisory Council', Google, https://www.google.com/advisorycouncil/

109. Mayer-Schönberger 2009, 171–99

110. Jonathan Zittrain, 'The Right to Be Forgotten Leaves Nagging Doubts', Financial Times, 13 July 2014, http://www.ft.com/intl/cms/s/0/c5d17a80-0910-11e4-8d27-00144feab7de.html#axzz3rrQrPPYr

111. quoted by Richard Waters in 'Adult Duties for Onetime Web Wunderkind', Financial Times, 30 May 2014

112. remarks at a conference on 'The "Right to Be Forgotten" and beyond', Oxford University, 12 June 2012

113. see the original tweet on 27 April 2010 at http://perma.cc/KY75-HGVY and the subsequent article by Tim Jones, 'Facebook's "Evil Interfaces"', Electronic Frontier Foundation, 29 April 2010, https://perma.cc/SKB9-WR5M?type=source

114. see the original 28 April 2010 tweet at http://perma.cc/23GG-TAYP and the subsequent article by Eliot van Buskirk, 'Report: Facebook CEO Mark Zuckerberg Doesn't Believe in Privacy', Wired, 28 April 2010, http://perma.cc/9GBF-TXVV

115. 'The Evolution of Privacy on Facebook', https://perma.cc/93CT-SRC7?type=image

116. see Kevin J. O'Brien, 'Austrian Law Student Faces Down Facebook', New York Times, 5 February 2012, http://www.nytimes.com/2012/02/06/technology/06iht-rawdata06.html?_r=0 and his website at http://europe-v-facebook.org/EN/en.html

117. Dominic Rushe, 'Facebook Reaches Deal with FTC over "Unfair and Deceptive" Privacy Claims', The Guardian, 29 November 2011, http://perma.cc/4YH8-RFNA

118. see Vindu Goel, 'Some Privacy, Please? Facebook, under Pressure, Gets the Message', New York Times, 22 May 2014, http://www.nytimes.com/2014/05/23/technology/facebook-offers-privacy-checkup-to-all-1-28-billion-users.html?_r=2 , and Facebook, 'Data Policy', https://www.facebook.com/about/privacy/

119. Kashmir Hill, 'Facebook Wants to Listen In on What You're Doing', Forbes, 22 May 2014, http://perma.cc/V8ZA-JZMH

120. for an informative, detailed technical account: Jimmy Su et al., 'A Little Bird Told Me: Personal Information Sharing in Angry Birds and Its Ad Libraries', FireEye, http://perma.cc/3DLJ-VQY6 . In January 2014, a senior excecutive of Rovio, the game-maker, claimed 2 billion downloads. Assuming that on average people do not download it more than twice, and some have done so since, I arrive at my estimate of 'more than 1 billion people'

121. see 'Erasing David', http://perma.cc/RY8Q-6HJ3

122. the guidelines were extended and updated in 2013; see 'OECD Guidelines on the Protection of Privacy and Transborder Flows of Personal Data', OECD, http://perma.cc/6WM5-4U7K

123. Ian Brown, 'Keeping Our Secrets, Shaping Internet Technologies for the Public Good', Oxford London Lecture, 18 March 2014, http://www.oii.ox.ac.uk/webcasts/?id=581

124. Collusion is a Mozilla Firefox add-on. See Sebastian Huempfer, 'Who Is Tracking the Trackers? Use "Collusion" to Find Out', Free Speech Debate, http://freespeech debate.com/en/2013/07/who-is-tracking-the-trackers-use-collusion-to-find-out/ , and the description at http://collusion.toolness.org

125. O'Hara et al. 2008, 72 and chapter 3 in general. Sebastian Anthony, '15-Year-Old Boy Arrested in Connection with TalkTalk Hack Has Been Released on Bail', ars technica, 27 October 2015, http://perma.cc/5Y58-W9QP ; Sophie Curtis, 'M&S Website Temporarily Suspended after Leaking Customers' Details', Daily Telegraph, 28 October 2015, http://www.telegraph.co.uk/technology/internet-security/11959667/MandS-web site-temporarily-suspended-after-leaking-customers-details.html; Ashley Armstrong, 'Morrisons Sued by 2,000 Staff over Data Breach', Daily Telegraph, 27 October 2015, http://www.telegraph.co.uk/finance/newsbysector/retailandconsumer/11957905/ Morrisons-sued-by-2000-staff-over-data-breach.html

126. Zuckerberg 2013

127. Boyd 2014, 64–65

128. see New Yorker, 5 July 1993, and 'On the Internet, Nobody Knows You're a Dog', Wikipedia, http://perma.cc/VKU5-JC4U

129. Manji 2011, xix , and 'Irshad Manji on Allah, Liberty and Love', Free Speech Debate, http://freespeechdebate.com/en/media/irshad-manji-on-allah-liberty-and-love/ . The quotation about 'Anonymous' comes from my notes of the subsequent discussion

130. DeNardis 2014, 235–36

131. see Emily Steel and April Dembosky, 'Facebook Raises Fears with Ad Tracking', Financial Times, 23 September 2012, http://www.ft.com/intl/cms/s/0/6cc4cf0a-0584-11e2 -9ebd-00144feabdc0.html#axzz3rracetFy

132. see Mayer-Schönberger et al. 2013

133. a useful summary is given by Nate Anderson, '"Anonymized" Data Really Isn't—and Here's Why Not', arstechnica, http://perma.cc/Z3N7-7TC3 . Sweeney's article was published in Journal of Law, Medicine and Ethics, no. 25, 1997, 98–110

134. Mayer-Schönberger et al. 2013, 154–55

135. see the paper by Arvind Narayanan and Vitaly Shmatikov, 'Robust De-anonymization of Large Datasets (How to Break Anonymity of the Netflix Prize Dataset)', University of Texas, 2008, and their useful FAQs at http://perma.cc/9PBE-5BW5 . For even more serious examples of the reidentification of supposedly anonymised medical data, see Nuffield Council on Bioethics 2015, 66–69

136. Ghonim 2012, chapters 3 and 4. He was the anonymous administrator of the Facebook page and used Tor to conceal his IP address

137. Josh Chin, 'China Is Requiring People to Register Real Names for Some Internet Services', Wall Street Journal, 4 February 2015, http://www.wsj.com/articles/china-to -enforce-real-name-registration-for-internet-users-1423033973 . For a timeline of the real-name registration, see Paul Bischoff, 'A Brief History of China's Campaign to Enforce Real-Name Registration Online', TechInAsia, http://perma.cc/LR54-AS7Z

138. see Timothy Garton Ash, 'Choices from an Uncrowned Queen', New York Review of Books, 6 June 2013, http://www.nybooks.com/articles/archives/2013/jun/06/burma-choices-uncrowned-queen/

139. see Goffman 1990

140. comment on 'Real Names vs Pseudonyms', Free Speech Debate, http://freespeech debate.com/en/discuss/real-names-vs-pseudonyms/ . See also Timothy Garton Ash, 'The Project', http://freespeechdebate.com/en/the-project/

141. see Katie Engelhart, 'Orlando Figes and the Anonymous Poison Pen', Free Speech Debate, http://freespeechdebate.com/en/case/orlando-figes-and-the-anonymous-poison-pen/

142. see Theo Merz, 'LivesOn Review: Can Twitter Make You Immortal?', Daily Telegraph, 16 August 2013, http://www.telegraph.co.uk/technology/mobile-app-reviews/10246708/LivesOn-review-can-Twitter-make-you-immortal.html

143. Mark 5:9, context in Olson 2013, 7–8, 81–83. On 'anonymous hacktivism', see also Anonymous 2013 and Coleman 2014

144. we asked the manufacturer of these masks how many had been sold, but they replied that 'Rubies is a privately run company and we do not disclose that sort of information'. Email, 30 July 2014

8. SECRECY

1. 'Gonzales defends NSA, rejects call for prosecutor', CNN, 17 January 2006, http://perma.cc/ZKG6-4QY4 . I owe this reference to Sagar 2013, 2. It is fair to point out that Gonzales claimed members of Congress had been briefed on such specific instances

2. Eliza Manningham-Buller, BBC Radio 4 Today programme, 27 December 2013

3. Chris Blackhurst, 'Edward Snowden's Secrets May Be Dangerous. I Would Not Have Published Them', The Independent, 13 October 2013, http://perma.cc/CQ6V-ZWJU

4. for some thoughts in this direction see Waldron 2012

5. see Elizabeth Becker, 'Washington Talk; Prickly Roots of "Homeland Security"', New York Times, 31 August 2002, http://www.nytimes.com/2002/08/31/us/washington-talk-prickly-roots-of-homeland-security.html

6. Rossijskaja Gazeta, Criminal Code of the Russian Federation, Article 275, amended by Article 1, paragraph 2, http://perma.cc/9V77-AB9C

7. Clarke et al. 2014, xvi, 1–4

8. PEN America, 'Chilling Effects: NSA Surveillance Drives U.S. Writers to Self-Censor', November 2013, http://perma.cc/HUZ9-W3A3 , 6. The actual figures were 28 percent for the first question and 24 percent for the second. It followed up with a survey of international writers: PEN America, 'Global Chilling: The Impact of Mass Surveillance on International Writers', January 2015, http://perma.cc/DH7U-3B2B

9. Jimmy Wales and Lila Tretikov, 'Stop Spying on Wikipedia Users', New York Times, 10 March 2015, http://www.nytimes.com/2015/03/10/opinion/stop-spying-on-wikipedia-users.html?_r=1

10. Tilly et al. 1975, 42, and a slightly different version in Tilly 1990, 67

11. Stone 2006, 4, summarising the argument of Stone 2004

12. Michael Howard, 'What's in a Name? How to Fight Terrorism', Foreign Affairs, Jan./ Feb. 2002, https://perma.cc/UAW9-PR5A

13. David Cole, 'Obama's Unauthorized War', New York Review of Books, 11 September 2014, http://www.nybooks.com/blogs/nyrblog/2014/sep/11/obama-isis-unauthorized-war/? insrc=wbll

14. see Agamben 2005

15. see the chapter by Andreas Busch in Leibfried et al., eds. 2015, 547–64, this on 558

16. summarised in Swire et al. 2011 and in more detail in Swire et al. 2012, 464–73

17. see the chapter by Andreas Busch in Leibfried et al., eds. 2015, 547–64, esp. 549–50

18. quoted in Stone 2004, 556

19. see Manav Bhushan, 'Satire or Sedition? Political Cartoons in India', Free Speech Debate, http://freespeechdebate.com/en/case/satire-or-sedition-political-cartoons-in -india/ , and Nivedita Menon, 'Arrested for Sitting during the National Anthem: Soli-darity Statement with Salman', Kafila, 24 August 2014, http://perma.cc/GYK9-VUMS

20. see Timothy Garton Ash, 'History Reclassified as State Secret: The Case of Xu Ze-rong', Free Speech Debate, http://freespeechdebate.com/en/case/history-reclassified -as-state-secret-the-case-of-xu-zerong-2/

21. quoted in Timothy Garton Ash, 'US Embassy Cables: A Banquet of Secrets', The Guardian, 28 November 2010, http://perma.cc/XJW8-MXMS . My source prefers to remain anonymous

22. see 'John Garton Ash—Obituary', Daily Telegraph, 16 July 2014, http://www.tele graph.co.uk/news/obituaries/10971430/John-Garton-Ash-obituary.html

23. see Deibert 2013 and Bartlett 2015

24. Cole et al., eds. 2013, 1

25. for the US judge's criticism of the 'unconscionable' way Drake was treated, see Scott Shane, 'No Jail Time in Trial over N.S.A. Leak', New York Times, 15 July 2011, http://www.nytimes.com/2011/07/16/us/16leak.html?_r=0 . To make your own judgement on his case and credibility, watch our interview: Thomas Drake, 'A Whistleblower's Argument', Free Speech Debate, http://freespeechdebate.com/en/ media/a-whistleblowers-argument/

26. Harding 2014, 294

27. the records were being collected under section 215 of the US Patriot Act. Privacy and Civil Liberties Oversight Board 2014, 11

28. both quoted by David Cole, '"We Kill People Based on Metadata"', New York Review of Books, 10 May 2014, http://www.nybooks.com/blogs/nyrblog/2014/may/10/ we-kill-people-based-metadata/

29. see this report, with video clip, which also usefully recalls some other such denials: Andy Greenberg, 'Watch Top U.S. Intelligence Officials Repeatedly Deny NSA Spy-ing on Americans over the Last Year (Videos)', Forbes, 6 June 2013, http://www.forbes .com/sites/andygreenberg/2013/06/06/watch-top-u-s-intelligence-officials-repeated ly-deny-nsa-spying-on-americans-over-the-last-year-videos/

30. see his comments at a discussion in Cairo on 12 February 2012, in Timothy Garton Ash, 'Can Europe and the Middle East Agree on the Terms of Freedom of Expression?', Free

Speech Debate, http://freespeechdebate.com/en/media/can-europe-and-the-middle
-east-agree-on-the-terms-of-freedom-of-expression/

31. see Suskind 2004. See also Timothy Garton Ash, 'The Time Has Come for a Final Report on the 43rd President of the US', The Guardian, 24 September 2008, http://perma.cc/6BTW-EQBM

32. see the dramatic accounts in Stothard 2003, 81–96, and Kampfner 2003, 298–309

33. U.S. National Intelligence Estimate (NIE) NIE 2006-02R, 'Trends in Global Terrorism: Implications for the United States', April 2006, http://perma.cc/RY7S-6YD7 . See also Timothy Garton Ash, 'If We Miss This Last Chance, Then Our Soldiers Will Have Died in Vain', The Guardian, 25 October 2006, http://perma.cc/G4B4-FYTA

34. see Neta C. Crawford, 'U.S. Costs of Wars through 2014: $4.4 Trillion and Counting', 25 June 2014, http://perma.cc/M7MD-XPWN for the justification of an estimate of $2.21 trillion

35. Presidential address on 10 September 2014, transcript at 'Transcript: President Obama on How U.S. Will Address Islamic State', NPR, http://www.npr.org/2014/09/10/347515100/transcript-president-obama-on-how-u-s-will-address-islamic-state

36. see 'Information on Country Legal Frameworks Pertaining to Freedom of Expression and Privacy in Telecommunications', Telecommunications Industry Dialogue, http://perma.cc/8M6D-MZGU . I am most grateful to Matthew Kirk of Vodafone for drawing this to my attention. Vodafone first did this on its own initiative in 2014: 'Country-by-Country Disclosure of Law Enforcement Assistance Demands', Vodafone, http://perma.cc/QM2P-8D2F

37. notes of conversations with Eliot Schrage, Facebook, Palo Alto, 15 September 2011, and Alex Macgillivray, Twitter, San Francisco, 20 September 2010

38. see Anthony May, '2013 Annual Report of the Interception of Communications Commissioner', http://perma.cc/ES3R-KUP8

39. see David Anderson, 'A Question of Trust. Report of the Investigatory Powers Review', June 2015, https://perma.cc/S4PW-BPHB?type=source , 8

40. Barendt 2007, 162 — there also the quotation from Kalven

41. at the 2014 British Conservative Party Conference, Home Secretary Theresa May said, 'I want to see new banning orders for extremist groups that fall short of the existing laws relating to terrorism. I want to see new civil powers to target extremists who stay within the law but still spread poisonous hatred'. Alan Travis, 'Theresa May Vows Tory Government Would Introduce "Snooper's Charter"', The Guardian, 30 September 2014, http://perma.cc/U7AP-DFJB . Something very close to this approach was subsequently announced by Prime Minister David Cameron in his July 2015 speech about extremism; see Lizzy Dearden, 'David Cameron Extremism Speech: Read the Transcript in Full', The Independent, 20 July 2015, http://perma.cc/JPC7-JDVN

42. Human Rights Committee 2011, paragraph 30

43. 'The Johannesburg Principles on National Security, Freedom of Expression and Access to Information', Article 19, 1966, http://perma.cc/6DW9-NSJR

44. 'Global Principles on National Security and the Right to Information (the Tshwane Principles)', http://perma.cc/YCP4-ZYA5

45. email from Margie Orford of South African PEN, 11 November 2015

46. Morton H. Halperin et al., 'Japan's Secrecy Law and International Standards', Paper prepared for the Open Society Foundations, 4 September 2014, http://perma .cc/7EVZ-DFDK

47. this is emphasised by a thoughtful retired British securocrat, David Omand; see Omand 2010, 281–85

48. 'Protecting Individual Privacy in the Struggle against Terrorists', National Research Council, 2008, http://perma.cc/7T9C-B4N2 esp. 8, 24, 86

49. I owe this reference to Sagar 2013, 190

50. quoted in Sagar 2013, 48

51. quoted in Zegart 2011, 8

52. conversation with the author, Palo Alto, 8 October 2014

53. this was a view heard, with varying degrees of enthusiasm, from an assemblage of senior people from the Western security establishment at a conference at the Ditchley Foundation on 'Intelligence, Security and Privacy' in May 2015. The proceedings, like all Ditchley conferences, were held under the Chatham House Rule (nothing may be attributed to any identifiable individual), but a good summary is given in this note by the foundation's director: 'Intelligence, Security and Privacy', http://perma.cc/5S5T-7VF5

54. see the chapter by Sudha Setty in Cole et al., eds. 2013, 57–71; this detail is on 68

55. see the chapter by Shiri Krebs in Cole et al., eds. 2013, 133–53

56. see the footage from his hotel room in Hong Kong in Laura Poitras's documentary film 'Citizenfour'

57. Harding 2014, 182

58. see Joss Wright, 'How Can You Tell What's Banned on the Internet?', Free Speech Debate, http://freespeechdebate.com/en/discuss/how-free-is-the-internet-in -liberal-democracies/

59. Kohn 2011, 201–12

60. Clarke et al. 2014, 225

61. SEC: Office of the Whistleblower, http://perma.cc/5DNQ-CZVB

62. '"Whistleblower" is not a bad word . . .', Whistleblowing International Network, http:// perma.cc/GM37-3B98

63. Glazer et al. 1989, 4

64. I follow the lucid account in Stone 2004, 500–16

65. quoted in Sagar 2013, 141

66. Alford 2001, 1

67. Sagar 2013, 147–48

68. Stone 2004, 514–15; but see also Kohn 2011, 53–54, where the point is made sharply

69. see Editorial, 'Eric Holder's Legacy', New York Times, 25 September 2014, http:// www.nytimes.com/2014/09/26/opinion/eric-holders-legacy.html?_r=0

70. 'Carter: Snowden's Leaks Good for Americans to Know', USA Today, 25 March 2014, http://www.usatoday.com/story/news/politics/2014/03/24/usa-today-capital-download -jimmy-carter-edward-snowden-probably-constructive/6822425/

71. Sagar 2013, 149–52

72. see 'SEC: Office of the Whistleblower: Frequently Asked Questions', http://perma .cc/USS4-X5VJ

73. Clarke et al. 2014, 144
74. Kohn 2011, 207–12
75. quoted in Glazer et al. 1989, 34
76. Abrams 2013, 289–92
77. US District Court for the Eastern District of Columbia, sworn affidavit dated 21 June 2011 in the case of US v Jeffrey Alexander Sterling (with some passages redacted), http://perma.cc/3VHS-H7UZ
78. see photograph and text in New York Times, 'The War Logs', 26 July 2010, A8
79. but see Matt Sledge, 'Bradley Manning Sentencing Testimony Suggests WikiLeaks Not Responsible for Any Deaths', Huffington Post, 8 March 2013, http://perma .cc/3SCZ-73DC
80. see Timothy Garton Ash, 'WikiLeaks Has Altered the Leaking Game for Good. Secrets Must Be Fewer, But Better Kept', The Guardian, 30 March 2011, http://perma .cc/6V73-QMSR
81. see the editorial 'The Times and Iraq', New York Times, 26 May 2004. See also Margaret Sullivan, 'The Disconnect on Anonymous Sources', New York Times, 12 October 2013, http://www.nytimes.com/2013/10/13/opinion/sunday/the-public-editor-the -disconnect-on-anonymous-sources.html , which reports that back in 2004 the use of anonymous sources had been the top concern of Times readers
82. see Margaret Sullivan, 'The Disconnect on Anonymous Sources', New York Times, 12 October 2013, http://www.nytimes.com/2013/10/13/opinion/sunday/the-public-editor -the-disconnect-on-anonymous-sources.html?_r=0
83. see the footage from his hotel room in Hong Kong in Laura Poitras's documentary film 'Citizenfour' at 1:03:37. Similarly, you can watch on freespeechdebate.com an interview with Thomas Drake, the earlier NSA whistleblower. If you do not conclude after watching that video—and then, if you want more, reading everything you can about him—that here was a patriotic, public-spirited person, grotesquely mistreated as a result, then you and I have different eyes. See Thomas Drake, 'A whistleblower's argument', Free Speech Debate, http://freespeechdebate.com/en/media/a-whistleblowers -argument/ . Even the former head of the NSA, Michael Hayden, wrote subsequently of 'overreach' in the prosecution of Drake, see Michael Hayden, 'Obama administration overreached on leak probes', CNN, 4 June 2013, http://perma.cc/QX9N-SGGR
84. Alford 2001, 36 and (on concealing his sources) 139–42
85. Alford 2001, xi
86. Bond 2005 reviews studies since the original experiments by Solomon Asch

9. ICEBERGS

1. Brown et al. 2013, 8
2. Deibert 2013, 29, and see 'Woman Who Cut Internet to Georgia and Armenia "Had Never Heard of Web"', Daily Telegraph, 11 April 2011, http://www.telegraph.co.uk/ news/worldnews/europe/georgia/8442056/Woman-who-cut-internet-to-Georgia-and -Armenia-had-never-heard-of-web.html
3. Deibert 2013, 40–42; DeNardis 2014, 116

4. DeNardis 2014, 155, 209, 22

5. Nye 2014, 4, and online at https://perma.cc/464Q-GQGG

6. see Rogier Creemers, 'Virtual Lines in the Sand: China's Demands for Internet Sovereignty', 6 October 2014, http://perma.cc/U9N6-HFW3

7. I owe this Latin word for 'internet' — *interrete* — to Oxford University's Public Orator, Richard Jenkyns, whose email wonderfully continued, 'The Vatican dictionary is too early to help, though the Vatican may indeed be the source for 'interrete', quo verbo utuntur Vicipaedia aliique fontes quos apud interrete ipsum reperire possis'. Email of 10 December 2014. Enjoy that if you can

8. the meeting was in 2012. See Alexander Klimburg, 'The Internet Yalta', Centre for a New American Security, 5 February 2013, http://perma.cc/58RW-MN93 . The official ITU list of the 89 is available at World Conference on International Telecommunications, 'Signatories of the Final Acts: 89', http://perma.cc/NA44-BBKW

9. the document, dated 30 September 2009, is online at 'Affirmation of Commitments by the United States Department of Commerce and the Internet Corporation for Assigned Names and Numbers', ICANN, http://perma.cc/LTT4-FB8C

10. see, for example, 'ICANN Update, by the Community, for the Community', ICANN, http://perma.cc/3YGU-VCCC , and ICANNnews, 'A Holiday Message from ICANN to Its Community', 18 December 2014, https://www.youtube.com/watch?v=UUTelKs Xlrc&feature=youtu.be

11. 'FAQ 2.2', ICANN, http://perma.cc/QB6X-NT6E

12. Michael Froomkin in Brown et al. 2013, 42

13. see '.WINE and .VIN: Where Does ICANN Stand?', ICANN, http://perma.cc/ A4MM-YYCF , and http://perma.cc/75LZ-EAJN

14. 'NTIA Announces Intent to Transition Key Internet Domain Name Functions', National Telecommunications & Information Administration, US Department of Commerce, http://perma.cc/56G2-46X8 . The transfer was not complete, and still facing resistance in the US Congress, as this book went to press

15. exquisite detail in DeNardis 2014, 49–50; see also the relevant page on the ICANN website: 'List of Root Servers', ICANN, http://perma.cc/G5HE-HG8Y

16. 'Russian MPs Back Law on Internet Data Storage', BBC News, 5 July 2014, http:// perma.cc/Y3W8-W4AZ

17. conversation with Michael Hayden, Palo Alto, 8 October 2014

18. Lanier 2011, 125

19. quoted in Tim Berners-Lee, 'An Online Magna Carta: Berners-Lee Calls for Bill of Rights for Web', The Guardian, 12 March 2014, http://perma.cc/22F4-AVKZ

20. see Wu 2003

21. Wu 2010, 202, makes this explicit. See also his seminal article: Wu 2003

22. thus Tim Wu, 'Net Neutrality: How the Government Finally Got It Right', New Yorker, 5 February 2015, http://perma.cc/SW5W-27QF

23. Van Schewick 2010 and Marsden 2010 helpfully show all the complexities

24. this was definitively established in the Supreme Court case of Ex parte Jackson 96 US 727 (1878)

25. see DeNardis 2014, chapter 6, for this point and lucidly explained technical detail

26. see Graham Reynolds, 'Netherlands Passes Europe's First Net Neutrality Legislation', Free Speech Debate, http://freespeechdebate.com/en/case/62696/

27. see Jordan 2010

28. although he ultimately rejects this argument, it is well stated by Jeremy Malcolm, 'Net Neutrality and the Global Digital Divide', Electronic Frontier Foundation, 24 July 2014, http://perma.cc/QN46-SVYP ; specifically in relation to India, see Manu Joseph, 'Another Take on Net Neutrality', New York Times, 15 April 2015, http://www .nytimes.com/2015/04/16/world/asia/another-take-on-net-neutrality.html?_r=0

29. see reports and analysis by Elise Hu, 'The White House Is Backing Strong Open Internet Rules', NPR, 10 November 2014, http://www.npr.org/sections/alltechconsid ered/2014/11/10/363013806/the-white-house-is-backing-the-internet-in-a-major-way , and '3.7 Million Comments Later, Here's Where Net Neutrality Stands', NPR, 17 September 2014, http://www.npr.org/sections/alltechconsidered/2014/09/17/349243335/3 -7-million-comments-later-heres-where-net-neutrality-stands . In the end, it was more than 4 million comments

30. quoted in David Crow, 'Strife in the Fast Lane', Financial Times, 16 November 2014, http://www.ft.com/cms/s/0/997ad3ee-6b23-11e4-ae52-00144feabdc0.html#axzz3s4 VCr5dH

31. the legendary libertarian Silicon Valley investor Peter Thiel even argued that internet monopolies, or near-monopolies, could be good for innovation; see Thiel 2014

32. Federal Communications Commission, 'In the Matter of Protecting and Promoting the Open Internet', 26 February 2015, http://perma.cc/R9H9-MWXG , and Tim Wu, 'Net Neutrality: How the Government Finally Got It Right', New Yorker, 5 February 2015, http://perma.cc/SW5W-27QF

33. http://www.thisisnetneutrality.org and the post on Jeremy Gillula et al., 'EFF Co-Launches Global Coalition on Net Neutrality, as the Battle for an Open Internet Heats Up', Electronic Frontier Foundation, 25 November 2014, https://perma.cc/ N9PK-UC29?type=source

34. the exact figure was 74 percent of 86 countries covered; see 'WebIndex Report 2014–15', WebIndex, http://perma.cc/D5TD-X5UF

35. see the account on Wikipedia itself: 'Internet Watch Foundation and Wikipedia', Wikipedia, http://perma.cc/9LZY-SRP6

36. United Nations Human Rights Council, 'Report of the Special Rapporteur on the Promotion and Protection of the Right to Freedom of Opinion and Expression, Frank La Rue', 16 May 2011, http://perma.cc/U4A6-8L5Y

37. see Deibert et al., eds. 2010, 283–84

38. see Claire Phipps, 'Lee Rigby Report: Facebook Accused of Failing to Flag Extremist Messages—as It Happened', The Guardian, 26 November 2014, http://perma .cc/6TLW-WBNZ , and 'Woolwich Murder: Facebook Criticism "Unfair", Former MI6 Director Says', BBC News, 26 November 2014, http://perma.cc/93KV-6K3Z , identifying Facebook as the site of the 'online exchange'

39. see also Virtual Centre of Excellence for Research in Violent Online Political Extremism, http://voxpol.eu

40. see Ian Brown and Douwe Korff, 'Digital Freedoms in International Law', 2012, https:// perma.cc/8ZQJ-SA57 , chapter 3 (including references and links in its footnotes)

41. 'Overview of the Public Sector', Wired, 2002, http://perma.cc/9SZG-W6S4

42. Citizen Lab, 'Planet Blue Coat: Mapping Global Censorship and Surveillance Tools', 15 January 2013, http://perma.cc/K882-HE28

43. letter to the author from Lauri Kivinen, Head of Corporate Affairs, Nokia Siemens Networks, 25 September 2009

44. see Moez Chakchouk, 'Tunisian Internet Agency Defends Net Neutrality', Free Speech Debate, http://freespeechdebate.com/en/media/tunisian-internet-agency -defends-net-neutrality/

45. see Max Gallien, 'Imported Repression in the Middle East', Free Speech Debate, http://freespeechdebate.com/en/discuss/imported-repression-in-the-middle-east/ . This links to an English version of the original document: https://perma.cc/GF8V -5UDG

46. for the Wassenaar Arrangement, see 'List of Dual-Use Goods and Technologies (WA-LIST (14) 2.) and Munitions List', Wassenaar, http://perma.cc/YJ56-BRBJ , but see also this critical view: Nate Cardozo and Eva Galperin, 'What Is the U.S. Doing about Wassenaar, and Why Do We Need to Fight It?', Electronic Frontier Foundation, 28 May 2015, http://perma.cc/6LH4-8XUA

47. comments during a panel organised by the Omidyar Network, London, 12 November 2014; see video here: Omidyar Network, 'Open Up? 2014: Data Collection and Sharing: Transparency and the Private Sector', http://vimeo.com/111748146

48. DeNardis 2014, 136, 53

49. quoted from 'algorithm', sense 2, in the *Oxford English Dictionary*

50. see Facebook Help Centre, 'How News Feed Works', Facebook, https://perma .cc/4UCM-P5XB?type=source

51. author's notes from a workshop on the 'Ethics of Data in Civil Society' organised by the Stanford Center on Philanthropy and Civil Society, Stanford University, September 2014 and see also Tufekci 2014

52. Craig Timberg, 'Research in India Suggests Google Search Results Can Influence an Election', Washington Post, 12 May 2014, http://perma.cc/7FWQ-HRXT . His methodology can be challenged on many points, and seems to assume an active will to manipulate on the part of the search engine

53. author's notes from a workshop on the 'Ethics of Data in Civil Society' organised by the Stanford Center on Philanthropy and Civil Society, Stanford University, September 2014

54. see, for example, the warning by Stephen Hawking: Rory Cellan-Jones, 'Stephen Hawking Warns Artificial Intelligence Could End Mankind', BBC News, 2 December 2014, http://perma.cc/VEC8-ZMXB

55. Eugene Volokh, 'First Amendment Protection for Search Engine Search Results', 20 April 2012, http://perma.cc/7YSD-9W6P . The title page states 'This White Paper was commissioned by Google but the views within it should not necessarily be ascribed to Google'

56. Sue Halpern, 'Mind Control and the Internet', New York Review of Books, 23 June 2011, http://www.nybooks.com/articles/archives/2011/jun/23/mind-control-and-internet/

57. see Kramer et al. 2013

58. Neier 1979, 5
59. email to the author, 11 February 2013, quoted with his kind permission
60. Lessig 2012, xii–xiii, 230–39, and see Figure 21
61. Eric L. Lewis, 'Who Are "We the People"?', New York Times Sunday Review, 4 October 2014, http://www.nytimes.com/2014/10/05/opinion/sunday/who-are-we-the-people .html?_r=1

10. COURAGE

1. Tucholsky 1975, 58. This comes in an essay first published in 1921
2. Twain, quoted in Bollinger 1986, 7
3. Mill 1991 [1859], 23
4. lyrics at 'The Reluctant Cannibal', http://perma.cc/AXF9-SVCX
5. Lewis 2007, 35–36
6. Thucydides 1943, 116
7. I closely follow the account in Gregg 2000, 62–67
8. Liu 2012, 313–26, quotations on 317 and 325–26
9. Elizabeth Flock, 'August Landmesser, Shipyard Worker in Hamburg, Refused to Perform Nazi Salute (Photo)', 7 February 2012, https://perma.cc/9HJ7-V9H7 , and see the photo at https://perma.cc/J8XT-PQLW
10. Khaled al-Johani, WhereIsKhaledEnglish, '"Where Is Khaled?" The English-Subtitled Interview', 5 April 2011, https://www.youtube.com/watch?v=mxinAxWxX08
11. Christopher Hitchens, 'Moderation or Death', London Review of Books, 26 November 1998, http://www.lrb.co.uk/v20/n23/christopher-hitchens/moderation-or-death
12. Ignatieff 1998, 333. Interestingly, Ignatieff consigns this to an endnote, although he discusses the issue of Berlin and courage carefully on 256–58
13. see 'Fathers and Children' in Berlin 1979, 261–305, this on 301
14. Hand 1963, 190
15. I explore this in my 2008 Isaiah Berlin Lecture at Wolfson College Oxford, 'Isaiah Berlin and the Challenge of Multiculturalism', https://podcasts.ox.ac.uk/series/ isaiah-berlin-lecture
16. Dahrendorf 2006, 84
17. Erasmus 2001, 63–64 (Adage I iii 7)
18. Erasmus 1989, 93
19. Dahrendorf 2006, 85. There also the quotation from Hutten's *Expostulation*
20. the exchange is translated in full in Erasmus et al. 1989
21. quoted in Lukes 2003, ix. Lukes attributes this to the poet Robert Frost
22. see his own account in Dahrendorf 2003, 62–78
23. quoted by Hugh Trevor-Roper in an essay reprinted in Erasmus 1989, this on 302
24. quoted by Dahrendorf 2006, 85
25. Isaiah Berlin, 'A Message to the 21st Century', New York Review of Books, 23 October 2014, http://www.nybooks.com/articles/archives/2014/oct/23/message-21st-century/
26. see Colquhoun 1986, 590–91

BIBLIOGRAPHY

Abrams, Floyd. 2013: *Friend of the Court: On the Front Lines with the First Amendment*. New Haven: Yale University Press.

Ackerman, Peter, and Duvall, Jack. 2003: *A Force More Powerful*. New York: Palgrave.

Aesop. 1998: *The Complete Fables*. Translated by Olivia and Robert Temple. London: Penguin.

Agamben, Giorgio. 2005: *State of Exception*. Translated by Kevin Attell. Chicago: University of Chicago Press.

Alford, C. Fred. 2001: *Whistleblowers: Broken Lives and Organizational Power*. Ithaca: Cornell University Press.

Anderson, Benedict R. 1983: *Imagined Communities: Reflections on the Origin and Spread of Nationalism*. London: Verso.

Anderson, Elizabeth, and Pildes, Richard H. 2000: 'Expressive Theories of Law: A General Restatement'. *University of Pennsylvania Law Review*, vol. 148, 1503–75. doi: 10.2307/3312748.

Anonymous. 2013: *A Brief History of Anonymous Hacktivism*. No place: No publisher.

Appiah, Kwame Anthony. 2008: *Cosmopolitanism: Ethics in a World of Strangers*. London: Allen Lane.

Appignanesi, Lisa, ed. 2005: *Free Expression Is No Offence*. London: Penguin.

Arendt, Hannah. 2006: *Between Past and Future: Eight Exercises in Political Thought*. London: Penguin.

Aristotle. 1996: *The Politics and the Constitution of Athens*. Edited by Stephen Everson. Cambridge, UK: Cambridge University Press.

Bacon, Francis. 1996: *The Major Works*. Edited by Brian Vickers. Oxford: Oxford University Press.

Bahr, Ehrhard, ed. 1974: *Was ist Aufklärung? Thesen und Definitionen*. Stuttgart: Philipp Reclam.

Baker, Philip, and Eversley, John. 2000: *Multilingual Capital: The Languages of London's Schoolchildren and Their Relevance to Economic, Social and Educational Policies*. London: Battlebridge.

Baldwin, James. 1993 [1963]: *The Fire Next Time*. New York: Vintage.

Baldwin, Peter. 2009: *The Narcissism of Minor Differences: How Europe and America Are Alike*. Oxford: Oxford University Press.

Baldwin, Peter. 2014: *The Copyright Wars: Three Centuries of Trans-Atlantic Battle*. Princeton: Princeton University Press.

Banaji, Mahzarin R., and Greenwald, Anthony G. 2013: *Blindspot: Hidden Biases of Good People*. New York: Delacorte.

Barendt, Eric. 2007: *Freedom of Speech*. Oxford: Oxford University Press.

Barendt, Eric. 2010: *Academic Freedom and the Law: A Comparative Study*. Oxford: Hart Publishing.

Barendt, Eric. 2011: 'Religious Hatred Laws: Protecting Groups or Belief?' *Res Publica*, vol. 17, 41–53. doi: 10.1007/s11158-011-9142-6.

Barker, William. 2001: *The Adages of Erasmus*. Toronto: University of Toronto Press.

Barrett, Cyril. 1991: *Wittgenstein on Ethics and Religious Belief*. Oxford: Blackwell.

Barrow, Robin. 2005: 'On the Duty of Not Taking Offence'. *Journal of Moral Education*, vol. 34, no. 3, 265–67. doi: 10.1080/03057240500211600.

Bartlett, Jamie. 2015: *The Dark Net: Inside the Digital Underworld*. London: Windmill Books.

Benesch, Susan. 2009: 'The New Law of Incitement to Genocide: A Critique and a Proposal'. http://www.ushmm.org/genocide/spv/pdf/benesch_susan.pdf.

Benesch, Susan. 2012: 'Words as Weapons'. *World Policy Journal*, vol. 29, no. 1, 7–12. doi: 10.1177/0740277512443794.

Benesch, Susan. 2014: *Countering Dangerous Speech: New Ideas for Genocide Prevention*. *Working Paper*. Washington DC: United States Holocaust Memorial Museum.

Benkler, Yochai. 2006: *The Wealth of Nations: How Social Production Transforms Markets and Freedom*. New Haven: Yale University Press.

Benner, Erica. 2009: *Machiavelli's Ethics*. Princeton: Princeton University Press.

Berlin, Isaiah. 1979: *Russian Thinkers*. Harmondsworth: Penguin Books.

Berlin, Isaiah. 1998: 'In Conversation with Steven Lukes'. *Salmagundi*, vol. 120, Fall 1998, 52–134. doi: http://www.jstor.org/stable/40549054.

Berlin, Isaiah. 2002: *Liberty*. Edited by Henry Hardy. Oxford: Oxford University Press.

Berners-Lee, Tim. 1999: *Weaving the Web: The Past, Present and Future of the World Wide Web by Its Inventor*. London: Orion Business.

Bibi, Asia, and Tollet, Anne-Isabelle. 2012: *Blasphemy: The True, Heartbreaking Story of a Woman Sentenced to Death over a Cup of Water*. London: Virago.

Biggar, Nigel. 2014: *In Defence of War*. Oxford: Oxford University Press.

Bleich, Erik. 2011: *The Freedom to Be Racist? How the United States and Europe Struggle to Preserve Freedom and Combat Racism*. Oxford: Oxford University Press.

Bollinger, Lee C. 1986: *The Tolerant Society*. Oxford: Oxford University Press.

Bollinger, Lee C. 2010: *Uninhibited, Robust and Wide-Open: A Free Press for a New Century*. Oxford: Oxford University Press.

Bond, Rod. 2005: 'Group Size and Conformity'. *Group Processes & Intergroup Relations*, vol. 8, no. 4, 331–54. doi: 10.1177/1368430205056464.

Borchgrevink, Aage. 2013: *A Norwegian Tragedy: Anders Behring Breivik and the Massacre on Utøya*. Translated by Guy Puzey. London: Polity.

Boyd, Danah. 2014: *It's Complicated: The Social Lives of Networked Teens*. New Haven: Yale University Press.

Boyd, Julian P., ed. 1950 [1787]: *The Papers of Thomas Jefferson. Volume 11*. Princeton: Princeton University Press.

Brand, Stewart. 2010: *Whole Earth Discipline: Why Dense Cities, Nuclear Power, Transgenic Crops, Restored Wildlands, Radical Science, and Geoengineering Are Necessary*. London: Penguin.

Brettschneider, Corey. 2012: *When the State Speaks, What Should It Say? How Democracies Can Protect Expression and Promote Equality*. Princeton: Princeton University Press.

Briggs, Rachel, and Feve, Sebastien. 2013: *Review of Programs to Counter Narratives of Violent Extremism*. London: Institute for Strategic Dialogue.

Broughton, John. 2008: *Wikipedia: The Missing Manual*. Beijing: O'Reilly.

Brown, Donald E. 1991: *Human Universals*. New York: McGraw-Hill.

Brown, Ian, ed. 2013: *Research Handbook on Governance of the Internet*. Cheltenham, UK: Edward Elgar.

Brown, Ian, and Korff, Douwe. 2012: 'Digital Freedoms in International Law: Practical Steps to Protect Human Rights Online'. Washington DC: Global Network Initiative.

Brown, Ian, and Korff, Douwe. 2014: 'Foreign Surveillance: Law and Practice in a Global Digital Environment'. *European Human Rights Review*, no. 3, 243–51.

Brown, Ian, and Marsden, Christopher. 2013: *Regulating Code: Good Governance and Better Regulation in the Internet Age*. Cambridge, MA: MIT Press.

Burckhardt, Jacob. 1965: *Briefe*. Berlin: Deutsche Buch-Gemeinschaft.

Buruma, Ian. 2006: *Murder in Amsterdam: The Death of Theo van Gogh and the Limits of Tolerance*. New York: Penguin.

Calhoun, Craig. 1992: *Habermas and the Public Sphere*. Cambridge, MA: MIT Press.

Cammack, Daniela. 2013: 'Aristotle on the Virtue of the Multitude'. *Political Theory*, vol. 4, no. 2, 175–202. doi: 10.2139/ssrn.2161069.

Carr, Nicholas. 2010: *The Shallows: What the Internet Is Doing to Our Brains*. New York: Norton.

Carter, Stephen L. 1998: *Civility: Manners, Morals, and the Etiquette of Democracy*. New York: Harper Perennial.

Casebourne, Imogen, Davies, Chris, Fernandes, Michelle, and Norman, Naomi. 2012: *Assessing the Accuracy and Quality of Wikipedia Entries Compared to Popular Online Encyclopedias: A Preliminary Comparative Study across Disciplines in English, Spanish and Arabic*. Brighton, UK: Epic.

Casper, Gerhard. 1971: *Redefreiheit und Ehrenschutz*. Karlsruhe: Müller.

Castells, Manuel. 2013: *Communication Power*. Oxford: Oxford University Press.

Chafee, Zechariah. 1946: *Free Speech in the United States*. 2nd ed. Cambridge, MA: Harvard University Press.

Clarke, Richard A., Morell, Michael J., Stone, Geoffrey R., Sunstein, Cass R., and Swire, Peter. 2014: *The NSA Report: Liberty and Security in a Changing World*. Princeton: Princeton University Press.

Coetzee, J. M. 1996: *Giving Offense: Essays on Censorship*. Chicago: University of Chicago Press.

Cole, David, Fabbrini, Federico, and Vedaschi, Arianna, eds. 2013: *Secrecy, National Security and the Vindication of Constitutional Law*. Cheltenham, UK: Edward Elgar.

Coleman, Gabriella. 2014: *Hacker, Hoaxer, Whistleblower, Spy: The Many Faces of Anonymous*. London: Verso.

Coleman, Stephen, Scott, Anthony, and Morrison, David E. 2009: *Public Trust in the News: A Constructivist Study of the Social Life of the News*. Oxford: Reuters Institute for the Study of Journalism.

Coliver, Sandra, ed. 1982: *Striking a Balance: Hate Speech, Freedom of Expression and Non-Discrimination*. London: Article 19.

Collier, Paul. 2008: *The Bottom Billion: Why the Poorest Countries Are Failing and What Can Be Done about It*. Oxford: Oxford University Press.

Collier, Paul, and Vicente, Pedro. 2013: 'Votes and Violence: Evidence from a Field Experiment in Nigeria'. *Economic Journal*, vol. 12, no. 4, 327–55. doi: 10.1111/ecoj.12109.

Colquhoun, Robert. 1986: *Raymond Aron. Volume 2. The Sociologist in Society 1955–1983*. London: Sage.

Corbin, Caroline Mala. 2009: 'The First Amendment Right against Compelled Listening'. *Boston University Law Review*, vol. 89, no. 3, 939–1016.

Cortese, Anthony T. 2008: *Provocateur: Images of Women and Minorities in Advertising*. Lanham, MD: Rowman & Littlefield.

Dahrendorf, Ralf. 2003: *Über Grenzen: Lebenserinnerungen*. Munich: Beck.

Dahrendorf, Ralf. 2006: *Versuchungen der Unfreiheit: Die Intellektuellen in Zeiten der Prüfung*. Munich: Beck.

Darnton, Robert. 2009: *The Case for Books: Past, Present and Future*. New York: Public Affairs.

Darnton, Robert. 2014: *Censors at Work: How States Shaped Literature*. New York: Norton.

Darwall, Stephen. 1977: 'Two Kinds of Respect'. *Ethics*, vol. 88, no. 1, 36–49.

Darwall, Stephen. 2013: *Honor, History and Relationships: Essays in Second-Personal Ethics II*. Oxford: Oxford University Press.

Davies, Nick. 2008: *Flat Earth News: An Award-Winning Reporter Exposes Falsehood, Distortion and Propaganda in the Global Media*. London: Vintage.

De Bary, Theodore, and Lufrano, Richard. 1999: *Sources of Chinese Tradition: Volume 2: From 1600 through the Twentieth Century*. New York: Columbia University Press.

Deibert, Ronald, Palfrey, John, Rohozinski, Rafal, and Zittrain, Jonathan, eds. 2010: *Access Controlled: The Shaping of Power, Rights, and Rule in Cyberspace*. Cambridge, MA: MIT Press.

Deibert, Ronald J. 2013: *Black Code: Inside the Battle for Cyberspace*. Toronto: Signal.

De Jong, Ferdinand. 2005: 'A Joking Nation: Conflict Resolution in Senegal'. *Canadian Journal of African Studies*, vol. 39, no. 2, 391–415. doi: 10.1080/00083968.2005.10751322.

Delgado, Richard, and Stefancic, Jean. 2004: *Understanding Words That Wound*. Boulder, CO: Westview.

DeNardis, Laura. 2014: *The Global War for Internet Governance*. New Haven: Yale University Press.

Dershowitz, Alan M. 2004: *America on Trial: Inside the Legal Battles That Transformed Our Nation*. New York: Grand Central Publishing.

Devlin, Patrick. 1959: *The Enforcement of Morals*. Oxford: Oxford University Press.

Diamond, Jared. 1993: *The Third Chimpanzee: The Evolution and Future of the Human Animal*. New York: Harper.

Diamond, Larry. 2010: 'Liberation Technology'. *Journal of Democracy*, vol. 21, no. 3, 69–83. doi: 10.1353/jod.0.0190.

Diamond, Milton, and Uchiyama, Ayako. 1999: 'Pornography, Rape and Sex Crimes in Japan'. *International Journal of Law and Psychiatry*, vol. 22, no. 1, 1–22. doi: 10.1016/S0160-2527(98)00035-1.

Domosławski, Artur. 2012: *Ryszard Kapuściński: A Life*. London: Verso.

Drèze, Jean, and Sen, Amartya. 2013: *An Uncertain Glory: India and Its Contradictions*. London: Allen Lane.

Dunbar, Robin. 1996: *Grooming, Gossip and the Evolution of Language*. London: Faber & Faber.

Dunbar, Robin. 2004: *The Human Story*. London: Faber & Faber.

Dunbar, Robin. 2014: *Human Evolution*. London: Pelican.

Ehrenfeld, Rachel. 2005: *Funding Evil: How Terrorism Is Financed and How to Stop It*. Chicago: Bonus.

Eisenstein, Elizabeth L. 1979: *The Printing Press as an Agent of Change: Communications and Cultural Transformations in Early-Modern Europe*. Cambridge, UK: Cambridge University Press.

Elias, Norbert. 2000: *The Civilizing Process: Sociogenetic and Psychogenetic Investigations*. Oxford: Blackwell.

Elson, Malte, and Ferguson, Christopher J. 2014: 'Twenty-Five Years of Research on Violence in Digital Games and Aggression: Empirical Evidence, Perspectives, and a Debate Gone Astray'. *European Psychologist*, vol. 19, no. 1, 33–46. doi: 10.1027/1016-9040/a000147.

Erasmus, Desiderius. 1989: *The Praise of Folly and Other Writings*. Translated by Robert M. Adams. London: Norton.

Erasmus, Desiderius, and Luther, Martin, eds. 1989: *Discourse on Free Will*. Translated by Ernst F. Winter. London: Bloomsbury.

Evans, Richard. 2002: *Telling Lies about Hitler: The Holocaust, History and the David Irving Trial*. London: Verso.

Feinberg, Joel. 1984: *Harm to Others: The Moral Limits of Criminal Law. Volume 1*. Oxford: Oxford University Press.

Feinberg, Joel. 1985: *Offense to Others: The Moral Limits of Criminal Law. Volume 2*. Oxford: Oxford University Press.

Feinberg, Joel. 1990: *Harmless Wrongdoing: The Moral Limits of the Criminal Law. Volume 3*. Oxford: Oxford University Press.

Feinberg, Joel, and Gross, Hyman. 1990: *Philosophy of Law*. 4th ed. Belmont, CA: Wadsworth.

Fenton, James. 2012: *Yellow Tulips: Poems 1968–2011*. London: Faber & Faber.

Feuz, Martin, Fuller, Matthew, and Stalder, Felix. 2011: 'Personal Web Searching in the Age of Semantic Capitalism: Diagnosing the Mechanism of Personalisation'. *First Monday*, vol. 16, no. 2. doi: 10.5210/fm.v16i2.3344.

Fielden, Lara. 2011: *Regulating for Trust in Journalism: Standards Regulation in the Age of Blended Media*. Oxford: Reuters Institute for the Study of Journalism.

Fischer, David Hackett. 2004: *Liberty and Freedom: A Visual History of America's Founding Ideas*. New York: Oxford University Press.

Fishkin, James S. 2009: *When the People Speak: Deliberative Democracy and Public Consultation*. Oxford: Oxford University Press.

Forsén, Björn, and Stanton, Greg R., eds. 1996: *The Pnyx in the History of Athens. Volume 2*. Helsinki: Papers and Monographs of the Finnish Institute at Athens.

Foucault, Michel. 2001: *Fearless Speech*. Los Angeles: Semiotext(e).

Foxman, Abraham H., and Wolf, Christopher. 2013: *Viral Hate: Containing Its Spread on the Internet*. London: Palgrave Macmillan.

Furedi, Frank. 2011: *On Tolerance: A Defence of Moral Independence*. London: Continuum.

Gagliardone, Iginio, Gal, Danit, Alves, Thiago, and Martinez, Gabriela. 2015: *Countering Online Hate Speech*. Paris: Unesco.

Galnoor, Itzhak, and Lukes, Steven. 1985: *No Laughing Matter: A Collection of Political Jokes*. London: Routledge.

Gant, Scott. 2007: *We're All Journalists Now: The Transformation of the Press and Reshaping of the Law in the Internet Age*. New York: Free Press.

Garton Ash, Timothy. 1989: *The Uses of Adversity: Essays on the Fate of Central Europe*. London: Penguin.

Garton Ash, Timothy. 1997: *The File: A Personal History*. New York: Vintage.

Garton Ash, Timothy. 1999: *History of the Present: Essays, Sketches and Despatches from Europe in the 1990s*. New York: Vintage.

Garton Ash, Timothy. 2005: *Free World: Why a Crisis of the West Reveals the Opportunity of Our Time*. London: Penguin.

Garton Ash, Timothy. 2009: *Facts Are Subversive: Political Writing from a Decade without a Name*. New Haven: Yale University Press.

Garton Ash, Timothy, ed. 2009: *Liberalisms in East and West*. Oxford: Oxford University.

Garton Ash, Timothy, Mortimer, Edward, and Öktem, Kerem. 2013: *Freedom in Diversity: 10 Lessons for Public Policy From Britain, Canada, France, Germany and the United States*. Oxford: Dahrendorf Programme for the Study of Freedom.

Ghonim, Wael. 2012: *Revolution 2.0: The Power of the People Is Greater Than the People in Power*. London: Fourth Estate.

Giles, Jim. 2005: 'Internet Encyclopedias Go Head to Head'. *Nature*, vol. 438, no. 15, 900–1. doi: 10.1038/438900a.

Givens, Terry L. 2007: *People of Paradox: A History of Mormon Culture*. Oxford: Oxford University Press.

Gladstone, Brooke. 2011: *The Influencing Machine*. New York: Norton.

Glazer, Myron Peretz, and Glazer, Penina Migdal. 1989: *The Whistleblowers: Exposing Corruption in Government and Industry*. New York: Basic.

Goffman, Erving. 1990: *The Presentation of Self in Everyday Life*. London: Penguin.

Goldacre, Ben. 2009: *Bad Science*. London: Fourth Estate.

Goldacre, Ben. 2012: *Bad Pharma: How Medicine Is Broken and How We Can Fix It*. London: Fourth Estate.

Goldsmith, Jack, and Wu, Tim. 2008: *Who Controls the Internet?* Oxford: Oxford University Press.

Gould, Jon B. 2005: *Speak No Evil: The Triumph of Hate Speech Regulation*. Chicago: University of Chicago Press.

Graham, Mark, Hale, Scott A., and Stephens, Monica. 2011: *Geographies of the World's Knowledge*. London: Convoco Foundation.

Green, Leslie. 1991: 'Freedom of Expression and Choice of Language'. *Law and Policy*, vol. 13, no. 3, 215–29. doi: 10.1111/j.1467-9930.1991.tb00067.x.

Greenwald, Glenn. 2014: *No Place to Hide: Edward Snowden, the NSA and the Surveillance State*. London: Hamish Hamilton.

Gregg, Pauline. 2000: *Free-Born John: A Biography of John Lilburne*. London: Phoenix Press.

Habermas, Jürgen. 1995: 'Reconciliation through the Public Use of Reason: Remarks on John Rawls's Political Liberalism'. *Journal of Philosophy*, vol. 92, no. 3, 109–31. doi: 10.2307/2940842.

Habermas, Jürgen. 2009: *Europe: The Faltering Project*. Cambridge, UK: Polity.

Hackett, Robert A., and Zhao, Yuezhi. 2005: *Democratizing Global Media: One World, Many Struggles*. Oxford: Rowman & Littlefield.

Hafner, Katie, and Lyon, Matthew. 2006: *Where Wizards Stay Up Late: The Origins of the Internet*. New York: Simon & Schuster.

Hald, Gert Martin, Malamuth, Neil, and Yuen, Carlin. 2010: 'Pornography and Attitudes Supporting Violence against Women: Revisiting the Relationship in Nonexperimental Studies'. *Aggressive Behavior*, vol. 36, no. 1, 14–20. doi: 10.1002/ab.20328.

Hallin, Daniel C., and Mancini, Paolo. 2004: *Comparing Media Systems: Three Models of Media and Politics*. Cambridge, UK: Cambridge University Press.

Hallin, Daniel C., and Mancini, Paolo, eds. 2012: *Comparing Media Systems beyond the Western World*. Cambridge, UK: Cambridge University Press.

Hand, Learned. 1963: *The Spirit of Liberty: Papers and Addresses of Learned Hand*. New York: Knopf.

Handley, Paul M. 2006: *The King Never Smiles: A Biography of Thailand's Bhumibol Adulyadej*. New Haven: Yale University Press.

Hansen, Mogens Herman. 1999: *The Athenian Democracy in the Age of Demosthenes: Structure, Principles, and Ideology*. London: Bristol Classical.

Harding, Luke. 2014: *The Snowden Files: The Inside Story of the World's Most Wanted Man*. London: Guardian.

Hare, Ivan, and Weinstein, Jeremy, eds. 2009: *Extreme Speech and Democracy*. Oxford: Oxford University Press.

Harrison, Joel. 2006: 'Truth, Civility, and Religious Battlegrounds: The Contest between Religious Vilification Laws and Freedom of Expression'. *Auckland University Law Review*, vol. 12, 71–96.

Hart, Adrian. 2009: *The Myth of Racist Kids: Anti-Racist Policy and Regulation of School Life*. London: Manifesto Club.

Hayek, Friedrich A. 1945: 'The Use of Knowledge in Society'. *American Economic Review*, vol. 35, no. 4, 519–30.

Hecht, Brent, and Gergle, Darren. 2010: 'The Tower of Babel Meets Web 2.0: User-Generated Content and Its Applications in a Multilingual Context'. *Proceedings of the SIGCHI Conference on Human Factors in Computing Systems*, 291–300. doi: 10.1145/1753326.1753370.

Heinze, Eric. 2016: *Hate Speech and Democratic Citizenship*. Oxford: Oxford University Press.

Hennessy, Peter. 2001: *The Prime Minister: The Office and Its Holders since 1945*. London: Penguin.

Herbert, George. 1995: *The Complete English Works*. Edited by Ann Pasternak Slater. London: Everyman.

Herodotus. 1998: *The Histories*. Translated by Robin Waterfield. London: Penguin.

Herz, Michael, and Molnár, Péter. 2012: *The Content and Context of Hate Speech: Rethinking Regulation and Responses*. Cambridge, UK: Cambridge University Press.

Hevia, James L. 2003: *English Lessons: The Pedagogy of Imperialism in Nineteenth-Century China*. Durham: Duke University Press.

Hirschman, Albert O. 1970: *Exit, Voice and Loyalty: Responses to Decline in Firms, Organizations and States*. Cambridge, MA: Harvard University Press.

Hirsi Ali, Ayaan. 2007: *Infidel: My Life*. London: Free Press.

Hobbes, Thomas. 2012 [1651]: *Leviathan. Volumes 1–3*. Edited by Noel Malcolm. Oxford: Oxford University Press.

Hobsbawm, Eric. 1994: 'The Historian between the Quest for the Universal and the Quest for Identity'. *Diogenes*, vol. 42, no. 168, 51–63. doi: 10.1177/039219219404216805.

Hollinger, David A. 2000: *Postethnic America: Beyond Multiculturalism*. New York: Basic.

Howe, Jeff. 2008: *Crowdsourcing: Why the Power of the Crowd Is Driving the Future of Business*. New York: Crown Business.

Huang, Max Ko-Wu. 2008: *The Meaning of Freedom: Yan Fu and the Origins of Chinese Liberalism*. Hong Kong: Chinese University Press.

Human Rights Committee, United Nations. 2011: *General Comment No. 34: Article 19: Freedoms of Opinion and Expression*. Geneva: United Nations.

Huntington, Samuel P. 1998: *The Clash of Civilizations and the Remaking of World Order*. London: Touchstone.

Hurrell, Andrew. 2013: 'Power Transitions, Global Justice and the Virtues of Pluralism'. *Ethics and International Affairs*, vol. 27, no. 2, 1–17. doi: 10.1017/S0892679413000087.

Husain, Ed. 2007: *The Islamist: Why I Joined Radical Islam in Britain, What I Saw Inside and Why I Left*. London: Penguin.

Ignatieff, Michael. 1998: *Isaiah Berlin: A Life*. London: Chatto and Windus.

Ignatieff, Michael. 2012: 'Reimagining a Global Ethic'. *Ethics & International Affairs*, vol. 26, no. 1, 7–19.

Ikenberry, John. 2011: *Liberal Leviathan: The Origins, Crisis, and Transformation of the American World Order*. Princeton: Princeton University Press.

Index. 2011: *Index on Censorship*. Vol. 40, no 2. Los Angeles: Sage.

Jack, Malcolm, ed. 2011: *Erskine May's Treatise on the Law, Privileges, Proceedings and Usage of Parliament*. 24th ed. London: LexisNexis.

Jacobs, Jane. 1993: *The Death and Life of Great American Cities*. New York: Modern Library.

Jarvis, Jeff. 2011: *Public Parts: How Sharing in the Digital Age Improves the Way We Work and Live*. New York: Simon & Schuster.

Jordan, Scott. 2010: 'The Application of Net Neutrality to Wireless Networks Based on Network Architecture'. *Policy & Internet*, vol. 2, no. 2, article 6. doi: 10.2202/1944-2866.1052.

Judt, Tony. 2010: *The Memory Chalet*. London: Heinemann.

Julius, Anthony. 2002: *Transgressions: The Offences of Art*. London: Thames & Hudson.

Julius, Anthony. 2003: *T. S. Eliot, Anti-Semitism, and Literary Form*. London: Thames & Hudson.

Kampfner, John. 2003: *Blair's Wars*. London: Free Press.

Kantorowicz, Alfred. 1959: *Deutsches Tagebuch. Volume 1*. Munich: Kindler Verlag.

Kapr, Albert. 1996: *Johann Gutenberg: The Man and His Invention*. Aldershot, UK: Scolar.

Katolikie Universiteit. 2009: *Independent Study on Indicators for Media Pluralism*. Leuven, Belgium: Katolikie Universiteit.

Keen, Andrew. 2007: *The Cult of the Amateur: How Today's Internet Is Killing Our Culture*. New York: Doubleday.

Kennedy, Randall. 2003: *Nigger: The Strange Career of a Troublesome Word*. New York: Vintage.

King, Gary, Pan, Jennifer, and Roberts, Margaret E. 2013: 'How Censorship in China Allows Government Criticism but Silences Collective Expression'. *American Political Science Review*, vol. 107, no. 2, 326–43. doi: 10.1017/s0003055413000014.

King, Gary, Pan, Jennifer, and Roberts, Margaret E. 2014: 'Reverse-Engineering Censorship in China: Randomized Experimentation and Participant Observation'. *Science*, vol. 345, no. 6199, 1–10. doi: 10.1126/science.1251722.

Kingston, Drew A., Malamuth, Neil, Fedoroff, Paul, and Marshall, William. 2009: 'The Importance of Individual Differences in Pornography Use: Theoretical Perspectives and Implications for Treating Sexual Offenders'. *Journal of Sex Research*, vol. 46, no. 2–3, 216–32. doi: 10.1080/00224490902747701.

Kirkpatrick, David. 2010: *The Facebook Effect: The Inside Story of the Company That Is Connecting the World*. New York: Simon & Schuster.

Klausen, Jytte. 2009: *The Cartoons That Shook the World*. New Haven: Yale University Press.

Koch, Henning, Hagel-Sørensen, Karsten, Haltern, Ulrich, and Weiler, Joseph, H. H., eds. 2010: *Europe: The New Legal Realism — Essays in Honour of Hjalte Rasmussen*. Copenhagen: DJØF.

Köckert, Matthias. 2007: *Die Zehn Gebote*. Munich: Beck.

Kohn, Stephen. 2011: *The Whistleblower's Handbook: A Step-by-Step Guide to Doing What's Right and Protecting Yourself*. Guilford, CT: Lyons.

Kołakowski, Leszek. 1982: *Religion*. London: Fontana.

Kołakowski, Leszek. 1990: *Modernity on Endless Trial*. Chicago: University of Chicago Press.

Koran, The. 2003: *The Koran*. Translated by N. J. Dawood. London: Penguin.

Kovach, Bill, and Rosenstiel, Tom. 2007: *The Elements of Journalism: What Newspeople Should Know and the Public Should Expect*. New York: Three Rivers.

Kramer, Adam D. I., Guillory, Jamie E., and Hancock, Jeffrey T. 2013: 'Experimental Evidence of Massive-Scale Emotional Contagion through Social Networks'. *Proceedings of the National Academy of Sciences of the United States of America*, vol. 111, no. 24, 8788–90. doi: 10.1073/pnas.1320040111.

Kundera, Milan. 1995: *Testaments Betrayed*. Translated by Linda Asher. London: Faber & Faber.

Kundera, Milan. 2005: *The Art of the Novel*. London: Faber & Faber.

Kurzweil, Ray. 2005: *The Singularity Is Near: When Humans Transcend Biology*. London: Duckworth.

Kymlicka, Will, and Patten, Alan, eds. 2003: *Language Rights and Political Theory*. Oxford: Oxford University Press.

Langton, Rae. 2009: *Sexual Solipsism: Philosophical Essays on Pornography and Objectification*. Oxford: Oxford University Press.

Lanier, Jaron. 2011: *You Are Not a Gadget*. New York: Vintage.

Lau, D. C. 1979: *Confucius: The Analects*. Translated with an Introduction by D. C. Lau. London: Penguin.

Law Commission. 2013: *Contempt of Court (1): Juror Misconduct and Internet Publications*. London: Stationery Office.

Leader Maynard, Jonathan, and Benesch, Susan. 2015: 'Dangerous Speech and Dangerous Ideology: An Integrated Model for Monitoring and Prevention'. *Genocide Studies and Prevention: An International Journal*, vol. 9, no. 3.

Leibfried, Stephan, Huber, Evelyne, Lange, Matthew, Levy, Jonah D., Nullmeier, Frank, and Stephens, John D., eds. 2015: *The Oxford Handbook of Transformations of the State*. Oxford: Oxford University Press.

Leist, Anton. 1993: 'Bioethics in a Low Key: A Report from Germany'. *Bioethics*, vol. 7, no. 2–3, 271–79.

Lessig, Lawrence. 2006: *Code: Version 2.0*. New York: Basic.

Lessig, Lawrence. 2012: *Republic, Lost: How Money Corrupts Congress—and a Plan to Stop It*. New York: Twelve.

Lester, Anthony. 2014: 'Two Cheers for the First Amendment'. *Harvard Law and Policy Review*, vol. 8, 701–18.

Lester, Anthony, Pannick, David, and Herberg, Jovan. 2009: *Human Rights Law and Practice*. 3rd ed. London: LexisNexis.

Levmore, Saul, and Nussbaum, Martha C., eds. 2010: *The Offensive Internet: Privacy, Speech and Reputation*. Cambridge, MA: Harvard University Press.

Levy, David A. L., and Nielsen, Rasmus Kleis. 2010: *The Changing Business of Journalism and Its Implications for Democracy*. Oxford: Reuters Institute for the Study of Journalism.

Lewis, Anthony. 2007: *Freedom for the Thought That We Hate: A Biography of the First Amendment*. New York: Basic.

Leys, Simon. 1997: *The Analects of Confucius*. Translation and Notes by Simon Leys. New York: Norton.

Li, Qiang. 1993: *The Social and Political Thought of Yen Fu*. Doctoral Thesis, University of London.

Liao, Han-Teng. 'Internet Users by Language: The Top 20 Languages Based on CLDR Version 25 Data'. Oxford Internet Institute, http://perma.cc/T9UW-8YDW.

Lieberman, Philip. 2007: 'The Evolution of Human Speech'. *Current Anthropology*, vol. 48, no. 1, 39–65.

Liebling, A. J. 1975: *The Press*. New York: Pantheon.

Linden, David J. 2015: *Touch: The Science of Hand, Heart, and Mind*. London: Viking.

Lipstadt, Deborah. 2006: *History on Trial: My Day in Court with a Holocaust Denier*. New York: Harper.

Liu, Xiaobo. 2012: *No Enemies, No Hatred: Selected Essays and Poems*. Edited by Perry Link, Tienchi Martin-liao and Xia Liu. Cambridge, MA: Harvard University Press.

Lloyd, John. 2004: *What the Media Are Doing to Our Politics*. London: Constable.

Lloyd, John. 2011: *Scandal! News International and the Rights of Journalism*. Oxford: Reuters Institute for the Study of Journalism.

Lovink, Geert. 2008: *Zero Comments: Blogging and Critical Internet Culture*. New York: Routledge.

Löwith, Karl. 1998: *Von Hegel zu Nietzsche: Der revolutionäre Bruch im Denken des 19. Jahrhunderts*. Hamburg: Meiner.

Lukes, Steven. 2003: *Liberals and Cannibals: The Implications of Diversity*. London: Verso.

Lukes, Steven. 2005: *Power: A Radical View*. 2nd ed. Basingstoke, UK: Palgrave Macmillan.

Lukianoff, Greg. 2012: *Unlearning Liberty: Campus Censorship and the End of American Debate*. New York: Encounter.

MacCulloch, Diarmaid. 2004: *Reformation: Europe's House Divided 1490–1700*. London: Penguin.

MacKinnon, Catharine A. 1993: *Only Words*. Cambridge, MA: Harvard University Press.

MacKinnon, Rebecca. 2012: *Consent of the Networked: The Worldwide Struggle for Internet Freedom*. New York: Basic.

Mahbubani, Kishore. 2013: *The Great Convergence: Asia, the West, and the Logic of One World*. New York: Public Affairs.

Malik, Kenan. 2009: *From Fatwa to Jihad: The Rushdie Affair and Its Legacy*. London: Atlantic.

Mancini, Paolo. 2011: *Between Commodification and Lifestyle Politics: Does Silvio Berlusconi Provide a New Model of Politics for the Twenty-First Century?* Oxford: Reuters Institute for the Study of Journalism.

Mancini, Paolo. 2012: 'Instrumentalisation of the Media vs. Political Parallelism'. *Chinese Journal of Communication*, vol. 5, no. 3, 262–80. doi: 10.1080/17544750.2012.701415.

Mandela, Nelson. 1995: *Long Walk to Freedom*. London: Abacus.

Manji, Irshad. 2011: *Allah, Liberty and Love: The Courage to Reconcile Faith and Freedom*. New York: Free Press.

Mann, Thomas. 1973: *Schriften zur Politik*. Frankfurt: Suhrkamp.

Margalit, Avishai. 1998: *The Decent Society*. Cambridge, MA: Harvard University Press.

Markoff, John. 2005: *What the Dormouse Said: How the Sixties Counter-Culture Shaped the Personal Computer Industry*. London: Penguin.

Marsden, Christopher T. 2010: *Net Neutrality: Towards a Co-Regulatory Solution*. London: Bloomsbury Academic.

Marshall, Paul, and Shea, Nina. 2011: *Silenced: How Apostasy and Blasphemy Codes Are Choking Freedom Worldwide*. Oxford: Oxford University Press.

Masani, Zareer. 2013: *Macaulay: Britain's Liberal Imperialist*. London: Bodley Head.

Maurer, Tim, and Morgus, Robert. 2014: 'Tipping the Scale: An Analysis of Global Swing States in the Internet Governance Debate'. *Internet Governance Papers*, vol. 7, no. 2.

Mayer-Schönberger, Viktor. 2009: *Delete: The Virtue of Forgetting in the Digital Age*. Princeton: Princeton University Press.

Mayer-Schönberger, Viktor, and Cukier, Kenneth. 2013: *Big Data: A Revolution That Will Transform How We Live, Work and Think*. London: Murray.

McGrath, Alister. 2007: *The Dawkins Delusion? Atheist Fundamentalism and the Denial of the Divine*. London: SPCK.

McLuhan, Marshall. 1962: *The Gutenberg Galaxy: The Making of Typographic Man*. Toronto: University of Toronto Press.

Mead, Walter Russell. 2002: *Special Providence: American Foreign Policy and How It Changed the World*. New York: Routledge.

Meiklejohn, Alexander. 1948: *Free Speech and Its Relation to Self-Government*. New York: Harper & Brothers.

Meili, Stephen. 2015: 'The Right to Not Hold a Political Opinion: Implications for Asylum in the United States and the United Kingdom'. *Columbia Human Rights Law Review*, vol. 46, no. 3. doi: 10.2139/ssrn.2668270.

Mill, John Stuart. 1991 [1859]: *On Liberty and Other Essays*. Oxford: Oxford University Press.

Milton, John. 1909 [1644]: *Areopagitica*. Oxford: Clarendon.

Mishra, Pankaj. 2013: *From the Ruins of Empire: The Revolt against the West and the Remaking of Asia*. London: Penguin.

Moggridge, Bill. 2010: *Designing Media*. Cambridge, MA: MIT Press.

Molnár, Péter, ed. 2015: *Free Speech and Censorship around the Globe*. Budapest: Central European University Press.

Montesquieu, Charles. 1989 [1748]: *The Spirit of the Laws*. Edited by Anne M. Cohler, Basia Carolyn Miller and Harold Samuel Stone. Cambridge, UK: Cambridge University Press.

Morozov, Evgeny. 2011: *The Net Delusion: The Dark Side of Internet Freedom*. New York: Public Affairs.

Mortimer, Edward. 1982: *Faith and Power: The Politics of Islam*. New York: Vintage.

Motherwell, Robert, ed. 1989: *The Dada Painters and Poets: An Anthology*. Cambridge, MA: Harvard University Press.

Moynihan, Ray. 2009: 'Court Hears How Drug Giant Merck Tried to "Neutralise" and "Discredit" Doctors Critical of Vioxx'. *British Medical Journal*, vol. 338, no. 2. doi: 10.1136/bmj.b1432.

Mueller, Milton M. 2004: *Ruling the Root: Internet Governance and the Taming of Cyberspace*. Cambridge, MA: MIT Press.

Mueller, Milton M. 2012: *Networks and States: The Global Politics of Internet Governance*. Cambridge, MA: MIT Press.

Mungello, David E. 1971: 'Leibniz's Interpretation of Neo-Confucianism'. *Philosophy East and West*, vol. 21, no. 1, 3–22. doi: 10.2307/1397760.

Murray, Douglas, and Verwey, Johan Pieter. 2008: *Victims of Intimidation: Freedom of Speech within Europe's Muslim Communities*. London: Centre for Social Cohesion.

Nagel, Thomas. 2002: *Concealment and Exposure and Other Essays*. Oxford: Oxford University Press.

Nair, Neeti. 2013: 'Beyond the "Communal" 1920s: The Problem of Intention, Legislative Pragmatism, and the Making of Section 295A of the Indian Penal Code'. *Indian Economic Social History Review*, vol. 50, no. 3, 317–40. doi: 10.1177/0019464613494622.

Nash, David. 1999: *Blasphemy in Modern Britain: 1789 to the Present*. Aldershot, UK: Ashgate.

Neier, Aryeh. 1979: *Defending My Enemy: American Nazis, the Skokie Case, and the Risks of Freedom*. New York: Dutton.

Neier, Aryeh. 2012: *The International Human Rights Movement: A History*. Princeton: Princeton University Press.

Neier, Aryeh. 2014: 'The Content and Context of Hate Speech: Rethinking Regulation and Responses'. *International Journal of Constitutional Law*, vol. 12, no. 3, 808–40. doi: 10.1093/icon/mou053.

Newman, Nic, and Levy, David A. L., eds. 2013: *Reuters Institute Digital News Report 2013: Tracking the Future of News*. Oxford: Reuters Institute for the Study of Journalism.

Newman, Nic, and Levy, David A. L., eds. 2014: *Reuters Institute Digital News Report 2014: Tracking the Future of News*. Oxford: Reuters Institute for the Study of Journalism.

Newman, Nic, Levy, David A. L., and Nielsen, Rasmus Kleis, eds. 2015: *Reuters Institute Digital News Report 2015: Tracking the Future of News*. Oxford: Reuters Institute for the Study of Journalism.

Nielsen, Michael. 2012: *Reinventing Discovery: The New Era of Networked Science*. Princeton: Princeton University Press.

Nissenbaum, Helen. 2010: *Privacy in Context: Technology, Policy, and the Integrity of Social Life*. Stanford: Stanford University Press.

Nuffield Council on Bioethics. 2015: *The Collection, Linking and Use of Data in Biomedical Research and Health Care: Ethical Issues*. London: Nuffield Council on Bioethics.

Nussbaum, Martha C. 2012: *The New Religious Intolerance: Overcoming the Politics of Fear in an Anxious Age*. Cambridge, MA: Harvard University Press.

Nye, Joseph S. 2011: *The Future of Power*. New York: Public Affairs.

Nye, Joseph S. 2014: 'The Regime Complex for Managing Global Cyber Activities'. *Global Commission on Internet Governance Paper Series*, no. 1.

O'Donovan, Oliver. 1999: *The Desire of the Nations: Rediscovering the Roots of Political Theology*. Cambridge, UK: Cambridge University Press.

O'Hara, Kieron, and Shadbolt, Nigel. 2008: *The Spy in the Coffee Machine: The End of Privacy as We Know It*. London: Oneworld.

O'Neill, Onora. 2002: *A Question of Trust: The BBC Reith Lectures*. Cambridge, UK: Cambridge University Press.

Ober, Josiah. 1998: *Political Dissent in Democratic Athens: Intellectual Critics of Popular Rule*. Princeton: Princeton University Press.

Ober, Josiah. 2008: *Democracy and Knowledge: Innovation and Learning in Classical Athens*. Princeton: Princeton University Press.

Ober, Josiah. 2013: 'Democracy's Wisdom: An Aristotelian Middle Way for Collective Judgment'. *American Political Science Review*, vol. 107, no. 1, 104–22. doi: 10.1017/S0003055412000627.

Ogas, Ogi, and Gaddam, Sai. 2012: *A Billion Wicked Thoughts: What the Internet Tells Us about Sexual Relationships*. New York: Plume.

Olson, Parmy. 2013: *We Are Anonymous: Inside the Hacker World of LulzSec, Anonymous, and the Global Cyber Insurgency*. London: Heinemann.

Omand, David. 2010: *Securing the State*. London: Hurst.

Orwell, George. 1987 [1938]: *Homage to Catalonia. Complete Works, Volume 6*. London: Secker & Warburg.

Orwell, George. 1987 [1949]: *Nineteen Eighty-Four. Complete Works, Volume 9*. London: Secker & Warburg.

Oz, Amos. 2012: *How to Cure a Fanatic*. London: Vintage.

Paine, Thomas. 2010 [1794]: *The Age of Reason*. New York: Merchant.

Painter, James. 2013: *India's Media Boom: The Good News and the Bad*. Oxford: Reuters Institute for the Study Journalism.

Pariser, Eli. 2011: *The Filter Bubble: What the Internet Is Hiding from You*. New York: Penguin.

Parker, Emily. 2014: *Now I Know Who My Comrades Are*. New York: Sarah Crichton.

Pearson, Roger. 2005: *Voltaire Almighty: A Life in Pursuit of Freedom*. London: Bloomsbury.

Petley, Julian, ed. 2013: *Media and Public Shaming*. London: Tauris.

Petley, Julian, and Richardson, Robin. 2011: *Pointing the Finger: Islam and Muslims in the British Media*. Oxford: Oneworld.

Pettegree, Andrew. 2014: *The Invention of News: How the World Came to Know About Itself*. New Haven: Yale University Press.

Pinker, Steven. 2011: *The Better Angels of Our Nature: Why Violence Has Declined*. London: Penguin.

Pinter, Harold. 1988: *Mountain Language: A Play*. London: Samuel French.

Plato. 2003: *The Last Days of Socrates*. London: Penguin.

Popper, Karl. 1966 [1945]: *The Open Society and Its Enemies*. London: Routledge & Kegan Paul.

Post, David G. 2009: *In Search of Jefferson's Moose: Notes on the State of Cyberspace*. New York: Oxford University Press.

Post, Robert C. 1986: 'The Social Foundations of Defamation Law: Reputation and the Constitution'. *California Law Review*, vol. 74, no. 3, 691–742. doi: 10.2307/3480391.

Post, Robert C. 1990: 'The Constitutional Concept of Public Discourse: Outrageous Opinion, Democratic Deliberation, and Hustler v. Falwell'. *Harvard Law Review*, vol. 103, no. 3, 610–86. doi: 10.2307/1341344.

Post, Robert C. 1995: *Constitutional Domains: Democracy, Community, Management*. Cambridge, MA: Harvard University Press.

Post, Robert C. 2007: 'Informed Consent to Abortion: A First Amendment Analysis of Compelled Physician Speech'. *Scholarship Series, paper 170*. doi: http://digitalcom mons.law.yale.edu/fss_papers/170.

Post, Robert C. 2012: *Democracy, Expertise, and Academic Freedom: A First Amendment Jurisprudence for the Modern State*. New Haven: Yale University Press.

Privacy and Civil Liberties Oversight Board. 2014: *Report on the Telephone Records Program Conducted under Section 215 of the USA Patriot Act and on the Operations of the Foreign Intelligence Surveillance Court*. Washington DC: Privacy and Civil Liberties Oversight Board.

Private Wealth Council. 2008: *Responsible Wealth Review: Privacy. Volume 2*. Vaduz, Liechtenstein: Private Wealth Council.

Prothero, Stephen. 2011: *God Is Not One: The Eight Rival Religions That Run the World*. New York: HarperOne.

Puhl, Rebecca M., and Heuer, Chelsea A. 2010: 'Obesity Stigma: Important Considerations for Public Health'. *American Journal for Public Health*, vol. 100, no. 6, 1019–28. doi: 10.2105/AJPH.2009.159491.

Rachbauer, Tamara. 2011: *Brockhaus und Wikipedia—Enzyklopädien im Wandel vom Statischen Nachschlagewerk zum Nutzergenerierten Lexikon*. Norderstedt: GRIN.

Radcliffe, Timothy. 2005: *What Is the Point of Being a Christian?* London: Bloomsbury.

Raine, Craig. 2006: *T. S. Eliot*. Oxford: Oxford University Press.

Rawls, John. 2006: *Political Liberalism*. New York: Columbia University Press.

Reagle, Joseph Michael Jr. 2010: *Good Faith Collaboration: The Culture of Wikipedia*. Cambridge, MA: MIT Press.

Ricoeur, Paul. 1992: *Oneself as Another*. Chicago: University of Chicago Press.

Roberts, Adam, and Garton Ash, Timothy. 2009: *Civil Resistance and Power Politics: The Experience of Non-Violent Action from Gandhi to the Present*. Oxford: Oxford University Press.

Roberts, Adam, Willis, Michael, McCarthy, Rory, and Garton Ash, Timothy. 2016: *Civil Resistance in the Arab Spring: Triumphs and Disasters*. Oxford: Oxford University Press.

Robertson, Geoffrey, and Nicol, Andrew. 2008: *Media Law*. 5th ed. London: Penguin.

Rodin, David. 2012: 'Toward a Global Ethic'. *Ethics & International Affairs*, vol. 26, no. 1, 33–42. doi: 10.1017/S0892679412000196.

Roehr, Bob. 2011: 'US Agency Seeks to Censor Influenza Research amid Biosecurity Fears'. *British Medical Journal*, vol. 343, no. 29, 1. doi: 10.1136/bmj.d8333.

Rosen, Michael. 2012: *Dignity: Its History and Meaning*. Cambridge, MA: Harvard University Press.

Roth, Philip. 2001: *The Human Stain*. London: Vintage.

Rowson, Martin. 2009: *Giving Offence*. London: Seagull.

Roy, Oliver. 2007: *Secularism Confronts Islam*. New York: Columbia University Press.

Rummel, R. J. 2004: *Death by Government*. New Brunswick, NJ: Transaction.

Rushdie, Salman. 2011: *Luka and the Fire of Life*. London: Vintage.

Rushdie, Salman. 2012: *Joseph Anton*. London: Cape.

Sacks, Jonathan. 2007: *The Home We Build Together: Recreating Society*. London: Continuum.

Sagar, Rahul. 2013: *Secrets and Leaks: The Dilemma of State Secrecy*. Princeton: Princeton University Press.

Sajó, András, ed. 2007: *Censorial Sensitivities: Free Speech and Religion in a Fundamentalist World*. Utrecht, The Netherlands: Eleven International.

Sambrook, Richard. 2012: *Delivering Trust: Impartiality and Objectivity in the Digital Age*. Oxford: Reuters Institute for the Study of Journalism.

Santayana, George. 1980 [1905]: *Reason in Common Sense*. New York: Dover.

Sassen, Saskia. 2001: *The Global City*. Princeton: Princeton University Press.

Saviano, Roberto. 2007: *Gomorrah*. Translated by Virginia Jewiss. London: Pan.

Scammell, Michael. 1981: 'How Index on Censorship Started'. *Index on Censorship*, vol. 10, no. 6, 6–71. doi: 10.1080/03064228108533275.

Scanlon, Thomas. 2003: *The Difficulty of Tolerance: Essays in Political Philosophy*. Cambridge, UK: Cambridge University Press.

Schauer, Frederick. 1982: *Free Speech: A Philosophical Enquiry*. Cambridge, UK: Cambridge University Press.

Schell, Orville, and Delury, John. 2013: *Wealth and Power: China's Long March to the Twenty-First Century*. New York: Random House.

Schiller, Friedrich. 2005 [1804]: *William Tell*. Translated by Francis Lamport. London: Libris.

Schmidt, Eric, and Cohen, Jared. 2013: *The New Digital Age: Reshaping the Future of People, Nations and Business*. New York: Knopf.

Schudson, Michael. 2008: *Why Democracies Need an Unlovable Press*. Cambridge, UK: Polity.

Schudson, Michael. 2011: *The Sociology of News*. New York: Norton.

Schultze, Harald. 1969: *Lessings Toleranzbegriff: Eine Theologische Studie*. Göttingen: Vandenhoek & Ruprecht.

Sedley, Stephen. 2011: *Ashes and Sparks: Essays on Law and Justice*. Cambridge, UK: Cambridge University Press.

Seierstad, Åsne. 2015: *One of Us: The Story of Anders Breivik and the Massacre in Norway*. Translated by Sarah Death. London: Virago.

Semelin, Jacques. 2007: *Purity and Destiny: The Political Uses of Massacre and Genocide*. Translated by Cynthia Schock. London: Hurst.

Sen, Amartya. 1985: *Commodities and Capabilities*. Amsterdam: North-Holland.

Sen, Amartya. 1999: *Development as Freedom*. Oxford: Oxford University Press.

Sen, Amartya. 2006: *Identity and Violence: The Illusion of Destiny*. London: Penguin.

Sennett, Richard. 2012: *Together: The Rituals, Pleasures and Politics of Cooperation*. London: Allen Lane.

Serres, Michel. 2012: *Petite Poucette*. Paris: Le Pommier.

Shamsie, Kamila. 2009: *Offence: The Muslim Case*. London: Seagull.

Sharp, Gene. 2005: *Waging Nonviolent Struggle: 20th Century Practice and 21st Century Potential*. Manchester, NH: Extending Horizons.

Shayegan, Daryush. 1992: *Cultural Schizophrenia: Islamic Societies Confronting the West*. Syracuse: Syracuse University Press.

Shils, Edward. 1997: *The Virtue of Civility: Selected Essays on Liberalism, Tradition and Civil Society*. Edited by Steven Grosby. Indianapolis: Liberty Fund.

Shteyngart, Gary. 2010: *Super Sad True Love Story*. London: Granta.

Sluiter, Ineke, and Rosen, Ralph M., eds. 2004: *Free Speech in Classical Antiquity*. Leiden: Brill.

Smith, Zadie. 2001: *White Teeth*. London: Penguin.

Solove, Daniel J. 2007: *The Future of Reputation: Gossip, Rumor, and Privacy on the Internet*. New Haven: Yale University Press.

Solzhenitsyn, Alexander. 1972: *'One Word of Truth Shall Outweigh the Whole World'. The Nobel Speech on Literature 1970*. London: Bodley Head.

Spar, Debra. 2001: *Ruling the Waves: From the Compass to the Internet, a History of Business and Politics along the Technological Frontier*. New York: Harcourt.

Stace, Walter T. 1990: *The Concept of Morals*. New York: Peter Smith.

Standage, Tom. 2007: *The Victorian Internet*. New York: Walker.

Starr, Paul. 2004: *The Creation of the Media: Political Origins of Modern Communications*. New York: Basic.

Stefancic, Jean, and Delgado, Richard. 1993: 'A Shifting Balance: Freedom of Expression and Hate-Speech Restriction'. *Iowa Law Review*, vol. 78, no. 1, 737–50.

Stepan, Alfred. 2012: 'Rituals of Respect: Sufis and Secularists in Senegal in Comparative Perspective'. *Comparative Politics*, vol. 44, no. 4, 379–401. doi: 10.5129/001041512801282960.

Stepan, Alfred, and Taylor, Charles, eds. 2014: *Boundaries of Toleration*. New York: Columbia University Press.

Stone, Geoffrey R. 2004: *Perilous Times: Free Speech in Wartime from the Sedition Act of 1798 to the War on Terrorism*. New York: Norton.

Stone, Geoffrey R. 2006: 'Civility and Dissent during Wartime'. *Human Rights*, vol. 33, no. 1, 2–4.

Stothard, Peter. 2003: *30 Days: A Month at the Heart of Blair's War*. London: HarperCollins.

Straus, Scott. 2007: 'What Is the Relationship between Hate Radio and Violence? Rethinking Rwanda's "Radio Machete"'. *Politics and Society*, vol. 35, 609–37.

Streckfuss, David. 2011: *Truth on Trial in Thailand: Defamation, Treason, and Lèse-Majesté*. London: Routledge.

Sunstein, Cass R. 2006: *Infotopia: How Many Minds Produce Knowledge*. Oxford: Oxford University Press.

Sunstein, Cass R. 2007: *Republic.com 2.0.* Princeton: Princeton University Press.

Sunstein, Cass R. 2009: *On Rumors: How Falsehoods Spread, Why We Believe Them, What Can Be Done.* London: Allen Lane.

Suskind, Ron. 2004: *The Price of Loyalty: George W. Bush, the White House, and the Education of Paul O'Neill.* New York: Simon & Schuster.

Sutherland, John. 1982: *Offensive Literature: Decensorship in Britain 1960–1982.* London: Junction.

Swire, Peter, and Ahmad, Kenesa. 2011: 'Going Dark' versus a 'Golden Age for Surveillance'. Center for Democracy and Technology, November 28, 2011.

Swire, Peter, and Ahmad, Kenesa. 2012: 'Encryption and Globalization'. *Columbia Science & Technology Law Review,* vol. 13, 416–81. doi: 10.2139/ssrn.1960602.

Taylor, Charles. 2007: *A Secular Age.* Cambridge, MA: Harvard University Press.

Thiel, Peter. 2014: *Zero to One: Notes on Startups, or How to Build the Future.* London: Virgin.

Thucydides. 1943: *The History of the Peloponnesian War.* Edited in translation by R. W. Livingstone. London: Oxford University Press.

Thürer, Daniel. 2009: *Völkerrecht als Fortschritt und Chance.* Baden-Baden: Nomos.

Tilly, Charles. 1990: *Coercion, Capital and European States, AD 990–1992.* Oxford: Blackwell.

Tilly, Charles, and Ardent, Gabriel, eds. 1975: *The Formation of Nation States in Western Europe.* Princeton: Princeton University Press.

Tomalin, Nicholas. 1975: *Reporting.* London: Andre Deutsch.

Tucholsky, Kurt. 1975: *Gesammelte Werke. Band 3: 1921–1924.* Reinbek: Rowohlt.

Tufekci, Zeynep. 2014: 'Engineering the Public: Big Data, Surveillance and Computational Politics'. *First Monday,* vol. 19, no. 7. doi: 10.5210/fm.v19i7.4901.

Van Schewick, Barbara. 2010: *Internet Architecture and Innovation.* Cambridge, MA: MIT Press.

Veen, Wim, and Vrakking, Ben. 2006: *Homo Zappiens: Growing Up in a Digital Age.* London: Network Continuum Education.

Volokh, Eugene. 2000: 'Freedom of Speech and Information Privacy: The Troubling Implications of a Right to Stop People from Speaking about You'. *Stanford Law Review,* vol. 52, no. 5, 1049–124. doi: 10.2139/ssrn.200469.

Wacks, Raymond. 2010: *Privacy: A Very Short Introduction.* Oxford: Oxford University Press.

Wade, Nicholas. 2009: *The Faith Instinct: How Religion Evolved and Why It Endures.* London: Penguin.

Wahid, Abdurrahman. 2001: 'Indonesia's Mild Secularism'. *SAIS Review,* vol. 21, no. 2, 25–28.

Waldron, Jeremy. 1992: 'Minority Cultures and the Cosmopolitan Alternative'. *University of Michigan Journal of Law Reform,* vol. 25, no. 3, 751–93.

Waldron, Jeremy. 1995: 'The Wisdom of the Multitude: Some Reflections on Book 3, Chapter 11 of Aristotle's Politics'. *Political Theory,* vol. 23, no. 4, 563–58.

Waldron, Jeremy. 2012: *The Harm in Hate Speech.* Cambridge, MA: Harvard University Press.

Waley, Arthur. 1938: *The Analects of Confucius*. London: Allen & Unwin.

Wallerstein, Immanuel. 2006: *European Universalism: The Rhetoric of Power*. New York: New Press.

Walzer, Michael. 1997: *On Toleration*. New Haven: Yale University Press.

Warburton, Nigel. 2009: *Free Speech: A Very Short Introduction*. Oxford: Oxford University Press.

Warraq, Ibn, ed. 2003: *Leaving Islam: Apostates Speak Out*. Amherst, NY: Prometheus.

Warren, Samuel D., and Brandeis, Louis D. 1890: 'The Right to Privacy'. *Harvard Law Review*, vol. 4, no. 5, 193–220. doi: 10.2307/1321160.

Watson, Burton. 2007: *The Analects of Confucius*. Translated by Burton Watson. New York: Columbia University Press.

Weinreich, Max. 1945: 'YIVO and the Problems of Our Time'. *Yivo-Bleter*, vol. 25, no. 1, 13.

Weizenbaum, Joseph. 1984: *Computer Power and Human Reason: From Judgment to Calculation*. London: Penguin.

Wekesa, Bob, and Zhang, Yanqiu. 2014: 'Live, Talk, Faces: An Analysis of CCTV's Adaption to the African Media Market'. *Stellenbosch University Discussion Paper*.

Wells, H. G. 1938: *World Brain*. New York: Doubleday.

Westin, Alan F. 1967: *Privacy and Freedom*. New York: Atheneum.

Whitman, James Q. 2000: 'Enforcing Civility and Respect: Three Societies'. *Yale Law Journal*, vol. 109, no. 6, 1279–398. doi: 10.2307/797466.

Whittle, Stephen, and Cooper, Glenda. 2009: *Privacy, Probity and Public Interest*. Oxford: Reuters Institute for the Study of Journalism.

Wilkie, Wendell L. 1943: *One World*. London: Cassell.

Wilkins, Jayne, Schoville, Benjamin J., Brown, Kyle S., and Chazan, Michael. 2012: 'Evidence for Early Hafted Hunting Technology'. *Science*, vol. 338, no. 6109, 942–46. doi: 10.1126/science.1227608.

Williams, Bernard, ed. 1981: *Obscenity and Film Censorship: An Abridgement of the Williams Report*. Cambridge, UK: Cambridge University Press.

Williams, Bernard. 2005: *In the Beginning Was the Deed: Realism and Moralism in Political Argument*. Selected, edited, and with an introduction by Geoffrey Hawthorn. Princeton: Princeton University Press.

Wittgenstein, Ludwig. 1980: *Culture and Value*. Edited by G. H. Wright. Oxford: Blackwell.

Wohlstetter, Albert. 1990–1991: 'Le fax vous rendra libres'. *Commentaire*, vol. 13, no. 52, 679–85. doi: 10.3917/comm.052.0679.

Wolff, Larry. 1994: *Inventing Eastern Europe: The Map of Civilization on the Mind of the Enlightenment*. Stanford: Stanford University Press.

Wu, Tim. 2003: 'Network Neutrality, Broadband Discrimination'. *Journal of Telecommunications and High Technology Law*, vol. 2, 141. doi: 10.2139/ssrn.388863.

Wu, Tim. 2010: *The Master Switch: The Rise and Fall of Information Empires*. London: Atlantic.

Wu, Tim. 2013: 'Machine Speech'. *University of Pennsylvania Law Review*, vol. 161, 1495–533.

Yanagizawa-Drott, David. 2014: 'Propaganda and Conflict: Evidence from the Rwandan Genocide'. *Quarterly Journal of Economics*, vol. 129, no. 4, 1947–94. doi: 10.1093/qje/qju020.

Yang, Guobin. 2009: *The Power of the Internet in China: Citizen Activism Online*. New York: Columbia University Press.

Zegart, Amy B. 2011: *Eyes on Spies: Congress and the United States Intelligence Community*. Stanford: Hoover Institution Press.

Zittrain, Jonathan. 2008: *The Future of the Internet*. London: Penguin.

Zuckerberg, Randi. 2013: *Dot*. London: Picture Corgi.

ACKNOWLEDGEMENTS

I have always liked travelling to new places, and I have ventured farther afield than ever, both geographically and intellectually, over the ten years that I have been engaged on this project. Setting out from the troubled shores of contemporary European history, I have found myself deep in unfamiliar forests of law, philosophy, computer science and evolutionary psychology, not to mention countries such as China, India and Egypt. I hope (but do not altogether expect) that academic colleagues expert in these areas will forgive me my trespassing. I could not have written this book without their help.

The phrase 'I have the privilege' has something stuffy and formulaic about it, like a gravy-stained master of ceremonies in a crumbling grand hotel, but it *is* a privilege to work in two great universities, Oxford and Stanford. Whatever the subject, from deliberative democracy in ancient Athens to the behavioural impact of computer games, the evolution of human speech or the Latin for 'internet', you generally find a colleague who turns out to be expert on it. And if you don't find them at the university, then there is someone in a think tank, NGO, newspaper, parliament or (somewhat more cagily) among those who work for the governments and giant information businesses that shape this connected world.

My first thanks therefore go to St Antony's College, Oxford, especially to its Warden, Margaret MacMillan, and its Fellows, who are specialists on every corner of the world; to the Hoover Institution, Stanford University, especially its successive Directors, John Raisian and Thomas Gilligan; to the immensely supportive staff of both institutions; and to the wider universities of which they are a part. I must also thank the New York Review of Books, the Guardian and an informal syndicate of newspapers around the world that print my commentaries on international affairs for allowing me to try out my ideas on their readers and for clarifying those ideas by editorial challenge. My argument about the assassin's veto, for example, was sharpened and refined in conversation with the incomparable Robert Silvers.

Amongst the many individuals to whom I owe specific intellectual debts are Richard Allan, Chinmayi Arun, Carol Atack, Clive Baldwin, Daniel Bell, Susan Benesch, Peter Berkowitz, Pratap Bhanu Mehta, Rajeev Bhargava, Monika Bickert, Nigel Biggar, Lee Bollinger, Jonathan Bright, Andreas Busch, Luigi Cajani, Agnes Callamard, Ryan Calo, Gerhard Casper, Ying Chan, Stephen Coleman, Sandra Coliver, Paul Collier, David Davis, Richard Dawkins, Faisal Devji, Larry Diamond, Marc-Antoine Dilhac, David Drummond, Robin Dunbar, Ronald Dworkin, David Edgar, David Erdos, Amir Eshel, Khaled Fahmy, James Fenske, Jo Fidgen, James Fishkin, Francis Fukuyama, Iginio Gagliardone, Sue Gardner, Nazila Ghanea, Jo Glanville, Mike Godwin, Arnab Goswami, Victoria Grand, Leslie Green, Paul Haahr, Scott Hale, Ivan Hare, Usama Hasan, Jonathan Heawood, Eric Heinze, Andrew Hurrell, Richard Jenkyns, Dominic Johnson, Ayşe Kadıoğlu, David Kennedy, Matthew Kirk, Henning Koch, Andrew Kohut, Markos Kounalakis, Steve Krasner, Anthony Lester, David Levy, Li Qiang, John Lloyd, Steven Lukes, Ken Macdonald, Alex Macgillivray, Noel Malcolm, Paolo Mancini, Erika Mann, Viktor Mayer-Schönberger, Jonathan Leader Maynard, Rory McCarthy, Andrew McLaughlin, Stephen Meili, Abbas Milani, Péter Molnár, Martin Moore, Evgeny Morozov, Edward Mortimer, Max Mosley, Turi Munthe, Norman Naimark, Victoria Nash, John Naughton, Aryeh Neier, Kalypso Nicolaïdis, Rasmus Kleis Nielsen, Peter Noorlander, Joseph Nye, Josiah Ober, Franz Josef Och, Kerem Öktem, Margie Orford, Richard Ovenden, David Pannick, Andrew Przybylski, Timothy Radcliffe, Jim Reed, Rob Reich, Michael Rosen, Alan Rusbridger, Jonathan Sacks, Sheryl Sandberg, Carol Sanger, Orville Schell, Eliot Schrage, Stephen Sedley, Soli Sorabjee, Philip Taubman, Daya Thassu, Mark Thompson, Lila Tretikov, Zeynep Tufekci, Barbara van Schewick, Jeremy Waldron, Jimmy Wales, Matt Walton, Nigel Warburton, Jeremy Weinstein, Rachel Whetstone, Kieran Williams, Rowan Williams, Justin Winslett, Tobias Wolff, Joss Wright, Tim Wu and Jonathan Zittrain.

This book draws heavily on the work of the Free Speech Debate research project which I have run at Oxford University, under the auspices of the Dahrendorf Programme for the Study of Freedom, since 2012. It has been a delight to work with an extraordinary array of Oxford graduate students, native speakers of the thirteen languages in which freespeechdebate.com is presented. Most of them are listed on the site, although we have had to exclude the names of some from countries where free speech is a dangerous business. They know who they are and that I am especially grateful to them.

So many members of the team contributed research assistance to the preparation of this book that I cannot thank them all individually, but four who have given extraordinary, resourceful and dedicated support, checking countless references and working through the whole text, are Dominic Burbidge, Sarah Glatte, Max Harris and Sebastian Huempfer. Dorian Singh, the research manager of the Dahrendorf Programme, has given unstinting support, with good humour in the face of all obstacles. I could not have finished it without them. I also owe much to our successive online editors, Maryam Omidi, Brian Pellot, Judith Bruhn and Michael Patefield, and our web developer, Simon Dickson. Jeff Edwards drew the maps and figures. Thanks also to Catherine Hueck for getting me straight and to Clive Roberts for getting me there.

Such a large project would not have been possible without generous funders, and I would like to thank the Fritt Ord Foundation, especially its successive directors, Erik Rudeng and Knut Olav Åmås; the Open Society Foundations, especially Aryeh Neier; the Aurea Foundation, especially Peter Munk, George Jonas and Rudyard Griffiths; Google (with a cast-iron guarantee of academic independence), especially Peter Barron, Bill Echikson and Verity Harding; and the Zeit Foundation (for the annual Dahrendorf Lecture and Colloquium), especially Michael Göring.

I am fortunate to enjoy the support of two exceptional literary agents, Gill Coleridge and Georges Borchardt. Bill Frucht has been a patient, stimulating and rigorous editor at Yale University Press, where the whole editorial and production team is exemplary. At Atlantic Books, Toby Mundy originally signed up for the book, with invigorating enthusiasm, while Will Atkinson and James Nightingale have expertly seen it through to fruition.

I am particularly grateful to five friends who read the whole typescript and greatly enriched it by their comments: Eric Barendt, Ian Brown, Ian McEwan, Adam Roberts and Michael Taylor. So did Danuta, Tom and Alec, to whom I owe so much else.

INDEX

Page numbers followed by 'f' indicate material in figures.